MW00651165

ASIAN AMERICAN HISTORY DAY BY DAY

ASIAN AMERICAN HISTORY DAY BY DAY

A REFERENCE GUIDE TO EVENTS

JONATHAN H. X. LEE

An Imprint of ABC-CLIO, LLC
Santa Barbara, California • Denver, Colorado

Library of Congress Cataloging-in-Publication Data

Names: Lee, Jonathan H. X., author.
Title: Asian American history day by day : a reference guide to events / Jonathan H. X. Lee.
Description: Santa Barbara, California : Greenwood, an Imprint of ABC-CLIO, LLC, [2018] | Includes bibliographical references and index.
Identifiers: LCCN 2018014677 (print) | LCCN 2018028819 (ebook) | ISBN 9780313399282 (ebook) | ISBN 9780313399275 (alk. paper)
Subjects: LCSH: Asian Americans—History.
Classification: LCC E184.A75 (ebook) | LCC E184.A75 L444 2018 (print) | DDC 973/.0495—dc23
LC record available at https://lccn.loc.gov/2018014677

ISBN: 978-0-313-39927-5 (print)
978-0-313-39928-2 (ebook)

22 21 20 19 18 1 2 3 4 5

This book is also available as an eBook.

Greenwood
An Imprint of ABC-CLIO, LLC

ABC-CLIO, LLC
130 Cremona Drive, P.O. Box 1911
Santa Barbara, California 93116-1911
www.abc-clio.com

This book is printed on acid-free paper ∞

Manufactured in the United States of America

I dedicate this volume to my father, Minh Quoc Lee,
and my son, Owen Edward Jinfa Quady-Lee.

Contents

Acknowledgments

There are many people to express my sincere gratitude to for the completion of this endeavor. First and foremost, I would like to thank all the good people at ABC-CLIO who invited me to take on this challenging volume. In particular, I wish to thank Kim Kennedy White, my editor for this project, who has been extraordinarily patient and understanding with me. Second, I wish to thank my colleagues at San Francisco State University who shared resources with me and answered my questions in their area of research. Third, to my students who remind me, every day, of the value and importance of this work in shaping their identity and cultivating their purpose. Fourth, I wish to thank my partner, Mark S. Quady, for providing me the time to conduct research and write. Lastly, I wish to thank all my colleagues in the field of Asian American studies, whose scholarship informed the content of this volume.

Introduction

Compared to the Indigenous, African Americans, and Lationas/os, the Asian American experience is relatively short—roughly 140 years. Although the historical experiences of Asian Americans are relatively short, it is rich and robust. In addition, it is diverse, multigenerational, and multidimensional. In *Asian American History Day by Day: A Reference Guide to Events*, I attempt to add to the promotion of Asian American cultures and document the Asian American experience. This volume showcases, highlights, and invites attention to significant historical events—national and transnational—as well as quotidian, everyday life. The experiences of Asian Americans in this volume include, but are not limited to, contributions to American history, polity, economy, society, education, science, technology, pop culture, music, sports, literature, arts, television, film, journalism, and much more. The events reveal struggle, pain, loss, violence, hope, determination, resistance, renewal, life, death, healing, growth, acceptance, and achievements by people—significant and not so significant. Asian American places, historical and contemporary, secular and sacred, are also documented to be remembered. Moreover, I include members of the Asian American community who have been marginalized and invisible—mixed-race, queer, and transgender Asian Americans. The completion of this volume makes clear the need for scholarship on new post-1965 Asian American communities and histories of Laotian, Hmong, Thai, Indonesian, Burmese, Tibetans, Nepali, Pakistani, and Sir Lankan Americans. I offer my sincere apology to anyone whose community is not represented or reflected in this volume. While I made diligent attempts to cover the mosaic of Asian American histories and cultures, I know I have not covered all, as I originally desired. I therefore invite students and others to take part in this important work of documenting and preserving the histories of Asian Americans. I also wish to point out that although the World Wide Web is a tremendous tool, web resources often come and go. During the time it took to research and write this volume, some websites I used disappeared, and were replaced with new ones during the production process. The availability of all websites used is not guaranteed, and this may cause some frustration for students. Nonetheless, I do hope this volume is useful, as a document that attests to the spirit of Asian Americans, whose contribution to the development of the United States—physical, geographic, cultural, economic, political, social—is attested to on the following pages. Asian Americans have played and continue to play a critical role in advancing civil rights, social justice, gender equality, and educational equity that holds institutions in the United States accountable to the ideals established in the Constitution and Bill of Rights. This work is not yet complete as the content of this volume reveals, in particular in the post–9/11 terrorist attack era and current rise of white supremacist, nativist, and xenophobic sentiments. Asian Americans have encountered these oppressive forces before, and Asian Americans are ready, as events in this volume illustrate, to fight back and claim this land as our land, not just for ourselves but for all Americans "yearning to breathe free."

January

January 1

1877

Labor leader Denis Kearney, an Irish immigrant, organizes anti-Chinese movement in San Francisco and leads violent attacks on the Chinese in San Francisco. He formed the Workingmen's Party of California alleging Chinese workers took lower wages, poorer conditions, and longer hours than white workers were willing to tolerate. The slogan "The Chinese Must Go" was being widely repeated. The Workingmen's Party successfully elected candidates to state office and will therefore influence California policies for decades.

Excerpt from Kearney's appeal to California for support to banish the Chinese from America's shores.

To add to our misery and despair, a bloated aristocracy has sent to China—the greatest and oldest despotism in the world—for a cheap working slave. It rakes the slums of Asia to find the meanest slave on earth—the Chinese coolie—and imports him here to meet the free American in the Labor market, and still further widen the breach between the rich and the poor, still further to degrade white Labor. . . .

These cheap slaves fill every place. Their dress is scant and cheap. Their food is rice from China. They hedge twenty in a room, ten by ten. They are wipped curs, abject in docility, mean, contemptible and obedient in all things. They have no wives, children or dependents. . . .

They are imported by companies, controlled as serfs, worked like slaves, and at last go back to China with all their earnings. They are in every place, they seem to have no sex. Boys work, girls work; it is all alike to them. . . .

California must be all American or all Chinese. We are resolved that it shall be American, and are prepared to make it so. May we not rely upon your sympathy and assistance?

With great respect for the Workingman's Party of California.

Dennis Kearney, President

H.L Knight, Secretary

Source: Kearney, Dennis and H. L. Knight. "Appeal from California. The Chinese Invasion. Workingmen's Address." *Indianapolis Times*, February 28, 1878.

Books

Kearney, Denis. *The Workingmen's Party of California: An Epitome of Its Rise and Progress.* San Francisco, CA: Bacon, 1878.

Shumsky, Neil Larry. *The Evolution of Political Protest and the Workingmen's Party of California.* Columbus: Ohio State University Press, 1992. Neil Shumsky examines the July 1877 riots in San Francisco, and the subsequent rise of the Workingmen's Party of California.

Websites

Carlsson, Chris. "The Workingmen's Party & the Denis Kearney Agitation." FoundSF.org. 1995. This site provides a historical overview of the Workingmen's Party. http://foundsf.org/index.php?title=The_Workingmen%E2%80%99s_Party_%26_The_Dennis_Kearney_Agitation. Accessed October 7, 2016.

"The Fight Begins at Home: Jewett Defends Asian Immigrants." History Matters: The U.S. Survey Course on the Web. This site provides the original newspaper editorial written by B.E.G. Jewett in defense of the Chinese immigrants and against anti-Chinese sentiment. http://historymatters.gmu.edu/d/5045. Accessed January 28, 2018.

1885

The first group of Japanese contract laborers leaves Japan to go work on the sugar plantations in Hawaii through the work of an American businessman and the Kingdom of Hawaii's minister to Japan. Robert Walker Irwin's major accomplishment as the top Hawaii representative to Japan was the immigration treaty between Japan and Hawaii, which resulted in significant Japanese immigration to Hawaii. On February 8, 1885, Irwin, along with 943 Japanese laborers, arrived in Honolulu aboard the Pacific Mail Steamship Company *City of Tokio*. Another 930 Japanese laborers arrived in Hawaii on June 17, 1885. By January 28, 1886, a formal emigration convention was signed by Japan and the Hawaiian government. This is known as the Irwin Convention, which remained in force until 1894. In effect for 10 years, a total of 28,691 (23,071 men, 5,487 women, 133 children) government-sponsored Japanese laborers went to work on sugar plantations on 3-year contracts. After 10 years, emigration business was turned over to private companies.

Under the convention, all emigration of Japanese to Hawaii was to be by contract (not to exceed three years), signed at Yokohama by the special agent of the Hawaiian board of immigration and the intending emigrants, and subject to approval by the Kenrei (governor) of Kanagawa. "During the continuance of any such contracts, the Hawaiian Government shall assume all the responsibilities of employer towards the emigrants, and shall consequently be responsible for the due and faithful performance of all the conditions of such contracts." The Hawaiian government agreed to furnish free steerage passage in first-class passenger steamers from Yokohama to Honolulu, and to employ during the continuance of the contracts "a sufficient number of Japanese physicians to attend the emigrants." The convention was to remain in force for five years, after which it could be terminated on six months notice by either country.

Source: Kuykendall, Ralph. *The Hawaiian Kingdom: 1874–1893, the Kalakaua Dynasty*. Vol. III. Honolulu: University of Hawaii Press, 1967, p. 170.

Books

Kuykendall, Ralph. *The Hawaiian Kingdom: 1874–1893, the Kalakaua Dynasty*. Vol. III. Honolulu: University of Hawaii Press, 1967. *The Hawaiian Kingdom* is a seminal work by a leading historian of Hawaii. This volume covers the history of Hawaii before Cook to the death of Kamehameha III.

Lueras, Leonard, ed. *Kanyaku Imin: A Hundred Years of Japanese Life in Hawaii*. Honolulu, HI: International Savings and Loan Association Ltd., 1985. *Kanyaku Imin* provides a pictorial history of Japanese life in Hawaii.

Websites

Japanese Overseas Migration Museum. 2015. This website provides historical overview of Japanese migration around the world. http://www.jomm.jp/ Japan International Cooperation Agency. Accessed August 30, 2017.

Ono, Philbert. "Robert Walker Irwin." This site provides a general biography of Irwin, along with photos of his life, family, and career. http://photoguide.jp/txt/Robert_Walker_Irwin. Updated January 9, 2017. Accessed August 30, 2017.

Also Noteworthy

1892

On this day, Ellis Island is opened. It would be the gateway to the United States for European immigrants.

1912

The Republic of China (Taiwan) is established, and Sun Yat Sen of the Kuomintang (the KMT or Nationalist Party) is proclaimed provisional president.

1928

The *Japanese American Courier*, the first Japanese American newspaper published entirely in English, is published by James Sakamoto

(March 22, 1903–December 3, 1955) in Seattle, Washington.

1946

Emperor Hirohito of Japan announces he is not a "god."

1972

Only 133,000 U.S. troops remain in South Vietnam.

1972

East West Bank, Chinese American bank, opens in Los Angeles.

1979

United States and China (People's Republic) begin diplomatic relations.

January 2

1945

The War Department announces that the exclusion orders against Japanese Americans are withdrawn after the Supreme Court rules in *Ex Parte Endo* (December 18, 1944) case that "loyal" citizens could not be detained without trial. The fact that the *Endo* case was brought at all, let alone appealed before the Supreme Court, was in some sense a matter of chance given its importance. Mitsuye Endo, a stenographer at the Department of Motor Vehicles in Sacramento, was one of a small group of Nisei state employees who were dismissed from their positions in early 1942. Following her removal to the Tanforan Assembly Center, Endo was contacted by American Civil Liberties Union (ACLU) lawyer James Purcell, who sought to challenge the arbitrary dismissal of the Nisei state employees. Although Endo either never met her lawyer or did so only on one occasion, she agreed to serve as a test case. Purcell's original intent was not to challenge confinement as such but for Endo to regain the civil service job from which she had been arbitrarily dismissed. Purcell determined, however, that the most rapid legal means to achieve this goal was by the circuitous route of challenging her confinement via a habeas corpus petition. Thus, Purcell charged the federal government with unlawful detention that deprived Mitsuye Endo of her right to return to her job. In bringing his petition, Purcell was supported not only by the ACLU but also by the Japanese American Citizens League, which had earned the enmity of many Nisei by declining to oppose mass wartime removal. Unlike the other challenges to Executive Order 9066, Endo's case did not involve a challenge to the initial removal but rather a larger question of liberty from arbitrary confinement.

Mitsuye Endo exemplified aggressive protest against the government. . . . On April 2, 1942, Mitsuye was dismissed from her California State government job without due process of law. In July 1942, she filed a petition for a writ of habeas corpus in the U.S. District Court, requesting to be released from the internment camp, thereby reclaiming her liberty. Three years and 11 days after the bombing of Pearl Harbor, on December 18, 1944, the U.S. Supreme Court ruled that the evacuation of Japanese-Americans was constitutional based on "military necessity." The Court further decided that any American citizen, like Mitsuye Endo, with undeniable loyalty should not be detained. Mitsuye Endo's actions proved crucial in influencing the Endo ruling, the army declared the West Coast exclusion orders revoked. Her independent efforts set a legal precedent. Mitsuye Endo's perseverance and determination influenced the fate of all Japanese-Americans.

Source: Arai, Ivy. "The Silent Significant Minority: Japanese-American Women, Evacuation, and Internment during World War II." In *Women and War in the Twentieth Century: Enlisted with or without Consent*, edited by Nicole Dombrowski, p. 231. New York: Garland Publishing, 1999.

Books

Robinson, Greg. *By Order of the President: FDR and the Internment of Japanese Americans*. Cambridge, MA: Harvard University Press, 2001. *By Order of the President* discusses the contradiction between Franklin D. Roosevelt's (FDR) image as humanitarian and preserver of democracy and the unjust internment of Japanese Americans during World War II.

Robinson, Greg. *A Tragedy of Democracy: Japanese Confinement in North America*. New York: Columbia University Press, 2009. *A Tragedy of Democracy* provides a comprehensive critical and transnational analysis of official government policy toward West Coast Japanese Americans in North America.

Websites

Ex Parte Endo (1944). JUSTIA U.S. Supreme Court. This site provides the full text for *Ex Parte Endo*. https://supreme.justia.com/cases/federal/us/323/283/case.html. Accessed January 13, 2017.

The Suyama Project. University of California, Los Angeles, Asian American Studies Center. This site provides summaries of Japanese American court cases that challenged unjust policies during World War II. http://www.suyamaproject.org/?p=56. Accessed August 31, 2017.

January 3

1852

The presence of Chinese in the Hawaiian Islands dates back to 1788, when the Kingdom of Hawaii was an independent nation. Widespread Chinese immigration began in 1852 when indentured servants escaping poverty in the provinces of Guangdong and Fujian went to Hawaii to work on sugar plantations. Smallpox had decimated the native Hawaiian population in early 1850s, creating a more urgent demand for laborers. Chinese immigrants were recruited to fill the void. Working under five-year contracts, Chinese plantation workers were paid in room, board, credit toward the cost of their passage from China, and an extra $3 a month. By 1882, almost half of the plantation laborers in Hawaii were Chinese.

Excerpt from Yee Yap, the United Chinese Society president, presenting a petition before a congressional hearing to petition for the importation of Chinese laborers to the territory of Hawaii on August 29, 1916.

Petition to the Administration of the Government of the United States of America for the Betterment, Conditions, and Admission of Chinese Laborers to the Territory of the Hawaiian Islands.

Gentlemen: In presenting this petition for your perusal, argument, discussion, and disposition, we are offering it for your consideration with the concurrence of the whole of the Chinese population of the Territory of Hawaii, and the desire that their prayer may be favorably granted. . . . From the years 1789 to 1852 the immigration of Chinese to these islands was not extensive, for we learn by an article printed in the Polynesian, a Hawaiian paper published in the early days, under date of August 24, 1850, that owing to growing industry of sugar cane it was necessary that labor suitable for this work be encouraged from some other country. And after due deliberation China was the country selected in which to look for this class of labor. In further records of the Polynesian we learn that in August, 1851, the Hawaiian Agricultural and Historical Society sent the ship Thetis, Capt. Cass, to China for laborers. In a few months the ship returned to Honolulu with 195 Chinese as agricultural laborers and in addition 20 boys as house servants. The experiment proved to be so satisfactory, since the laborers turned out to be industrious, that Capt. Cass was again sent out with his ship to China in July, 1852, for an additional 100 laborers. From 1852 to 1864 Chinese immigration was encouraged, and during that period 704 Chinese landed at Honolulu. At that time many Chinese merchants in San Francisco began to establish their business here. . . .

These facts now placed before you are not intended as asking for privileges for the Chinese to the whole of the United States but for the benefit of the Territory of Hawaii only.

Source: "Statement of W. H. Hindle and Petition from United Chinese Society of Hawaii." *Labor Conditions in Hawaii*, Hearings before a Subcommittee of the Committee on the Territories. House of Representatives, Sixty-Fourth Congress. Washington: Government Printing Office. August 29, 1916.

Books

McKeown, Adam. *Chinese Migrant Networks and Cultural Change: Peru, Chicago, Hawaii, 1900–1936*. Chicago, IL: University of Chicago Press, 2001. Historian Adam McKeown offers a transnational approach to the research on Chinese migrant laborers.

Takaki, Ronald. *Pau Hana: Plantation Life and Labor in Hawaii, 1835–1920*. Honolulu: University of Hawaii Press, 1983. Historian Ronald Takaki provides a history of plantation life as experienced by the laborers.

Websites

Char, Tin-Yuke, and Wai Jane. "The First Chinese Contract Laborers in Hawaii, 1852." *Hawaiian Journal of History* 9 (1975): 128–134. This article discusses the history and origins of early Chinese migrants in Hawaii. This article is available at eVols, an open-access, digital repository for the University of Hawaii. https://evols.library.manoa.hawaii.edu/bitstream/10524/131/2/JL09144.pdf. Accessed January 28, 2018.

Glick, Clarence. "The Voyage of the 'Thetis' and the First Chinese Contract Laborers Brought to Hawaii." *Hawaiian Journal of History* 9 (1975): 135–140. Notable resource on Captain Cass's voyages in search of Chinese laborers. This article is available at eVols, an open-access, digital repository for the University of Hawaii. https://evols.library.manoa.hawaii.edu/bitstream/handle/10524/330/JL09151.pdf?sequence=2. Accessed January 28, 2018.

Also Noteworthy

2009

Anh Quang "Joseph" Cao, a Vietnamese American, is elected to the U.S. Representative for Louisiana's Second Congressional District from 2009 to 2011.

2011

Jean Quan is sworn in as the first female mayor of Oakland, California.

2012

Yiaway Yeh is elected by city council to serve as mayor of Palo Alto, California. He was the first Chinese American to hold this office.

2013

Mazie Keiko Hirono (b. November 3, 1947) assumes office as U.S. senator from Hawaii. She is known as the first Asian American woman, first Buddhist, and first Japan-born elected to the U.S. Senate.

January 4

1919

Albert F. Judd, a former territorial senator, launches a Japanese school-control law campaign that appears in the *Pacific Commercial Advertiser*. Known as the Judd proposal, it was a forerunner of laws restricting the activities of Japanese language schools, requiring licenses for all teachers in Japanese schools, approval of textbooks, and placement under the supervision of the Department of Public Instruction. Although introduced, the bill died in session.

Measure Provides for Regulation and Inspection of Schools Conducted in Foreign Tongues to Insure Their American Ideals

Honolulu, March 12—The long expected bill to regulate foreign language schools in the territory, and place them under the exclusive jurisdiction of the department of public instruction, was introduced in the house on Tuesday by Representative Lorrin Andrews. In a way the measure is a drastic one, and some heads of foreign language schools have asserted that, if the measure passes, their institutions cannot exist. Little or no weight is attached to this protest by the Honolulu Star-Bulletin in editorial comment yesterday.

In full, the measure reads as follows:

Section 1. The term "Foreign Language School" as used in this act, shall be construed to mean any school academy in any language alien to the English or Hawaiian languages.

Section 2. That it shall be unlawful for any person, association or institution to conduct any foreign language school in the territory of Hawaii unless a license so to do shall first been obtained from the department of public instruction of the Territory of Hawaii, and no such license shall be issued except as hereinafter ordered.

Section 3. The department of public instruction before issuing such license shall first ascertain that such school shall pursue a course of study . . . to inculcate in the pupils and principles of the form of government and, as for as practicable, having regard to the age and mental capacity of such pupils, included in such course of study shall be American history, economics, geography and literature.

Section 4. The department of public instruction shall have power to determine the text books to be used by such foreign language schools, and no text book shall be used by such schools until the same has been approved and it use authorized by the department of public instruction, and no such approval and authorization shall be given where it appears that such text book is calculated to extol or exploit the ideals or principles of a government foreign to the government of the United States, or is not, for other cause, suitable for the training of youths for American citizenship.

Section 8. Any person, association or institution that shall conduct a foreign language school, and any person who shall instruct in such school, where a license has not been first had and obtained as in this act provided, shall be guilty of a misdemeanor and upon conviction thereof may be fined not exceeding $500 or by imprisonment not exceeding six months, or by both such fine and imprisonment.

Source: *Maui News*, March 14, 1919, pp. 1 and 3.

Books

Asato, Noriko. *Teaching Mikadoism: The Attack on Japanese Language Schools in Hawaii, California, and Washington, 1919–1927*. Honolulu: University of Hawaii Press, 2006. *Teaching Mikadoism* explores Japanese language schools in Hawaii, California, and Washington from within the Japanese American communities and generations and anti-Japanese forces that argued Japanese language schools teach Mikadoism to Japanese American children as part of Japan's attempt to colonize the United States.

Morimoto, Toyotomi. *Japanese Americans and Cultural Continuity: Maintaining Language and Heritage*. New York: Garland Publishing, 1997. *Japanese Americans and Cultural Continuity* examines Japanese language education among Japanese in the United States and in other overseas communities.

Websites

"Japanese Schools in Hawaii." Hawai'i Digital Newspaper Project. This site provides a history of Japanese schools in Hawaii with links to primary documents. https://sites.google.com/a/hawaii.edu/ndnp-hawaii/Home/historical-feature-articles/japanese-schools-in-hawaii. Accessed February 4, 2018.

Nakamura, Kelli. "Japanese Language Schools." *Densho Encyclopedia*, June 10, 2015. This essay provides an overview history of Japanese language schools and Nisei, second-generation Japanese Americans, attitudes toward them. http://encyclopedia.densho.org/Japanese_language_schools/. Accessed February 4, 2018.

Also Noteworthy

1965

President Lyndon B. Johnson reaffirms the United States' support of South Vietnam in the fight against communist forces in his State of the Union speech.

January 5

1976

On this day, the Khmer Rouge proclaims the Constitution of Democratic Kampuchea. The Khmer Rouge regime lasted from April 1975 through January 1979. It would become one of the most radical and brutal periods in world history. Under the leadership of a Paris-educated school teacher, Pol Pot (formerly Saloth Sar), and Chinese Khmer Khieu Samphan (president of Democratic Kampuchea from 1976 to 1979), the Khmer Rouge attempted to transform Cambodian society into a Maoist peasant agrarian cooperative. Under their rule, urban dwellers, merchants, ethnic Chinese and ethnic Vietnamese Cambodians, along with other elites of Cambodian society, were either executed or sent to labor and reeducation camps. In total, nearly 2 million Cambodians were killed in this autogenocide. As a result, a massive global movement of Cambodian refugees fled Cambodia: upward of 150,000 would resettle in the United States, changing the demographic composition of the Asian American communities.

Most resettled Cambodians are ethnic Khmer, but they include Cambodians who have Chinese, Lao, Thai, or Vietnamese ancestry. Although most Khmer refugees were formerly subsistence rice farmers in Cambodia, some were prominent in business, government, and the military and a few were urban students and workers. The approximately 150,000 Khmer refugees resettled in the United States after the mid-1970s included Theravada Buddhists, Muslims, Christians, Mahayana Buddhists, and practitioners of tribal religions. The majority of Khmer refugees were resettled in urban areas, and many continue to live there. Long Beach, California, has the largest population of people of Cambodian ancestry outside Cambodia, and communities of Khmer reside in other urban centers across the country, particularly in southern California, eastern Massachusetts, and the Puget Sound region of the Pacific Northwest. Over the decades, Cambodian Americans have increased in number, scattering to even more suburbs and towns. By 2010, over 275,000 people of Khmer descent resided in America (United States Census 2011).

Source: Mortland, Carol. *Cambodian Buddhism in the United States.* Albany: State University of New York Press, 2017, p. 1.

Books

Chandler, David. *Brother Number One: A Political Biography of Pol Pot*. Boulder, CO: Westview Press, 1999. *Brother Number One* offers a comprehensive biography of Pol Pot that covers various aspects of his life: from childhood to education to his rise to power.

Chandler, David. *Voices from S-21: Terror and History in Pol Pot's Secret Prison*. Berkeley: University of California Press, 1999. *Voices from S-21* is a history of the Khmer Rouge secret prison, genocide agenda, and ideology.

Websites

Dy, Khamboly. *A History of Democratic Kampuchea (1975–1979)*. Phnom Penh, Cambodia: The Documentation Center of Cambodia, 2007. This site provides a full PDF of *A History of Democratic Kampuchea* that provides a detailed and concise historical narrative of the Khmer Rouge period with photos, maps, and sidebars with key information. http://www.d.dccam.org/Projects/Genocide/DK_Book/DK_History--EN.pdf. Accessed August 31, 2017.

Selected Documents of the Khmer Rouge. This site provides archival primary documents related to the Khmer Rouge, such as the National Anthem, Manifesto, and Minutes from meetings, and so on collected in *Selected Documents of the Khmer Rouge*, published in 1970. https://archive.org/details/SelectedDocumentsOfTheKhmerRouge. Accessed August 31, 2017.

Also Noteworthy

1942

All Japanese American men of draft age are classified as 4-C, "enemy aliens" by the War Department.

January 6

1942

On this day, Jose Cabalfin Calugas serves as a member of the Philippine Scouts during World War II. When a battery gun position was bombed by the enemy until it was put out of commission, Calugas voluntarily ran 1,000 yards through a shell-swept area to put the gun back into action and fired effectively at the Japanese forces, all through constant heavy enemy fire. He became one of two Filipino Americans to receive a Medal of Honor.

Tribute to the Late Capt. Jose Calugas. Hon. Bob Filner of California, in the House of Representatives. Tuesday, February 3, 1998.

Mr. FILNER. Mr. Speaker and colleagues, I rise today to pay tribute to Captain Jose Calugas, who passed away on January 18, 1998. Captain Calugas was the only Filipino World War II veteran to receive the Congressional Medal of Honor. Jose Calugas was a true hero! On January 16, 1942, he was a mess sergeant who voluntarily ran 1,000 yards across a shell-swept area to take command of a gun position where all the cannoneers had been killed or wounded. Organizing a volunteer squad of 16 men, he placed the gun back in commission and fired effectively against the enemy although this position was under constant and heavy fire. Born December 29, 1904 in the Philippines, he entered military service in the Philippine Scouts in 1930. Captured by the enemy forces after the fall of Bataan in 1942, Calugas survived the infamous Bataan Death March and more than two years as a prisoner of war. He remained in the United States Army after the war, and retired with the rank of Captain in 1957. He received his Bachelors Degree in Business Administration at the University of Puget Sound and worked for Boeing Aircraft in Seattle until his retirement in 1972. Upon receiving the Medal of Honor, Calugas, a naturalized United States citizen, said: When the situation confronted me, I did not have any hesitation to fight and give my life for the cause of freedom and my country. I feel great being an American. I am proud to be such and I humbly say thank you. Besides the Congressional Medal of Honor, Calugas was awarded many additional military decorations, including the Asiatic Pacific Campaign Medal, the Distinguished Unit Citation with 1st and 2nd Oak Leaf Cluster, the Philippine Liberation Ribbon, the World War II Victory Medal, and an Ex-Prisoner of War Medal. He also received many civilian awards, including the Honorary Citizen Award of Tacoma, Washington, the Key to the City of Tacoma, and the Medal of Honor Permanent Car License Plate Recipient, presented by then Governor of Washington, Dixy Lee Ray. He is survived by his wife, four children, 11 grandchildren and 5 great-grandchildren. It is an honor to acknowledge the life and bravery of Captain Jose Calugas and his courageous action under fire to preserve the freedoms we all hold dear.

Source: Congressional Record—Extensions of Remarks (February 3, 1998). Government Publishing Office. https://www.gpo.gov/fdsys/pkg/CREC-1998-02-03/pdf/CREC-1998-02-03-pt1-PgE70-2.pdf#page=1. Accessed February 4, 2018.

Books

Olson, John. *The Philippine Scouts*. La Mesa, CA: The Philippine Scouts Heritage Society, 1996.

Whitman, John W. *Bataan: Our Last Ditch: The Bataan Campaign, 1942*. New York: Hippocrene Books.

Websites

Beers, Carole. "Jose Calugas, Medal of Honor Winner, 'Death March' Survivor." *Seattle Times*, September 1, 2017. This article provides details of Calugas's heroism and service during World War II. http://community.seattletimes.nwsource.com/archive/?date=19980124&slug=2730347. Accessed August 31, 2017.

Calugas, Jose, Jr. "My Father." This site is a detailed biography of Jose Calugas, written by his son. http://www.us-japandialogueonpows.org/Calugas.htm. Accessed August 31, 2017.

Also Noteworthy

1967

The United States launches a 10-day sweep of the Mekong River delta known as "Operation Deckhouse Five." It was carried out by U.S. Marine Corps and Republic of Vietnam Marine Corps.

2003

The National Center for Transgender Equality is founded in Washington, D.C., and serves Asian Pacific Islander transgender Americans.

January 7

1985

The Filipino American National Historical Society (FANHS) is chartered by the state of Washington. Founded earlier in 1982, in Seattle, Washington, by Dorothy Laigo Cordova, the FANHS is a community-based organization whose goal is to promote, preserve, and disseminate Filipino American history and culture. Fred Cordova, historian, joined the effort and served as the organization's first president. FANHS was recognized as a primary organization in documenting Filipino American history.

Fourteen young Filipinos traveled to Virginia Beach, VA to learn about the legacy of Filipino Americans in the United States by attending the 8th national conference of the Filipino American National Historical Society (FANHS). The group joined approximately 275 other participants—scholars, historians, authors, filmmakers, educators, archivists, community researchers, student activists, and community members—eager to share their research, resources, expertise, and personal experiences.

They met authors, playwrights, and poets such as Jeannie Barroga, Dr. Fred Cordova, Dr. Joan May Cordova, Timoteo Cordova, Oscar Penaranda, Emil Guillermo, Emily Lawsin, Dawn Mabalon, Rex Navarette, and many others.

The FANHS conference identifies voices and experiences relevant to the past, present and future. For Filipino Americans, it was a rare opportunity to reaffirm, renew, and remember the commitment of preserving, promoting and evolving from the Pinay/Pinoy legacies of the past.

The youth who attended are part of the Filipino American National Historical Society—Oregon Chapter, which included a group from Portland Community College: Tiffany Aquino, Cheryll Fernandez, Ricci Lim, Jason Shirey, Julie Ann Yambao, and Joy Yoro. Joining the college students were John Duran of Franklin High School; Jackie Fernandez, a nurse at OHSU; Jonathan Friolo, a designer at Adidas International; Carol Lalangan; Wil Olandria, of Fred Meyer Corporation, Emily Rice, a recent graduate from Wheaton College; Patrick Villaflores, a recent graduate of Cleveland High School; and this reporter.

Source: Oliveros, Claire. "FANHS Conference 2000: Young Pinoys Seek Out History." *Asian Reporter*, July 24, 2000. https://search-proquest-com.jpllnet.sfsu.edu/docview/368189794?accountid=13802. Accessed September 1, 2017.

Books

Cordova, Fred. *Filipinos: Forgotten Asian Americans. A Pictorial Essay, 1763–circa 1963*. Dubuque, IA: Kendall/Hunt Publishing Company, 1983. Historian and activist Fred Cordova presents historical photographs of the Filipino American experience.

Posadas, Barbara. *The Filipino Americans*. Westport, CT: Greenwood Press, 1999. *The Filipino Americans* provides a general history of the Filipino American experience.

Websites

Filipino American National Historical Society. 2017. This is the web page for the headquarter of FANHS. http://www.fanhs-national.org/history.html. Accessed January 27, 2018.

Filipino American National Historical Society Stockton Chapter. 2009. FANHS maintains 34 local chapters throughout the United States. Each chapter maintains a web page with local activities and history. http://fanhsstockton.com/fanhs_museum. Accessed January 28, 2018.

Also Noteworthy

1979

North Vietnamese troops drive out Pol Pot and the Khmer Rouge from Cambodia.

2002

In Salt Lake City, Utah, James Herrick, a 32-year-old, is sentenced to four years in prison for attempting to set fire to a Pakistani American family restaurant in September 2001.

2010

Edwin Mah Lee (May 5, 1952–December 12, 2017) is elected mayor of San Francisco by the board of supervisors.

The Japanese community in Hawaii, however, distinguished between the Okinawans and the Naichi *(Mainland) Japanese from the four main islands of Japan proper. The Okinawans themselves used the term* Uchinanchu *to identify themselves as a distinct ethnic group apart from the* Naichi *Japanese. . . . On January 8, 1900 . . . twenty-six men entered Hawaii as the first Okinawan immigrants. The second labor group from Okinawa was composed of 40 young farmers . . . they arrived in Honolulu on April 6, 1903. The records indicate that in 1904, 206 Okinawa men migrated to Hawaii; in 1905, 1,200 men; in 1906, 4,500 men; and in 1907, 2,500. Thus, during this period the Okinawa immigrants totaled approximately 8,500 constituting about one-fifth of the total Japanese immigrants of 44,000. . . .*

Today most Okinawa immigrants in Hawaii are prosperous as owners of leading restaurants, dairy farms, bakeries, and flower farms. A notable characteristic of the Okinawans in Hawaii has been their ability to organize and work in groups with a strong sense of social solidarity. The network of family ties as well as place of origin in Okinawa has played important roles in the successful development of many business enterprises. Second generation Okinawans have been highly successful in such fields as dentistry, insurance, and real estate, and have made important contributions to Hawaii as political, financial, and cultural leaders of the community.

Source: Matsumoto, Y. Scott. "Okinawa Migrants to Hawaii." *Hawaiian Journal of History* 16 (1982): pp. 124–125 and 130–131.

January 8

1900

Twenty-six men from Okinawa arrive in Hawaii aboard the SS *City of China* from Yokohama. They were taken to the Ewa Plantation where they worked. Hawaii maintains the oldest and largest overseas Okinawan community. In many publications and census, Okinawans are conflated with Japanese Americans, so their exact population is difficult to ascertain. However, Okinawan Americans maintain a distinct ethnic identity.

Books

Ethnic Studies Program, University of Hawaii at Manoa, ed. *Uchinanchu, A History of Okinawans in Hawaii*. Honolulu: Ethnic Studies Program, University of Hawaii at Manoa, 1981. This volume is based on15 oral histories to document the experiences of Okinawans in Hawaii.

Nakasone, Ronald, ed. *Okinawan Diaspora*. Honolulu: University of Hawaii Press, 2002. *Okinawan Diaspora* uses primary data and oral histories to examine the history and experience of Okinawan Americans vis-à-vis Japan from the 19th century to 20th century.

Websites

Center for Oral History. University of Hawaii at Manoa. August 2010. This is the website for the oral history project at the University of Hawaii that started in 1976. It contains a database of oral histories that are searchable by ethnic group. http://ethnicstudies.manoa.hawaii.edu/center-for-oral-history/ Accessed June 14, 2018.

"Okinawans in Hawaii." The Samurai Archives: Samurai Wiki. March 2017. This site provides a comprehensive historical overview of Okinawan American history in Hawaii. https://wiki.samurai-archives.com/index.php?title=Okinawans_in_Hawaii. Accessed September 1, 2017.

January 9

1901

Joseph and Mary Tape successfully sue the San Francisco school board to enroll their Chinese daughter, Mamie, in a public school. On January 9, 1885, Superior Court justice McGuire announced the decision in favor of Joseph and Mary Tape. On appeal, the California Supreme Court upheld the lower court decision on March 3, 1885. Shortly after the decision, the San Francisco school board lobbied for a separate school system for Chinese and other "Mongolian" children. A bill passed through the California State Legislature giving the school board the authority to create an Oriental Public School in San Francisco. In 1885, San Francisco built a new segregated "Oriental School" in response to the Mamie Tape case.

One fine day in September 1884, Mary took Mamie to register for school at the Spring Valley Primary School on Union Street. Perhaps she believed that her highly acculturated, English-speaking family, Americans "except in features" in Mary's own inimitable phrasing, would protect them from Chinese exclusion, the act passed just 2 years prior. But Miss Hurley, the principal, refused to admit little Mamie, who, despite speaking fluent English and being dressed in a pretty checkered pinafore with a ribbon in her braids, had features that marked her as Chinese. The principal seemed undeterred by the new state law that entitled all children in the state to a public education, confident, indeed, that she was upholding the views of her boss, school superintendent Andrew Jackson Moulder, already known for his racist views.

Source: Hu-DeHart, Evelyn. "An Asian American Perspective on Segregated Schooling, *Brown v. Board*, and Affirmative Action." In *Race, Equity, and Education: Sixty Years from Brown*, edited by Pedro Noguera, Jill Pierce, and Roey Ahram, p. 127. New York: Springer International Publishing, 2016.

Books

Ngai, Mae. *The Lucky Ones: One Family and the Extraordinary Invention of Chinese America.* Princeton, NJ: Princeton University Press, 2012. This book uncovers the story of the Tape family and argues that they are the first middle-class Chinese American family.

Odo, Franklin, ed. "Letter from Mary Tape, April 8, 1885." In *The Columbia Documentary History of the Asian American Experience*, edited by Franklin Odo, 72–73. New York: Columbia University Press, 2002. This edited volume reproduces a letter Mary Tape writes to the school board.

Websites

The National Women's History Museum. Chinese American Women: A History of Resilience and Resistance. "Tape v. Hurley." The site provides an essay with citations from archival newspaper that brings forth Mary Tape's voice in her struggle for equality for her daughter. http://www.mixedracestudies.org/wordpress/?tag=national-womens-history-museum. Accessed June 14, 2018.

"Separate Is Not Equal: *Brown v. Board of Education.*" Smithsonian National Museum of American History. This site provides historical background to the decision and impact of *Brown v. Board of Education*. It contains a photo of the Tape family and a summary of this struggle for educational equality. http://americanhistory.si.edu/brown/history/2-battleground/detail/tape-family.html. Accessed January 28, 2018.

Also Noteworthy

1901

Peter Ryu, the first recorded Korean immigrant, reaches Hawaii on the *Kongkong Maru*, a Japanese ship.

1966

On this day, professor of sociology William Petersen publishes "Success Story, Japanese-American Style" in the *New York Times Magazine*. Shortly afterward, *U.S. News and World Report* published "Success Story of One Minority in the U.S." (December 26, 1966). Together, the image of Asian Americans as a racialized stereotype as a "model minority" emerged and continues to persist today.

2017

Dat Tan Nguyen (b. September 25, 1975) is elected to the College Football Hall of Fame by the National Football Foundation.

January 10

1862

Amasa Leland Stanford was an American tycoon and politician. Along with his wife, Jane, he founded Leland Stanford Junior University on November 11, 1885. He served one two-year term as Republican governor of California (1862–1863). Stanford was president of the Central Pacific Railroad company that built the western portion of the First Transcontinental Railroad over the Sierra Nevada mountains that linked California, Nevada, and Utah. During the gold rush, anti-Chinese sentiment was the major political issue, and Stanford accepted the prevailing racist mood of the time and lobbied for the restriction of Chinese immigration. In his inaugural address as governor of California, Leland Stanford promised to protect the state from "the dregs of Asia."

Excerpt from Leland Stanford's inaugural address as the eighth governor of California.

While the settlement of our State is of the first importance, the character of those who shall become settlers is worthy of scarcely less consideration. To my mind it is clear, that the settlement among us of an inferior race is to be discouraged, by every legitimate means. Asia, with her numberless millions, sends to our shores the dregs of her population. Large numbers of this class are already here; and, unless we do something early to check their immigration, the question, which of the two tides of immigration, meeting upon the shores of the Pacific, shall be turned back, will be forced upon our consideration, when far more difficult than now of disposal. There can be no doubt but that the presence of numbers among us of a degraded and distinct people must exercise a deleterious influence upon the superior race, and, to a certain extent, repel desirable immigration. It will afford me great pleasure to concur with the Legislature in any constitutional action, having for its object the repression of the immigration of the Asiatic races.

Source: California State Library. "The Governors' Gallery." 2016. http://governors.library.ca.gov/addresses/08-Stanford.html. Accessed February 4, 2018.

Books

Sandmeyer, Elmer Clarence. *The Anti-Chinese Movement in California*. Urbana: University of Illinois Press, 1973. This book was originally published in 1939 and was the first study of the anti-Chinese movement in the American West. See Chapter 2, "The Bases of Anti-Chinese Sentiment," and Chapter 3, "California Anti-Chinese Agitation Prior to 1876," for historical background.

Tutorow, Norman, Evie LaNora Tutorow, and George Deukmejian. *The Governor: The Life and Legacy of Leland Stanford, a California Colossus*. Vol. II. Glendale, CA: Arthur H. Clark Company, 2004. This biography is the most comprehensive resource on Leland Stanford that contains historical documents, notes, photographs, and maps.

Websites

"Jane Stanford Timeline." Stanford University. This web page offers a detailed chronology of Stanford University. https://www.stanford.edu/about/history/. Accessed June 14, 2018.

The Leland Stanford Junior University. The Act of the Legislature of California. The Grant of Endowment. Address of Leland Stanford to the Trustees. Minutes of the First Meeting of the Board of Trustees. 1885. Entire text is available at archive.org. https://archive.org/details/lelandstanfordju00stanrich. Accessed January 28, 2018.

Also Noteworthy

1930

The Northern Monterey Chamber of Commerce passes an anti-Filipino resolution to discourage hiring Filipino laborers.

January 11

1943

The Republic of China agrees to the Sino-British New Equal Treaty and the Sino-American New Equal Treaty. The Sino-American New Equal Treaty is also known as the Sino-American Treaty for Relinquishment of Extraterritorial Rights in China. After the United States declared war on Japan on December 8, 1941, the governments of the United States and the United Kingdom decided that it would be to their advantage to end extraterritoriality and unequal treaties with China. Extraterritoriality exempted American and English subjects residing in China from being subject to Chinese laws. It was a form of colonial control in China since the Opium Wars. The period of unequal treaties between the United States and China is between 1842 and 1946. The shift in U.S.-China foreign relations during World War II influenced how Chinese Americans were viewed and treated in the United States, because the shared enemy was Japan and Japanese.

Treaty between the United States of America and the Republic of China for the Relinquishment of Extraterritorial Rights in China and the Regulation of Related Matters

The terms of the Treaty are summarized as follows:

Article I: Section 1 declared mutual peace and friendship between China and the U.S. Section 2 provided for the mutual exchange and recognition of diplomats with reciprocal rights, privileges, exemptions, and immunities generally recognized under international law.

Article II: Section 1 authorized nationals of each country to enter territories in the other country to reside, travel, and carry on trade subject to any applicable laws and regulations in the host country and without unreasonable interference and without requiring any travel documents other than either valid passports or other official identification documents issued by the other country. Section 2 authorized nationals of each country to engage in a broad range of enumerated activities in the territories of the other country subject to any applicable laws and regulations of the host country to the same extent that the laws and regulations apply to nationals of the host country except the practice of a profession reserved exclusively to nationals of the host country. Section 3 required that, under Sections 1 and 2, each country must treat nationals of the other country no less favorably than the nationals of a third country. Section 4 declares that the Treaty does not affect each country's existing and future immigration laws except that such laws may not prevent the nationals of either country from entering, traveling, and residing in the territories of the other country to carry on trade between both countries or engaging in related commercial activity on less favorable terms than those afforded by the country to nationals of a third country engaging in the same activities in relation to the third country. Section 4 also declares that the geographic zones for immigration established by the U.S. in Section 3 of the Immigration Act of 1917 shall not prevent Chinese people and people of Chinese descent from being admitted into the U.S.

Article III: Section 1 broadly defined "corporations and associations." Section 2 declared that all corporations and associations of one of the countries shall have their status recognized in the territories of the other country, regardless of whether they have an established presence there, and may establish branch offices and fulfill their functions in the other country as authorized by treaty or as consistent with the laws and regulations of the host country. Section 3 requires each of the countries to permit all corporations and associations of the other country to engage in a broad set of enumerated activities within the host country's territories without interference to the same extent as those of the host country except as otherwise limited by the host country's laws. Section 3 further specified that all corporations and associations of China shall be treated the same in each U.S. state, territory, or possession as others of another U.S. state, territory, or possession. Section 4 requires each of the countries to treat all corporations and associations of the other country no less favorably than those of a third country.

Source: Bevans, Charles, compiler. *Treaties and Other International Agreements of the United States of America 1776–1949*. Washington, DC: Department of State Publication, 1971, pp. 739–741.

Books

Feis, Herbert. *The China Tangle: The American Effort in China from Pearl Harbor to the Marshall Mission*. Princeton, NJ: Princeton University Press, 1953. *The China Tangle* describes what the U.S. government tried to do in and with China during and after World War II.

Wang, Dong. *China's Unequal Treaties: Narrating National History*. Lanham, MD: Lexington Books, 2005. *China's Unequal Treaties* discusses how China shifts its narratives of unequal treaties with the United States and the United Kingdom to gain national unity, international independence, and political authority.

Websites

"Extraterritoriality—China." *Encyclopedia of the New American Nation*. 2017. This site summarizes the history and consequences of extraterritorial policies in China. http://www.americanforeignrelations.com/E-N/Extraterritoriality-China.html. Accessed September 1, 2017.

Hull, Cordell. "China's External Relations—A History." This site provides the full text of the *Treaty between the United States of America and the Republic of China for the Relinquishment of Extraterritorial Rights in China and the Regulation of Related Matters*, in addition to a history of China's foreign relations with other countries, chronology, and bibliography. http://www.chinaforeignrelations.net/node/215. Accessed September 1, 2017.

Also Noteworthy

1942

On this day, the Japanese forces capture Kuala Lumpur, Malaysia, and attack Tarakan in Borneo, Netherlands Indies.

2011

Edwin Mah Lee is appointed by the board of supervisors as the 43rd mayor of San Francisco, California. He served as interim mayor until he won the election on November 8, 2011. He was sworn in on January 8, 2012. Lee was the first Chinese American mayor in San Francisco's history. Lee was born in Seattle, Washington. He received a bachelor's degree from Bowdoin College and a law degree from the University of California at Berkeley.

January 12

1883

Anti-Chinese agitation in Montana was heating up and expressed economically through boycotts. For example, restaurants and other businesses would advertise that they did not "employ Chinese" laborers. An example of this is seen in a French restaurant's advertisement in the *Butte Daily Miner* on this day that reads "No Chinese Employed." By 1884, labor unions in Butte, Montana, attempted to drive out the Chinese immigrants. This was again attempted in 1891–1892 and then later in 1896 during another nationwide depression. The labor unions called for a boycott of Chinese-owned businesses as well as businesses employing Chinese, scapegoating them for the poor economic conditions. They used flyers to promote the boycott, as well as to advertise which establishment to avoid.

Boycott

A General Boycott has been declared upon all CHINESE and JAPANESE Restaurants, Tailor Shops and Wash Houses. Also all persons employing them in any capacity. All Friends and Sympathizers of Organized Labor will assist us in this fight against the lowering Asiatic standards of living and of morals.

America vs. Asia

Progress vs. Retrogression

Are the considerations involved.

By Order Of Silver Bow Trades and Labor Assembly and Butte Miners' Union.

Source: National Archives and Records Administration. Image of flyer available at https://www.archives.gov/education/lessons/chinese-boycott/images/union-flyer-01.gif. Accessed February 4, 2018.

Books

Cassel, Susie Lan, ed. *The Chinese in America: A History from Gold Mountain to the New Millennium*. Walnut Creek, CA: AltaMira Press, 2002. This edited volume provides a collection of essays that covers multiple aspects of the Chinese experience in the United States.

Pfaelzer, Jean. *Driven Out: The Forgotten War against Chinese Americans*. Berkeley: University of California Press, 2007. Jean Pfaelzer uses primary documents, such as newspaper articles, to narrate the societal impact of the anti-Chinese movement from 1848 into the 20th century.

Websites

"Anti-Asian Boycott, 1897." Records of Rights. National Archives. This site provides archival flyers and affidavits and images from the National Archives at Seattle. http://recordsofrights.org/events/15/anti-asian-boycott. Accessed January 28, 2018.

"Teaching with Documents: Affidavit and Flyers from the Chinese Boycott Case." The U.S. National Archives and Records Administration. This site provides information on the history of the Chinese in America, in particular in Butte, Montana, in addition to an archive of historic Union boycott flyers. The flyers reveal that this anti-Chinese/anti-Asian phenomenon was occurring in other states. https://www.archives.gov/education/lessons/chinese-boycott/. Accessed January 28, 2018.

Also Noteworthy

2002

Justin Lin's *Better Luck Tomorrow* is released. It is a film about Asian American overachievers who engage in crime and break the model minority stereotype.

January 13

1903

One hundred and twenty Korean men, women, and children arrive at Honolulu Harbor on the SS *Gaelic*. This marked the beginning of Korean immigration to the United States. Their arrival was in response to the sugar planters wanting "new Asian" laborers because Chinese and Japanese laborers were organizing for higher wages and better living conditions.

The SS Gaelic *eased into her berth at Honolulu Harbor, carrying the first Korean immigrants recruited to work on Hawai'i's sugar plantations. There were 56 men, 21 women, and 25 children. In the next two years more than seven thousand others, including six hundred women, would join this small band of pioneers. In 1905, the Korean government—upset about the alleged mistreatment of Korean workers in Mexico and pressured by the Japanese, who controlled Korea under a protectorate treaty—stopped workers from going abroad.*

The first leg of the ocean journey was a short trip from a Korean port city to Japan, where the immigrants boarded a large ship bound for Honolulu. During the twenty-two-day ordeal from Kobe or Yokohama, people were packed like cattle into a large cargo hold; bunk beds were stacked three high. The smell of vomit permeated the ship. Until 1924, picture brides made the same journey, and though conditions had improved, the seasickness and homesickness were the same. On many of the voyages, a minister or a so-called Bible woman accompanied the immigrants, giving comfort and spiritual sustenance to the weary travelers. By the time the ships docked in Honolulu, many immigrants had been converted to Christianity.

Upon landing, the travelers were divided into groups and sent to sugar plantations on various islands. Like the Chinese and Japanese immigrants before them, the Koreans were kept together in one camp, the bachelors living in dormitories and the families in one-room apartments. Cooking was done in community kitchens. Women who had never worked before now toiled in the cane fields with the men, and did the cooking and laundry as well.

Source: Arinaga, Esther Kwon. "The First Wave Pioneers: An Introduction." *Manoa* 14, no. 2 (2002–2003): pp. 30–31.

Books

Chang, Roberta, and Wayne Patterson. *The Koreans in Hawai'i: A Pictorial History 1903–2003*. Honolulu: University of Hawaii Press, 2003. *The Koreans in Hawai'i* provides hundreds of photographs to narrate the story of Korean immigrant experience in Hawaii, and by extension, the United States.

Murabayashi, Duk Hee Lee, compiler. *Korean Passengers Arriving at Honolulu, 1903–1905*. Honolulu: Center for Korean Studies, University of Hawaii at Manoa, 2001. *Korean Passengers Arriving at Honolulu* provides a comprehensive list of Koreans who arrived at Honolulu between 1903 and 1905 based on records of the Immigration and Naturalization Service passenger manifests for inbound vessels.

Websites

"A Brief History of Korean Americans." National Association of Korean Americans. 2017. This site provides a useful general history of Korean immigration to the United States, with links to primary documents important to Korean American history. http://www.naka.org/resources/history.asp. Accessed January 28, 2018.

Young-Sik, Kim. "A Brief History of the US-Korean Relations Prior to 945." 2008. This site provides an overview history of U.S.-Korean foreign policies and Korean immigration to the United States. http://www.freerepublic.com/focus/f-news/943949/posts. Accessed September 1, 2017.

Also Noteworthy

1996

Marking the culmination of a decade of work by San Diego's Chinese American community, the Chinese Mission Building, originally constructed in 1927, is officially dedicated as a Chinese American museum and cultural center.

January 14

1942

Five and a half weeks after Japan's attack on Pearl Harbor, which triggered the United

States' entry into World War II, President Franklin D. Roosevelt issues Presidential Proclamation No. 2537, requiring "aliens" from World War II enemy countries—Italy, Germany, and Japan—to register with the U.S. Department of Justice. Registered individuals were issued a Certificate of Identification for "Aliens of Enemy Nationality." Proclamation No. 2537 came on the heels of the Alien Registration Act of 1940 and facilitated the beginning of widespread illegal internment of Japanese Americans. Proclamation No. 2537 was issued on the pretense of national security and permitted the arrest, detention, and internment of "enemy aliens" who violated restrictive wartime policies and curfews. A month later, President Roosevelt would sign the War Department's Executive Order 9066, which authorized the physical removal of all Japanese Americans into internment campus. Executive Order 9066 subsequently authorized the removal of 111,155 Japanese citizens and resident aliens from the three Pacific coast states and Arizona.

By the end of January, 1942, the prospects for tolerant or even moderate treatment of Japanese Americans had all but disappeared. The ultimate fate of alien Japanese was foreshadowed by the announcement of the Justice Department that along with alien Germans and Italians they were to be removed from various prohibited zones, and that their freedom of movement in still other areas would be curtailed. The position of American citizens of Japanese descent, theoretically more secure, was almost equally precarious. Regarded generally as "descendants of the Japanese enemy," they found their status as citizens more and more in jeopardy. The confusion of alien ancestry with alien status was compounded in the public mind as newspapers referred indiscriminately to all Japanese—whether citizens or aliens, enemy forces or peaceful residents—as "Japs." An increasing number of organization and prominent individuals were urging the evacuation of citizens as well as aliens, and the cry of "once a Jap always a Jap" was heard on all sides.

Source: tenBroek, Jacobus, Edward Barnhart, and Floyd Matson. *Prejudice, War and the Constitution: Causes and Consequences of the Evacuation of the Japanese Americans in World War II*. Berkeley: University of California Press, 1954, p. 81.

Books

Robinson, Greg. *After Camp: Portraits in Midcentury Japanese American Life and Politics*. Berkeley: University of California Press, 2012. *After Camp* provides a series of case studies to examine the life, development, and legacy of wartime internment on Japanese Americans after World War II.

Robinson, Greg. *By Order of the President: FRD and the Internment of Japanese Americans*. Cambridge, MA: Harvard University Press, 2001. *By Order of the President* explains the contradictory personality and history of President Franklin D. Roosevelt who, on the one hand, fought for democracy and human rights and, on the other hand, for unjust treatment and internment of Japanese Americans during his administration.

Websites

Franklin: Access to the FDR Library's Digital Collections. The University of Illinois at Urbana-Champaign. 2011. This web page contains large digitized versions of President Franklin D. Roosevelt's executive orders and proclamations. http://www.fdrlibrary.marist.edu/archives/collections/franklin/?p=collections/findingaid&id=507. Accessed September 1, 2017.

Kale, Shelly. "This Day in History: Precedent for a Muslim Registry? Presidential Proclamation No. 2537." California Historical Society, January 14, 2017. This site provides a historical overview of events leading up to and after the passage of Proclamation No. 2537. In addition, it provides historical documents and images. http://californiahistoricalsociety.blogspot.com/2017/01/this-day-in-history-precedent-for.html. Accessed September 1, 2017.

Also Noteworthy

2008

In New Hyde Park, New York, David Wood, a 36-year-old, attacks a 63-year-old Sikh American man outside his temple. He was charged with a hate crime.

January 15

1997

Gary Faye Locke delivers his inaugural address on this day as governor of Washington. Locke became the first Chinese American governor in U.S. history when he won the general election for governor of Washington in 1996. Locke was born on January 21, 1950, in Seattle, Washington, and is a third-generation Chinese American whose paternal lineage is from Taishan, China.

I am humbled by the honor of serving as your governor. And I am deeply grateful to all those who have made our American tradition of freedom and democracy possible.

I also want to express my gratitude to members of my family, and to introduce them to you. First I'd like you to meet my father, Jimmy Locke, who fought in World War II and participated in the Normandy invasion. I'd like you to meet my mother, Julie, who raised five children, learned English along with me when I started kindergarten, and who returned to school at Seattle Community College when she was nearly 60. . . . And finally, it is my greatest pleasure to introduce Washington's new First Lady, Mona Lee Locke. This truly is a wonderful day for the Locke family.

One of my ancestors—a distant cousin, actually—was a merchant who immigrated to Olympia in 1874 and became a leader of the Chinese-American community just a few blocks from this state capitol. He acted as a bridge between the Chinese and white communities, and became friends with the other downtown merchants, and with the sheriff, William Billings.

In 1886, an anti-immigrant, anti-Chinese mob threatened to burn down the Chinese settlement here. But what happened next is a story that every Washington resident ought to know: Sheriff Billings deputized scores of Olympia's merchants and civic leaders. And those citizen deputies stood between the angry mob and the Chinese neighborhood at Fifth and Water streets. Faced by the sheriff and the leading citizens of Olympia, the mob gradually dispersed. Not a single shot was fired, nor a single Chinese house burned.

For the Locke family, that incident helped establish a deep faith in the essential goodness of mainstream American values:

- *The values that reject extremism and division, and embrace fairness and moral progress;*
- *The value of working together as a community; and*
- *The values of hard work, hope, enterprise and opportunity.*

Just a few years after that Olympia show of courage, my grandfather came to America to work as a "house boy" for the Yeager family, who lived in a house that's still standing, less than a mile from here.

His purpose was to get an education, and so the Yeager family agreed to teach him English in return for his work. Like everyone else in our family, my grandfather studied and worked hard, and he eventually became the head chef at Virginia Mason Hospital in Seattle. . . .

Our family history is more the norm than the exception. . . . There are millions of families like mine, and millions of people like me—people whose ancestors dreamed the American Dream and worked hard to make it come true. And today, on Martin Luther King's birthday, we are taking another step toward that dream.

In the 108 years since Washington became a state, we have gone from riding horses to flying in jets; from sending telegrams to sending e-mail; and from woodstoves to microwave ovens. Can anyone even guess what the next hundred years will bring? . . .

To keep the American Dream alive in a high-tech and unpredictable future, we have to raise our sights, and our standards. . . .

The principles that will guide me in this quest for higher standards—and the principles that will guide my response to legislative proposals—are clear and simple.

- *My first principle is that education is the great equalizer that makes hope and opportunity possible. That's why I am passionately committed to developing a world-class system of education.*

In the last century, the drafters of our Constitution made the education of children the "paramount duty" of the state. But learning is not just for kids anymore. For the next century, the paramount duty of this state will be to create an education system for lifelong learning—a system that every person regardless of age can plug into for basic skills, professional advancement or personal enrichment.

- *My second principle is to promote civility, mutual respect and unity, and to oppose measures that divide, disrespect, or diminish our humanity. I want our state to build on the mainstream values of equal protection and equal opportunity, and to reject hate, violence and bigotry. And I want our state to be known as a place where elected officials lead by example.*
- *My third principle is to judge every public policy by whether it helps or hurts Washington's working families. Everyone who works hard and lives responsibly ought to be rewarded with economic security, the opportunity to learn and to advance in their chosen field of work, and the peace of mind that comes from knowing that the essential services their families need—like health care insurance and child care—will be affordable and accessible. And every senior citizen who has spent a lifetime contributing to the freedom and prosperity we enjoy deserves dignity and security.*
- *My fourth principle is to protect our environment, so that future generations enjoy the same natural beauty and abundance we cherish today. . . .*

As most of you already know, Mona and I are expecting our first child in March. So in very rapid succession, I will be blessed with two titles that carry immense responsibility and immense honor: Governor and Dad.

As the advent of fatherhood gets closer, I am more and more conscious that everything I do as governor—and everything we do together—we do for our children.

Our child will be a child of the 21st Century. He or she will come of age in a world that we can scarcely imagine. But it is his or her world that we must now work together to create. For our children and yours, I want to foster a new century of personal responsibility, of community, and of hope and optimism.

Please help me carry on the Locke family tradition of focusing on those three crucial values: get a good education, work hard, and take care of each other.

With your hand in partnership, and with an abiding faith in the essential goodness of the people of our great state, I want to devote the next four years to making the American Dream come true for children whose faces we have yet to see.

Thank you.

Source: Governor Gary Locke. Washington State Office of the Governor, 2004. http://www.digitalarchives.wa.gov/GovernorLocke/speeches/speeches.asp. Accessed January 28, 2018.

Also Noteworthy

1930

Toshiko Inaba, a 20-year-old *kibei* (a Japanese American born in the United States but educated in Japan), is deported back to Japan, for marrying an alien ineligible for citizenship while in Japan. She was denied admission to San Francisco on September 3, 1928, and was detained at Angel Island Immigration Station, until she lost her appeal.

1963

The Chinese Historical Society of America in San Francisco Chinatown is established to document and preserve the history of the Chinese experience in the United States.

1998

President Bill Clinton awards the Presidential Medal of Freedom to Fred Korematsu.

2012

Khasokhas Weekly, a Nepali weekly magazine, based in New York City, is launched. It was founded by Kishor Panthi, a Nepali American journalist.

January 16

1767

The French play, written by Voltaire, *Orphan of China* (*L'Orphelin de la Chine*) is performed by European actors at the Southwark Theatre in Philadelphia on this day. It played in New York at the John Street Theatre in 1768. This was the first documented case of European (white) actors playing Chinese parts, known as "yellowface" in the United States.

Yellowface, a term used primarily during the twentieth century to describe the ways in which white actors portrayed Asians, manifested degrading images of Chinese immigrants on the stage—images that were also appearing in contemporary political cartoons and magazine covers. As with blackface, which emerged in the 1830s as a popular way to parody African Americans, dialect, makeup, posture, and costuming comprised yellowface; when combined, these items marked the Chinese body as inferior and foreign. The combination of these devices did not necessarily create a unilateral anti-Chinese image; both allure and repulsiveness coexisted in these performances. . . . As a result, Chinese and Chinese Americans, and by extension all persons of Asian descent, were vital to the conception of American culture and the boundaries of racial and national identity.

Source: Moon, Krystyn. *Yellowface: Creating the Chinese in American Popular Music and Performance, 1850s–1920s.* New Brunswick, NJ: Rutgers University Press, 2005, p. 6.

Books

Chan, Anthony. *Perpetually Cool: The Many Lives of Anna May Wong (1905–1961).* Lanham, MD: Scarecrow Press, 2003. *Perpetually Cool* is a biography of Chinese American actress Anna May Wong. See Chapter 10 for a discussion of the history of yellowface.

Lee, Esther Kim. *A History of Asian American Theatre*. Cambridge: Cambridge University Press, 2006. *A History of Asian American Theatre* examines the history and development of Asian American theater and issues of cultural nationalism, identity politics, and the racialization of Asian American subjects.

Websites

Padgett, Ken. Yellowface: Racist Asian Stereotypes. Yellow-face.com. This site provides a historical discussion of yellowface in film and television, along with images. https://yellow-face.com/yellowface-film-and-tv.htm. Accessed September 1, 2017.

Tang, Roger. Asian American Theatre Revue: Asian American Theatre Timeline. 2010. This site provides a useful chronology of the history of Asian American theater with important notes on Asian American challenge to yellowface. http://www.aatrevue.com/Timeline.html. Accessed September 1, 2017.

Also Noteworthy

2010

In Murfreesboro, Tennessee, a sign marking the future site of an Islamic center is spray-painted with the words "not welcome."

January 17

1874

On this day, Chang Bunker dies while in his sleep. Eng, his brother, would die shortly thereafter. They were the famous Siamese twins Chang and Eng. They were the first Thais to arrive in the United States. For four decades they toured the United States and the world. They were born in 1811 to Chinese parents. Before going to the United States, the twins were successful entrepreneurs in Siam (now Thailand). Captain Abel Coffin contracted to manage the twins' touring schedule. After three years with Coffin, the brothers took over their own careers as a touring curiosity until they earned enough money to purchase a plantation and slaves in North Carolina. They were granted U.S. citizenship in 1839. They died in January 1874.

They are united to each other by a ligature or band, about three and a half inches in length, and eight in circumference, formed at the extremity of the breast bone of each, and extending downwards to the abdomen. The upper part of the band is a strong cartilaginous substance; the lower part is soft and fleshy, and contains a tube or cavity, presumed to be about an inch and a half in circumference. Great difference of opinion exists among medical men, concerning the contents of this cavity.

On the lower edge of the band, exactly in the centre, is situated the umbilicus or navel, there being but one in common between them. If the band by which the bodies are connected be touched in the centre, both are equally sensible of it; but if half an inch from the centre, it is only felt by one.

The question of the probable success of an attempt to separate the twins by a surgical operation, has, naturally enough, been often discussed amongst professional men. In the United States and England, the Faculty, with very few exceptions, thought it would be attended with fatal results; whilst on the continent of Europe every medical man who had an opportunity of examining them, declared that there would be no more chance of their surviving such an operation, than of surviving the cutting off their heads. The twins can only walk in one position, but the flexibility of the cartilage is so great, that they can readily turn those shoulders outwards which are close together when they walk; indeed, it is probable, that if attention had been paid to the subject, they might have been taught to walk either way. Eng is 5 feet 2 inches in height, and Chang one inch shorter; but to obviate the inconvenience arising from this, Chang has soles to his boots sufficiently thick to raise him on a level with his brother. Although they stand so close together, yet they do not seem to be at all in each other's way, and whatever movement is made by one is responded to so immediately by the other, that it seems as if they were moved by the same impulse. They never thwart or oppose each other in any way, and it may therefore be set down as certain, that they present one of the few, if not indeed the only case, in which two persons have lived together twenty-five years, without even one little quarrel. They can run very fast for a short distance, and have some-times walked eight or ten miles when they have had something to interest them; they also can swim very well for a short distance.

They generally have a very good appetite, and almost invariably partake of the same food.

They have adopted the American style of dress in every thing except the hair, which is three feet in length, and is worn by them braided in the Chinese style; in doing which, in washing, dressing, or in any other occupation, they require no assistance, each acting for himself with as perfect ease as would one individual. They appear to be as nearly as possible alike in their friendship for particular persons, and also in their preference of places; and in their dislikes they are equally as uniform.

While in bed they are not confined to any particular position, but rest on either side, as may best suit their convenience, generally, however, with their faces towards each other.

They usually sleep quite soundly, and almost invariably awake at the same moment.

They seldom speak one to the other; but this is not very surprising, when it is recollected that they have always been placed in the same circumstances, and that their sphere of observation has been bounded by the same limits. They play chess and draughts tolerably well, but it affords them no amusement to play these games in opposition to each other. They have learned to read and write sufficiently to amuse themselves during their hours of relaxation. They can drive a carriage with perfect ease, and prefer taking exercise in a gig to any other mode of conveyance, and although they have been upset very often, yet they have never received the least hurt.

Source: A Few Particulars Concerning Chang-Eng, the United Siamese Brothers. Published under their direction. New York: Printed by J. M. Elliott, 1836, pp. 12–13.

Books

Orser, Joseph. *The Lives of Chang and Eng: Siam's Twins in Nineteenth-Century America.* Chapel Hill: University of North Carolina Press, 2014. Historian Joseph Orser wrote this biography of Chang and Eng's history through antebellum America, their family lives in North Carolina, their fame, and the shifting racial and cultural landscape of 19th-century American culture and society.

Wu, Cynthia. *Chang and Eng Reconnected: The Original Siamese Twins in American Culture.* Philadelphia, PA: Temple University Press, 2012. American studies professor Cynthia Wu traces the history of Chang and Eng through the terrain of American culture, representations of race, disability, and science vis-à-vis nation-building ideologies and narratives.

Websites

Eng and Chang Bunker: Original Siamese Twins Exhibit, Mount Airy, North Carolina. This site provides a timeline of the twins' life, along with historical background, and images. Surry Arts Council. 2016. http://www.surryarts.org/siamesetwins/index.html. Accessed January 28, 2018.

Eng & Chang Bunker: The Siamese Twins collection. This site presents original primary source material on Chang and Eng Bunker, from the special collections in Wilson Library at the University of North Carolina at Chapel Hill. http://dc.lib.unc.edu/cdm/compoundobject/collection/bunkers/id/504/rec/2. Accessed January 28, 2018.

1893

Queen Liliuokalani, the last native ruler of an independent Hawaii, is deposed in a bloodless coup d'état by five American nationals, one English national, and one German national. All were living and doing business in Hawaii and opposed her efforts to establish a new constitution. President Grover Cleveland refused to annex Hawaii because he felt the Americans in the sugar industry engineered the overthrow and that the Hawaiian people did not want revolution.

FROM this moment dates my official title of Liliuokalani, that being the name under which I was formally proclaimed princess and heir apparent to the throne of my ancestors. Now that this important matter had been decided by those whom the constitution invests with that prerogative, it became proper and necessary for me to make a tour of the islands to meet the people, that all classes, rich and poor, planter or fisherman, might have an opportunity to become somewhat acquainted with the one who some day should be called to hold the highest executive office. The first journey undertaken was that of encircling the island on which the capital city of Honolulu is situated; we therefore started from our home to make the trip around the coast-line of Oahu, a tour of nearly one hundred and fifty miles, following the roads which wind along on the brink of the ocean. This we proposed to do on horseback; although my carriage, where I could rest if required, accompanied the party. Our cavalcade was a large one; my immediate companions being my husband, General J. O Dominis, governor of the island, and my sister, the Princess Likelike, wife of Hon. A. S. Cleghorn, who was attended by her personal suite. But large numbers are no discouragement to Hawaiian hospitality, especially under the additional inspiration of the love and loyalty to their chiefs; so the people opened their doors with an "Aloha nui loa" *to us in words and acts, and wherever we went a grand reception awaited us on arrival. Our route was first to the eastward, past Diamond Head, Koko Head to the point of Makapur, then turning to the northward and around to*

Waimanalo, where we found ourselves the guests of Ah Kua, a very wealthy Chinaman, who owned a large plantation there devoted to the cultivation of rice. Intelligence of our approach must have travelled faster than we had ridden; for as soon as our cavalcade drew near to this estate we were greeted with a discharge of firecrackers and bombs, let off to do honor to the presence of the heir to the throne and her companions. There was no cessation of the salutes during the feast of good things which had been spread by Ah Kau for our refreshment, to which and to the professions of loyalty on the part of our host, we did ample justice. From thence we proceeded to Maunawili, the beautiful residence of Mr. and Mrs. Edwin Boyd, whose doors were already opened for our reception; and here we spent the night and remained an entire day, enjoying the entertainment prepared for us, which can be described in no better terms than by saying that we received a royal welcome indeed. Our progress continued on the day following through Kaneohe, our noonday rest being at the house of Judge Pii, where a generous lunch awaited us on the moment of our arrival. The people of that entire district had congregated to do us honor, and showed us in every way that there was no doubt or disloyalty in their hearts. Yet, while still at Kaneohe, a letter was received by the Princess Likelike from her husband, in which that gentleman advised his wife to return to Honolulu, and stated it was his opinion that if it was the purpose of my tour to meet the people and cultivate their love, the time spent on the route would be wasted because they were all zealous partisans of Queen Emma. My sister acquainted me with these views of her husband, and asked my advice as to her course. I did not wish to influence her in any way, and therefore left it to her option to continue the journey with me, or to take Mr. Cleghorn's advice. But we had already advanced far enough on our pathway amongst the people to prove that her husband had made a great mistake, for no heir to the throne could have been more royally received by all than I had been. The princess had not failed to notice this, and as we proceeded it was still more apparent; the most zealous of Queen Emma's people, now that the question had been officially decided, hastened to do us honor. So, after due consideration, Princess Likelike decided that she would not return. A decision she had no after occasion to regret, and was one which made me very glad; for she was welcomed and showered with marks of favor by the very adherents of Queen Emma, of whose disappointment she had been warned by her husband. It would be tiresome to others, perhaps, should I go on and describe with minute particulars the steps of our party as they passed around the island. From place to place the reception was the same, cheerful, hearty, and enthusiastic,—Kahuku, Waialua, Makahao, Waianae, and so on to our latest stopping-place, which was with Mr. James Campbell and his sweet wife at Honouliuli. He had the advantage of a little more time in his preparations for our reception than was possible to some of our other places of rest, and had spared no pains to give us an ovation in every way worthy of himself and his amiable companion. The result was a manifestation of kind feelings and generous hospitality such as, even at this distant day, cannot, no, nor ever will be, effaced from my memory. From thence we started for Honolulu; and as it was noised abroad that the party would enter the city, there was scarcely space for our cavalcade to pass between the throngs of people which lined our way. From Leleo to Alakea Street it was a mass of moving heads, through which only slowly could our carriages, horses, and outriders pass. It was understood and accepted as a victorious procession; and out of sympathy for the disappointed dowager queen, our people refrained from noisy demonstrations and loud cheering, and instead the men removed their hats, and the women saluted as we passed.

Source: Liliuokalani. *Hawaii's Story by Hawaii's Queen*. Boston: Lee and Shepard, 1898.

Books

Allen, Helena. *The Betrayal of Liliuokalani: Last Queen of Hawaii 1838–1917*. Honolulu: Mutual Publishing, 1982. *The Betrayal of Liliuokalani* focuses on the overthrow of the queen and the impact on the Hawaiian people.

Iaukea, Sydney. *The Queen and I: A Story of Dispossessions and Reconnections in Hawaiʻi*. Berkeley: University of California Press, 2012. *The Queen and I* details the internal intergenerational conflicts in Liliuokalani's time.

Websites

Blatty, David. "Liliuokalani Biography." The Biography.com website. A&E Television Networks, 2015. This site contains a biography, video documentary, and discussion on significant events in Liliuokalani's life. http://www.biography.com/people/liliuokalani-39552. Accessed October 9, 2016.

Liliuokalani. *Hawaii's Story by Hawaii's Queen.* Boston: Lee and Shepard, 1898. Full digital text is available at http://digital.library.upenn.edu/women/liliuokalani/hawaii/hawaii.html. Accessed January 28, 2018.

Also Noteworthy

1907

Ten-year-old Keikichi Aoki is denied admissions to the San Francisco's Redding School because state law provides for a segregated Oriental school.

1989

A gunman shoots and kills five Southeast Asian schoolchildren and wounds 29 other children and one teacher at Cleveland School massacre, in Stockton, California.

1999

A Vietnam video store owner starts a large-scale anticommunism protest after he puts up a flag of Communist Vietnam and photograph of Ho Chi Minh in Little Saigon, Westminster, California.

2013

The San Francisco International Asian American Film Festival (SFIAAFF) announces about changing its name to CAAMFest (Center for Asian American Media Fest). SFIAAFF was founded in 1982 as a joint production of Asian CineVision and the Center for Asian American Media.

January 18

1778

On this day, English explorer Captain James Cook becomes the first European to discover the Hawaiian Islands when he sails by Oahu. He landed on Waimea, on the Kauai, two days later, and named it Sandwich Islands, in honor of John Montagu, who was one of his patrons, and the Earl of Sandwich. The Hawaiians welcomed Cook and his crew. They were also fascinated by his ship and use of iron. Cook resupplied his ship by trading his metal, and his crew traded iron for sex. Cook returned to Hawaii two years later, harboring safely in Hawaii's Kealakekua Bay. The Hawaiians treated Cook and his crew as if they were divine, until one of the crew members died, exposing the Europeans as mortals. Among Hawaiians, Cook is not viewed favorably or as a heroic figure, but rather, as a racist who introduced syphilis to the Hawaii.

When Cook arrived off Kauai in January 1778, his advent coincided with the annual "feast" of Lono, lasting four months roughly from mid-September to mid-January. All the signs were there: the appearance of the Pleiades, the wondrous seabird in which Cook/Lono travelled, the powerful sticks that thundered. Cook's very regime of sexual abstinence helped, for the priests (as mentioned) had devised sexual intercourse as the acid test of whether the travelers were gods or men. The fact that his followers were men did not preclude Cook's being an avatar of Lono; the only thing that raised doubts was the venereal disease the strangers left in their wake—hardly something a god such as Lono would visit on them—and the killing of a man, which seemed more redolent of Ku, the god of war. Nevertheless, on balance, Cook's earlier visit seemed to fit the Lono matrix. The sailors told the Hawaiians that they had come from Tahiti, and in the traditional myth of Lono he had sailed away from Hawaii to Kahiki (Tahiti) after striking his wife in a fit of jealousy, promising that he would return some day. Now, on the second visit, there were even stronger circumstantial pointers. Once again he had arrived in the Makahiki season, when warfare was forbidden, hard work banned, games and sports held, censuses held and taxes collected. Lono's symbol was a long staff bearing a banner of tapa attached to a crosspiece and thus very like the yard of a ship's mast. Traditionally, when Lono came there would be terrible storms, and these had duly manifested themselves during the terrible seven weeks from late November to 17 January. The legend also said that when Lono returned, he would sail slowly round the big island of Hawaii and come to haven at Kealakekua Bay—exactly what Cook had done.

Source: McLynn, Frank. *Captain Cook: Master of the Seas*. New Haven, CT: Yale University Press, 2011, pp. 377–378.

Books

Horwitz, Tony. *Blue Latitudes: Boldly Going Where Captain Cook Has Gone Before*. New York: Henry Holt and Co., 2003. *Blue Latitudes* is a biography of Captain James Cook and his voyages through the Pacific Ocean.

Thomas, Nicholas. *Cook: The Extraordinary Voyages of Captain James Cook*. New York: Walker & Company, 2003. *Cook: The Extraordinary Voyages of Captain James Cook* is a thorough history of James Cook's voyages, his ambition, and legacy of European contact among indigenous populations in Australia, New Zealand, and Hawaii.

Websites

Captain Cook Society. 2017. This site provides a biography of Cook, chronology, primary documents, images, and historical accounts of Cook's three voyages. http://www.captaincooksociety.com/home. Accessed January 28, 2018.

The Wisconsin Historical Society provides a detailed chronology of James Cook's voyage. http://www.captaincooksociety.com/home/detail/the-third-voyage-1776-1780. Accessed January 28, 2018.

January 19

1920

Pablo Manlapit, head of the Filipino Labor Union, unilaterally issues an order for Filipinos to strike and urges the Japanese to join them. By February 1, during a united strike that included 8,300 Filipinos and Japanese strikers, 77 percent of the entire plantation workforce on Oahu brought the plantation to a stop. The strike lasted six months.

In August, 1919, Manlapit organized the Filipino Labor Union (or Filipino Federation of Labor) after at least four months of agitation. The union's sphere of influence was limited to Oahu. Unlike the Federation of Japanese Labor, a grass-roots organization with strong community, professional, business, and monetary support, the Filipino union developed from the top down and lacked any middle-class support. After founding the union, Manlapit conducted a vigorous drive to organize Filipinos in the cane fields. . . .

By 1920 the basic labor issue was that of wages. Postwar inflation had set prices 40 to 50 percent higher but prewar wages of 77¢ a day still prevailed. Changes in wages, the bonus system, and working conditions were demanded. On January 19, 1920, after HSPA rejection of their demands, Manlapit called his union out on strike on five plantations. Some 2,600 workers (and 300 more of other nationalities) struck at Aiea, Waipahu, Ewa, Waialua, and Kahuku. Manlapit had previously asked for support from the Japanese union, which had been making similar protests to the HSPA. On February 2, the entire Japanese work force of these five plantations, in addition to Waimanalo, joined the striking Filipinos.

Source: Sharma, Miriam. "Labor Migration and Class Formation among the Filipinos in Hawaii, 1906–1946." In *Labor Immigration under Capitalism: Asian Workers in the United States before World War II*, edited by Lucie Cheng and Edna Bonacich, pp. 595–596. Berkeley: University of California Press, 1984.

Books

Asher, Robert, and Charles Stephenson, eds. *Labor Divided: Race and Ethnicity in United States Labor Struggles, 1835–1960.* Albany: State University of New York Press, 1990. *Labor Divided* offers a comparative analysis and history of working-class labor struggles in the United States. See Ronald Takaki's Chapter 2, "Ethnicity and Class in Hawaii: The Plantation Labor Experience, 1835–1920."

Kerkvliet, Melinda Tria. *Unbending Cane: Pablo Malapit, a Filipino Labor Leader in Hawai'i.* Honolulu: Office of Multicultural Student Services, University of Hawaii, 2002. *Unbending Cane* is a complete history of Filipino labor leader Pablo Malapit.

Websites

"Filipino American Farmworker History Timeline." Welga! Filipino American Labor Archives and University of California at Davis. This site provides a detailed timeline and online access to the archives. http://welgadigitalarchive.omeka.net/. Accessed October 30, 2016.

"History of Labor in Hawai'i." Center for Labor Education & Research. University of Hawaii—West O'ahu. This site offers a historical overview of labor struggles in Hawaii. https://www.hawaii.edu/uhwo/clear/home/HawaiiLaborHistory.html. Accessed October 30, 2016.

1920

The 1913 California Alien Land Law is amended to close a loophole that permitted Asian immigrants to own or lease land under the names of their native-born children.

The 1920 amendment to the 1913 Webb Act closed the loopholes that had allowed the growth of Japanese agriculture in California. While the new law did not trigger the complete demise of Japanese farming, it made many Japanese families dependent on white landowners, leaving "a legacy of stagnation and powerlessness." The California law, along with similar measures passed by state legislatures throughout the American West . . . had the effect of establishing a "racial cartel in the agricultural property and contract market" that denied Asian immigrants economic rights and prevented "everyday interracial association and intimacy." Under the 1920 law, aliens ineligible for naturalized citizenship could not lease agricultural land at all, nor could they acquire land under the names of American-born minors or land corporations. As a result, between 1920 and 1925, the amount of land Japanese owned in California dropped from close to 75,000 acres to about 42,000 acres, and Japanese-leased lands declined from 192,150 acres to just over 76,000 acres. In contrast to the Alien Land Law of 1913, the 1920 legislation produced a significant decline in Japanese American farming.

Source: Tsu, Cecilia. *Garden of the World: Asian Immigrants and the Making of Agriculture in California's Santa Clara Valley.* Oxford: Oxford University Press, 2013, p. 129.

Books

Buchanan, Paul. *Race Relations in the United States: A Chronology, 1896–2005.* Jefferson, NC: McFarland & Company, Inc., Publishers, 2005. *Race Relations in the United States* offers a comparative and comprehensive summary of policies and events in U.S. history that inform the construction of race. See page 23 for discussion of California's Alien Law Land.

Daniels, Roger. *The Politics of Prejudice: The Anti-Japanese Movement in California and the Struggle for Japanese Exclusion.* Berkeley: University of California Press, 1962. *The Politics of Prejudice* is a historical study of the anti-Japanese prejudice in California from the late 19th century to 1924.

Websites

"The Alien Land Act of 1913." The New Castle: The Future as History. May 31, 2015. This site discusses the history of alien land laws and their impact. http://www.thenewcastle.org/blog/2015/5/31/the-alien-land-act-of-1913. Accessed October 20, 2016.

"Tells Japan's Side of California Case. State's Attitude Inconsistent with Our Previous Acts of Friendship, New Consul Says." *New York Times*, June 30, 1913. This site provides a historical newspaper article that discusses opposition to California's Alien Land Law from a Japanese perspective. http://query.nytimes.com/mem/archive-free/pdf?res=990CE5DD153FE633A25753C3A9609C946296D6CF. Accessed October 20, 2016.

Also Noteworthy

1977

Iva Toguri D'Aquino (July 4, 1916–September 26, 2006), also known as Tokyo Rose, is pardoned by President Gerald Ford. Tokyo Rose, an American, was accused and convicted of eight counts of treason related to her participation in the English language propaganda broadcasts transmitted by Radio Tokyo to Allied soldiers in the South Pacific during World War II.

January 20

1881

Hawaiian king David Kalakaua begins his diplomatic nine-month trip around the world. He departed Honolulu Harbor aboard the steamship *City of Sydney*. He met with rulers and perhaps wanted to find more laborers for Hawaii's plantations. He also wanted to learn the ways of other rulers to better protect his own people. He first went to San Francisco and then Japan, China, Siam (now Thailand), Burma (now Myanmar), India, Egypt, Italy, Belgium, Germany, Austria, France, Spain, Portugal, and England. The *Pacific Commercial Advertiser* published a column of this trip and then turned them all into a book.

Excerpt from "Introduction" in *King Kalakaua's Tour Round the World* (October 1881).

King Kalakaua is the first and only Monarch who has made the tour of the world; and his journey was undertaken for the greatest and noblest purpose, that could animate a King. Looking to ancient times, we find a King of Ithaca who undertook an expedition to settle a point of honor, that affected his neighbor; or an Alexander who marched through Asia to leave a track of desolation behind; and in modern times, we see an adventuring Charles of Sweden, while madly seeking to destroy his neighbors, meet with his own destruction; or a Shah of Persia, traveling to squander barbaric wealth, and to display barbaric tastes; or an Emperor of Brazil, an enlightened and humane man; but who goes abroad to attend scientific congresses and gratify his taste for scientific lore; whereas our Hawaiian King,—our enlightened and humane Pacific Monarch, goes abroad solely for the purpose of benefitting his Kingdom, to promote the welfare of his people; and to make good the noble motto, and device, proclaimed at his accession,—"Hooulu Lahui !"—INCREASE THE NATION!

Source: *King Kalakaua's Tour Round the World: A Sketch of Incidents of Travel, with a Map of the Hawaiian Islands*. Honolulu: Prepared and published by the P.C. Advertiser Co., October 1881.

Books

Allen, Helena. *Kalakaua: Renaissance King*. Honolulu, HI: Mutual Publishing, 1994. This book discusses the life and accomplishments of Hawaii's last king who attempted to revive the Hawaiian population by restoring traditional Hawaiian culture.

Burns, Eugene. *The Last King of Paradise*. New York: Pellegrini and Cudahy, 1952. This volume provides a history of Hawaii through a critical biography of King David Kalakaua.

Websites

Damitio, Vago. "Royal Vagabond—King David Kalakaua—The Merrie Monarch." Vagobond: Real Life Travel. April 6, 2014. This site provides a detailed biography of King Kalakaua with photographs. https://www.pinterest.ca/pin/121104677450191280/. Accessed June 14, 2018.

Kim, Alice. "King Kalakaua's Travels around the World." Hawai'i Digital Newspaper Project. This site contains a short historical account of King Kalakaua's travels and a digital archive of newspapers that covered his voyage. https://sites.google.com/a/hawaii.edu/ndnp-hawaii/Home/historical-feature-articles/king-kalakaua-s-travels-around-the-world. Accessed January 28, 2018.

Also Noteworthy

2001

Elaine Lan Chao is sworn in as the 24th U.S. secretary of labor in the George W. Bush administration for two terms.

January 21

1910

On this day, the U.S. government opens an immigration state on Angel Island in the San Francisco Bay. Angel Island is commonly referred to as the "Ellis Island of the West." The Exclusion Act prohibited passengers on ships to disembark until immigration officials inspected and approved them. From 1898 to 1910, immigration inspection at San Francisco occurred on the Pacific Mail Steamship dock in a dilapidated two-story shed. It was infamous for being unsanitary, overcrowded, unsafe, and easy to escape from. As a result, in 1904, Congress appropriated $250,000 to build a Bureau of Immigration Station Angel Island. Approximately 100,000 Chinese migrants entered the United States through San Francisco from 1910 to 1940. Nearly half were admitted directly from their ships, and the other half were detained on Angel Island. Angel Island enforced immigration policies that targeted Asians for exclusion.

Chinese were first subjected to a primary inspection on the steamship that had carried them. After receiving identification numbers, new arrivals were sent to the hospital for a medical examination. There the staff examined their bodies for physical defects and even measured their body parts to determine their ages. . . .

Chinese immigrants found these examinations extremely humiliating. They were unaccustomed to being naked in front of strangers, let alone forced to provide stool samples on demand so that the hospital staff could test for disease. "When the doctor came, I had to take off all my clothes. It was so embarrassing and shameful," Lee Puey You recalled in 1939. She was held for 20 months and then sent back to China. She later told interviewers that she cried a "bowlful of tears" on Angel Island. . . .

To combat the "paper son" system, Angel Island officials gave particularly strong scrutiny to cases involving families. As a routine part of the interrogations, prospective immigrants were questioned about a wealth of minute details concerning their family histories, relationships, and everyday life in the home villages—things immigration officials believed should be common knowledge to all parties.

Source: Lee, Erika. "'The Chinese Must Go!'" *Reason* 47, no. 10 (2016): pp. 42–49.

Books

Barde, Robert. *Immigration at the Golden Gate: Passenger, Ships, Exclusion, and Angel Island.* Westport, CT: Praeger, 2008. *Immigration at the Golden Gate* demonstrates various aspects of how newcomers experience immigration on the West Coast.

Lee, Erika, and Judy Yung. *Angel Island: Immigrant Gateway to America.* Oxford: Oxford University Press, 2010. Historians Erika Lee and Judy Yung tell the full history of the Asian immigrants and their experiences on Angel Island through oral histories and copious research.

Websites

Angel Island Conservancy. This site discusses the history of Angel Island, the paper sons phenomenon, and Chinese immigration during the era of exclusion. http://angelisland.org/history/united-states-immigration-station-usis/. Accessed October 14, 2016.

"U.S. Immigration Station, Angel Island San Francisco Bay, California." National Park Service.

U.S. Department of the Interior. This site documents the history of Angel Island immigration station with photographs. https://www.nps.gov/nr/travel/Asian_American_and_Pacific_Islander_Heritage/US-Immigration-Station-Angel-Island.htm. Accessed October 14, 2016.

1974

The U.S. Supreme Court in *Lau v. Nichols* rules that school districts with children who speak little English must provide them with bilingual education. The Court said, "The failure of the San Francisco school system to provide English language instruction to approximately 1,800 students of Chinese ancestry who do not speak English, or to provide them with other adequate instructional procedures, denies them a meaningful opportunity to participate in the public educational program and thus violates 601 of the Civil Rights Act of 1964."

U.S. Supreme Court Decision of 1974: Lau v. Nichols. *This decision places an obligation on school districts to remove language barriers that have the effects of excluding children from full participation in public education. The* Lau v. Nichols *case was responsible for the U.S. bilingual education system as we know it. In the decision, the Supreme Court declared that it was the responsibility of the school, and not the parents, to teach children in their native languages. Prior to this time, most Americans believed that it was primarily the responsibility of the parents to maintain their children's native tongue.* Lau v. Nichols *changed that entire orientation of the schools toward language minority students.*

Source: Jeynes, William. *American Educational History: School, Society, and the Common Good.* Los Angeles: Sage, 2007, p. 296.

Books

Gonzalez, Josue, ed. *Encyclopedia of Bilingual Education*. Los Angeles, CA: Sage, 2008. *Encyclopedia of Bilingual Education* is a complete general reference that covers issues and topics related to bilingual education.

Olivas, Michael, and Ronna Schneider, eds. *Education Law Stories*. New York: Foundation Press, 2008. *Education Law Stories* covers major landmark court cases dealing with educational issues. Chapter 5 focuses on *Lau v. Nichols*.

Websites

Bon, Susan. Lau v. Nichols. Education Law. This site provides the legal summary of *Lau v. Nichols* that includes a discussion of its background, facts of the case, and court ruling. http://usedulaw.com/362-lau-v-nichols.html. Accessed January 17, 2017.

Lau v. Nichols (1974). JUSTIA U.S. Supreme Court. This site provides the full text for the *Lau v. Nichols* ruling. https://supreme.justia.com/cases/federal/us/414/563/case.html. Accessed January 17, 2017.

Also Noteworthy

1910

Angel Island Immigration Station, located in the San Francisco Bay, begins operation and stays open until November 5, 1940. During this period, the immigration station, or detention facility, held hundreds of thousands of immigrants from China, Japan, India, and the Philippines.

1976

Miyako Oriental Foods is founded at 404 Towne Avenue, Los Angeles, California.

1977

President Jimmy Carter extends a full and unconditional pardon to nearly 10,000 men who evaded the Vietnam War draft.

2009

Steven Chu is sworn in as the 12th U.S. secretary of energy in President Barack Obama's administration.

January 22

2009

On this day, *Gran Torino*, the first mainstream American film to feature Hmong Americans, opens in Australia and New Zealand. The film had a limited release earlier in North America on December 12, 2008, and then on January 2009, it opened worldwide. *Gran Torino* publicized the Laotian refugee community's problems, such as youth gang activity. The film is about the relationship between a disgruntled Korean War veteran, Walt Kowalski (Clint Eastwood), and his young neighbor, Thao Vang Lor (Bee Vang). Thao attempted to steal Walt's 1972 Ford Gran Torino, as an initiation into a Hmong gang. The two eventually developed a friendly relationship as Walt attempts to assist Thao out of the gang. Critics of the film argued that it represents Walt, a white male, as a Christ-like figure who saves a minority. Fans argued that it provides a realistic representation of Hmong American youth gangs.

The ongoing elaboration of Hmong American hyperviolence in popular discourse took spectacular form in Clint Eastwood's 2008 feature Gran Torino. *Alongside the menace of armed Hmong men, however, emerged other figures of masculinity and femininity to be explored further here. The production, rumored to be the last film in which Eastwood would act, authenticated the Hmong types it purveyed through its casting and publicizing of purportedly "natural" actors. In search of Hmong actors for ten leads and supporting roles, Warner Brothers worked through Hmong community organizations in Fresno, St. Paul, and Detroit to hold open casting calls. Hundreds turned out. Amazingly, all but one of those eventually chosen were first-time actors. Euphoric at their role in this history-making venture, they threw themselves into creating credible characters and improvising Hmong language lines on camera. . . .*

Gran Torino's *story predictably centers on Eastwood's character, Walt Kowalski, a grumpy Korean War veteran of Polish descent estranged from his own family after his wife's death. The action is propelled by the contest between a hapless newcomer Hmong family and a predatory Hmong street gang who struggle over the soul of a teenage boy. Eastwood's character gets drawn into his neighboring Hmong family after their teenage son Thao tries to steal his vintage Gran Torino vehicle on a dare from the gang. Eastwood then becomes a paternal figure toward the boy when he exacts physical labor as payback for the attempted theft. Not only does he tutor Thao in masculine forms of work, but he presumes to "man up" the boy, liberating him from the effeminacy apparently imposed on him by his domineering mother and sister (and implicitly his race). Eventually, Walt becomes more and more of a white savior trying to intervene to keep the boy from the gang.*

Source: Schein, Louisa, Va-Megn Thoj, Bee Vang, and Ly Chong Thong Jalao. "Beyond *Gran Torino*'s Guns: Hmong Cultural Warriors Performing Genders." *positions: east asia cultures critique* 20, no. 3 (2012): pp. 768–769.

Books

Chan, Sucheng. *Hmong Means Free: Life in Laos and America.* Philadelphia, PA: Temple University Press, 1994.

Hein, Jeremy. *Ethnic Origins: The Adaptation of Cambodian and Hmong Refugees in Four American Cities.* New York: Russell Sage Foundation, 2006.

Websites

Hamlin, Andrew. "'Gran Torino' Falls Short on Depiction of Hmong." *Northwest Asian Weekly* 28, no. 2 (January 3–9, 2009). This essay is a critique of *Gran Torino*'s depiction of the Hmong American community. http://nwasianweekly.com/2008/12/%E2%80%98gran-torino%E2%80%99-falls-short-on-depiction-of-hmong/. Accessed September 1, 2017.

Reyes-Ortiz, Krissy. "Gran Torino Actor Reveals Behind-the-Scenes Racism." Bottom Line. University of California, Santa Barbara. January 25, 2011. This essay shares

Hmong American cast members' perception of racism during the filming of *Gran Torino*. https://thebottomline.as.ucsb.edu/2011/01/gran-torino-actor-reveals-behind-the-scenes-racism. Accessed September 1, 2017.

Also Noteworthy

1941

Time magazine publishes an article entitled "How to Tell Your Friends from the Japs" that explains arbitrary racial distinctions between a person of Chinese heritage and a person of Japanese heritage.

1943

During World War II in the Pacific, the Allied forces get its first land victory in the war when Japanese resistance ended in New Guinea.

1973

The U.S. Supreme Court rules in *Roe v. Wade* decision, in a 7–2 ruling, that legalizes abortion, using a trimester approach.

2008

In Blaine, Minnesota, three men use bottles of combustible liquid to set fire in a convenience store. The word "Arab" was spray-painted on the store.

January 23

1930

On this day, anti-Filipino riot in Watsonville, California, involving disputes between Filipino American farm workers and local residents opposed to immigration ends. The riot started on January 19, when groups of white vigilantes attacked Filipino clubs and dance halls. Many have argued that this riot resulted due to Filipino men interacting with white women, or rather, white female entertainers at the Palm Beach Filipino Club in Watsonville. Fermin Tobera, a 22-year-old laborer, was killed, and seven suspects were arrested, but none was convicted of any crime. However, besides the sexual fear of Filipino men on white women, the riot revealed the conflict and hostility of Filipino laborers who competed with white laborers. This economic conflict resulted in labor arguments and anti-Chinese and anti-Japanese rhetoric use to incite vigilante violence against those two Asian communities earlier. Moreover, similar to earlier anti-Chinese and anti-Japanese movements, anti-Filipino sentiments were used by white politicians to pander support. The Watsonville anti-Filipino riot caused great anger and resentment among Filipinos in the Philippines. As such, they declared it "National Humiliation Day."

His name was Fermin Tobera, a lettuce picker. Dead by gunshot through the heart. He was 22.

Exactly 59 years ago this January, Tobera became the first casualty in what is known as the Watsonville race riots, the violent series of events which resulted from anti-Filipino prejudice in Northern California's farm belt.

Tobera was one of the first Filipino immigrant who came to this country as recruited field workers in the 1920s. A number of them became service workers—janitors, houseboys and bellhops. . . .

Fermin Tobera was a "manong," the term today commonly used by Filipinos—especially those who rediscovered their roots in the 1970s and 1980s—to refer to their pioneers. Manong literally translates to "brother" or "cousin" in Ilocano, the language spoken in northern Philippines, the region of the majority of the first Filipino Americans. . . .

In January 1930 a band of white youths charged into the dance halls and labor crew barracks, and put to an end Tobera's short life and dreams. To the killers' minds the Filipinos were taking away their women, and their jobs.

The San Francisco Chronicle screamed the tragedy in its January 26, 1930 headline "Race Riot Menace Spreads to L.A." The story told of white lawmakers' revilement of Filipinos.

Source: Querol, Cherie. "Filipinos Recall Watsonville Riots of a Half Century Ago." *Asian Week*, January 13, 1989.

Books

DeWitt, Howard. *Anti-Filipino Movements in California: A History, Bibliography and Study Guide.* San Francisco, CA: R and E Research Associates, 1976. *Anti-Filipino Movements in California* covers various aspects of the history of Filipino laborers in California and anti-Filipino history with a comprehensive bibliography.

DeWitt, Howard. *Violence in the Fields: California Filipino Farm Labor Unionization during the Great Depression.* Saratoga, CA: Century Twenty One Publishing, 1980. *Violence in the Fields* offers a comprehensive history of Filipino laborers in California.

Websites

"Depression Era: 1930s: Watsonville Riots." Picture This: California Perspectives on American History. Oakland Museum of California. This essay provides a historical overview of intersection of the Great Depression and racial conflicts in the United States, in particular, through a focused discussion of the anti-Filipino riots at Watsonville, California. http://picturethis.museumca.org/timeline/depression-era-1930s/watsonville-riots/info. Accessed January 12, 2017.

Jones, Donna. "Riots in 1930 Revealed Watsonville Racism: California Apologizes to Filipino Americans." *Santa Cruz Sentinel*, September 4, 2011. This article discusses the history of the riots, their legacy, and reconciliation between the Filipino American community and the state of California. http://www.santacruzsentinel.com/article/ZZ/20110904/NEWS/110908006. Accessed January 12, 2017.

January 24

1848

Gen. John A. Sutter discovers gold at Coloma. At the beginning of 1849, there were only 54 "Chinamen" in California. They arrived wanting to be miners, but many would become a source of cheap labor for railroads, mines, fisheries, farms, orchards, canneries, garment and cigar factories, and so on along the Pacific coast. By 1876, there were 151,000 in the United States, and 116,000 in California.

Excerpt from Gen. John A. Sutter's personal account of discovering gold and its impact on his life. Published in *Hutchings' California Magazine* in November 1857.

It was in the first part of January, 1848, when the gold was discovered at Coloma, where I was then building a saw-mill. The contractor and builder of this mill was James W. Marshall, from New Jersey. In the fall of 1847, after the mill seat had been located, I sent up to this place Mr. P. L. Wimmer with his family, and a number of laborers, from the disbanded Mormon Battalion; and a little later I engaged Mr. Bennet from Oregon to assist Mr. Marshall in the mechanical labors of the mill. Mr. Wimmer had the team in charge, assisted by his young sons, to do the necessary teaming, and Mrs. Wimmer did the cooking for all hands. . . .

So soon as the secret was out my laborers began to leave me, in small parties first, but then all left, from the clerk to the cook, and I was in great distress; only a few mechanics remained to finish some very necessary work which they had commenced, and about eight invalids, who continued slowly to work a few teams, to scrape out the mill race at Brighton. The Mormons did not like to leave my mill unfinished, but they got the gold fever like everybody else. After they had made their piles they left for the Great Salt Lake. So long as these people have been employed by me they have behaved very well, and were industrious and faithful laborers, and when settling their accounts there was not one of them who was not contented and satisfied. . . .

By this sudden discovery of the gold, all my great plans were destroyed. Had I succeeded for a few years before the gold was discovered, I would have been the richest citizen on the Pacific shore; but it had to be different. Instead of being rich, I am ruined, and the cause of it is the long delay of the United States Land Commission of the United States Courts, through the great influence of the squatter lawyers. Before my case will be decided in Washington, another year may elapse, but I hope that justice will be done me by the last tribunal—the Supreme Court of the United States. By the Land Commission and the District Court it has been decided in my favor. The Common Council of the city of Sacramento, composed partly of squatters, paid Adelpheus Felch, (one of the late Land Commissioners, who was engaged by the squatters during his office), $5,000, from the fund of the city, against the will of the tax-payers, for which amount he has to try to defeat my just and old claim from the Mexican government, before the Supreme Court of the United States in Washington.

Source: Sutter, John. "The Discovery of Gold in California." The Virtual Museum of the City of San Francisco. http://www.sfmuseum.org/hist2/gold.html. Accessed January 28, 2018.

Books

Brands, H. W. *The Age of Gold: The California Gold Rush and the New American Dream.* New York: Random House, 2008. Historian H. W. Brands offers a readable account of the gold rush and the early history of the state of California.

Sederquist, Betty. *Coloma: Images of America.* Charleston, SC: Arcadia Publishing, 2012. This volume provides historic images of the gold rush in Coloma.

Websites

The California Department of Parks and Recreation produces a pamphlet that provides a timeline of main events, images, and maps of the discovery of gold at Marshall Gold Discovery State Historic Park. https://www.parks.ca.gov/pages/484/files/MarshallGoldFinalWebLayout032615.pdf. Accessed February 4, 2018.

The Virtual Museum of the City of San Francisco provides various primary sources related to the gold rush. The archive includes eyewitness accounts of gold discovery, newspaper coverage, images, and a detailed chronology of the gold rush. http://www.sfmuseum.org/hist2/gold.html. Accessed January 28, 2018.

Also Noteworthy

1985

Ellison Shoji Onizuka (June 24, 1946–January 28, 1986) is the first Japanese American and first Asian American to become an astronaut on the space shuttle *Discovery*. Onizuka embarked on a second expedition on January 28, 1986, but shortly after lifting off, the space shuttle *Challenger* broke apart. Onizuka, along with six other astronauts, died.

1992

Psi Chi Omega, an Asian American interest fraternity, is established at the University of California, San Diego.

2007

In Newark, New Jersey, a mosque is set on fire.

January 25

1901

On this day, the Chinese Consolidated Benevolent Association in San Francisco is formally registered with the state of California. However, it was established in 1882. One of the objectives was to provide leadership in the Chinese community to fight against anti-Chinese legislation. The Chinese in New York established Chinese Consolidated Benevolent Association in 1883.

The Chinese Consolidated Benevolent Association (CCBA), or Zhonghua Huiguan, was founded in San Francisco following passage of the Chinese Exclusion Act (1882) to facilitate the need for a more unified and inclusive approach to state and national political discrimination. The CCBA initially differed from other ethnic associations in the immigrant community because it represented a unification of organizations and was dedicated to fighting social segregation, halting anti-Chinese legislation, lobbying politicians, and pursing lawsuits against discriminatory laws. Since its inception, a number of consolidated benevolent associations have been established throughout the United States in locations such as New York, Boston, Philadelphia, New England, and Los Angeles. However, these newer organizations have often deferred to the original in San Francisco. Throughout its existence the CCBA has argued against the Geary Act (1892), sought to repeal the Exclusion Act, lobbied to reform U.S. immigration legislation, defended civil rights, and actively supported Taiwanese nationalism.

Source: Morton, Sean. "Chinese Consolidated Benevolent Association." In *Chinese Americans: The History and Culture of a People*, edited by Jonathan H.X. Lee, p. 167. Santa Barbara, CA: ABC-CLIO, 2016.

Books

Kuah-Pearce, Khun Eng, and Evelyn Hu-Dehart, eds. *Voluntary Organizations in the Chinese Diaspora*. Hong Kong: Hong Kong University Press, 2006. This volume provides an overview of Chinese voluntary organizations among the overseas Chinese communities. See Zhou Min and Rebecca Kim's Chapter 10, "The Paradox of Ethnicization and Assimilation: The Development of Ethnic Organizations in the Chinese Immigrant Community in the United States."

Lai, Him Mark. 2004. *Becoming Chinese American: A History of Communities and Institutions*. Walnut Creek, CA: AltaMira Press, 2004. This volume is a collection of essays by historian Him Mark Lai on the history of the Chinese in America. See Chapter 3, "The Chinese Consolidated Benevolent Association/Huiguan System."

Websites

Chinese Consolidated Benevolent Association. September 8, 2016. This site provides a history of the CCBA, in addition to current news, personnel, members, and events. http://www.ccbanyc.org/eaboutus.html. Accessed June 14, 2018.

Lai, Him Mark. "Historical Development of the Chinese Consolidated Benevolent Association/Huiguan System." The Him Mark Lai Digital Archive. Chinese Historical Society of America. The article, originally published in *Chinese America: History and Perspectives*, 1987, pp. 13–15, is available on this site. http://himmarklai.org/digitized-articles/1986-1990/historical-development-of-the-chinese-consolidated-benevolent-association/. Accessed January 28, 2018.

January 26

1942

The *Hearst Newspapers* on the West Coast launches a vilifying attack on Japanese Americans and begins the public outcry for a mass exclusion policy. William Randolph Hearst promoted the idea of a "yellow peril" that described a threat of Japanese immigration, and by extension, Asian immigration, as a precursor to a Japanese-cum-Asian invasion of the United States. In the early 1900s, Mr. Hearst believed that a Japanese invasion was imminent.

The incarceration of Japanese Americans during World War II was a culmination of a long history of anti-Chinese and anti-Japanese sentiment on the West Coast. The agitation was in part due to special interest and white supremacy groups such as the Native Sons of the Golden West, the American Legion, the Japanese Exclusion League and the American Federation of Labor in California, but the press of the day played a large part in whipping up racial tension and a contagious lynch-mob hysteria.

Perhaps most influential in perpetuating the prejudice against Asian Americans were the writings of the Hearst and McClatchy newspapers, both of which advocated the exclusion of Americans of Japanese and Chinese ancestry in vicious "Yellow Peril" campaigns. The inflammatory editorials and news columns roused outrage among white Californians and led to the perception that Japanese Americans were responsible for the attack on Pearl Harbor.

Recently, on the 50th anniversary of the signing of Executive Order the San Francisco Examiner, one of the most vituperative of the sheets calling for exclusion and internment of Japanese Americans following Pearl Harbor, apologized in an editorial:

. . . The commemoration of the 50th anniversary offers us—individually and collectively—an opportunity to reflect on our past and remember the lessons learned. The Examiner takes this occasion to apologize to the Japanese American community for our wrong judgment 50 years ago.

Newspapers are the products of human beings—reflecting all their shortcomings as well as their talents, their myopia as well as their broader vision.

Source: Sherry, Linda. "Hearst Publication Publicly Apologizes to Japanese Americans for Rabble-Rousing 50 Years Ago." *Asian Week*, February 28, 1992.

Books

Daniels, Roger. *The Politics of Prejudice: The Anti-Japanese Movement in California and the Struggle for Japanese Exclusion*. Berkeley: University of California Press, 1962. *The Politics of Prejudice* discusses various aspects of anti-Japanese racism in California history.

Roxworthy, Emily. *The Spectacle of Japanese American Trauma: Racial Performativity and World War II*. Honolulu: University of Hawaii Press, 2008. *The Spectacle of Japanese American Trauma* argues that U.S. anti-Japanese policies during World War II impacted the lives of Japanese Americans after the war.

Websites

"A More Perfect Union. Japanese Americans & the U.S. Constitution." Smithsonian National Museum of American History. This site provides a general chronology of Japanese American history and a chronology of anti-Japanese activities in the United States. http://amhistory.si.edu/perfectunion/resources/history.html#IMMIGRATION. Accessed September 1, 2017.

"Yellow Peril." Densho Digital Repository. 2017. This site provides digital images of Hearst Newspapers' anti-Japanese publications. http://ddr.densho.org/browse/topics/185/. Accessed September 1, 2017.

January 27

1908

Seventy South Asians are driven out of Live Oak, California, by a white mob for not being able to "observe the laws of decency." The town formed a vigilante group to remove all South Asian farm workers. They marched to their camp, burned it down, beat and terrorized the farmworkers, and drove them out of the town. Efforts to obtain justice through the courts failed because white witnesses provided alibis for the accused.

In the initial years of their migration, Indians in the US were often the targets of racially motivated campaigns: students were hazed in universities, while bunkhouses of Indian workers were attacked by white laborers. Protests against "Hindus" buying land for farming coincided with campaigns opposed to Asiatic immigration that described the Asians as the "Yellow Peril" and Indians as a "Tide of Turbans." Political parties and exclusivist organizations, along with a section of the media, seem to have fanned the fires of this hatred. Indians were described as people willing to take up jobs for cheap wages, thus taking away the work of local labor. Whites in Marysville, California drove out Indians from Live Oak. A mob attacked houses occupied by 70 Hindus who had been discharged from the Southern Pacific Transportation Company. In Bellingham, Washington, violent white mobs expelled Sikhs in September 1907. The Asiatic Exclusion League, which emerged as the most significant organization aimed at preventing and opposing the entry of Asians into the US, directed some of its attacks at Indians.

Source: Janardhanan, Vinod. "Political Participation of the Indian Diaspora in the USA." *Journal of International and Global Studies* 5, no. 1 (2013): p. 17.

Books

Leonard, Karen Isaksen. *The South Asian Americans*. Westport, CT: Greenwood Press, 1997. This volume discusses various aspects of the South Asian American history experience and community development.

Singh, Pashaura, and Louis Fenech, eds. *The Oxford Handbook of Sikh Studies*. Oxford: Oxford University Press, 2014. See Chapter 43 by Jaideep Singh, "Sikhs as a Racial and Religious Minority in the US."

Websites

Cahn, David. "The 1907 Bellingham Riots in Historical Context." Seattle Civil Rights & Labor History Project. University of Washington. 2008. This site provides a detailed history of this riot, historical photographs, and link to *Present in All That We Do*, a documentary film about this riot. http://depts.washington.edu/civilr/bham_history.htm. Accessed October 14, 2016.

"Sikhism in America." The Pluralism Project. Harvard University. 2017. This site provides a detailed chronology of Sikh American history. http://pluralism.org/timeline/sikhism-in-america/. Accessed September 1, 2017.

Also Noteworthy

1973

All warring parties in the Vietnam War sign a cease-fire. It was signed in Paris by Henry Kissinger and Le Duc Tho.

2017

President Donald Trump signs Executive Order 13769, titled "Protecting the Nation from Foreign Terrorist Entry into the United States," popularly referred to as the "Muslim ban."

January 28

1943

The War Department restores the rights of Nisei Japanese Americans to volunteer in a segregated combat unit in the army. The Nisei embraced the policy enthusiastically, but their Issei relatives were disheartened because they were not allowed to volunteer. As such, the overall morale of Japanese Americans was low. Even though, nearly 10,000 Nisei from Hawaii volunteered. Another 1,200 volunteered from the mainland. The majority of the volunteers were living at internment camps during that time.

War Department policy toward Nisei enlistment took a dramatic turn in January 1943, when the War Department announced the formation of an all-volunteer Nisei combat unit, the 442d Regimental Combat Team (RCT). The War Department did not mention that many of the volunteers would be assigned not to the 442d RCT but to the Military Intelligence Service (MIS). Hawaii Nisei greeted the announcement with great enthusiasm. War Department planners hoped for 1,500 volunteers, but 10,000 rushed to enlist. Grown men wept when turned away for medical reasons or age. The Hawaiian Department raised the quota to 2,500, the maximum local authorities would allow given Hawaii's manpower shortage, and agreed to permit 20 percent of Nisei soldiers serving in noncombat units in Hawaii to volunteer. Eventually 2,686 Hawaii Nisei enlisted and sailed for the mainland with great fanfare on 4 April 1943.

Source: McNaughton, James. *Nisei Linguists: Japanese Americans in the Military Intelligence Service during World War II*. Washington, DC: Department of the Army, 2007, p. 133.

Books

Ng, Wendy. *Japanese American Internment during World War II: A History and Reference Guide.* Westport, CT: Greenwood Press, 2002. *Japanese American Internment during World War II* provides a variety of resources, such as a chronology, biographies, primary documents, and narrative history to assist readers in understanding the Japanese American internment experience during World War II.

Robinson, Greg. *By Order of the President: FRD and the Internment of Japanese Americans.* Cambridge, MA: Harvard University Press, 2001. *By Order of the President* addresses history of various policies related to Japanese Americans during World War II.

Websites

Niiya, Brian. "Japanese Americans in Military during World War II." *Densho Encyclopedia,* March 5, 2014. This essay provides a comprehensive history of Japanese American military history. http://encyclopedia.densho.org/Japanese_Americans_in_military_during_World_War_II/. Accessed September 1, 2017.

Wakamatsu, Peter. "442nd Regimental Combat Team." 2017. This site is dedicated to the history and preservation of primary archival documents related to the 442nd Regimental Combat Team. http://www.the442.org/activation.html. Accessed September 2, 2017.

January 29

1979

On this day, President Jimmy Carter meets with deputy premier of China, Deng Xiaoping, and signs new historic accords that reversed decades of U.S. opposition to the People's Republic of China. Later this year, the United States granted full diplomatic recognition to the People's Republic of China. Owing to Deng leadership, China's economy grew, and Chinese citizens became wealthier and enjoyed more personal and cultural freedoms. China continued to be an authoritative one-party state. The renewal of U.S.-China diplomacy would impact the Chinese American community and, eventually, demographic developments within the community.

At the invitation of the President of the United States of America and Mrs. Carter, the Vice-Premier of the State Council of the People's Republic of China Deng Xiaoping and Madame Zhuo Lin are on an official visit to the United States which lasts from January 29 to February 4, 1979. Vice-Premier Deng and President Carter held talks on questions of mutual interest in Washington. Accompanying Vice-Premier Deng in the talks were Vice-Premier Fang Yi, Foreign Minister Huang Hua and others. Accompanying President Carter in the talks were Vice President Mondale, Secretary of State Cyrus Vance, Assistant to the President for National Security Affairs Zbigniew Brzezinski and others.

The talks were cordial, constructive and fruitful. The two sides reviewed the international situation and agreed that in many areas they have common interests and share similar points of view. They also discussed those areas in which they have differing perspectives. They reaffirm that they are opposed to efforts by any country or group of countries to establish hegemony or domination over others, and that they are determined to make a contribution to the maintenance of international peace, security and national independence. The two sides consider that the difference in their social systems should not constitute an obstacle to their strengthening friendly relations and cooperation. They are resolved to work toward this end, and they firmly believe that such cooperation is in the interest of their two peoples and also that of peace and stability in the world and the Asia-Pacific region in particular.

Vice-Premier Deng Xiaoping on behalf of the Government of the People's Republic of China and President Carter on behalf of the United States Government signed an Agreement on Cooperation in Science and Technology and a Cultural Agreement. Vice-Premier Fang Yi and the President's Science Adviser Frank Press signed and exchanged letters of understanding on cooperation between the two countries in education, agriculture and space. Vice-Premier Fang Yi and Secretary of Energy James Schlesinger signed an Accord between the two countries on Cooperation in the Field of High Energy Physics. Foreign Minister Huang Hua and Secretary of State Cyrus Vance signed an Agreement on the Mutual Establishment of Consular Relations and the Opening of Consulates General in each other's country.

Each side agreed to facilitate the accreditation of resident journalists by the other side.

The two sides agreed to conclude trade, aviation, and shipping agreements. These will be discussed during the visits to the People's Republic of China by Secretary of the Treasury Michael Blumenthal and Secretary of Commerce Juanita Kreps.

On behalf of the Chinese Government and Premier Hua Guofeng, Vice-Premier Deng Xiaoping extended an invitation to President Carter to visit China at a time convenient to him. President Carter accepted this invitation. President Carter extended an invitation to Premier Hua Guofeng to visit the United States. Vice-Premier Deng Xiaoping accepted this invitation on behalf of Premier Hua Guofeng. The specific time for these visits by the top leaders of the two countries will be discussed and decided upon at a later time.

Source: Carter, Jimmy. "Visit of Vice Premier Deng of China Joint Press Communiqué." February 1, 1979. Online by Gerhard Peters and John T. Woolley. The American Presidency Project. http://www.presidency.ucsb.edu/ws/?pid=31546. Accessed March 1, 2018.

Books

Dillon, Michael. *Deng Xiaoping: The Man Who Made Modern China*. London: I.B. Tauris, 2015. *Deng Xiaoping* tells the story of Deng's achievement in liberalizing China's economy and the impact of his brutal suppression of the democracy movement at Tiananmen Square.

Vogel, Ezra. *Deng Xiaoping and the Transformation of China*. Cambridge, MA: Harvard University Press, 2011. Ezra Vogel examines the impact of Deng Xiaoping's economic, social, and technological reforms and transformations.

Websites

"China Policy." Office of the Historian, Bureau of Public Affairs. U.S. Department of State. This site provides an overview history of U.S.-China foreign policy, leading to the historic meeting between Carter and Deng, and its legacy. https://history.state.gov/milestones/1977-1980/china-policy. Accessed September 2, 2017.

"The Establishment of Sino-U.S. Diplomatic Relations and Vice Premier Deng Xiaoping's Visit to the United States." Ministry of Foreign Affairs of the People's Republic of China. 2014. This essay narrates the issues and history of the Carter–Deng meeting, from a Chinese perspective. http://www.fmprc.gov.cn/mfa_eng/ziliao_665539/3602_665543/3604_665547/t18007.shtml. Accessed September 2, 2017.

Also Noteworthy

1886

Before Washington enters statehood, it passes Alien Land Law policy that prohibited anyone who cannot become a naturalized citizen from the right of land ownership. The law was, in large part, an anti-Chinese measure that allowed cities to deny Chinese licenses for laundries.

1942

Attorney General Francis Biddle issues orders to establish "prohibited zones" from which "enemy aliens" are excluded. Americans of Japanese, German, and Italian ancestry were removed from these areas.

1943

The War Department establishes a registration program, and the War Relocation Authority starts to administer a loyalty questionnaire to all internees over 17 years old by February 3.

1989

The Asian American Music Society is founded as a nonprofit organization dedicated to the continued appreciation of all music.

January 30

1875

On this day, the United States and Hawaii sign Reciprocity Treaty. The treaty was a free-trade agreement between the United States and the Kingdom of Hawaii starting in September 1876. In return, the United States gained lands in the area known as Pu'u Loa that would later house the Pearl Harbor naval base. The treaty led to large investment by Americans in sugar plantations in Hawaii. The treaty was signed on January 30, 1875, ratified by the Kingdom of Hawaii on April 17, 1875, and ratified by the United States on May 31, 1875. The treaty foreshadowed the annexation of Hawaii.

Those for ratifying the treaty said that the strategic location of the Islands would help protect the west coast of the United States militarily. They also felt Hawai'i's location would promote American commercial interests in the Pacific and in Asia. Perhaps the most convincing argument, however, was that if the United States rejected the treaty, Hawai'i—which in 1873 already exported more than a third of its sugar to Australia, New Zealand, and western Canada—would turn to the British colonies for similar treaty and become a part of the British commercial system. With this in mind, the U.S. Senate ratified the Reciprocity Treaty. It went into effect in 1876.

Source: Menton, Linda, and Eileen Tamura. *A History of Hawai'i*. Honolulu: University of Hawaii Press, 1999, p. 64.

Books

Kauanui, J. Kēhaulani. *Hawaiian Blood: Colonialism and the Politics of Sovereignty and Indigeneity*. Durham, NC: Duke University Press, 2008. *Hawaiian Blood* critically examines the arbitrary correlation between ancestry and race as imposed by the U.S. government.

Menton, Linda, and Eileen Tamura. *A History of Hawai'i*. Honolulu: University of Hawaii Press, 1999. This book covers many aspects of the history of Hawaii.

Websites

"A Guide to the United States' History of Recognition, Diplomatic, and Consular Relations, by Country, since 1776: Hawaii." Office of the Historian, Bureau of Public Affairs. U.S. Department of State. This site offers a list and summary of all diplomatic documents related to Hawaii. https://history.state.gov/countries/hawaii. Accessed January 28, 2018.

Monet, Sam. "Treaty of Reciprocity between the United States of America and the Hawaiian Kingdom." Hawaii Resource Library. This site provides the full text of the treaty. http://www.hawaii-nation.org/treaty1875.html. Accessed October 8, 2016.

Also Noteworthy

January 30–31

1968

During the Tet holiday, Lunar New Year, the Viet Cong, under General Vo Nguyen Giap, captures part of the U.S. Embassy in Saigon for six hours. They launched an attack on more than 100 other South Vietnamese cities and towns and caused many U.S. casualties. American forces were able to recapture most areas, and beaten by the Viet Cong, but it was a major setback for the United States, and by extension, a disastrous blow of public support for the war.

January 31

2007

On this day, U.S. congressman Michael Honda (D-San Jose, CA) introduces House

Resolution 121, "Relative to the War Crimes Committed by the Japanese Military during World War II." The resolution urged the government of Japan to issue an apology and provide reparations to surviving "comfort women" who were forced into sexual slavery by the Imperial Japanese Army in occupied territories before and during World War II.

Why comfort women? There were several reasons why the Japanese military decided that comfort stations were necessary. As mentioned previously, Japanese military leaders were very concerned about the rape of civilians by members of the Japanese armed forces—but not out of concern for those civilians. For good strategic reasons, they believed that the antagonism of civilians in occupied territories towards their conquerors was exacerbated by such behaviour. They also believed that a ready supply of women for the armed forces would help to reduce the incidence of rape of civilians. Was the exploitation of women in military-controlled comfort stations effective in preventing widespread random sexual violence by Japanese soldiers? The initiator of the Japanese army comfort women system, General Okamura, reflecting on the Japanese invasion of Wuhan in 1938, stated that random sexual violence occurred in spite of the fact that the Japanese forces had groups of comfort women attached to them. He admitted, therefore, that his scheme was a failure. Until it was revised in February 1942, the Japanese Imperial Army Criminal Law (Article 86, Clause 2) stated that army personnel who committed rape at the same time as looting would be punished by between seven years and life imprisonment. Here rape was regarded as a secondary crime, incidental to looting. It was also a general trend in the Japanese Imperial forces that looting and rape, in particular during combat operations, were not only tolerated but even encouraged by many troop commanders as a means of arousing the fighting spirit in their men. Therefore, it is not surprising that only a small number of soldiers were convicted of rape under this code of conduct each year. In 1939, 15 men were found guilty of looting, rape and manslaughter. Only four soldiers in 1940 and a mere two men in 1941 were convicted of the same crimes. This Japanese official military data looks absurd when it is compared with actual evidence, such as various testimonies presented at the Tokyo War Crimes Tribunal regarding the Rape of Nanjing.

Source: Tanaka, Yuki. *Japan's Comfort Women: The Military and Involuntary Prostitution during War and Occupation*. London: Routledge, 2001, pp. 28–29.

Books

Hicks, George. *The Comfort Women: Japan's Brutal Regime of Enforced Prostitution in the Second World War*. New York: W.W. Norton & Company, Inc., 1997. George Hicks utilizes testimonies of survivors to paint a shockingly graphic abuse of Korean comfort women by the Japanese military during World War II.

Soh, C. Sarah. *The Comfort Women: Sexual Violence and Postcolonial Memory in Korea and Japan*. Chicago, IL: University of Chicago Press, 2009. Sociologist C. Sarah Soh employs historical research and interviews with survivors to investigate how Japanese colonialism and Korean patriarchy informed the fate of Korean comfort women.

Websites

Soh, C. Sarah. The Comfort Women Project. San Francisco State University. 2002. This site provides a historical overview to the comfort women issue and provides multidimensional analysis on the complexity of seeking justice for Korean comfort women. https://web.archive.org/web/20061209130115/http://online.sfsu.edu/~soh/comfortwomen.html. Accessed September 2, 2017.

Wright, Dustin. "Inserting America into Japanese History Woes." Japan Policy Research Institute. 2007. This article discusses the history of comfort women and other war crimes committed by the Japanese military during World War II and also critiques H. Res. 121 for omitting and ignoring U.S. war crimes and U.S. participation in the comfort women program. http://jpri.org/publications/workingpapers/wp112.html. Accessed September 2, 2017.

February

February 1

1901

The Japanese community, religious and business leaders in the San Francisco Bay Area, establish the Japanese Benevolent Society of California (Kashu Nihonjin Jikei Kai) to address the needs of the poor, sick, injured Japanese immigrants and provide a proper burial site for those who passed away. By August 2, the state of California granted the Japanese Benevolent Society of California its nonprofit status, and by the end of the year, it was able to raise more than the $1,400 needed to purchase two acres of land in Colma, California, to use as a cemetery. Exactly one year to the day after the property was acquired, on March 17, 1903, the Jodo Shinshu cleric, Rev. Nishijima Kakuryo (1873–1942), officiated at the opening of the cemetery. Over the years, Japanese Benevolent Society of California also served as a unifying force in the Japanese American community by bringing together the Buddhist, Shinto, and Christian religious organizations, and by participating in local historical, cultural, and memorial events that honor the Japanese heritage in the United States.

Over 100 people gathered at the Japanese Cemetery in Colma, Calif., on Memorial Day to pay tribute to Japanese Americans buried there.

The Japanese Benevolent Society of California (Jikei Kai), a nonprofit organization that has encouraged relations between the Japanese government and the Japanese community of the Bay Area, organized the 57th annual Memorial Day service.

The cemetery was founded in 1901 by members of the Japanese community in San Francisco. The Japanese Benevolent Society has received numerous donations for maintaining the grounds, including grants from Emperor Meiji of Japan in 1906 and Emperor Hirohito in 1937.

The cemetery's Japanese American historical walk offers facts to visitors about the prewar community. A traditional Japanese garden greets visitors and is decorated with imported stone lanterns. The cemetery contains 2,000 gravesites and over 5,000 interments.

There are monuments dedicated to George Ushijima, the "Potato King"; statesman Ayao Hattori, who was sent to alleviate anti-Japanese sentiment in the U.S.; Kyutaro Abiko, publisher of the Nichi Bei Times *and pioneer of Yamato Colony; the Santa Fe Railroad workers; and Dr. Ernest Sturge, a Quaker and physician who devoted his life to work among the Japanese.*

Consul General Yasumasa Nagamine said that two of the first Japanese to come to America in 1852 are buried there.

Source: "Remembering Japanese Buried at Colma Cemetery." *AsianWeek*, May 30, 2008, 8.

Books

Kimura, Yukiko. *Issei: Japanese Immigrants in Hawaii*. Honolulu: University of Hawaii Press, 1988. See Chapter 11, "Major Organizations and Institutions," for a discussion of the history of the Japanese Benevolent Society in Hawaii and its hospital.

Smith, Bradford, Sylvia Shue, Jennifer Lisa Vest, and Joseph Villarreal. *Philanthropy in Communities of Color*. Bloomington: Indiana University Press, 1999. See Chapter 7, "Japanese," for a discussion of various philanthropic organizations in the Japanese American communities, including a discussion of the Japanese Benevolent Society in the United States.

Websites

"Japanese Fishermen's Benevolent Society Building Exhibit." Steveston Historical Society. 2015. This site discusses a branch of the Japanese Benevolent Society in Steveston, British

Columbia, Canada. http://historicsteveston.ca/japanese-fishermens-benevolent-society-building-exhibit/. Accessed June 14, 2018.

Jikei Kai. 2006. This is the official web page for the Japanese Benevolent Society. http://www.jikei-kai.org/. Accessed September 2, 2017.

Also Noteworthy

1909

Korean National Association is established in California to serve as a quasi-governing body for all Korean Americans and to provide leadership to the independence movement.

1943

The 442nd Regimental Combat Team is activated by the U.S. Army. It is comprised of the 100th Battalion from Hawaii and Japanese American volunteers from the continental United States.

2003

Kalpana Chawla, an Indian American research scientist and astronaut, dies as a result of the space shuttle *Columbia* disintegrating while reentering the earth's atmosphere over Texas.

February 2

1966

On this day, the Immigration and Naturalization Service (INS) ends its Chinese Confession Program that started in 1956 as a means for the government to curtail immigration document fraud among Chinese immigrants. Since the passage of the Chinese Exclusion Act of 1882, Chinese laborers were legally barred from immigrating to the United States. When exclusion policies were enforced, Chinese immigrants falsified documents to gain entry into the United States by claiming family relations of exempted classes or descendants of U.S. citizens. Chinese exclusion policies lasted for 61 years, when it ended in 1943, but Chinese immigrants continued to falsify documents as a means to sponsor family members in China over the United States.

This excerpt is from an oral history of San Francisco Chinatown resident Laura Lai.

Most of the members of Mun Ching were immigrant youth from China. They viewed the establishment of socialism in China with hope for an end to the poverty, oppression, foreign domination, and political corruption that had existed in China for decades. During the anti-Communist hysteria of the 1950s, membership in left-wing Chinese organizations declined sharply. Mun Ching, which still had forty to fifty members, decided to move away from progressive politics and do cultural activities instead. It promoted and performed the music, songs, folk dances, and plays coming out of mainland China. It also provided a tutorial program for immigrant high school students, offered use of a library, and encouraged the study of science and technical skills. Him Mark was one of the few American-born members and served as president from 1951 to 1959. The FBI questioned and harassed all the members of Mun Ching for many years, and eventually over half lost their citizenship. Four were indicted and tried in court. The Confession Program was the main avenue used by the FBI to go after the members.

When the FBI knocked on the door and demanded to speak to Laura, Him Mark told them they could not. He told them, "I speak for Laura," and shielded her from their harassment. Laura's family and friends did not want to take part in the Confession Program. Nor did Him Mark's family; his father was a paper son. But because of the Confession Program, Laura did lose her citizenship, which left her with no legal status in the United States. She described what happened: I lost my citizenship for ten years. My father came over as a paper son, and I came over as his legal daughter. As long as he was safe, I was safe. My father had two paper brothers, one older and one younger; my father was in the middle. The older paper brother lived in Sacramento and was tricked by the immigration officer. The officer asked him, why was he protecting his brothers. He then tricked him by saying that his brothers had already confessed, so he should just tell the truth. So the brother told the officer everything, and afterwards he called my father, but by then it was too late. Everything was out. This confession brought so much trouble for Laura's father that he went back to Hong Kong in 1961. Her mother stayed in the United States because she was very sick with diabetes and her daughter-in-law, Jane, was taking care of her. But after one year of separation, she wanted to join her husband in Hong Kong. She was so sick that she had to be in a wheelchair. Laura still did not have her citizenship, and neither did any of her brothers. Him Mark was the only one with a passport who could take her to Hong Kong on the airplane.

Source: Dere, Jean. "Born Lucky: The Story of Laura Lai." In *Chinese America: History & Perspectives—The Journal of the Chinese Historical Society of America*, p. 34. San Francisco, CA: Chinese Historical Society of America with UCLA Asian American Studies Center, 2011.

Books

Lai, Mark. 2004. *Becoming Chinese American: A History of Communities and Institutions*. Walnut Creek, CA: AltaMira Press, 2004.

Zhao, Xiaojian. *Remaking Chinese America: Immigration, Family, and Community, 1940–1965*. New Brunswick, NJ: Rutgers University Press, 2002.

Websites

"Chinese Confession Program." Museum of Chinese in America. 2016. This site provides basic historical facts about the Chinese Confession Program. http://www.mocanyc.org/learn/timeline/chinese_confession_program. Accessed September 2, 2017.

"Register of Chinese Confession Program Investigation Case Files, 1957–1968." National Archives Catalog. This site provides complete information on the confessions obtained through the Chinese Confession Program. https://catalog.archives.gov/id/1565956. Accessed September 2, 2017.

Also Noteworthy

1924

Legionarios Del Trabajo, a Filipino fraternal organization, is established in San Francisco. At its zenith, it has a membership of 3,000, and lodges in all the states, including Hawaii and Alaska.

2002

In Cooper City, Florida, a Muslim mosque and a school are ransacked.

February 3

1994

President William Clinton announces the lifting of the 19-year-old trade embargo with the Republic of Vietnam. The embargo was established in 1975, after the withdrawal of U.S. forces from Vietnam, that marked the end of the Vietnam War. Besides improving economic relations between the United States and Vietnam, President Clinton also wanted to uncover the fate of American prisoners of war (POWs) and missing in action (MIA) who remained unaccounted for after the war. In 2000, six years after lifting the embargo, President Clinton became the first American head of state to visit Vietnam since before the war. Twelve years after lifting the embargo, 325 American servicemen were accounted for, but thousands remain missing. The embargo also impacted Vietnamese Americans' relations with their Vietnamese kin in Vietnam.

President William Clinton's Memorandum on Lifting the Trade Embargo on Vietnam (February 3, 1994)

Subject: *Lifting of the Embargo against Vietnam*

I hereby direct the Secretary of the Treasury to take all appropriate actions to authorize prospectively all trade and financial dealings with Vietnam, and the Secretary of Commerce to exempt Vietnam from existing controls implementing the embargo. Vietnamese assets in the United States or within the possession or control of persons subject to U.S. jurisdiction and that are now blocked should remain blocked until further notice.

In discharging these responsibilities, you are directed to consult with the heads of other Executive departments and agencies as may be appropriate.

WILLIAM J. CLINTON

Source: Clinton, William. "Memorandum on Lifting the Trade Embargo on Vietnam." February 3, 1994. The American Presidency Project. University of California, Santa Barbara. http://www.presidency.ucsb.edu/ws/?pid=49254. Accessed September 2, 2017.

Books

Hershberger, Mary. *Traveling to Vietnam: American Peace Activists and the War.* Syracuse, NY: Syracuse University Press, 1998. *Traveling to Vietnam* chronicles Vietnam War peace activists and their role in Washington's normalization with Vietnam.

Stern, Lewis. *Defense Relations between the United States and Vietnam: The Process of Normalization, 1977–2003.* Jefferson, NC: McFarland & Company, Inc., 2005. Lewis Stern traces the development of U.S.-Vietnam relations since the Vietnam War, with particular attention to the 1990s.

Websites

"Clinton Lifts Trade Embargo against Vietnam." In *CQ Almanac 1994*, 50th ed., 467–468. Washington, DC: Congressional Quarterly, 1995. This site provides an article published in the *Congressional Quarterly* that details President Clinton's announcement on lifting the trade embargo on Vietnam. http://library.cqpress.com/cqalmanac/cqal94-1102509. Accessed September 2, 2017.

Richter, Paul, and Michael Ross. "Clinton Lifts Vietnam Embargo to 'Resolve the Fate' of MIAs." *Los Angeles Times*, February 4, 1994. This article discusses Clinton's reasons for lifting the embargo on Vietnam. http://articles.latimes.com/1994-02-04/news/mn-19139_1_vietnam-veteran. Accessed September 2, 2017.

February 4

1899

This day marks the beginning of the Philippine-American War. The Philippine Islands become a protectorate of the United States under the Treaty of Paris ending the Spanish-American War. The United States acquired the Philippines for $20 million. This was a war between U.S. occupation forces and the Philippines and Filipino insurgents (Filipino Nationalist Army) led by General Emilio Aguinaldo y Famy. The war was officially declared over on July 4, 1902.

Filipinos expected American sympathy and support, for they aspired to establish a self-governing and constitutional republic like that of the Americans. But when the First Philippine Commission, or Schurman Commission, reviewed the Malolos Constitution, it pronounced it inadequate for violating "so many of the vital principles laid down by Hamilton and Madison in the Federalist." To the Schurman Commission, which was constituted in January 1899 and named for its chairman, Cornell University president Jacob Gould Schurman, the misunderstanding reflected in the Filipino charter bespoke a lack of capacity that disqualified them from sovereignty. The Schurman Commission was sent to the Islands prior to the outbreak of the Philippine-American War at Admiral Dewey's behest to help defuse escalating tensions between the American military government and the revolutionaries. . . . [I]t laid the groundwork . . . to map, bound, count, and thus systematically make knowable the new colonial terrain's geography, population, and resources. In so doing, it established the process for generating the abstract institutionalized colonial knowledge that supplied proof of Filipino incapacity to justify American rule, consolidate the colonial state, and warrant America's civilizing interventions.

Source: Anastacio, Leia Castañeda. *The Foundations of the Modern Philippine State: Imperial Rule and the American Constitutional Tradition, 1898–1935*. Cambridge: Cambridge University Press, 2016, p. 28.

Books

Shaw, Angel Velasco, and Luis H. Francia, eds. *Vestiges of War: The Philippine-American War and the Aftermath of an Imperial Dream 1899–1999*. New York: New York University Press, 2002. Essays in this volume provide perspectives on American colonialism in the Philippines through critiques, visual arts, photographs—archival and current—plays, and poetry.

Silbey, David. *A War of Frontier and Empire: The Philippine-American War, 1899–1902*. New York: Hill and Wang, 2007. *A War of Frontier and Empire* is a military history that critically examines the Philippine-American War as an insurgency, a revolution, a guerrilla and conventional war.

Websites

Dumindin, Arnaldo. "Philippine-American War, 1899–1902." 2006. This site provides comprehensive historical data on the Philippine-American War with photographs and links to historical archival materials. http://www.filipinoamericanwar.com/. Accessed October 12, 2016.

"Philippine-American War, 1899–1902." Office of the Historian, Bureau of Public Affairs. U.S. Department of State. This site provides a historical background to the Philippine-American War. https://history.state.gov/milestones/1899-1913/war. Accessed January 28, 2018.

Also Noteworthy

1942

The U.S. Army designates "restricted areas" in which enemy aliens (people of Japanese, German, and Italian ancestry) must observe curfew and are limited in their travel—they are not allowed to travel more than five miles from their homes in these restricted areas.

February 5

1917

On February 5, 1917, the U.S. Congress passes the Immigration Act of 1917. The most stringent law to date, it established a literacy requirement for immigrants over 16 years of age and restricted the entry of "undesirables" from other countries including idiots, alcoholics, poor, criminals, beggars, any person suffering attacks of insanity, aliens who have a physical disability that will restrict them from earning a living in the United States, polygamists, anarchists, prostitutes, and contract laborers. The Immigration Act of 1917 restricted immigration of anyone born in a geographically defined "Asiatic Barred Zone" excluding the Japanese and Filipinos. The Gentlemen's Agreement already restricted immigration of Japanese laborers, and the Philippines was an American colony so they were considered American nationals and had unrestricted entry. On December 14, 1916, President Woodrow Wilson had vetoed, but Congress overrode his veto. The act prohibited immigration from all of Asia and India by drawing an imaginary line from the Red Sea in the Middle East all the way through the Ural Mountains: people living east of the line were not allowed entry to the United States. This act also includes a literacy test requirement. Immigrants from China and Japan were not named because they were already excluded from the United States through the Chinese Exclusion Act of 1882 and Gentlemen's Agreement of 1907. The "Barred Zone" Act was amended in 1946, with the enactment of the Luce-Celler Bill. At that time, Asian Indians were allowed to enter the United States, but the quota was set at 100 persons per year.

CHAP. 29.—An Act to regulate the immigration of aliens to, and the residence of aliens in, the United States.

Be it enacted by the Senate and House of Representatives of the United States of America in Congress assembled, That the world "alien" wherever used in this Act shall include any person not a native-born or naturalized citizen of the United States; but this definition shall not be held to include Indians of the United States not taxed or citizens of the island under the jurisdiction of the United States . . . unless otherwise provided for by existing treaties, persons who are natives of islands not possessed by the United States adjacent to the Continent of Asia, situate south of the twentieth parallel latitude north, west of the one hundred and sixtieth meridian of longitude east from Greenwich, and north of the tenth parallel of latitude south, or who are natives of any country, province, or dependency situate on the Continent of Asia west of the one hundred and tenth meridian of longitude east from Greenwich and east of the fiftieth meridian of longitude east from Greenwich and south of the fiftieth parallel of latitude north, except that portion of said territory situate between the fiftieth and the sixty-fourth meridians of longitude east from Greenwich and the twenty-fourth and thirty-eighth parallels of latitude north, and no alien now in any way excluded from, or prevented from entering, the United States shall be admitted to the United States. The provision next foregoing, however, shall not apply to person of the following status or occupations: Government officers, ministers or religious teachers, missionaries, lawyers, physicians, chemists, civil engineers, teachers, students, authors, artists, merchants, and travelers for curiosity or pleasure, nor to their legal wives or their children under sixteen years of age who shall accompany them or who subsequently may apply for admission to the United States, but such person or their legal wives or foreign-born children who fail to maintain in the United States a status or occupation placing them within the excepted classes shall be deemed to be in the United States contrary to law, and shall be subject to deportation as provided in section nineteen of this Act.

Source: The Statutes at Large of the United States of America. Volume 39, Part I. Washington, DC: Government Printing Office, 1917.

Books

Hing, Bill Ong. *Defining America through Immigration Policy*. Philadelphia, PA: Temple University Press, 2004. *Defining America* is a comparative analysis of the intersection of race and U.S. immigration policies.

Tichenor, Daniel. *Dividing Lines: The Politics of Immigration Control in America*. Princeton, NJ: Princeton University Press, 2002. *Dividing Lines* explores various aspects of the history of the immigration debate in the United States.

Websites

Lyon, Cherstin. "Immigration Act of 1917." *Densho Encyclopedia*, July 17, 2015. This site provides a historical overview and discussion of the significance of the 1917 Immigration Act. http://encyclopedia.densho.org/Immigration%20Act%20of%201917/. Accessed October 20, 2016.

"1917 Immigration Act." U.S. Immigration Legislation Online. The University of Washington—Bothell Library. This site provides a summary of the act, a discussion of its significance, in addition to the full text. http://library.uwb.edu/static/USimmigration/1917_immigration_act.html. Accessed October 20, 2016.

Also Noteworthy

2012

A Sikh gurdwara in Sterling, Michigan, is defaced with profanities and references to 9/11.

February 6

1886

Starting on this day, and lasting until February 9, a race riot erupts in Seattle, Washington, fueled by anti-Chinese sentiment and fierce labor competition. A white mob, affiliated with the Knights of Labor, forced more than 200 Chinese residents from the city.

In the early fall of 1885, agitators began to hold meetings here. It was their intention to drive out the Chinese of Seattle about the time a similar occurrence had been planned to take place elsewhere. After the arrest of several men accused of killing a number of Chinese hop pickers while they were asleep in their tents in World's Hop Yard in Issaquah Valley, there was an assemblage in Seattle called an Anti-Chinese Congress which promulgated a manifesto that all Chinese inhabitants in the towns and localities represented should be compelled to depart, and committees were appointed to personally give warning to the Chinese inhabitants of Seattle, Tacoma and other places, to leave on or prior- to the first day of November. . . .

On Sunday morning (Feb. 7th), about 11 o'clock, the old University and M. E. Church bells sounded the signals. At a meeting the previous evening a committee had been appointed to take charge of the removal of the Chinese. They proceeded to the Chinese quarters with wagons, ordered the Orientals to pack up, then, with the aid of the rioters, placed them and their baggage onto wagons and drove them to the dock at the foot of Main St., the intention being to load them onto the Str. "Queen," which was expected from San Francisco any hour. Upon the arrival of Capt. Alexander with the "Queen" at Port Townsend, he first learned of the situation at Seattle, and when he arrived at the Ocean Dock he ran out the hot-water hose, declaring he would scald all persons attempting to force their way onto the ship. They willingly kept at a distance.

But the City was completely in the hands of the mob. The Acting Chief-of-Police Murphy and nearly all of the police force were aiding in the lawless acts.

Source: Kinnear, George. *Anti-Chinese Riots at Seattle, Wn., February 8, 1886.* Twenty-Fifth Anniversary of Riots. Seattle, Washington (February 8, 1911), pp. 3–5. https://archive.org/details/AntiChineseRiotsAtSeattle1886. Accessed March 7, 2017.

Books

Lutz, J. Brenda, and James M. Lutz. *Terrorism in America*. New York: Palgrave Macmillan, 2007. *Terrorism in America* argues that since the birth of the nation, terrorism has existed in America. It provides examples of instances when Americans acted as terrorists or were victims of it.

Pomper, Steve. *It Happened in Seattle: Remarkable Events That Shaped History*. Kearney, NE: Morris Book Publishing, 2010. *It Happened in Seattle* is a collection of stories about events that shaped the history of Seattle. See "Remove Yourselves from the Northwest—1886."

Websites

"Anti-Chinese Riot at Seattle." *Harper's Weekly*, March 6, 1886, p. 155 (illustrated article). This site provides the entire article, along with the illustrations. http://immigrants.harpweek.com/chineseamericans/Items/Item095L.htm. Accessed January 28, 2018.

Crowley, Walt. "Anti-Chinese Activism—Seattle." HistoryLink.org Essay 1057. May 2, 1999. This is a general essay on the history of anti-Chinese movement in Seattle with images and resources. http://www.historylink.org/File/1057. Accessed January 28, 2018.

February 7

1965

The Viet Cong attacks Camp Holloway, helicopter facility for the U.S. Air Force base at Pleiku, South Vietnam, killing 8 Americans and wounding another 126. Additionally, the Viet Cong destroyed nine helicopters and a transport plane and damaged nearly a dozen helicopters and six light observation planes. This attack was a turning point to further U.S. military involvement in Vietnam, as President Johnson ordered the evacuation of about 2,000 dependents of U.S. personnel in South Vietnam; he said, "It has become clear that Hanoi has undertaken a more aggressive course of action. . . . We have no choice but to clear the decks and make absolutely clear our continued determination to back South Vietnam in its fight to maintain its independence."

While the attacks on Pleiku and Qui Nhon led the administration to escalate its air war against the North, they also highlighted the vulnerability of the bases that American planes would be using for the bombing campaign. In an effort to provide greater security for these installations, Johnson sanctioned the dispatch of two Marine battalions to Danang in early March. The troops arrived on 8 March, though Johnson endorsed the deployment prior to the first strikes themselves. Like other major decisions he made during the escalatory process, it was not one Johnson came to without a great deal of anxiety. As he expressed to longtime confidant Senator Richard Russell (D-Georgia), LBJ understood the symbolism of "sending the Marines" and their likely impact on the combat role the United States was coming to play, both in reality and in the minds of the American public.

The bombing, however, was failing to move Hanoi or the Vietcong in any significant way. By mid-March, therefore, Johnson began to consider additional proposals for expanding the American combat presence in South Vietnam. By 1 April, he had agreed to augment the 8 March deployment with two more Marine battalions; he also changed their role from that of static base security to active defense, and soon allowed preparatory work to go forward on plans for stationing many more troops in Vietnam. In an effort to achieve consensus about security requirements for those troops, key personnel undertook a review in Honolulu on 20 April. Out of that process came Johnson's decision to expand the number of U.S. soldiers in Vietnam to eighty-two thousand.

Source: Coleman, David, and Marc Selverstone. "Lyndon B. Johnson and the Vietnam War." Presidential Recordings Digital Edition. Miller Center, University of Virginia. 2014. http://prde.upress.virginia.edu/content/Vietnam#fnref0. Accessed January 28, 2018.

Books

Tilford, Earl. *Crosswinds: The Air Force's Setup in Vietnam*. Dallas: Second Texas A&M University Press, 1993. *Crosswinds* analyzes the reason why increased U.S. bombing of Vietnam failed to produce the results U.S. military generals hoped for.

Van de Mark, Brian. *Into the Quagmire: Lyndon Johnson and the Escalation of the Vietnam War*. New York: Oxford University Press, 1995.

Websites

Bos, Carole. "Vietnam—Pleiku and Camp Holloway Attack." AwesomeStories.com. October 7, 2013. This site provides media footage of the attack at Camp Holloway, courtesy of the U.S. National Archives. https://www.awesomestories.com/asset/view/Vietnam-Pleiku-and-Camp-Holloway-Attack. Accessed September 3, 2017.

"The United States of America Vietnam War Commemoration." Department of Defense. http://www.vietnamwar50th.com. 2015. This site provides detailed historical coverage of the attack at Camp Holloway and all other events related to the Vietnam War. http://www.vietnamwar50th.com/education/week_of_february_11/. Accessed September 3, 2017.

Also Noteworthy

1990

Alpha Kappa Delta Phi, an Asian American interest sorority, is founded at the University of California, Berkeley.

February 8

1908

The Chinese Primary Public School of Subjects of the Great Qing Empire is opened in San Francisco. In 1907, the Chinese government directed Leong Chin Kwai (Liang Qinggui), commissioner of education, to oversee the establishment of a Chinese school in the United States. He arrived in San Francisco in 1908 to support the establishment of the Chinese Primary School of Subjects on the second and third stories of the Chinese Consolidated Benevolent Association headquarters building. Tuition was covered by the Chinese government, while students bear the cost of books. The school employed five teachers, and the curriculum focused on teaching the Chinese classics, music, ethics, language, history, geography, mathematics, rhetoric, calligraphy, singing, and gymnastics. The Chinese American community in San Francisco's Chinatown enthusiastically supported the school as a means to modernize Chinatown and China.

During the early 1900s the Chinese imperial government, bowing to demands for reform, ordered modernization of the Chinese education system. In 1902 the court issued the Qinding xuetang zhangcheng *(Imperially mandated regulations for schools) ordering that xuetang (modern schools) based on Western models be established in the various provinces. In 1905 Dai Hongci, one of five officials ordered by the imperial government to travel abroad on an extended inspection trip to learn from the West, stopped briefly in San Francisco. . . .*

Shortly afterward, Liang Qinggui presented a memorial to the throne proposing that Chinese in America be encouraged to establish modern schools and making the point that Chinese in America who were better educated would benefit both Chinese American society and China herself. At the beginning of 1907, the Qing emperor appointed Liang commissioner to proceed to North America to accomplish this task. Liang arrived in San Francisco in the spring of 1908, when the community was still recovering from the 1906 earthquake and fire and the Daqing Shuyuan had been forced to suspend operations temporarily. Liang worked with a committee appointed by the Chinese Consolidated Benevolent Association (CCBA) to establish the Daqing Qiaomin Gongli Xiaoxuetang (Chinese Primary School of Subjects of the Great Qing Empire) which opened on February 8, 1909. The school was housed on the second and third stories of the CCBA headquarters building, with the CCBA occupying the ground floor.

Due to insufficient funds the school administration abandoned its original intent to include both Chinese and Western (social and natural sciences) subjects in the curriculum and chose instead to focus on teaching selected Chinese subjects. These included Chinese classics, cultivation of moral character, Chinese language, Chinese history and geography, Chinese calligraphy, gymnastics, and singing. The initial enrollment was 104 students.

Source: Lai, Him Mark. "Retention of the Chinese Heritage: Chinese Schools in America before World War II." *Chinese America: History and Perspectives*, 2000, p. 12.

Books

Jorae, Wendy. *The Children of Chinatown: Growing Up Chinese American in San Francisco, 1850–1920*. Chapel Hill: The University of North Carolina Press, 2009. *The Children of Chinatown* focuses on the history of Chinese American children in San Francisco Chinatown. See Chapter 4, "Challenging Segregation Chinese Children at School," for details about the Chinese Primary Public School of Subjects of the Great Qing Empire in the lives of Chinese American children.

Lai, Him Mark. 2004. *Becoming Chinese American: A History of Communities and Institutions*. Walnut Creek, CA: AltaMira Press, 2004. See Chapter 8, "The Mission of Commissioner Liang Qinggui," for concise historical background of the Chinese Primary Public School of Subjects of the Great Qing Empire in San Francisco Chinatown.

Websites

Guan, Kenneth. Translated by Mandy Huang. "A Brief History of Central Chinese High School in America." http://www.cchsia.org. This site provides a historical overview of the Chinese Primary Public School of Subjects of the Great Qing Empire with historical photographs. http://www.cchsia.org/schoolhisEn.html. Accessed September 3, 2017.

Lai, Him Mark. "Retention of the Chinese Heritage: Chinese Schools in America before World War II." *Chinese America: History and Perspectives*, 2000, 10–31. The Him Mark Lai Digital Archive. Chinese Historical Society of America. This article examines Chinese schools in America before WWII. https://himmarklai.org/digitized-articles/1996-2000/01-retention-of-the-chinese-heritage/. Accessed January 28, 2018.

Also Noteworthy

1886

The Seattle anti-Chinese riot erupts as Chinese residents in Seattle, Washington Territory, are driven out of town by an angry mob who wanted to restore law and order by expelling the Chinese from the city.

February 9

1971

Asian American students, members of the Oriental Student Union at Seattle Central Community College, protest the administration's racial demographics and demand Asian American representation in the administration. Of the school's 90 administrators, 87 were white and 3 were African American. On March 9, 1971, the administration agreed to hire an Asian American to their rank.

On a cold snowy morning 27 years ago, 17 Asian-American students from Seattle Central Community College and the University of Washington jumped out of two vans, walked into the Seattle Central Community College Administrative Building at 8 A.M., and closed it down. The takeover of the administrative building had two purposes: To protest discrimination at Seattle Central Community College; And to force SCCC administration to hire Asians in administrative positions. Over a three-month period prior to the takeover, college officials told student leaders from the Oriental Student Union:

"No Asians had ever applied for administrative positions".
"Asians were not qualified".
"Asian candidates were overqualified".
"You should be happy to know we just hired an Asian janitor".

By 10 A.M. more than 100 Asian students joined the demonstration. By 4:30 P.M. a police tactical squad had arrested several demonstrators. After a month of negotiations, the college finally agreed to hire Asians in administrative positions. That fall Frank Fujii was hired, and in later years the administration hired other Asians including Dr. Peter Koo as President of North Seattle Community College. This event sparked the Asian American movement in Seattle. More importantly, the individuals who participated in it have not forgotten their community, have helped pave the way for others and have given back many times more than they have received.

Source: Sugiyama, Al. "History Lessons." *International Examiner*, April 3, 1998, p. 3.

Books

Ancheta, Angelo. *Race, Rights, and the Asian American Experience*. New Brunswick, NJ: Rutgers University Press, 2006. *Race, Rights, and the Asian American Experience* traces the racial discourse in the United States by critiquing the black-white model of race and race relations.

Maeda, Daryl. *Rethinking the Asian American Movement*. London: Routledge, 2011. See Chapter 2, "Campus Activism," for analysis of the role of student activists in the Asian American civil rights movement.

Website

"Oriental Student Union Sit-In." Seattle Civil Rights & Labor History Project. University of Washington. 2017. This site narrates the history of the Oriental Student Union at Seattle Central Community College protest in 1971 with historical photographs. http://depts.washington.edu/civilr/aa_osu.htm. Accessed September 3, 2017.

Weiland, Kathryn, Amilcar Guzman, and KerryAnn O'Meara. "Politics, Identity, and College Protest: Then and Now." *About Campus* 18 (May–June 2013): 2–9. This article provides a comparative analysis of student protests among minority college students. http://journals.sagepub.com/doi/full/10.1002/abc.21114. Accessed June 14, 2018.

February 10

2015

Fresh off the Boat, a television series about a Chinese American family, based on Eddie Huang's best-selling memoir of the same title, airs in its prime-time slot.

Set in Florida during the 90s, the show explores Huang's childhood as his family navigates the cultural challenges of settling into a city that is predominantly white. What this television show aims to do is examine Anglo Americans and the cultural dynamics from an Asian perspective—for once, the white person is the Other. The show stars Randall Park, Constance Wu, and Hudson Yang. Park is most recently known for playing the exaggerated version of Kim Jong Un in the irreverent comedy "The Interview," while Wu is a newcomer to the small screen. The two adults play Huang's father and mother respectively while Yang plays the young Eddie Huang.

"Fresh Off the Boat" is the first sitcom to star an all Asian starring cast since comedienne Margaret Cho's sitcom "All-American Family," which aired for one season from 1994–1995. That is 20 years since we've last had a show about Asians on American television. It doesn't need to be repeated that this show is important and that there will inevitably be a range of reactions from all corners of our community. This is what happens when you have a lack of representation in the media. . . .

Race and cultural conflicts obviously play a central role in storylines. In one pivotal moment in the pilot, an African American boy calls Huang (Yang) a chink during a school lunch. Huang fought television executives to keep this scene. I cannot imagine how difficult it must have been to keep "chink" in a network television show. Huang famously penned an essay lambasting the show's staff and network executives for tearing apart his autobiography and the original story he wanted to tell, but concluded that the show had a greater purpose, which is to serve as a vehicle of getting Asian representation into the media.

Source: Nguyen, Vivian. "Fresh off the Boat." *Northwest Asian Weekly*, February 14, 2015, pp. 1, 15.

Books

Huang, Eddie. *Fresh Off the Boat: A Memoir*. New York: Spiegel & Grau, 2013. Eddie Huang's memoir inspired *Fresh off the Boat*, the sitcom series.

Lee, Jonathan H. X., ed. *Chinese Americans: The History and Culture of a People*. Santa Barbara, CA: ABC-CLIO, 2016. Part 4 of *Chinese Americans* covers various aspects of Chinese Americans and popular culture in the United States, including an entry of Eddie Huang's *Fresh off the Boat*.

Websites

Fresh off the Boat. Official web page. abc.go.com. This site is the official web page for the show. http://abc.go.com/shows/fresh-off-the-boat. Accessed January 28, 2018.

Lee, Ashley. "ABC's 'Fresh off the Boat': What the Critics Are Saying." *Hollywood Reporter*, February 4, 2015. This site reproduces all the reviews of *Fresh off the Boat*. http://www.hollywoodreporter.com/live-feed/fresh-boat-review-abc-what-770083. Accessed September 3, 2017.

Also Noteworthy

2010

In Nashville, Tennessee, an Islamic center is defaced with the words "Muslims Go Home" and a crusade-style cross.

February 11

1903

One thousand Japanese and 200 Mexican laborers become the charter members of the Japanese Mexican Labor Association in Oxnard, California. Kozaburo Baba serves as the association's president. This is the first farmworkers' union in California, but the American Federation of Labor refused to recognize a nonwhite union.

Cited in many accounts of labor and ethnic history, the 1903 Oxnard, California sugar beet workers' strike has by now become a familiar story. When Anglo farmers and the American Beet Sugar Company conspired to lower piece rates for beet thinning and eliminate Japanese and Mexican labor contractors, 200 Mexican farmworkers and 1000 Japanese farmworkers joined together, formed the Japanese-Mexican Labor Association (JMLA), launched the first big multiethnic agricultural labor strike in California, and on March 30 forced growers to restore the original arrangements and disband the Western Agricultural Contracting Company (WACC), their company-sponsored labor contracting business.

Flushed with victory, JMLA leaders then petitioned the American Federation of Labor to charter their organization as Sugar Beet Farm Laborer's Union of Oxnard (SBFLU), but in June withdrew their application after Samuel Gompers extended membership to Mexican sugar beet workers but not to Asians. Refusing to abandon the Asians, the fledgling farmworker union immediately fell apart, expiring so completely that . . . review of newspaper accounts of labor activities in Ventura County through 1910 failed to uncover further mention of the JMLA after its success in April 1903.

Source: Street, Richard Steven. "The 1903 Oxnard Sugar Beet Strike: A New Ending." *Labor History* 39, no. 2 (May 1998): p. 193.

Books

Barajas, Frank. *Curious Unions: Mexican American Workers and Resistance in Oxnard, California, 1898–1961*. Lincoln: University of Nebraska Press, 2012. *Curious Unions* explores the ways in which the Mexican community forged relationships and partnerships with other ethnic groups in Oxnard during the labor movement in the first half of the 20th century.

Daniel, Cletus. *Bitter Harvest: A History of California Farmworkers, 1870–1941*. Berkeley: University of California Press, 1982. *Bitter Harvest* employs extensive primary sources to narrate a history of California's farmworkers and agriculture industry.

Websites

Preserving California's Japantowns. "Oxnard." This site provides a history of the Japanese American community in Oxnard, California, discusses the Japanese Mexican Labor Association, and has historic photographs of the community. http://www.californiajapantowns.org/oxnard.html. Accessed October 12, 2016.

Quintana, Maria, and Oscar Rosales Castañeda. "Asians and Latinos Enter the Fields." Seattle Civil Rights & Labor History Project. University of Washington. Although this site focuses on the labor movement in the state of Washington, it provides general comparative perspective and history of the Asian and Latino labor movement. http://depts.washington.edu/civilr/farmwk_ch4.htm. Accessed October 12, 2016.

Also Noteworthy

2015

American Chef Mei Lin wins *Top Chef: Boston* (Season 12).

February 12

1864

Lo Sun is Edward Day Cohota's (d. 1935) Chinese name. Lo Sun was renamed and given the last name Cohota, after the ship that carried him to the United States at the tender age of four. On this day, he enlisted in the 23rd Massachusetts Volunteer Infantry. Cohota fought in the Union's army during the Civil War and continued to serve in the army for 30 years. Nevertheless, Cohota was denied naturalization, because he was Chinese. In response, he said, "I, if anyone, have earned the right to be pronounced a citizen of the United States."

Edward Day Cohota's middle and last names are clearly derived from Sargent S. Day, the sea captain who "adopted" him, and the ship Cohota, which brought him from China to Massachusetts. . . .

Cohota himself told reporters that he "was born in Scow Jow, 60 miles from Shanghai [and] left China when he was about five years old. His father was then dead, having been drowned in a flood of the Yangstee Klong. [He] wandered down to the docks and was there picked up as a stray [by Captain Day]. This was about the year 1852."

During the sixteen months of service in Company I, Cohota fought with Grant at Cold Harbor, Petersburg, and Appomatox. He seems to have been extraordinarily lucky. The Battle of Drury's Bluff on May 16, 1864, was fought in dense fog. . . . Yet Cohota came out of the battle with "seven bullet holes thro' clothes. None touched his flesh." Then, at the Battle of Cold Harbor, Virginia, on Friday June 3, 1864, where Union troops suffered seven thousand casualties in a single hour, "a Confederate minie ball parted his hair permanently when it grazed his scalp." But he was not otherwise hurt. . . .

[W]hen he tried to take up a homestead in 1912, he was notified that "he was not a citizen of this country and could never become a citizen and therefore could never prove up his homestead."

Cohota protested: "I have fought in the country's service as a soldier, and I served in its regular army from which I was retired for long continued honorable service of over thirty years, and I believe that I, if anyone, have earned the right to be pronounced a citizen of the United States and enjoy all of its rights and privileges."

Source: McCunn, Ruthanne Lum. "Chinese in the Civil War: Ten Who Served." 1995, pp. 153–154.

Books

Carol A. Shively, ed. *Asians and Pacific Islanders and the Civil War.* Washington, DC: National Park Service, U.S. Department of the Interior, 2015. This book, part of a series, commemorates the 150th anniversary of the Civil War and documents the stories of Asian and the Pacific Islander Americans who fought for the Union or the Confederacy during the American Civil War.

McCunn, Ruthanne Lum. *Chinese Yankee: A True Story from the Civil War.* San Francisco, CA: Design Enterprises of San Francisco, 2014. *Chinese Yankee* documents the story of Chinese American Thomas Sylvanus (Ah Yee Way) who joined the Freedom Army during the American Civil War.

Websites

House Resolution 1069 (109th): Honoring Edward Day Cohota, Joseph L. Pierce, and other veterans of Asian descent who fought in the Civil War. Govtrack.us. 2006. This site provides the full resolution to commemorate Asian American Civil War veterans. https://www.govtrack.us/congress/bills/109/hres1069/text. Accessed September 3, 2017.

Kwok, Gordon. "Edward Day Cohot." Association to Commemorate the Chinese Serving in the American Civil War. 2005. This site documents the life of Edward Day Cohot and research related to him. https://sites.google.com/site/accsacw/Home/cohota. Accessed September 3, 2017.

1982

San Francisco proclaims this day "Ruth Asawa Day" to honor Japanese American artists known for her sculptures. Ruth Asawa (January 24, 1926–August 5, 2013) was an American sculptor. Asawa was born in Norwalk, California. During World War II, her father, Umakichi Asawa, was interned at a camp in New Mexico.

Artist Ruth Asawa Lanier was born on January 24, 1926, in Norwalk, California. She grew up on a truck farm, where her parents sometimes worked eighteen-hour days. From 1942 to 1943, along with thousands of other Japanese Americans who were removed from the Pacific Coast under the pretext that they were a threat to national security, she was interned in Santa Anita Assembly Center (formerly a racetrack) in Arcadia, California, and Rohwer, Arkansas. It was at Santa Anita that Lanier seriously began to develop her craft mentored by Nisei (second generation Japanese American) Disney Studio veterans. Lanier graduated from high school at Rohwer and attended Milwaukee State Teachers College from 1943 to 1946, majoring in art. From 1946 to 1949 she attended Black

Mountain College, an experimental college with an art centered curriculum in North Carolina.

From 1946 to the present Lanier has lived and worked in San Francisco, California. Her work has centered on bas-relief sculptures and fountains, generally utilizing cast bronze or glass fiber-reinforced concrete. Some of her important commissioned pieces include "Andrea," a cast bronze fountain in Ghirardelli Square, San Francisco (1966); a cast bronze fountain at the Hyatt on Union Square, commissioned by the Hyatt Corporation of America (1970–1973); a glass fiber-reinforced concrete bas-relief wall at the San Francisco Parc Fifty Five Hotel (formerly the Ramada Renaissance; 1984); "Aurora," a stainless steel fountain at Bayside Plaza, San Francisco, commissioned by Hampshire Properties (1986); a glass fiber-reinforced concrete bas-relief fountain at Old Courthouse Square, Santa Rosa, California, commissioned by the Santa Rosa Redevelopment and Housing Agency (1987); a cast bronze fountain at Beringer Winery, St. Helena, California (1988); and the Japanese American Internment Memorial Sculpture, a cast bronze bas-relief sculpture commissioned by the City of San Jose, County of Santa Clara, and the local Japanese American community (1994).

Source: Fugita, Stephen. "Ruth Asawa Lanier." In *Distinguished Asian Americans: A Biographical Dictionary*, edited by Dorothy C. L. Cordova, Chung H. Chuong, Robert H. Hyung Chan Kim, Franklin Ng, and Jane Singh, pp. 175–176. Westport, CT: Greenwood, 1999.

Books

Cornell, Daniell, Ruth Asawa, and M.H. De Young Memorial Museum, ed. *The Sculpture of Ruth Asawa: Contours in the Air*. Berkeley: University of California Press, 2006. *The Sculpture of Ruth Asawa* catalogs the life and work of Ruth Asawa: it was created to accompany the first complete retrospective of her career as an artist.

San Francisco Museum of Art. *Ruth Asawa: A Retrospective View*. San Francisco, CA: San Francisco Museum of Art, 1973. This volume reviews the life and work of Ruth Asawa and contains photographs of her works of art.

Websites

Archer, Sarah. "Maker to Market: Ruth Asawa Reappraised." This site provides an essay that was originally published in the *Journal of Modern Craft* 8, no. 2 (November 2015) that details Asawa's artwork and life history. https://www.sarah-archer.com/essays-content/2017/3/28/maker-to-market-ruth-asawa-reappraised. Accessed September 3, 2017.

Ruth Asawa. Estate of Ruth Asawa. 2016. This is the official site of Ruth Asawa with images of her works of art, exhibitions, videos, and other resources. http://www.ruthasawa.com/. Accessed September 3, 2017.

Also Noteworthy

1912

China's last emperor Pu Yi is forced to abdicate, or give up, his throne.

2018

Chloe Kim, snowboarder, wins a gold medal in the half-pipe at the 2018 Pyeongchang Winter Olympics. Kim is an American of Korean descent, who is the daughter of Korean immigrants who settled in Southern California.

February 13

2012

Jeremy Shu-How Lin (b. August 23, 1988) trademarks the term "Linsanity" by submitting an application with the U.S. Patent and Trademark Office to own the term. Lin is a Chinese American of Taiwanese background who is a professional basketball player of the National Basketball Association. Lin grew up in Northern California where he and his family attended Chinese Church in Christ where services in both English and Mandarin are offered. He is known for being open about his Christian religious beliefs and has given God credit for his successes as an NBA player.

Before Jeremy Lin started his professional career, his unusual ethnic (Asian) and educational (Harvard) background made him appear in the Sports Illustrated *for the first time in his senior year in February 2010. Lin's NBA career started as a Golden State Warrior as a non-draftee free agent in 2010. He was a marginal player when playing for the Warriors and eventually got waived by the team. Houston Rockets signed him yet waived him again in December 2011. Even though the New York Knicks claimed him off waiver later, he did not obtain prominent playing time until February 4, 2012, against the New Jersey Nets, when some starters went down with injuries. He contributed immediately with 25 points, 7 assists, 5 rebounds and 2 steals and helped the team to win, 99–92. Since then, the craze of Linsanity has spread across major New York press. For example, Lin has featured on the cover of the sports page of* Newsday *on 20 of 21 days since February 6. He was also the cover story for* Sports Illustrated *for two consecutive issues. The usual sports news void between the Super Bowl and March Madness was filled by Linsanity.*

Source: Chiang, Ying, and Tzu-hsuan Chen. "Adopting the Diasporic Son: Jeremy Lin and Taiwan Sport Nationalism." *International Review for the Society of Sports* 50, no. 6 (2015): p. 711.

Books

Dalrymple, Timothy. *Jeremy Lin: The Reason for the Linsanity*. New York: Center Street, 2012. Timothy Dalrymple chronicles the sport's career of Jeremy Lin based on interviews with Lin, basketball experts, Asian American leaders, and so on.

Gutman, Bill. *Jeremy Lin: The Incredible Rise of the MBA's Most Unlikely Superstar*. New York: Sports Publishing, 2012.

Websites

The Jeremy Lin Foundation. This site is the official website for the Jeremy Lin Foundation to seek love and serve youth through empowerment and leadership development. http://www.jeremylinfoundation.org/. Accessed January 28, 2018.

The official website of Jeremy Lin. 2017. This site provides news and updates on Lin. https://www.jlin7.com/. Accessed January 28, 2018.

Also Noteworthy

2011

In Yorba Linda, California, a group of 100 protesters sneer at Muslim Americans, including small children, entering a fund-raiser event with statements such as "Muhammad was a child molester!" and "Go back home! Terrorists!"

February 14

1942

General John L. DeWitt sends a memo to Secretary of War Henry Stimson recommending the removal of all immigrants and citizens of Japanese ancestry from the West Coast. DeWitt was the commanding general of the Western theater of operations in San Francisco, with the responsibility of West Coast security. Stimson relied on DeWitt's assessment, while President Roosevelt relied on the recommendations of Stimson.

Excerpt from General DeWitt's memo to Secretary Stimson.

In the war in which we are now engaged racial affinities are not severed by migration. The Japanese race is an enemy race and while many second and third generation Japanese born on United State soil, possessed of United States citizenship, have become "Americanized," the racial strains are undiluted. To conclude otherwise is to expect that children born of white parents on Japanese soil sever all racial affinity and become loyal Japanese subjects, ready to fight and, if necessary, to die for Japan in a war against the nation of their parents. That Japan is allied with Germany and Italy in this struggle is not ground for assuming that any Japanese, barred from assimilation by convention as he is, though born and raised in the United States, will not turn against this nation when the final test of loyalty comes. It, therefore, follows that along the vital Pacific Coast over 112,000 potential enemies, of Japanese extraction, are at large today. . . .

DeWitt condensed his opinion of a policy he hand opposed, allowing American soldiers of Japanese ancestry into the excluded areas, by telling the reporters that "a Jap is a Jap." . . .

Under General DeWitt's guidance from the Presidio, the War Department moved toward the momentous exclusion of American citizens from the West Coast without any thoughtful, thorough analysis of the problems, if any, of sabotage and espionage on the West Coast or of realistic solutions to those problems.

Source: Commission on Wartime Relocation and Internment of Civilians. 1982. Personal Justice Denied. National Archives, pp. 66–67. Full text is available at https://www.archives.gov/research/japanese-americans/justice-denied. Accessed February 4, 2018.

Books

Daniels, Roger, Sandra Taylor, Harry Kitano, and Leonard Arrington, eds. *Japanese Americans: From Relocation to Redress*. Seattle: University of Washington Press, 1992. This anthology covers various aspects of Japanese American World War II internment and relocation, and postwar redress movement.

Reeves, Richard. *Infamy: The Shocking Story of the Japanese American Internment in World War II*. New York: Henry Holt and Company, 2015. Historian Richard Reeves tells the dark chapter in American history as the simultaneous collision of racism, xenophobia, greed, and the hunger for revenge. *Infamy* provides a complete overview of the Japanese American World War II experience and postwar redress and civil rights achievements.

Websites

Conn, Stetson. "The Decision to Evacuate the Japanese from the Pacific Coast." The Virtual Museum of the City of San Francisco. 2017. This essay provides historical details and military arguments behind the decision to evacuate and intern Japanese Americans during World War II. http://www.sfmuseum.org/hist6/conn.html. Accessed September 3, 2017.

Yenne, Bill. "Fear Itself: The General Who Panicked the West Coast." Historynet.com. 2017. This essay analyzes DeWitt's motivation and the consequences of his advocacy for the evacuation of Japanese Americans from the West Coast. http://www.historynet.com/fear-itself-the-general-panicked-west-coast.htm. Accessed September 3, 2017.

February 15

2006

Toby Dawson (b. November 30, 1978) wins a bronze medal in freestyle mogul skiing during the 2006 Turin Winter Olympics. Dawson is the first Asian American medalist in the Olympic sport of skiing. Originally, he was born in Busan, South Korea, and given the birth name Kim Bong-seok, and was later adopted by a couple in Vail, Colorado, who worked as ski instructors. After the 2006 Olympics, Dawson reunited with his birth father in South Korea.

In February 2007, Toby Dawson, a Korean American adoptee who won the bronze medal for the US Olympic team at the Torino Winter Games in the men's freestyle mogul competition, was reunited with his Korean father and younger brother, bringing an end to the most media-saturated birth family search in South Korean adoption history. Dawson was given a hero's welcome in South Korea, and during the same week that he met his father, he was named honorary PR ambassador to represent South Korea to the International Olympic Commission (IOC) in its bid for the 2018 Pyongchang Winter Olympic Games. Dawson's reunion with his birth father, staged as a press conference at the Lotte Hotel in downtown Seoul, melded seamlessly with Dawson's performance of filial loyalty to the nation, through his newly minted role as ambassador and representative of South Korea on the global stage. In fact, Dawson's role as an "ambassador" on behalf of the South Korean state actualized what had been, up until that point, a largely rhetorical gesture on the part of diplomats and government officials who frequently addressed adoptees as "cultural ambassadors" or "civil diplomats." Adoptees, they optimistically asserted, were ideally positioned to function as bridges connecting South Korea to their Western adoptive nations in an age of globalization.

Source: Kim, Eleana. "Human Capital: Transnational Korean Adoptees and the Neoliberal Logic of Return." *Journal of Korean Studies* 17, no. 2 (Fall 2012): p. 302.

Books

Dawson, Toby, and Lena Dawson. *Twenty-Two Years for Twenty-Two Seconds*. Self-Published. Amazon.com, CreateSpace, 2010. Toby Dawson recounts his journey from adopted Korean boy to American Olympic medalist, who subsequently reunites with his birth father in Korean.

Kim, Youna, ed. *The Routledge Handbook of Korean Culture and Society*. London: Routledge, 2017. See Rachel Miyung Joo's Chapter 20, "Transnational Sport and Expressions of Global Koreanness," for discussion that includes Toby Dawson's adoption and reunion with his birth father in Korea.

Websites

Kiszla, Mark. "Awesome Dawson." *Denver Post*, February 15, 2006. This article examines the complex racial identity struggles that Toby Dawson negotiated while growing up in a transracial family with white Euro-American parents. http://www.denverpost.com/2006/02/15/awesome-dawson/. Accessed September 3, 2017.

Kyung, Oh Jun. "New Documentary on Korean-American Olympian, 'Toby Dawson—Lost and Found.'" Korea.net. April 21, 2011. This site provides a trailer to the documentary, in addition to an overview of Toby Dawson's adoption story and journey. http://www.korea.net/NewsFocus/Society/view?articleId=86287. Accessed September 3, 2017.

Also Noteworthy

2005

California Assembly Bill 420 is introduced to address decreased resources and funding for Filipino language education in California public schools due to the passage of No Child Left Behind Act in 2002.

February 16

1946

Ho Chi Minh writes letter to President Harry S. Truman asking for support of the United States in Vietnam's independence. The United States did not respond to his letter. Many critics of President Truman have argued this was a missed opportunity between the United States and Vietnam that may have averted the Vietnam War. Ho Chi Minh had high hopes of getting support from the United States to maintain Vietnam's independence.

The letter was never answered and was not declassified until 1972

DEAR MR. PRESIDENT:

I avail myself of this opportunity to thank you and the people of the United States for the interest shown by your representatives at the United Nations Organization in favour of the dependent peoples.

Our VIETNAM people, as early as 1941, stood by the Allies' side and fought against the Japanese and their associates, the French colonialists.

From 1941 to 1945 we fought bitterly, sustained by the patriotism, of our fellow-countrymen and by the promises made by the Allies at YALTA, SAN FRANCISCO and POTSDAM.

When the Japanese were defeated in August 1945, the whole Vietnam territory was united under a Provisional Republican Government, which immediately set out to work. In five months, peace and order were restored, a democratic republic was established on legal bases, and adequate help was given to the Allies in the carrying out of their disarmament mission.

But the French Colonialists, who betrayed in wartime both the Allies and the Vietnamese, have come back, and are waging on us a murderous and pitiless war in order to reestablish their domination. Their invasion has extended to South Vietnam and is menacing us in North Vietnam. It would take volumes to give even an abbreviated report of the crisis and assassinations they are committing every day in this fighting area.

This aggression is contrary to all principles of international law and the pledge made by the Allies during World War II. It is a challenge to the noble attitude shown before, during, and after the war by the United States Government and People. It violently contrasts with the firm stand you have taken in your twelve-point declaration, and with the idealistic loftiness and generosity expressed by your delegates to the United Nations Assembly, MM. BYRNES, STETTINIUS, AND J.F. DULLES.

The French aggression on a peace-loving people is a direct menace to world security. It implies the complicity, or at least the connivance of the Great Democracies. The United Nations ought to keep their words. They ought to interfere to stop this unjust war, and to show that they mean to carry out in peacetime the principles for which they fought in wartime.

Our Vietnamese people, after so many years of spoliation and devastation, is just beginning its building-up work. It needs security and freedom, first to achieve internal prosperity and welfare, and later to bring its small contribution to world-reconstruction.

These security and freedom can only be guaranteed by our independence from any colonial power, and our free cooperation with all other powers. It is with this firm conviction that we request of the United Sates as guardians and champions of World Justice to take a decisive step in support of our independence.

What we ask has been graciously granted to the Philippines. Like the Philippines our goal is full independence and full cooperation with the UNITED STATES. We will do our best to make this independence and cooperation profitable to the whole world.

I am Dear Mr. PRESIDENT,
Respectfully Yours,
(Signed) Ho Chi Minh

Source: "Letter from Ho Chi Minh to President Harry S. Truman, 02/28/1946." National Archives. https://www.archives.gov/historical-docs/todays-doc/?dod-date=228. Accessed October 15, 2016.

Books

Bowman, John Stewart. *The Vietnam War: An Almanac*. New York: World Almanac Publication, 1985. *The Vietnam War: An Almanac* is a detailed chronological resource on the history of Vietnam leading to the development of the Vietnam War and its aftermath.

Duiker, William. *Ho Chi Minh: A Life*. New York: Hachette Books, 2012. *Ho Chi Minh: A Life* is a complete historical biography of Ho Chi Minh.

Websites

"Letter from Ho Chi Minh to President Harry S. Truman, 02/28/1946." National Archives. This site provides the digital download of the archival document. https://www.archives.gov/historical-docs/todays-doc/?dod-date=228. Accessed January 13, 2017.

"Messages to America: The Letters of Ho Chi Minh." History Is a Weapon. This site contains letters written by Ho Chi Minh to the United States from 1945 to 1969. http://www.historyisaweapon.com/defcon2/hochiminh/. Accessed January 13, 2017.

Also Noteworthy

2011

Lisa J. Ling (b. August 30, 1973) premieres her show, *Our America with Lisa*, on OWN: The Oprah Winfrey Network and airs for five seasons.

February 17

2009

On this day, President Barack Obama signs the Stimulus Bill that includes a provision that provides veterans benefits to Filipino veterans. Senator Daniel Akaka (D-Hawaii) sponsored the Filipino veterans' compensation bill during the 100th Congress (January 3, 2007–January 3, 2009). The provision passed by President Obama includes compensation for the veterans in the form of lump-sum payments in the amounts of $15,000 for the veterans with U.S. citizenship and $9,000 for those with Philippine citizenship. This provision is entitled the World War II Filipino Veterans Equity Compensation Act and is argued to be reparations for the legacy of the 1946 Rescission Act.

Excerpt is from Chris Lu, former assistant to President Barack Obama and cabinet secretary.

Filipino Americans have been an important part of our nation's diverse history. Since their first documented arrival in Morro Bay, California in October 1587, Filipino Americans have made remarkable contributions to every sector of American life, including government, business, and the military.

Indeed, in 1941, more than 250,000 Filipino soldiers responded to President Roosevelt's call-to-arms and later fought under the American flag during World War II. Many made the ultimate sacrifice as both soldiers in the U.S. Army Forces in the Far East and as guerilla fighters during the Imperial Japanese occupation of the Philippines. Later, many of these brave individuals became proud United States citizens. For over 60 years, Filipino veterans and community advocates have fought to obtain compensation for those who served with American soldiers during World War II.

President Obama recognizes the extraordinary contribution made by Filipino veterans. The American Recovery and Reinvestment Act of 2009, which the President signed into law, contained a provision creating the Filipino Veterans Equity Compensation Fund. Eligible veterans who are U.S. citizens receive a one-time payment of $15,000; eligible veterans who are not U.S. citizens receive a one-time payment of $9,000. The Department of Veterans Affairs established a process, in collaboration with the Department of Defense, to determine eligibility to receive payments from the Fund.

To date, we are pleased that over 18,000 claims have been approved. However, we also have heard from many Filipino veterans who have been impeded from filing claims or believe their claims were improperly denied.

To address their concerns, the White House Initiative on Asian Americans and Pacific Islanders, in collaboration with the Office of Management and Budget, has launched an Interagency Working Group comprised of officials from the Department of Veterans Affairs, the Department of Defense, and the National Archives and Record Administration. The Interagency Working Group will be tasked with analyzing the process faced by these Filipino veterans in demonstrating eligibility for compensation in order to ensure that all applications receive thorough and fair review. This is part of the Obama Administration's ongoing efforts to honor the contributions of all veterans in their service to our country.

Chris Lu is Assistant to the President and Cabinet Secretary. He is also Co-Chair of the White House Initiative on Asian Americans and Pacific Islanders.

Source: Lu, Chris. "Honoring Filipino World War II Veterans for Their Service." The White House: President Barack Obama. October 17, 2012. https://obamawhitehouse.archives.gov/blog/2012/10/17/honoring-filipino-world-war-ii-veterans-their-service. Accessed January 28, 2018.

Books

Posadas, Barbara. *The Filipino Americans*. Westport, CT: Greenwood Press, 1999. *The Filipino Americans* covers various aspects of the Filipino American experience.

Woods, Damon. *The Philippines: A Global Studies Handbook*. Santa Barbara, CA: ABC-CLIO, 2006. See Part 1 of *The Philippines* for discussion related to Filipino veterans.

Websites

Center for Minority Veterans. U.S. Department of Veterans Affairs. 2017. This site provides information of the World War II Filipino Veterans Equity Compensation Fund and includes the report funds allocated and distributed. https://www.va.gov/centerforminorityveterans/fvec.asp. Accessed September 3, 2017.

The Filipino Veterans Recognition and Education Project. 2017. This site seeks to raise awareness of the history of Filipino veterans who served during World War II and their struggle for recognition for their service. https://www.filvetrep.org/. Accessed September 3, 2017.

February 18

1979

David Oyama leads a group of 15–20 actors to protest against the Public Theater in New York, for racist casting practice of casting "non-Asian actors in Asian roles without an equal opportunity for Asian actors to be casted in non-Asian roles." The protest was successful in getting the theater to put more effort into casting and hiring Asian American actors, playwrights, and directors. The following year, David Henry Hwang's *FOB*, premiered at the Public Theater and won an Obie Award.

Books

Lee, Esther Kim. *A History of Asian American Theatre*. Cambridge: Cambridge University Press, 2006. *A History of Asian American Theatre* covers the history of Asian American theater from 1965 to 2005.

Zia, Helen. *Asian American Dreams: The Emergence of an American People*. New York: Farrar, Straus, and Giroux, 2000. See Chapter 5, "Gangsters, Gooks, Geishas, and Geeks," for a discussion of the development of Asian American theater and David Oyama's inspired protest of yellowface at the Public Theater.

Websites

Fraser, Gerald. "Asian-American Actors Get Pledge from Papp." *New York Times* Archives, February 22, 1979, p. 26. This site provides the *New York Times* article that details Joseph Papp's reaction and resolution of the protest by Asian American actors at the Public Theater. http://www.nytimes.com/1979/02/22/archives/asianamerican-actors-get-pledge-from-papp.html?mcubz=0. Accessed September 3, 2017.

Wang, Catherine. "Behind the Curtains: The Evolution and Impact of Asian Americans in Theatre." USC US-China Institute. January 17, 2017. This essay critically analyzes the development of Asian American theater. http://china.usc.edu/behind-curtains-evolution-and-impact-asian-americans-theatre. Accessed September 3, 2017.

February 19

1862

While the origins of the term "coolie" are unclear, historians agree that by the 18th century it was used in reference to Asian Indian and Chinese contract laborers. The increased suppression of the international slave trade and the permanent end of slavery within the British Empire pushed sugar planters in the Caribbean to turn to import Chinese "coolie" labor under terms of a contract. From 1847 to 1862, most Chinese contract laborers bound for Cuba were shipped on American vessels. An estimated 6,000 laborers arrived per year. Although planters and their allies argued that "coolieism" represented a departure from slavery, laborers lived under brutal conditions. The terms of the contract were often not honored, and like slaves, many men worked in gangs under the command of a strict overseer. Despite the distinction between contract labor and voluntary migration, the term "coolie" came to be applied broadly to label most Chinese immigrant laborers in the United States. The "coolie" stereotype would later be used by 19th-century American nativists seeking to stop the influx of Chinese migrants to the U.S. West Coast.

CHAP. XXVII—An Act to prohibit the "Coolie Trade" by American Citizens in America Vessels.

Be it enacted by the Senate and House of Representatives of the United States of America in Congress assembled, That no citizen or citizens of the United States, or foreigner coming into or residing within the same, shall, for himself or for any other person whatsoever, either as master, factor, owner, or otherwise, build, equip, load, or otherwise prepare, any ship or vessel, or any steamship or stem-vessel, registered, enrolled, or licensed, in the United States, or any port within the same, for the purpose of procuring from China, or from any part or place therein, or from any other port or place the inhabitants or subjects of China, known as "coolies," to be transported to any foreign country, port, or place whatever, to be disposed of, or sold, or transferred, for any term of years or for any time whatever, as servants or apprentices, or to be held to service or labor. And if any ship or vessel, steamship, or steam-vessel, belonging in whole or in part to citizens of the United States, and registered, enrolled, or otherwise licensed as aforesaid, shall be employed for the said purposes, or in the "coolie trade," so called, or shall be caused to procure or carry from China or elsewhere, as aforesaid, any subjects of the Government of China for the purpose of transporting or disposing of them as aforesaid, every such ship or vessel, steamship, or steam-vessel, her tackle, apparel, furniture, and other appurtenances, shall be forfeited to the United States, and shall be liable to be seized, prosecuted, and condemned in any of the circuit courts or district courts of the United States for the district where the said ship or vessel, steamship or steam-vessel, may be found, seized or carried.

SEC. 2 And be it further enacted, That every person who shall so build it out, equip, load or otherwise prepare, or who shall send to sea, or navigate, as owner, master, factor, agent, or otherwise, any ship or vessel, steamship, or steam-vessel, belonging in whole or in part to citizens of the United States, or registered, enrolled, or licensed within the same, or at any port thereof, knowing or intending that the same shall be employed in that trade or business aforesaid, contrary to the true intent and meaning of this act, or in anywise aiding or abetting therein, shall be severally liable to be indicted therefor, and, on conviction thereof, shall be liable to a fine not exceeding two thousand dollars and be imprisoned not exceeding one year.

SEC. 3. And be it further enacted, That if any citizen or citizens of the United States shall, contrary to the true intent and meaning of this act, take on board of any vessel, or receive or transport any such persons as are above described in this act, for the purpose of disposing of them as aforesaid, he or they shall be liable to be indicted therefore, and, on conviction thereof, shall be liable to a fine not exceeding two thousand dollars and be imprisoned not exceeding one year.

SEC. 4. And be it further enacted, That nothing in this act hereinbefore contained shall be deemed or construed to apply to or affect any free and voluntary emigration of any Chinese subject, or to any vessel carrying such person as passenger on board the same: Provided, however, That a permit or certificate shall be prepared and signed by the consul or consular agent of the United States residing at the port from which such vessel may take her departure, containing the name of such person, and setting forth the fact of his voluntary emigration from such vessel; but the same shall not be given until such consul or consular agent shall be first personally satisfied by evidence produced of the truth of the facts therein contained.

SEC. 5. And be it further enacted, That all the provisions of the act of Congress approved February twenty-second, eighteen hundred and forty-seven, entitled "An act to regulate the carriage of passengers in merchant vessels," and all the provisions of the act of Congress approved March third, eighteen hundred and forty-nine, entitled "An act to extend the provisions of all laws now in force relating to the carriage of passengers in merchant vessels and the regulation thereof," shall be extended and shall apply to all vessels owned in whole or in part by citizens of the United States, and registered, enrolled, or licensed within the United States, propelled by wind or by steam, and to all masters thereof, carrying passengers or intending to carry passengers from any foreign port or place without the United States to any other foreign port or place without the United States; and that all penalties and forfeitures provided for in said act shall apply to vessels and masters last aforesaid.

SEC. 6. And be it further enacted, That the President of the United States shall be and he is hereby, authorized and empowered, in such way and at such time as he shall judge proper to the end that the provisions of this act may be enforced according to the true intent and meaning thereof, to direct and order the vessels of the United States, and the masters and commanders thereof, to examine all vessels navigated or owned in whole or in part by citizens of the United States, and registered, enrolled, or licensed under the laws of the United States, wherever they may be, whenever, in the judgment of such master or commanding officer thereof, reasonable cause shall exist to believe that such vessel has on board, in violation of the provisions of this act, any subjects of China known as "coolies," for the purpose of transportation; and upon sufficient proof that such vessel is employed in violation of the provisions of this act, to cause such vessel to be carried, with her officers and crew, into any port or district within the United States, and delivered to marshal of such district, to be held and disposed of according to the provisions of this act.

SEC. 7. And be it further enacted, That this act shall take effect from and after six months from the day of its passage.

APPROVED, February 19. 1862.

Source: Sanger, George P., ed. *The Statutes at Large, Treaties and Proclamations of the United States of America*. Boston, MA: Little, Brown and Company, 1863.

Books

Meagher, Arnold. *The Coolie Trade: The Traffic in Chinese Laborers to Latin America, 1847–1874*. Philadelphia, PA: Xlibris LLC, 2008. Historian Arnold Meagher provides a comprehensive history of the Chinese coolie trade in Latin America and includes a board discussion of the Chinese immigration to California.

Yun, Lisa. *The Coolie Speaks: Chinese Indentured Laborers and African Slaves in Cuba*. Philadelphia, PA: Temple University Press, 2008. English and Asian American studies professor Lisa Yun employs the written and oral testimonies of nearly 3,000 Chinese laborers in Cuba to provide a "coolie narrative" that reveals aspects of indentured life.

Websites

"California's Anti-Coolie Tax." Chinatown San Francisco. This site provides the full text for California's anti-coolie tax, passed on April 26, 1862. http://www.sanfranciscochinatown.com/history/1862anticoolietax.htm. Accessed January 28, 2018.

"1862 Anti-coolie Law." U.S. Immigration Legislation Online. The University of Washington-Bothell Library. This site provides a summary of the legislation, along with the original text. http://library.uwb.edu/Static/USimmigration/1862_anti_coolie_law.html. Accessed June 14, 2018.

1923

The U.S. Supreme Court in the *U.S. v. Bhagat Singh Thind* upholds the 1790 Naturalization Act and declares South Asians ineligible for naturalized citizenship. Thind immigrated to the United States in 1913 and attended the University of California. He served in the U.S. Army during World War I, becoming an acting sergeant before his honorable discharge in 1919. In 1920, Thind received his citizenship papers from the U.S. District Court in Oregon. However, because he was a vocal advocate for India's independence, federal government officials looked for a way to deport him in order to maintain their relationship with Great Britain. The Bureau of Immigration took Thind to court in an attempt to "denaturalize" him, claiming that he was not "white," as stipulated in the Naturalization Law of 1790. The U.S. Supreme Court upheld the claim for the federal agency, arguing that the definition of race had to be based on the understanding of "common man." Thus, while Thind was classified as an Aryan and Caucasian ethnographically, he was not white. The Court held that the term "white person" meant an immigrant from Northern or Western Europe. Following the *Thind* decision, immigration officials successfully canceled the naturalization certificates of other Asian Indians residing in the United States. In 1935, Congress passed a law allowing all veterans of World War I to naturalize. Thind petitioned immediately, and a federal court in New York granted his petition. In 1936, 13 years after the Supreme Court decision, Thind became a U.S. citizen.

Excerpt from *U.S. v. Bhagat Singh Thind*. Decided on February 19, 1923

Mr. Justice SUTHERLAND delivered the opinion of the Court.

The appellee was granted a certificate of citizenship by the District Court of the United States for the District of Oregon, over the objection of the Naturalization Examiner for the United States. A bill in equity was then filed by the United States, seeking a cancellation of the certificate on the ground that the appellee was not a white person and therefore not lawfully entitled to naturalization. The District Court, on motion, dismissed the bill (In re Bhagat Singh Thind, 268 Fed. 683), and an appeal was taken to the Circuit Court of Appeals. No question is made in respect of the individual qualifications of the appellee. The sole question is whether he falls within the class designated by Congress as eligible. . . .

What we now hold is that the words "free white persons" are words of common speech, to be interpreted in accordance with the understanding of the common man, synonymous with the word "Caucasian" only as that word is popularly understood. As so understood and used, whatever may be the speculations of the ethnologist, it does not include the body of people to whom the appellee belongs. It is a matter of familiar observation and knowledge that the physical group characteristics of the Hindus render them readily distinguishable from the various groups of persons in this country commonly recognized as white. The children of English, French, German, Italian, Scandinavian, and other European parentage, quickly merge into the mass of our population and lose the distinctive hallmarks of their European origin. On the other hand, it cannot be doubted that the children born in this country of Hindu parents would retain indefinitely the clear evidence of their ancestry. It is very far from our thought to suggest the slightest question of racial superiority or inferiority. What we suggest is merely racial difference, and it is of such character and extent that the great body of our people instinctively recognize it and reject the thought of assimilation.

Source: *United States Reports, Volume 261: Cases Adjudged in the Supreme Court.* Washington, DC: Government Printing Office, 1923.

Books

Almaguer, Tomas. *Racial Fault Lines: The Historical Origins of White Supremacy in California.* Berkeley: University of California Press, 1994. *Racial Fault Lines* is an ethnic history of California that explores the development of white supremacy as public and institutional discourse.

Berg, Manfred, and Martin Geyer, eds. *Two Cultures of Rights: The Quest for Inclusion and Participation in Modern America and Germany.* Cambridge: Cambridge University Press, 2002. *Two Cultures of Rights* comparatively discusses critical issues in the history for civil rights in America and Germany. See Roger Daniels's Chapter 1, "Asian Americans: Rights Denied and Attained."

Websites

Dr. Bhagat Singh Thind. This site provides comprehensive information on Bhagat Singh Thind: it contains photos, discussion on his life, and the history and significance of *US v. Bhagat Singh Thind.* http://www.bhagatsinghthind.com/about_thind.php. Accessed October 26, 2016.

"United States v. Bhagat Singh Thind". www.pbs.org. This site provides a legal summary of the decision and analysis of its significance. http://www.pbs.org/rootsinthesand/i_bhagat2.html. Accessed October 26, 2016.

1942

The bombing of Pearl Harbor by Japanese forces on the morning of December 7, 1941, marked a bitter turning point in Japanese American history. President Franklin D. Roosevelt signs Executive Order 9066 in February 19, 1942, authorizing the exclusion of Japanese—including Okinawan—Americans from the West Coast. The order granted the federal government ability to create military zones, including the authority to remove individuals—mostly American citizens and residents of Japanese descent—from areas that there deemed threats to national security. Immediately after Pearl Harbor, the Federal Bureau of Investigation (FBI) identified and captured Japanese American community leaders from California, Oregon, and Washington—states that were designated critical zones of national security. These early detainees, arrested by the FBI as early as December 1941, were sent to facilities such as the Department of Justice internment camp in Santa Fe, New Mexico, Crystal City, Texas, and Fort Missoula, Montana. They were held without bail, without being formally charged, and without knowing what crime they were being accused of committing.

Excerpt from Executive Order 9066,

Now, therefore, by virtue of the authority vested in me as President of the United States, and Commander in Chief of the Army and Navy, I hereby authorize and direct the Secretary of War, and the Military Commanders whom he may from time to time designate, whenever he or any designated Commander deems such action necessary or desirable, to prescribe military areas in such places and of such extent as he or the appropriate Military Commander may determine, from which any or all persons may be excluded, and with respect to which, the right of any person to enter, remain in, or leave shall be subject to whatever restrictions the Secretary of War or the appropriate Military Commander may impose in his discretion. The Secretary of War is hereby authorized to provide for residents of any such area who are excluded therefrom, such transportation, food, shelter, and other accommodations as may be necessary, in the judgment of the Secretary of War or the said Military Commander, and until other arrangements are made, to accomplish the purpose of this order. The designation of military areas in any region or locality shall supersede designations of prohibited and restricted areas by the Attorney General under the Proclamations of December 7 and 8, 1941, and shall supersede the responsibility and authority of the Attorney General under the said Proclamations in respect of such prohibited and restricted areas.

I hereby further authorize and direct the Secretary of War and the said Military Commanders to take such other steps as he or the appropriate Military Commander may deem advisable to enforce compliance with the restrictions applicable to each Military area hereinabove authorized to be designated, including the use of Federal troops and other Federal Agencies, with authority to accept assistance of state and local agencies.

I hereby further authorize and direct all Executive Departments, independent establishments and other Federal Agencies, to assist the Secretary of War or the said Military Commanders in carrying out this Executive Order, including the furnishing of medical aid, hospitalization, food, clothing, transportation, use of land, shelter, and other supplies, equipment, utilities, facilities, and services.

This order shall not be construed as modifying or limiting in any way the authority heretofore granted under Executive Order No. 8972, dated December 12, 1941, nor shall it be construed as limiting or modifying the duty and responsibility of the Federal Bureau of Investigation, with respect to the investigation of alleged acts of sabotage or the duty and responsibility of the Attorney General and the Department of Justice under the Proclamations of December 7 and 8, 1941, prescribing regulations for the conduct and control of alien enemies, except as such duty and responsibility is superseded by the designation of military areas hereunder.

Franklin D. Roosevelt
The White House,
February 19, 1942.

Source: Executive Order 9066, February 19, 1942; General Records of the U.S. Government; Record Group 11; National Archives. https://www.archives.gov/historical-docs/todays-doc/?dod-date=219. Accessed January 13, 2017.

Books

Daniels, Roger. *Prisoners without Trial: Japanese Americans in World War II*. New York: Hill and Wang, 1993. *Prisoners without Trial* covers various historical aspects of the internment of Japanese Americans during World War II.

Irons, Peter. *Justice at War: The Story of the Japanese American Internment Cases*. Berkeley: University of California Press, 1993. *Justice at War* is a critical historical analysis of the U.S. government's suppression, alteration, and destruction of evidence that could have convinced the U.S. Supreme Court to strike down the internment order.

Websites

Niiya, Brian. "Executive Order 9066." *Densho Encyclopedia*, August 25, 2015. This site provides a general historical overview of Executive Order 9066, and how it was enforced, and its immediate impact on the Japanese American community. http://encyclopedia.densho.org/Executive_Order_9066/. Accessed January 13, 2017.

"'Suffering under a Great Injustice': Ansel Adams's Photographs of Japanese-American Internment at Manzanar." Library of Congress. This site provides a historical account of the impact of Executive Order 9066 and specific details about the Manzanar internment camps with historic photographs by acclaimed photographer Ansel Adams. https://www.loc.gov/teachers/classroommaterials/connections/manzanar/history2.html. Accessed January 13, 2017.

1976

On this day, President Gerald Ford rescinds Executive Order 9066, 34 years after World War II. After World War II, Japanese Americans worked hard to restore their lives and recover from the devastation of having been imprisoned without due process and charged with any crimes. Many did not want to talk about their experiences. Nisei became notorious for keeping their wartime experiences from their sansei children. However, it is the Sansei generation who will fight for their rights, and the rights of their elders to be recognized and treated as fully American!

The social and political climate during the postwar period was one of civil rights and ethnic pride. While the Japanese American Citizens League (JACL) was disparaged for cooperating with the U.S. government in all of their policies during World War II, lawyers and lobbyists for the JACL worked diligently to overturn laws banning interracial marriage, legalizing segregation, and restricting rights to citizenship and immigration based on race.

AN AMERICAN PROMISE

By the President of the United States of America

A PROCLAMATION

In this Bicentennial Year, we are commemorating the anniversary dates of many of the great events in American history. An honest reckoning, however, must include a recognition of our national mistakes as well as our national achievements. Learning from our mistakes is not pleasant, but as a great philosopher once admonished, we must do so if we want to avoid repeating them.

February 19th is the anniversary of a sad day in American history. It was on that date in 1942, in the midst of the response to the hostilities that began on December 7, 1941, that Executive Order No. 9066 was issued, subsequently enforced by the criminal penalties of a statute enacted March 21, 1942, resulting in the uprooting of loyal Americans. Over one hundred thousand persons of Japanese ancestry were removed from their homes, detained in special camps, and eventually relocated.

The tremendous effort by the War Relocation Authority and concerned Americans for the welfare of these Japanese-Americans may add perspective to that story, but it does not erase the setback to fundamental American principles. Fortunately, the Japanese-American community in Hawai'i was spared the indignities suffered by those on our mainland.

We now know what we should have known then—not only was that evacuation wrong, but Japanese-Americans were and are loyal Americans. On the battlefield and at home, Japanese-Americans—names like Hamada, Mitsumori, Marimoto, Noguchi, Yamasaki, Kido, Munemori and Miyamura—have been and continue to be written in our history for the sacrifices and the contributions they have made to the well-being and security of this, our common Nation.

The Executive order that was issued on February 19, 1942, was for the sole purpose of prosecuting the war with the Axis Powers, and ceased to be effective with the end of those hostilities. Because there was no formal statement of its termination, however, there is concern among many Japanese-Americans that there may yet be some life in that obsolete document. I think it appropriate, in this our Bicentennial Year, to remove all doubt on that matter, and to make clear our commitment in the future.

Now, Therefore, I, Gerald R. Ford, *President of the United States of America, do hereby proclaim that all the authority conferred by Executive Order No. 9066 terminated upon the issuance of Proclamation No. 2714, which formally proclaimed the cessation of the hostilities of World War II on December 31, 1946.*

I call upon the American people to affirm with me this American Promise—that we have learned from the tragedy of that long-ago experience forever to treasure liberty and justice for each individual American, and resolve that this kind of action shall never again be repeated.

In Witness Whereof, *I have hereunto set my hand this nineteenth day of February in the year of our Lord nineteen hundred seventy-six, and of the Independence of the United States of America the two hundredth.*

GERALD R. FORD

Source: Gerald R. Ford: "Proclamation 4417—An American Promise." February 19, 1976. Ford Library Museum.gov. https://fordlibrarymuseum.gov/library/speeches/760111p.htm. Accessed January 17, 2017.

Books

Hosokawa, Bill. *JACL in Quest of Justice: The History of the Japanese American Citizens League.* New York: William Morrow, 1982. *JACL in Quest of Justice* details the history of Japanese American Citizens League's effort to get redress for the internment of Japanese Americans during World War II.

Murray, Alice. *Historical Memories of the Japanese American Internment and the Struggle for Redress.* Stanford, CA: Stanford University Press, 2008. *Historical Memories of the Japanese American Internment* analyzes the competing narratives and representations of the history of the Japanese American internment experience by the Japanese American community, media, government, activists, and academics.

Websites

Japanese American Citizens League (JACL). *The Japanese American Experience: Lesson in American History. Curriculum and Resource Guide.* 5th ed. 2011. This JACL publication provides a general history of the Japanese American historical experience during World War II, with a comprehensive chronology, images, and discussion of the post–World War II redress movement. https://jacl.org/wordpress/wp-content/uploads/2015/01/covers.pdf. Accessed January 17, 2017.

Yang, Alice. "Redress Movement." *Densho Encyclopedia*, June 15, 2014. This site provides a complete historical narrative of the Redress Movement with links to photographs and archival documents. http://encyclopedia.densho.org/Redress_movement/. Accessed January 17, 2017.

Also Noteworthy

2002

In Palermo, New York, Mitchel Trumble, a 18-year-old, is charged with felony criminal mischief as a hate crime for participating in the vandalism and destruction of a Sikh temple.

2009

Diana Chang (1924–2009), a Chinese American novelist, poet, and artist, dies. Chang's first and best-known novel, *The Frontiers of Love*, was published in 1956 and received critical acclaim.

February 20

1928

On this date, the U.S. Court of Appeals, Ninth Circuit, in *Lam Mow v. Nagle, Commissioner of Immigration*, rules that children born of Chinese parents on American vessels traveling on the high seas are not considered to be born in the United States and are thus not citizens. This affirms the decision in *Wong Kim Ark v. United States* (1898), which limits citizenship to a person of Chinese descent to being born on actual U.S. soil. This birthright citizenship is a guarantee of the Fourteenth Amendment but is limited to the territorial boundaries of the United States, and a ship is not a part of that boundary. Even though the child's parents have resided in the United States, were permitted to work, and were returning from a visit to China, the parents are not citizens/nationals of the United States, and therefore, the child is a subject and national of China.

Lam Mow v. Nagle, Commissioner of Immigration (9th Cir. 1928)

Circuit Court of Appeals, Ninth Circuit.

February 20, 1928.

Stephen M. White, of San Francisco, Cal., for appellant.

Geo. J. Hatfield, U. S. Atty., and T. J. Sheridan, Asst. U. S. Atty., both of San Francisco, Cal., for appellee.

Before GILBERT, RUDKIN, and DIETRICH, Circuit Judges.

DIETRICH, Circuit Judge.

This appeal is from a judgment dismissing a petition for a writ of habeas corpus by one Lam Mow or Lam Korea, a person of the Chinese race who seeks to prevent the enforcement of an order of the Department of Labor excluding him from admission to the United States upon the alleged ground of his alienage. There is no dispute about the facts, and the single question for consideration is whether a child born on a merchant vessel of American registry, on the high seas, of parents of the Chinese race and subjects of China, but domiciled in the United States, to which country they are returning from China at the time of the child's birth, is a citizen of the United States.

The petitioner's contention is that a child so born comes within the scope of section 1 of article 14 of the Constitution of the United States which provides that "all persons born or naturalized in the United States, and subject to the jurisdiction thereof, are citizens of the United States." The meaning of this provision and the general subject of citizenship, both by birth and by naturalization, are elaborately discussed in United States v. Wong Kim Ark, 169 U.S. 649, 18 S. Ct. 456, 42 L. Ed. 890, where it is definitely held, in effect, that if the petitioner here had been born within an area of land over which the United States exercises dominion as a sovereign power, he would be a citizen though of alien parentage. The real point in issue is therefore limited to the inquiry whether such a birth upon an American merchant vessel at sea is birth "in the United States" within the meaning of the Constitution.

Undoubtedly petitioner's theory that a merchant ship is to be considered a part of the territory of the country under whose flag she sails finds a measure of support in statements made in some of the decided cases and in texts upon international law. But no one of the decisions brought to our attention involved the precise question here presented, and the general statement, or its equivalent, that a vessel upon the high seas is deemed to be a part of the territory of the nation whose flag she flies, must be understood as having a qualified or figurative meaning. Manifestly in a physical sense that must be true. In view of recent decisions of the Supreme Court, elaboration upon this point is thought to be unnecessary. Scharrenberg v. Dollar S. S. Co., 245 U.S. 122, 127, 38 S. Ct. 28, 62 L. Ed. 189; Cunard S. S. Co. v. Mellon, 262 U.S. 100, 122, 43 S. Ct. 504, 67 L. Ed. 894, 27 A. L. R. 1306. In the latter case the court had under consideration the territorial coverage of the clause "United States and all territories subject to the jurisdiction thereof" in the Eighteenth Amendment. Speaking of defendants' contention that by this language the Prohibition Law extends to domestic merchant ships outside the waters of the United States, the court said:

"In support of their contention the defendants refer to the statement sometimes made that a merchant ship is a part of the territory of the country whose flag she flies. But this, as has been aptly observed, is a figure of speech, a metaphor. Scharrenberg v. Dollar S. S. Co., 245 U.S. 122, 127, 38 S. Ct. 28, 62 L. Ed. 189; In re Ross, 140 U.S. 453, 464, 11 S. Ct. 897, 35 L. Ed. 581; 1 Moore, International Law Digest, § 174; Westlake, International Law (2d Ed.) p. 264; Hall, International Law (7th Ed., Higgins)

sec. 76; Manning, Law of Nations (Amos) p. 276; Piggott, Nationality, pt. II, p. 13. The jurisdiction which it is intended to describe arises out of the nationality of the ship, as established by her domicile, registry and use of the flag, and partakes more of the characteristics of personal than of territorial sovereignty. See The Hamilton, 207 U.S. 398, 403, 28 S. Ct. 133, 52 L. Ed. 264; American Banana Co. v. United Fruit Co., 213 U.S. 347, 355, 29 S. Ct. 511, 53 L. Ed. 826, 16 Ann. Cas. 1047; 1 Oppenheim, International Law (3d Ed.) §§ 123–125, 128. It is chiefly applicable to ships on the high seas, where there is no territorial sovereign; and as respects ships in foreign territorial waters it has little application beyond what is affirmatively or tacitly permitted by the local sovereign. 2 Moore, International Law Digest, §§ 204, 205; Twiss, Law of Nations (2d Ed.) § 166; Woolsey, International Law (6th Ed.) § 58; 1 Oppenheim, International Law (3d Ed.) §§ 128, 146, 260. The defendants further contend that the Amendment covers foreign merchant ships when within the territorial waters of the United States. Of course, if it were true that a ship is a part of the territory of the country whose flag she carries, the contention would fail. But, as that is a fiction, we think the contention is right."

And it was further said:

"Various meanings are sought to be attributed to the term 'territory' in the phrase 'the United States and all territory subject to the jurisdiction thereof.' We are of opinion that it means the regional areas of land and adjacent waters over which the United States claims and exercises dominion and control as a sovereign power. The immediate context and the purport of the entire section show that the term is used in a physical and not a metaphorical sense that it refers to areas or districts having fixity of location and recognized boundaries. See United States v. Bevans, 3 Wheat. 336, 390, 4 L. Ed. 404. It now is settled in the United States and recognized elsewhere that the territory subject to its jurisdiction includes the land areas under its dominion and control, the ports, harbors, bays and other enclosed arms of the sea along its coast and a marginal belt of the sea extending from the coast line outward a marine league, or three geographic miles [citing cases]. This, we hold, is the territory which the amendment designates as its field of operation; and the designation is not of a part of this territory, but of 'all' of it."

We find no substantial reason for holding the phrase of the Fourteenth Amendment, "in the United States," was intended to have a wider scope.

It is said upon behalf of the petitioner that under this view we would have an absurd and unjust result in that appellant and others similarly situated would have no political status and would be in the position of a man without a country. But such conclusion does not necessarily follow. In Inglis v. Sailor's Snug Harbor, 3 Pet. 99, 155, 70 L. Ed. 617, Mr. Justice Story said:

"Two things usually concur to create citizenship; First, birth locally within the dominions of the sovereign; and secondly, birth within the protection and obedience, or, in other words, within the ligeance of the sovereign. That is, the party must be born within a place where the sovereign is, at the time, in full possession and exercise of his power, and the party must also, at his birth, derive protection from, and consequently owe obedience or allegiance to, the sovereign, as such de facto. There are some exceptions, which are founded upon peculiar reasons, and which, indeed, illustrate and confirm the general doctrine. Thus, a person who is born on the ocean is a subject of the prince to whom his parents then owe allegiance; for he is still deemed under the protection of his sovereign, and born in a place where he has dominion in common with all other sovereigns. So the children of an ambassador are held to be subjects of the prince whom he represents, although born under the actual protection and in the dominions of a foreign prince."

And the language was quoted with apparent approval in United States v. Wong Kim Ark, 169 U.S. 649, 659, 18 S. Ct. 456, 42 L. Ed. 890. In that view appellant is not without a country, but was born in allegiance to and under the protection of the Chinese government, with such temporary qualification only of the rights and obligations of that sovereignty as are recognized by the law of nations during the time the nationals of one country are being carried on the ships of another on the high seas. Moreover, if we resort to considerations as inconvenient as an aid to construction, we are inclined to think that in a comprehensive view the weight of such argument is against appellant's contention.

The judgment is affirmed.

Source: *Lam Mow v. Nagle, Commissioner of Immigration*. JUSTIA U.S. Supreme Court. This site provides the full text of *Lam Mow v. Nagle, Commissioner of Immigration*. http://law.justia.com/cases/federal/appellate-courts/F2/24/316/1496936/. Accessed January 28, 2018.

Books

McWhirter, Robert. *The Citizenship Flowchart*. Chicago, IL: American Bar Association, 2007. *The Citizenship Flowchart* provides comprehensive Q & A discussions on topics related to U.S. citizenship and naturalization.

Sohn, Louis, Kristen Juras, John Noyes, and Erik Franckx, eds. *Law of the Sea in a Nut Shell*. St Paul, MN: West Academic Publishing Co., 1984. *Law of the Sea in a Nut Shell* is a comprehensive guide that summarizes the international laws of the sea. In addition, it covers relevant historical jurisprudence of the United States.

Websites

Eng, Mike. "Perspectives: Birthright Citizenship; Chinese Americans Have Stake in Safeguarding This Right." Asian Americans Advancing Justice: Asian Law Caucus. This essay discusses this history and contemporary significances of birthright citizenship guaranteed by the Fourteenth Amendment. http://www.advancingjustice-alc.org/news_and_media/perspectives-birthright-citizenship-chinese-americans-have-stake-in-safeguarding-this-right/. Accessed January 12, 2017.

Kiel, Kim. "The Dauntless Incident: Should a United States Public Vessel Be Declared a 'Floating Piece' of United States Territory for Citizenship Purposes?" *University of Miami Inter-American Law Review* 21 (1989): 121–141. University of Miami Law School Institutional Repository. This article discusses the history and implication of court cases related to U.S. citizenship and the sea. http://repository.law.miami.edu/umialr/vol21/iss1/5. Accessed January 12, 2017.

Also Noteworthy

1920

The Korean School of Aviation is established in Willows, California.

1971

John Okada (September 23, 1923–February 20, 1971), author of *No-No Boy* (1957), dies.

1994

Pi Delta Psi, an Asian American cultural fraternity, is founded at Binghamton University in Binghamton, New York.

2007

In Ballard, Washington, Brian D. Lappin, a 35-year-old white man, and Nicole A. Kirk, a 25-year-old white woman, yell racial slurs at a Yemeni American deli owner and his employee, calling them terrorists before assaulting the owner.

2012

Jeremy Lin appears on the cover of *Sports Illustrated*.

2014

Julie Chu wins silver medal with the U.S. women's national ice hockey team at the Winter Olympics in Sochi, Russia.

February 21

1972

President Richard M. Nixon visits China. It was an important step toward formally normalizing diplomatic relations with the People's Republic of China. This allows many Americans to see images of China for the first time since the communist victory in 1949.

It also influenced the image of Chinese Americans and impacted Chinese and Chinese American transnational linkages.

The former Deputy Foreign Secretary, Guo Jiading, told the three of us why no assurance of a meeting by President Nixon with Chairman Mao was tendered. The reason was not for matters of foreign policy but for the feebleness of the Chairman's health. Throughout the fall of 1971 Mao was bed ridden, surrounded by nurses, oxygen tanks, and ventilation equipment.

Yet when the president's plane touched down in Beijing on February 21, 1972, Mao summoned the strength to struggle out of bed, ordering the removal of the nurses and the medical gear he issued the command "Bring Nixon here now."

Nixon in Leaders *described him on that first meeting "robust, earthy, exuding an animal magnetism." Nixon recalled in 1977 that Mao said "I see where your friend Chiang Kai-shek called me a bandit."*

After the translation Nixon said "What does the Chairman call Chiang Kai-shek?" Nixon stated Mao said "Well, uh, I call him a bandit too." Then Chou En-lai said "We just abuse each other." Then both Mao and Chou threw their heads back and laughed.

Nixon then said "You are aware of my sentiments in regard to communism. I am considered to be a rightist."

Then Mao said "I like rightists. I like Prime Minister Heath. I voted for you."

Nixon then said "Sometimes those on the right can do things which those on the left can only talk about. I could do it because no one could question my so called anti-communist credentials."

At the end of the meeting, Mao had to be helped to stand up for the handshake.

Yet it was the proffered outstretched handshake President Nixon was extending as he descended the airplane steps to greet Premier Chou that would be forever etched in their collective memory. Secretary of State John Foster Dulles, in 1954 at the Geneva Conference, had refused to take Chou En-lai's hand and that snub still rankled the Chinese. Nixon, who had done his diplomatic homework, understood that and was determined to begin the opening of relations with the People's Republic with this symbolic and dramatic shaking of hands.

On their ride from the airport into the city, Premier Chou said to President Nixon, "Your handshake came over the vastest ocean in the world—twenty-five years of no communication."

Source: Humes, James, and Jarvis Ryals. *"Only Nixon": His Trip to China Revisited and Restudied.* Lanham, MD: University Press of America, 2009, p. 75.

Books

Chang, Gordon. *Friends and Enemies: The United States, China, and the Soviet Union, 1948–1972.* Stanford, CA: Stanford University Press, 1990. *Friends and Enemies* critiques bilateral Sino-U.S. relation analysis and urges a triangular Sino-U.S.-Soviet approach to understand the complex foreign policy of the 1950s–1960s.

Tudda, Chris. *A Cold War Turning Point: Nixon and China, 1969–1972.* Baton Rouge: Louisiana State University Press, 2012. *A Cold War Turning Point* employs deep archival research to reveal new details between Nixon's administration and the Chinese government that impacted 20th-century international relations.

Websites

The Opening of China. Richard Nixon Foundation, Library, Museum. 2017. This site provides a detailed chronology of events that culminates in the normalization of U.S.-Sino relations. https://www.nixonfoundation.org/exhibit/the-opening-of-china/. Accessed September 3, 2017.

"Rapprochement with China, 1972." Milestones in the History of U.S. Foreign Relations. Office of the Historian. Bureau of Public Affairs. U.S. Department of State. This site provides a historical overview and legacy of Nixon's visit to China and includes historical photographs of Nixon meeting Chairman Mao Zedong. https://history.state.gov/milestones/1969-1976/rapprochement-china. Accessed September 3, 2017.

Also Noteworthy

1907

The Japan America Society of Southern California is established.

1942

The Tolan Committee, or the House Select Committee Investigating National Defense Migration, begins hearings to investigate problems related to "enemy aliens" (people with Japanese, German, and Italian ancestry) on the West Coast.

1956

Xuefei Jin, who writes using the pen name Ha Jin, is born on February 21, 1956, in Liaoning, China. He received a doctorate in English from Brandeis University in 1992. He published a book of poetry, *Between Silences* (1990), and *Waiting* (1999) for which he received a PEN/Faulkner Award.

2002

In Norwalk, California, James Scott Yungkans, a 37-year-old, is sentenced to a year in jail and placed on three years' probation for threatening a store clerk of Middle Eastern descent.

February 22

1784

The *Empress of China* (a.k.a. Chinese Queen) leaves New York. It was built in Boston in 1783 and is the first American ship to sail from the United States to China. The ship departed New York on February 22, 1784, and returned on May 11, 1785. The success of this voyage encouraged others to invest in further trade with China and is the cornerstone for beginning U.S.-China relations.

The ship left Canton on Dec. 28, 1784 and arrived in New York Harbor on May 11, 1785, with 800 chests of tea, 20,000 pairs of nankeen trousers and a huge quantity of porcelain. Newspapers announced her return, and her cargo was sold in stores up and down the East Coast. That's where they learned the real money of the trip was made in the sale of Chinese export goods to Americans. All told, the voyage earned a 25 percent return on investment, not as much as hoped, but enough to spawn a new era of commerce with China. [Samuel] Shaw gave a complete report of the voyage to John Jay, the U.S. foreign minister. Jay shared his findings with Congress, whose members felt "a peculiar satisfaction in the successful issue of this first effort of the citizens of America to establish a direct trade with China." For the next 60 years, the China trade would make New England merchants very, very wealthy. In Boston alone the China trade enriched George Cabot, John Perkins Cushing, Thomas Handasyd Perkins, Robert Bennet Forbes, Israel Thorndike and Russell Sturgis. Gideon Nye from North Fairhaven, Mass., made his fortune in the China Trade. And in Salem, trade with China made rich men of Elias Hasket Derby, Abiel Abbot Low and Joseph Peabody. The wealth generated by the China trade can best be seen in Salem's Chestnut Street District, part of the Samuel McIntire Historic District, the Salem Maritime National Historic Site and the Peabody-Essex Museum.

Source: "The Boatload of Ginseng That Launched the China Trade." New England Historical Society. 2016. http://www.newenglandhistoricalsociety.com/boatload-ginseng-launched-china-trade/. Accessed December 15, 2016.

Books

Giunta, Mary, and J. Dane Hartgrove, eds. *Documents of the Emerging Nation: U.S. Foreign Relations, 1775–1789*. Wilmington, DE: Scholarly Resources Books, 1998. This book contains diplomatic memos, private letters, and other historical documents in U.S. diplomatic history. See "The Far East Trade," pp. 237–238, for document related to the *Empress of China*.

Smith, Philip Chadwick Foster. *The Empress of China*. Philadelphia, PA: Philadelphia Maritime Museum, 1984. This volume narrates the story of the voyage largely from two journals, that of John Green and Samuel Shaw, two men who served on the ship. In addition, it provides an exhibition of material artifacts from the cargo on the ship.

Websites

Inghram, Matthew. "Chinese Porcelain." The Fred W. Smith National Library for the Study of George Washington at Mount Vernon. 2018. This essay reflects on the legacy of U.S.-China relations and Chinese porcelain of that period. https://www.mountvernon.org/library/digitalhistory/digital-encyclopedia/article/chinese-porcelain/. Accessed June 14, 2018.

"Two Hundred Years of U.S. Trade with China (1784–1984)." *Asia for Educators*. Columbia University, 2009. This article provides historical background to this historic voyage that set the stage for U.S.-China relations. http://afe.easia.columbia.edu/special/china_1750_us.htm. Accessed June 14, 2018.

Also Noteworthy

1877

Kanichi Miyama becomes the first legal Japanese immigrant to the United States to be baptized, and soon he was instrumental in creating the Fukuinkai (Gospel Society), which was the first voluntary Japanese organization in the United States. In addition to promoting Christian teachings and values, the Fukuinkai also hosted English lessons and several secular workshops to help the Japanese immigrants settle into their new surroundings.

1921

Caballeros De Demas-Alang, a Filipino fraternal organization, is established in San Francisco.

2006

Riverside Community College in California renames a street on campus after Miné Okubo (June 27, 1912–February 10, 2001), an American artist and author of Japanese ancestry who was interned at Tanforan and Topaz internment camps. She published *Citizen 13660* (1946)—her graphic book about life in the camps.

February 23

1944

The Renunciation Act of 1944 is passed by the U.S. House of Representatives and then passed by the Senate on June 23, 1944, and signed into law by President Franklin D. Roosevelt on July 1, 1944. Japanese Americans who gave up their citizenship included Nisei (second generation) and Kibei (American-born second-generation Japanese Americans who were educated in Japan) and are referred to as "renunciants."

When the amended act went into effect in July 1944, the expectation was that the extreme pro-Japanese Tule Lake internees would be most eager to renounce their allegiance to the United States, and so ease the way for them to return to Japan. But, surprisingly, only 144 internees took up the renunciation offer. . . . The renunciation act got out of hand after December 18, 1944, when word reached Tule Lake that all the internment camps were scheduled to be closed within a year and the internees would be forced to return to a hostile world outside. Rumors spread that the government would either deport alien parents and separate them from their citizen children or force entire families out to fend for themselves in hostile white communities. Pro-Japanese forces at the camp capitalized on these anxieties, ratcheting up the already considerable pressure they were bringing to bear on camp residents to renounce their citizenship. . . . Contrary to all expectation, the announcement of the closing of the internment camps set off mass renunciations at Tule Lake. Between December 1944 and January 1945, approximately six thousand people at Tule Lake renounced their citizenship. . . . When the initial "hysteria" subsided, and the renunciants had a chance to consider what they had done, they realized the enormity of their action and wished to undo it. . . . The renunciants attempted to enlist the help of other attorneys from all parts of the country, but they had no success. . . . The JACL wanted nothing to do with the renunciants.

Source: Srikanth, Rajini. *Constructing the Enemy: Empathy/Antipathy in U.S. Literature and Law.* Philadelphia, PA: Temple University Press, 2012, pp. 89–91.

Books

Collins, Donald. *Native American Aliens: Disloyalty and the Renunciation of Citizenship by Japanese Americans during World War II.* Westport, CT: Greenwood Press, 1985. *Native American Aliens* explores the history and impact of the renunciation law and contends that Japanese American renunciation was based on misinformation instead of disloyalty.

Tamura, Eileen. *In Defense of Justice: Joseph Kurihara and the Japanese American Struggle for Equality*. Urbana: University of Illinois Press, 2013. See Chapter 8, "Renunciation."

Websites

"From a Silk Cocoon: A Japanese American Renunciation Story." This site discusses renunciants at Tule Lake internment camp. http://www.fromasilkcocoon.com/renunciant.html. Accessed February 5, 2018.

Lyon, Cherstin. "Denaturalization Act of 1944/Public Law 78–405." *Densho Encyclopedia*, May 15, 2017. This essay offers a historical overview of the renunciation law and its impact on the Japanese American community. http://encyclopedia.densho.org/Denaturalization%20Act%20of%201944/Public%20Law%2078-405/. Accessed February 5, 2018.

Also Noteworthy

2014

The Dalai Lama, the spiritual leader of Tibetan Buddhism, blesses the Tibetan Association of Northern California's office in Richmond, California.

2016

Christine Diane Teigen (b. November 30, 1985) is an American model of Norwegian and Thai ancestries. Her cookbook *Cravings* is released on this day and becomes a *New York Times* bestseller.

February 24

1907

On this day, the Gentlemen's Agreement between the United States and Japan is concluded in the form of a Japanese note agreeing to deny passports to laborers who want to migrate to the United States. The Gentlemen's Agreement of 1907–1908 between the United States and Japan arose as a solution to a situation instigated by the segregationist policies of the San Francisco Board of Education. On October 11, 1906, the San Francisco Board of Education ordered the segregation of all Asian children into separate public schools. Since Chinese children were already restricted to segregated schools, it was understood that the order targeted the Japanese population. Roughly 93 ethnic Japanese students were ordered to attend the racially segregated Chinese school. The Chinese school was located in an area that had been devastated by the San Francisco earthquake and fires of that year. All but two families objected and refused to send their children to the segregated school. Some families retained an Issei (first-generation Japanese) attorney to file a legal challenge to the segregation order.

Both the Roosevelt administration and the Japanese Foreign Ministry were aware of their delicate political relationship and worked to ensure its stability despite the brewing crisis in San Francisco and growing anti-Japanese sentiment in California. The Gentlemen's Agreement presented itself as a compromise for both nations: in exchange for the rescinding of the San Francisco segregation order, the Japanese government agreed to restrict the immigration of Japanese laborers to the continental United States. Returning laborers, and parents, wives, and children of laborers already residing in the United States, were allowed to immigrate.

Although the Roosevelt administration intended the executive agreement to curb the growing Japanese population, it actually led to a steady increase in numbers. As part of the agreement, all Issei residents of the United States were required to register with the Japanese Foreign Ministry. With the assistance of the Japanese consulate general, community leaders organized Japanese associations to help with the bureaucratic processes of registration. They also assisted in processing applications to bring Japanese women into the United States as "picture brides." As a result of this loophole, the Issei were able to form families and escape the extreme gender imbalance that plagued the Chinese community.

Theodore Roosevelt Executive Order

Whereas, by the act entitled "An Act to regulate the immigration of aliens into the United States," approved February 20, 1907, whenever the President is satisfied that passports issued by any foreign government to its citizens to go to any country other than the United States or to any insular possession of the United States or to the Canal Zone, are being used for the purpose of enabling the holders to come to the continental territory of the United States to the detriment of labor conditions therein, it is made the duty of the President to refuse to permit such citizens of the country issuing such passports to enter the continental territory of the United States from such country or from such insular possession or from the Canal Zone;

And Whereas, upon sufficient evidence produced before me by the Department of Commerce and Labor, I am satisfied that passports issued by the Government of Japan to citizens of that country or Korea and who are laborers, skilled or unskilled, to go to Mexico, to Canada and to Hawai'i, are being used for the purpose of enabling the holders thereof to come to the continental territory of the United States to the detriment of labor conditions therein;

I hereby order that such citizens of Japan or Korea, to-wit: Japanese or Korean laborers, skilled and unskilled, who have received passports to go to Mexico, Canada or Hawai'i, and come therefrom, be refused permission to enter the continental territory of United States.

It is further ordered that the Secretary of Commerce and Labor be, and he hereby is, directed to take, thru the Bureau of Immigration and Naturalization such measures and to make and enforce such rules and regulations as may be necessary to carry this order into effect.

THEODORE ROOSEVELT
The White House,
Signed March 14, 1907.

Source: *The Complete Executive Orders of Theodore Roosevelt.* http://www.theodore-roosevelt.com/trexecutiveorders.html. Accessed January 28, 2018.

Books

Daniels, Roger. *The Politics of Prejudice: The Anti-Japanese Movement in California and the Struggle for Japanese Exclusion*. Berkeley: University of California Press, 1962. *The Politics of Prejudice* is a historical study of the anti-Japanese prejudice in California from the late 19th century to 1924.

Neu, Charles. *An Uncertain Friendship: Theodore Roosevelt and Japan, 1906–1909*. Cambridge, MA: Harvard University Press, 1967. *An Uncertain*

Friendship details a Japanese American political crisis during the last three years of Roosevelt's presidency.

Websites

"Gentlemen's Agreement." History.com. This site provides a discussion on the history of the Gentlemen's Agreement and its impact on U.S.-Japan relation. There are also links to short video clips. http://www.history.com/topics/gentlemens-agreement. Accessed October 14, 2016.

Imai, Shiho. "Gentlemen's Agreement." *Densho Encyclopedia*, March 19, 2013. This site provides a history of the Gentlemen's Agreement with links to relevant related topics. http://encyclopedia.densho.org/Gentlemen%27s_Agreement/. Accessed October 14, 2016.

Also Noteworthy

2013

Director Ang Lee wins Academy Award for Best Director for *Life of Pi* (2012).

February 25

1940

Frank Chin, controversial writer, literary critic, and editor, is born in Berkeley, California. He spent most of his childhood in Oakland, Chinatown. In 1972, he became the first Asian American playwright to have a play produced as a mainstream New York theater production at the American Place Theatre. Chin wrote *Chickencoop Chinaman* (1971) and won the East West Players in Los Angeles playwriting contest. Chin's second play, *The Year of the Dragon* (1974), was staged at the American Place Theatre. Chin published *The Chinaman Pacific & Frisco R.R. Co.* (1988), a collection of short stories and was awarded the American Book Award. In the early 1990s, Chin published two novels *Donald Duk* (1991) and *Gunga Din Highway* (1994). Among Asian American literature scholars, he is dubbed the "Godfather" of Asian American writing. He coedited the Asian American literary anthology *Aiiieeeee!* (1974) and *The Big Aiiieeeee!* (1991). In addition, Chin is considered a pioneer in Asian American theater, in part, because he founded the Asian American Theatre Workshop, which became the Asian American Theater Company in San Francisco, in 1973.

Excerpt from an interview between Robert Murray Davis and Frank Chin, on December 20, 1996.

Davis: Donald Duk, your first published novel, seemed to be a real departure for you. If I hadn't known you wrote it, I'm not sure I could have picked it out as your work, because it seemed very different from the kind of thing that you have done before. While it had some of the old Chin bite, it was less personal, more subdued. Did you do that consciously?

Chin: Sure. At the time Donald Duk came out, all of the Asian American stuff was autobiographies that I despised. All pushing the idea that we're all victims, all pushing the idea of the Chinese family or the Japanese family in America as dysfunctional. Talking about the big change to become Americanized. That's the only kind of thing that had ever been published in Chinese America, the White supremacist autobiography saying how fucked up it is being Chinese in America, that it doesn't work. So I saw a big gap. If there was all this rebellion going on, what were they rebelling against? Where was the portrait of the functioning Chinese-American family? How did all these people grow up in America-I am fifth generation-without committing suicide? If everyone despised Chinatown that much, why was there a Chinatown? How did the sucker survive? I saw instantly two gaps that had to be filled. One, they needed a book or several books of Chinese children's stories or Chinese fairy tales. Two, there needed to be a kind of Asian American Catcher in the Rye, an adolescent book dealing with being an Asian American adolescent or pubescent in this case. So I very consciously set out to fill these gaps.

Source: Davis, Robert. "West Meets East: A Conversation with Frank Chin." *Amerasia Journal* 24, no. 1 (1998): p. 88.

Books

Kim, Daniel. *Writing Manhood in Black and Yellow: Ralph Ellison, Frank Chin, and the Literary Politics of Identity*. Stanford, CA: Stanford University Press, 2005. See Chapter 3, "The Legacy of Fu-Manchu: Orientalist Desire and the Figure of the Asian 'Homosexual,'" for a critical analysis of Frank Chin's work vis-à-vis racial stereotypes and Orientalist ideologies.

Yin, Xiao-huang. *Chinese American Literature since the 1850s*. Champaign: University of Illinois Press, 2000. *Chinese American Literature since the 1850s* examines the origins and development of Chinese American literature written in English and Chinese.

Websites

Chin, Frank. Frank Chin blog site. 2017. This site contains videos, images, and writings of, about, and by Frank Chin. https://chintalks.blogspot.com/. Accessed September 3, 2017.

"Sleuthing Out 'Charlie Chan.'" *On Point with Tom Ashbrook*. August 3, 2010. This site provides a debate between Yunte Huang and Frank Chin, on the radio show, *On Point with Tom Ashbrook*, regarding the Chinese American stereotype of Charlie Chan. http://onpoint.legacy.wbur.org/2010/08/27/charlie-chan. Accessed September 3, 2017.

Also Noteworthy

1942

The navy orders 500 Japanese American families to evacuate their homes and businesses in 48 hours on Terminal Island, in San Pedro, California.

1946

The U.S. Supreme Court rules in *Duncan v. Kahanamoku*, 327 U.S. 304 (1946) that provost court justice and the military's usurpation of the civilian government in Hawaii during World War II was illegal.

1981

Lambda Phi Epsilon, an Asian American interest fraternity, is established at the University of California, Los Angeles.

February 26

1885

As the transatlantic trade in African slaves gradually came to be outlawed over the course of the 19th century, and as freed slaves in the Caribbean and the Americas began to demand higher pay for their work (or refused to work at all for their former masters), colonial plantation apparatuses found that their survival would depend upon the recruitment of more cheap labor. The trade in "indentured" Chinese labor, more commonly referred to as the "coolie trade," was one such type of recruitment. The 1885 Alien Contract Labor Law (a.k.a. Foran Act) prohibited American individuals or organizations from entering into labor contracts with individuals prior to their immigration to the United States and prohibited ship captains from transporting migrants under labor contracts.

CHAP. 164.—An act to prohibit the importation and migration of foreigners and aliens under contract or agreement to perform labor in the United States, its Territories, and the District of Columbia.

Be it enacted by the Senate and House of Representatives of the United States of America in Congress assembled, That from and after the passage of this act it shall be unlawful for any person, company, partnership, or corporation, in any manner whatsoever, to prepay the transportation, or in any way assist or encourage the importation or migration of any alien or aliens, any foreigner or foreigners, into the United States, its Territories, or the District of Columbia, under contract or agreement, parol or special, express or implied, made previous to the importation or migration of such alien or aliens, foreigner or foreigners, to perform labor or service of any kind in the United States, its Territories, or the District of Columbia.

Source: The Statutes at Large of the United States of America from December, 1883 to March, 1885. Washington, DC: Government Printing Office, 1885.

Books

LeMay, Michael. *U.S. Immigration: A Reference Handbook*. Santa Barbara, CA: ABC-CLIO, 2004. Political scientist Michael LeMay documents U.S. immigration laws in this authoritative volume.

Steinfeld, Robert J. *Coercion, Contract, and Free Labor in the Nineteenth Century*. Cambridge: Cambridge University Press, 2001. This volume examines the nature of wage labor in 19th-century America.

Websites

"1885 Contract Labor Law." U.S. Immigration Legislation Online. The University of Washington-Bothell Library. This site provides a summary of the legislation, along with the original text. http://library.uwb.edu/static/USimmigration/1885_contract_labor_law.html. Accessed October 20, 2016.

Orth, Samuel. "The Alien Contract Labor Law." *Political Science Quarterly* 22 (March 1, 1907), 49–60. This article is available at archive.org. It provides an analysis of the Alien Contract Labor Law, its history, development, evolution, and its legal implications. https://archive.org/stream/jstor-2140911/2140911#page/n0/mode/2up. Accessed March 7, 2017.

Also Noteworthy

1921

Arizona passes an Alien Land Law.

1930

Los Angeles Superior Court judge J. K. Smith rules that Filipinos are of the "Mongolian race," which invalidates more than 100 interracial marriages since 1921.

February 27

1880

Medical doctor Hugh Huger Toland dies. Toland was a prominent figure in the development of the public panic of the Chinese medical threat during the beginning of the anti-Chinese sentiment in the United States. He characterized Chinatown as a public health sanitary nuisance.

Although many physicians were ambivalent about regulating prostitution, some energetically developed knowledge about the effects of the Chinese prostitute on society. In the mid-1870s, at the height of the anti-Chinese political debate, physicians expressed fears about the spread of syphilis from Chinese prostitutes to the white population. During the California State Senate investigation of Chinese immigration in 1876, the senators questioned physicians about the prevalence of syphilis among Chinese prostitutes and the ramifications of white society. The most famous testimony came from Dr. Hugh Huger Toland, a member of the San Francisco Board of Health and founder of Toland Medical College (which subsequently became the University of California Medical School). Dr. Toland reported that he had examined white "boys eight and ten years old" with venereal diseases contracted at "Chinese houses of prostitution." These boys neglected their condition and hid it from their parents. When Toland diagnosed the disease as syphilis, the boys enlisted his assistance to "conceal their condition from their parents." Toland estimated that "nine-tenths" of all syphilis cases in white boys and young men were attributable to Chinese prostitutes: "When these persons come to me I ask them where they got the disease, and they generally tell me that they have been with Chinawomen. They think diseases contracted from Chinawomen are harder to cure than those contracted elsewhere, so they tell me as a matter of self-protection. I am satisfied from my experience, that nearly all boys in town, who have venereal disease, contracted it in Chinatown. They have no difficulty there, for the prices are so low that they go whenever they please. The women do not care how old the boys are, whether five years old or more, as long as they have money."

Source: Shah, Nayan. *Contagious Divides: Epidemics and Race in San Francisco's Chinatown*. Berkeley: University of California Press, 2001, pp. 85–86.

Books

Craddock, Susan. *City of Plagues: Disease, Poverty, and Deviance in San Francisco*. Minneapolis: University of Minnesota Press, 2000. *City of Plagues* scrutinizes public health and the construction of race in 19th–20th-century San Francisco.

Risse, Guenter. *Plague, Fear, and Politics in San Francisco's Chinatown*. Baltimore, MD: The Johns Hopkins University Press, 2012. Physician and historian Guenter Risse probes the public health crisis vis-à-vis race, politics, and fear mongering of Chinese residents in Chinatown.

Websites

Hugh Huger Toland (1806–1880). A History of UCSF. University of California, San Francisco. This site provides a brief biography and image of Dr. Toland. http://history.library.ucsf.edu/toland.html. Accessed September 3, 2017.

Trauner, Joan. "Chinese as Medical Scapegoats, 1870–1905: Historical Essay." FoundSF. This essay is a digital reproduction of the original published in the *California History Magazine*, 1978. http://www.foundsf.org/index.php?title=Chinese_as_Medical_Scapegoats,_1870-1905. Accessed September 3, 2017.

Also Noteworthy

2012

Jeremy Lin appears on the covers of both *Time* and *Sports Illustrated*, two major magazines in the United States. Jeremy Lin joined Michael Jordan and Dirk Nowitzki as the only NBA players to make the cover of *Sports Illustrated* twice in a row.

February 28

1947

An antigovernment uprising in Taiwan that was violently suppressed by the Chinese Nationalist government (Kuomintang), still headquartered on mainland China, kills thousands of civilians beginning on this day. This incident is commonly referred to as the February 28 Massacre, or 228 (Er Er Ba) in Chinese. The protest developed into a series of uprisings across the island that left more than 30,000 people dead. The Nationalist government's suppression of the protest ushered in the search for leaders of the independence movement, known as White Terror, that resulted in imprisonment and execution of thousands of Taiwanese intellectuals who challenged their rule. After Chinese Communist defeated the Chinese Nationalist, the Kuomintang imposed martial law in Taiwan. In the wake of the 228 Massacre, Taiwanese survivors fled and established dissident communities in the United States, Canada, Europe, and Japan.

As early as the evening of 28 February 1947, Governor Chen Yi delivered a message to the central authorities in Nanjing, claiming that the unrest on Taiwan had been staged and orchestrated by local communists and Taiwanese criminals. This telegram helped to set the stage for the official explanation of the incident, which remained largely unchanged until the late 1980s: from the perspective of the ruling KMT regime, the incident was depicted as an abortive attempt to overthrow the local authorities on Taiwan, and it was only due to resolute military intervention that the island—in the words of a sympathetic author—had been saved from "becoming Red even before the mainland." . . . Quite interestingly, however, the KMT did not make any attempt to substantiate this historical evaluation and to establish the memory of 228 as Taiwan's salvation from communist encroachment—a propagandistic strategy which would, after all, have been theoretically feasible. On the contrary, 228 was turned into a strictly taboo topic politically, so that even mention of the incident could have led to draconian punishment. The KMT regime made a determined—and partly successful—effort to erase all memory of 228 from Taiwanese society.

Source: Fleischauer, Stefan. "Perspectives on 228: The '28 February 1947 Uprising' in Contemporary Taiwan." In *Taiwanese Identity in the 21st Century: Domestic, Regional and Global Perspectives*, edited by Gunter Schubert and Jens Damm, p. 36. London: Routledge, 2011.

Books

Lai, Tse-han, Ramon Hawley Myers, and Wou Wei. *A Tragic Beginning: The Taiwan Uprising of February 28, 1947*. Palo Alto, CA: Stanford University Press, 1991. *A Tragic Beginning* is a history of the 228 Massacre.

Shackleton, Allan. *Formosa Calling: An Eyewitness Account of Conditions in Taiwan during the February 28th, 1947 Incident*. Upland, CA: Taiwan Publishing Company, 1998. *Formosa Calling* provides a firsthand account of the 228 Massacre.

Websites

Shattuck, Thomas. "Taiwan's White Terror: Remembering the 228 Incident." Foreign Policy Research Institute. February 27, 2017. This essay discusses the history and legacy of 228 in Taiwan. https://www.fpri.org/article/2017/02/taiwans-white-terror-remembering-228-incident/. Accessed March 1, 2013.

Teon, Aris. "The 228 Incident—The Uprising That Changed Taiwan's History." *Greater China Journal*, February 27, 2017. This essay is a well-researched historical overview of the 228 Massacre. https://china-journal.org/2017/02/27/the-228-incident-the-uprising-that-changed-taiwans-history/. Accessed September 3, 2017.

1948

Steven Chu, a Chinese American physicist, a 1997 Nobel Prize recipient in Physics, and the 12th U.S. secretary of energy, is born in St. Louis to father Ju Chin Chu, a chemical engineering professor at Washington University, and mother, Ching Chen Li. As secretary of energy, Chu focused on the development of renewable energy technologies to combat global climate change.

Excerpt of Steven Chu's written testimony in confirmation process to be President-Elect Obama's Secretary of Energy (January 13, 2009).

Excerpt from written testimony of Steven Chu during nomination process:

Question 1. How do you see a cap and trade market being designed? Do you support a cost containment mechanism? Do you support the inclusion of off-sets and, if so, what eligibility criteria do you believe should apply to those projects? Should property rights be extended to the holder of permits-to-emit under a cap and trade program?

Answer. President-elect Obama has proposed a cap-and-trade program to reduce greenhouse gas emissions, but the details of that program will not be developed until after the new Administration takes office. At that time, the issues of environmental targets and timetables, cost containment, offsets, linkages to other nations' commitments, and the many other program elements and options will be fully examined. The President-elect has said that he plans to work with Congress to develop an effective, bipartisan program.

Question 2. What role do you see the Department of Energy playing in the administration of a cap and trade program, if enacted?

Answer. President-elect Obama has proposed a cap-and-trade program to reduce greenhouse gas emissions, but the details of that program will not be developed until after the new Administration takes office. One of the most promising ways to meet both our climate change and energy goals without harming consumers is to develop the next generation of technologies that will enable us to transform the way we produce and use energy in America. If confirmed, I look forward to helping to lead that effort.

Question 3. Many areas of the United States, and the world, are already experiencing climatic change. How important do you believe adaptation will be, in terms of dealing with the issue of climate change in the very near future and going forward?

Answer. Mitigation actions to reduce greenhouse gas emissions are the most important steps that the United States must take. But most climate scientists believe that additional warming is built into the system, and therefore adaptation will also be important, especially in the Arctic and other areas that are feeling dramatic effects sooner.

Question 4. At least week's hearing on energy security, we discussed the imposition of a carbon tax as a straight-forward and transparent option in our efforts to combat climate change. Last year, the now-nominee for the Office of Management and Budget testified as Director of the Congressional Budget Office that a carbon tax could be as much as five times more efficient than a stringent cap and trade program. What are your thoughts on a carbon tax in lieu of a cap and trade program?

Answer. President-elect Obama has stated his preference for a cap-and-trade system, which has several advantages over a carbon tax. Advantages of a cap-and-trade system include more certainty about achieving the desired level of greenhouse gas reductions, and the possibility of linkages between domestic and international cap and-trade systems.

Question 5. A desire to transition away from our current energy mix and towards lower carbon energy sources, while incredibly important, is also very expensive. If confirmed, what level of coordination do you intend to pursue on climate change matters with the National Economic Council?

Answer. I expect that the National Economic Council will be a close partner of the Department of Energy and other agencies in the Administration's work on energy and climate change issues.

Source: Chu Nomination. Hearing before the Committee on Energy and Natural Resources U.S. Senate. 111th Congress. First Session to Consider the Nomination of Steven Chu to Be Secretary of Energy. January 13, 2009. Washington, DC: U.S. Government Printing Office, 2009, pp. 67–68.

Books

Daynes, Byron, Glen Sussman, and Jonathan P. West. *American Politics and the Environment*. 2nd ed. Albany: State University of New York Press, 2016. See Chapter 6 "Executive Agencies and the Environment: Personal Profile: Steven Chu: The Scientist in Charge Case Study: EPA Regulations of Carbon Emissions" for personal profile of Steven Chu and discussion of policies on climate change.

Gradziuk, Artur, and Ernest Wyciszkiewicz, eds. *Energy Security and Climate Change: Double Challenge for Policymakers*. Warsaw, Poland: Polski Instytut Spraw Miedzynarodowych, 2009. See Jennifer Bovair's "U.S. Energy and Climate Policy: Managing Expectations."

Websites

Bullis, Kevin. "Q & A: Steven Chu." *MIT Technology Review*, May 14, 2009. Besides providing an overview of Steven Chu, this site offers Chu's responses to questions about nuclear power post Yucca Mountain and why fuel-cell cars have no future. https://www.technologyreview.com/s/413475/q-a-steven-chu/. Accessed September 4, 2017.

Chu, Steven. "Letter from Secretary Steven Chu to Energy Department Employees." Department of Energy. February 1, 2013. In this open letter, Secretary of Energy Steven Chu highlights his accomplishments and announces his decision to not serve a second term. https://energy.gov/articles/letter-secretary-steven-chu-energy-department-employees. Accessed September 4, 2017.

Also Noteworthy

1849

The gold rush begins in California with the arrival of prospectors looking to strike it rich and many Chinese laborers looking for high wages in mining camps.

2007

Teddy Zee, Hollywood producer of Chinese ancestry, launches an interactive news magazine show called *MashBox* for Asian American cable network Myx TV.

March

March 1

1919

Known as the March 1st Movement, also known as the Samil Movement, Koreans in Korea protest Japanese occupation with a nationwide nonviolent demonstration. It marked the start of the Korean independence movement as Korean nationalists rose up against their Japanese colonizers. Subsequently, Korean American nationalists formed the Korean Congress on April 14–15, 1919, in Philadelphia at the Little Theatre to advocate for Korean independence. In the United States, Philip Jaisohn, the first Korean American to become a citizen, collaborated with Henry Chung and Syngman Rhee to advocate for Korean independence from overseas. The result was a transnational movement with a Korean Provisional Government established in Shanghai, China, and galvanized Koreans in America to organize for Korean independence.

Korean nationalism in the United States reached another important turning point in 1919 after the cause of Korean independence was rejected at the Paris Peace Conference that concluded World War I and former Korean King Kojong died. On March 1, 1919, Korean political and religious leaders gathered in Seoul to proclaim Korea's independence. The "March First Movement" would become a massive anticolonial uprising involving an estimated one million people. The Japanese tried to repress the nationwide demonstrations with brutal violence. Thousands of Koreans were killed and almost 20,000 were arrested. However, Koreans abroad in the continental United States, Hawai'i, Manchuria, Siberia, and China carried on the movement.

On [April 15,] the Korean National Association held the first Korean Liberty Congress in Philadelphia. Korean nationalists in the United States had long identified with American political ideologies and institutions in the cause of Korean independence. At this crucial moment, Korean American nationalists chose the United States' "cradle of history" to launch their own declaration. Two hundred representatives from twenty-seven organizations in the United States and Mexico as well as a few from Europe were there to witness the public Proclamation of Independence of Korea and to recognize the newly established Korean Provisional Government. Prominent American supporters joined leading Korean nationalists at the rally. The conference ended with a massive march through Philadelphia to Independence Hall, where the Proclamation of Independence of Korea was read and the representatives formally ask the U.S. government to recognize the new government.

Source: Lee, Erika. *The Making of Asian America: A History*. New York: Simon & Schuster, 2015, p. 148.

Books

Choe, Yong-ho, ed. *From the Land of Hibiscus: Koreans in Hawai'i, 1903–1950*. Honolulu: University of Hawaii Press, 2007. See Do-Hyung Kim and Yong-ho Choe's "The March First Movement of 1919 and Koreans in Hawaii."

Corfield, Justin. *Historical Dictionary of Pyongyang*. London: Anthem Press, 2013. See entry on "March 1st Movement" that details the history of this political protest and its significance in Korea's independence movement.

Websites

Davis, Susan. "The March First Movement." Koreasociety.org. This document is curriculum resource for teaching about the March 1st Movement. http://www.koreasociety.org/doc_view/550-the-march-first-movement-grades-7-12. Accessed September 4, 2017.

Kim, Han-Kyo. "Declaration of Independence (March 1, 1919)." Primary Source Document with Questions. Asia for Educators. Columbia University. This site provides the translation of the March 1, 1919, Proclamation for Independence. http://afe.easia.columbia.edu/ps/

korea/march_first_declaration.pdf. Accessed September 4, 2017.

Also Noteworthy

1920

The Japanese Foreign Ministry stops issuing passports to picture brides. Only women who are accompanying their husbands to the United States are issued passports.

2000

Alpha Psi Rho, an Asian/Pacific Islander interest fraternity, is founded at San Diego State University.

2018

While out for a walk in their neighborhood in Long Beach, California, Tony Kao and his wife and daughter, all American born, are targets of a racist rant by Tarin Frances Olson, a professor and counselor at Golden West College, who shouts at them to "Go back to your home country." In an interview with the media following the incident, Olsen says, "If you would like to have a full normal interview about the displacement of European-Americans, then I gladly am available to enlighten the public."

March 2

1889

Jodo Shinshu priest Soryu Kagai arrives in Honolulu, surveys the Japanese immigrant community, and later, establishes Buddhist groups among the Japanese laborers on the plantations.

Given the dynamics of immigration and the characteristics of the early Japanese American population, the initial formation of Jodo Shinshu Buddhism did not stem from a missionary effort in which priests set out to spread the Buddhist religion, but form requests from Japanese laborers in Hawaii and California. . . . In keeping with the historical sequence of the immigration, the first organized Jodo Shinshu presence in American-influenced territory was in Hawaii. In 1889, the Rev. Soryu Kagai arrived in Honolulu and began to establish Buddhist groups among the Japanese workers on the plantations. . . . As the recruitment of Japanese laborers to the islands continued, the population of Buddhists continued to grow through the 1890s, culminating in the construction of the first Japanese Buddhist temple in Hawaii in 1897. The founding of this temple marks the establishment of an independent Jodo Shinshu organization in Hawaii. This initial separation from the parent Jodo Shinshu body in Japan remains to this day, and by this same token, even after Hawaii because a US state in 1959, the Hawaiian organization retained only informal affiliation with the mainland organization and maintained its own leadership and clergy.

Source: Nishimura, Arthur. "The Buddhist Mission of North America 1898–1942: Religion and Its Social Functions in an Ethnic Community." In *North American Buddhists in Social Context*, edited by Paul David Numrich, p. 93. Leiden, the Netherlands: Brill, 2008.

Books

Hasegawa, Atsuko, and Nancy Shiraki. *Hōsha: A Pictorial History of Jōdo Shinshū Women in Hawaii*. Honolulu: The Hawaii Federation of Honpa Hongwanji, 1989. *Hōsha* offers an introduction to the history of Jodo Shinshu in Hawaii and the role of Japanese American women through historic photographs.

Williams, Duncan Ryuken, and Tomoe Moriya. *Issei Buddhism in the Americas*. Urbana: University of Illinois Press, 2010. *Issei Buddhism in the Americas* documents the history of Japanese Buddhism in the Americas.

Websites

"Buddhism in America." The Pluralism Project, Harvard University. This site provides a timeline of Buddhism in America, along with case studies of Buddhist temples in the United States. http://pluralism.org/timeline/buddhism-in-america/. Accessed October 9, 2016.

Honpa Hongwanji Buddhist Women's Association. This site contains the history of this association, photographs, newsletters, and more. http://www.hawaiibwa.org/. Accessed October 9, 2016.

Also Noteworthy

1942

General DeWitt issues Public Proclamation No. 1 designating military areas in Washington, Oregon, California, and Arizona and states that "enemy aliens" (people of Japanese, German, or Italian ancestry) might be excluded from these areas.

1995

Jerry Chih-Yuan Yang (b. November 6, 1968) and David Filo (b. April 20, 1966) incorporate Yahoo, one of the pioneers of the early Internet era in the 1990s. Yang served as CEO until November 17, 2008.

March 3

1875

The Page Law, enacted on March 3, 1875, is the first piece of U.S. legislation to attempt to directly regulate immigration. It reflected a growing anti-Asian sentiment in the United States and also marked a growing expansion of federal power following settlement of states' rights issues during the Civil War (1861–1865). Prostitution followed the influx of a large number of Chinese male laborers who came to California as a result of the 1849 gold rush and, later, the building of the transcontinental railroad. Although the female prostitutes on the West Coast were of various races and ethnicities, Chinese prostitutes predominated because of the growing bachelor community of Chinese men. Alarmed at the growing rate of laboring Chinese men and women, President Ulysses S. Grant called for immigration legislation in December 1874. California representative Horace F. Page, a Republican, sponsored the legislation that restricted the entry of contract labor and prostitutes from "China, Japan, or any Oriental country" that was not "free and voluntary." As a result of this piece of legislation, along with the 1882 Chinese Exclusion Law, a great majority of Chinese male laborers remained spouseless and turned to their bachelor communities for support and camaraderie.

CHAP.141—An act supplementary to the acts in relation to immigration.

SEC. 3. That the importation into the United States of women for the purpose of prostitution is hereby forbidden; and all contracts and agreements in relation thereto, made in advance or in pursuance of such illegal importation and purposes, are hereby declared void; and whoever shall knowingly or willfully hold, or attempt to hold, any woman to such purposes, in pursuance of such illegal importation and contract or agreement, shall be deemed guilty of a felony, and, on conviction thereof, shall be imprisoned not exceeding five years and pay a fine not exceeding five thousand dollars.

SEC. 4. That if any person shall knowingly and willfully contract, or attempt to contract, in advance or in pursuance of such illegal importation, to supply to another the labor of any coolie or other person brought into the United States in violation of section two thousand one hundred and fifty-eight of the Revised Statutes, or of any other section of the laws prohibiting the coolie-trade or of this act, such person shall be deemed guilty of a felony, and, upon conviction thereof, in any United States court, shall be fined in a sum not exceeding five hundred dollars and imprisoned for a term not exceeding one year.

SEC. 5. That it shall be unlawful for aliens of the following classes to immigrate into the United States, namely, persons who are undergoing a sentence for conviction in their own country of felonious crimes other than political or growing out of or the result of such political offenses, or whose sentence has been remitted on condition of their emigration, and women "imported for the purposes of prostitution." Every vessel arriving in the United States may be inspected under the direction of the collector of the port at which it arrives, if he shall have reason to believe that any such obnoxious person are on board; and the officer making such inspection shall certify the result thereof to the master or other person in charge of such vessel, designated in such certificate the person or persons, if any there be, ascertained by him to be of either of the classes whose importation is hereby forbidden. When such inspection is required by the collector as aforesaid, it shall be unlawful, without his permission, for any alien to leave any such vessel arriving in the United States from a foreign country until the inspection shall have been had and the result certified as herein provided; and at no time thereafter shall any alien certified to by the inspecting officer—as being of either of the classes whose immigration is forbidden by this section, be allowed to land in the United States, except in obedience to a judicial process issued pursuant to law.

Source: The Statutes at Large of the United States. Volume 18, Part 3. Washington, DC: Government Printing Office, 1875.

Books

Wegars, Priscilla. *Polly Bemis: A Chinese American Pioneer.* Cambridge, ID: Backeddy Books, 2003. Historical archaeologist Priscilla Wegars provides a history of Polly Bemis, a family Chinese American woman pioneer who lived in Idaho in the late 19th and early 20th century.

Yung, Judy. *Unbound Feet: A Social History of Chinese Women in San Francisco.* Berkeley: University of California Press, 1995. Historian Judy Yung employs oral histories to document the history of Chinese women in the United States.

Websites

Barde, Robert. "An Alleged Wife: One Immigrant in the Chinese Exclusion Era." *Prologue Magazine* 36, no. 1 (Spring 2004). In this issue, Robert Barde presents history and biography of Quok Shee, a Chinese woman who was interrogated on Angel Island. http://www.archives.gov/publications/prologue/2004/spring/alleged-wife-1.html. Accessed July 7, 2017.

"Chinese American Women: A History of Resilience and Resistance." The National Women's History Museum. 2008. This site provides historical information on the Chinese women experience and their contribution in the United States. https://archive.is/8SZ58. Accessed October 7, 2016.

Also Noteworthy

1931

An amendment to Cable Act declares that no American-born woman who was stripped of her citizenship (by marrying an alien ineligible to citizenship) can be denied the right of naturalization at a later date.

March 4

1942

The 1st Filipino Battalion is created on March 4, 1942, and activated on April 1, 1942, at Camp San Luis Obispo, California, under the direction of the California National Guard. On July 13, 1942, it was elevated as the First Filipino Infantry Regiment at the California Rodeo Grounds in Salinas, California, from which Japanese Americans were evacuated to isolated concentration camps. The battalion was comprised of volunteers of Filipinos from the United States and also by soldiers of the Philippine army and Philippine Scouts. The Filipino volunteers from the United States were mainly immigrant farm and cannery workers but also included a few Filipinos who had attained a college education.

On 3 January 1942, one day after Manila fell to Japanese forces, the National Headquarters of the Selective Services System formally announced congressional legislation permitting Filipinos, as volunteers and as draftees, to serve in the armed forces. In California, 16,000 Filipinos, almost half the immigrant community's population, enlisted. In April 1942, at the height of the joint U.S.-Filipino defense of Bataan and Corregidor, the First Filipino Infantry Battalion, a segregated unit of the U.S. Army, was formed at Camp San Luis Obispo. As news spread about the destruction of the Philippine fortresses and the Japanese occupation of the islands, the number of Filipino recruits swelled. Three months later, the First Filipino Infantry Regiment and Band, under the command of Colonel Robert H. Offley and staffed by 143 commissioned officers, 6 warrant officers, and more than 3,000 soldiers, absorbed the initial, smaller Filipino company. Before the end of the year, the Second Filipino Infantry Regiment was formed at Camp Cooked, California. About 7,000 Filipinos served in these units. Vincent Mendoza, a migrant laborer who eventually joined one of the Filipino divisions, remembered how during their training "lots of Americans come and see us. One time we went down to have a parade in Los Angeles in the street and we ended down there in City Hall and the Chamber of Commerce. We fired our weapon[s]. . . . Oh boy, how the American[s] liked it."

Source: Espana-Maram, Linda. *Creating Masculinity in Los Angeles's Little Manila: Working-Class Filipinos and Popular Culture, 1920s–1950s*. New York: Columbia University Press, 2006, pp. 152–153.

Books

Baldoz, Rick. *The Third Asiatic Invasion: Migration and Empire in Filipino America, 1898–1946.* New York: New York University Press, 2011. *The Third Asiatic Invasion* critically explores the history of Filipinos in the United States through politics of immigration, race, and questions of citizenship.

Crouchett, Lorraine Jacobs. *Filipinos in California: From the Days of the Galleons to the Present.* El Cerrito, CA: Downey Place Publishing House, Inc., 1983. *Filipinos in California* is a comprehensive history of the Filipino American experience in California.

Websites

Fabros, Alex. "California and Second World War: California's Filipino Infantry." www.militarymuseum.org. California State Military Department. February 8, 2016. This essay provides a historical overview of the first and second Filipino infantry regiments during World War II. http://www.militarymuseum.org/Filipino.html. Accessed September 4, 2017.

"History of the US Army's 1st Filipino Regiment and 2nd Filipino Battalion." U.S. Army Center of Military History. May 13, 2011. This site provides a historical overview of the Filipino Regiment and Battalion, along with links for the Yearbook of the First Filipino Regiment's training in California, and other resources related to this subject. http://www.history.army.mil/html/topics/apam/filipino_regt/filipino_regt.html. Accessed September 4, 2017.

Also Noteworthy

1939

Indian political exile and independence activist Lala Har Dayal dies in Philadelphia.

1981

Asian American journalists meet to discuss the formation of the Asian American Journalists Association.

1997

Morinaga Nutritional Foods opens a tofu plant in Tualatin, Oregon.

March 5

2006

Director Ang Lee (b. October 23, 1954) wins the Academy Award for Best Director for *Brokeback Mountain* (2005).

Brokeback Mountain—After the Academy Awards

The peace on Lee's face as he won the Academy Award for Best Director belied the controversy that had surrounded Brokeback Mountain *both prior to and following the awards ceremony. Immediately following the Best Director win,* Brokeback Mountain *went on to lose to* Crash *(2004) for Best Picture of 2005. It was a startling upset—*Brokeback Mountain *had been heavily favored to win—so unexpected that even the* Crash *producers were visibly caught by surprise. . . .* Brokeback Mountain*'s loss stirred up a new wave of controversy almost immediately. For example, after the ceremony, just minutes after Lee won his Best Director award, reporters in the postshow interviews bombarded him with questions about whether* Brokeback Mountain*'s loss was a snub against homosexuals. It was a familiar topic—James Schamus and Ang Lee, as well as the principal actors, Heath Ledger and Jake Gyllenhaal, had continually dealt with the homosexuality controversy since the film had been released. In this case, without taking the reporter's bait, Lee replied with utter grace: "You're asking me a question and I don't know the answer. . . . Congratulations to the Crash filmmakers."*

Source: Dilley, Whitney. *The Cinema of Ang Lee: The Other Side of the Screen*. London: Wallflower Press, 2015, p. 13.

Books

Fuller, Karla, ed. *Ang Lee: Interviews*. Jackson: University Press of Mississippi, 2016. *Ang Lee: Interviews* is a collection of interviews with Ang Lee discussing his films.

Wilson, Flannery. *New Taiwanese Cinema in Focus: Moving within and beyond the Frame*. Edinburgh: Edinburgh University Press, 2014. See Chapter 5, "The Chinese/Hollywood Aesthetic of Ang Lee: 'Westernized', Capitalist . . . and Box Office Gold."

Websites

"Ang Lee." Turner Classic Movies. 2010. This site provides a full biography of Ang Lee, along with a list of all his films. http://www.tcm.com/tcmdb/person/110811%7C0/Ang-Lee/. Accessed September 4, 2017.

"Ang Lee: Breaking Down 'Brokeback Mountain.'" Day to Day. (December 23, 2005). NPR. Ang Lee is interviewed about making *Brokeback Mountain*. https://www.npr.org/templates/story/story.php?storyId=5066480. Accessed June 14, 2018.

Also Noteworthy

1923

Nisei Americans (second-generation Japanese Americans) establish the American Loyalty League of Fresno, California, to demonstrate their loyalty and allegiance to the United States in response to anti-Japanese sentiment.

1999

The Masjid al-Huda mosque is attacked in Minneapolis, Minnesota.

2010

A group of Cambodian (Khmer) women hold their first "kick-off" meeting to establish Devata Giving Circle, a Cambodian American philanthropic organization comprised of Cambodian (Khmer) women working together to raise funds to advance leadership and human rights for Cambodian American women and girls.

March 6

1900

San Francisco City health officer autopsies a deceased Chinese man and finds organisms in the body that looked like plague. In April 1901, a cleanup campaign of Chinatown was undertaken, scouring almost 1,200 houses and 14,000 rooms. By May 19, 1900, San Francisco orders the quarantine and compulsory inoculation to all Japanese and Chinese upon discovery of the bubonic plague victim in Chinatown.

Our curtain opens on the morning of March 6, 1900, when the lifeless body of Wing Chung Ging, a forty-one-year-old Chinese lumberyard owner who had been a resident of San Francisco for sixteen years, was transported from the cellar of the dingy Globe Hotel in Chinatown to another location in preparation for embalming and burial. Had the Chinese physicians who attended to Wing chosen not to report this death, San Francisco's bubonic plague drama might have unfolded very differently. As it was, since only a white physician could issue a death certificate and burial permit, the doctors had decided to call in a white practitioner. Aware that Wing had been ill for some time and confident that his was yet another routine death from either a sexually transmitted disease or typhoid or some combination of the two, the Chinese doctors saw no risk in taking this action. What Wing's corpse revealed, however, was the strong possibility that he had died from bubonic plague. This discovery triggered yet another sad episode in the history of Chinese relations with Americans and sparked a public health crisis in San Francisco rarely encountered before or since.

Source: Echenberg, Myron. *Plague Ports: The Global Urban Impact of Bubonic Plague, 1894–1901*. New York: New York University Press, 2007, pp. 214–215.

Books

Chase, Marilyn. *The Barbary Plague: The Black Death in Victorian San Francisco*. New York: Random House, 2004. *The Barbary Plague* uncovers the history of the bubonic plague in late Victorian San Francisco through interlocking discussions of public health policies, race, and geography.

Shah, Nayan. *Contagious Divides: Epidemics and Race in San Francisco's Chinatown*. Berkeley: University of California Press, 2001. *Contagious Divides* is a public health history that examines racial formation among Chinese immigrants and public health policies surrounding the bubonic plague in San Francisco.

Websites

Anderson, Elizabeth. "Plague in the Continental United States, 1900–76." *Public Heath Reports* 93, no. 3 (May–June 1978): 297–301. This article covers the history of the plague in the United States. https://www.ncbi.nlm.nih.gov/pmc/articles/PMC1431896/pdf/pubhealthrep00142-0091.pdf. Accessed October 12, 2016.

"Bubonic Plague Hits San Francisco: 1900–1909." PBS. This site provides a general history of the plague in San Francisco with photographs. http://www.pbs.org/wgbh/aso/databank/entries/dm00bu.html. Accessed October 12, 2016.

Also Noteworthy

1879

California's second constitution prevents municipalities, corporations, and county and state government from employing people of Chinese ancestry. It says, "No Chinamen or Mongolian shall be employed, directly or indirectly, in any capacity or any public works, or in or about any buildings, or institutions, or grounds, under the control of this State." *Nev. Laws* 1879 (March 6), 81, ch. 74, section 1.

2004

In Lubbock, Texas, anti-Islamic and pro-American slogans are tagged on an Islamic center and burglarized. Four teenagers are charged with the burglary.

March 7

2017

Asian American Equal Pay Day launches a social media campaign to bring attention to Asian American women's wage gap.

On March 7th we observe Asian American Equal Pay Day. Please join in on social media to raise awareness of how AAPI communities experience the wage gap and increase visibility of AAPI work and wealth disparities that are often rendered invisible in mainstream conversations about the wage gap.

CORE MESSAGE Wage disparities experienced by many Asian American and Pacific Islander (AAPI) women and gender non-conforming people are made invisible due to the model minority myth. AAPI communities deserve equal pay for equal work and need research, advocacy, and policies that acknowledge the diversity of needs that exist across our communities.

Source: National Asian Pacific American Women's Forum. Sample Tweets & Messaging. http://www.napawf.org/uploads/1/1/4/9/114909119/asian-american-equal-pay-day_social-media-guide_short-version-2.28.17.pdf. Accessed February 5, 2018.

Books

Lee, Jennifer, and Min Zhou. *The Asian American Achievement Paradox*. New York: Russell Sage Foundation, 2015. *The Asian American Achievement Paradox* examines the racial stereotype of Asian Americans as a "model minority" and the complex historical, cultural, and institutional variables that confer success on some Asian American communities and not others.

Woo, Deborah. *Glass Ceilings and Asian Americans: The New Face of Workplace Barriers*. Walnut Creek, CA: AltaMira Press, 2000. *Glass Ceilings and Asian Americans* analyzes Asian American employment issues vis-à-vis discrimination in the workplace.

Websites

"Equal Pay Day Social Media Kit 2017." National Organization for Women. This site provides the social media talking points for Asian American women's equal pay. https://now.org/leaderdoc/equal-pay-days-social-media-kit-2017/. Accessed February 5, 2018.

"It's 2017 and AAPI Women Still Aren't Getting Equal Pay for Equal Work." Reappropriate: Asian American Feminism, Politics, and Pop Culture! March 7, 2017. This site provides quantitative data to argue for Asian American women's equal pay. http://reappropriate.co/2017/03/its-2017-and-aapi-women-still-arent-getting-equal-pay-for-equal-work-aapiequalpay/. Accessed February 5, 2018.

Also Noteworthy

2016

Season 8 of *RuPaul's Drag Race* airs and Kim Chi (born Sang-Young Shin, on August 8, 1987), a Korean American drag queen from Chicago, Illinois, is one of the 12 contestants. Kim Chi would go on to become runner-up in the reality television contest.

March 8

1921

Washington State legislature passes Alien Land Law.

In Washington State, similar alliances between politicians, the American Legion, and the Anti-Japanese League combined to push for a tightening of their alien land laws, leading the Washington State Legislature to pass in 1921and 1923 further anti-alien land laws that prohibited not only land ownership by aliens who had not declared in good faith their intention to become U.S. citizens, but also prohibited their leasing, renting, and sharecropping of land. The laws also disqualified aliens from acting as trustee, executor, administrator, or guardian of an estate that included land. Lands held by such aliens were to be escheated to the state. Japanese were thus by state law dispossessed of their land in Washington except on the Yakama Indian Reservation, where state law did not apply to federally administered land.

It was clear to exclusionists that federal intervention was necessary to completely remove Japanese from farming in Washington. The Yakama Indian Reservation was seen as pivotal in securing a federal anti-Japanese land policy, not just state law. Exclusionists stepped up their calls for formal prohibition against leasing reservation lands to Japanese. Although federal laws did indeed prohibit land ownership of federal lands by aliens, it did not prohibit the leasing of such lands by aliens. Exclusionists groups such as the Grange and the American Legion pressured the Department of Interior, under Secretary Albert B. Fall, to make federal leasing policy governing reservation land conform to the Washington State anti-alien law laws.

Source: Nomura, Gail. "Becoming 'Local' Japanese: Issei Adaptive Strategies on the Yakama Indian Reservation, 1906–1923." In *Nikkei in the Pacific Northwest: Japanese Americans and Japanese Canadians in the Twentieth Century*, edited by Louis Fiset and Gail Nomura, p. 58. Seattle: University of Washington Press, 2005.

Books

Allerfeldt, Kristofer. *Race, Radicalism, Religion, and Restriction: Immigration in the Pacific Northwest, 1890–1924*. Westport, CT: Praeger, 2003. Kristofer Allerfeldt researches the development of anti-Asian policies in the Pacific Northwest from 1890 to 1924.

Ichioka, Yuji. *The Issei: The World of the First Generation Japanese Immigrants, 1885–1924*. New York: The Free Press, 1990. Historian Yuji Ichioka details the history of the Issei in the United States.

Websites

Grant, Nicole. "White Supremacy and the Alien Land Laws of Washington State." Seattle Civil Rights & Labor History Project. University of Washington. 2008. This essay discusses the history of Alien Land Laws in Washington. http://depts.washington.edu/civilr/alien_land_laws.htm. Accessed September 4, 2017.

Lyon, Cherstin. "Alien Land Law." *Densho Encyclopedia*, May 23, 2014. This essay provides detailed historical overview of Alien Land Laws in the United States. http://encyclopedia.densho.org/Alien%20land%20laws/. Accessed October 12, 2016.

Also Noteworthy

1965

The first American combat troops arrive in Vietnam.

1970

Prince Norodom Sihanouk is ousted as Cambodia's chief of state in a bloodless coup backed by the United States, by pro-western Lt. Gen. Lon Nol, premier and defense minister, and First Deputy Premier Prince Sisowath Sirik Matak.

2006

Chloe Dao (b. June 15, 1972) wins season 2 of *Project Runway*.

March 9

1945

Japanese forces occupy French Indochina (Vietnam, Cambodia, and Laos) and declare its independence. This would later end France colonization of Vietnam, Cambodia, and Laos and open the way for U.S. intervention to stop the spread of communism, and eventually lead to the development of the Vietnam War.

The Japanese Coup d'Etat

On March 9 the Japanese occupation forces effected a coup d'état *throughout Indochina in which French military units were disarmed and interned along with French colonial authorities and influential French civilians. The Japanese action was intended to forestall an anticipated Indochinese uprising by Gaullist sympathizers after the Allies' liberation of France and the demise of the Vichy government in 1944. It was probably one of the greatest strokes of luck ever to befall a group of revolutionaries. Vietnam, with the exception of Cohin China, was declared independent as were Laos and Cambodia, all under Japanese tutelage. The Vietnamese emperor Bao Dai, a puppet under the French administration, formed another puppet government under the Japanese to administer Annam and Tonkin from the imperial capital of Hue while the Japanese retained full control of Cochin China.*

Source: Haycraft, William. *Unraveling Vietnam: How American Arms and Diplomacy Failed in Southeast Asia*. Jefferson, NC: McFarland & Company, Inc., 2005, p. 18.

Books

Khanh, Huynh Kim. *Vietnamese Communism 1925–1945*. Ithaca, NY: Cornell University Press, 1982. *Vietnamese Communism* is a focused study of the history of Vietnam's communist movement and its victory.

Smith, T. O. *Vietnam and the Unravelling of Empire: General Gracey in Asia 1942–1951*. New York: Palgrave Macmillan, 2014. Historian T. O. Smith traces the history of decolonization of French Indochina. See Chapter 3, "The Power Vacuum: Vietnam 1945," for discussion related to Vietnam.

Websites

Budge, Kent. "French Indochina." *The Pacific War Online Encyclopedia*, 2014. This essay provides a concise and detailed account of the Japanese invasion of French Indochina, and the subsequent liberation of Vietnam, Cambodia, and Laos from French colonization. http://pwencycl.kgbudge.com/F/r/French_Indochina.htm. Accessed September 4, 2017.

"Japanese Seizure of French Indochina." Current Intelligence Study Number 4. Office of Strategic Service. Research and Analysis Branch. March 30, 1945. www.cia.gov. This file is a CIA analysis of the Japanese *coup d'état* of French Indochina. https://www.cia.gov/library/readingroom/docs/DOC_0000709429.pdf. Accessed September 4, 2017.

Also Noteworthy

March 9–10, 1945

From March 9 to March 10, the U.S. bombs ignited a massive firestorm in Tokyo, killing upward of 120,000 civilians.

2004

In Davis, California, a white man points a gun at a Middle Eastern man at a gas station while making threatening remarks.

March 10

1959

On this day, nearly 300,000 Tibetans surround Norbulingka Palace, to stop the Dalai Lama from going to China with the People Liberation Army. By March 17, the Dalai Lama, members of his government, and roughly 80,000 Tibetans, fled to India. They sought political asylum from India, Nepal, and Bhutan and announced the formation of a Tibetan government in exile. This is a major reason for the resettlement of Tibetan refugees in the United States.

The exodus of Tibetans in 1949 was fueled by the Chinese occupation of Tibet: though the majority resettled in neighboring India, some made their way to the United States as political refugees. According to the 1990 U.S. Census, there were 2,185 Tibetans residing in the United States. There might have been earlier Tibetans (as well as Mongolians and Nepali immigrants) before 1949, but since they were classified as "Other Asian" by the U.S. Immigration Bureau, it is not possible to ascertain the exact figure. Most, if not all, Tibetan Americans have entered the United States as refugees. The Refugee Act of 1980 makes it possible for individuals to enter the United States as refugees if there are humanitarian concerns. Arrangement[s] for their transportation to the United States are usually organized through the International Organization for Migration, which also facilitated the resettlement of post–Vietnam War Cambodian, Laotian, and Vietnamese refugees from 1975 to the 1990s. The Immigration and Naturalization Service admits the refugees officially to the United States at the point of entry, and relies on support by VOLAGs to assist the new arrival with housing, schooling, and employment. As part of the Immigration Act of 1990, 1,000 displaced Tibetans were given special immigrant visas and have since resettled throughout the United States. Tibetans, classified as "citizens" of China, were not eligible to participate in the 1998 DV99 diversity lottery. While 40 percent of the Tibetan American population resides in Southern California, many communities have been established in other urban centers such as New York City; Washington, D.C.; Seattle, Washington; and Portland, Oregon. Tibetan Americans have formed strong communities in Northern California as well, primarily in Berkeley.

Source: Lee, Jonathan H. X. *History of Asian Americans: Exploring Diverse Roots*. Santa Barbara, CA: ABC-CLIO, 2015, pp. 169–170.

Books

Bernstorff, Dagmar, and Hubertus von Welck, ed. *Exile as Challenge: The Tibetan Diaspora*. Hyderabad, India: Orient Longman, 2003. *Exile as Challenge: The Tibetan Diaspora* is a comprehensive study of the global Tibetan diaspora. See Chapter 12 "Exiled Tibetans in Europe and North America" for a discussion of the Tibetan diaspora in Europe and North America.

Hess, Julia. *Immigrant Ambassadors: Citizenship and Belonging in the Tibetan Diaspora*. Stanford, CA: Stanford University Press, 2009. Anthropologist Julia Hess provides a study of Tibetan American community formation and identity vis-à-vis politics and globalization. See Chapter 5, "The Tibetan U.S. Resettlement Project: The Lottery, the 'Lucky 1,000,' and Immigrant Ambassadors."

Websites

Chang, Momo. "Little Tibet by the Bay." *Monthly: The East Bay's Premier Magazine of Culture and Commerce*, December 2016. Journalist Momo Chang discusses the history of Tibetan immigration to the United States and the formation of the Tibetan American community in Richmond, California. http://www.themonthly.com/feature1612.html. Accessed September 4, 2017.

Miller, Olivia. "Tibetan Americans." Countries and Their Cultures. 2017. This essay provides an overview of Tibetan immigration history and community formation in the United States. http://www.everyculture.com/multi/Sr-Z/Tibetan-Americans.html. Accessed September 4, 2017.

March 11

1976

The movie adaptation of Jeanne Wakatsuki Houston and James D. Houston's memoir, *Farewell to Manzanar* (1973), airs on NBC. The question of loyalty to the United States or to Japan is a core theme in *Farewell to Manzanar*. The memoir begins with the attack on Pearl Harbor and Papa quietly burning a flag of Japan that he brought with him from Hiroshima. Jeanne recalls seeing her father, Ko Wakatsuki, or "Papa," burn documents, "anything that might suggest he still had some connection with Japan." Papa is arrested and imprisoned for his "disloyalty," and the rest of Jeanne's family, along with all Japanese American families, is relocated to internment camps. The conflicted attitudes among internees, including Jeanne's family, toward the loyalty questionnaire, a survey in which internees were asked to swear loyalty to the United States, reflected the struggle to come to terms with one's place in a country that asked for loyalty and yet treated Japanese Americans with distrust.

Excerpt from *Farewell to Manzanar*, where Jeanne Wakatsuki recalls her first night at Manzanar internment camp.

A Different Kind of Sand.

We woke early, shivering and coated with dust that had blown up through the knotholes and in through the slits around the doorway. During the night Mama had unpacked all our clothes and heaped them on our beds for warmth. Now our cubicle looked as if a great laundry bag had exploded and then been sprayed with fine dust. A skin of sand covered the floor. I looked over Mama's shoulder at Kiyo, on top of his fat mattress, buried under jeans and overcoats and sweaters. His eyebrows were gray, and he was starting to giggle. He was looking at me, at my gray eyebrows and coated hair, and pretty soon we were both giggling. I looked at Mama's face to see if she thought Kiyo was funny. She lay very still next to me on our mattress, her eyes scanning everything—bare rafters, walls, dusty kinds—scanning slowly, and I think the mask of her face would have cracked had not Woody's voice just then come at us through the wall. He was rapping on the planks as if testing to see if they were hollow.

Source: Houston, Jeanne Wakatsuki, and James D. Houston. *Farewell to Manzanar: A True Story of Japanese American Experience during and after the World War II Internment*. Boston, MA: Houghton Mifflin, 1973, pp. 21–22.

Books

Cooper, Michael. *Remembering Manzanar: Life in a Japanese Relocation Camp*. New York: Clarion Books, 2002. Historian Michael Cooper uses internees' life writings to narrate the history and story of the Japanese Americans forced to live behind barbed wire.

Houston, Jeanne Wakatsuki, and James D. Houston. *Farewell to Manzanar: A True Story of Japanese American Experience during and after the World War II Internment*. Boston, MA: Houghton Mifflin, 1973.

Websites

Houston, Jeanne Wakatsuki. Interview. Online video. Japanese American National Museum, Discover Nikkei. 2006. This site provides an interview recording of Jeanne Wakatsuki in which she discusses her life and reflects on *Farewell to Manzanar*. http://www.discovernikkei.org/en/interviews/profiles/61/. Accessed September 4, 2017.

Wakida, Patricia. "Farewell to Manzanar (film)." *Densho Encyclopedia*, February 27, 2018. This essay discusses the film adaptation of *Farewell to Manzanar* and its impact. http://encyclopedia.densho.org/Farewell_to_Manzanar_%28film%29/. Accessed September 4, 2017.

Also Noteworthy

1886

Anandibai Gopalrao Joshi (March 31, 1865–February 26, 1887) graduates with a medical degree from Philadelphia's Woman's Medical College in Pennsylvania. Dr. Joshi is the first Hindu woman to receive a medical degree in the United States.

1912

Supreme Court rules in *Tang Tun v. Edsell* that Tang Tun and his bride are ordered to be deported, even though there is evidence that Tang Tun was born in the United States. The decision effectively denied Chinese immigrants' recourse to the court, as the court argued that consideration for deportation lies in the authority of the inspector and secretary of commerce and that the court should be left out of that process.

1942

The Wartime Civil Control Administration (WCCA) is established for "the execution of duties and responsibilities imposed upon the Commanding General, Western Defense Command," including the exclusion of civilians from the West Coast.

March 12

2007

Samdech Preah Maha Ghosananda, popularly referred to as the "Gandhi of Cambodia," a Theravada Buddhist monk who played a key role in reestablishing Buddhism in Cambodia after the fall of the Khmer Rouge, dies, at the age of 81, in Northampton, Massachusetts. Maha Ghosananda publicized the plight of the Cambodian people at many international forums and founded a number of temples in the United States. He was nominated for the Nobel Peace Prize three times in the 1990s.

When the Khmer Rouge era ended, the response of the Cambodian Buddhist leadership, particularly Samdech Preah Maha Ghosananda, was to focus on the healing of the wounds of the people and the reconciliation of the four mutually hostile camps within Cambodia which were fully capable of continuing armed hostilities.

To help with the healing of the people's wounds, Maha Ghosananda entered the refugee campus reciting the Metta Sutta *and verse 5 of the* Dhammapada . . . *as people wept. He urged people to let go of the past and move forward in their lives. The Cambodian people generally bore in mind the teachings of karma and forewent seeking revenge as they saw this as only prolonging the cycle of suffering, and they did not want themselves, or their children, to suffer any further. Maha Ghosananda led the Dhammayietra movement which accompanied refugees home, visited isolated villages still threatened by violence, and supported the voting that made the institution of a new government possible.*

Source: King, Sallie. "A Buddhist Perspective." In *Sharing Wisdom: Benefits and Boundaries of Interreligious Learning,* edited by Alon Goshen-Gottstein, p. 59. Lanham: Lexington Books, 2017.

Books

Hunt, Scott. *The Future of Peace: On the Front Lines with the World's Great Peacemakers*. San Francisco, CA: HarperSanFrancisco, 2002. See Chapter 6, "Maha Ghosananda: The Gandhi of Cambodia."

Marston, John Amos, and Elizabeth Guthrie, eds. *History, Buddhism, and New Religious Movements in Cambodia*. Honolulu: University of Hawaii Press, 2004. This anthology provides fresh research on the issue of the religion, institution, history, and government in Cambodia.

Websites

"Venerable Preah Maha Ghosananda." Khmer-Buddhist Educational Assistance Project. This site provides a full biography of Maha Ghosananda's life, activism, and legacy with images and links to a video interview. http://www.keap-net.org/venerablemahagho.html. Accessed September 4, 2017.

Venerable Santi. *Somdech Preah Maha Ghosananda: The Buddha of the Battlefields*. 2007. This site provides an online biography of Maha Ghosananda. http://www.ghosananda.org/bio_book.html. Accessed September 4, 2017.

Also Noteworthy

1997

House Foods America Corporation opens America's largest tofu factory in Garden Grove, California.

2006

Jeff Adachi's documentary *The Slanted Screen* (2006), examining the portrayal of Asian men in film and television, is released.

March 13

1977

The Organization of Chinese American Women (OCAW) elects its first inaugural executive board members.

Founded in 1977 by Pauline Tsui, Julia Chang Bloch, and Jeanie Jew, the Organization of Chinese American Women (OCAW) functions as a nonprofit clearing house for Asian and Pacific Islander American women. The OCAW lobbies federal authorities on a variety of issues, including increasing Asian American leadership role models, improving immigration laws for undocumented immigrants, and sponsoring congressional bills.

Source: Lamphier, Peg. "Organization of Chinese American Women." In *Women in American History: A Social, Political, and Cultural Encyclopedia and Document Collection*, edited by Peg Lamphier and Rosanne Welch, p. 208. Santa Barbara, CA: ABC-CLIO, 2017.

Books

Tsui, Pauline, ed. *History of the Organization of Chinese American Women*. Honolulu: University of Hawaii Press, 2014. *History of the Organization of Chinese American Women* covers the contributions and achievements of OCAW from 1977 to 2009.

Wei, William. *The Asian American Movement*. Philadelphia, PA: Temple University Press, 1993. See Chapter 3, "Race versus Gender: The Asian American Women's Movement."

Websites

Organization of Chinese American Women. Official web page. http://www.ocawwomen.org/about/. Accessed February 5, 2018.

Organization of Chinese American Women, Silicon Valley Chapter. This site provides OCAW newsletter. http://www.ocaw-svc.org/. Accessed February 5, 2018.

March 14

1907

President Theodore Roosevelt signs Executive Order (EO) 589 prohibiting Japanese with passports from Hawaii, Mexico, or Canada reentry to the United States. EO 589 impacts Japanese and Korean immigration from Hawaii to the continental United States. On February 13, 1913, President Harry S. Truman issued Executive Order 10009—Revoking in Part Executive Orders No. 589 of March 14, 1907, and No. 1712 of February 24, 1913.

Unfortunately for the planters, immigration did not resume, a consul was never appointed (providing Japan with an excuse to halt Korean emigration to Hawai'i), and Koreans continued to depart for California, with more than 450 departing in 1906. In 1907, the number dropped sharply to 150 only because President Theodore Roosevelt issued Executive Order 589 in March of that year prohibiting Japanese and Koreans in Hawai'i from moving to the mainland. With only a trickle moving thereafter, it is fair to say that the U.S. government did what the planters had not been able to do—stop the flow to the mainland. Between 1903, when the Koreans first arrived in Hawai'i, and 1907, when Roosevelt issued the Executive order, about 1,100 Koreans left Hawai'i for the West Coast. For the planters, what appeared to be the solution to their loss was dashed the following year, 1908, when Japan and the United States negotiated the Gentlemen's Agreement, effectively depriving the planters of immigrant labor from Japan (and Korea) and forcing them to turn to the Philippines in what would be the final major wave of labor immigration to Hawai'i, lasting until 1931.

Source: Patterson, Wayne. *The Ilse: First-Generation Korean Immigrants in Hawai'i, 1903–1973*. Honolulu: University of Hawaii Press, 2000, p. 27.

Books

Chang, Robert. *Disoriented: Asian Americans, Law, and the Nation-State*. New York: New York University Press, 1999. *Disoriented* examines the interconnection between race and law, historically, and in contemporary political discourses surrounding affirmative action and civil rights.

Lee, Erika, and Judy Yung. *Angel Island: Immigrant Gateway to America*. Oxford: Oxford University Press, 2010. See Chapter 5, "'A People without a Country': Korean Refugee Students and Picture Brides."

Websites

Executive Order 589. "Regulating the Entrance of Japanese or Korean Laborers into U.S. Territories." Papers of Theodore Roosevelt. The American Presidency Project. 2017. This site provides the full text of EO 589, along with other papers of Roosevelt's presidency. http://www.presidency.ucsb.edu/theodore_roosevelt.php. Accessed September 4, 2017.

President Harry S. Truman issued Executive Order 10009—Revoking in Part Executive Orders No. 589 of March 14, 1907, and No. 1712 of February 24, 1913. The American Presidency Project. 2017. This site provides the full text of EO 10009. http://www.presidency.ucsb.edu/ws/?pid=78225. Accessed September 4, 2017.

March 15

1884

A branch of the Japanese Fujinkai (Women's Association) opens in Oakland, California. Fujinkai are related to Jodo Shinshu sect of Japanese Buddhist tradition and established in all Japanese American communities as a mutual assistance organization where Japanese American women contributed to their family and community at large. It also became a major variable in the preservation of Jodo Shinshu Japanese American Buddhist cultural heritage.

Like the other associations (such as kumi*), the* fujinkai *played a crucial role when a member of one of the Buddhist temples passed away. The main function of the* fujinkai *at such times was to ensure that the families of the deceased were well taken care of during the ritual ceremonies. They also helped to prepare the corpse for the funeral ritual, which involved cleaning and dressing the body.*

Other fujinkai *activities included significant charitable works, which included the implementation of numerous projects for religious and language education purposes, as well as raising money for particular causes. For example . . . in Kona . . . the* fujinkai *collected $0.25 from each family in order to send comfort bags to Japanese soldiers in China.*

When members of the Kona Hongwanji and the Kona Daifukuji temple were interviewed, they described the fujinkai *members as strong, intelligent, and hardworking women who supported their temples. Several unpublished documents relating to the history of the temples in Kona District attest to the* fujinkai*'s cohesive connection with the Japanese community in Kona.*

Source: Abe, David. *Rural Isolation & Dual Cultural Existence: The Japanese-American Kona Coffee Community*. New York: Palgrave Macmillan, 2017, p. 147.

Books

Hasegawa, Atsuko, and Nancy S. Shiraki, eds. *Hosha: A Pictorial History of Jodo Shinshu Women in Hawaii*. Taipei: The Hawaii Federation of Honpa Hongwanji, 1989. This rare volume provides historical and modern images of the Jodo Shinshu women in Hawaii.

Nakano, Mei. *Japanese American Women: Three Generations 1890–1990*. Berkeley, CA: Mina Press Publishing, 1990. *Japanese American Women* documents "herstories" of Japanese American women and their contributions to the Japanese American community.

Websites

"Buddhist Women's Association." San Jose Buddhist Church Betsuin. 2003. This site provides a history of the San Jose Buddhist Women's Association that included historical photographs. http://sjbetsuin.com/buddhist-womens-association-bwa/history/. Accessed September 4, 2017.

Nakamura, Kelli. "Fujinkai." *Densho Encyclopedia*, May 24, 2016. This essay covers the historical development and significance of the Fujinkai in Japanese American communities. http://encyclopedia.densho.org/Fujinkai/. Accessed September 4, 2017.

Also Noteworthy

1994

Sigma Psi Zeta, an Asian American interest sorority, is established at the University of Albany, New York.

March 16

1900

President William McKinley appoints William Howard Taft to head the Second Philippine Commission.

One January 20, 1899, President McKinley appointed the First Philippine Commission (the Schurman Commission), a five-person group headed by Dr. Jacob Schurman, president of Cornell University, and including Admiral Dewey and General Otis, to investigate conditions in the islands and make recommendations. In the report . . . the commissioners acknowledged Filipino aspirations for independence; they declared, however, that the Philippines was not ready for it. . . .

The Second Philippine Commission (the Taft Commission), appointed by McKinley on March 16, 1900, and headed by William Howard Taft, was granted legislative as well as limited executive powers. Between September 1900 and August 1902, it issued 499 laws. A judicial system was established, including a Supreme Court, and a legal code was drawn up to replace antiquated Spanish ordinances. A civil service was organized. The 1901 municipal code provided for popularly elected presidents, vice presidents, and councilors to serve on municipal boards. . . . After military rule was terminated on July 4, 1901, the Philippine Constabulary gradually took over from United States army units the responsibility for suppressing guerrilla and bandit activities.

From the very beginning, United States presidents and their representatives in the islands defined their colonial mission as tutelage: preparing the Philippines for eventual independence.

Source: *Philippines Country Study Guide: Volume 1. Strategic Information and Developments.* Washington, DC: International Business Publications, 2013, pp. 64–65.

Books

Lurie, Jonathan. *William Howard Taft: The Travails of a Progressive Conservative.* Cambridge: Cambridge University Press, 2012. *William Howard Taft* is a biographical study of Taft that focuses on his career as both president and chief justice of the United States. See Chapter 3 "Roosevelt and Taft in the Philippines, 1900–1904" for a discussion of his time in the Philippines.

Philippines Country Study Guide: Volume 1. Strategic Information and Developments. Washington, DC: International Business Publications, 2013. This volume provides detailed historical information on all aspects of the history of the Philippines.

Websites

Miller Center of Public Affairs, University of Virginia. "William Taft (1857–1930)." This site provides essays by Taft, in addition to historical essays about Taft, his career, its impact, and photographs. http://millercenter.org/president/taft. Accessed October 12, 2016.

"The Taft Commission." Philippine History. 2005–2016. This site provides information on the Taft Commission, as well as chronology of Philippine history, current demographic statistics, and historic photographs. http://www.philippine-history.org/taft-commission.htm. Accessed October 12, 2016.

Also Noteworthy

2006

Jade Snow Wong (January 21, 1922–March 16, 2006), author of *Fifth Chinese Daughter* (1950), dies of cancer at age 84.

March 17

1980

President Jimmy Carter signs the Refugee Act into law. Under this act, the Office of Refugee Resettlement was established. It also adopted the definition of "refugee" used in the UN Protocol and provide regular and emergency admissions of refugees. Many refugees from Cambodia, Loas, and Vietnam will enter the United States through this act.

Only a meager 17,000 slots are allocated for persons who meet the universal standard of persecution set forth by the UN convention and the 1967 protocol. This standard was incorporated into the Refugee Act of 1980 and was intended to be the standard for United States refugee admissions. When the Refugee Act was being drafted, the House Judiciary Committee report emphasized that "the plight of the refugees themselves as opposed to national-origin or political considerations should be paramount in determining which refugees are to be admitted to the United States." The ideological and geographical biases included in all previous refugee legislation were to be jettisoned, the domestic definition was to be linked to the international definition, and the humanitarian and nondiscriminatory aspects of the law were to be emphasized. This has not happened in either refugee or asylee admissions. Since the passage of the Refugee Act, the prime beneficiaries of the controlling troika of interests have been Southeast Asians, Cubans, émigrés from Eastern Europe, the USSR, and now the former Soviet Union and its republics. In the years since its passage, the major provisions of the Refugee Act, ideologically neutral admissions and a fair asylum policy, have never been implemented.

Source: Zucker, Norman, and Naomi Zucker. *Desperate Crossings: Seeking Refuge in America.* New York: M.E. Sharpe, 1996, p. 43.

Books

Chan, Yuk Wah, ed. *The Chinese/Vietnamese Diaspora: Revisiting the Boat People*. New York: Routledge, 2011. *The Chinese/Vietnamese Diaspora* explores Chinese Vietnamese refugee displacement and examines their global resettlement.

Haines, David. *Refugees in America in the 1990s: A Reference Handbook*. Westport, CT: Greenwood Press, 1996. *Refugees in America in the 1990s* includes coverage of the history of refugees from Southeast Asia, resettlement policies, and community formations.

Websites

Carter, Jimmy. "Refugee Act of 1980 Statement on Signing S. 643 into Law." The American Presidency Project. University of California, Santa Barbara. 2018. The full text of President Carter's remarks after signing the act is available. http://www.presidency.ucsb.edu/ws/?pid=33154. Accessed February 5, 2018.

Refugee Act of 1980. National Archives Foundation. 2018. This site provides historical background to the passage of the act, as well as its significance, and provides a digital image of the document. https://www.archivesfoundation.org/documents/refugee-act-1980/. Accessed February 5, 2018.

Also Noteworthy

2003

In Boca Raton, Florida, George Aboujawdeh, a 46-year-old, is sentenced to one month in prison after repeatedly setting fire to a sign announcing the new site of an Islamic community center and mosque.

March 18

1942

On this day, President Roosevelt issues Executive Order 9102, establishing the War Relocation Authority (WRA) for the purposes of relocating Japanese Americans named in Order 9066. In total, 112,000 Japanese Americans were forced to leave their homes and properties and move into government detention facilities, euphemistically called "Assembly Centers" and "Relocation Centers." They were sent to 10 camps located in far-flung regions; each housed 10,000–20,000 Japanese Americans: Rohwer and Jerome, Arkansas; Gila River and Poston, Arizona; Manzanar and Tule Lake, California; Amache, Colorado; Minidoka, Idaho; Topaz, Utah; and Heart Mountain, Wyoming.

Executive Order 9102 Establishing the War Relocation Authority

By virtue of the authority vested in me by the Constitution and statutes of the United States, as President of the United States and Commander in Chief of the Army and Navy, and in order to provide for the removal from designated areas of persons whose removal is necessary in the interests of national security, it is ordered as follows:

1. *There is established in the Office for Emergency Management of the Executive Office of the President the War Relocation Authority, at the head of which shall be a Director appointed by and responsible to the President.*
2. *The Director of the War Relocation Authority is authorized and directed to formulate and effectuate a program for the removal, from the areas designated from time to time by the Secretary of War or appropriate military commander under the authority of Executive Order No. 9066 of February 19, 1942, of the persons or classes of persons designated under such Executive Order, and for their relocation, maintenance, and supervision.*
3. *In effectuating such program the Director shall have authority to*

   (a) *Accomplish all necessary evacuation not undertaken by the Secretary of War or appropriate military commander, provide for the relocation of such persons in appropriate places, provide for their needs in such manner as may be appropriate, and supervise their activities.*
   (b) *Provide, insofar as feasible and desirable, for the employment of such persons at useful work in industry, commerce, agriculture, or public projects, prescribe the terms and conditions of such public employment, and safeguard the public interest in the private employment of such persons.*
   (c) *Secure the cooperation, assistance, or services of any governmental agency.*
   (d) *Prescribe regulations necessary or desirable to promote effective execution of such program, and, as a means of coordinating evacuation and relocation activities, consult with the Secretary of War with respect to regulations issued and measures taken by him.*
   (e) *Make such delegations of authority as he may deem necessary.*
   (f) *Employ necessary personnel, and make such expenditures, including the making of loans and grants and the purchase of real property, as may be necessary, within the limits of such funds as may be made available to the Authority.*

4. *The Director shall consult with the United States Employment Service and other agencies on employment and other problems incident to activities under this Order.*
5. *The Director shall cooperate with the Alien Property Custodian appointed pursuant to Executive Order No. 9095 of March 11, 1942, in formulating policies to govern the custody, management, and disposal by the Alien Property Custodian of property belonging to foreign nationals removed under this Order or under Executive Order No. 9066 of February 19, 1942; and may assist all other persons removed under either of such Executive Orders in the management and disposal of their property.*
6. *Departments and agencies of the United States are directed to cooperate with and assist the Director in his activities hereunder. The Departments of War and Justice, under the direction of the Secretary of War and the Attorney General, respectively, shall insofar as consistent with the national interest provide such protective, police, and investigational services as the Director shall find necessary in connection with activities under this Order.*
7. *There is established within the War Relocation Authority the War Relocation Work Corps. The Director shall provide, by general regulations, for the enlistment in such Corps, for the duration of the present war, of persons removed under this Order or under Executive Order No. 9066 of February 19, 1942, and shall prescribe the terms and conditions of the work to be performed by such Corps, and the compensation to be paid.*
8. *There is established within the War Relocation Authority a Liaison Committee on War Relocation, which shall consist of the Secretary of War, the Secretary of the Treasury, the Attorney General, the Secretary of Agriculture, the Secretary of Labor, the Federal Security Administrator, the Director of Civilian Defense, and the Alien*

Property Custodian, or their deputies, and such other persons or agencies as the Director may designate. The Liaison Committee shall meet at the call of the Director and shall assist him in his duties.

9. *The Director shall keep the President informed with regard to the progress made in carrying out this Order, and perform such related duties as the President may from time to time assign to him.*
10. *In order to avoid duplication of evacuation activities under this Order and Executive Order No. 9066 of February 19, 1942, the Director shall not undertake any evacuation activities within military areas designated under said Executive Order No. 9066, without the prior approval of the Secretary of War or the appropriate military commander.*
11. *This Order does not limit the authority granted in Executive Order No. 8972 of December 12, 1941; Executive Order No. 9066 of February 19, 1942; Executive Order No. 9095 of March 11, 1942; Executive Proclamation No. 2525 of December 7, 1941; Executive Proclamation No. 2526 of December 8, 1941; Executive Proclamation No. 2527 of December 8, 1941; Executive Proclamation No. 2533 of December 19, 1941; or Executive Proclamation No. 2537 of January 14, 1942; nor does it limit the functions of the Federal Bureau of Investigation.*

Source: Roosevelt, Franklin D. "Executive Order 9102 Establishing the War Relocation Authority." March 18, 1942. The American Presidency Project. University of California, Santa Barbara. http://www.presidency.ucsb.edu/ws/?pid=16239. Accessed January 28, 2018.

Books

Robinson, Greg. *By Order of the President: FDR and the Internment of Japanese Americans*. Cambridge, MA: Harvard University Press, 2001. *By Order of the President* discusses the contradiction between FDR's image as humanitarian and preserver of democracy and the unjust internment of Japanese Americans during World War II.

Robinson, Greg. *A Tragedy of Democracy: Japanese Confinement in North America*. New York: Columbia University Press, 2009. *A Tragedy of Democracy* provides a comprehensive critical and transnational analysis of official government policy toward West Coast Japanese Americans in North America.

Websites

"Historic Documents." Manzanar National Historic Site, California. National Park Service. This site provides archival documents related to the internment of Japanese Americans during World War II. https://www.nps.gov/manz/learn/historyculture/historic-documents.htm. Accessed January 13, 2017.

Robinson, Greg. "War Relocation Authority." *Densho Encyclopedia*, May 6, 2015. This site provides a detailed historical overview of the War Relocation Authority with a discussion of its impact and legacy, accompanied by links to historical images, and archival documents. http://encyclopedia.densho.org/War_Relocation_Authority/. Accessed January 13, 2017.

Also Noteworthy

1901

The Supreme Court rules in *Sung v. U.S.* that the prohibition against unreasonable searches and seizures, cruel and unusual punishment, and the right to a jury trial does not apply to deportation hearings.

March 19

1970

The day before, Lon Nol (November 13, 1913–November 17, 1985), with support from the United States, led a bloodless *coup d'état* that ousted Prince Norodom Sihanouk (October 31, 1922–October 15, 2012). On this day, Premier Lon Nol declares a state of emergency and suspends four articles of the constitution, permits arbitrary arrest, and bans public assembly. By April 1970, Lon Nol abolished the monarchy and established the Khmer Republic. Days later, Sihanouk established a government in exile, the National United Front of Kampuchea, seeking support from his old enemy, the Khmer Rouge. This move surprised many, because for years, Sihanouk had denounced and suppressed their activities and had even derisively dubbed them "Khmer Rouge" (Red Khmer). Little did he know that he was laying the foundation for the Khmer Rouge victory that would come five years later.

Lon Nol was a Sihanouk loyalist until the night before the coup that overthrew Sihanouk, when Prince Sisowath Sirik Matak cajoled and threatened him into making common cause with the plotters. "When did you stop being a faithful servant of Sihanouk?" a report asked Lon Nol at his first press conference after the prince's overthrow. "On the eighteenth of March at one o'clock," the prime minister answered unhesitatingly. That was the hour of the parliament's vote to depose the chief of state. And Sihanouk had no argument with that. The quality that Sihanouk most prized in Lon Nol, whom he had appointed prime minister and chief of staff and who had served him in a wide range of ministerial and military jobs, was his unquestioning loyalty.... Members of Lon Nol's entourage, among them Lon Non, told me that it was only when Lon Nol came reluctantly to believe, not long before the coup d'etat, that Sihanouk had sold out to the Vietnamese that Lon Nol began to lend an ear to criticisms of the prince. He voiced none himself.

Kamm, Henry. *Cambodia: Report from a Stricken Land.* New York: Arcade Publishing, 1998, pp. 93–94.

Books

Brinkley, Joel. *Cambodia's Curse: The Modern History of a Troubled Land.* New York: PublicAffairs, 2011. Pulitzer Prize–winning journalist, Joel Brinkley, explores the legacy of the Khmer Rouge–era historical terror in the people of Cambodia, today.

Osborne, Milton. *Sihanouk: Prince of Light, Prince of Darkness.* Honolulu: University of Hawaii Press, 1994. *Sihanouk* traces the complete life and political career of Norodom Sihanouk.

Websites

Becker, Elizabeth, and Seth Mydans. "Norodom Sihanouk, Cambodian Leader through Shifting Allegiances, Dies at 89." *New York Times*, October 14, 2012. This article is a retrospective on the life and political career of Norohom Sihanouk. http://www.nytimes.com/2012/10/15/world/asia/norodom-sihanouk-cambodian-leader-through-shifting-allegiances-dies-at-89.html?mcubz=0. Accessed September 4, 2017.

Kerr, Peter. "Lon Nol, 72, Dies; Led Cambodia in Early 1970's." *New York Times*, November 18, 1985. This article provides a retrospective on Lon Nol's life. http://www.nytimes.com/1985/11/18/world/lon-nol-72-dies-led-cambodia-in-early-1970-s.html?mcubz=0. Accessed September 4, 2017.

Also Noteworthy

2003

President George Bush announces the launch of Operation Iraqi Freedom, which begins the war in Iraq.

March 20

1900

Two hundred and forty-six Japanese and 111 Chinese passengers arrive in San Francisco on the SS *Hong Kong Maru.*

Japanese Are Pouring into San Francisco

The Toyo Kisen Kaisha's steamer Hongkong Maru *arrived from the Orient late Wednesday night and was sent into quarantine yesterday morning. As soon as Dr. Kinyoun learned that the plague was dying out in Honolulu he allowed the cabin passengers to land.*

The vessel was held for fumigation, however, and will probably dock to-day....

In the steerage the Japanese mail boat has three Europeans, 246 Japanese and 111 Chinese passengers. The influx of Japanese into California has been something wonderful of late.

Every steamer from the Orient brings them into the United States in hundreds, and in consequence every vessel from the Sound has her steerage crowded with them. The Walla Walla *brought in over a hundred, while the* City of Puebla, *due here Sunday, has near two hundred aboard.*

The demand for Japanese labor has increased with leaps and bounds within the last few months. The Highbinder Wars among the Chinese have paralyzed that class of labor, and the "little brown men" from Japan are wanted in their place. On its face, however, it looks very much like contract labor coming into California.

Source: "Ship Passengers, Sea Captains." The Maritime Heritage Project, San Francisco, 1846–1899. http://www.maritimeheritage.org/. Accessed October 13, 2016.

Books

Matthews, Frederick. *American Merchant Ships, 1850–1900.* Mineola, NY: Dover Publications, 2012. *American Merchant Ships* is a complete history of 322 19th-century merchant vessels that includes photographs, images, stories, and meticulous details about the vessels.

Uchinanchu: A History of Okinawans in Hawaii. Honolulu: Ethnic Studies Program, University of Hawaii, 1981. *Uchinanchu* examines many aspects of Okinawan immigration to Hawaii through oral histories.

Websites

Japanese American Citizens League. This site provides information on many aspects of Japanese immigration history to the United States. https://jacl.org/asian-american-history/. Accessed October 13, 2016.

The Maritime Heritage Project, San Francisco 1846–1899. This site is related to immigration in the 1800s, family history, maritime history and studies, and California studies. http://www.maritimeheritage.org/. Accessed October 13, 2016.

Also Noteworthy

1946

Tule Lake "Segregation Center" is the last internment camp to close.

1969

The student-led protest at San Francisco State University ends with a settlement to establish the country's first and still only School (now College) of Ethnic Studies. Asian American Studies is one of the programs, along with American Indian Studies, Black Studies (now Africana Studies), and La Raza Studies (now Latina/o Studies).

March 21

1910

A "race riot" between white and "East Indian" laborers leaves two Sikhs injured at St. Johns, Oregon. In the wake of that riot, almost 200 residents and the town's mayor and police chief were charged with rioting by the Portland district attorney. Only one man was convicted.

Punjabis began arriving in Oregon through direct immigration to the United States and through the fluid border with Canada. It is easy to imagine that Punjabis displaced by the Bellingham and Vancouver riots found their way south, swelling existing Punjabi settlements or creating new ones. It is also easy to envision mill operators in out-of-the-way towns along the Columbia River greedily hiring these newly arrived men, as labor was chronically short in this land rich with trees. The largest community of Punjabis developed in Astoria but was amplified by others in The Dalles,

Hood River, Bridal Veil, Winans, Portland, St. Johns, Linnton, Goble, Clatskanie, Rainier, John Day, and Seaside.

Oregon was not free of hostility toward Asian Indians. Newspapers in both Portland and Astoria ran their share of stories promoting the exclusionist myth of the "Hindu invasion," along with reports on the riots against the Punjabis in Bellingham, Everett, and Vancouver. In Boring, just outside Portland, an Asian Indian man was shot to death on Halloween 1907, the victim of a hate crime. Asian-exclusion societies gained some coverage in the daily press and took some nominal organizational forms in both Portland and Astoria. Communal violence occurred as well, most notably in St. Johns . . . nearly three hundred men moved on Punjabi laborers' homes, ransacked them, beat and robbed the men, and drove out those still at work in the mill. All the Punjabi men left St. Johns that night.

Source: Ogden, Johanna. "Ghadar, Historical Silences and Notions of Belonging: Early 1900s Punjabis of the Columbia River." *Oregon Historical Quarterly* 113, no. 2 (Summer 2012): p. 173.

Books

Shah, Nyan. *Stranger Intimacy: Contesting Race, Sexuality, and the Law in the North American West.* Berkeley: University of California Press, 2011. *Stranger Intimacy* studies the ways that the United States and Canada worked together to exclude Asian immigrants during the first half of the 20th century.

Sohi, Seema. *Echoes of Mutiny: Race, Surveillance & Indian Anticolonialism in North America.* Oxford: Oxford University Press, 2014. *Echoes of Mutiny* looks at the history of South Asian immigrants during the early 20th century who migrated to the Pacific Coast of North America, and despite encounters with racist exclusionary policies, forged a transnational anticolonial movement from abroad.

Websites

Ogden, Johanna. "East Indians of Oregon and the Ghadar Party." *Oregon Encyclopedia*, March 11, 2016. This essay is an overview of South Asian history in Oregon. https://oregonencyclopedia.org/articles/east_indians_of_oregon_and_the_ghadar_party/#.Wa5QUsiGO70. Accessed September 5, 2017.

Ogden, Johanna. "Social and Political Lives of Punjabi Settlers of the Columbia River, Oregon 1910–1920." Canadian Sikh Centre. This conference paper discusses the history of Punjabi Sikhs in Oregon. http://www.canadiansikhcentre.com/wp-content/uploads/2013/04/Social-and-Political-Lives-of-Punjabi-Settlers-of-the-Columbia-River-Oregon-1910-1920-Johana-Ogden.pdf. Accessed September 5, 2017.

Also Noteworthy

1921

The Korean Residents Association (Yuomindan) is established by a group of Korean residents in Hawaii to assist Syngman Rhee's work to achieve Korean independence.

1942

Congress passes Public Law 503 to punish anyone defying orders to carry out Executive Order 9066.

Manzanar, California, Assembly Center opens; it is in operation until June 2.

2003

In Burbank, Illinois, Eric K. Nix, a 24-year-old, throws a fireworks device into a Palestinian Muslim family's van. He is convicted of arson and committing a hate crime in 2006.

March 22

2002

On this day, Cambodia and the United States enter into a repatriation agreement. The agreement broadly established that Cambodia would fully cooperate in the repatriation of their nationals from the United States. Changes to immigration policy made deportation mandatory for all legal permanent residents who were sentenced to a year or more for aggravated felonies, moral turpitude, or use of controlled substances. Judge's discretion for individual cases was also removed. The Cambodian American community, and some 1,400 young men and women who had been ordered deported to Cambodia, for the first time faced the prospect of the forced return of family members to the country that they had fled just four decades earlier. Cambodian Americans are most concerned that the repatriated Cambodian Americans may face serious human rights abuses such as imprisonment and torture. At a minimum, most of them have limited knowledge of Cambodia and its social norms. They would be going there with little or no family support, and many would be leaving behind most if not all of their immediate families. Many of the repatriated Cambodian Americans have limited Khmer language skills, and most are illiterate in written Khmer.

My name is Andrew Thi. I was born on February 10, 1975 in Battambang, Cambodia. It was bad there, all the genocide and war. If the Communists saw you, they would put you in jail or kill you on sight. My family did what we had to do to escape to a Thai refugee camp where we began the long process to immigrate to the U.S. It was a long wait, but worth it. In 1981, my parents, three sisters and I arrived in San Francisco and made our home in Oakland. . . .

High school is when it really began. We went from stealing clothes to stealing cars for money and to get around. I wasn't in an organized gang; we would sell that parts to people. I taught my Hayward friends how to steal cars, and when they were caught by the cops they blamed me. That was so weak; they snitched on me. I wanted to go up there and snatch them. . . .

I wasted my youth. I wanted fun and excitement, I wanted to be independent and in control, but it cost me five years in prison. . . .

Since getting out of custody, I don't fool with the law anymore. I do landscaping with my dad four days a week. I pay taxes. I have no complaints . . . I still check in quarterly with INS. I can potentially be deported back to Cambodia whenever they call my name. Every time I check in, I wonder if they're going to take me in, especially now that they want to know about my ancestors, village, and relatives—I know nothing. It would be hard if I go back, since I have no family there. . . .

Source: Hing, Bill. *Deporting Our Souls: Values, Morality, and Immigration Policy*. Cambridge: Cambridge University Press, 2006, pp. 83–87.

Books

Barrett, Kimberly, and William George, eds. *Race, Culture, Psychology & Law*. Thousand Oaks, CA: Sage Publications, 2005. See Dori Cahn and Jay Stansell's Chapter 16, "From Refugee to Deportee: How U.S. Immigration Law Failed the Cambodian Community."

Lee, Jonathan H.X., ed. *Cambodian American Experiences: Histories, Communities, Cultures, and Identities*. Dubuque, IA: Kendall and Hunt Publishing Company, 2010. *Cambodian American Experiences* covers the history and contemporary challenges of the Cambodian American community, including the issue of "forced return."

Websites

"Deported from U.S., Cambodians Fight Immigration Policy." *PBS NewsHour*, May 8, 2017. This site contains a video that documents Cambodian American deportees, along with an interview with a Cambodian American who was deported back to Cambodia. http://www.pbs.org/newshour/bb/deported-u-s-cambodians-fight-immigration-policy/. Accessed September 5, 2017.

Ten, Soksreinith. "Cambodians Face Deportations to Homeland They've Never Known." Voice of America. February 10, 2017. This essay chronicles the experiences of a Cambodian American who was deported back to Cambodia. https://www.voanews.com/a/cam

bodians-face-deportations-to-homeland-they-never-knew/3718283.html. Accessed September 5, 2017.

March 23

1908

Chang In-hwan (Jang In-hwan), a Korean independence activist, shoots and kills Durham Stevens who supported Japanese occupation of Korea. The Korean Women's Association is established in San Francisco.

San Francisco, March 26.—Durham White Stevens, the diplomat who was shot by the Korean, In Whan Chang, Monday morning, died late last night at the St. Francis Hospital after an operation which disclosed a more serious condition of his wounds than had been apprehended by the surgeons.

At his bedside, besides the doctors, was the Japanese Consul General, Chozo Koike.

"This is most unfortunate, a great loss to Japan, Korea, and this country," were his words as he left the hospital.

Until yesterday morning every hope had been entertained for Mr. Steven's recovery, but at 10 o'clock symptoms of inflammation appeared. At 6 o'clock he was taken to the operating room and placed under an anesthetic. Only once during the evening did Mr. Stevens show any signs of returning consciousness. He died shortly after 11 o'clock.

Mr. Stevens leaves two sisters in Atlantic City, who were informed of his death last night. Consul General Koike reported the death to his Government.

In Whan Chang, the Korean, when informed of the death of his victim, received the news with manifest delight.

Source: "Stevens Is Dead; Japanese Mourn: American Diplomat Succumbs to the Wounds Inflicted by Korean Fanatic." *New York Times*, March 27, 1908.

Books

Dudden, Alexis. *Japan's Colonization of Korea: Discourse and Power*. Honolulu: University of Hawaii Press, 2004. *Japan's Colonization of Korea* investigates the colonial history of Korea under Japanese occupation, and how Japan legitimated its occupation, to itself, Korea, and the international community.

Patterson, Wayne. *The Korean Frontier in America: Immigration to Hawaii, 1896–1910*. Honolulu: University of Hawaii Press, 1988. *The Korean Frontier in America* covers the history of Korean migration to Hawaii and the mainland United States, and U.S.-Korean relations.

Websites

Jung, Sung-ki. "Independent Activist Jang In-hwan Honored." *Korean Times*, March 3, 2008. This newspaper article discussion Jang In-hwan's assignation of Durham Stevens, and his memorialization in South Korea. http://www.koreatimes.co.kr/www/news/special/2008/04/178_20010.html. Accessed October 14, 2016.

Korean National Association. This site provides a history of the Korean independence movement, along with historic photographs of key individuals, events, and places. http://koreannationalassn.com/home.html. Accessed October 14, 2016.

Also Noteworthy

1942

The first Civilian Exclusion Order is issued by General DeWitt and demands that all persons of Japanese ancestry "evacuate" Bainbridge Island, Washington before March 30, 1942.

March 24

1934

In the late 1920s and early 1930s, it became clear that the only effective way to exclude Filipinos would be to make the Philippines an independent sovereign nation. Among manufacturers, this was a relatively popular position since they perceived a competition from sugar, cordage, coconut, and tobacco entering the United States from the Philippines duty free. Consequently, the U.S. Congress passed the Tydings-McDuffie Act (also known as the Philippines Independence Act), which President Roosevelt signed into law on March 24, 1934. It became effective for immigration purposes on May 1, 1934. As of this date, Filipinos were considered aliens, and only 50 were allowed to enter the country annually, although Section 8 allowed Hawaiian sugar planters an exemption to import more Filipino laborers to the islands if they could demonstrate a need. In exchange for limiting Filipino migration to 50 a year, the Philippines would become an independent nation by 1946.

Excerpt from the Philippine Independence Act, also known as the Tydings-McDuffie Act

AN ACT TO PROVIDE FOR THE COMPLETE INDEPENDENCE OF THE PHILIPPINE ISLANDS, TO PROVIDE FOR THE ADOPTION OF A CONSTITUTION AND A FORM OF GOVERNMENT FOR THE PHILIPPINE ISLANDS, AND FOR OTHER PURPOSES.

(1) *For the purposes of the Immigration Act of 1917, the Immigration Act of 1924 [except section 13 (c)], this section, and all other laws of the United States relating to the immigration, exclusion, or expulsion of aliens, citizens of the Philippine Islands who are not citizens of the United States shall be considered as if they were aliens. For such purposes the Philippine Islands shall be considered as a separate country and shall have for each fiscal year a quota of fifty. This paragraph shall not apply to a person coming or seeking to come to the Territory of Hawai'i who does not apply for and secure an immigration or passport visa, but such immigration shall be determined by the Department of the Interior on the basis of the needs of industries in the Territory of Hawai'i.*

(2) *Citizens of the Philippine Islands who are not citizens of the United States shall not be admitted to the continental United States from the Territory of Hawai'i (whether entering such territory before or after the effective date of this section) unless they belong to a class declared to be non-immigrants by section 3 of the Immigration Act of 1924 or to a class declared to be nonquota immigrants under the provisions of section 4 of such Act other than subdivision (c) thereof, or unless they were admitted to such territory under an immigration visa. The Secretary of Labor shall by regulations provide a method for such exclusion and for the admission of such excepted classes.*

Source: *The Statutes at Large of the United States of America*. Volume 48, Part 1. Washington, DC: Government Printing Office, 1934.

Books

Hing, Bill Ong. *Making and Remaking Asian America through Immigration Policy: 1850–1990*. Stanford, CA: Stanford University Press, 1993. *Making and Remaking Asian America through Immigration Policy* is a comprehensive discussion of how U.S. immigration policies have influenced the demographic, economic, and social development of six Asian American communities in the United States.

Jenkins, Shirley. *American Economic Policy toward the Philippines*. Stanford, CA: Stanford University Press, 1954. *American Economic Policy toward the Philippines* explores critical aspects between U.S. and Philippine relations through American economic policies.

Websites

Baldoz, Richard. "The Nativist Origins of Philippines Independence." *Truthout*, April 1, 2014. http://www.truth-out.org/news/item/22826-the-nativist-origins-of-philippines-independence. Accessed January 12, 2017.

"March 18–24, 1934: President Franklin Roosevelt Signs the Philippines Independence Act." The Schiller Institute. March 2012. This site provides a historical narrative and discussion of the impact of the Tydings–McDuffie Act. It includes historical images. http://www.schillerinstitute.org/educ/hist/eiw_this_week/v5n12_mar18_1934.html. Accessed January 12, 2017.

Also Noteworthy

1877

Five Chinese workers are massacred in a woodchopper's camp two miles from Chico, California.

1942

Public Proclamation No. 3 extends travel restrictions, curfew, and contraband protocols to Japanese Americans.

1990

An Wang (b. February 7, 1920), Chinese American computer engineer, inventor, and cofounder of Wang Laboratories, a computer company, dies of cancer in Lincoln, Massachusetts.

March 25

1985

On this day, Chinese Cambodian Dr. Haing S. Ngor wins the Oscar for best supporting actor for his role in *The Killing Fields*. Ngor was born in Samrong Young, Cambodia, on March 22, 1940. Before the Khmer Rouge captured control of Cambodia on April 17, 1975, Ngor was a middle-class skilled surgeon and gynecologist in Phnom Penh. Shortly afterward, Ngor, along with 2 million other inhabitants, were forced into labor camps and were forced to endure systematic inhumane torture. While in the camps, his wife, My-Huoy, died after giving birth. Although a gynecologist, Ngor was unable to treat his wife because he would have been exposed and killed. For three years, eight months, and 20 days, between 1975 and 1979, nearly 2 million Cambodians perished from mass starvation, forced labor, torture, slavery, ethnic cleansing, and senseless killing. After four years in the "death camps," Ngor and his niece Sophia Ngor took refuge in Thailand, where he worked as a medical doctor until resettling in the United States on August 30, 1980. Ngor did not resume his medical career in the United States and did not remarry.

Ngor was cast to play the role of journalist Dith Pran in the film *The Killing Fields* (1984), arguably the first major international call for attention to the Cambodian situation. In his debut role, Ngor won the Global Globe Award and an Academy Award for Best Supporting Actor. He is the first Asian American male actor to win the Academy Award for a supporting performance. Overnight, Ngor became the face of Cambodia to the world. On February 25, 1996, Ngor was murdered in a dark alley outside his apartment in Los Angeles Chinatown. It is unknown whether his murder was a botched robbery or an international conspiracy. Two years after his death, in 1998, a Los Angeles jury found three Chinese American gang members guilty of murder on the same day Pol Pot died quietly in a tiny jungle village, never having faced charges for his heinous crimes. His is an inspiring survivor's story of reconciliation with the horrors of genocide, a story that ends mysteriously with his murder in 1996. His legacy in making public the horrific acts of senseless murder continues to assist the reconciliation and collective healing for Cambodia and Cambodians today.

Haing S. Ngor Oscar acceptance speech:

This unbelievable, but so is my entire life. I wish to thank all member of Motion Picture Academy for this great honor. I thank David Puttnam, Roland Joffé for giving me this chance to act for the first time in The Killing Fields. *And I share this award to my friend Sam Waterston, Dith Pran, Sydney Schanberg, and also Pat Golden, that casting lady who found me for this role. And I thank Warner Bros. for helping me tell my story to the world, let the world know what happened in my country. And I thank God Buddha that tonight I'm even here. Thank you very much. Thank you.*

Source: Academy Awards Acceptance Speech Database. http://aaspeechesdb.oscars.org/link/057-2/. Accessed January 17, 2017.

Books

Ngor, Haing, and Roger Warner. *Survival in the Killing Fields*. New York: Carroll & Graf Publishers, 2003. *Survival in the Killing Fields* is a memoir of Haing Ngor; the book ends with coauthor Warner sharing personal insights into the life and passion of Ngor.

Ngor, Haing, with Roger Warner. *A Cambodian Odyssey*. Basingstoke, UK: Palgrave Macmillan Publishing Company, 1987. *A Cambodian Odyssey* details Haing Ngor's life and survival in the Killing Fields, and the suffering and devastation of the Khmer Rouge autogenocide and the Cambodian struggle to recover in its wake.

Websites

The Dr. Haing S. Ngor Foundation. This site maintains comprehensive resources about Haing Ngor, including this biography, publications, films, photographs, and links to interviews and other media related to Ngor. http://www.haingngorfoundation.org/. Accessed January 17, 2017.

Ebert, Roger. "The Day Haing S. Ngor Won the Oscar." RogerEbert.com Interviews. March 24, 1985. This is an interview of Haing Ngor by acclaimed film critic Roger Ebert that discusses the Killing Fields, Ngor's experience, and the film *The Killing Fields*. http://www.rogerebert.com/interviews/the-day-haing-s-ngor-won-the-oscar. Accessed January 17, 2017.

Also Noteworthy

1944

Beginning on this day, and until early May, 63 Japanese Americans had been arrested for their refusal to report for their preinduction physicals until their citizenship rights had been clarified and restored. Their case, *U.S. v. Shigeru Fujii, et al.*, was the largest mass trial in Wyoming's history.

1994

Wat Dhammararam Buddhist Temple Association, a Cambodian/Khmer American Buddhist temple, is officially declared legally incorporated in Stockton, California. It was established earlier, as a temple, on August 18, 1982.

2002

In Tallahassee, Florida, Charles Franklin, a 51-year-old, is charged with burglary and criminal mischief for vandalizing a local mosque.

March 26

1790

The 1790 Naturalization Act is the first statute in the United States to codify naturalization law. This act effectively restricted citizenship to free white men, barring slaves, indentured servants, and most women. This implied that Africans and, later, Asian immigrants, who began to arrive in large numbers to the United States during the 19th century, were not eligible to naturalize. Following the end of the Civil War and the abolishment of slavery, Congress created new legislation that gave "aliens of African nativity and persons of African descent" access to citizenship. Racial barriers to naturalization remained for Asians, effectively marking them as "aliens ineligible for citizenship."

Excerpt from "An act to establish a uniform Rule of Naturalization" (United States Congress, March 26, 1790).

Be it enacted by the Senate and House of Representatives of the United States of America, in

Congress assembled, That any Alien being a free white person, who shall have resided within the limits and under the jurisdiction of the United States for the term of two years, may be admitted to become a citizen thereof on application to any common law Court of record in any one of the States wherein he shall have resided for the term of one year at least, and making proof to the satisfaction of such Court that he is a person of good character, and taking the oath or affirmation prescribed by law to support the Constitution of the United States, which Oath or Affirmation such Court shall administer, and the Clerk of such Court shall record such Application, and the proceedings thereon; and thereupon such person shall be considered as a Citizen of the United States. And the children of such person so naturalized, dwelling within the United States, being under the age of twenty one years at the time of such naturalization, shall also be considered as citizens of the United States. And the children of citizens of the United States that may be born beyond Sea, or out of the limits of the United States, shall be considered as natural born Citizens: Provided, that the right of citizenship shall not descend to persons whose fathers have never been resident in the United States: Provided also, that no person heretofore proscribed by any States, shall be admitted a citizen as aforesaid, except by an Act of the Legislature of the State in which such person was proscribed.

United States Congress, "An act to establish a uniform rule of Naturalization; and to repeal the act heretofore passed on that subject" (January 29, 1795).

For carrying into complete effect the power given by the constitution, to establish a uniform rule of naturalization throughout the United States:

SEC. 1. Be it enacted by the Senate and House of Representatives of the United States of America, in Congress assembled, That any alien, being a free white person, may be admitted to become a citizen of the United States, or any of them, on the following conditions, and not otherwise:—

First. He shall have declared, on oath or affirmation, before the supreme, superior, district, or circuit court of some one of the states, or of the territories northwest or south of the river Ohio, or a circuit or district court of the United States, three years, at least, before his admission, that it was bona fide, his intention to become a citizen of the United States, and to renounce forever all allegiance and fidelity to any foreign prince, potentate, state, or sovereignty whatever, and particularly, by name, the prince, potentate, state or sovereignty whereof such alien may, at that time, be a citizen or subject.

Secondly. He shall, at the time of his application to be admitted, declare on oath or affirmation before some one of the courts aforesaid, that he has resided within the United States, five years at least, and within the state or territory, where such court is at the time held, one year at least; that he will support the constitution of the United States; and that he does absolutely and entirely renounce and abjure all allegiance and fidelity to any foreign prince, potentate, state, or sovereignty whatever, and particularly by name, the prince, potentate, state, or sovereignty, whereof he was before a citizen or subject; which proceedings shall be recorded by the clerk of the court.

Thirdly. The court admitting such alien shall be satisfied that he has resided within the limits and under the jurisdiction of the United States five years; and it shall further appear to their satisfaction, that during that time, he has behaved as a man of a good moral character, attached to the principles of the constitution of the United States, and well disposed to the good order and happiness of the same.

Fourthly. In case the alien applying to be admitted to citizenship shall have borne any hereditary title, or been of any of the orders of nobility, in the kingdom or state from which he came, he shall, in addition to the above requisites, make an express renunciation of his title or order of nobility, in the court to which his application shall be made; which renunciation shall be recorded in the said court.

SEC. 2. Provided always, and be it further enacted, That any alien now residing within the limits and under the jurisdiction of the United States may be admitted to become a citizen on his declaring, on oath or affirmation, in some one of the courts aforesaid, that he has resided two years, at least, within and under the jurisdiction of the same, and one year, at least, within the state or territory where such court is at the time held; that he will support the constitution of the United States; and that he does absolutely and entirely renounce and abjure all allegiance and fidelity to any foreign prince, potentate, state, or sovereignty whatever, and particularly by name the prince, potentate, state, or sovereignty, whereof he was before a citizen or subject; and moreover, on its appearing to the satisfaction of the court, that during the said term of two years, he has behaved as a man of good moral character, attached to the constitution of the United States, and well disposed to the good order and happiness of the same; and when the alien applying for admission to citizenship, shall have borne any hereditary title, or been of any of the orders of nobility in the kingdom or state from which he came, on his moreover making in the court an express renunciation of his title or order of nobility, before he shall be entitled to such admission; all of which proceedings, required in this proviso to be performed in the court, shall be recorded by the clerk thereof.

SEC. 3. And be it further enacted, that the children of persons duly naturalized, dwelling within the United States, and being under the age of twenty-one years, at the time of such naturalization, and the children of citizens of the United States, born out of the limits and jurisdiction of the United States, shall be considered as citizens of the United States: Provided, That the right of citizenship shall not descend to persons, whose fathers have never been resident of the United States: Provided also, That no person heretofore proscribed by any state, or who has been legally convicted of having joined the army of Great Britain during the late war, shall be admitted a citizen as foresaid, without the consent of the legislature of the state, in which such person was proscribed.

SEC. 4. And be it further enacted, That the Act intituled, "An act to establish an uniform rule of naturalization," passed the twenty-sixth day of March, one thousand seven hundred and ninety, be, and the same is hereby repealed.

Source: *1790 Naturalization Act.* The Library of Congress, American Memory. A Century of Lawmaking for a New Nation: U.S. Congressional Documents and Debates, 1774–1875. It provides original images of the legal documents. http://memory.loc.gov/cgi-bin/ampage?collId=llsl&fileName=001/llsl001.db&recNum=226. Accessed January 28, 2018.

Books

LeMay, Michael, and Elliott R. Barkan, eds. *U.S. Immigration and Naturalization Laws and Issues: A Documentary History*. Westport, CT: Greenwood Press, 1999. Historians Michael LeMay and Elliott Barkan provide 150 primary documents related to immigration and naturalization in U.S. history.

Pinder, Sherrow. *Whiteness and Racialized Ethnic Groups in the United States: The Politics of Remembering*. Lanham, MD: Lexington Books, 2012. Political scientist Sherrow Pinder examines the history and legal development of whiteness in America.

Websites

1790 Naturalization Act. The University of Washington, Bothell Library. The complete text is available at http://library.uwb.edu/guides/USimmigration/1790_naturalization_act.html. Accessed October 5, 2016.

PBS RACE—The Power of an Illusion. Go Deeper: Race Timeline. This timeline explores the different rules and definitions of "whites" and race in American history. 2003. http://www.pbs.org/race/000_About/002_03_d-godeeper.htm. Accessed October 5, 2016.

Also Noteworthy

1974

The Asian Center for Theology and Strategies (ACTS) is incorporated as a 501(c)(3) nonprofit entity in the state of California. ACTS was initially based at Mills College and then moved to the Pacific School of Religion campus in Berkeley, California.

2006

Family Guy episode 22 of season 4 "Sibling Rivalry" written by Cherry Chevapravatdumrong (also known as Cherry Cheva) airs on television. Chevapravatdumrong is an American author of Thai ancestry who is executive producer of *Family Guy*.

March 27

1933

Since 1880, California Civil Code Section 60 prohibited marriages between a white person and "negros," "mulattos," and/or "Mongolians." Salvador Roldan was a Filipino engaged to Marjorie Rogers, a white British woman. In August 1931, their marriage license was rejected by the Los Angeles County clerk. On March 27, 1933, the California District Court of Appeal rules in *Salvador Roldan v. Los Angeles County* that Filipinos are part of the "Malay" race, not "Mongolian," and therefore, upholds lower court ruling that Filipinos can marry whites. However, shortly afterward, the California legislature amended the Civil Code to include "Malay" among the "races" prohibited from marrying whites. It was ratified by both the state senate and the assembly and then was signed by Governor James Rolph on April 5, 1933. The new law banned Filipinos from marrying whites until 1948, when the California Supreme Court ruled the state's antimiscegenation statute unconstitutional because it violates the Fourteenth Amendment's due process and equal protection clauses.

The couple petitioned for a writ of mandate soon after, which was eventually granted by Superior Court Judge Walter Gates. Not surprisingly county counsels L. E. Lampton and Everett Mattoon filed an injunction with the state appeals court, hoping to get Gates's decision reversed. U.S. Webb and Associate Attorney General Frank English also filed an amicus curiae brief on behalf of the appellants, supporting the county clerk's contention that Filipinos were members of the Mongolian race. The legal maneuvering in this case centered on two interrelated issues: the contested racial status of Filipinos and the statutory intent of the California legislature regarding Sections 60 and 69 of the state civil code.

To determine the first question, the court reviewed scientific and popular opinion pertaining to the racial identification of Filipinos. . . . Importantly, the court also noted that the U.S. Congress's own widely referenced publication the Dictionary of Race or Peoples *listed Filipinos under the "Brown or Malay" race. These sources tended to support Roldan and Rogers's contention that Filipinos fell outside the purview of the California prohibition.*

County and state officials sought to contravene the petitioner's argument by citing the work of Ales Hrdlicka, a contemporary anthropologist who claimed that Filipinos belonged to the "yellow-brown race or Mongoloid race." . . .

Although the verdict in the Roldan *appeal signaled a legal victory for California's Filipino community, only a few individuals got to take advantage of the ruling.*

Source: Baldoz, Rick. *The Third Asiatic Invasion: Empire and Migration in Filipino America, 1898–1946.* New York: New York University Press, 2011, pp. 98–101.

Books

Gross, Ariela. *What Blood Won't Tell: A History of Race on Trial in America.* Cambridge, MA: Harvard University Press, 2008. *What Blood Won't Tell* investigates the legal history of racial identity and citizenship rights.

Moran, Rachel. *Interracial Intimacy: The Regulation of Race and Romance.* Chicago, IL: University of Chicago Press, 2003. *Interracial Intimacy* explores the history of interracial intimacy policies in the United States.

Websites

Chan, Ken. "10 Shocking Cases That Will Change Your Understanding of American History." JUSTIA U.S. Supreme Court. May 30, 2014. This article discusses 10 critical cases that define Asian American racial classification and citizenship rights. *Roldan v. Los Angeles County* is listed as number six. https://lawblog.justia.com/2014/05/30/10-shocking-cases-will-change-understanding-american-history/. Accessed January 12, 2017.

Roldan v. Los Angeles County. Casetext, Inc. 2016. This site provides for the full text for *Roldan v. Los Angeles County*. https://casetext.com/case/roldan-v-los-angeles-county. Accessed January 12, 2017.

Also Noteworthy

1942

Second War Powers Act repeals the confidentiality of census data, allowing the Federal Bureau of Investigation (FBI) to use this information to round up Japanese Americans and change naturalization restrictions to allow persons serving the U.S. military during World War II to become naturalized.

Santa Anita, California, Assembly Center opens; it is in operation until October 27.

1986

United Commercial Bank, a Chinese American bank, opens in San Francisco.

March 28

1898

Wong Kim Ark was born in San Francisco, California, in 1873 to Chinese "resident alien" parents. When his parents returned to China in 1890, Ark followed for a temporary visit. Upon his return, the collector of customs permitted Ark's reentry to the United States on the basis of his place of birth. Four years later, Wong Kim Ark again took a trip to China. Upon his attempted return in the summer of 1895, Ark was detained at the Port of San Francisco and denied reentry because the collector of customs declared that he was not a citizen of the United States.

Ark contended that his birth in San Francisco legally entitled him to the full privileges of U.S. citizenship and filed a writ of habeas corpus. In 1898, Ark's case was heard by the U.S. Supreme Court. While Ark and his supporters argued that the Fourteenth Amendment granted citizenship to all born on American soil, a concept known as *jus soli*, the dissenters claimed that this only pertained to those not held subject to any other foreign power. Since Ark's parents were subjects of the emperor of China and unable to naturalize into the United States, dissenters used the logic of *jus sanguinis* (inheriting citizenship through blood) to claim that Wong Kim Ark himself was a subject of China. With a vote of 6–2 in favor of Wong Kim Ark, the Supreme Court ruled that the fundamental rule of citizenship by birth would extend to children of resident aliens born in the United States.

GRAY, J., Opinion of the Court

MR. JUSTICE GRAY, after stating the case, delivered the opinion of the court.

. . . It is conceded that, if he is a citizen of the United States, the acts of Congress, known as the Chinese Exclusion Acts, prohibiting persons of the Chinese race, and especially Chinese laborers, from coming into the United States, do not and cannot apply to him.

The question presented by the record is whether a child born in the United States, of parents of Chinese descent, who, at the time of his birth, are subjects of the Emperor of China, but have a permanent domicil and residence in the United States, and are there carrying on business, and are not employed in any diplomatic or official capacity under the Emperor of China, becomes at the time of his birth a citizen of the United States by virtue of the first clause of the Fourteenth Amendment of the Constitution,

All persons born or naturalized in the United States, and subject to the jurisdiction thereof, are citizens of the United States and of the State wherein they reside.

The evident intention, and the necessary effect, of the submission of this case to the decision of the court upon the facts agreed by the parties were to present for determination the single question stated at the beginning of this opinion, namely, whether a child born in the United States, of parent of Chinese descent, who, at the time of his birth, are subjects of the Emperor of China, but have a permanent domicil and residence in the United States, and are there carrying on business, and are not employed in any diplomatic or official capacity under the Emperor of China, becomes at the time of his birth a citizen of the United States. For the reasons above stated, this court is of opinion that the question must be answered in the affirmative.

Order affirmed.

Source: *United States v. Wong Kim Ark*, 169 U.S. 649 (1898).

Books

Martin, David, and Peter Schuck, eds. *Immigration Stories*. New York: Foundation Press, 2005. *Immigration Stories* examines the U.S. Supreme Court's ruling on immigration and the "plenary power doctrine." See Lucy E. Salyer's Chapter 3, "Wong Kim Ark: The Context over Birthright Citizenship."

Moran, Rachel, and Devon Carbado, eds. *Race Law Stories*. New York: Thomson Reuters/Foundation Press, 2008. *Race Law Stories* provides historical context for legal decisions related to race. See Erika Lee's Chapter 3, "Birthright Citizenship, Immigration, and the U.S. Constitution: The Story of *United States v. Wong Kim Ark*."

Websites

"United States v. Wong Kim Ark 169 U.S. 649 (1898)." JUSTIA U.S. Supreme Court. This site contains the full text of *United States v. Wong Kim Ark*. https://supreme.justia.com/cases/federal/us/169/649/case.html. Accessed October 11, 2016.

"Wong Kim Ark Day." *Chinese American Forum* 26, no. 1 (July 2010). This essay provides a history of the case, along with a discussion of its significance. http://caforumonline.net/CAFHandlerPDF.ashx?ID=334. Accessed January 27, 2018.

1942

Minoru Yasui was born in Oregon to Issei parents in 1916. On March 28, 1942, Yasuri deliberately breaks the curfew by walking around downtown Portland after hours. Yasuri turned himself in for arrest at the Portland police station to test the discriminatory curfew policies issued by General John L. DeWitt. Yasui was an attorney and member of the Oregon bar association and was an army second lieutenant in the infantry reserve. Executive Order 9066 limited the movement of Japanese Americans to home and work by establishing a curfew between 9:00 P.M. and 6:00 A.M. Through Public Proclamation Number 3 issued on March 24, 1942, the curfew was justified as a means of securing the country from risk of espionage and acts of sabotage. Yasui waived his rights to a trial by jury and was found guilty: he was fined $5,000 by a federal judge and sentenced to one year in the Multnomah County Jail in Portland. He was transferred to the Minidoka War Relocation Center at Idaho in 1944. While serving his sentence, he filed an appeal to the Ninth Circuit Court, which later went to the Supreme Court: the Supreme Court ruling, authored by Chief Justice Harlan Fiske Stone, upheld the constitutionality of the curfew and the War Powers Act.

Yasui's training as an attorney was the backdrop for his challenges to the curfew and evacuation orders. He believed that the orders were unconstitutional as applied to U.S. citizens. He believed it was his responsibility to take measures to show the rights and wrongs of the government. In an interview conducted with him later, he stated,

> *It was my feeling and belief, then and now, that no military authority had the right to subject any United States citizen to any requirement that does not equally apply to all other U.S. citizens. Moreover, if a citizen believes that the sovereign state is committing an illegal act, it is incumbent upon that citizen to take measures to rectify such error.... [I]t seemed to me then and now that if the government unlawfully curtails the rights of any person, the damage is done not only to that individual person but to the whole society. If we believe in America, if we believe in equality and democracy, if we believe in*

law and justice, then each of us, when we see or believe such errors are being made, has an obligation to make every effort to correct them.

Source: Ng, Wendy. *Japanese American Internment during World War II: A History and Reference Guide*. Westport, CT: Greenwood Press, 2002, p. 81.

Books

Kim, Hyung-chan, ed. *Distinguished Asian Americans: A Biographical Dictionary*. Westport, CT: Greenwood Press, 1999. See entry on "Minoru Yasui" by Steven Fugita.

Maki, Mitchell, Harry Kitano, and Sarah Berthold. *Achieving the Impossible Dream: How Japanese Americans Obtained Redress*. Urbana: University of Illinois Press, 1999. *Achieving the Impossible Dream* covers many aspects of Japanese Americans who worked to get an apology from the U.S. government and achieve compensation for the unlawful internment of their community during World War II.

Websites

Asakawa, Gil. "Minoru Yasui." *Densho Encyclopedia*, 2017. This site provides an essay on the life and legacy of Minoru Yasui, with images and links to archival documents. http://encyclopedia.densho.org/Minoru_Yasui/. Accessed January 13, 2017.

Minoru Yasui v. United States (1943). U.S. Supreme Court. FindLaw. 2017. This site provides the text to the ruling in *Minoru Yasui v. United States*. http://caselaw.findlaw.com/us-supreme-court/320/115.html. Accessed January 13, 2017.

Also Noteworthy

California State Senator Leland Yin Yee (b. November 20, 1948) is voted out of the California State Senate as a result of gun running and criminal charges against him. On July 1, 2015, Yee pleases guilty to a felony racketeering count in relation to money laundering, public corruption, and bribery. On February 24, 2016, Yee was sentenced to five years in federal prison.

March 29

1905

Philip Ahn, Korean American actor, is born. Ahn was the first Asian American actor to receive a star on the Hollywood Walk of Fame. As a Korean American actor, he was cast to play many Chinese and Japanese characters. He is best known for his role as Master Kan on the television series *Kung Fu* (1972). He passed away in Los Angeles on February 28, 1978, after lung surgery.

Like explicit yellowface, implicit yellowface involves both stage and social actors looking, sounding, and acting according to some notion of normativized, authentic standard of Asianess. . . . Philip Ahn's make-up, costuming, and accent "played a pivotal role in Orientalizing" him. . . . Thus, implicit yellowface requires that actors meet a predefined and arbitrary notion of authenticity and downplay their own existential identities and experiences. In addition to their being made up to look Oriental, implicit yellowface includes Asian and Asian American actors playing ethnic groups other than those they themselves know most intimately. . . . For example, in the film Daughter of Shanghai *(1937), because of rules prohibiting on-stage romantic acting between Asian American actors and white actors, there occurred the unusual circumstance of two Asian American romantic leads. . . . Nevertheless, the relationship between Anna May Wong's character and that of Philip Ahn remains a form of yellowface, since Ahn, who is Korean American and son of a key Korean anti-Japanese colonial figure, plays a Chinese American in the film. . . . Ahn often played both Chinese and Japanese characters . . . to support Korean nationalism and Korean resistance to Japanese violence and domination, when Ahn took on the role of evil Japanese characters he played them as powerfully as he could. In other films . . . Ahn took the opportunity, provided to him by the assumption that all Asian languages are the same, to speak Korean, while people assumed he was speaking Chinese.*

Source: Ono, Ken, and Vincent Pham. *Asian Americans and the Media*. Cambridge: Polity Press, 2009, pp. 54–55.

Books

Chung, Hye Seung. *Hollywood Asian: Philip Ahn and the Politics of Cross-Ethnic Performance*. Philadelphia, PA: Temple University Press, 2006.

Dave, Shilpa, LeiLani Nishime, and Tasha Oren, eds. *East Main Street: Asian American Popular Culture*. New York: New York University Press, 2005. See Hey Seung Chung's Chapter 8, "Between Yellophillia and Yellowphobia: Ethnic Stardom and the (Dis)Orientalized Romantic Couple in *Daughter of Shanghai* and *King of Chinatown*."

Websites

Cuddy, Philip. "Philip Ahn: Born in America." The Philip Ahn Admiration Society. 1996. This is a complete biographic essay on Philip Ahn's life and career as an actor. http://www.philipahn.com/pacessay.html. Accessed September 5, 2017.

"Philip Ahn, Actor in Character Roles." *New York Times*, March 4, 1978. *New York Times Archives*. This article discusses Philip Ahn's life and legacy. http://www.nytimes.com/1978/03/04/archives/philip-ahn-actor-in-character-roles-played-many-oriental-villains.html?mcubz=0. Accessed September 5, 2017.

Also Noteworthy

2007

Governor of Hawaii, Linda Lingle, declares this day Peter Aquino Aduja (October 19, 1920–February 19, 2007) Day. Aduja is the first Filipino American elected to public office in the United States and served as a representative in the Hawaii Legislature in 1954.

March 30

1981

Architect and sculptor Maya Lin submits winning design for the Vietnam Veterans Memorial in Washington, D.C. There were more than 1,400 submissions and a prize of $20,000.

Out of 1,421 designs, a jury of architects and landscape designers chose the design of Maya Ying Lin, who graduated from college this spring as the one that will memorialize the Vietnam war

Like everything else she'd done in architecture classes, this project was an abstract solution to be solved in the mind, drawn out, and handed in. Her own personal image of a memorial is an abstract one: "It's not resolved. It's not specific details of the Vietnam war. . . . It's a personal solution and a statement on my part and I submitted it with no chance of winning. I only did it because I wanted to say this." . . .

After she had settled into a scruffy brown armchair, explaining in a level but impersonal voice that now the interviews were down to one a day, she began to tell how the memorial will look . . . the two 200-foot walls, sunk 10 feet in the ground with the names of those lost in chronological order, meeting where the walls meet, where the beginning and ending dates of the war are engraved. As I began to visualize the massive slabs of black granite with their somber rows of names, those little cheery gestures took on considerable power.

She denies this power, saying of her design, "It was just a nice thing." A nice thing to the jury, too, which wrote in its statement that "entry number 1026" was the one which should be built. "All who come here can find it a place of healing," they commented.

Source: Lewis, Maggie. "Vietnam War Memorial; 'Violence Healed Over by Time.'" *Christian Science Monitor*, August 6, 1982.

Books

Doubek, Robert. *Creating the Vietnam Veterans Memorial: The Inside Story*. Jefferson, NC: McFarland & Company, 2015. *Creating the Vietnam Veterans Memorial* provides a behind-the-scenes history of the Vietnam Veterans Memorial.

Hagopian, Patrick. *The Vietnam War in American Memory: Veterans, Memorials, and the Politics of Healing*. Amherst: University of Massachusetts Press, 2009. *The Vietnam War in American Memory* discusses the role of Vietnam War veterans in shaping public memory and healing.

Websites

Klein, Christopher. "The Remarkable Story of Maya Lin's Vietnam Veterans Memorial." Biography. November 10, 2015. This essay details the inspiration behind Maya Lin's Vietnam Veterans Memorial. https://www.biography.com/news/maya-lin-vietnam-veterans-memorial. Accessed September 5, 2017.

Maya Lin: Artist, Architect, & Memorial Designer. Makers Profile. 2017. This site provides a video that shows Maya Lin reflecting on the Vietnam Veterans Memorial and the controversy of her winning the competition. https://www.makers.com/maya-lin. Accessed September 5, 2017.

Also Noteworthy

1927

The Filipino Federation of America is organized in Hawaii, to gain U.S. citizenship rights for Filipinos.

1942

Two hundred and twenty-seven Japanese Americans are ordered to leave Bainbridge Island, Washington, with six days' notice; the majority of the internees were interned at Manzanar, California, while some were later transferred to Minidoka, Idaho.

2008

Dith Pran, Cambodian photojournalist for the *New York Times* whose life is portrayed in the film *The Killing Fields* (1984), passes away in New Jersey.

March 31

1854

The Treaty of Kanagawa, also known as the Perry Convention, was the first treaty between the United States and Japan. It was also the latter's first treaty with a Western nation and marked the end of Japan's period of isolation (1639–1854). This document set the tone for the tension-filled Japan-U.S. relationship in the 20th century.

With the support of leaders such as Oda Nobunaga, Catholic missionaries were able to foster a thriving community of converts in 14th-century Japan. However, after Nobunaga's death, his successor, Toyotomi Hideyoshi, launched the anti-foreign, anti-Christian policy that culminated in the Tokugawa exclusion edicts. Japan's closed-door policy was fully implemented by the third Tokugawa shogun, Iemitsu, in 1639. It was forcibly brought to an end in 1854 with the signing of the Treaty of Kanagawa.

As the United States began to expand beyond its continental boundaries and become heavily involved in maritime trade, it became increasingly determined to bring Japan's two-century-old policy of self-imposed isolation to a close. In 1953, U.S. president Fillmore sent Commodore Matthew C. Perry to Tokyo with the latest steam-powered warships to pressure the Tokugawa government into an agreement that would protect the rights of American whalers, provide for coaling ports, and create a trade relationship. Perry successfully secured two coaling ports and protection for American whalers. In 1858, the U.S. consul achieved Perry's final objective: establishing a commercial treaty.

The United States of America and the empire of Japan, desiring to establish firm, lasting and sincere friendship between the two nations, have resolved to fix, in a manner clear and positive by means of a treaty or general convention of peace and amity, the rules which shall in future be mutually observed in the intercourse of their respective countries; for which most desirable object the President of the United States has conferred full powers on his commissioner, Matthew Calbraith Perry, special ambassador of the United States to Japan and the august sovereign of Japan has given similar full powers to his commissioners, Hayashi-Daigaku-no-kami, Ido, Prince of Tsus-Sima; Izawa, Prince of Mmimasaki; and Udono, member of the Board of Revenue.

And the said commissioners after having exchanged their said full powers and duly considered the premises, have agreed to the following articles:

Article I

There shall be a perfect, permanent and universal peace, and a sincere and cordial amity, between the United States of American on the one part and between their people, respectfully, (respectively,) without exception of persons or places.

Article II

The port of Simoda, in the principality of Idzu and the port of Hakodadi, in the principality of Matsmai are granted by the Japanese as ports for the reception for American ships, where they can be supplied with wood, water, provisions and coal, and other articles their necessities may require, as far as the Japanese have them. The time for opening the first named port is immediately on signing this treaty; the last named port is to be opened immediately after the same day in the ensuing Japanese year.

Note—A tariff of prices shall be given by the Japanese officers of the things which they can furnish, payment for which shall be made in gold, and silver coin.

Article III

Whenever ships of the United States are thrown or wrecked on the coast of Japan, the Japanese vessels will assist them, and carry their crews to Simoda or Hakodadi and hand them over to their countrymen appointed to receive them. Whatever articles the shipwrecked men may have preserved shall likewise be restored and the expenses incurred in the rescue and support of Americans and Japanese who may thus be thrown up on the shores of either nation are not to be refunded.

Article IV

Those shipwrecked persons and other citizens of the United States shall be free as in the other countries and not subjected to confinement but shall be amenable to just laws.

Article V

Shipwrecked men and other citizens of the United States, temporarily living at Simoda and Hakodadi, shall not be subject to such restrictions and confinement as the Dutch and Chinese are at Nagasaki but shall be free at Simoda to go where they please within the limits of seven Japanese miles from a small island in the harbor of Simoda, marked on the accompanying chart hereto appended; and shall in like manner be free to go where they please at Hakodadi, within limits to be defined after the visit of the United States squadron to that place.

Article VI

If there be any other sort of goods wanted or any business which shall require to be arranged, there shall be careful deliberation between the particles in order to settle such matters.

Article VII

It is agreed that ships of the United States resorting to the ports open to them, shall be permitted to exchange gold and silver coin and articles of goods for other articles of goods under such regulations as shall be temporarily established by the Japanese government for that purpose. It is stipulated, however that the ships of the United States shall be permitted to carry away whatever articles they are unwilling to exchange.

Article VIII

Wood, water provisions, coal and goods required shall only be procured through the agency of

Japanese officers appointed for that purpose, and in no other manner.

Article IX

It is agreed, that if, at any future day, the government of Japan shall grant to any other nation or nations privileges and advantages which are not herein granted to the United states and the citizens thereof, that these same privileges and advantages shall be granted likewise to the United States and to the citizens thereof without any consultation or delay.

Article X

Ships of the United States shall be permitted to resort to no other ports in Japan but Simoda and Hakodadi, unless in distress or forced by stress of weather.

Article XI

There shall be appointed by the government of the United States consuls or agents to reside in Simoda at any time after the expiration of eighteen months from the date of the signing of this treaty; provided that either of the two governments deem such arrangement necessary.

Article XII

The present convention, having been concluded and duly signed, shall be obligatory, and faithfully observed by the United States of America, and Japan and by the citizens and subjects of each respective power; and it is to be ratified and approved by the President of the United States, by and with the advice and consent of the Senate thereof, and by the august Sovereign of Japan, and the ratification shall be exchanged within eighteen months from the date of the signature therefore, or sooner if practicable.

In faith, whereof, we, the respective plenipotentiaries of the United States of America and the empire of Japan aforesaid have signed and sealed these presents.

Done at Kanagawa, this thirty-first day of March, in the year of our Lord Jesus Christ one thousand eight hundred and fifty-four and of Kayei the seventh year, third month and third day.

Source: Miller, Hunter, ed. *Treaties and Other International Acts of the United States of America*. Vol. VI. Washington, DC: Government Printing Office, 1942.

Books

Auslin, Michael. *Negotiating with Imperialism: The Unequal Treaties and the Culture of Japanese Diplomacy*. Cambridge, MA: Harvard University Press, 2004. Historian Michael Auslin argues that Japan's modern history began in 1858 when it signed an "unequal" commercial treaty with the United States. This volume examines Japanese diplomacy after this event.

Chaurasia, R. S. *History of Japan*. New Delhi: Atlantic Publishers, 2003. This volume is a complete history of Japan. See Chapter 3, "Western Contact with Japan," for a discussion of the Treaty of Kanagawa and Perry's mission to open Japan's door to the West.

Websites

Griffiths, Ben. "Commodore Perry's Expedition to Japan." This site provides a readable and concise summary of events leading to the Treaty of Kanagawa and the impact of the treaty on Japan-U.S. relation. http://www.grifworld.com/perryhome.html#who. Accessed October 6, 2016.

National Archives & Records Administration. This site provides historical background and impact analysis of the Treaty of Kanagawa, in addition to the digital images of the original print document. http://www.archives.gov/exhibits/featured_documents/treaty_of_kanagawa/. Accessed October 6, 2016.

1883

Saint Malo, a small fishing village at St. Bernard Parish, Louisiana, on the shore of Lake Borgne, is the first recorded settlement of

"Manilamen" or "Tagalas" in America. Saint Malo was established in 1763 by Filipinos who escaped the Spanish galleon ships during the Manila Galleon Trade. Saint Malo was destroyed by the New Orleans Hurricane of 1915.

Excerpt from Lafcadio Hearn's description of Saint Malo, published in March 31, 1883.

Out of the shuddering reeds and bannerettted grass on either side rise the fantastic houses of the Malay fishermen, posed upon slender supports above the marsh, like cranes or bitterns watching for scaly prey. Hard by the slimy mouth of the bayou extends a strange wharf, as ruined and rotted and unearthly as the timbers of the spectral ship in the "rim [sic] of the Ancient Mariner." Odd craft huddle together beside it, fishing-nets make cobwebby drapery about the skeleton timber work, green are the banks, green the water is, green also with fungi every beam and plank and board and shingle of the houses upon stilts. All are built in true manila style, with immense hat shaped eaves and balconies, but in wood; for it had been found that palmetto and woven cane could not withstand the violence of the climate.

Source: Hearn, Lafcadio. "Saint Malo: A Lacustrine Village in Louisiana." *Harper's Weekly*, March 31, 1883, pp. 196–199.

Books

Bronner, Simon J., ed. *Lafcadio Hearn's America: Ethnographic Sketches and Editorials*. Lexington: The University Press of Kentucky, 2002. In 1877, Lafcadio Hearn went to New Orleans to write a series of articles and was later hired by Harper Publishing Co.

Espina, Marina E. *Filipinos in Louisiana*. New Orleans, LA: A. F. Laborde & Sons, 1988. Educator and local historian, Marina Espina, worked as a librarian at the University of New Orleans and conducted research on the Filipinos in Louisiana.

Websites

The Library of Congress, Prints and Photographs Online Catalog contains photographs of Saint Malo by Charles E. Whitney that were published in *Harper's Weekly* in 1883. http://www.loc.gov/pictures/resource/cph.3b15665/. Accessed January 28, 2018.

Mateo, Grace. "The Filipino-American Historical Society of Hawai'i and Operation Manong Present . . ." The Philippine History Site. An online project funded by the Hawaii Committee for the Humanities, the Filipino-American Society of Hawaii, and the University of Hawaii's Office of Multicultural Student Services. See section on "Filipino Migration to the United States." 1991–2001. http://opmanong.ssc.hawaii.edu/Filipino/index.html. Accessed March 7, 2018.

April

April 1

1945

An 82-day "Battle of Okinawa" begins when 182,000 U.S. troops land in Okinawa. The United States lost 116 planes, three aircraft carriers were damaged, and 50,000 combat troops of the 10th Army were damaged too. To this day, Okinawa is a site of U.S. military bases and mobilizes a transnational resistance to remove the U.S. military from Okinawa that brings together Okinawan and Okinawan Americans.

Results

When Okinawa was finally declared secure, the cost had been horrific. Some 150,000 Okinawans died, approximately one third the island's population. An additional 10,000 Koreans, used by the Japanese military as slave labor, died as well. Of the 119,000 or so Japanese soldiers, as many as 112,000 were killed in the battle or forever sealed inside a collapsed cave or bunker. Aside from the human cost, most of the physical aspects of Okinawan culture were razed. Few buildings survived the 3 months' fighting. Collectively, the defenders lost more dead than the Japanese suffered in the two atomic bombings combined. The United States lost 13,000 dead: almost 8,000 on the island and the remainder at sea; another 32,000 were wounded. The loss of life on both sides, particularly among the Japanese civilians, caused immense worry in Washington. New President Harry Truman was looking at the plans for a proposed assault on the Japanese main islands, and the casualty projections were unacceptable. Projections numbered the potential casualties from 100,000 in the first 30 days to as many as 1 million attackers, and the death count for the Japanese civilians would be impossible to calculate. If they resisted as strongly as did the citizens of Okinawa—and the inhabitants of the home islands would be even more dedicated to defending their homeland—Japan would become a wasteland. It was already looking like one in many areas. The U.S. bombing campaign, in place since the previous September, was burning out huge areas of Japanese cities. How much longer the Japanese could have held out in the face of the fire bombing is a matter of much dispute; some project that, had the incendiary raids continued until November, the Japanese would have been thrown back to an almost Stone Age existence. The problem was this: no one in the west knew exactly what was happening in Japan. The devastation could be estimated, but the resistance could not.

Thus, with the casualties of the Okinawa battle fresh in his mind, when Truman learned of the successful testing of an atomic bomb, he ordered its use. This is a decision debated since 6 August 1945, the date of the bombing of Hiroshima, and even before. Just what was known of Japanese decision making processes before that date is also argued to this day. Was the Japanese government in the process of formulating a peace offer, in spite of the demand for unconditional surrender the Allies had decided upon in February 1943? If they were doing so, did anyone in the west know about it? Who knew what, when they knew it, and what effect that knowledge had or may have had on Truman's decision making is a matter of much dispute. Whatever the political ramifications of the atomic bomb on the immediate and postwar world, Truman's decision was certainly based in no small part on the nature of the fighting on Okinawa. Truman wrote just after his decision, "We'll end the war sooner now. And think of the kids who won't be killed." Horrible as the effects of the two atomic bombs were, the number of casualties in Hiroshima and Nagasaki as compared with the potential number an invasion could have caused is small indeed.

Source: Tucker, Spencer. *Battles That Changed American History: 100 of the Greatest Victories and Defeats*. Santa Barbara, CA: ABC-CLIO, 2014, p. 248.

Books

Feifer, George. *The Battle of Okinawa: The Blood and the Bomb*. Guilford, CT: Lyons Press, 2012. *The Battle of Okinawa* examines the experiences and impact of the battle on the American invaders, Japanese soldiers, and Okinawan natives.

Sloan, Bill. *The Ultimate Battle: Okinawa 1945—The Last Epic Struggle of World War II*. New York: Simon & Schuster, 2007. *The Ultimate Battle* is a complete history of the Battle of Okinawa.

Websites

"Battle for Okinawa." Preceden. 2018. This site contains photographs and links to additional resources about the Battle of Okinawa, with descriptions and explanations. https://www.preceden.com/timelines/317234-battle-of-okinawa. Accessed June 14, 2018.

Hammel, Eric. "Battle of Okinawa: Summary, Fact, Pictures and Causalities." HistoryNet.com. June 12, 2006. This essay is a detailed history of the Battle of Okinawa. http://www.historynet.com/battle-of-okinawa-operation-iceberg.htm. Accessed September 5, 2017.

Also Noteworthy

1921

Texas enacts Alien Land Law.

2006

In Waco, Texas, a white man yells anti-Muslim and racial slurs and attacks a female Muslim student at Baylor University.

April 2

1895

The Planters' Labor and Supply Company reorganizes under the name Hawai'ian Sugar Planters' Association (HSPA). Its goal is the "advancement, improvement and protection of the sugar industry of Hawai'i, the support of an Experiment Station, the maintenance of a sufficient supply of labor for the sugar plantations of Hawai'i and the development of agriculture in general."

The Experiment Station, HSPA, was established on April 2, 1895, with the arrival of Dr. Walter Maxwell in Hawaii. Dr. Maxwell previously worked in Germany with sugar beets, with the U.S. government sugar station in Schuyler, Nebraska, and with the Louisiana sugarcane industry. Maxwell's arrival in Hawaii was the culmination of nearly ten years of discussion within the Hawaiian sugar industry on the need for scientific expertise to assist the growers in maximizing yields in the fledgling sugar industry which had had its start in the early 1800s.

The establishment of an experiment station was not a spur-of-the- moment decision. At the first convention (1882) of the Planters' Labor and Supply Company, it was resolved, "that the trustees be requested to consider the advisability of employing a thoroughly competent chemist to reside on these Islands, and do such chemical work as may be for the advantage of planters and manufactures." . . . At the 1896 meeting of HSPA, Dr. Maxwell reported that he had obtained land for the Experiment Station on Keeaumoku Street and further reported that he planned experiments on fertilization to observe the action of potash, phosphoric acid, and nitrogen and also to note the action of these chemicals in different combinations.

Source: *Hawaiian Planters' Record*. Vol. 61, November 3, 2009, p. 11. Kunia: Hawaii Agriculture Research Center. http://www.harc-hspa.com/uploads/2/6/1/7/26170270/hawnplant_-_new_edit_9-12-11.pdf. Accessed March 1, 2018.

Books

Kurashige, Lon. *Two Faces of Exclusion: The Untold History of Anti-Asian Racism in the United States*. Chapel Hill: University of North Carolina Press, 2016. *Two Faces of Exclusion* examines the opposition to anti-Asian exclusion policies during the beginning of Asian migration to the United States. See Chapter 3,

"Eye of the Storm: The Laboring of Exclusion, 1882–1904."

Takaki, Ronald T. *Pau Hana: Plantation Life and Labor in Hawaii*. Honolulu: University of Hawaii Press, 1983. Historian Ronald Takaki provides a history of plantation life as experienced by the laborers.

Websites

The Hawaiian Sugar Planters' Association Plantation Archives. This site contains primary documents from plantation records for Kauai, Oahu, Maui, and Hawaii. University of Hawaii at Manoa. http://www2.hawaii.edu/~speccoll/hawaiihspa.html. Accessed October 11, 2016.

Nakamura, Kelli. "Hawaiian Sugar Planters' Association." *Densho Encyclopedia*, February 26, 2014. This web page provides a history of the Hawaiian Sugar Planters' Association in Hawaii. http://encyclopedia.densho.org/Hawaiian%20Sugar%20Planters%27%20Association/. Accessed October 11, 2016.

1917

President Woodrow Wilson asks Congress to declare war on Germany. The United States soon formally entered World War I. During World War I, several thousand Chinese, Japanese, Korean, and Filipino immigrants joined the U.S. military and served with distinction on the battlefields for America. On December 19, 1918, Judge Horace W. Vaughn of the U.S. District Court for Hawaii ruled that Japanese, Chinese, and Korean veterans of World War I were eligible for naturalization under the act of May 9, 1918. As a result, 398 Japanese, 99 Koreans, and 4 Chinese were granted citizenship by November 14, 1919. Unfortunately, their citizenship was revoked by the *Toyota v. United States* decision on May 25, 1925. Asian American veterans who served in World War I would be eligible for naturalization in 1935 when Congress passed the Nye-Lea Act, which permitted only 500 Asian veterans of World War I to become naturalized citizens.

During WWI, the government offered naturalization to any alien who served in the armed forces during the war. This statute, however, clashed with those that denied citizenship for Asians on the basis of race, thus pitting two concepts of political membership against each other: martial and racial. During the 1920s, when nativism peaked, the racial conception was dominant, despite the war-born assertiveness of Asian veterans who argued that their wartime patriotism placed upon the government and society a moral obligation to treat them with greater respect. In 1935, however, Congress, under pressure from the American Legion (which argued that "these Japanese boys are veterans just like the rest of us"), passed the Nye-Lea Act, which awarded citizenship (in the formal sense) to Asian veterans of that war. "The powerful appeal of militaristic patriotism," . . . "provided an unexpected opening for Asians who fought in the world war and supplied the only successful argument for their naturalization before the racial prerequisite for citizenship was repealed in 1952." Formal citizenship, however, did not prevent the interning of Japanese-Americans during WWII, but that war, like the first, provided yet another opportunity to demonstrate loyalty and courage.

Source: Diamant, Neil. *Embattled Glory: Veterans, Military Families, and the Politics of Patriotism in China, 1949–2007*. Lanham, MD: Rowman & Littlefield Publishers, 2009, pp. 27–28.

Books

Kurashige, Lon. *Two Faces of Exclusion: The Untold History of Anti-Asian Racism in the United States*. Chapel Hill: University of North Carolina Press, 2016. *Two Faces of Exclusion* discusses various aspects of U.S. legal racial construction of "Asian" Americans. See Chapter 6 "Silver Lining: New Deals for Asian Americans, 1924–1941" for discussion on how Asian Americans challenged racial policies and practices.

Lien, Pei-Te. *Making of Asian America through Political Participation*. Philadelphia, PA: Temple University Press, 2001. *Making of Asian America* comparatively examines Asian American political participation in the United States.

Websites

"Asian-Americans & Pacific Islanders in the United States Army." U.S. Army. This site provides a history of Asian American participation in U.S. military history. https://www.army.mil/asianpacificamericans/. Accessed October 20, 2016.

Niiya, Brian. "Tokutaro Slocum." *Densho Encyclopedia*, November 15, 2017. This essay chronicles the life of Japanese American World War I veteran and citizenship activist. http://encyclopedia.densho.org/Tokutaro%20Slocum/. Accessed March 2, 2018.

Also Noteworthy

1942

State of California fires all Japanese Americans in the state's civil service.

1998

Alpha Sigma Rho, an Asian American interest sorority, is founded at the University of Georgia.

April 3

1975

In South Vietnam, Operation Babylift begins as an attempt to save thousands of "orphans" as U.S. forces withdraw from Vietnam. As the United States was losing the war, Operation Babylift was an attempt to display the United States as moral victors, saving orphans of war; however, many of the babies lifted were not orphans. The initial mission resulted in a plane crash that killed 180 people, including 78 children and 35 military attachés. The children, once in America, were adopted out to families. Many of the children were "Amerasians" (born of Vietnamese mother and American soldier father).

Operation Babylift . . . was heralded by some as an heroic humanitarian effort. However, critics rebuked it as a "media relations effort . . . to give Americans a positive spin on its role in the war" or a well-intended, albeit misguided, attempt to rescue children who were either not orphans or would be better off remaining in Vietnam; some even denounced it as kidnapping. . . .

Operation Babylift was . . . the largest mass overseas evacuation of children. . . . Responding to pressure from humanitarian organizations working in Vietnam, President Ford announced on 3 April 1975 that $2m had been allocated for 30 flights to airlift infants and children out of Saigon. . . . Although reports vary, 2500–3000 children were evacuated, with the majority flown to the USA and the remaining to Canada, Australia and Europe. . . . Tragically the first flight crashed, killing 180 of its passengers. Despite the devastating loss, a fleet of military and commercial transport planes evacuated children in coordination with adoption and aid agencies until 26 April. . . . Controversy and criticism resulted in lawsuits and public condemnation. Gloria Emerson . . . characterized Operation Babylift as a "successful propaganda effort". A Yale psychologist, Edward Zigler . . . questioned US motivations, observing, "We've been ripping [the children] right out of their culture, their community." Similarly . . . ethics and religion professors denounced Babylift as immoral, raising concerns that the children might not be orphans. . . . Tran Tuong Nhu, a Vietnamese American who helped care for the newly arrived children, was startled to learn that many of the "orphans" had living parents. . . . When her concerns went unaddressed by adoption agencies and federal government officials, a class action lawsuit was filed. . . . Nonetheless, lawsuits were filed by family members who made it to the USA. Over 30 years later, debate and controversy surround Operation Babylift, especially in the light of the implementation of the Hague Convention's protocol to protect children in intercountry adoption.

Source: Bergquist, Kathleen Ja Sook. "Operation Babylift or Babyabduction? Implications of the Hague Convention on the Humanitarian Evacuation and 'Rescue' of Children." *International Social Work* 52, no. 5 (August 24, 2009): pp. 622–623.

Books

Lee, Sabine. *Children Born of War in the Twentieth Century*. Manchester: Manchester University Press, 2017. See Chapter 4, "*Bui Doi*: The Children of the Vietnam War."

Sachs, Dana. *The Life We Were Given: Operation Babylift, International Adoption, and the Children of War in Vietnam*. Boston, MA: Beacon Press, 2010. *The Life We Were Given* addresses the unresolved implications and realities of Operation Babylift from the perspectives of birth mothers, adoptees, orphanage workers, military personnel, doctors, and adoptive families.

Websites

Martin, Allison. "The Legacy of Operation Babylift." Adopt Vietnam. 2000. This is a historical essay about Operation Babylift that includes a discussion of its legacy. http://www.adoptvietnam.org/adoption/babylift.htm. Accessed September 5, 2017.

"Operation Babylift." Gerald Ford Museum. This site provides historic images of Operation Babylift, along with descriptions and explanation. https://www.fordlibrarymuseum.gov/museum/exhibits/babylift/photography/. Accessed September 5, 2017.

Also Noteworthy

1969

President Richard Nixon's administration will "Vietnamize" the Vietnam War.

April 4

1900

Japanese sugar plantation workers at the Pioneer Mill in Lahaina, Maui, go on strike and win a nine-hour workday and most of their other demands. This strike led to the development of other strikes through the islands.

On April 4 Japanese workers at the Pioneer Mill in Lahaina struck. Upset over the deaths of three mill hands who had been crushed under a collapsed sugar pan, the laborers blamed management carelessness for the accident and refused to work. The strikers seized virtual control of the mill, as well as the town. According to an investigator, "the strikers for 10 days continued to meet, to parade in town under Japanese flags, to drill, and even, unhindered by anyone, demolished the house and property of a store clerk who would not give them credit." The Lahaina strikers successfully forced the manager to yield to most of their demands, including $500 payments to the relatives of each of the accident victims and a nine-hour day for all workers. Meanwhile Japanese laborers at the nearby Olowalu Plantation also went out on strike and secured even greater concessions from their manager: the discharge of all but one luna, abolition of the docking system, a shorter word day, and $1000 to cover their expenses while on strike. Shortly after the strikes at Lahaina and Olowalu, the president of the Planters' Association of Maui warned the HSPA trustees: "Labor strikes have already begun on Maui, and we have received information from various sources that as soon as the U.S. laws governing this country go into effect the Japanese will strike for higher wages." Japanese laborers on the Spreckelsville Plantation also struck, demanding the termination of all labor contracts. Swinging clubs and throwing stones, two hundred strikers fought a posse of sixty policemen and lunas armed with black snake whips. Though the strikers were "most thoroughly black snaked" and forced to retreat to their camps, they won the cancellation of their labor contracts.

Source: Takaki, Ronald. *Pau Hana: Plantation Life and Labor in Hawaii*. Honolulu: University of Hawaii Press, 1983, pp. 148–149.

Books

Beechert, Edward. *Working in Hawaii: A Labor History*. Honolulu: University of Hawaii Press, 1985. *Working in Hawaii* covers the history of plantation labor in Hawaii.

Kodama-Nishimoto, Michi, Warren Nishimoto, and Cynthia Oshiro, eds. *Hanahana: An Oral History Anthology of Hawaii's Working People.* Honolulu: Ethnic Studies Oral History Project, University of Hawaii, 1984. *Hanahana* contains oral histories of plantation workers that include their strikes.

Websites

"CLEAR Timeline of Hawai'i Labor History." Center for Labor Education and Research, University of Hawaii, West Oahu. This site offers a detailed timeline of labor history and relations in Hawaii from pre-1870 to 2000. https://www.hawaii.edu/uhwo/clear/home/Timeline.html#1900. Accessed September 5, 2017.

"Labor Strikes." Hawaii Digital Newspaper Project. This site provides a chronology of labor strikes in Hawaii, along with historic photographs. https://sites.google.com/a/hawaii.edu/ndnp-hawaii/Home/subject-and-topic-guides/labor-strikes. Accessed September 5, 2017.

Also Noteworthy

1903

Thirty-five laborers from Okinawa arrive in Honolulu aboard the SS *Hong Kong Maru*.

1968

Civil rights leader Dr. Martin Luther King Jr. is assassinated at the Lorraine Motel in Memphis, Tennessee.

1975

Operation Babylift begins airlifting 2,000 Vietnamese "orphans" out of Vietnam in an attempt to gain American public support for the Vietnam War. During the operation, a World Airways C-5A crashed, killing 150 "orphans" and 50 adults. Later reports of the "orphans" reveal many belonged to loving families and were talked into giving up their babies for a better future out of war-torn Vietnam.

April 5

1929

Chi Alpha Delta, an Asian American interest sorority, receives charter at the University of California, Los Angeles.

Founded in 1928 at the University of California, Los Angeles, Chi Alpha Delta was the first Japanese American and Asian American sorority in the United States. Asian American sororities were to become so popular that by 1959, another sorority, Theta Kappa Phi, had been founded on the same campus. Chi Alpha Delta attracted membership of approximately 60 sorors each year, and by 1960 the predominately Japanese American sorority had attracted other Asian ethnic women as members. Through food and fashion, the women of Chi Alpha Delta carved a gendered, ethnicized, and generational identity that vacillated between Asian-ethnic and distinctively American. For example, the women of Chi Alpha Delta prepared and served "international" foods on a regular basis. For a social with Sigma Phi Omega, the University of Southern California Asian American sorority, the menu was American with a Mexican entrée: tamales, dill pickles, salad, rolls, punch, sherbert, cookies, and coffee. Magazines like Scene normalized "American" food for parties and provided daughters of immigrant women a venue to pick up on the knowledge of choosing, preparing, and presenting such foods.

Source: Lim, Shirley. "Hell's a Poppin': Asian American Women's Youth Consumer Culture." In *Asian American Youth: Culture, Identity, and Ethnicity*, edited by Jennifer Lee and Min Zhou, p. 106. New York: Routledge, 2004.

Books

Lim, Shirley. *A Feeling of Belonging: Asian American Women's Public Culture 1930–1960.* New York: New York University Press, 2006. See Chapter 1, "'A Feeling of Belonging': Chi Alpha Delta, 1928–1941," for discussion of the sorority's early history.

Torbenson, Craig, and Gregory Parks, eds. *Brothers and Sisters: Diversity in College Fraternities and Sororities.* Madison, WI: Fairleigh Dickinson

University Press, 2009. See Edith Wen-chu Chen's Chapter 3, "Asian Americans in Sororities and Fraternities: In Search of a Home and Place."

Websites

Chi Alpha Delta. Official web page. https://chialphadelta.com/. Accessed February 5, 2018.
Chi Alpha Delta Alumnae. Official alumnae web page. http://www.chialphadeltaalumnae.com/. Accessed February 5, 2018.

Also Noteworthy

1969

Anti-Vietnam War demonstrations take place in more than 30 cities across the United States.

April 6

1903

The U.S. Supreme Court holds in *Kaoru Yamataya v. Thomas M. Fisher* that immigrants have right to appeal their deportation if their procedural due process has been violated.

Kaoru Yamataya v. Thomas M. Fisher *No. 171. Argued February 24, 1903. Decided April 6, 1903.*

This case presents some questions arising under the act of Congress relating to the exclusion of certain classes of alien immigrants.

On the 11th day of July, 1901, appellant, a subject of Japan, landed at the port of Seattle, Washington; and on or about July 15th, 1901, the appellee, an immigrant inspector of the United States, having instituted an investigation into the circumstances of her entering the United States, decided that she came here in violation of law, in that she was a pauper and a person likely to become a public charge,—aliens of that class being excluded altogether from this country by the act of March 3d, 1891 (26 Stat. at L. 1085, chap. 551, U. S. Comp. Stat. 1901, p. 1294).

The evidence obtained by the inspector was transmitted to the Secretary of the Treasury, who, under date of July 23d, 1901, issued a warrant addressed to the immigrant inspector at Seattle, reciting that the appellant had come into the United States contrary to the provisions of the above act of 1891, and ordering that she be taken into custody and returned to Japan at the expense of the vessel importing her.

The inspector being about to execute this warrant, an application was presented in behalf of the appellant to the district court of the United States for the district of Washington, northern division, for a writ of habeas corpus. The application alleged that the imprisonment of the petitioner was unlawful, and that she did not come here in violation of the act of 1891, or of any other law of the United States relating to the exclusion of aliens.

The writ having been issued, a return was made by the inspector, stating that he had found upon due investigation and the admissions of the appellant that she was a pauper and a person likely to become a public charge, and had "surreptitiously, clandestinely, unlawfully, and without any authority come into the United States;" that, "in pursuance of said testimony, admissions of the petitioner, Kaoru Yamataya, evidence, facts, and circumstances," he had decided that she had no right to be within the territory of the United States, and was a proper person for deportation; all which he reported to the proper officers of the government, who confirmed his decision, and thereupon the Secretary of the Treasury issued his warrant, requiring the deportation of the appellant. That warrant was produced and made part of the return.

The return of the inspector was traversed, the traverse admitting that the inspector had investigated the case of the petitioner, and had made a finding that she had illegally come into this country, but alleging that the investigation was a "pretended" and an inadequate one; that she did not understand the English language, and did not know at the time that such investigation was with a view to her deportation from the country; and that the investigation was carried on without her having the assistance of counsel or friends, or an opportunity to show that she was not a pauper or likely to become a public charge. The traverse alleged that the petitioner was not in the United States in violation of law.

A demurrer to the traverse was sustained, the writ of habeas corpus was dismissed, and the appellant was remanded to the custody of the inspector. From that order the present appeal was prosecuted.

Messrs. Vere Goldthwaite, Harold Preston, *and* Walter A. Keene *for appellant.*

[Argument of Counsel from pages 88–92 intentionally omitted]

Assistant Attorney General Hoyt for *appellee.*

[Argument of Counsel from pages 92–94 intentionally omitted]

Mr. Justice Harlan delivered the opinion of the court:

Source: Kaoru Yamataya v. Thomas M Fisher, 189 US 86 April 6, 1903.

Books

Chuman, Frank. *The Bamboo People: The Law and Japanese-Americans.* Del Mar, CA: Publisher's Inc., 1976. *The Bamboo People* is a legal history of Japanese Americans since 1869.

Zolberg, Aristide. *A Nation by Design: Immigration Policy in the Fashioning of America.* Cambridge, MA: Harvard University Press, 2006. *A Nation by Design* is a comprehensive overview of U.S. immigration policy history.

Websites

"The Japanese Immigrant Case (Yamataya v. Fisher) case brief." Law School Case Briefs. 2014. This site contains the case synopsis, facts, discussion, and conclusion. http://www.lawschoolcasebriefs.net/2013/11/the-japanese-immigrant-case-yamataya-v.html. Accessed September 5, 2017.

Kaoru Yamataya v. Fisher (1903). FindLaw. 2017. The full text of ruling is available here. http://caselaw.findlaw.com/us-supreme-court/189/86.html. Accessed September 5, 2017.

Also Noteworthy

2004

As a reaction to the commuter-train bombing in Spain, two women and a man attack a Muslim woman, yanking on her headscarf and calling Muslim people violent at Tampa, Florida.

2007

The Namesake (2007), a film based on Jhumpa Lahiri's novel of the same name—directed by Mira Nair and screenplay written by Sooni Taraporevala—is released.

2016

Khairuldeen Makhzoomi, an American of Iraqi descent, and a senior at the University of California, Berkeley, is kicked off a Southwest Airlines flight for speaking Arabic after another passenger complained. On February 13, 2018, Makhzoomi, the San Francisco Bay Area office of the Council on American-Islamic Relations (CAIR-SFBA), and the law firm of Walkup, Melodia, Kelly & Schoenberger filed a federal lawsuit against Southwest Airlines.

April 7

1954

Responding to the defeat of the French by the Viet Minh at Dien Bien Phu, President Dwight D. Eisenhower coins one of the most well-known Cold War phrases when he suggests that the fall of French Indochina to the communists could generate a "domino" effect in Southeast Asia. The "domino theory" will dominate U.S. thinking and foreign policy about Vietnam and Southeast Asia for the next decade.

President Dwight D. Eisenhower News Conference (April 7, 1954)

Q. Robert Richards, Copley Press: *Mr. President, would you mind commenting on the strategic importance of Indochina for the free world? I think there has been, across the country, some lack of understanding on just what it means to us.*

The President: *You have, of course, both the specific and the general when you talk about such things. First of all, you have the specific value of a locality in its production of materials that the world needs.*

Then you have the possibility that many human beings pass under a dictatorship that is inimical to the free world.

Finally, you have broader considerations that might follow what you would call the "falling domino" principle. You have a row of dominoes set up, you knock over the first one, and what will happen to the last one is the certainty that it will go over very quickly. So you could have a beginning of a disintegration that would have the most profound influences.

Now, with respect to the first one, two of the items from this particular area that the world uses are tin and tungsten. They are very important. There are others, of course, the rubber plantations and so on.

Then with respect to more people passing under this domination, Asia, after all, has already lost some 450 million of its peoples to the Communist dictatorship, and we simply can't afford greater losses.

But when we come to the possible sequence of events, the loss of Indochina, of Burma, of Thailand, of the Peninsula, and Indonesia following, now you begin to talk about areas that not only multiply the disadvantages that you would suffer through the loss of materials, sources of materials, but now you are talking about millions and millions of people.

Finally, the geographical position achieved thereby does many things. It turns the so-called island defensive chain of Japan, Formosa, of the Philippines and to the southward; it moves in to threaten Australia and New Zealand.

It takes away, in its economic aspects, that region that Japan must have as a trading area or Japan, in turn, will have only one place in the world to go—that is, toward the Communist areas in order to live.

So, the possible consequences of the loss are just incalculable to the free world.

Source: Public Papers of the Presidents Dwight D. Eisenhower, 1954, pp. 381–390. The Public Papers of the Presidents of the United States. https://quod.lib.umich.edu/p/ppotpus?cginame=text-idx;id=navbarbrowselink;page=browse. Accessed January 14, 2017.

Books

Kaufman, Burton, and Diane Kaufman. *Historical Dictionary of the Eisenhower Era*. Lanham, MD: Scarecrow Press, 2009. *Historical Dictionary of the Eisenhower Era* examines significant individuals, organizations, policies, historical events, economic issues, critical issues, and themes during the Eisenhower presidency.

Welch, David. *Painful Choices: A Theory of Foreign Policy Change*. Princeton, NJ: Princeton University Press, 2005. *Painful Choices* is a sophisticated discussion of political theory and U.S. foreign policy that includes a discussion of the history, implication, and analysis of the "Domino Theory."

Websites

"Domino Theory." History. 2017. This site provides a general historical background of the "Domino Theory" and its significance and impact during the Cold War on U.S. foreign policies. http://www.history.com/topics/cold-war/domino-theory. Accessed January 14, 2017.

"The Quotable Quotes of Dwight D. Eisenhower." National Park Service. This site provides quotes by President Dwight Eisenhower accompanied by a brief discussion of its significance. https://www.nps.gov/features/eise/jrranger/quotes2.htm. Accessed January 14, 2017.

Also Noteworthy

1900

Congress creates a civil government for Puerto Rico, establishing the island as an American territory without all the rights of American citizenship.

1921

Delaware enacts Alien Land Law.

1965

The United States offers North Vietnam economic aid in exchange for peace, but the offer is summarily rejected.

1971

President Richard Nixon appoints Herbert Young Cho Choy (January 6, 1916–March 10, 2004) to the U.S. Court of Appeal for the Ninth Circuit. Choy is the first Korean American (and Asian American) appointed as a federal judge.

April 8

1997

The Court of Appeals rules unanimously that California's Proposition 209, known as California Civil Rights Initiative, does not violate the U.S. Constitution and therefore nullifies Judge Henderson's preliminary injunction. Proposition 209 amended the state constitution to prohibit state government institutions from considering race, sex, or ethnicity in the areas of public employment, contracts, and education. It passed in the November 5, 1996, election with over 54 percent of the vote.

Exit Polls: Asian American Voting Patterns

Strong support for affirmative action, growing political participation, and the importance of bilingual voting materials were key finds [in the exit polls]. It was evident that Asian Americans supported affirmative action and had voted strongly against Proposition 209—which was to eliminate affirmative action policies in government and public schools. . . . Supporters of Proposition 209 used Asian Americans as an example of a group that would be discriminated against by affirmative action, and when Asian American organizations such as the Japanese American Citizens League and the NAPALC spoke in favor of affirmative action they were criticized for not reflecting the sentiments of their communities. As Art Takei of the Asian Pacific American Labor Alliance said, "The first thing this is going to do is raise eyebrows and destroy some of the myths that we tend to be conservative and mainstream." . . . A seventy-one-year-old voter stated as he left the Geen Mun Neighborhood Center, a senior service facility in San Francisco's Chinatown, "I'm Chinese . . . I voted against Proposition 209 because it is unfair to Chinese. I have more than ten grandchildren and I care about their future, so I voted against 209."

Source: Saito, Leland. *Race and Politics: Asian Americans, Latinos, and Whites in a Los Angeles Suburb.* Urbana: University of Illinois Press, 1998, p. 99.

Books

Ancheta, Angelo. *Race, Rights, and the Asian American Experience.* New Brunswick, NJ: Rutgers University Press, 1998. See Chapter 2, "Discrimination and Antidiscrimination Law," for a discussion related to Proposition 209.

Curry, George, ed. *The Affirmative Action Debate.* Cambridge: Perseus Publishing, 1996. See Theodore Hsien Wang and Frank Wu's "Beyond the Model Minority Myth."

Websites

"Prop 209." American Civil Rights Institute. 2014. This site provides data related to how Californians voted on Prop. 209, including the ballot summaries, and chronology of lawsuits against Prop. 209. http://acri.org/prop-209/. Accessed September 5, 2017.

"Proposition 209." The California Online Voter Guide. General Election 1996. This site provides the full text for Proposition 209, with links for support and opposition. https://www.calvoter.org/voter/elections/archive/96gen/props/209.html. Accessed September 5, 2017.

Also Noteworthy

1902

The Fresno Buddhist Church is dedicated.

April 9

2015

The Panama Hotel in Seattle, Washington, is designated as a National Treasure by the National Trust for Historic Preservation.

Ironically, it also may be necessary to reexamine historic properties long recognized as significant in the heritage of various ethnic communities because of features that were overlooked when they were originally documented, as the example of Seattle's Panama Hotel doubly illustrates. A single-room occupancy workingman's hotel built in 1910, the Panama is one of many contributing structures to Seattle's International District. As has been common practice in many places, the surveys conducted in preparation for the historic district nomination did not extend into the building's interiors. As a result, the district nomination overlooked two significant features in the Panama Hotel's basement. One is an extraordinarily well-preserved example of an urban furo, *or Japanese American bathhouse. . . . The other more haunting feature is a significant number of fully packed trunks stored by Japanese Americans on the eve of internment which were never reclaimed. . . . Important cultural resources such as these have no recognition or protection unless they are documented in the preservation planning tools of cultural resource managers. The example of the Panama Hotel suggests that state and local preservation planning initiatives can bring long-overlooked ethnic cultural resources into public view, building new constituencies for their protection.*

Source: Dubrow, Gail. "Feminist and Multicultural Perspectives on Preservation Planning." In *Making the Invisible Visible: A Multicultural Planning History*, edited by Leonie Sandercock, pp. 61–62. Berkeley: University of California Press, 1998.

Books

Fiset, Louis, and Gail Nomura, eds. *Nikkei in the Pacific Northwest: Japanese Americans and Japanese Canadians in the Twentieth Century*. Seattle: University of Washington Press, 2005. See Gail Dubrow's Chapter 6, "'The Nail That Sticks Up Gets Hit': The Architecture of Japanese American Identity in the Urban Environment, 1885–1942."

Meeks, Stephanie. *The Past and Future City: How Historic Preservation Is Reviving America's Communities*. Washington, DC: Island Press, 2000. *The Past and Future City* discusses various aspects of historic preservation and highlights examples of successes.

Websites

Broom, Jack. "Seattle's Panama Hotel Deemed a National Treasure." *Seattle Times*, July 27, 2015. This article details the history and significance of the Panama Hotel and its historic preservation efforts. https://www.seattletimes.com/seattle-news/seattles-panama-hotel-deemed-a-national-treasure/. Accessed February 5, 2018.

Historic Panama Hotel Bed & Breakfast. Official web page with history. http://www.panamahotel.net/. Accessed February 5, 2018.

April 10

1971

On this day, the U.S. table tennis team arrives in China for a 10-day visit, becoming the first group of Americans in over 20 years to get a peek behind the "Bamboo Curtain." Ping-pong diplomacy was successful and resulted in opening the U.S.-China relationship, leading the United States to lift the embargo against China.

Books

Griffin, Nicholas. *Ping-Pong Diplomacy: The Secret History behind the Game That Changed the World*. New York: Scribner, 2014. *Ping-Pong Diplomacy* is a rich and complex history of ping-pong diplomacy that argues ping-pong was always political and tied to Communism, and strategically employed by Mao Zedong.

Itoh, Mayumi. *The Origin of Ping-Pong Diplomacy: The Forgotten Architect of Sino-U.S. Rapprochement*. New York: Palgrave Macmillan, 2011. *The Origin of Ping-Pong Diplomacy* is a comprehensive treatment of the factors behind ping-pong diplomacy that sheds light on today's complex U.S.-Japan-China international relations.

Websites

Andrews, Evan. "How Ping-Pong Diplomacy Thawed the Cold War." www.History.com. April 8, 2016. This essay is a detailed history of ping-pong diplomacy and its significance in world history with historical photographs . http://www.history.com/news/ping-pong-diplomacy. Accessed January 16, 2018.

Cauffman, Charlie. "Ping-Pong Diplomacy: How People Coming Together Established Sino-America Détente." Richard Nixon Foundation Library Museum. 20148. This essay provides a historical overview of ping-pong diplomacy and its significances in "thawing" the Cold War. There are photographs and links to related archival documents. https://www.nixonfoundation.org/2017/09/ping-pong-diplomacy-people-coming-together-established-sino-america-detente/. Accessed January 16, 2018.

Also Noteworthy

2002

In Oswego, New York, Joshua Centrone, William J. Reeves, and Mitcheal W. Trumball, all 18-year-olds, and Cassie Hudson, a 19-year-old, are charged with a hate crime for burning a Sikh temple in September 2001.

April 11

1943

Japanese American internee James Hatsuki Wakasa is shot and killed by military police at Topaz War Relocation Center while allegedly trying to escape. It is later concluded that he was killed while inside the fence.

But it was not only on the battlefield that Japanese-Americans lost their lives. At least nine people were shot and killed by prison guards at the internment camps for getting too close to the fence. At Topaz, sixty-three-year-old man was shot and killed by military police in April 1944. The MP said James Hatsuki Wakasa, an Issei, was trying to crawl under the fence and ignored warnings from the guard towers above the camp. The sentry who shot him was a disabled Pacific war veteran. But Wakasa was shot in the chest and would have been facing the guard, so it was hard for residents to understand how he could have been crawling away. Most believed instead that he was confused and did not hear or understand the guard's warnings. Court-martial proceedings were held for the guard, but he was found not guilty.

Source: Yellin, Emily. *Our Mothers' War: American Women at Home and at the Front during World War II*. New York: Free Press, 2004, p. 275.

Books

Ng, Wendy. *Japanese American Internment during World War II: A History and Reference Guide*. Westport, CT: Greenwood Press, 2002. Ng's volume covers various aspects of Japanese American internment, along with primary documents, photographic essays, and biographies of personalities behind the internment program.

Taylor, Sandra. *Jewel of the Desert: Japanese American Internment at Topaz*. Berkeley: University of California Press, 1993. *Jewel of the Desert* is based on interviews with survivors of Topaz, archives, and historical newspapers to document the life of Japanese Americans in the face of extreme prejudice.

Websites

Russell, Nancy. "James Hatsuaki Wakasa." *Densho Encyclopedia*, July 8, 2015. This essay is a history of James Hatsuaki Wakasa's killing. http://encyclopedia.densho.org/James_Hatsuaki_Wakasa/. Accessed February 5, 2018.

Topaz. Remembrance Project. Japanese American National Museum. 2012. This site provides a history to the shooting, along with art based on the event. http://www.remembrance-project.org/camps/topaz.html?referrer=https://www.google.com/. Accessed February 5, 2018.

Also Noteworthy

2009

First International Lao New Year Festival is held at San Francisco's Civic Center.

April 12

1975

President Gerald Ford orders the U.S. military to evacuate U.S. citizens from Cambodia, through "Operation Eagle Pull."

On April 12, 1975, U.S. Ambassador John Gunther Dean ordered the evacuation of the remaining 82 U.S. personnel plus 159 Cambodians and 35 other nationals who had been employed by the U.S. embassy. While Lon Nol was evacuated, several prominent leaders, including Prime Minister Long Boret and Prince Sirik Matak, stayed behind in the hope that they could play some role in national reconciliation, but they were killed by the KR [Khmer Rouge]. There were no clamoring mobs, as in Vietnam, seeking places on U.S. helicopters. Although rumors of the KR's brutality had reached Phnom Penh, most Cambodians awaited their arrival stoically. On April 17, the KR, dressed in black peasant garb, marched into Phnom Penh. To show their independence of Vietnam, they timed their victory two weeks before north Vietnamese forces entered Saigon.

Source: Poole, Peter. *Politics and Society in Southeast Asia*. Jefferson, NC: McFarland & Company, 2009, p. 53.

Books

Cornfield, Justin. *The History of Cambodia*. Santa Barbara, CA: ABC-CLIO, 2009. *The History of Cambodia* is a complete history of Cambodia. See Chapter 6 "The Khmer Republic (1970–1975)" for discussion related to the U.S. evacuation from Cambodia.

Hunt, Ira. *Losing Vietnam: How America Abandoned Southeast Asia*. Lexington: The University Press of Kentucky, 2013. *Losing Vietnam* argues that congressional budget cuts negatively impacted the U.S. military and State Department, leading to defeat.

Websites

Gray, Denis. "Former US Ambassador Describes When the US 'Abandoned Cambodia and Handed It over to the Butcher.'" *Business Insider*, April 10, 2015. Former U.S. ambassador John Gunther Dean reflects on the U.S. evacuation of Cambodia. https://www.businessinsider.com/former-us-ambassador-describes-when-the-us-abandoned-cambodia-and-handed-it-over-to-the-butcher-2015-4 Accessed August 1, 2018.

"Operation Eagle Pull before the Fall of Phnom Penh." Moments in U.S. Diplomatic History. Association for Diplomatic Studies and Training. 2017. This essay provides a detailed history of Operation Eagle Pull, with historic photographs. http://adst.org/2013/04/operation-eagle-pull-before-the-fall-of-phnom-penh/#.WbAuEMiGO70. Accessed September 6, 2017.

Also Noteworthy

1966

Aveline and Michio Kushi, Japanese teachers of macrobiotics, found Erewhon, a small macrobiotic and natural foods retail store in Boston, Massachusetts. Over the decades, they introduce Americans to miso, Kikkoman, shoyu, and tempeh.

2002

In Madison, Wisconsin, Thomas D. Iverson, a 45-year-old, is sentenced to two years and three months in prison for making threatening calls to a man of Middle Eastern descent in September 2001.

April 13

1850

On April 13, 1850, the first California state legislature passes the first Foreign Miners Tax

Law, levying $20 per month tax on each foreigner engaged in mining. It also set the stage for discrimination against the Chinese because Chinese immigrants were not allowed to become naturalized and therefore subject to this tax. A revolt resulted, and it was repealed in 1851. The Foreign Miners Tax Law was reenacted in 1852. In 1854, California amended the law to exempt naturalized citizens from paying the Foreign Miners Tax. This clearly discriminated against Chinese, since they were prohibited from naturalization and had no option but to pay the Foreign Miner's Tax.

Excerpt from Chapter 97. An act for the better regulation of the Mines, and the government of Foreign Miners.

The People of the State of California, represented in Senate and Assembly, do enact as follows:

1. *No person who is not a native or natural born citizen of the United States, or who may not have become a citizen under the treaty of Guadalupe Hidalgo (all native California Indians excepted), shall be permitted to mine in any part of this State, without having first obtained a license so to do according to the provisions of this Act. . . .*
6. *Every person required by the first section of this Act to obtain a license to mine, shall apply to the Collector of Licenses to foreign miners, and take out a license to mine, for which he shall pay the sum of twenty dollars per month; and such foreigners may from time to time take out a new license, at the same rate per month, until the Governor shall issue his proclamation announcing the passage of a law by Congress, regulating the mines of precious metals in this State.*
7. *If any such foreigner or foreigners shall refuse or neglect to take out such license by the second Monday of May next, it shall be the duty of the Collector of Licenses to foreign miners of the county in which such foreigner or foreigners shall be, to furnish his or their names to the Sheriff of the county, or to any Deputy Sheriff, whose duty it shall be to summon a posse of American citizens, and, if necessary, forcibly prevent him or them from continuing such mining operations.*
8. *Should such foreigner or foreigners, after having been stopped by a Sheriff or Deputy Sheriff from mining in one place, seek a new location and continue such mining operations, it shall be deemed a misdemeanor, for which such offender or offenders shall be arrested as for a misdemeanor, and he or they shall be imprisoned for a term not exceeding three months, and fined not more than one thousand dollars.*
9. *Any foreigner who may obtain a license in conformity with the provisions of this Act, shall be allowed to work the mines anywhere in this State, under the same regulations as citizens of the United States.*

Source: *The Statutes of California Passed at the First Session of the Legislature*. San Jose, CA: J. Winchester, State Printer, 1850.

Books

Pfaelzer, Jean. *Driven Out: The Forgotten War against Chinese Americans*. Berkeley: University of California Press, 2007. Jean Pfaelzer uses primary documents, such as newspaper articles, to narrate the societal impact of the anti-Chinese movement from 1848 into the 20th century.

Sandmeyer, Elmer. *The Anti-Chinese Movement in California*. Chicago: University of Illinois Press, 1991. This book studies the anti-Chinese movement in the West, much of it in California.

Websites

California State Assembly. Office of the Chief Clerk. This site provides the full text of the Foreign Miners Tax of 1850. http://clerk.assembly.ca.gov/content/statutes-and-amendments-codes-1850?archive_type=statutes. Accessed October 6, 2016.

A History of the Chinese in California: A Syllabus. With Thomas Chinn and Philip Choy. San Francisco: Chinese Historical Society of

America, 1969. This publication by historian Him Mark Lai and others provides a discussion of Chinese exclusion acts from 1882 to 1904. It is published by the Chinese Historical Society of America and is available at the Him Mark Lai digital archive. http://himmarklai.org/wordpress/wp-content/uploads/A-History-of-the-Chinese-in-CA-A-Syllabus-Part-I.pdf. Accessed October 6, 2016.

Also Noteworthy

1971

Norman Mineta becomes the first Japanese American mayor in San Jose, California.

April 14–16

1919

Philip Jaisohn organizes the Korean Liberty Congress in Philadelphia during April 14–16, 1919. Jaisohn made a symbolic link between the Korean and American declarations of independence. In addition, activities and speeches during the Congress advocated American democracy, Christianity, and the Korean people's faith to those ideals and values. It was clear that American support was critical in their quest for independence. To achieve this goal, prominent American religious and academic personalities were invited to speak on behalf of the Korean people and against Japanese occupation. The content of their speeches linked American democracy, freedom, and Christianity together and asserted that the United States had a moral obligation to assist Korea in its battle against tyranny.

Dr. Philip Jaisohn, as temporary chairman, called the Congress to order at 9.30 o'clock A. M.

Introductory Address

By Dr. Philip Jaisohn: Ladies and gentlemen, you are here on a very solemn and momentous mission. You are here to deal with questions and problems that will have a very far-reaching effect not only upon 20,000,000 of Koreans, but it will have an indirect influence upon the peoples of China, Japan and Eastern Russia. Their combined population is approximately 600,000,000 souls, or nearly one-third of the total population of the world. Korea is small in area, but owing to her geographical situation she plays a very important part in that part of Asia. So it is evident that you will have to do some very clear thinking and that you will have to take some firm and decisive steps tending to bring about permanent peace in the Orient, that democracy and Christianity may be firmly established in the continent of Asia.

Whenever we assemble on a great mission of this kind it is proper and it is our duty to ask the guidance, help and protection of God, who rules the whole world, and from whom only we can receive perfect wisdom, strength and courage. Therefore I will ask Rev. Dr. Floyd W. Tomkins, rector of Holy Trinity Church, Philadelphia, to offer a prayer.

Prayer by Rev. Floyd W. Tomkins

Dr. Jaisohn: There is no nation in the world whom the Koreans love more than the United States of America, excepting only their own country. There is a good reason for this: Ever since Korea was opened to foreign intercourse, while the Koreans have found that most of the foreign nations were there for the purpose of self-exploitation or political aggrandizement, with America it has not been so. On the contrary, America sent missionaries by hundreds; they brought the Bible, with which they gave this oppressed and unfortunate people a new hope and a new courage in this life. The Evangelical efforts of these missionaries were followed by hospitals, schools, science, arts, music and the spirit of independence and democracy. Thus came those American pioneers and missionaries. Is it any wonder then that the Koreans love America? We will therefore with the opening of this Congress sing the national hymn of the country which they love, next to Korea. I will therefore ask all to rise and sing "America" with that true spirit of love and veneration.

Source: First Korean Congress Held in the Little Theatre 17th and Delancey Streets. April 14, 15, 16. Philadelphia, 1919, pp. 3–4.

Books

Hurh, Won Moo. *The Korean Americans*. Westport, CT: Greenwood Press, 1998. *The Korean Americans* covers the history of Korean migration and their experiences in the United States and community formation and demographics.

Lee, Chong-Sik. *The Politics of Korean Nationalism*. Berkeley: University of California Press, 1965. *The Politics of Korean Nationalism* provides a complete history of Korean nationalism.

Websites

Coffman, Tom. "An Interactive Classroom on the Korean American Experience." 2003. This site provides interactive curriculum on Korean American history that includes short text, videos, images, timelines, lesson plans, and resources. http://www.koreanamericanstory.org/arirang/flash/main/index.htm. Accessed October 20, 2016.

Stucke, Walter. "The First Korean-American." *Groove Korea*, February 19, 2013. This site provides a historical overview of Dr. Philip Jaisohn and his legacy. http://groovekorea.com/article/first-korean-american/. Accessed October 20, 2016.

Also Noteworthy

April 14

2003

In Frederick, Maryland, a 10-year-old Muslim girl is harassed repeatedly at school because of her religion.

April 15

1967

Anti-Vietnam War protest begins at the UN Building to demand an end to the war and lead to the creation of Vietnam Veterans against the War.

On April 15, 1967, a crowd estimated at 100,000 to 125,000 people marched from Central Park to the United Nations Building to demand an end to the American military operations in Vietnam. American troop strength by this time stood at about 410,000; approximately 8,000 U.S. military personnel had died in the line of duty. There already were more than 500,000 Vietnam veterans who had served with military units in South Vietnam and now were back in the United States. Protest organizers invited twenty Vietnam veterans to lead the parade. The veterans accepted and carried a banner which read, "Vietnam Veterans Against the War." Following the march, six of them formed an organization by that name. Rather than the traditional veterans' issues of compensation and treatment for wounds, their principal bone of contention was the war itself. Vietnam Veterans Against the War (VVAW) demanded an immediate withdrawal of all American troops from Vietnam; they wanted to "bring their brothers home." They became the first group of American veterans to formally and publicly oppose the war in which they fought while it was still in progress.

Source: Scott, Wilbur. *Vietnam Veterans since the War: The Politics of PTSD, Agent Orange, and the National Memorial*. Norman: University of Oklahoma Press, 2003, pp. 1–2.

Books

Hunt, Andrew. *The Turning: A History of Vietnam Veterans against the War*. New York: New York University Press, 1999. *The Turning* is history of the Vietnam veteran's movement that transformed the antiwar efforts in the United States.

Stacewicz, Richard. *Winter Soldiers: An Oral History of the Vietnam Veterans against the War*. New York: Twayne Publishers, 1997. *Winter Soldiers* reveals the difficulties and challenges faced by Vietnam War veterans who publicly protested the Vietnam War.

Websites

Vietnam Veterans against the War. Official web page. http://www.vvaw.org/. Accessed February 5, 2018.

Vietnam War Protests. History.com. 2010. This site provides a history of anti-Vietnam War protests that includes videos. http://www.history.com/topics/vietnam-war/vietnam-war-protests. Accessed February 5, 2018.

April 16

2007

Cho Seung-hui, a Korean American undergraduate student at the Virginia Polytechnic Institute and State University in Blacksburg, Virginia, commits mass murder, kills 32 people, and wounds 17 others with two semiautomatic pistols.

On the morning of April 16, 2007, Seung-Hui Cho, wielding two semiautomatic handguns—a 9 mm Glock 19 and a .22-caliber Walther P22—killed thirty-two students and faculty members at Virginia Tech. His first two victims were shot in West Ambler Johnston Residence Hall at approximately 7:15 A.M. The two bodies were discovered by the Virginia Tech Police Department roughly nine minutes later. In the interval between the double homicide and the attack on Norris Hall, Cho went back to his dorm room in Harper Residence Hall to change his clothes. At 9:01 A.M., from the downtown Blacksburg Post Office, he mailed a package to NBC and a letter to Virginia Tech's Department of English. Between 9:15 and 9:30 A.M., he chained shut three of the main doors to Norris Hall, attaching bomb threats to them. Cho then proceeded to the second floor where he opened fire. It was the second period of the day and classes had not been suspended, though an e-mail had been sent by the Virginia Tech administration at 9:26 A.M. notifying faculty, staff, and students that there had been a shooting in a dorm. The students who were killed or injured were in classes in Intermediate French, Elementary German, and Advanced Hydrology. A Solid Mechanics class, taught by a seventy-six-year-old Holocaust survivor Professor Liviu Librescu, was also attacked, but most of the students escaped when Professor Librescu braced himself against the door and told students to jump out of the second-floor window. Students in a fifth class, Issues in Scientific Computing, successfully barricaded the door preventing Cho from entering. In roughly eleven minutes, Cho fired approximately 174 rounds of ammunition, returning several times to classrooms he had already attacked. Courageous students and faculty did their best to escape from the barrage of bullets, some risking their own lives to try to save others, but Cho was determined to obliterate everyone he saw. During his murderous rampage in Norris Hall, student Seung-Hui Cho never uttered a word.

Source: Roy, Lucinda. *No Right to Remain Silent: What We've Learned from the Tragedy at Virginia Tech*. New York: Three Rivers Press, 2009, pp. 1–2.

Books

Agger, Ben, and Timothy Luke, eds. *Tragedy and Terror at Virginia Tech: There Is a Gunman on Campus*. Lanham, MD: Rowman & Littlefield Publishers, 2008. *Tragedy and Terror at Virginia Tech* is a collection of essays that critically examines the massacre at Virginia Tech vis-à-vis the gun control debate, mental illness, normalization of violence and terror, public and campus reactions, and mass shooting at schools.

Gumpert, Matthew. *The End of Meaning: Studies in Catastrophe*. Newcastle upon Tyne, England: Cambridge Scholars Publishing, 2012. See Chapter 17, "Generic Violence: Massacre at Virginia Tech."

Websites

Friedman, Emily. "Va. Tech Shooter Seung-hui Cho's Mental Health Records Released." abcNews.go.com. August 19, 2009. This article highlights Seung-Hui Cho's mental health issues. http://abcnews.go.com/US/seung-hui-chos-mental-health-records-released/story?id=8278195. Accessed February 6, 2018.

Seung-Hui Cho Biography. Biography.com. October 14, 2014. A biography of his early life and his massacre at Virginia Tech. https://www.biography.com/people/seung-hui-cho-235991. Accessed February 6, 2018.

Also Noteworthy

1907

Korean American newspaper, the *New Korean World*, begins publication at San Francisco, California.

1971

The first National Asian American Studies conference takes place in Los Angeles. It takes place from April 16 to April 18.

2007

Kiran Carrie Chetry (b. August 26, 1974), an American television broadcast journalist of Nepali ancestry, serves as coanchor of CNN's *American Morning*.

April 17

1952

The California Supreme Court declares California's Alien Land Law of 1913 unconstitutional in *Sei Fujii v. State of California*. The 1913 law had been used to prevent Asian immigrants from owning property, regardless of their length of residence in the United States. The Japanese American Citizens League lobbied to place a measure on the general ballot to repeal the act. It won by popular vote on November 6, 1956.

The subject of Sei Fujii v. The State of California *was California's Alien Land Law of [1913]. Racial discrimination against Japanese residents had prompted the creation of this law, which prohibited non-US citizens from owning land in the state of California. But due to restrictive federal naturalization laws Japanese residents were not permitted to become US citizens, and therefore a Japanese person could* never *own land in California, because under the Alien Land Law, he or she was "not qualified or permitted to acquire, possess, enjoy, use, cultivate, occupy or transfer real property or any interest therein in the State of California, or to have in whole or in part the beneficial use thereof."*

Born in 1882, Sei Fujii was a business owner who, after graduating from USC Law School, started and ran a bilingual Japanese newspaper called the California Daily News. *Although he had been a California resident for approximately forty years, under California's Alien Land Law he was unable to own land title in California. After the state of California seized his property, Fujii appealed, challenging the constitutionality of the Alien Land Law, by arguing that it arbitrarily discriminated against him based solely on his race.*

On review of the case, Justice Emmett Wilson of the California Court of Appeal, Second District, produced a decision on April 24, 1950 that was unlike any decision to have ever come out of a court in the United States. As opposed to looking towards the dictates of domestic law, the US Constitution, or precedents in US case law, the Court held that the Alien Land Law was invalid because it ran afoul of the United Nations Charter.

Source: Roberts, Christopher. *The Contentious History of the International Bill of Human Rights*. Cambridge: Cambridge University Press, 2015, p. 111.

Books

Brilliant, Mark. *The Color of America Has Changed: How Racial Diversity Shaped Civil Rights Reform in California, 1941–1978*. New York: Oxford University Press, 2012. *The Color of America Has Changed* is a history of the multiracial dimensions of the civil rights movement in California.

Chuman, Frank. *The Bamboo People: The Law and Japanese-Americans*. Del Mar, CA, Publisher's Inc., 1976. *The Bamboo People* is a legal history of the Japanese Americans.

Websites

Robinson, Greg. "Fujii v. California." *Densho Encyclopedia*, September 4, 2014. This essay provides historical overview of the case, along with its impact and significance. http://encyclopedia.densho.org/Fujii_v._California/. Accessed September 6, 2017.

Sei Fujii v. State of California. JUSTIA U.S. Law. The full text for this case is available at http://law.justia.com/cases/california/supreme-court/2d/38/718.html. Accessed September 6, 2017.

Also Noteworthy

1975

The Communist Party of Kampuchea (CPK), otherwise known as the Khmer Rouge, takes control of Cambodia. The CPK created the state of Democratic Kampuchea in 1976 and ruled the country until January 1979. While in power, the Khmer Rouge committed a genocide of its own people: the numbers of Cambodians who died under the Khmer Rouge remains a topic of debate. Vietnamese sources say 3 million, while others estimate 1–2 million deaths.

2000

PraCh Ly, American hip-hop artist of Cambodian ancestry, releases his first album *DALAMA*, "the end'n is just the beginn'n."

April 18

1906

San Francisco earthquake and fire destroy Chinatown. The city of San Francisco wanted to rebuild the Chinatown six miles away at Hunter's Point. Chinatown was near the municipal government, and authorities concluded it was no place for a Chinese ghetto. The Chinese would not move: two years after the disaster, 15,000 Chinese returned to Chinatown that contained new buildings inspired by Chinese palatial and temple architecture. This made Chinatown more unique and exotic than before. Ironically, the positive note of the disaster was the destruction of government documents, including birth certificates, which open the way for Chinese immigrants to come as "paper sons" claiming birthrights. This resulted in large-scale detention of Chinese migrants on Angel Island as well.

Despite the abundance of exclusionary laws, many Chinese nevertheless found ways to circumvent them. Crossing the border from Mexico was one common practice. The 1906 San Francisco earthquake and fire, moreover, gave the Chinese an immigration reprieve. Official birth records had been destroyed by the fire, and many Chinese oldtimers in San Francisco took the opportunity to claim citizenship, saying that their American birth records had been destroyed. This opened up a new avenue for the younger generation, who could then claim to be the foreign-born, unmarried children of American citizens, a category unaffected by the exclusionary laws. Actually, many of the oldtimers had married shortly before coming, and had left their brides in China. Another practice was to come as a "paper son," assuming a false identity and claiming to be the offspring of an American citizen. As the early Chinese population was overwhelmingly Cantonese, the immigrants who came through these methods were from the same Cantonese locale. Hence, the Saamyup and Seiyup population distribution in America did not dramatically change, although the Seiyup immigrants, being mostly laborers, were the major target of the exclusion.

Source: Hom, Marlon. *Songs of Gold Mountain: Cantonese Rhymes from San Francisco Chinatown.* Berkeley: University of California Press, 1987, p. 14.

Books

Morris, Charles, ed. *The 1906 San Francisco Earthquake and Fire: As Told by Eyewitnesses.* Mineola, NY: Dover Publications, 2015. Charles Morris offers a comprehensive historical account of the earthquake and fire through tales of people who experienced it.

Pan, Erica Ying Zi. *The Impact of the 1906 Earthquake on San Francisco's Chinatown.* New York: Peter Lang, 1995. This volume discusses many aspects of the history and impact of the earthquake and fire on San Francisco's Chinatown.

Websites

"Earthquake and Fire Newspaper Clippings." The Virtual Museum of the City of San Francisco. This site provides links to multiple archival newspaper articles covering the 1906 earthquake and fire, in addition to articles related to the treatment of the Chinese residents. http://www.sfmuseum.org/press/clip.html. Accessed October 13, 2016.

"1906 Earthquake: Chinese Displacement." Presidio of San Francisco. National Park Service. This site provides a history of the earthquake and its impact on the Chinese American community in Chinatown. There are images and links to other resources related to the 1906 disaster. https://www.nps.gov/prsf/learn/historyculture/1906-earthquake-chinese-treatment.htm. Accessed October 13, 2016.

1925

The Chinese Hospital, the first of its kind devoted to the health needs of the immigrant Chinese community in San Francisco, opens.

The Chinese Hospital is the only hospital in the United States that seeks to serve the Chinese American community. Its roots date back to 1899 when the Tung Wah Dispensary opened its door in San Francisco's Chinatown. By the early 1920s, the Tung Wah Dispensary was not able to meet the growing health-care demands of the Chinese American community, and other medical providers in San Francisco denied service to the Chinese residents due to anti-Chinese sentiments and racism. To meet the health-care needs of the Chinese residents, the Chinese Hospital Association, a nonprofit public benefit corporation, was created in 1923 comprising 15 community organizations. The Chinese Hospital Association's Board of Trustees raised funds for construction of a new hospital at 835 Jackson Street, and the Chinese Hospital opened its doors with 60 acute beds on April 18, 1925. In the mid-1970s, the Chinese Hospital's Board of Trustees raised funds to construct a new hospital that opened on September 29, 1979, at 845 Jackson Street, next door to the original Chinese Hospital. Today, the Chinese Hospital is undergoing another transformation as it is being rebuilt with 21st-century medical technologies to meet the needs of the community. The new hospital plans were contested as historic preservationists advocated that the old structure or parts of the old structure be saved from demolition. However, the Chinese Hospital and its supporters argued that the historical importance of the Chinese Hospital lies in its missions to serve the immediate immigrant Chinese communities. The new hospital will be better equipped to meet the growing needs of the residents. For decades, the Chinese Hospital has served the health-care needs of the communities whose lives are tied in the fabric of Chinatown.

Source: Lee, Jonathan H. X. "Chinese Hospital, San Francisco." In *Chinese Americans: The History and Culture of a People*, edited by Jonathan H. X. Lee, p. 178. Santa Barbara, CA: ABC-CLIO, 2016.

Books

Lai, Mark. *Becoming Chinese American: A History of Communities and Institutions*. Walnut Creek, CA: AltaMira Press, 2004. This volume is a collection of essays by historian Him Mark Lai on the history of the Chinese in America.

Yoo, Grace, Mai-Nhung Le, and Alan Odo, eds. *Handbook of Asian American Health*. New York: Springer, 2013. *Handbook of Asian American Health* is a comprehensive collection of articles related to Asian American health. See Laureen Hom's Chapter 26, "Early Chinese Immigrants Organizing for Healthcare: The Establishment of the Chinese Hospital in San Francisco."

Websites

Chinese Hospital. 2016. This is the official web page for the Chinese Hospital in San Francisco's Chinatown. They provide a history and mission statement of the hospital, along with photographs. http://www.chinesehospital-sf.org/mission-vision-values. Accessed October 26, 2016.

"Chinese Hospital." Chinatown San Francisco. This site provides a historical summary of the Chinese Hospital in San Francisco's Chinatown with photographs of the old and new facilities. http://www.sanfranciscochinatown.com/attractions/chinesehospital.html. Accessed October 26, 2016.

Also Noteworthy

1874

The Weaverville Joss House (The Temple among the Trees beneath the Clouds), a historic Chinese Taoist temple in Weaverville, California, is dedicated by the early Chinese pioneers.

1975

The Inter-Agency Task Force is created to coordinate all U.S. government activities in evacuating U.S. citizens as well as selected Vietnamese from South Vietnam.

April 19

1983

Fred Toyosaburo Korematsu sues the U.S. federal government in order to have his earlier conviction vacated. Due to the statute of limitations, the only legal principle his group of young lawyers could employ was the little-known or little-used *writ of coram nobis* (our error), through which cases may be heard when there is extensive evidence that the government intentionally provided deceptive information and/or omitted relevant information in papers before the court.

Twenty years ago, in a crowded federal courtroom for the Northern District of California, Fred Korematsu uttered a simple request: "I would like to see the government admit that they were wrong and do something about it so this will never happen again to any American citizen of any race, creed, or color." Korematsu and his team of young lawyers were there that day to argue for vacating his 1942 conviction for disobeying military wartime exclusion and detention orders, and to end the public stigma of disloyalty imprinted by the original Korematsu decision onto the Japanese American community. Unearthed documents had revealed that no military necessity existed to justify the incarceration, and that government decision makers knew this at the time, and later lied about it to the Supreme Court. On that day, November 19, 1983, forty years after the United States Supreme Court upheld his conviction, Judge Marilyn Hall Patel reversed Korematsu's conviction, acknowledging the "manifest injustice" done to him and to all those interned.

Source: Serrano, Susan, and Dale Minami. "Korematsu v. United States: A Constant Caution in a Time of Crisis." Asian *American Law Journal* 10, no. 1 (January 2003): p. 37. https://scholarship.law.berkeley.edu/cgi/viewcontent.cgi?article=1084&context=aalj. Accessed February 6, 2018.

Books

Daniels, Roger. *The Japanese American Cases: The Rule of Law in Time of War.* Lawrence: University of Kansas Press, 2013. *The Japanese American Cases* examines the convictions of Min Yasui, Gordon Hirabayashi, Fred Korematsu, and Mitsuye Endo and the redress movement during the 1980s.

Irons, Peter. *Justice Delayed: The Record of the Japanese American Internment Cases.* Middletown, CT: Wesleyan University Press, 1989. *Justice Delayed* is a detailed study of the Fred Korematsu case.

Websites

Imai, Shiho. "Korematsu v. United States." *Densho Encyclopedia*, July 29, 2015. This essay discusses the history of the case, as well as its significance. http://encyclopedia.densho.org/Korematsu_v._United_States/. Accessed February 6, 2018.

Niiya, Brian. "Coram Nobis Cases." *Densho Encyclopedia*, August 20, 2015. This essay discusses the three major writ of coram nobis cases associated with the Japanese American redress movement. http://encyclopedia.densho.org/Coram_nobis_cases/. Accessed February 6, 2018.

Also Noteworthy

1962

Cathay Bank, a Chinese American bank, opens in Los Angeles.

2004

In Dover Township, New Jersey, windows at an Islamic center are broken, walls tagged with swastikas and sexually explicit slurs and anti-Semitic slurs are scrawled on two doors.

April 20

1942

One hundred forty-one South American civilians of Japanese ancestry arrive at San Francisco aboard the *Etolin* and *Acadia*, at the request of the U.S. government who wanted to employ them for future prisoner exchanges. By 1934, a total of 2,100 persons, mostly from Peru, were transported into U.S. custody and placed into internment camps in Texas and New Mexico.

Between April 1942 and April 1945, approximately 1,800 Peruvian Japanese were interned in the United States. They represented 80 percent of all the Latin-American Japanese interned here. The deportation-internment program involving the Latin-American Japanese was totally unrelated to the relocation-internment program of the War Relocation Authority. The Immigration and Naturalization Service held the people from Latin America in Texas, at Kenedy in a one-time CCC campus; at Seagoville in a federal reformatory for women; and at Crystal City in a migrant labor camp.

As soon as the first shipment of enemy aliens arrived from Panama, the question of keeping the internee families together quickly entered U.S.-Peruvian relations. When the State Department and the Peruvian Foreign Office agreed that family unity should be preserved, one was left to wonder how much of the decision stemmed from elementary humanitarianism and how much reflected the expedient control of even larger numbers of aliens. After all, the U.S. ambassador in Lima, R. Henry Norweb, had declared, "We may be able to assist the Peruvian Government by making available information and suggestions based upon our handling of Japanese residents of the United States."

The embassy staff in Lima included John K. Emmerson. . . . Thirty-five years later he would declare, "During my period of service in the embassy we found no reliable evidence of planned or contemplated acts of sabotage, subversion, or espionage." Nonetheless, Japanese assets were frozen and successive issues of the American blacklist targeted more businesses. Fears multiplied as the Japanese witnessed the increasing alignment of Peru with American wartime aims. As the press mounted attacks on the Japanese, the Peruvian police fashioned lists of prospective deportees that encouraged the solicitation and acceptance of bribes in return for the opportunity to escape deportation temporarily.

Source: Gardiner, C. Harvey. "The Latin-American Japanese and World War II." In *Japanese Americans from Relocation to Redress*, edited by Roger Daniels, Sandra Taylor, and Harry Kitano, p. 143. Seattle: University of Washington Press, 1991.

Books

Connell, Thomas. *America's Japanese Hostages: The World War II Plan for a Japanese Free Latin America*. Westport, CT: Praeger, 2002. *America's Japanese Hostages* examines the history of the Latin American Japanese internees.

Gardiner, C. Harvey. *Pawns in a Triangle of Hate: The Peruvian Japanese and the United States*. Seattle: University of Washington Press, 1981. *Pawns in a Triangle of Hate* studies the history of the Peruvian Japanese relocation and internment during World War II.

Websites

Adachi, Nobuko. "Racial Journeys: Justice, Internment and Japanese-Peruvians in Peru, the United States, and Japan." *The Asia-Pacific Journal* 5, no. 9 (September 3, 2007): 1–11. This article covers multiple aspects of the Japanese

Peruvian relocation and internment during World War II, its legacy, and the journey of internees to find justice and reconciliation. http://apjjf.org/-Nobuko-Adachi/2517/article.html. Accessed September 6, 2017.

Mak, Stephen. "Japanese Latin Americans." *Densho Encyclopedia*, 2017. This essay offers a complete historical overview of the Japanese Latin American relocation and detention during World War II, with accompanying photos and archival documents. http://encyclopedia.densho.org/Japanese_Latin_Americans/. Accessed September 6, 2017.

Also Noteworthy

1942

Tulare, California, Assembly Center opens; it is in operation until September 4.

April 21

1913

The Hindu Association of the Pacific Coast, or the Ghadar Party, is established in Astoria, Oregon. It started as loose social and political gatherings to promote India's independence from British colonial occupation since 1907. The headquarter of the Ghadar Party was in San Francisco.

Many of the Indian land workers who started coming to the U.S. in the late nineteenth century brought their economic and political frustrations as colonial subjects with them. Their experiences in the U.S.—at times financially beneficial yet tempered with racism and discrimination—compounded with the subjugated political life they lived in India. These agricultural workers' political participation in the U.S. ranged from organized labor activity—including involvement with the Industrial Workers of the World—to forming the Hindu Association of the Pacific Coast, more commonly known as the Ghadar Party, an organization that advocated and instigated armed rebellion against the British in India. These immigrant Indian agricultural workers were minority subjects of different states, had potentially conflicting class interests yet coalesced to engage in various revolutionary struggles transnationally.

Source: Cahill, Kevin. *Considering Class: Essays on the Discourse of the American Dream.* Munster, Germany: Lit Verlag, 2007, p. 63.

Books

Leonard, Karen Isaksen. *The South Asian Americans*. Westport, CT: Greenwood Press, 1997. *The South Asian Americans* covers various aspects of South Asian history and immigration to the United States.

Puri, Harish. *Ghadar Movement to Bhagat Singh: A Collection of Essays*. Ludhiana, India: Unistar Books, 2012. *Ghadar Movement to Bhagat Singh* is a history of the Ghadar movement in the United States.

Websites

Bhatia, Nishtha. "India's Ghadar Party Born in San Francisco." FoundSF.org. This essay discusses the history of the Ghadar Party in San Francisco with historic photographs. http://www.foundsf.org/index.php?title=India%27s_Ghadar_Party_Born_in_San_Francisco. Accessed September 6, 2017.

Singh, Inder. "Gadar—Overseas Indians Attempt to Free India from British Serfdom." Frontlines of Revolutionary Struggle. This essay discusses the history of the Ghadar movement in Canada and the United States. https://revolutionaryfrontlines.wordpress.com/2013/04/02/1913-the-gadar-party-and-the-roots-of-indias-armed-anti-british-colonial-struggle-in-san-francisco/. Accessed September 6, 2017.

April 22

1912

Yung Wing, a prominent Chinese scholar, dies on this day. In 1842, three Chinese students arrive in New York City for schooling. One of them was Yung Wing (1828–1912), a native of Pedro Island, near Macau. Yung and two other Chinese students came to the United States in 1842 to study at Monson Academy, Monson, Massachusetts. He became a Christian while studying at the academy. In 1848, he entered Yale University and graduated in 1854. Yung was a prominent scholar and an educator and was the head of the Chinese Educational Mission to the United States, having shepherded a number of Chinese students to study in the United States. In 1875, when the anti-Chinese sentiment was high in California and other states, the Chinese government appointed Yung along with Chen Lanpin, imperial commissioners to the United States, Peru, and Spain. They were responsible for promoting friendly relations and protecting Chinese nationals abroad.

Excerpt from "Preface" of Yung Wing's *My Life in China and America* (1909).

The first five chapters of this book give an account of my early education, previous to going to America, where it was continued, first at Monson Academy, in Monson, Massachusetts, and later, at Yale College.

The sixth chapter begins with my reentrance into the Chinese world, after an absence of eight years. Would it not be strange, if an Occidental education, continually exemplified by an Occidental civilization, had not wrought upon an Oriental such a metamorphosis in his inward nature as to make him feel and act as though he were a being coming from a different world, when he confronted one so diametrically different? This was precisely my case, and yet neither my patriotism nor the love of my fellow-countrymen had been weakened. On the contrary, they had increased in strength from sympathy. Hence, the succeeding chapters of my book will be found to be devoted to the working out of my educational scheme, as an expression of my undying love for China, and as the most feasible method to my mind, of reformation and regeneration to her.

With the sudden ending of the Educational Commission, and the recall of one hundred and twenty students who formed the vanguard of the pioneers of modern education in China, my educational work was brought to a close.

Of the survivors of these students of 1872, a few by dint of hard, persistent industry, have at last come forth to stand in the front ranks of the leading statesmen of China, and it is through them that the original Chinese Educational Commission has been revived, though in a modified form, so that now, Chinese students are seen flocking to America and Europe from even the distant shores of Sinim for a scientific education.

Source: Wing, Yung. *My Life in China and America*. New York: Henry Holt Company, 1909.

Books

Liel Leibovitz, and Matthew Miller. *Fortunate Sons: The 120 Chinese Boys Who Came to America, Went to School, and Revolutionized an Ancient Civilization*. New York: W.W. Norton, 2011. This volume discusses the history of the 120 Chinese boys who were sent to the United States for a "western" education, against the backdrop of anti-Chinese sentiments and a nation seeking to modernize.

Wing, Yung. *My Life in China and America*. New York: Henry Holt Company, 1909.

Websites

This Yale Obituary Record provides a summary of Yung Wing's time at Yale as well as his achievements after. http://mssa.library.yale.edu/obituary_record/1859_1924/1911-12.pdf. Accessed October 6, 2016.

The Yung Wing Project. This project is dedicated to the research and primary documentation of Yung Wing and the Chinese Educational Mission. http://ywproject.x10.mx/. Accessed October 6, 2016.

Also Noteworthy

2003

In Brooklyn, New York, Max Abrahamowitz, a 29-year-old, assaults a Muslim woman while yelling racial slurs at her.

2004

In Denton, Texas, a window and glass door of an Islamic Society are shot out with a gun.

April 23

1975

President Gerald Ford announces, in a speech at Tulane University, that the Vietnam War is "finished."

Each time that I have been privileged to visit Tulane, I have come away newly impressed with the intense application of the student body to the great issues of our time, and I am pleased tonight to observe that your interest hasn't changed one bit.

As we came into the building tonight, I passed a student who looked up from his book and said, "A journey of a thousand miles begins but with a single step." To indicate my interest in him, I asked, "Are you trying to figure out how to get your goal in life?" He said, "No, I am trying to figure out how to get to the Super Dome in September." [Laughter] *Well, I don't think there is any doubt in my mind that all of you will get to the Super Dome. Of course, I hope it is to see the Green Wave [Tulane University] have their very best season on the gridiron. I have sort of a feeling that you wouldn't mind making this another year in which you put the Tigers [Louisiana State University] in your tank.*

When I had the privilege of speaking here in 1968 at your "Directions '68" forum, I had no idea that my own career and our entire Nation would move so soon in another direction. And I say again, I am extremely proud to be invited back.

I am impressed, as I undoubtedly said before—but I would reiterate it tonight—by Tulane's unique distinction as the only American university to be converted from State sponsorship to private status. And I am also impressed by the Tulane graduates who serve in the United States Congress: Bennett Johnston, Lindy Boggs, Dave Treen.

Eddie Hebert, when I asked him the question whether he was or not, and he said he got a special degree: Dropout '28. [Laughter]

But I think the fact that you have these three outstanding graduates testifies to the academic excellence and the inspiration of this historic university, rooted in the past with its eyes on the future.

Just as Tulane has made a great transition from the past to the future, so has New Orleans, the legendary city that has made such a unique contribution to our great America. New Orleans is more, as I see it, than weathered bricks and cast-iron balconies. It is a state of mind, a melting pot that represents the very, very best of America's evolution, an example of retention of a very special culture in a progressive environment of modern change.

On January 8, 1815, a monumental American victory was achieved here—the Battle of New Orleans. Louisiana had been a State for less than three years, but outnumbered Americans innovated, outnumbered Americans used the tactics of the frontier to defeat a veteran British force trained in the strategy of the Napoleonic wars.

We as a nation had suffered humiliation and a measure of defeat in the War of 1812. Our National Capital in Washington had been captured and burned. So, the illustrious victory in the Battle of New Orleans was a powerful restorative to our national pride.

Yet, the victory at New Orleans actually took place two weeks after the signing of the armistice in Europe. Thousands died although a peace had been negotiated. The combatants had not gotten the word. Yet, the epic struggle nevertheless restored America's pride.

Today, America can regain the sense of pride that existed before Vietnam. But it cannot be achieved by refighting a war that is finished as far as America is concerned. As I see it, the time has come to look forward to an agenda for the future, to unify, to bind up the Nation's wounds, and to restore its health and its optimistic self-confidence.

In New Orleans, a great battle was fought after a war was over. In New Orleans tonight, we can begin a great national reconciliation. The first engagement must be with the problems of today, but just as importantly, the problems of the future. That is why I think it is so appropriate that I find myself tonight at a university which addresses itself to preparing young people for the challenge of tomorrow.

I ask that we stop refighting the battles and the recriminations of the past. I ask that we look now at what is right with America, at our possibilities and our potentialities for change and growth and achievement and sharing. I ask that we accept the responsibilities of leadership as a good neighbor to all peoples and the enemy of none. I ask that we strive to become, in the finest American tradition, something more tomorrow than we are today.

Instead of my addressing the image of America, I prefer to consider the reality of America. It is true that we have launched our Bicentennial celebration without having achieved human perfection, but we have attained a very remarkable self-governed society that possesses the flexibility and the dynamism to grow and undertake an entirely new agenda, an agenda for America's third century.

So, I ask you to join me in helping to write that agenda. I am as determined as a President can be to seek national rediscovery of the belief in ourselves that characterized the most creative periods in our Nation's history. The greatest challenge of creativity, as I see it, lies ahead.

We, of course, are saddened indeed by the events in Indochina. But these events, tragic as they are, portend neither the end of the world nor of America's leadership in the world.

Let me put it this way, if I might. Some tend to feel that if we do not succeed in everything everywhere, then we have succeeded in nothing anywhere. I reject categorically such polarized thinking. We can and we should help others to help themselves. But the fate of responsible men and women everywhere, in the final decision, rests in their own hands, not in ours.

America's future depends upon Americans—especially your generation, which is now equipping itself to assume the challenges of the future, to help write the agenda for America.

Earlier today, in this great community, I spoke about the need to maintain our defenses. Tonight, I would like to talk about another kind of strength, the true source of American power that transcends all of the deterrent powers for peace of our Armed Forces. I am speaking here of our belief in ourselves and our belief in our Nation.

Abraham Lincoln asked, in his own words, and I quote, "What constitutes the bulwark of our own liberty and independence?" And he answered, "It is not our frowning battlements or bristling seacoasts, our Army or our Navy. Our defense is in the spirit which prized liberty as the heritage of all men, in all lands everywhere."

It is in this spirit that we must now move beyond the discords of the past decade. It is in this spirit that I ask you to join me in writing an agenda for the future.

I welcome your invitation particularly tonight, because I know it is at Tulane and other centers of thought throughout our great country that much consideration is being given to the kind of future Americans want and, just as importantly, will work for. Each of you are preparing yourselves for the future, and I am deeply interested in your preparations and your opinions and your goals. However, tonight, with your indulgence, let me share with you my own views.

I envision a creative program that goes as far as our courage and our capacities can take us, both at home and abroad. My goal is for a cooperative world at peace, using its resources to build, not to destroy.

As President, I am determined to offer leadership to overcome our current economic problems. My goal is for jobs for all who want to work and economic opportunity for all who want to achieve.

I am determined to seek self-sufficiency in energy as an urgent national priority. My goal is to make America independent of foreign energy sources by 1985.

Of course, I will pursue interdependence with other nations and a reformed international economic system. My goal is for a world in which consuming and producing nations achieve a working balance.

I will address the humanitarian issues of hunger and famine, of health and of healing. My goal is to achieve—or to assure basic needs and an effective system to achieve this result.

I recognize the need for technology that enriches life while preserving our natural environment. My goal is to stimulate productivity, but use technology to redeem, not to destroy our environment.

I will strive for new cooperation rather than conflict in the peaceful exploration of our oceans and our space. My goal is to use resources for peaceful progress rather than war and destruction.

Let America symbolize humanity's struggle to conquer nature and master technology. The time has now come for our Government to facilitate the individual's control over his or her future—and of the future of America.

But the future requires more than Americans congratulating themselves on how much we know and how many products that we can produce. It requires new knowledge to meet new problems. We must not only be motivated to build a better America, we must know how to do it.

If we really want a humane America that will, for instance, contribute to the alleviation of the world's hunger, we must realize that good intentions do not feed people. Some problems, as anyone who served in the Congress knows, are complex. There are no easy answers. Willpower alone does not grow food.

We thought, in a well-intentioned past, that we could export our technology lock, stock, and barrel to developing nations. We did it with the best of intentions. But we are now learning that a strain of rice that grows in one place will not grow in another; that factories that produce at 100 percent in one nation produce less than half as much in a society where temperaments and work habits are somewhat different.

Yet, the world economy has become interdependent. Not only food technology but money management, natural resources and energy, research and development—all kinds of this group require an organized world society that makes the maximum effective use of the world's resources.

I want to tell the world: Let's grow food together, but let's also learn more about nutrition, about weather forecasting, about irrigation, about the many other specialties involved in helping people to help themselves.

We must learn more about people, about the development of communities, architecture, engineering, education, motivation, productivity, public health and medicine, arts and sciences, political, legal, and social organization. All of these specialties and many, many more are required if young people like you are to help this Nation develop an agenda for our future—your future, our country's future.

I challenge, for example, the medical students in this audience to put on their agenda the achievement of a cure for cancer. I challenge the engineers in this audience to devise new techniques for developing cheap, clean, and plentiful energy, and as a byproduct, to control floods. I challenge the law students in this audience to find ways to speed the administration of equal justice and make good citizens out of convicted criminals. I challenge education, those of you as education majors, to do real teaching for real life. I challenge the arts majors in this audience to compose the great American symphony, to write the great American novel, and to enrich and inspire our daily lives.

America's leadership is essential. America's resources are vast. America's opportunities are unprecedented.

As we strive together to prefect a new agenda, I put high on the list of important points the maintenance of alliances and partnerships with other people and other nations. These do provide a basis of shared values, even as we stand up with determination for what we believe. This, of course, requires a continuing commitment to peace and a determination to use our good offices wherever possible to promote better relations between nations of this world.

The new agenda, that which is developed by you and by us, must place a high priority on the need to stop the spread of nuclear weapons and to work for the mutual reduction in strategic arms and control of other weapons. And I must say, parenthetically, the successful negotiations at Vladivostok, in my opinion, are just a beginning.

Your generation of Americans is uniquely endowed by history to give new meaning to the pride and spirit of America. The magnetism of an American society, confident of its own strength, will attract the good will and the esteem of all people wherever they might be in this globe in which we live. It will enhance our own perception of ourselves and our pride in being an American. We can, we—and I say it with emphasis—write a new agenda for our future.

I am glad that Tulane University and other great American educational institutions are reaching out to others in programs to work with developing nations, and I look forward with confidence to your participation in every aspect of America's future.

And I urge Americans of all ages to unite in this Bicentennial year, to take responsibility for themselves as our ancestors did. Let us resolve tonight to rediscover the old virtues of confidence and self-reliance and capability that characterized our forefathers two centuries ago. I pledge, as I know you do, each one of us, to do our part.

Let the beacon light of the past shine forth from historic New Orleans and from Tulane University and from every other corner of this land to illuminate a boundless future for all Americans and a peace for all mankind.

Thank you very much.

President Gerald R. Ford—April 23, 1975

Source: Ford, Gerald. "Address at a Tulane University Convocation." April 23, 1975. Online by Gerhard Peters and John T. Woolley. The American Presidency Project. University of California, Santa Barbara. http://www.presidency.ucsb.edu/ws/?pid=4859. Accessed March 10, 2018.

Books

Duong, Van Nguyen. *The Tragedy of the Vietnam War: South Vietnamese Officer's Analysis*. Jefferson, NC: McFarland & Company, 2008. *The Tragedy of the Vietnam War* is a memoir written by an officer of the South Vietnamese army.

Langston, Thomas. *The Cold War Presidency: A Documentary History*. Washington, DC: CQ Press, 2007. *The Cold War Presidency* is a chronological documentary history of presidents of the Cold War period, with analytical summaries and original documents.

Websites

"Ford Says That War Is Finished for America." www.History.com. 2009. This essay provides background of the historical situation of the Vietnam War on the day President Ford declared an end to the U.S. war in Vietnam. http://www.history.com/this-day-in-history/ford-says-that-war-is-finished-for-america. Accessed September 6, 2017.

"When President Ford Declared an End to the War in Vietnam." *Newsweek*, April 23, 2015. This essay reflects on the end of the Vietnam War and President Ford's speech at Tulane. http://www.newsweek.com/when-president-ford-declared-end-war-vietnam-321235. Accessed September 6, 2017.

Also Noteworthy

2005

Jawed Karim (b. October 28, 1979), an American Internet entrepreneur of German and Bangladeshi ancestries, cofounder of YouTube, uploads the first video "Me at the Zoo." His YouTube cofounders are Chad Hurley and Steven Men Chen (b. August 18, 1978).

April 24

1796

On this day, Andreas Everardus van Braam Houckgeest (1739–1801), a Dutchman who was formerly Canton Agent for the Dutch East India Company, comes to the United States from China with cargo of Chinese arts and five Chinese servants. He settled in Philadelphia, organized the first exhibit on Chinese art in America, and authored the first book on China, published in the United States, in 1797–1798.

A Dutch merchant, Andreas Everardus van Braam Houckgeest, who had spent years in China in the service of the Dutch East India Company, settled in Philadelphia in 1796, bought a farm on the Delaware near Bristol, and built a fifteen-room house called "China's Retreat," where he lived surrounded by the curiosities he had brought back with him and waited upon by Chinese servants and a Malay housekeeper. A description of his visit to the court of the Ch'ien Lung emperor was published in Philadelphia by Moreau de Saint-Méry in two handsome volumes in 1797–1798. His collection of Chinese art was soon sent across the Atlantic and sold at Christie's in London in February 1799. Other objects of Oriental workmanship arrived in Philadelphia. Exhibition pieces from the East Indies and China appeared in the accession book of the Peale Museum, and mementos of Asia accumulated in homes up and down the Delaware.

Source: Weigley, Russell. *Philadelphia: A 300-Year History*. New York: W.W. Norton & Company, 1982, p. 212.

Books

Blussé, Leonard. *Visible Cities: Canton, Nagasaki, and Batavia and the Coming of the Americans.* Cambridge, MA: Harvard University Press, 2008. *Visible Cities* chronicles the economic and cultural transformation of three cities during the 18th century.

Liu, Yong. *The Dutch East India Company's Tea Trade with China: 1757–1781.* Leiden, the Netherlands: Brill, 2007. This volume investigates history, politics, and economics of the Dutch East India Company's trade with China.

Websites

Haddad, John Rogers. *The Romance of China: Excursions to China in U.S. Culture: 1776–1876.* Columbia University Press. This site provides an online book that discusses the history of Western voyages into China, using primary sources. Andreas Everardus van Braam Houckgeest's excursions are examined. http://www.gutenberg-e.org/haj01/index.html. Accessed October 12, 2016.

Jarus, Owen. "American's Visit to China's Forbidden City Revealed in Old Journal." LiveScience, May 28, 2014. This site discusses Andreas Everardus van Braam Houckgeest's journal and details some of the things in it. It includes images and photographs. http://www.livescience.com/45917-american-visit-to-china-forbidden-city.html. Accessed October 12, 2016.

April 25

1898

The U.S. Congress formally declares war on Spain. The U.S. military engaged the Spaniards in Cuba, Puerto Rico, and Manila Bay. On December 1898, the Treaty of Paris was signed and ended the Spanish-American War. Although Cuba's independence was recognized by the United States, Puerto Rico, Guam, and the Philippines fell under U.S. control.

At the time of the Spanish-American war, General Emilio Aguinaldo was in Singapore where he had negotiations with the American consul general, Mr. E. Spencer Pratt, regarding the Americans' offer to support the Philippines in fighting the Spaniards. The United States would then recognize Philippine independence after the deaf of Spain. Pratt advised Aguinaldo to meet with Commodore Dewey who was then based in Hong Kong, if he were to join the latter should he sail for the Philippines.

*General Aguinaldo rushed to Hong Kong but missed Commodore Dewey who had already sailed to Manila to destroy the Spanish Fleet. Dewey proceeded at once to Manila with his fleet consisting of our armored cruises—*Olympia, Baltimore, Boston *and* Raliegh *and two gunboats—*Concord *and* Petrel.

The Battle of Manila Bay began on May 1, 1989 at 5:40 A.M. and ended at noon. Admiral Patricio Montojo of the Spanish forces incurred heavy causalities with 160 of his men killed and 210 wounded. The Spanish forces consisting of twelve ships, including the flagship Reina Castilla were subdued. The U.S. naval squadron had no fatal causalities. None of the ships was heavily damaged.

This battle made Dewey an instant hero. The Congress promoted him to rear admiral and later admiral. However, the U.S. naval squadron could not attempt to occupy Manila in the absence of ground troops, which did not arrive until about three months later.

Source: Halili, Maria. *Philippine History.* Manila: Rex Book Store, 2004, pp. 155–156.

Books

Jones, Gregg. *Honor in the Dust: Theodore Roosevelt, War in the Philippines, and the Rise and Fall of America's Imperial Dream.* New York: New American Library, 2012. See Part 2, "Imperial Glory," for details related to U.S. imperialism in the Philippines.

Silbey, David. *A War of Frontier and Empire: The Philippine-American War, 1899–1902.* New York: Hill and Wang, 2007. *A War of Frontier and Empire* is a complete military history of the Philippine-American War.

Websites

"The Philippine-American War, 1899–1902." Office of the Historian, Bureau of Public Affairs. U.S. Department of State. This essay provides historical overview of the war and discussion of Emilio Aguinaldo and President Theodore Roosevelt. https://history.state.gov/milestones/1899-1913/war. Accessed September 6, 2017.

"Spanish-American War and the Philippine-American War, 1898–1902." Golden Gate: National Recreation Area California. February 28, 2015. This essay discusses the historical significance of San Francisco's Presidio during the Spanish-American War and the Philippine-American War. https://www.nps.gov/goga/learn/historyculture/spanish-american-war.htm. Accessed September 6, 2017.

Also Noteworthy

2014

Maulik Navin Pancholy (b. January 18, 1974), an American actor of Indian ancestry, is appointed to President Barack Obama's Advisory Commission of Asian Americans and Pacific Islanders.

April 26

1858

California State legislature passes "An Act to Prevent the Further Immigration of Chinese or Mongolians." The act is an exclusion law that prohibited Chinese or Mongolian to enter the state except when driven ashore by weather or unavoidable accident. The penalty for violation of this act was a fine of $400–$600, or imprisonment from six months to a year, or both. This act was struck down by an unpublished opinion of the state Supreme Court in 1862.

Excerpt from An Act to Prevent the Further Immigration of Chinese or Mongolians to this State.

Section 1. On and after the 1st day of October, A.D. 1858, any person or persons of the Chinese or Mongolian races, shall not be permitted to enter this State, or land therein, at any port or part thereof, and it shall be unlawful for any man, or person, whether caption or commander, or other person, in charge of, or interested in, or employed on board of, or passenger upon, any vessel, or vessels, of any nature or description whatsoever, to knowingly allow or permit any Chinese or Mongolian on and after such time to enter any of the ports of the State, to land therein, or at any place or places within the borders of This State. . . .

Section 2. The landing of each and every Chinese or Mongolian person or persons shall be deemed and held as a distinct and separate offence, and punished accordingly.

Source: *Reports of the Immigration Commission: Immigration Legislation*. Presented by Mr. Dillingham. Washington, DC: Government Printing Office, December 5, 1910.

Books

Heizer, Robert, and Alan Almquist. *The Other Californians: Prejudice and Discrimination under Spain, Mexico, and the United States to 1920*. Berkeley: University of California Press, 1971. This is a social history of non-European peoples in California's past as revealed through racist attitudes and discriminatory legislation against them. See Chapter 7, "The Early Legal Status of the Chinese."

McClain, Charles, ed. *Chinese Immigrants and American Law*. New York: Garland Publishing, Inc. 1991. See Shirley Hune's Chapter 4, "Politics of Chinese Exclusion: Legislative-Executive Conflict 1876–1882."

Websites

"Anti-Chinese Movement and Chinese Exclusion." This site provides brief and concise historical background on topics related to the anti-Chinese movement. University of California, Berkeley. Bancroft Library. http://bancroft.berkeley.edu/collections/chineseinca/antichinese.html. Accessed March 7, 2017.

"Local and State Anti-Chinese Legislation." The Chinese Experience in 19th Century

America. University of Illinois. This site provides teachers with lesson plans on topics related to Chinese American immigration history. http://teachingresources.atlas.illinois.edu/chinese_exp/process03.html. Accessed March 7, 2017.

Also Noteworthy

1862

California State Legislature passes an "anti-coolie tax" or "police tax" of $2.50 a month on every Chinese and Mongolians. The goal of the act is to protect white labor from Chinese labor and to discourage the immigration of Chinese labor into the state.

1917

Renowned Chinese American architect, Ieoh Ming (I.M.) Pei, is born. Pei is best known for his work on large-scale institutional and high-profile projects, such as the Grand Louvre in Paris, the East Building of the National Gallery of Art in Washington, the John Fitzgerald Kennedy Library in Boston, and the Bank of China Tower in Hong Kong.

April 27

1942

The War Relocation Authority isolation center for "troublemakers" is moved from Moab, Utah, to Leupp, Arizona.

Even more striking . . . however, is [Dillon] Myer's unabashed description of an isolation center for select Japanese American U.S. citizens whom administrators lacked evidence to charge with any crime. Myer described a situation in which WRA administrators were not bound by law or even clear criteria for singling out "troublemakers" who could be expelled from the WRA camps and incarcerated in what amounted to a maximum security prison. The WRA established this camp, the Moab isolation center in Utah, shortly after the so-called Manzanar Riot—a disturbance in the Manzanar relocation center in December 1942 that had erupted within the context of dissatisfaction with camp conditions and a drive to recruit Japanese American linguists into the army. And as Myer predicted in his testimony, although the Moab isolation center was closed in April 1943, its role was taken up first by the Leupp isolation center in Arizona and later by the stockade that was established inside the Tule Lake relocation center.

Source: Fijitani, Takashi. *Race for Empire: Koreans as Japanese and Japanese as Americans during World War II.* Berkeley: University of California Press, 2011, p. 151.

Books

Drinnon, Richard. *Keeper of Concentration Camps: Dillon S. Myer and American Racism*. Berkeley: University of California Press, 1987. *Keeper of Concentration Camps* connects Japanese American relocation and internment to the removal and confinement of Native Americans. See Chapter 6, "Troublemakers."

Kashima, Tetsuden. *Judgment without Trial: Japanese American Imprisonment during World War II.* Seattle: University of Washington Press, 2003. *Judgment without Trial* contends that long before Japan attacked Pearl Harbor, the U.S. government looked into plans for forced removal and internment of Japanese Americans. It also examines internment camps in the Justice and War Department for "enemy aliens" from the continental United States and Alaska, Hawaii, and Latin America.

Websites

Burton, J., M. Farrell, F. Lord, and R. Lord. "Citizen Isolation Centers." Confinement and Ethnicity: An Overview of World War II Japanese American Relocation Sites. National Park Service. September 1, 2000. This site provides a history of isolation centers and internment campus, along with photographs. https://www.nps.gov/parkhistory/online_books/anthropology74/ce14.htm. Accessed February 6, 2018.

Hansen, Arthur. "Moab/Leupp Isolation Centers (detention facility)." *Densho Encyclopedia*, January 16, 2018. This essay is a concise history of isolation centers with annotated timeline of each location. http://encyclopedia.densho.org/Moab/Leupp_Isolation_Centers_%28detention_facility%29/. Accessed February 6, 2018.

Also Noteworthy

1942

Salinas, California, Assembly Center opens; it is in operation until July 4.

1965

Chinatrust Bank (United States) opens in Los Angeles.

1972

The first national conference on Asian American mental health takes place from April 27 to April 29 at San Francisco.

April 28

1855

California passes a capitation tax (a.k.a. head tax, Chinese Police Tax, Passenger Tax) whereby ship owners were charged a tax of $50 for every Chinese immigrant on their vessel who lands in California. It is a tax on the person, as opposed to a tax in an economic transaction or income. The act was passed to discourage ship owners from assisting Chinese immigration.

Excerpt from "An Act to Discourage the Immigration to this State of Persons Who Cannot Become Citizens Thereof." April 28, 1855.

Section 1. The master, owner, or consignee of any vessel, arriving in any of the ports of this State from any foreign State, country, or territory, having on board any persons who are incompetent by the laws of the United States or the laws and constitution of this State to become citizens thereof are hereby required to pay a tax, for each such person, of fifty dollars. . . .

Section 3. In the event of the non-payment of said tax within three days after the arrival of said vessel, or within three days after demand for said tax, said Commissioner, Mayor or chief officer of any city, town or village, shall commence suit in the name of the State against the master, owner or consignee, or all of them for said tax before any court of competent jurisdiction in said town or city; and the commencing of said suit shall constitute a lien upon such vessel for the amount of said tax, and it shall be forever liable for the same.

Source: *The Statutes of California, Passed at the Sixth Session of the Legislature.* Sacramento, CA: B. B. Redding, State Printer, 1855.

Books

McClain, Charles. *In Search of Equality. The Chinese Struggle against Inequality in Nineteenth-Century America.* Berkeley: University of California Press, 1996. Legal scholar Charles McClain examines Chinese efforts to fight legalized racial discrimination. He focuses mainly on case studies in San Francisco.

Motomura, Hiroshi. *Americans in Waiting: The Lost Story of Immigration and Citizenship in the United States.* New York: Oxford University Press, 2006. Law professor Hiroshi Motomura reflects on the relationship between immigration and citizenship and challenges conventional conception that immigration is a path toward citizenship.

Websites

"Anti-Chinese Movement and Chinese Exclusion." This site provides brief and concise historical background on topics related to the anti-Chinese movement. University of California, Berkeley. Bancroft Library. http://bancroft.berkeley.edu/collections/chineseinca/antichinese.html. Accessed March 7, 2017.

"The Chinese Experience in 19th Century America." University of Illinois. This site provides a timeline of California's anti-Chinese legislations. http://teachingresources.atlas.illinois.edu/chinese_exp/resources/resource_2_4.pdf. Accessed March 7, 2017.

Also Noteworthy

1942

Puyallup, Washington, Assembly Center opens; it is in operation until September 12. Tanforan, California, Assembly Center opens; it is in operation until October 13.

April 29

1878

California Circuit Court ruling *In Re: Ah Yup* declares that Chinese are not white and therefore ineligible to naturalization rights. Before this case, another Chinese immigrant was successful in his request for naturalization in New York. Although the political rhetoric was deeply anti-Chinese, there were some who advocated for the Chinese, such as Republican senator Charles Sumner of Massachusetts, who argued naturalization was a right for all immigrants, irrespective of race. In his decision, Sawyer concluded, ". . . that congress retained the word 'white' in the naturalization laws for the sole purpose of excluding the Chinese from the right of naturalization."

Asians first tested America's racist definition of citizenship in a California federal court in 1878 in the case In re Ah Yup. *One of three litigants, Ah Yup, was joined by Li Huang and Leong Lan in what Circuit Judge Lorenzo Sawyer called "the first application made by a native Chinaman for naturalization." In truth, though, several Chinese had applied for citizenship three years earlier in 1875, when Hong Chung, Chock Wong, and Chin Tin appeared before the California state senate to explain that they sought American citizenship because, in the words of Hong Chung, "American man make no good laws for Chinaman. We make good laws for Chinaman citizens." In the 1878 case, Ah Yup and his co-litigants claimed that Asians were included under the category "white," a strategy that was followed by all subsequent claims almost without exception, and Judge Sawyer, in ruling against Chinese naturalization, employed the argument that formed the crux of later decisions that the Chinese, by everyday speech and scientific evidence, were "nonwhite."*

Source: Okihiro, Gary. *Common Ground: Reimagining American History*. Princeton, NJ: Princeton University Press, 2001, p. 48.

Books

Miller, Marion, ed. *Great Debates in American History: From the Debates in the British Parliament on the Colonial Stamp Act (1764–1765) to the Debates in Congress at the Close of the Taft Administration (1912–1913)*. New York: Current Literature Publishing Company, 1913. This volume provides primary historical source documents. See Chapter 5 on the "Chinese Exclusion" for documents related to debates surrounding the issue of Chinese Exclusion.

Zhao, Xiaojian, and Edward J. W. Park, eds. *Asian Americans: An Encyclopedia of Social, Cultural, Economic, and Political History*. Santa Barbara, CA: ABC-CLIO, 2013. See entry by John S. W. Park, "Ah Yup, In Re (1878)," pp. 8–9.

Websites

"This Month in History: In re Ah Yup, April 29, 1878." Smithsonian Asian Pacific American Center. This site provides background and description of the case, along with links for other related artifacts in the collection. http://smithsonianapa.org/now/this-month-in-history-in-re-ah-yup-rules-chinese-ineligible-for-naturalized-citizenship-on-april-29-1878/. Accessed March 1, 2018.

This site provides *In Re: Ah Yup* (1878). Public. Resource.Org. https://law.resource.org/pub/us/case/reporter/F.Cas/0001.f.cas/0001.f.cas.0223.pdf. Accessed March 1, 2018.

1902

The Scott Act indefinitely extends the systems of Chinese exclusion and surveillance, which were created in the Chinese Exclusion Act 1882 and Geary Act 1892. It also maintained the domestic certificate registration program for all Chinese residents in the United States.

CHAP. 641.—An Act to prohibit the coming into and to regulate the residence within the United States, its Territories, and all territory under its jurisdiction, and the District of Columbia, of Chinese and person of Chinese descent.

Be it enacted by the Senate and House of Representatives of the United States of America in Congress assembled, That all laws now in force prohibiting and regulating the coming of Chinese persons, and persons of Chinese descent, into the United States, and the residence of such persons therein, including sections five, six, seven, eight, nine, ten, eleven, thirteen, and fourteen of the Act entitled "An Act to prohibit the coming of Chinese laborers into the United States" approved September thirteenth, eighteen, hundred and eighty-eight, be, and the same are hereby, re-enacted, extended, and continued so far as the same are not inconsistent with treaty obligation, until otherwise provided by law, and said laws shall also apply to the island territory under the jurisdiction of the United States, and prohibit the immigration of Chinese laborers, not citizens of the United States, from such island territory to the mainland territory of the United States, whether in such island territory at the time of cession or not, and form one portion of the island territory of the United States to another portion of said island territory: Provided, however, That said laws shall not apply to the transit of Chinese laborers from one island to another island of the same group; and any islands within the jurisdiction of any State or the District of Alaska shall be considered a part of the mainland under this section.

SEC. 2. That the Secretary of the Treasury is hereby authorized and empowered to make and prescribe, and from time to time to change, such rules and regulations not inconsistent with the laws of the land as he may deem necessary and proper to execute the provisions of this Act and the Acts hereby extended and continued and of the treaty of December eighth, eighteen hundred and ninety-four, between the United States and China, and with the approval of the President to appoint such agents as he may deem necessary for the efficient execution of said treaty and said Acts.

SEC. 3. That nothing in the provisions of this Act or any other Act shall be constructed to prevent, hinder, or restrict any foreign exhibitor, representative, or citizen of any foreign nation, or the holder, who is a citizen of any foreign nation, of any concession or privilege from any fair or exposition authorized by Act of Congress from bringing into the United States, under contract, such mechanics, artisans, agents, or other employees, natives of their respective foreign countries, as they or any of them may deem necessary for the purpose of making preparation for installing or conducting any business authorized or permitted under or by virtue of or pertaining to any concession or privilege which may have been or may be granted by any said fair or exposition in connection with such exposition, under such rules and regulations as the Secretary of the Treasury may prescribe, both as to the admission and return of such person or persons.

SEC. 4. That it shall be the duty of every Chinese laborer, other than a citizen, rightfully in, and entitled to remain in any of the insular territory of the United States (Hawaii excepted) at the time of the passage of this Act, to obtain within one year thereafter a certificate of residence in the insular territory wherein he resides, which certificate shall entitle him to residence therein, and upon failure to obtain such certificate as herein provided he shall be, deported from such insular territory; and the Philippine Commission is authorized and required to make all regulations and provisions necessary for the enforcement of this section in the Philippine Islands, including the form and substance of the certificate of residence so that the same shall clearly and sufficiently identify the holder thereof and enable officials to prevent fraud in the transfer of the same: Provided, however, That if said Philippine Commission shall find that it is impossible to complete the registration herein provided for within one year from the passage of this Act, said Commission is hereby authorized and empowered to extend the time for such registration for a further period not exceeding one year.

Approved, April 26, 1902.

Source: The Statutes at Large of the United States of America. Vol. XXV. Washington, DC: Government Printing Office, 1889.

Books

Gold, Martin. *Forbidden Citizens: Chinese Exclusion and the U.S. Congress: A Legislative History*. Alexandria, VA: TheCapitol.Net, Inc., 2012. *Forbidden Citizens* is a comprehensive work that covers the history of anti-Chinese politics, debates, and legislation from the U.S. Congress. See Chapter 7, "The Scott Act of 1888."

Kermit Hall, James Ely, and Joel Grossman, eds. *The Oxford Companion to the Supreme Court of the United States*. Oxford: Oxford University Press, 2005. This book is an essential guide for judges, lawyers, academics, journalists, and anyone interested in the impact of the Court's decisions on American society.

Websites

Chin, Philip. "Enforcing Chinese Exclusion, The Scott Act of 1888, Part 2." This essay discusses the history of the Scott Act, as well as the social-political milieu of the period. http://www.chineseamericanheroes.org. Accessed October 12, 2016.

"1902 Scott Act." The University of Washington-Bothell Library. "US Immigration Legislation Online." This site provides a summary of the legislation, along with the original text. http://library.uwb.edu/static/USimmigration/1902_scott_act.html. Accessed October 12, 2016.

1992

Korean businesses were looted and burned as a result of riots in Los Angeles due to outrage over Rodney King verdict. On March 3, 1991, a group of four policemen beat Rodney King after pulling him over for speeding. The police claimed King was resisting arrest and proceeded to beat him for roughly 15 minutes, resulting in a fractured skull, broken bones and teeth, and permanent brain damage. The beating was filmed and released to the media. The policemen are found "not guilty" on April 29, 1992, which fuels the anxiety and frustration of protestors. Minutes after the verdict, a riot erupts in South Central Los Angeles. The riots last five days, resulting in the death of 53 people, and over $1 billion in damages.

The aftershock of the L.A. riots has deeply affected thousands of Koreans. Many shopkeepers say that the police arrived too late to prevent looters from plundering their stores. One Korean grocer who lost his small store to looters bitterly described how the police responded to the crisis: "Basically, the orders were to draw a line, to cord off the affluent neighborhoods . . . and the police, well they came out 'big' when it was safe, and retreated in the face of real danger."

At the local, state, and federal levels, aid was distributed through community agencies but often failed to help the 2,300 burned, looted, or damaged businesses, even though their damages amounted to half the city's total losses, nearly one billion dollars. The SBA (Small Business Administration), FEMA (Federal Emergency Management Agency), insurance companies, and others did not meet the demands of the Korean store owners. Instead, they sent letters and forms that further frustrated and confused the non-English speaking immigrants. . . .

Many merchants who had lost their stores packed up and returned to Korea where they would be able to work without the fear of another Sa-ee-gu. Since 1992, 1,000 to 3,000 L.A. Korean residents have returned to Korea each year. Still, 200,000 have remained in Los Angeles County and hope to get back on their feet and return to normal living.

The riots have shown Korean Americans that nothing, not even 112-hour work weeks, can guarantee financial stability. The American Dream of success as many once knew it has since evaporated with the smoke of riotfires. . . . The name of the game is survival, and like many other minorities, survival is what Koreans learned throughout our history.

Source: Kim, Laura. "A Korean American Perspective of Korean-Black Relations and the Los Angeles Riots." *Korea Times*, April 30, 1998, p. 8.

Books

Abelmann, Nancy, and John Lie. *Blue Dreams: Korean Americans and the Los Angeles Riots*. Cambridge, MA: Harvard University Press, 1997. *Blue Dreams* critically analyzes the Los Angeles riots from the intersection of historical, political, and economic factors vis-à-vis race, class, culture, and community.

Kim, Kwang, ed. *Koreans in the Hood: Conflict with African Americans*. Baltimore: Johns Hopkins University Press, 1999. *Koreans in the Hood* is a collection of critical essays that examines Korean American and African American relations in Los Angeles, Chicago, and New York City.

Websites

"LA Riots." South Central History. This site provides a detailed history of riots that have occurred in South Central Los Angeles, including a day-by-by chronology of the 1992 Los Angeles riots. http://www.southcentralhistory.com/la-riots.php. Accessed January 17, 2017.

"Los Angeles Riots Fast Facts." CNN, April 8, 2016. This site provides facts related to the damages caused by the riots, in addition to a detailed chronology of events leading up to the riots, during the riots, and after the riots. http://www.cnn.com/2013/09/18/us/los-angeles-riots-fast-facts/. Accessed January 17, 2017.

Also Noteworthy

1989

Le Ly Hayslip's memoir *When Heaven and Earth Changed Places* (1989) is published by Doubleday. It is adapted into a movie by Oliver Stone, *Heaven & Earth* (1993).

April 30

1900

The Hawaiian Organic Act makes all U.S. laws applicable to Hawaii, thus ending contract labor in the islands. Under this act, the Chinese in Hawaii are required to apply for certificates of residence, and they are prohibited from entering any other U.S. territory or the mainland.

Chapter 339.—An Act to provide a government for the Territory of Hawaii.

Be it enacted by the Senate and House of Representatives of the United States of America in Congress assembled,

Chapter 1. General Provisions.

§ 1. Definitions

That the phrase "the laws of Hawaii," as used in this Act without qualifying words, shall mean the constitution and laws of the Republic of Hawaii, in force on the twelfth day of August, eighteen hundred and ninety-eight, at the time of the transfer of the sovereignty of the Hawaiian Islands to the United States of America.

The constitution and statute laws of the Republic of Hawaii then in force, set forth in a compilation made by Sidney M. Ballou under the authority of the legislature, and published in two volumes entitled "Civil Laws" and "Penal Laws," respectively, and in the Session Laws of the Legislature for the session of eighteen hundred and ninety-eight, are referred to in this Act as "Civil Laws," "Penal Laws," and "Session Laws."

§ 2. Territory of Hawaii

That the islands acquired by the United States of America under an Act of Congress entitled "Joint resolution to provide for annexing the Hawaiian Islands to the United States," approved July seventh, eighteen hundred and ninety-eight, shall be known as the Territory of Hawaii.

§ 3. Government of the Territory of Hawaii

That a Territorial government is hereby established over the said Territory, with its capital at Honolulu, on the island of Oahu.

§ 4. Citizenship

That all persons who were citizens of the Republic of Hawaii on August twelfth, eighteen hundred and ninety-eight, are hereby declared to be citizens of the United States and citizens of the Territory of Hawaii.

And all citizens of the United States resident in the Hawaiian Islands who were resident there on or since August twelfth, eighteen hundred and ninety-eight and all the citizens of the United States who shall hereafter reside in the Territory of Hawaii for one year shall be citizens of the Territory of Hawaii.

§ 5. United States Constitution

That the Constitution, and, except as otherwise provided, all the laws of the United States, including laws carrying general appropriations, which are not locally inapplicable, shall have the same force and effect within the said Territory as elsewhere in the United States; Provided, That sections 1841 to 1891, inclusive, 1910 and 1912, of the Revised Statutes, and the amendments thereto, and an act entitled "An act to prohibit the passage of local or special laws in the Territories of the United States, to limit Territorial indebtedness, and for other purposes," approved July 30, 1886, and the amendments thereto, shall not apply to Hawaii. Annotations.

§ 6. Laws of Hawaii

That the laws of Hawaii not inconsistent with the Constitution or laws of the United States or the provisions of this Act shall continue in force, subject to repeal or amendment by the legislature of Hawaii or the Congress of the United States.

Source: Organic Act: An Act to Provide a Government for the Territory of Hawaii (Act of April 30, 1900, C 339, 31 Stat 141).

Books

Lee, Anne. *The Hawaii State Constitution*. Oxford: University of Oxford Press, 2011. *The Hawaii State Constitution* is a legal history of the state of Hawaii. Part I covers the history of the state constitution and the Organic Act.

Van Dyke, Jon M. *Who Owns the Crown Lands of Hawai'i*. Honolulu: University of Hawaii Press, 2007. Law professor Jon M. Van Dyke examines the history and legal issues regarding Hawaii's "crown lands," sovereignty, and native Hawaiian birthrights.

Websites

Lyon, Cherstin. "Organic Act." *Densho Encyclopedia*, July 29, 2015. This site provides an essay that details the history and impact of the 1900 Organic Act. http://encyclopedia.densho.org/Organic%20Act/. Accessed October 12, 2016.

"Organic Act." Hawaiian Independence. This site provides the complete text for the Organic Act of 1900. http://www.hawaii-nation.org/organic.html. Accessed October 12, 2016.

Also Noteworthy

1942

Turlock Assembly Center in Turlock, California, one of fifteen temporary assembly centers, begins processing Japanese American detainees. Detainees from Turlock were then transferred to the Gila River internment camp in the Arizona desert. The last inmate leaves Turlock on August 12.

1975

President Gerald Ford reports that a force of 70 evacuation helicopters and 865 marines had evacuated about 1,400 U.S. citizens and 5,500 third country nationals and South Vietnamese from landing zones near the U.S. Embassy in Saigon and the Tan Son Naut Airfield.

Fall of Saigon. The aftermath of the fall of Saigon on April 30, 1975, results in a large influx of refugees to the United States.

2006

Hines E. Ward Jr. (b. March 8, 1976), best known as a National Football League player, announces the establishment of the Hines Ward Helping Hand Foundation with a $1 million endowment, in partnership with the Pearl S. Buck Foundation, to assist mixed-race children. Ward was born in Seoul, South Korea, to a Korean mother, Young-hee Kim, and an African American G.I., Hines Ward Sr. When he was a year old, his family moved to Atlanta, Georgia. In 2010, President Barack Obama appointed him to the President's Advisory Commission of Asian Americans and Pacific Islanders, further promoting his reputation as an advocate for Asian Americans.

May

May 1

1817

On this day, the Foreign Mission School officially commences. It was established by the Board of Foreign Missions in 1816 with the expressed goal to teach "heathen" youths from around the world to become Christian missionaries in their own cultures. In 1818, Wong Arce, Ah Lan, Ah Lum, Chop Ah See, and Lieaou Ah-See were the first Chinese students to receive any education in the United States, when they enrolled at the Foreign Mission School in Cornwall, Connecticut. Lieaou Ah-See became the first Chinese Protestant convert in America.

Excerpt from "Biography of Rev. Herman Daggett (1789–1832)." He served as the second principal of the Foreign Mission School in Cornwall, Connecticut.

The school of which Mr. Daggett now became the head, consisted of youth and children from various Pagan nations. Though they were only about thirty in number, there were natives of Sumatra, China, Bengal, Hindostan, Mexico, New Zealand; of the Society Islands and Marquesas Islands; of the Isles of Greece and of the Azores; there were specimens also of various North American Indian tribes—Cherokees, Choctaws, Osages, Oneidas, Tuscaroras, Senecas, and the tribe of St. Regis in Canada.

Source: Sprague, William. *Annals of the American Pulpit*. Vol. II. New York: Robert Carter & Brothers, 1859, p. 293.

Books

Demos, John. *The Heathen School: A Story of Hope and Betrayal in the Age of the Early Republic*. New York: Alfred A. Knopf, 2014. For historical background on missionary schools, this volume by historian John Demos explores the racial construction in the United States through Christian evangelism and schools designed to civilize the "heathens."

Rhoads, Edward. *Stepping Forth into the World: The Chinese Educational Mission to the United States*. Hong Kong: Hong Kong University Press, 2011. Edward Rhoads is a historian of the late 19th- and early 20th-century China. In this book, he documents this history and experience of Chinese missionary students and other Chinese students during a period of extreme anti-Chinese racism and sentiment.

Websites

Lai, Him Mark, Thomas Chinn, and Philip Choy. *A History of the Chinese in California: A Syllabus*. San Francisco, CA: Chinese Historical Society of America, 1969. This publication by historian Him Mark Lai and others provides a concise history of the Chinese in the United States. It was published by the Chinese Historical Society of America and is available at the Him Mark Lai digital archive. http://himmarklai.org/wordpress/wp-content/uploads/A-History-of-the-Chinese-in-CA-A-Syllabus-Part-I.pdf. Accessed January 29, 2018.

This site provides historical documents, images, and records of the Foreign Mission School from 1817 to 1826. It includes a Chinese Friendship Album, produced in 1824 by Henry Martyn A'lan (Wu Lan in Cantonese), a student at Cornwall's Foreign Mission school. http://www.cornwallhistoricalsociety.org/exhibits/foreign_mission_school.html. Accessed January 29, 2018.

1898

U.S. Commodore George Dewey's U.S. Asiatic Squadron annihilates the Spanish fleet at the Battle of Manila Bay. By August 13, 1898, Spain surrenders to the United States. On December 10, Spain ceded the Philippines and Guam to the United States with the Treaty of Paris, which ended the Spanish-American War. This was the start of Filipino migration to the United States.

Filipino migrants would start to immigrate to the United States in large numbers because they were colonial subjects of the United States.

The Battle of Manila Bay was the decisive naval engagement of the Spanish-American War. Commodore George Dewey's U.S. . . .

[On] April 27, the American ships departed Chinese waters. They made landfall at Cape Bolineau, Luzon, at daybreak on April 30. Dewey detached the Boston and Concord, later reinforced by the Baltimore, to make a quick reconnaissance of Subic Bay. The Americans soon determined that the Spanish squadron was not in evidence. Reportedly, Dewey was pleased at the news and remarked, "Now we have them."

Dewey then ordered his ships to steam to Manila Bay, which the squadron entered on the night of April 30. Dewey chose to ignore the threat of mines and the fortifications guarding the entrance to the bay. He selected Boca Grande channel and the ships steamed in single file with as few lights as possible. Not until the squadron had passed El Fraile rock did the Spanish discover the American presence. Both sides then exchanged a few shots but without damage. The American ships were now in the bay. Detaching his two supply ships and the McCulloch, *Dewey proceeded ahead, although he did not intend to engage the Spanish until dawn.*

Source: Springer, Paul, and Spencer Tucker. "Spanish-American and Philippine American Wars Battles." In *U.S. Leadership in Wartime: Clashes, Controversy, and Compromise*, edited by Spencer Tucker, p. 395. Santa Barbara, CA: ABC-CLIO, 2009.

Books

Barnes, Mark. *The Spanish-American War and Philippines Insurrection, 1898–1902: An Annotated Bibliography*. New York: Routledge, 2011. *The Spanish-American War and Philippines Insurrection* provides a timeline and history of the Spanish-American War and Philippine Insurrection, along with an annotated bibliography of scholarship on this topic.

O'Toole, G.J. A. *The Spanish War: An American Epic 1898*. Combined Books, 1996. New York: W.W. Norton & Company, 1984. *The Spanish War* discusses various aspects of the Spanish-American War and its historical, cultural, ideological, and geopolitical impact.

Websites

"Battle of Manila Bay." History.com. This site provides a summary of the battle, along with videos. http://www.history.com/topics/battle-of-manila-bay. Accessed October 11, 2016.

"The Battle of Manila Bay, 1898." EyeWitness to History. 2011. This site provides an eyewitness account of the Battle of Manila Bay. www.eyewitnesstohistory.com. Accessed October 11, 2016.

Also Noteworthy

1992

On this day, a few hundred young Korean Americans organize a "peace rally" in the heart of Koreatown, Los Angeles, California, to call for peace in the city and to end violence and destruction in their community.

May 2

2011

Raja Gemini, stage name of Sutan Amrull (b. June 14, 1974), becomes the first Asian American drag queen to win *RuPaul's Drag Race* in season three.

RAJA GEMINI sewed, danced, cat-walked and lip-synced her way to victory on season three of Logo TV's RuPaul's Drag Race*—beating out 12 other fierce and fabulous contenders on the drag-queen competition show in 2011.*

Born Sutan Amrull, the 39-year-old Los Angeles native had already made his name in Hollywood as both a makeup artist for celebrity clients like Tyra Banks and Adam Lambert as well as a renowned L.A. drag performer before the drag legend RuPaul crowned him the queen with the most charisma, uniqueness, nerve and talent.

Since then, the Dutch-Indonesian chameleon has headlined drag shows at clubs across the country, while working on followups to his first pop single, "Diamond Crowned Queen" and blogging at artofraja.com.

Source: Kawana, Lauren. "Long Live Raja." *Hyphen Magazine*, no. 27 (Summer 2013): p. 9.

Books

Daems, Jim, ed. *The Makeup of RuPaul's Drag Race: Essays on the Queen of Reality Shows*. Jefferson, NC: McFarland & Company Inc., Publishers, 2014. *The Makeup of RuPaul's Drag Race* is a collection of critical essays that examines the intersection of drag, race, trans, and LGBTQQI politics.

Han, C. Winter. *Geisha of a Different Kind: Race and Sexuality in Gaysian America*. New York: New York University Press, 2015. *Geisha of a Different Kind* is a study of race and sexuality among Asian American queer communities. See Chapter 4, "Asian Girls Are Prettier: How Drag Queens Saved Us."

Websites

Raja Gemini. Official Facebook page. This site provides a short biography of Raja Gemini, photographs, and latest news. https://www.facebook.com/RajaOfficial/. Accessed February 6, 2018.

"Talking Life, Love and Demons with Raja Gemini, Drag Superstar." *Vice*. This is an interview with Raja Gemini that explores her personal and professional life. https://partners.vice.com/diesel/makelovenotwalls/news/talking-life-love-and-demons-with-raja-gemini-drag-superstar/. Accessed February 6, 2018.

Also Noteworthy

1942

Portland, Oregon, Assembly Center opens; it is in operation until September 10.

1953

The day is declared Korean Day in the United States, and Americans are encouraged to make donations of money and materials to assist war-torn Korea and Koreans.

May 3

1965

On this day, Cambodia announces that it will end diplomatic relations with the United States. On February 7, 1950, the United States formally recognized the Kingdom of Cambodia, which was still colonized by France. The government of Cambodia ended diplomatic relations with the United States because it held the United States responsible for the cross-border air attacks by South Vietnam that killed Cambodian civilians. Diplomatic relations between the two countries were reestablished on July 2, 1969, and by August 16, 1969, a U.S. Embassy was reopened in Phnom Penh.

By the early 1960s [Prince Norodom] Sihanouk's foreign policy was also being increasingly influenced by his anger toward the hostile policies of the United States and the pro-U.S. governments in Thailand and South Vietnam. The Khmer Serei (Free Khmer) guerrillas, whom he believed correctly were backed by the U.S. Central Intelligence Agency (and who were led by Sihanouk's long-standing political rival Son Ngoc Thanh), were broadcasting anti-Sihanouk propaganda from Thailand and South Vietnam. In August 1963 Sihanouk broke diplomatic relations with South Vietnam. In November of that year he terminated all U.S. military assistance programs in Cambodia. In December 1963 Sihanouk signed the country's first military assistance agreement with China. On May 3, 1965, Sihanouk broke diplomatic relations with the United States.

Source: Morris, Stephen. *Why Vietnam Invaded Cambodia: Political Culture and the Causes of War*. Stanford, CA: Stanford University Press, 1999, p. 40.

Books

Drachman, Edward, and Alan Shank. *Presidents and Foreign Policy: Countdown to Ten Controversial Decisions*. Albany: State University of New York Press, 1987. See Chapter 5, "President Nixon's Decision to Order an Incursion into Cambodia."

Young, Marilyn, and Robert Buzzanco, eds. *A Companion to the Vietnam War*. Oxford: Blackwell Publishing, 2002. See Chapter 12, Kenton Clymer, "A Casualty of War: The Break in American Relations with Cambodia, 1965."

Websites

"A Guide to the United States' History of Recognition, Diplomatic, and Consular Relations, by Country, since 1776: Cambodia." Office of the Historian, Bureau of Public Affairs. U.S. Department of State. This site provides a detailed chronology of U.S.-Cambodian relations. https://history.state.gov/countries/cambodia. Accessed September 30, 2017.

"Southeast Asia: Cambodia Ends U.S. Ties." Facts on File News Service. 2011. This site provides concise historical background for Prince Norodom Sihanouk's decision to end diplomatic relations with the United States. http://web.stanford.edu/group/tomzgroup/pmwiki/uploads/1806-1969-05-05-FoF-a-OEP.pdf. Accessed September 30, 2017.

Also Noteworthy

2006

Two hundred Indian Americans from across the United States attend a White House briefing led by Karl Rove on the importance of the U.S.-India Civil Nuclear Agreement for both the United States and India. The group traveled to Washington, D.C., to meet the members of Congress from their respective areas to lobby for the passage of U.S.-India Civil Nuclear Agreement.

May 4

1987

On this day, President Ronald Reagan issues proclamation of Asian Pacific American Heritage Week.

Proclamation 5674—Asian/Pacific American Heritage Week, 1987.

By the President of the United States of America

A Proclamation

Like all Americans, those of Asian and Pacific descent share twin heritages—the rich cultural legacy of the lands of their forebears and the liberty that is the birthright of every American. Drawing on the values and traditions of their homelands and the promise of this land of opportunity, Asian and Pacific Americans have long helped build and strengthen our Nation. They have also gallantly defended our country and our freedom in time of war.

Through the years, many of the indelible contributions by Asian and Pacific Americans to our land have come from immigrants. These quiet heroes and heroines have known oppression and poverty in their native lands and have courageously struggled to reach the United States and make a new life for themselves and their children. Their story is America's story, and their spirit is America's spirit.

Every American can be profoundly grateful for the achievements of Asian and Pacific Americans. Their hard work, creativity, and intelligence have inspired their fellow citizens and added new dimensions to our national life.

Now, Therefore, I, Ronald Reagan, *President of the United States of America, by virtue of the authority vested in me by the Constitution and the laws of the United States, do hereby proclaim the week beginning May 3, 1987, as Asian/Pacific American Heritage Week. I call upon the people of the United States to observe this week with appropriate ceremonies and activities.*

In Witness Whereof, *I have hereunto set my hand this 4th day of May, in the year of our Lord nineteen hundred and eighty-seven, and of the Independence of the United States of America the two hundred and eleventh.*

RONALD REAGAN

Source: Reagan, Ronald. "Proclamation 5647—Asian/Pacific American Heritage Week, 1987." May 4, 1987. Online by Gerhard Peters and John T. Woolley. The American Presidency Project. http://www.presidency.ucsb.edu/ws/?pid=34218. Accessed January 17, 2017.

Books

Lee, Jonathan H.X., and Kathleen Nadeau, eds. *Encyclopedia of Asian American Folklore and Folklife*. Santa Barbara, CA: ABC-CLIO, 2011. In this three-volume reference, Dawn Lee Tu's entry on Asian Pacific American Heritage Week discusses Asian Pacific Heritage Month from a folklore studies perspective: see pp. 63–64.

Zhao, Xiaojian, and Edward Park, eds. *Asian Americans: An Encyclopedia of Social, Cultural, Economic, and Political History*. Santa Barbara, CA: Greenwood, 2013. The entry on Asian Pacific American Heritage Week is authored by Dawn Lee Tu, an expert on this topic, on pp. 118–119.

Websites

"About Asian/Pacific American Heritage Week." The Library of Congress. This site explains history and purpose of Asian Pacific American Heritage Week. http://asianpacificheritage.gov/about/. Accessed January 17, 2017.

"Asian/Pacific American Heritage Week." The Law Library of the Library of Congress. This site provides an overview of Asian Pacific American Heritage Month, in addition to links to all legislation related to it. https://www.loc.gov/law/help/commemorative-observations/asian.php. Accessed January 17, 2017.

Also Noteworthy

2002

In Alexandria, Virginia, Michael Woolls, a 24-year-old, is charged with assault and attempted assault, motivated by racial basis, and destruction of property after throwing a brick through the car window of a Middle Eastern man.

May 5

1892

The 1882 Chinese Exclusion law expires, and is extended for an additional 10 years with the passing of the 1892 Geary Act. The Geary Act established an internal passport system that applied to all Chinese residing in the United States. According to the law, all Chinese residents had to apply for and carry with them a certificate of residence. Any Chinese person who is caught without his or her registration certificate is subject to immediate deportation or imprisonment for one year of hard labor. Chinese government officials abroad and immigrants in the United States denounced the law.

Jee Gam, a baptized Chinese Christian and leader in the community published the following critique of the Geary Act.

I am a Chinaman and a Christian. I am not any less Chinese for being a follower of Christ. My love of Jesus has intensified rather than belittled my love for my native country. I am proud of China, for it is a great country. I admire her, for she has a wonderful future. What a glorious nation she will be when she embraces Christianity! . . .

I am in some sense also American, for I have lived in America almost twice as long as in China. I love this country. I teach my children who are native-born Americans to sing the National hymns. And just as I rejoice in whatever is honorable to America, and commend her example to my countrymen, so I am pained when unjust and oppressive laws are permitted to be placed upon her statute books. Such a law as the Geary Act seems to me to be one which dishonors America, as well as injures my countrymen and native land. . . .

[The] Act is an oppression of the weak. China is a great and powerful nation, but not just now in condition to fight a power like America.

Source: Yung, Judy, Gordon H. Chang, and H. Mark Lai, eds. *Chinese American Voices: From the Gold Rush to the Present*. Berkeley: University of California Press, 2006, p. 86.

Books

Kanstroom, Daniel. *Deportation Nation: Outsiders in American History*. Cambridge, MA: Harvard University Press, 2007. In *Deportation Nation* legal scholar Daniel Kanstroom shows that deportation has been a legal tool to control immigrants in the United States.

Parker, Kunal. *Making Foreigners: Immigration and Citizenship Law in America, 1600–2000*. Cambridge: Cambridge University Press, 2015. Law professor Kunal Parker conceptualizes the history of U.S. immigration and citizenship law from the colonial period to the beginning of the 21st century through comparative analysis of minority communities, women, and the poor.

Websites

Bily, Cynthia. "Geary Act of 1892." Immigration to the United States. This site discusses the significance of the Geary Act in U.S. immigration history. http://immigrationtounitedstates.org/514-geary-act-of-1892.html. Accessed October 9, 2016.

"1892 Geary Act." U.S. Immigration Legislation Online. The University of Washington-Bothell Library. This site provides the full text for the Geary Act, along with a summary of its significance. http://library.uwb.edu/static/usimmigration/1892_geary_act.html. Accessed October 9, 2016.

Also Noteworthy

1943

Korean nationalist and anti-Japanese spy Kilsoo Kenneth Haan predicts Japan's attack of Crescent City, California, that would take place before the end of the year. American intelligence and military ignored him.

May 6

1843

While commanding a whaling ship, the *John Howland* in the Pacific, Captain William Whitfield rescued five shipwrecked Japanese sailors. In November 1841, four of the rescued Japanese sailors disembarked at the port of Oahu. Manjiro Nakahama stayed on board and went with Whitfield to Fairhaven, Massachusetts. On May 6, 1843, the *John Howland* sails into New Bedford harbor. Manjiro Nakahama would attend school in New England and adopt the same Western name: John Manjiro. Later on, John Manjiro would serve as an interpreter for Commodore Matthew Perry. John Manjiro indirectly influenced the treaty negotiations between Japan and Commodore Perry, which ended the 250 years of Japanese isolation from the world.

Letter from Manjiro to Whitfield, March 12, 1847. This letter illustrates the close relationship between John Manjiro and Captain William Whitfield.

Respected Friend,

I will take the pen to write you a few lines and let you know that I am well and hope you were the same. First thing I will tell you about the home, the time I left. Well sir your boy, William, is well all the summer but the cold weather sets in he will smart a little cunning creature I ever saw before. He will cry after me just as quick as he would to his mother. Your wife and Amelia and Mr. Bonny's family and your neighborhoods they all well when I last saw them.

Source: This letter is reprinted from Bernard, Donald R. *The Life and Times of John Manjiro*. New York: McGraw-Hill, 1992.

Books

Bernard, Donald. *The Life and Times of John Manjiro*. New York: McGraw-Hill, 1992. This book is a well-documented history of the story of John Manjiro.

Nagakuni, Junya, and Junji Kitadai, trans. *Drifting toward the Southeast: The Story of Five Japanese Castaways*. New Bedford, MA: Spinner Publication, 2003. This is a translation of Hyoson Kiryaku's autobiographical account of John Manjiro's historic voyage in the United States.

Websites

"Manjiro Nakahama." Fairhaven, MA Office of Tourism. 2018. This site provides historical information on Manjiro Nakahama with photographs and links to additional resources. http://fairhaventours.com/manjiro-nakahama/. Accessed June 14, 2018.

The Manjiro Society is an international educational and cultural organization that seeks to foster mutual understanding between the people of the United States and Japan. This page is dedicated to the "first" encounter of Japan and the United States through the life of John Manjiro. http://www.manjiro.org/society.html. Accessed January 29, 2018.

1882

On this day, President Chester A. Arthur ends free immigration into the United States with the enactment of the Chinese Exclusion Act. The initial 1882 law suspended entry of Chinese laborers for a period of 10 years but exempted certain classes including diplomats, tourists, teachers, students, and merchants. The exclusion law did not apply to Chinese laborers who already resided in the United States before November 1880 and those who arrived up to 90 days after its passing. It also prohibited federal and state courts from naturalizing Chinese immigrants, marking them as "aliens ineligible for citizenship." The initial law was amended several times in order to address loopholes and further curb Chinese immigration. Although an 1884 amendment required Chinese immigrants residing in the United States to obtain a certificate for reentry before traveling internationally, an amendment that passed just four years later voided all previously issued certificates and prevented the reentry of roughly 20,000 laborers.

An Act to Execute Certain Treaty Stipulations Relating to Chinese

Whereas, in the opinion of the Government of the United States the coming of Chinese laborers to this country endangers the good order of certain localities within the territory thereof: Therefore,

Be it enacted by the Senate and House of Representatives of the United States of America in Congress assembled, That from and after the expiration of ninety days next after the passage of this act, and until the expiration of ten years next after the passage of this act, the coming of Chinese laborers to the United States be, and the same is hereby, suspended; and during such suspension it shall not be lawful for any Chinese laborer to come, or having so come after the expiration of said ninety days, to remain within the United States.

SEC. 2. That the master of any vessel who shall knowingly bring within the United States on such vessel, and land or permit to be landed, any Chinese laborer, from any foreign port or place, shall be deemed guilty of a misdemeanor, and on conviction thereof shall be punished by a fine of not more than $500 for each and every such Chinese laborer so brought, and may be also imprisoned for a term not exceeding one year.

SEC. 3. That the two foregoing sections shall not apply to Chinese laborers who were in the United States on the 17th day of November, 1880, or who shall have come into the same before the expiration of ninety days next after the passage of this act. . . .

SEC. 4. That for the purpose of properly identifying Chinese laborers who were in the United States on the 17th day of November, 1880, or who shall have come into the same before the expiration of ninety days next after the passage of this act, and in order to furnish them with the proper evidence of their right to go from and come to the United States of their free will and accord, as provided by the treaty between the United States and China dated November 17, 1880, the collector of customs of the district from which any such Chinese laborer shall depart from the United States shall, in person or by deputy, go on board each vessel having on board any such Chinese laborer and cleared or about to sail from his district for a foreign port, and on such vessel make a list of all such Chinese laborers, which shall be entered in registry-books to be kept for that purpose, in which shall be stated the name, age, occupation, last place of residence, physical marks or peculiarities, and all facts necessary for the identification of each of such Chinese laborers, which books shall be safely kept in the custom-house; and every such Chinese laborer so departing from the United States shall be entitled to, and shall receive, free of any charge or cost upon application therefor, from the collector or his deputy, at the time such list is taken a certificate, signed by the collector or his deputy and attested by his seal of office, in such form as the Secretary of the Treasury shall prescribe, which certificate shall contain a statement of the name, age, occupation, last place of residence, personal description, and facts of identification of the Chinese laborer to whom the certificate is issued, corresponding with the said list and registry in all particulars. . . .

SEC. 5. That any Chinese laborer mentioned in section four of this act being in the United States, and desiring to depart from the United States by land, shall have the right to demand and receive, free of charge or cost, a certificate of identification similar to that provided for in section four of this act to be issued to such Chinese laborers as may desire to leave the United States by water; and it is hereby made the duty of the collector of customs of the district next adjoining the foreign country to which said Chinese laborer desires to go to issue such certificate, free of charge or cost, upon application by such Chinese laborer, and to enter the same upon registry-books to be kept by him for the purpose, as provided for in section four of this act.

SEC. 6. That in order to the faithful execution of articles one and two of the treaty in this act before mentioned, every Chinese person other than a laborer who may be entitled by said treaty and this act to come within the United States, and who shall be about to come to the United States, shall be identified as so entitled by the Chinese Government in each case, such identity to be evidenced by a certificate issued under the authority of said government, which certificate shall be in the English language or (if not in the English language) accompanied by a translation into English, stating such right to come, and which certificate shall state the name, title, or official rank, if any, the age, height, and all physical peculiarities, former and present occupation or profession, and place of residence in China of the person to whom the certificate is issued and that such person is entitled conformably to the treaty in this act mentioned to come within the United States . . .

SEC. 7. That any person who shall knowingly and falsely alter or substitute any name for the name written in such certificate or forge any such certificate, or knowingly utter any forged or fraudulent certificate, or falsely personate any person named in any such certificate, shall be deemed guilty of a misdemeanor; and upon conviction thereof shall be fined in a sum not exceeding $1,000, and imprisoned in a penitentiary for a term of not more than five years.

SEC. 8. That the master of any vessel arriving in the United States from any foreign port or place shall, at the same time he delivers a manifest of the cargo, and if there be no cargo, then at the time of making a report, of the entry of the vessel pursuant to law, in addition to the other matter required to be reported, and before landing, or permitting to land, any Chinese passengers, deliver and report to the collector of customs of the district in which such vessels shall have arrived a separate list of all Chinese passengers taken on board his vessel at any foreign port or place, and all such passengers on board the vessel at that time. . . .

SEC. 9. That before any Chinese passengers are landed from any such vessel, the collector, or his deputy, shall proceed to examine such passengers, comparing the certificates with the list and with the passengers; and no passenger shall be allowed to land in the United States from such vessel in violation of law. . . .

SEC. 11. That any person who shall knowingly bring into or cause to be brought into the United States by land, or who shall knowingly aid or abet the same, or aid or abet the landing in the United States from any vessel of any Chinese person not lawfully entitled to enter the United states, shall be deemed guilty of a misdemeanor, and shall, on *conviction thereof, be fined in a sum not exceeding $1,000, and imprisoned for a term not exceeding one year.*

SEC. 12. That no Chinese person shall be permitted to enter the United States by land without producing to the proper officer of customs the certificate in this act required of Chinese persons seeking to land from a vessel. . . .

SEC. 13. That this act shall not apply to diplomatic and other officers of the Chinese Government traveling upon the business of that government, whose credentials shall be taken as equivalent to the certificate in this act mentioned, and shall exempt them and their body and household servants from the provisions of this act as to other Chinese persons.

SEC. 14. That hereafter no State court or court of the United States shall admit Chinese to citizenship; and all laws in conflict with this act are hereby repealed.

SEC. 15. That he words "Chinese laborers," wherever used in this act, shall be construed to mean both skilled and unskilled laborers and Chinese employed in mining.

Approved, May 6, 1882.

Source: The Statutes at Large of the United States of America. Vol. XXII. Washington, DC: Government Printing Office, 1883.

Books

Lee, Erika. *At America's Gates: Chinese Immigration during the Exclusion Era, 1882–1943.* Chapel Hill: University of North Carolina Press, 2004. Historian Erika Lee offers a transnational analysis on Chinese immigration history during the period of Chinese exclusion.

Soennichsen, John. *The Chinese Exclusion Act of 1882.* Santa Barbara, CA: Greenwood, 2011. This book traces the complete history and evolution of the Chinese Exclusion Act.

Websites

"The Chinese Exclusion Act (1882)." Ourdocuments.gov. U.S. National Archives & Records Administration. This site provides a digital image of the original act, along with a historical account of the passage of the act, and its subsequent evolution. https://www.ourdocuments.gov/doc.php?flash=true&doc=47. Accessed February 10, 2018.

"Chinese Immigration and the Chinese Exclusion Acts." Office of the Historian, Bureau of Public Affairs, U.S. Department of State. This site provides a historical background that led to the passage of the act. https://history.state.gov/milestones/1866-1898/chinese-immigration. Accessed February 10, 2018.

Also Noteworthy

1893

Three Chinese laborers are arrested for not carrying registration cards, in violation of Section 6 of the Geary Act. As a result, the men were ordered to be deported by the federal district court judge. A petition for *writ of habeas corpus* was filed for each man. The court dismissed the writs and ordered the men to be detained by the federal marshal. The cases were consolidated and appealed to the U.S. Supreme Court, in what is known as *Fong Yue Ting v. United States*, 149 U.S. 698 (1893).

1896

The U.S. Supreme court upholds the "separate but equal" concept in its decision on *Plessy v. Ferguson*. The decision legalizes "Jim Crow" laws for nearly 60 years.

1942

Merced, California, Assembly Center opens; it is in operation until September 15. Fresno, California, Assembly Center opens; it is in operation until October 30.

2013

Cecilia Chiang is awarded the 2013 James Beard Foundation Lifetime Achievement Award.

May 7

1843

Five Japanese subjects arrive in the United States. They were rescued at sea by an American whaler ship *John Howland* commanded by Captain William H. Whitfield. Among them was 14-year-old Manjiro Nakahama (January 27, 1827–November 2, 1898), also known as John Manjiro, or John Mung. After his rescue, he was educated at the Oxford School in Fairhaven, Massachusetts. He studied English and navigation and later signed on to the whaler *Franklin*, commanded by Captain Ira Davis. In 1860, he served as interpreter/translator for the first official Japanese delegation to the United States. In 1898, he died in Japan.

In July 1853, four black warships of the American navy under the command of Commodore Matthew Calbraith Perry appeared in Uraga Bay near Edo. . . . At that time, Manjiro may have been the only Japanese who was fluent in English and well-informed about the United States. Eight days after Commodore Perry's departure, the shogunate summoned Manjiro to Edo to work for the central government. He was given a higher samurai rank and made a retainer of the Shogun, which allowed him to have a family name. In the rigid class system of the Tokugawa period, only samurai had surnames while commoners such as merchants, craftsmen, and farmers had only given names. With a surname, a samurai could carry two swords and acquired a privileged status that he could pass on to his descendants. Manjiro chose the surname "Nakahama," after his hometown.

Source: Halloran, Fumiko Mori, Japanese Cultural Center of Hawaii, and the Joseph Heco Society of Hawaii. "John Manjiro: Whaler, Navigator, and Interpreter." In *Nakahama Manjiro's Hyosen kiryaku: A Companion Book*. Produced for the exhibition "Drifting: Nakahama Majiro's Tale of Discovery: An Illustrated Manuscript Recounting Ten Years of Adventure at Sea." Philadelphia, PA: Rosenbach Museum & Library, 1999, p. 21.

Books

Bernard, Donald. *The Life and Times of John Manjiro*. New York: McGraw-Hill, 1992. *The Life and Times of John Manjiro* is a well-documented and written history of the life of John Manjiro.

Kiryaku, Hyoson. *Drifting toward the Southeast: The Story of Five Japanese Castaways*. Translated by Junya Nagakuni and Junji Kitadai. New Bedford, MA: Spinner Publications, 2003. *Drifting toward the Southeast* provides comprehensive narrative of John Manjiro's life and legacy. It is a translated work, with maps, images, and photos.

Websites

Kingdon, Amorina. "Manjiro Nakahama: From Castaway to Samurai." This article published in *Hakai Magazine* provides images of John Manjiro's drawing and a detailed historical narrative of his life. https://www.hakaimagazine.com/article-short/manjiro-nakahama-castaway-samurai. Accessed August 31, 2017.

The Manjiro Society for International Exchange. This web page provides an introduction to John Manjiro with useful information and resources. http://www.manjiro.org/society.html. Accessed August 31, 2017.

1900

The first large-scale anti-Japanese protest takes place in San Francisco. It was organized by various labor groups. By 1905, the *San Francisco Chronicle* conducted an anti-Japanese campaign, warning of the invasion of Asiatics and the peril the state will face as a result.

Convention Meets To-Day to Protest Against Japs.

Delegates from labor organizations and civic and commercial bodies from all over the Convention proposed by the union labor interests of San Francisco. The convention is recognized as the most important held in California since the convention to protest against the unrestricted immigration of Chinese and will have a strong bearing upon the anti-Asiatic agitation which is gaining ground all over the country.

Delegates From Labor and Civic Bodies All Over State to Attend.

The meeting of the Anti-Japanese Convention at Lyric Hall this afternoon will mark an important epoch in the history of San Francisco, of California, and in fact of the whole country. No movement of recent years has been more important to the vital interests of the country than the agitation against the unrestricted immigration of a non-assimilative horde of Asiatics.

While the labor unions, the wage-earners of California, have taken the initiative in the movement, the question is one which affects every American, irrespective of occupation or affiliation. It is an admitted fact that the Japanese form a more dangerous element than the Chinese or the most undesirable immigrants from any other part of the globe. That assemblage will be a representative one admits of no doubt. Almost every organization having the welfare of the community at heart will be represented by duly accredited delegates.

Source: "Convention Meets To-Day to Protest against Japs." *San Francisco Chronicle*, May 7, 1905.

Books

Chuman, Frank. *The Bamboo People: The Law and Japanese-Americans*. Del Mar, CA: Publisher's Inc., 1976. *The Bamboo People* discusses the history and various core legal principles of the law and Japanese Americans.

Daniels, Roger. *The Politics of Prejudice: The Anti-Japanese Movement in California and the Struggle for Japanese Exclusion*. Berkeley: University of California Press, 1962. *The Politics of Prejudice* is a historical study of the anti-Japanese prejudice in California from the late 19th century to 1924.

Websites

Kamiya, Gary. "Chinatown School Was at Center of Anti-Japanese Crusade in S.F." *SF Gate*, August 22, 2014. This article discusses the anti-Japanese movement in California, its historical legacy, and provides archival images. http://www.sfgate.com/bayarea/article/Chinatown-school-was-at-center-of-anti-Japanese-5706859.php#photo-6760616. Accessed October 12, 2016.

Lyon, Cherstin. "Alien Land Law." *Densho Encyclopedia*, May 23, 2014. This site provides a historical overview of Alien Land Laws and other forms of anti-Japanese racism in the United States. http://encyclopedia.densho.org/Alien%20land%20laws/. Accessed October 12, 2016.

Also Noteworthy

1905

A Japanese and Korean Exclusion League is organized in San Francisco, California.

1942

Pinedale, California, Assembly Center opens; it is in operation until July 23. Pomona, California, Assembly Center opens and is in operation until August 24. Mayer, Arizona, Assembly Center opens and is in operation until June 2.

1945

Nazi Germany surrenders unconditionally to the Allies: Japan fights on alone.

2012

Vietnamese American Judge Jacqueline H. Nguyen is confirmed as the U.S. Ninth Circuit Court of Appeals judge by a U.S. Senate vote of 91–3. She is President Barack Obama's third nomination to the U.S. Ninth Circuit, a federal appellate court—one level below the U.S. Supreme Court and the largest of the nation's 13 Circuits of Appeal. The jurisdiction of the Ninth Circuit Court of Appeals includes the states of California, Arizona, Nevada, Oregon, Washington, Idaho, Montana, Alaska, and Hawaii. Judge Nguyen would fill a new appellate seat in San Francisco, California.

May 8

1957

Ngo Dinh Diem, South Vietnamese president, arrives in the United States on a state visit and is recognized for his success.

> *[Ngo Dinh] Diem's American tour was the high point of his presidency among his American benefactors. He enjoyed for greater popularity within the United States than he did in his own country. Diem was invited to address a joint session of Congress. Diem enjoyed a tickertape parade in his honor down Broadway and attended a private Mass celebrated by Cardinal Spellman. He was feted at public gatherings as the gutsy leader had overcome the inveterate political fragmentation of Saigon to create a strong, stable government, a showcase of freedom. He was the patriotic Vietnamese leader who was more than a match for Ho Chi Minh. South Vietnam was offered to the world as a model of enlightened U.S. foreign policy in action. The South Vietnamese had established a free society and were holding the line against the further spread of Communism in Indochina. Diem was the leader of his people fighting on the front lines of freedom, stemming the Communist tide.*
>
> *Source*: Moss, George. *Vietnam: An American Ordeal*. 6th ed. London: Routledge, 2016, pp. 68–69.

Books

Elkind, Jessica. *Aid under Fire: Nation Building and the Vietnam War*. Lexington: The University Press of Kentucky, 2016. *Aid under Fire* is a history of U.S. nation building in Vietnam during the decade preceding the full-scale ground war in Vietnam.

Jacobs, Seth. *America's Miracle Man in Vietnam: Ngo Dinh Diem, Religion, Race, and U.S. Intervention in Southeast Asia*. Durham, NC: Duke University Press, 2004. *America's Miracle Man in Vietnam* argues that Diem, from the very beginning, was an American creation, which doomed his attempt to establish a government to fail.

Websites

"New York Hails Vietnam's President Diem (1957)." Youtube.com. Posted 2014. This site provides archival video footage of Diem being hailed at the parade in New York during his state visit. https://www.youtube.com/watch?v=8Rj8-qxROFc. Accessed September 30, 2017.

"President Ngo Dinh Diem of South Vietnam Addressed a Joint Meeting of Congress." History, Art & Archives. U.S. House of Representatives. This site provides an overview of Ngo's speech and is companied by photos and links for further research. http://history.house.gov/HistoricalHighlight/Detail/35131?ret=True. Accessed September 30, 2017.

Also Noteworthy

1942

Marysville, California, Assembly Center opens; it is in operation until June 29, 1942.

1950

Chiang Kai-shek asks the United States for weapons.

May 9

1909

In response to low wages, poor working conditions, and long hours, thousands of Japanese laborers working on Oahu's sugar plantations go on strike. The strikers were supported by laborers from other plantation with donations of food and money. During the strike, opponents called those demanding wage increases "agitators," "irresponsible men," "opportunists," and "outlaws"; similarly, those who were against the strike were called "planters' dogs," "planters' pigs," "insurgents," "traitors," and "Czarist spies." The strikers and their families were expelled from the plantations and eventually returned to work.

Like a fire racing across dry cane fields, one of the most massive and sustained strikes in the history of Hawaii swept through the plantations of Oahu in 1909. On the night of May 9, several hundred Japanese laborers gathered at the Aiea Plantation mill camp to demand higher wages. Throughout the evening, "worked up by the beating of empty kerosene tins," the discontented laborers discussed the need for action. At five o'clock in the morning, they decided to strike and three "banzais" thundered through the camps. Two days later Japanese laborers on the nearby Waipahu Plantation followed the lead of the Aiea strikers. Suddenly the strike spread from plantation to planation—Waialua on the 19th, Kahuku on the 22d, Waianae on the 23d, Ewa on the 24th, and Waimanalo on the 26th. Altogether seven thousand Japanese laborers acted collectively in a struggle which became known as the "Great Strike."

The strike of 1909 was indeed a great one. Where earlier strikes were usually protests against mistreatment from lunas, the 1909 strike had a definite and singular economic focus: higher wages. Where earlier strikes were confined to individual plantations, the 1909 strike involved all of the major plantations on Oahu. Where earlier strikes lasted only a few days, the 1909 strike was a protracted four-month long conflict. Finally, where earlier strikes were usually spontaneous actions, the 1909 strike was well organized, spearheaded by an articulate and educated leadership, an influential network of Japanese newspaper, and effective inter-island strike support system.

Source: Takaki, Ronald. *Pau Hana: Plantation Life and Labor in Hawaii*. Honolulu: University of Hawaii Press, 1983, p. 153.

Books

Duus, Masayo Umezawa. *The Japanese Conspiracy: The Oahu Sugar Strike of 1920*. Translated by Beth Cary and adapted by Peter Duus. Berkeley: University of California Press, 1999. *The Japanese Conspiracy* provides a historical discussion of labor strikes in Hawaii, with particular focus on the strike of 1920.

Okihiro, Gary. *Cane Fires: The Anti-Japanese Movement in Hawai'i, 1865–1945*. Philadelphia, PA: Temple University Press, 1991. *Cane Fires* is a well-researched history of anti-Japanese movements in the United States, with an emphasis on Hawaii.

Websites

"History of Labor in Hawai'i." University of Hawaii at West Oahu. Center for Labor Education & Research. This site provides a historical overview of labor history in Hawaii that includes Japanese immigration and laborer strikes. https://www.hawaii.edu/uhwo/clear/home/HawaiiLaborHistory.html. Accessed September 5, 2017.

"Labor Strikes." Hawai'i Digital Newspaper Project. This site provides a chronological discussion of labor strikes in Hawaii and links to an archive of historical newspaper covering the strikes. https://sites.google.com/a/hawaii.edu/ndnp-hawaii/Home/subject-and-topic-guides/labor-strikes. Accessed September 5, 2017.

May 10

1869

On this day, known as "Golden Spike Day," the Transcontinental Railroad is officially completed. After digging 13 tunnels through solid granite in the Sierras, after losing more than a thousand of Chinese workers to snow avalanches and other hazards never mentioned in the labor contracts, the first transcontinental railroad is completed. Ninety percent of the laborers who built the Central Pacific section from California to Utah were Chinese immigrants. Ten thousand Chinese laborers became unemployed, and many found work in agriculture.

On May 10, 1869 the transcontinental railroad was officially completed with the ceremonial driving of the golden spike. It activated a telegraph that sent the message of the line's completion to the great cities of the east. That night the actual golden spike was carefully removed and replaced with a regular iron spike, lest the historical artifact be stolen.

Source: Carlisle, Rodney, ed. *Handbook of Life in America, Volume III. The Civil War and Reconstruction 1860 to 1876*. New York: Facts on File, 2009, p. 121.

Books

Annian, Huang, ed. *The Silent Spikes: Chinese Laborers and the Construction of North American Railroads*. Translated by Zhang Juguo. Beijing: China Intercontinental Press, 2006. This is one of the books that specifically focuses on the history and contribution of the Chinese laborers who built the transcontinental railroad.

Williams, John. *A Great and Shining Road: The Epic Story of the Transcontinental Railroad*. Lincoln: University of Nebraska Press, 1988. Historian John Williams writes the story of the mammoth undertaking, science, political courage, engineering, and industry and heroism of the laborers who accomplished the completion of the railroad.

Websites

"Chinese-American Contribution to Transcontinental Railroad." Central Pacific Railroad Photographic History Museum. This site provides historic photos, in addition to historical quotes from primary sources, and links to multimedia materials. http://cprr.org/Museum/Chinese.html. Accessed January 29, 2018.

"Chinese Railroad Workers in North American Project." Stanford University. This site provides comprehensive historical information on the history of Chinese railroad workers. It contains a digital archive, oral histories, photographs, and much more useful information for anyone interested on this topic. http://web.stanford.edu/group/chineserailroad/cgi-bin/wordpress/. Accessed January 29, 2018.

1886

Yick Wo is a Chinese laundryman who is jailed for operating a laundry in a wooden building because it violated a San Francisco statute. However, for over 22 years, previous fire and safety revealed no violations. In *Yick Wo v. Hopkins*, the U.S. Supreme Court, in a unanimous opinion, invoked the Equal Protection Clause of the Fourteenth Amendment to protect Chinese laundry owners against an ordinance that on its face was race neutral but was applied in a prejudicial manner.

Mr. JUSTICE MATTHEWS delivered the opinion of the court.

In the case of the petitioner, brought here by writ of error to the Supreme Court of California, our jurisdiction is limited to the question whether the plaintiff in error has been denied a right in violation of the Constitution, laws, or treaties of the United States. The question whether his imprisonment is illegal under the constitution and lass of the State is not open to us. And although that question might have been considered in the Circuit Court in the application made to it, and by this court on appeal from its order, yet judicial propriety is best consulted by accepting the judgment of the State court upon the points involved in that inquiry. . . .

That, however, does not preclude this court from putting upon the ordinances of the supervisors of the county and city of San Francisco an independent construction, for the determination of the question whether the proceedings under these ordinances and in enforcement of them are in conflict with the Constitution and laws of the United States necessarily involves the meaning of the ordinance, which, for that purpose, we are required to ascertain and adjudge. . . .

The Fourteenth Amendment to the Constitution is not confined to the protection of citizens. It says:

"Nor shall any State deprive any person of life, liberty, or property without due process of law; nor deny to any person within its jurisdiction the equal protection of the laws."

These provisions are universal in their application to all persons within the territorial jurisdiction, without regard to any differences of race, of color, or of nationality, and the equal protection of the laws is a pledge of the protection of equal laws. It is accordingly enacted by § 1977 of the Revised Statutes, that "all persons within the jurisdiction of the United States shall have the same right in every State and Territory to make and enforce contracts, to sue, be parties, give evidence, and to the full and equal benefit of all laws and proceedings for the security of persons and property as is enjoyed by white citizens and shall be subject to like punishment, pains, penalties, taxes, licenses, and exactions of every kind, and to no other."

The questions we have to consider and decide in these cases, therefore, are to be treated as invoking the rights of every citizen of the United States equally with those of the strangers and aliens who now invoke the jurisdiction of the court.

It is contended on the part of the petitioners that the ordinances for violations of which they are severally sentenced to imprisonment are void on their face as being within the prohibitions of the Fourteenth Amendment, and, in the alternative, if not so, that they are void by reason of their administration, operating unequally so as to punish in the present petitioners what is permitted to others as lawful, without any distinction of circumstances—an unjust and illegal discrimination, it is claimed, which, though not made expressly by the ordinances, is made possible by them. . . .

The present cases, as shown by the facts disclosed in the record, are within this class. It appears that both petitioners have complied with every requisite deemed by the law or by the public officers charged with its administration necessary for the protection of neighboring property from fire or as a precaution against injury to the public health. No reason whatever, except the will of the supervisors, is assigned why they should not be permitted to carry on, in the accustomed manner, their harmless and useful occupation, on which they depend for a livelihood. And while this consent of the supervisors is withheld from them and from two hundred others who have also petitioned, all of whom happen to be Chinese subjects, eighty others, not Chinese subjects, are permitted to carry on the same business under similar conditions. The fact of this discrimination is admitted. No reason for it is shown, and the conclusion cannot be resisted that no reason for it exists except hostility to the race and nationality to which the petitioners belong, and which, in the eye of the law, is not justified. The discrimination is, therefore, illegal, and the public administration which enforces it is a denial of the equal protection of the laws and a violation of the Fourteenth Amendment of the Constitution. The imprisonment of the petitioners is, therefore, illegal, and they must be discharged. To this end,

The judgment of the Supreme Court of California in the case of Yick Wo, and that of the Circuit Court of the United States for the District of California in the case of Wo Lee, are severally reversed, and the cases remanded, each to the proper court, with directions to discharge the petitioners from custody and imprisonment.

Source: Yick Wo v. Hopkins, 118 U.S. 356 (1886).

Books

McClain, Charles, ed. *Chinese Immigrants and American Law.* New York: Garland Publishing, Inc., 1991. See Charles McClain's Chapter 7, "The Chinese Struggle for Civil Rights in Nineteenth-Century America: The First Phase, 1850–1870."

Szmanko, Klara. *Visions of Whiteness in Selected Works of Asian American Literature.* Jefferson, NC: McFarland & Company, 2015. Chapter 2, "Demonic and Oxymoronic Whiteness in Maxine Hong Kingston's *China Men*," discusses *Yick Wo v. Hopkins.*

Websites

Yick Wo and the Equal Protection Clause. The Constitution Project. This site contains a 20-minute documentary on *Yick Wo v. Hopkins.* In addition, it provides an essay that covers the history and legacy of the case. 2016. http://www.theconstitutionproject.com/portfolio/yick-wo-and-the-equal-protection-clause/. Accessed October 8, 2016.

Yick Wo v. Hopkins (1886). JUSTIA U.S. Supreme Court. This site provides the full text of the ruling. https://supreme.justia.com/cases/federal/us/118/356/case.html. Accessed January 29, 2018.

1905

China begins a nationwide boycott against U.S. products to protest anti-Chinese discrimination in the United States. Chinese Americans supported the boycott with donations.

In addition, they sent vivid descriptions of life in the United States under anti-Chinese legislation and sentiments. The boycott expressed opposition to the injustice of Chinese exclusion policies and the exploitation and ingratitude toward the Chinese laborers for their contribution to the development of America. It was also a transnational event that meaningfully linked the Chinese to Chinese Americans politically, and more importantly, developed into a moment of national awareness for the Chinese in China. It was the moment when modern Chinese nationalism emerged and played an important part in China-U.S. relations moving forward.

The significance of the 1905 boycott stems not from its impact on the U.S. policy of Chinese exclusion, which was minimal, but from its transformation of China's political landscape and of the political consciousness of the Chinese people. The anti-American boycott of 1905–1906 marked the beginning of mass politics and modern nationalism in China. Never before had shared nationalistic aspirations mobilized Chinese across the world in political action, joining the cause of Chinese migrants with the fate of the Chinese nation. All Chinese could sympathize with Chinese immigrants detained for months in wooden sheds, stripped and examined for diseases, questioned harshly, and often deported, their chances for a decent livelihood lost. That image personalized the impact of foreign powers over Chinese people, and, by extension, over China.

Millions of Chinese in China and abroad were moved by the boycott action, which they learned about in newspapers or novels if they could read or in speeches, plays, and songs if they could not. Boycott rallies attracted thousands. Merchants stopped buying and selling American products, or if they refused, boycott committees put on the pressure. . . .

From the very beginning of the movement, the boycott ideology linked China's weakness with American imperialism.

Source: Larson, Jane Leung. "The 1905 Anti-American Boycott as a Transnational Chinese Movement." *Chinese America: History & Perspectives*, 2007, p. 191.

Books

Cassel, Susie Lan, ed. *The Chinese in America: A History from Gold Mountain to the New Millennium.* Walnut Creek, CA: AltaMira Press, 2002. *The Chinese in America* is a complete history of Chinese immigration to the United States since the mid-1800s that focuses on politics and the contemporary racism that still impacts the Chinese American communities.

Gries, Peter Hays. China's New Nationalism: Pride, Politics, and Diplomacy. Berkeley: University of California Press, 2004. *China's New Nationalism* explores various aspects of China-U.S. and China–Japan relations.

Websites

Foster, John. "The Chinese Boycott." *Atlantic Monthly* 97, no. 1 (January 1906): 118–127. This site provides a historic account of the boycott published in the *Atlantic* in 1906. http://www.theatlantic.com/past/docs/unbound/flashbks/china/foster.htm. Accessed October 13, 2016.

Zhang, Yunqiu. "Chinese Boycott of 1905." Immigration to the United States. This site provides a historical overview of the Chinese boycott of 1905 and a discussion of its significance. http://immigrationtounitedstates.org/421-chinese-boycott-of-1905.html. Accessed October 13, 2016.

Also Noteworthy

1906

The Korean Presbyterian Church of Los Angeles is founded by a group of Korean residents.

2004

In Miami, Florida, a Muslim mosque is broken into and ransacked.

May 11

1937

Taiwanese Buddhist nun and philanthropist, Cheng Yen, is born. Dharma Master Cheng

Yen, along with a group of 30 followers, founded Tzu Chi in Hualien, Taiwan, in 1966. Currently, Tzu Chi is the largest civil organization in Taiwan. In 1993, the Tzu Chi Foundation established its Free Clinic in Alhambra, California. The clinic is a general health care facility providing medical assistance to financially disadvantaged residents in Los Angeles. It incorporates traditional Chinese healing with Western medicine and Buddhist philosophies of compassion to serve clients without regard to age, sex, race, class, or religious affiliation.

Tzu Chi's mission is focused on charity, medicine, education, and culture. As such, Tzu Chi is intimately involved in providing social, educational, charitable, and medical relief to the underprivileged and underserved throughout and beyond Taiwan, reaching the United States and other parts of Asia, including mainland China. Tzu Chi has been especially proficient at providing disaster relief after typhoons, floods, and earthquakes. The provision of international relief started in 1991, when the American branch of Tzu Chi in Los Angeles helped victims of a cyclone in Bangladesh. After the serious earthquake in Taiwan on September 21, 1999, Tzu Chi relief workers did most of the early rescue work as government officials dallied over who had jurisdiction. In addition, Tzu Chi has continuously provided medical and charitable relief to areas in Southeast Asia following the December 26, 2004, tsunamis and earthquake. Tzu Chi U.S.A. became a national player in relief work following the terrorist attacks of 9/11 in New York City and in the aftermath of Hurricane Katrina that shattered the Gulf Coast. In the United States alone, there are a total of 49 Tzu Chi branches, including three free clinics.

Source: Lee, Jonathan H.X. "Tzu Chi Foundation U.S.A." In *Asian American Religious Cultures*, edited by Jonathan H.X. Lee, Fumitaka Matsuoka, Edmond Yee, and Ronald Y. Nakasone, p. 927. Santa Barbara: ABC-CLIO, 2015.

Books

Huang, C.J. *Charisma and Compassion: Cheng Yen and the Buddhist Tzu Chi Movement*. Cambridge, MA: Harvard University Press, 2009. *Charisma and Compassion* provides detailed information about Dharma Master Cheng Yen and the Tzu Chi organization worldwide.

Laliberté, André. *The Politics of Buddhist Organizations in Taiwan, 1989–2003: Safeguard the Faith, Build a Pure Land, Help the Poor*. New York: Routledge, 2004. *The Politics of Buddhist Organizations in Taiwan* discusses Tzu Chi's history and development in Taiwan.

Websites

Tzu Chi USA. 2017. This is the official website of Tzu Chi USA. It provides essays on its history, mission, and access to its journals and publications. https://www.tzuchi.us/. Accessed September 30, 2017.

Tzu Chi USA Facebook. This is the Facebook account for Tzu Chi USA that provides up-to-date activities at various Tzu Chi USA locations. https://www.facebook.com/TzuChiUSA/. Accessed September 30, 2017.

Also Noteworthy

2004

In Omaha, Nebraska, a 33-year-old man leaves two threatening voice messages on an Islamic center's answering machine.

May 12

1961

Vice President Lyndon B. Johnson meets with South Vietnamese president Ngo Dinh Diem in Saigon during his two-week tour of South and Southeast Asia. Johnson refers to Diem as "the Churchill of Asia" while assuring Diem that he is crucial to U.S. objectives in Vietnam, and its larger mission of curtailing the spread of communism in Southeast Asia.

"Joint Communique, Saigon, May 13, 1961"

Lyndon B. Johnson, Vice President of the United States, has just completed a visit to the Republic of

Viet-Nam, on behalf of President Kennedy and on invitation of President Ngo Dinh Diem. The enthusiastic welcome he received in Viet-Nam reflected a deep sense of common cause in the fight for freedom in Southeast Asia and around the world. This recognition of mutual objectives resulted in concrete understandings between the Republic of Viet-Nam and the United States. It is clear to the Government and the people of Viet-Nam and to the United States that the independence and territorial integrity of Viet-Nam are being brutally and systematically violated by Communist agents and forces from the north. It is also clear to both Governments that action must be strengthened and accelerated to protect the legitimate rights and aspirations of the people of free Viet-Nam to choose their own way of life. The two Governments agreed that this is the basic principle upon which their understandings rest. The United States, for its part, is conscious of the determination, energy and sacrifices which the Vietnamese people, under the dedicated leadership of President Ngo Dinh Diem, have brought to the defense of freedom in their land. The United States is also conscious of its responsibility and duty, in its own self-interest as well as in the interest of other free peoples, to assist a brave country in the defense of its liberties against unprovoked subversion and Communist terror. It has no other motive than the defense of freedom. The United States recognizes that the President of the Republic of Viet-Nam, Ngo Dinh Diem, who was recently reelected to office by an overwhelming majority of his countrymen despite bitter Communist opposition, is in the vanguard of those leaders who stand for freedom on the periphery of the Communist empire in Asia. Free Viet-Nam cannot alone withstand the pressure which this Communist empire is exerting against it. Under these circumstances—the need of free Viet-Nam for increased and accelerated emergency assistance and the will and determination of the United States to provide such assistance to those willing to fight for their liberties—it is natural that a large measure of agreement on the means to accomplish the joint purpose was found in high-level conversations between the two Governments. Both Governments recognize that under the circumstances of guerrilla warfare now existing in free Viet-Nam, it is necessary to give high priority to the restoration of a sense of security to the people of free Viet-Nam. This priority, however, in no way diminishes the necessity, in policies and programs of both Governments, to pursue vigorously appropriate measures in other fields to achieve a prosperous and happy society.

Source: Department of State Bulletin 36 (June 19, 1961): pp. 956–957.

Books

Tucker, Spencer, ed. *The Encyclopedia of the Vietnam War: A Political, Social, and Military History*. Santa Barbara, CA: ABC-CLIO, 2011. *The Encyclopedia of the Vietnam War* is a comprehensive resource for students studying the Vietnam War.

Willbanks, James, ed. *Vietnam War: The Essential Reference Guide*. Santa Barbara, CA: ABC-CLIO, 2013. *Vietnam War: The Essential Reference Guide* examines the Vietnam War and discusses its relevance today.

Websites

Cosmas, Graham. *History of the Joint Chiefs of Staff. The Joint Chiefs of Staff and the War in Vietnam: 1960–1968. Part 2*. Washington, DC: Office of the Chairman of the Joint Chiefs of Staff, 2012. This is a comprehensive government publication of U.S. policy documents related to the Vietnam War. http://www.jcs.mil/Portals/36/Documents/History/Vietnam/Vietnam_1960-1968_P002.pdf. Accessed September 4, 2017.

Lindsay, James. "The Vietnam War in Forty Quotes." Council on Foreign Relations. April 30, 2015. This site provides a historical narrative on U.S. policy during the Vietnam War through primary source quotes. https://www.cfr.org/blog/vietnam-war-forty-quotes. Accessed September 4, 2017.

Also Noteworthy

1999

Police officers arrest a man parked in front of the Colorado Islamic center, who possessed bomb-making materials, semiautomatic guns, and other ammunitions, who was planning an attack on the site.

2003

In Bensalem, Pennsylvania, three boys, two white 13-year-olds and one black 12-year-old, attack an 8-year-old boy of Middle Eastern descent while calling him "you Saddam Hussein helper" and telling him to "go back to Iraq."

2004

In Miami, Florida, swastikas and vulgarities are tagged at an Islamic school.

2007

In Little Falls, New Jersey, David Liscio, a 32-year-old, is charged with harassment and making terroristic threats and biased intimidation after he shouted racial slurs at a Latino Muslim American woman.

May 13

1942

On this day, Gordon K. Hirabayashi, a Nisei, and his Quaker lawyer, Art Barnet, present themselves at the Seattle FBI office. Because of his American citizenship and Christian religious principles, Gordon Hirabayashi believed that both the curfew and mass detention were unnecessary, discriminatory, and unjust. He decided to resist both orders, on principle, and retained a lawyer. Hirabayashi's decision caught the attention of progressive Seattle community leaders, and quickly his stand garnered the status of a test case with support on the part of religious and political sympathizers. With the support of the Gordon Hirabayashi Defense Committee, made up of progressive supporters in the University District, the initial trial proceeded. Lawyer Frank Walters argued the Fifth Amendment right of due process was violated by the exclusion order, emphasizing that Gordon had never been accused of posing a danger in terms of espionage or sabotage, the two ostensible reasons for the exclusion proclamation. He moved that the Court dismiss the indictment on the grounds that the defendant had been deprived of liberty and property without due process of law. Furthermore, Gordon and his lawyer charged that Executive Order (EO) 9066, Proclamations 2 and 3, and Civilian Exclusion Order #57 of the military commander, as well as Public Law #503, were all unconstitutional and void. The judge pronounced Gordon guilty of each offense charged in the two counts of the indictment. His trial lasted just one day. Although he was imprisoned, the charges against Hirabayashi were amended to include violation of the curfew order. A lower court found him guilty on both charges and sentenced him to 90 days in prison. Hirabayashi appealed the verdict and appeared before the court of appeals on February 19, 1943, exactly one year after EO 9066. Although the court avoided issuing opinions on the legality of evacuation, it ruled unanimously that Congress had the right to make and enforce curfew laws.

Hirabayashi prepared a two-page written statement, "Why I Refuse to Register for Evacuation."

Hirabayashi writes:

Over and above any man-made creed or law is the natural law of life—the right of human individuals to live and to creatively express themselves. No man was born with the right to limit that law. Nor, do I believe, can anyone justifiably work himself to such a position.

Down through the ages, we have had various individuals doing their bit to establish more securely these fundamental rights. They have tried to help society see the necessity of understanding those fundamental laws; some have succeeded to the extent of having these natural laws recorded. Many have suffered unnatural deaths as a result of their convictions. Yet, today, because of the efforts of some of these individuals, we have recorded in the laws of our nation certain rights for all men and certain additional rights for citizens. These fundamental moral rights and civil liberties are included in the Bill of Rights, U.S. Constitution and other legal records. They guarantee that these fundamental rights shall not be denied without due process of law.

The principles or the ideals are the things which give value to a person's life. They are the qualities which give impetus and purpose toward meaningful experiences. The violation of human personality is the violation of the most sacred thing which man owns.

This order for the mass evacuation of all persons of Japanese descent denies them the right to live. It forces thousands of energetic, law-abiding individuals to exist in a miserable psychological and a horrible physical atmosphere. This order limits to almost the full extent the creative expressions of those subjected. It kills the desire for a higher life. Hope for the future is exterminated. Human personalities are poisoned. The very qualities which are essential to a peaceful, creative community are being thrown out and abused. Over 60 percent are American citizens, yet they are denied on a wholesale scale without due process of law the civil liberties which are theirs.

If I were to register and cooperate under those circumstances, I would be giving helpless consent to the denial of practically all of the things which give me incentive to live. I must maintain my Christian principles. I consider it my duty to maintain the democratic standards for which this nation lives. Therefore, I must refuse this order for evacuation.

Let me add, however, that in refusing to register, I am well aware of the excellent qualities of the army and government personnel connected with the prosecution of this exclusion order. They are men of the finest type, and I sincerely appreciate their sympathetic and honest efforts. Nor do I intend to cast any shadow upon the Japanese and the other Nisei who have registered for evacuation. They have faced tragedy admirably. I am objecting to the principle of this order, which denies the rights of human beings, including citizens. [May 13, 1942]

Source: Gordon K. Hirabayashi letter titled "Why I Refused to Register for Evacuation." May 13, 1942. University of Washington, University Libraries, Digital Collection. http://digitalcollections.lib.washington.edu/cdm/ref/collection/pioneerlife/id/21356. Accessed March 7, 2017.

Books

Hirabayashi, Gordon, James Hirabayashi, and Lane Ryo Hirabayashi. *A Principled Stand: The Story of Hirabayashi v. United States*. Seattle: University of Washington Press. 2013. *A Principled Stand* is a memoir of Gordon Hirabayashi's account of his family's history, internment, and his protest of World War II policies of internment.

Irons, Peter. *Justice at War: The Story of the Japanese American Internment Cases*. Berkeley: University of California Press, 1993. *Justice at War* reveals the U.S. government's attempt to suppress, alter, and destroy critical evidence that could have persuaded the U.S. Supreme Court to strike down the World War II internment order.

Websites

Hirabayashi, Gordon. "Gordon Hirabayashi: Why I Refused to Register for Japanese Evacuation." Crosscut.com. April 11, 2013. This essay is Gordon Hirabayashi's reflection on his act of civil disobedience in protest of unjust wartime policies to intern Japanese Americans. http://crosscut.com/2013/04/principled-stand-recounts-wwii-politics-pacific-no/. Accessed October 4, 2017.

Ikeda, Tom. "Japanese Americans in Seattle." Discover Kikkei: Japanese Migrants and Their Descendants. Japanese American National Museum. 2017. This site provides historical background of the Japanese American community and history in Seattle, including a detailed discussion of Gordon Hirabayashi's act of civil disobedience with archival photos, links to videos of Hirabayashi, and other resources. http://www.discovernikkei.org/en/journal/2013/11/25/japanese-americans-seattle/. Accessed October 4, 2017.

Also Noteworthy

1889

The U.S. Supreme Court decides, in *Chae Chan Ping v. U.S.*, that despite the Burlingame Treaty of 1868, the United States could freely prevent Chinese from immigrating to the United States. Thus, the decision upholds constitutionality of Chinese exclusion law.

1913

Korean nationalist organization Hungsadan (Corps for the Advancement of Individuals), also known as the Young Korean Academy, is established in San Francisco. Its purpose was to improve the lives of Koreans living overseas so that they can provide leadership for the restoration of Korea's sovereignty.

1942

The War Relocation Authority and the Wartime Civil Control Administration permit recruitment of seasonal farm laborers at assembly and war relocation centers. During May 20–21, the first internees left for sugar beet fields in eastern Oregon.

May 14

1905

The Asiatic Exclusion League is established in San Francisco by 67 labor unions. Eventually over 200 labor unions joined the league to restrict Asian immigration to the United States. The Asiatic Exclusion League met at Council Hall, 316 14th St., San Francisco, California, on January 5, 1908, to discuss concerns about "the invasion of the Pacific Coast, especially California, by Japanese laborers, together with the methods used by them in gaining admission to the mainland of the United States."

The Japanese Invasion

The fruits of the various Chinese Restriction Acts were enjoyed by the people of the Pacific Coast for a very short time because, immediately following the decrease in the number of Chinese coolies, another evil closely followed upon their retreating footsteps. This evil—the Japanese—crept in so easily, so gradually, so secretly, that its danger was not fully recognized by the people at large until after the year 1890. It is true that in the middle eighties, industrial strife had been precipitated by the employment of large numbers of Japanese in the Coast shipping and mines of British Columbia, and it was hoped that the defeat of the ship owners by the Coast Seamen's Union would cause the elimination of that class of labor from among us. The hope was vain. The daily press, from time to time, would call attention to the arrival of Japanese laborers, but they would quietly move to the farming districts where they attracted but little attention, until the white laborers who had been in the habit of obtaining employment throughout the interior, were confronted with, to them, an appalling condition—seeking employment and being refused the same, while gangs of Japanese were busily engaged performing the work which had formerly, and of right, been performed by the actual and prospective American citizen.

Source: Proceedings of the Asiatic Exclusion League. San Francisco, CA: Organized Labor Print, January 1908, p. 10.

Books

Daniels, Roger. *The Politics of Prejudice: The Anti-Japanese Movement in California and the Struggle for Japanese Exclusion.* Berkeley: University of California Press, 1962. *The Politics of Prejudice* examines anti-Japanese sentiment, policies, and racism in California from the late 19th century to 1924. It argues that the anti-Japanese political climate and policies set the stage for the unlawful incarceration of Japanese Americans during World War II.

Osborne, Thomas. *Pacific Eldorado: A History of Greater California.* Chichester, England: John Wiley & Sons, Ltd, 2013. *Pacific Eldorado* covers the entire span of California history, with a focus on the maritime world of the Pacific Basin.

Websites

"Asiatic Coolie Invasion." Virtual Museum of the City of San Francisco. This site provides a history of the Asiatic Exclusion League, established in San Francisco, and contains primary documents, images, and other useful archival materials. http://www.sfmuseum.org/1906.2/invasion.html. Accessed October 13, 2016.

"Finding Aid to the Asiatic Exclusion League Records." Labor Archives and Research Center. San Francisco State University. Online Archive of California. This site contains information on the Asiatic Exclusion League's archival, with a historical description. http://www.oac.cdlib.org/findaid/ark:/13030/c89k4c1p/entire_text/. Accessed October 13, 2016.

Also Noteworthy

1900

Hawaii becomes a U.S. territory, and Sanford Dole is appointed its first governor.

1997

The Laos and Hmong Veterans of America Memorial is dedicated in Washington, D.C.

May 15

1893

Fong Yue Ting v. U.S. upholds the constitutionality of Geary Act. In this ruling the U.S. Supreme Court declared that Congress had the power to exclude noncitizens from entering as well as deport them from the United States. The Court upheld a law that required a noncitizen seeking to avoid deportation to produce a "credible white witness" to vouch for their physical presence in the United States prior to a certain time. The Chinese community had raised money to bring this before the Court to test the Geary Act.

On May 6, 1893, Fong Yue Ting, Wong Quan, and Lee Joe became the main litigants in what would become a landmark Supreme Court decision in immigration and constitutional law. That was the day U.S. Marshal John W. Jacobus arrested them for failure to comply with the Geary Act of 1892, which required all resident Chinese laborers to register with the government. The same day, Judge Addison Brown of the U.S. District Court for the Southern District of New York ordered the three Chinese resident aliens to be deported, but they were released by the circuit court pending an appeal to the U.S. Supreme Court. Only nine days later, the Supreme Court decided their case, upholding the constitutionality of the Geary Act and, in the process, granting the federal government sweeping power to deport resident aliens with few, if any, procedural restrictions. . . .

All three were Chinese laborers who had come . . . in the late 1870s, before the Chinese exclusion law was passed. They lived in New York City; Fong Yue Ting gave his address as 1 Mott Street in the heart of the Chinese enclave. The records are silent as to their specific occupations . . . or the paths their lives took after they lost.

Source: Salyer, Lucy. "Fong Yue Ting: The Chinese Campaign for Civil Rights." In *100 Americans Making Constitutional History: A Biographical History*, edited by Melvin Urofsky, p. 62. Washington, DC: CQ Press, 2004.

Books

Dowling, Julie, and Jonathan Xavier Inda, ed. *Governing Immigration through Crime: A Reader*. Palo Alto, CA: Stanford University Press, 2013. See chapter by Jennifer Chacón, "The Security Myth: Punishing Immigrants in the Name of National Security."

Law, Anna. *The Immigration Battle in American Courts*. Cambridge: Cambridge University Press, 2010. Constitutional professor of American law Anna Law traces the history of immigration cases from the U.S. Supreme Court and U.S. Courts of Appeals.

Websites

"Fong Yue Ting v. United States, 149 U.S. 698 (1893)." JUSTIA U.S. Supreme Court. The full text of this case is available here. https://supreme.justia.com/cases/federal/us/149/698/case.html. Accessed October 9, 2016.

Lewis, Thomas Tandy. "Fong Yue Ting v. United States." Immigration to the United States. This site discusses the history and significance of *Fong Yue Ting v. U.S.* http://immigrationtounitedstates.org/503-fong-yue-ting-v-united-states.html. Accessed October 9, 2016.

Also Noteworthy

1861

John Tomney (d. 1863) enlists in New York City to fight for the Union Army in First Regiment Excelsior Brigade, Company D, making him one of the earliest volunteers. He is the only Chinese solider known to have been killed in action during the American civil war. Military records indicate he was 18 years old and of Chinese descent.

2008

Dance of the Dragon, the Bruce Lee story, is released, starring Chinese Hawaiian actor Jason Scott Lee (b. November 19, 1966).

2015

The Cambodian American Heritage Museum & Killing Fields Memorial obtains 501(c)(3) status in Chicago, Illinois.

May 16

1924

Written at a time when fear over anarchism and Bolshevism was widespread, the Immigration Act of 1924, also known as the Johnson-Reed Act, reflects nativist sentiment and restricts immigration from southern Europe and the Mediterranean through the use of national origins quotas. The 1924 law stated that number of immigrants to be admitted annually was limited to 2 percent of the foreign-born individuals of each nationality residing in the United States in 1890. Although the act itself contained no specific mention of the Japanese, it effectively ended Issei immigration and impacted future relations between the United States and Japan.

Although they were not named specifically, the act contained a provision prohibiting the immigration to the United States of any "aliens ineligible for citizenship," as determined by the 1790 Naturalization Act. As Chinese and Asian Indians had already been excluded by previous legislation, it was understood that the Japanese were being singled out and targeted. The 1924 act served as the culmination of the legal decisions aimed at restricting Japanese immigration and the ability to naturalize.

The Japanese community in the United States and the Meiji government staged public protests and rallies against the passing of the act. Despite the international outrage, President Calvin Coolidge signed the bill into law on May 26, 1924. It would not be until the passing of the Immigration and Nationality Act of 1952 that Japanese would become eligible for admission into the United States (with the exception of war brides of American servicemen post–World War II.)

To the Chinese the Act of 1924 was but another form of persecution and "gratuitous affront" added to a condition that was already severe enough.... [T]he Act of 1924 did not repeal the Chinese Exclusion Act of 1882. Consequently, the Chinese are now subjected to the rules and regulations connected with the two systems of exclusion. For over forty years, the Chinese had battled with the administrative authorities against what they considered to be the unjust and unnecessarily severe enforcement of the Exclusion Law. Directly after the Immigration Act of 1924 went into effect, the Chinese Chamber of

Commerce of San Francisco addressed a letter to the president of the Chamber of Commerce of the United States in which they presented their objections to being included in the new law intended primarily for the Japanese.

After referring to their "graceful" acceptance of America's exclusion policy for the last forty-two years and stating "that the Chinese people have always been reasonable in the realization that the influx of the Oriental coolie classes . . . would subject white laborers to a competition . . . and would . . . lower the standard of living in this county," they proceeded to argue that the Exclusion Law . . . had accomplished its purpose of keeping out Chinese coolies.

Source: McKenzie, Roderick. *Oriental Exclusion: The Effect of American Immigration Laws, Regulations and Judicial Decisions upon the Chinese and Japanese on the American Pacific Coast*. New York: J. S. Ozer, 1971, pp. 42–43.

Books

Brawley, Sean. *The White Peril: Foreign Relations and Asian Immigration to Australasia and North America 1919–78*. Sydney: University of New South Wales Press, 1995. *The White Peril* chronicles the history of Asian exclusion and foreign policy among Australia, New Zealand, Canada, and the United States. See Chapter 13 "The US Immigration Act, 1924" for discussion of the 1924 Immigration Act.

Hirobe, Izumi. *Japanese Pride, American Prejudice: Modifying the Exclusion Clause of the 1924 Immigration Act*. Stanford, CA: Stanford University Press, 2001. *Japanese Pride, American Prejudice* is a history of the unsuccessful attempt to change the 1924 Immigration Act to promote good relations between the United States and Japan in the 1920s through 1930s.

Websites

"The Immigration Act of 1924 (The Johnson-Reed Act)." Office of the Historian, Bureau of Public Affairs. U.S. Department of State. This site provides a historical overview of the Johnson-Reed Act. https://history.state.gov/milestones/1921-1936/immigration-act. Accessed October 26, 2016.

"1924 Immigration Act." U.S. Immigration Legislation Online. The University of Washington-Bothell Library. This site provides a history of the 1924 Immigration Act and a discussion of its significance and impact. http://library.uwb.edu/static/usimmigration/1924_immigration_act.html. Accessed October 26, 2016.

1942

Similar to Minoru Yasui, Gordon Hirabayashi is arrested for breaking the curfew. Hirabayashi also challenged the exclusion of Japanese Americans from the West Coast. He argued that his Fifth Amendment rights to "due process under the law" were violated by the exclusion and curfew orders. His case would be the first case to challenge the laws based on race because it only applied to Japanese Americans. His lawyers argued that he was a citizen of the United States, was born in the United States, had no ties to Japan, had never been to Japan, and had no relations with anyone from Japan. However, the court ruled that national security was paramount during times of war. The curfew order, the court argued, was a "protective measure." The court was able to avoid more complex legal issues with exclusion, registration, and relocation by focusing their ruling on Hirabayashi's violation of the curfew law.

Books

Hirabayashi, Gordon, James Hirabayashi, and Lane Ryo Hirabayashi. *A Principled Stand: The Story of Hirabayashi v. United States*. Seattle: University of Washington Press. 2013. *A Principled Stand* is memoir of Gordon Hirabayashi with photographs and archival documents.

Lyon, Cherstin. *Prisons and Patriots: Japanese American Wartime Citizenship, Civil Disobedience, and Historical Memory*. Philadelphia, PA: Temple University Press, 2011. *Prisons and Patriots* examines Japanese American protest and dissent during World War II.

Websites

Hirabayashi v. United States 320 U.S. 81 (1943). JUSTIA U.S. Supreme Court. This site provides the full text for the U.S. Supreme Court decision in *Hirabayashi v. United States*. https://supreme.justia.com/cases/federal/us/320/81/case.html. Accessed January 13, 2017.

Lyon, Cherstin. "Gordon Hirabayashi." *Densho Encyclopedia*, July 14, 2015. This site provides an essay that covers Hirabayashi's family history, his act of civil disobedience during World War II, his sentence, and his role in the fight for civil rights for Japanese Americans during and after the war. http://encyclopedia.densho.org/Gordon_Hirabayashi/. Accessed January 13, 2017.

Also Noteworthy

1885

The First Japanese Presbyterian Church of San Francisco is established. They later established the Japanese YMCA on August 27, 1886.

1919

The League of the Friends of Korea is organized by Flyod W. Tomkins to keep the American public abreast of the conditions in Korea and advocate for Korean Christians.

1990

Daniel Akaka is appointed to the U.S. Senate for Hawaii following the death of Senator Spark Matsunaga. He is the first Native Hawaiian Chinese American to serve in the U.S. Senate.

May 17

1868

The *Scioto* sets sail from Yokohama, Japan, for Hawaii, carrying 153 Japanese laborers headed for the sugar plantations. They are the first large group of migrants from Japan and are known as *gannenmono*.

> *Between May 9 and May 16 [Eugene] Van Reed frantically wrote letters to Higashikuze, Terashima, and other officials trying to get the* bakufu*—issued passports returned to him. He also wanted the new officials to explicitly approve agreements previously made by* bakufu *authorities allowing the Japanese to immigrate to Hawaii. If they did not, he demanded a refund of the money he paid for the charter of the* Scioto *and his expenses in recruiting the laborers. Terashima had two meeting with Van Reed and told him the new Japanese government wanted one of the treaty powers to guarantee the return of the Japanese laborers at the end of the three-year period because Japan and Hawaii had yet to sign a treaty.... On the morning of May 16, the* Scioto *was ready to sail. The caption received his departure papers from the British consul and, despite the lack of an agreement between Van Reed and the new government, the* Scioto *was cleared by Japanese customs house officials at Yokohama.... Still the ship did not sail, even though Van Reed was likely to suffer from its continued presence. The longer the* Scioto *waited, the greater the chances the new government would prevent the ship from sailing altogether.... Nevertheless, he sent three letters to government officials on May 16 warning them that the ship would sail the next morning with the Japanese on board unless they took actions to stop it and refund his money. By 9:00 A.M. on May 17, he had received no reply to his letters and so ordered the ship to depart. After final preparations, the* Scioto *set sail at 2:00 P.M.*
>
> *Source*: Van Sant, John. *Pacific Pioneers: Japanese Journeys to America and Hawaii, 1850–80*. Urbana: University of Illinois Press, 2000, pp. 104–105.

Books

Beechert, Edward. *Working in Hawaii: A Labor History*. Honolulu: University of Hawaii Press, 1985. *Working in Hawaii* focuses on 19th- and early 20th-century labor history in Hawaii.

Takaki, Ronald. *Pau Hana: Plantation Life and Labor in Hawaii*. Honolulu: University of Hawaii Press, 1983. *Pau Hana* is a detailed history of life on the plantations of Hawaii.

Websites

"Gannen mono—The First Overseas Emigrants." Japanese Emigration to Brazil. National Diet Library, Japan. 2014. This essay provides historical background to early Japanese migration to Hawaii and Brazil. http://www.ndl.go.jp/brasil/e/s1/s1_1.html. Accessed February 6, 2018.

Ichise, Laura. "The History of Japanese Immigration to the United States." KCC Alterna—TV News. This article provides general history of Japanese immigration to the United States and Hawaii. http://www2.hawaii.edu/~sford/alternatv/s05/articles/laura_history.html. Accessed February 6, 2018.

Also Noteworthy

2014

Allison Sansom (b. July 7, 1994), a Thai German American from Eagle Rock, Los Angeles, California, known in Thailand by her Thai name, Pimbongkod Chankaew, is the first Thai American to become the Miss Universe Thailand. During the competition, Pimbongkod won first runner-up, but when Weluree Ditsayabut, who won the crowned, resigned her title, Pimbongkod replaced her. She goes on to represent Thailand at Miss Universe 2014.

2016

John Chiang (b. July 31, 1962) announces his campaign for governor of California in 2018.

May 18

1946

The *Nichi Bei Times* (*Nichi Bei Shimbun*) publishes its first issue post–World War II. *Nichi Bei Times* was first published in 1899 when Abiko Kyutrao and four other friends merged two Japanese language newspapers they had acquired. The paper was forced to close operation when the staff was sent to internment camps in April 1942.

The first newspaper of that name, the Nichi Bei Shimbun, *founded by Issei businessman Kyutaro Abiko in 1899, was the oldest and, by consensus, the best of the vernacular journals serving the prewar West Coast Japanese community. Shut down during the mass wartime removal, Shichinosuke Asano revived it in 1946 under the name* Nichi Bei Times, *publishing separate weekly editions in English and Japanese into the new millennium.*

Source: Robinson, Greg. *The Great Unknown: Japanese American Sketches*. Boulder: University Press of Colorado, 2016, pp. xvi–xvii.

Books

Lee, Jonathan H. X., ed. *Japanese Americans: The History and Culture of a People*. Santa Barbara, CA: ABC-CLIO, 2017. See Part 2 for essays related to Japanese immigrant press and the *Nichi Bei Times*.

Mansfield-Richardson, Virginia. *Asian Americans and the Mass Media: A Content Analysis of Twenty United States Newspapers and a Survey of Asian American Journalists*. New York: Routledge, 2014. *Asian Americans and the Mass Media* is a comparative study of Asian American newspapers in the United States that includes specific discussion of Japanese American publications.

Websites

Drennan, Justine. "Nichi Bei Times Decides to Close; Nonprofit Hopes to Continue Legacy." Discover Nikkei: Japanese Migrants and Their Descents. April 25, 2011. This article discusses the closure of *Nichi Bei Times*. http://www.discovernikkei.org/en/journal/2011/4/25/nichi-bei-times-close/. Accessed February 6, 2018.

"Nichi Bei Times." http://www.californiajapantowns.org. This provides a short historical outline history of *Nichi Bei Times*. http://www.californiajapantowns.org/sf/nicheibeitimes.html. Accessed February 6, 2018.

May 19

1913

California State Legislature passed the Webb Act or Alien Land Act. This act prohibits "aliens ineligible to citizenship" from buying land or leasing it for longer than three years. In 1913, five anti-alien land bills were introduced in the California Assembly and two in the Senate. Despite the Japanese government's protest and U.S. Secretary of State William Jennings Bryan's cross-country trip to pressure California's lawmakers not to pass the legislation, Governor Hiram Johnson signs the bill into law on May 19, 1913. Although the Alien Land Law of 1913 prohibited "aliens ineligible for citizenship" from owning land and possessing long-term land leases, it was understood that it was meant to exclude Japanese immigrants from land ownership in California. Issei families navigated around the law, with some purchasing land through a white intermediary and others forming corporations to purchase land on behalf of the immigrants. Many families chose to purchase land in the name of their U.S.-born citizen children. Although the Alien Land Law of 1913 prohibited long-term land leases of more than three years, this practice actually increased, as European American landowners realized larger financial returns from farms cultivated by Japanese tenants.

§ 1. All aliens eligible to citizenship under the laws of the United States may acquire, possess, enjoy, use, cultivate, occupy, transfer, transmit and inherit real property, or any interest therein, in this state, and have in whole or in part the beneficial use thereof, in the same manner and to the same extent as citizens of the United States, except as otherwise provided by the laws of this state.

§ 2. All aliens other than those mentioned in section one of this act may acquire, possess, enjoy, use, cultivate, occupy and transfer real property, or any interest therein, in this state, and have in whole or in part the beneficial use thereof, in the manner and to the extent, and for the purposes prescribed by any treaty now existing between the government of the United States and the nation or country of which such alien is a citizen or subject, and not otherwise....

§ 7. Any real property hereafter acquired in fee in violation of the provisions of this act by any alien mentioned in Section 2 of this act, ... shall escheat as of the date of such acquiring, to, and become and remain the property of the state of California....

The intent of the law was to restrict land ownership by Japanese immigrants. However, by assigning ownership of land to second generation children, born in the United States and thus citizens, or by the use of extended leases the law could be evaded. The result was Proposition 1 on the California ballot in 1920:

Proposition 1: Permits acquisition and transfer of real property by aliens eligible to citizenship, to same extent as citizens except as otherwise provided by law; permits other aliens, and companies, associations and corporations in which they hold majority interest, to acquire and transfer real property only as prescribed by treaty, but prohibiting appointment thereof as guardians of estates of minors consisting wholly or partially of real property or shares in such corporations; provides for escheats in certain cases; requires reports of property holdings to facilitate enforcement of act; prescribes penalties and repeals conflicting acts.

Source: The Statutes of California and Amendments to the Codes Passed at the Fortieth Session of the Legislature, 1913. Sacramento, CA: Superintendent of State Printing, 1913.

Books

Buchanan, Paul. *Race Relations in the United States: A Chronology, 1896–2005.* Jefferson, NC: McFarland & Company, Inc., Publishers, 2005. *Race Relations in the United States* offers a comparative and comprehensive summary policies and events in U.S. history that inform the construction of race. See page 23 for discussion of California's Alien Land Law.

Daniels, Roger. *The Politics of Prejudice: The Anti-Japanese Movement in California and the Struggle for Japanese Exclusion.* Berkeley: University of

California Press, 1962. *The Politics of Prejudice* is a historical study of the anti-Japanese prejudice in California from the late 19th century to 1924.

Websites

"The Alien Land Act of 1913." May 31, 2015. The New Castle: The Future as History. This site discusses the history of alien land laws and their impact. http://www.thenewcastle.org/blog/2015/5/31/the-alien-land-act-of-1913. Accessed October 20, 2016.

"Tells Japan's Side of California Case. State's Attitude Inconsistent with Our Previous Acts of Friendship, New Consul Says." *New York Times*, June 30, 1913. This site provides a historical newspaper article that discusses opposition to California's Alien Land Law form a Japanese perspective. http://query.nytimes.com/mem/archive-free/pdf?res=990CE5DD153FE633A25753C3A9609C946296D6CF. Accessed October 20, 2016.

1921

President Warren G. Harding, pressured by the Immigration Restriction League, signs the Johnson Act, also known as the Emergency Quota Act of 1921, or the Immigration Act of 1921, into law. It is the first quota immigration act that limited the annual number of immigrants to 3 percent of the number of foreign-born persons of most nationalities living in the United States in 1910.

The news in 2012 that the number of non-white babies born in the United States had outstripped the number of white babies spurred heated blog activity on the Internet. The development had been projected since the 1970s, in part because of US policies. . . . In the United States, the legislation that had the greatest impact on national ethnic composition was the Immigration and Nationality Act of 1965. . . . Between 1920 and 1965, legal immigration averaged approximately 206,000 people per year. Before 1965, immigrants came to America for a variety of reasons, and most of these came from Northern Europe. In 1921, the United States guaranteed that this trend would continue—at least for a time. Addressing the fear that America was becoming more diverse, Congress passed the 1921 Emergency Quota Law. The objective of this act was to impose quotas based on the country of birth. Annual allowable quotas for each country were calculated at 3 percent of the total number of foreign-born people from that country in the 1910 US census. This meant that 70 percent of all immigrants in the immediate future would come from Great Britain, Ireland, and Germany. The ethnic status quo was ensured—at least until 1965.

Source: Lackey, Jill. *American Ethnic Practices in the Twenty-First Century: The Milwaukee Study.* Lanham, MD: Lexington Books, 2013, p. 81.

Books

Briggs, Vernon. *Mass Immigration and the National Interest: Policy Directions for the New Century.* Armonk: M. E. Sharpe, 2003. *Mass Immigration and the National Interest* discusses the complex interaction among immigration, labor, history, and the discourse of America's "national interest."

Higham, John. *Strangers in the Land: Patterns of American Nativism*. New Brunswick, NJ: Rutgers University Press, 1963. *Strangers in the Land* is a history of American nativism vis-à-vis ethnic prejudice, power, violence, and race.

Websites

"First Quota Law—1921." MaltaMigration.com. This site provides a historical overview of the 1921 Emergency Quota Law. http://www.maltamigration.com/history/exodus/chapter4-3.shtml. Accessed October 26, 2016.

"1921 Emergency Quota Law." U.S. Immigration Legislation Online. The University of Washington-Bothell Library. This site provides a summary of the 1921 Emergency Quota Law with a discussion of its significance and a link to the full text. http://library.uwb.edu/static/USimmigration/1921_emergency_quota_law.html. Accessed October 26, 2016.

Also Noteworthy

1928

Congressman Richard J. Welch and Senator Hiram Johnson of California introduce a House bill designed to exclude Filipinos from the United States.

1941

The Viet Minh, the League for the Independence of Vietnam, is founded.

1981

Wat Mongkolratanaram, a Thai Buddhist temple, is registered in Tampa, Florida.

May 20

1869

On this day, a group of 22 samurai and their families come to San Francisco and eventually find their way to the Gold Hill (Coloma) region of California, near Sacramento. There, with the help of a benefactor, John Henry Schnell, the Japanese purchased the land from Charles Graner and established the Wakamatsu Tea and Silk Farm Colony on 600 acres. They planted tea seeds and mulberry shoots from Japan. Unfortunately, the agricultural experiment failed by 1871 due to the dry soil and weather of California.

Excerpt from "Arrival of Japanese Immigrants," *Daily Alta California* 21, no. 7008 (May 27, 1869).

It should be understood that the Japanese conduct themselves with dignity; but they are prompt to repel insult and imposition. They cannot safely be treated as Chinamen often are. They come with their families; they bring skill and industry to develop our resources. Herr Schnell means to buy Government land, not in the valleys, which are unsuited, but in the cheaper hill or mountain lands. These gravelly loams are best adopted to the healthiest growth of silkworms and to the finer qualities of silk; and especially is it an axiom, "Hills for the fine teas, dales for the coarse." He knew that we were overstocked with common mulberry trees in nursery, with very few set out for permanent plantation; so he has brought his own trees. He does not intend to feed worms till his trees, now three years old, have another full year's growth. The Japanese do not esteem either eggs or cocoons fed, like ours, on cuttings scarce rooted in the nursery. . . . Herr Schnell would reel out California cocoons this year if he could find them of merchantable quality.

Source: "Arrival of Japanese Immigrants." *Daily Alta California* 21, no. 7008 (May 27, 1869). California Digital Newspaper Collection. http://cdnc.ucr.edu/cgi-bin/cdnc. Accessed October 7, 2016.

Books

Meyer, Evelene. *Wakamatsu Tea and Silk Farm Colony*. North Charleston, SC: CreateSpace Independent Publishing, 2016. Community historian Evelene Meyer discusses the history of the Wakamatsu Tea and Silk Farm Colony and its designation as a California State Historic Park.

Shurtleff, William, and Akiko Aoyagi, compiler. *History of Soybeans and Soyfoods in Japan, and in Japanese Cookbooks and Restaurants Outside Japan (701 CE to 2014)*. Lafayette, LA: Soyinfo Center, 2014. There are limited publications in English on this subject. This volume provides a detailed history of the Wakamatsu colony.

Websites

American River Conservancy. "Wakamatsu: A Rich, Diverse History." 2009. This site provides a historical account of the Wakamatsu colony, a list of archival newspaper articles, images, and links for the preservation of the site. http://www.arconservancy.org/site/c.psKZL3PFLrF/b.7719191/k.2889/Wakamatsu_Tea_and_Silk_Colony_Farm_historic_site_of_the_first_Japanese_Colony_in_the_United_States.htm. Accessed October 7, 2016.

Yoshikawa, Sean. *Imagining Home: CCSF Oral History Project*. "The First Japanese Immigrants to America: A Story of the Lost Samurais in

California." December 23, 2015. This site provides useful historical background of Japanese immigration to the United States and history of the Wakamatsu colony based on local newspaper publications, images, and oral histories. https://ccsforalhistoryproject.wordpress.com/2015/12/23/249/. Accessed October 7, 2016.

Also Noteworthy

1848

The Treaty of Guadalupe Hidalgo is signed between the United States and Mexico. As a result, Mexico transferred almost half of its territory to the United States, including parts of California, Colorado, Nevada, and Utah as well as Arizona, New Mexico, and Texas.

May 21

1975

The Bok Kai Temple, a historic Chinese temple in Marysville, California, that dates back to 1854 is listed on the U.S. National Register of Historic Places.

The importance of the Bok Kai Temple in the history of the Chinatown in Marysville cannot be overemphasized. This is the one institution that has held the Chinese people together for the last 150 years. It continues to play that role today, as the Bok Kai Festival is one of the largest community celebrations in town. The Bok Kai Temple in Marysville is unlike other Chinese temples in larger Chinatowns. Most Chinese temples in California were built by a single association or organization and thus open only to members. In Marysville, the Chinese long ago agreed to band together and build one temple that would be used by all. As a result, many worshippers, including many new immigrants to America, have come to Marysville to worship at the temple.

Source: Tom, Brian, Lawrence Tom, and the Chinese American Museum of Northern California. *Marysville's Chinatown*. Charleston, SC: Arcadia Publishing, 2008, p. 33.

Books

Ho, Chuimei, and Bennet Bronson. *Three Chinese Temples in California: Weaverville, Oroville, Marysville*. Bainbridge Island, WA: Chinese in Northwest America Research Committee, 2016. *Three Chinese Temples in California* is a history of historic Chinese temples and their material artifacts.

Miller, James, ed. *Chinese Religions in Contemporary Societies*. Santa Barbara, CA: ABC-CLIO, 2006. See Jonathan H.X. Lee's Chapter 10, "Contemporary Chinese American Religious Life," for a discussion that includes the Bok Kai Temple.

Websites

Bok Kai Temple. This is the official website with history and photographs. 2013. http://www.bokkaitemple.com/. Accessed February 6, 2018.

The Marysville Bok Kai Parade. 2013. This is the official website of the parade. It provides history and images of the historic parade. https://www.bokkaiparade.com/. Accessed February 6, 2018.

Also Noteworthy

1945

The Hawaii legislature passes the Hawaii Employment Relations Act—the "Little Wagner Act"—which accords agricultural workers the same organizing rights as industrial workers.

1995

Omega Phi Gamma, an Asian American interest fraternity, is established at the University of Texas at Austin.

May 22

1882

On this day, the U.S.-Korea Treaty of 1882 is signed. It is also known as the Treaty of

Chemulpo (Incheon), and it was the first treaty between Korea and a Western nation. Modeled after the "unequal treaties" between Western powers and East Asian countries during the period of European colonial expansion, the U.S.-Korea Treaty of 1882 reflects the multifaceted political conditions of the Korean nation caught amid China, Japan, Russia, and the United States. The treaty made possible the first wave of immigration from Korea to the United States and its territories, most notably Hawaii.

The official introduction of Protestantism to Korea began after the ratification of the American-Korean Treaty in 1882. The Hermit Kingdom thus finally ended 250 years of self-imposed isolation from the world by signing its first foreign treaty of "amity and commerce" with the United States. American Protestant missionaries found their way to Korea in succession: Dr. Horace Newton Allen, a Presbyterian medical missionary, arrived first in Chemulpo (Inchon) in 1884, eventually opened Korea's first modern hospital (Severance Hospital in Seoul), and became an early resident minister of the American legation. He was instrumental in persuading King Kojong to send Korean laborers to sugar plantations in Hawaii to relieve the labor shortage there. . . . When the recruitment process for the emigrant laborers was not moving fast, American missionaries were asked to help: "It took Reverend George H. Jones' persuasive sermon to entice his congregation members to fill the first ship which left Inchon port on December 22, 1902, arriving in Honolulu on January 13, 1903."

Source: Hurh, Won Moo. *The Korean Americans: The New Americans*. Westport, CT: Greenwood Publishing Company, 1998, p. 22.

Books

Choy, Bong Youn. *Koreans in America*. Chicago, IL: Nelson Hall, 1979. *Koreans in America* covers various aspects of the Korean experience in America.

Kim, Hyung-chan, and Wayne Patterson. *The Koreans in America, 1882–1974*. Dobbs Ferry, NY: Oceana Publications, 1974. *The Koreans in America* is a comprehensive history of the Korean American experience from the mid-19th to 20th centuries.

Websites

Morse, David. "Unequal Treaties: The Treaty of Chemulpo." Korea Society. This is a lesson plan for teaching on the topic of the U.S-Korea Treaty of 1882 that includes the full text of the treaty. http://www.koreasociety.org/doc_view/548-unequal-treaties-grades-9-12. Accessed September 6, 2017.

"Treaty between the United States of America and the Kingdom of Chosen." Library of Congress. This site provides the full text of the treaty. https://www.loc.gov/law/help/us-treaties/bevans/b-korea-ust000009-0470.pdf. Accessed September 6, 2017.

Also Noteworthy

2002

In Evansville, Indiana, John Joseph Kirkwood, a 28-year-old, is sentenced to four years in prison for driving his car into an Islamic center.

2007

In Lynn Haven, Florida, Thomas E. Plaisted is charged with battery after spiting on a Muslim child and shoving another at a fast-food restaurant.

May 23

1942

In February 23, 1942, Japanese American students at the University of Hawaii formed the Varsity Victory Volunteers (VVV or "Triple V"), which went on to become a symbol of Japanese American dedication to the war effort. By January 1943, the VVV disbanded and members joined the 442nd Regimental Combat Team or the Military Intelligence Service as Japanese language experts.

Although the War Department once again set to work on a plan to satisfy the president, his orders were defeated, not only by the enormous difficulties of the tasks, but by countervailing forces from Hawaii itself. With support from non-Japanese allies such as FBI chief Robert Shivers, Colonel Kendall Fielder of Army Intelligence, and Hung Wai Ching of the Morale Section, local Japanese organized to claim their place in the war effort. Most notably, in the days following the discharge of Nisei recruits from the Territorial Guard, local Japanese inspired by Ching organized public meetings and circulated petitions to General Emmons requesting alternate service as volunteer laborers. As a result, in late February 1942 Emmons approved the creation of the Corps of Engineers Auxiliary, a work battalion attached to the Thirty-Fourth Combat Engineers. The unit, dubbed the "Varsity Victory Volunteers," quickly attracted 169 enlistees, mostly Nisei college students who had formerly served in the Territorial Guard. The work the unit performed, amid the tropical heat of the islands, was arduous—clearing brush, building roads, quarrying rocks, painting buildings, and fixing fences.

Source: Robinson, Greg. *A Tragedy of Democracy: Japanese Confinement in North America.* New York: Columbia University Press, 2009, p. 119.

Books

Duus, Masayo Umezawa. *Unlikely Liberators: The Men of the 100th and 442nd.* Translated by Peter Duus. Honolulu: University of Hawaii Press, 1987. See Chapter 3, "Go for Broke," for details related to the VVV.

Odo, Franklin. *No Sword to Bury: Japanese Americans in Hawai'i during World War II.* Philadelphia, PA: Temple University Press, 2004. *No Sword to Bury* tells the story of the VVV during wartime Hawaii.

Websites

Odo, Franklin. "Varsity Victory Volunteers." *Densho Encyclopedia*, March 19, 2013. This essay is a detailed history of the VVV and their significance during World War II. http://encyclopedia.densho.org/Varsity_Victory_Volunteers/. Accessed January 15, 2018.

"Varsity Victory Volunteers Part of UH Legacy." University of Hawaii News. February 27, 2015. This site provides a historical background of VVV, videos, and photographs. https://www.hawaii.edu/news/2015/02/27/varsity-victory-volunteers-part-of-uh-legacy/. Accessed January 15, 2018.

Also Noteworthy

1908

The Korean Women's Association is established in San Francisco.

May 24

1975

The Indochina Migration and Refugee Assistance Act is passed. The act reimburses state governments for the expenses of state resettlement programs for Vietnamese refugees. Under this act, more than 130,000 refugees from Vietnam, 4,600 from Cambodia, and 800 from Laos entered the United States. This first wave consisted of refugees who were members of the social and political elites: they spoke English, were generally educated and westernized, had political connections, and came from wealthy background. They included high-ranking soldiers, professionals, civic service workers, and those who had worked with American personnel or companies, ethnic Vietnamese who were educated in the United States, and individuals with family ties in the United States. The first wave was mainly Roman Catholics and ethnic Vietnamese. Their resettlement was well funded in part due to America's sense of moral responsibility for the displacement of the Vietnamese refugees.

To enable the United States to render assistance to, or in behalf of, certain migrants and refugees.

Be it enacted by the Senate and House of Representatives of the United States of America in Congress assembled. That this Act may be cited as "The Indochina Migration and Refugee Assistance Act of 1975".

SEC. 2. (a) Subject to the provisions of subsection (b) there are hereby authorized to be appropriated, in addition to amounts otherwise available for such purposes. $55,000,000 for the performance of functions set forth in the Migration and Refugee Assistance Act of 1962 (76 Stat. 121), as amended, with respect to aliens who have fled from Cambodia or Vietnam, such sums to remain available in accordance with the provisions of subsection (b) of this section.

(b) None of the funds authorized to be appropriate by this Act shall be available for the performance of functions after June 30, 1976, other than for carrying out the provisions of clauses (3), (4), 5), and (6) of section 2(b) of the Migration and Refugee Assistance Act of 1962, as amended. None of such funds shall be available for obligation for any purpose after September 30, 1977.

SEC. 3. In carrying out functions utilizing the funds made available under this Act, the term "refugee" as defined in section 2(b)(3) of the Migration and Refugee Assistance Act of 1962, as amended, shall be deemed to include aliens who (A) because of persecution or fear of persecution on account of race, religion, or political opinion, fled from Cambodia or Vietnam; (B) cannot return there because of fear of persecution on account of race, religion, or political opinion; and are in urgent need of assistance for the essentials of life.

SEC. 4. (a) The President shall consult with and keep the Committees on the Judiciary, Appropriations, and International Relations of the House of Representatives and the Committees of Foreign Relations, Appropriations and Judiciary of the Senate fully and currently informed of the use of funds and the exercise of functions authorized in this Act.

(b) Not more than thirty days after the date of enactment of this Act, the President shall transmit to such Committees a report describing fully and completely the status of refugees from Cambodia and South Vietnam. Such report shall set forth, in addition—

(1) a plan for the resettlement of those refugees remaining in receiving or staging centers;

(2) the number of refugees who have indicated an interest in returning to their homeland or being resettled in a third country, together with (A) a description of the plan for their return or resettlement and the steps taken to carry out such return or resettlement, and (B) any initiatives that have been made with respect to the Office of the High Commissioner for Refugees of the United Nations; and

(3) a full and complete description of the steps the President has taken to retrieve and deposit in the Treasury as miscellaneous receipts all amounts previously authorized and appropriated for assistance to South Vietnam and Cambodia but not expended for such purpose, exclusive of the $98,000,000 of Indochina Postwar Reconstruction funds allocated to the Department of State for movement and maintenance of refugees prior to the date of enactment of this Act. . . .

Approved May 23, 1975.

Source: United States Statutes at Large Containing Laws and Concurrent Resolutions Enacted during the First Session of the Ninety-Fourth Congress, 1975. Vol. LXXXIX. Washington, DC: Government Printing Office, 1977.

Books

Do, Hien Duc. *The Vietnamese Americans*. Westport, CT: Greenwood Press, 1999. *The Vietnamese Americans* covers various aspects of Vietnamese American history, community formation, identity, and cultural adaption.

Haines, David. *Refugees in America in the 1990s: A Reference Handbook*. Westport, CT: Greenwood Press, 1996. *Refugees in America in the 1990s* provides comparative analysis of refugee resettlement, history, and communities in the United States: Chapter 14 focuses on Vietnamese refugees.

Websites

Bily, Cynthia. "Indochina Migration and Refugee Assistance Act of 1975." Immigration to the United States. 2015. This site provides an essay that discusses the background and impact of the Indochina Migration and

Refugee Assistance Act of 1975. http://immigrationtounitedstates.org/607-indochina-migration-and-refugee-assistance-act-of-1975.html. Accessed January 17, 2017.

Zong, Jie, and Jeanne Batalova. "Vietnamese Immigrants in the United States." Migration Policy Institute. June 8, 2016. This site provides an essay that covers the history of Vietnamese refugee migration to the United States with demographic charts and graphs. http://www.migrationpolicy.org/article/vietnamese-immigrants-united-states. Accessed January 17, 2017.

Also Noteworthy

1988

Porntip Nakhirunkanok, Thai American beauty queen, is crowned Miss Universe.

May 25

1887

Around this time, a gang of white horse thieves robbed a Chinese mining camp, killed them, and brutally mutilated their bodies and threw them into the river. Their killing spree continued the next day as 8 additional Chinese miners were killed. Then another 13. Accounts of the death toll vary, but more than 30 Chinese miners were slain over the course of two days. This is known as the Snake River Massacre in Oregon.

Excerpt from newspaper article originally published in the Wallowa *Signal* and then reprinted in the *Oregon Scout*. It describes the 1887 Snake River Massacre.

The Wallowa Signal of the 13th says: "Three weeks ago we published an account of a massacre of Chinamen on Snake river just above the mouth of the Imnaha, and while in main the facts were true as we published them, we are now in possession of the entire matter as it actually occurred.

A party of men consisting of Bruce Evans, J. T. Canfield, Homer LaRue, Robert McMillan, Carl Hughes, H. Maynard and Frank Vaughn entered into an agreement last spring, now nearly a year ago, to murder these Chinese miners for the gold dust which they thought they possessed, and agreed that if any of the parties divulged it the rest should kill him; but Hughes did not like the idea of committing the deed at all and would have no hand in the matter, but at this time was stopping with the parties who committed the deed.

As near as we can learn, about a year ago now, all the men named above except Hughes went down to the Chinese camp and opened fire on them, killing them all, ten in number, and then put the bodies of all except two into a boat which the Chinamen had and scuttled it. They then secured all the money and gold dust they could find, amounting to between $4,000 and $5,000, which was given to Canfield to sell for coin, and after he got possession of it, he skipped the country, and the rest of the parties got nothing.

The Grand Jury took hold of the matter, but, of course, it is not known just what they found out, but Vaughn has made a confession in accord with the above and we are satisfied the matter is about straight. All the parties have left the country except Vaughn and Hughes.

Wednesday evening Hughes was arrested and taken to jail. What will be done with Vaughn we do not know, but, as he has turned states [sic] evidence, we suppose he will be held as a witness against the others, but as they are all gone except Hughes there is little probability that they will ever be brought to justice."

Source: "The Chinese Murderers." *Oregon Scout* 4, no. 43 (April 20, 1888). The original article is available as a digital download from the University of Oregon Libraries' Historic Oregon Newspapers database. http://oregonnews.uoregon.edu/lccn/sn93051670/1888-04-20/ed-1/seq-1/. Accessed January 29, 2018.

Books

Nokes, Gregory. *Massacred for Gold: The Chinese in Hells Canyon*. Corvallis: Oregon State University Press, 2009. In this book, Gregory Nokes, a reporter for the Associated Press and the *Oregonian*, uncovers the long-lost history of the massacre and its aftermath.

Pfaelzer, Jean. *Driven Out: The Forgotten War against Chinese Americans*. Berkeley: University of California Press, 2007. This volume offers one of the most complete records of the systematic attempt to "drive out" the Chinese from the American West.

Websites

Allen, Cain. "News Article, the Chinese Murderers." Oregon Historical Society. 2005. This site provides a summary of the original newspaper article and the image of the archival article. https://oregonhistoryproject.org/articles/historical-records/news-article-the-chinese-murderers/. Accessed January 29, 2018.

Nokes, Gregory. "Chinese Massacre at Deep Creek." The Oregon Encyclopedia. A Project of the Oregon Historical Society and Portland State University. 2016. This essay is a history of the massacre, its impact, and legacy. https://oregonencyclopedia.org/articles/chinese_massacre_at_deep_creek/. Accessed January 29, 2018.

1925

The U.S. Supreme Court in *Hidemitsu Toyota v. U.S.* rules that a "person of the Japanese race, born in Japan, may not legally be naturalized." In 1922, the U.S. Supreme Court confirmed in *Takao Ozawa v. United States* that Japanese immigrants were not eligible to become naturalized citizens. Takao Ozawa immigrated to the United States in 1894 as a student, graduated from Berkeley High School, and then attended the University of California at Berkeley. He was a self-described "assimilated" American who primarily spoke English in his home. In October 1914, Ozawa applied for citizenship in the U.S. District Court in Hawaii. The court rejected his application on the grounds that he was of the Japanese race and not white. Ozawa filed a law suit that gradually made its way to the U.S. Supreme Court. The court's ruling in November 1922 declared that first-generation Japanese Americans, or natives of Japan, the Issei, are ineligible of becoming naturalized citizens. Hidemitsu Toyota tested whether service in America's armed forces during World War I made him eligible for naturalization. Toyota enlisted in the Coast Guard in 1913 and served during wartime. He petitioned for naturalization under a 1918 act allowing alien war veterans who had been honorably discharged to become naturalized citizens. Toyota's naturalization bid was successful, but the government filed to revoke his citizenship in the First Circuit Court of Appeals. The Supreme Court upheld that decision and contended that there was no reason to enlarge the categories of aliens eligible for naturalization under existing statutes.

Excerpt from *Hidemitsu Toyota v. United States.* Decided on May 25, 1915.

Mr. Justice BUTLER delivered the opinion of the Court.

Hidemitsu Toyota, a person of the Japanese race, born in Japan, entered the United States in 1913. He served substantially all the time between November of that year and May, 1923, in the United States Coast Guard Service. This was a part of the naval force of the United States nearly all of the time the United States was engaged in the recent war. He received eight or more honorable discharges, and some of them were for service during the war. May 14, 1921, he filed his petition for naturalization in the United States District Court for the District of Massachusetts. The petition was granted, and a certificate of naturalization was issued to him. This case arises on a petition to cancel the certificate on the ground that it was illegally procured. Section 15, Act of June 29, 1906, c. 3592, 34 Stat. 596, 601 (Comp. St. § 4374). It is agreed that if a person of the Japanese race, born in Japan, may legally be naturalized under the seventh subdivision of section 4 of the Act of June 29, 1906, as amended by the Act of May 9, 1918, c. 69, 40 Stat. 542 (Comp. St. 1918, Comp. St. Ann. Supp. 1919, § 4352), or under the Act of July 19, 1919, c. 24, 41 Stat. 222 (Comp. St. Ann. Supp. 1923, § 4352aaa), Toyota is legally naturalized. The District Court held he was not entitled to be naturalized, and entered a decree canceling his certificate of citizenship. 290 F. 971. An appeal was taken to the Circuit Court of Appeals, and that court under section 239, Judicial Code (Comp. St. § 1216), certified to this court the following questions: (1) Whether a person of the Japanese race, born in Japan, may legally be naturalized under the seventh subdivision of section 4 of the Act of June 29, 1906, as amended by the Act of May 9, 1918; and (2) whether such subject may legally be naturalized under the Act of July 19, 1919. The material provisions of these enactments are printed in the margin.

Source: United States Reports, Volume 268, Cases Adjudged in the Supreme Court. Washington, DC: Government Printing Office, 1926.

Books

Higham, John. *Strangers in the Land: Patterns of American Nativism*. New Brunswick, NJ: Rutgers University Press, 1963. *Strangers in the Land* is a history of American nativism vis-à-vis ethnic prejudice, power, violence, and race.

Weil, Patrick. *The Sovereign Citizen: Denaturalization and the Origins of the American Republic*. Philadelphia: University of Pennsylvania Press, 2013. *The Sovereign Citizen* investigates the formation and construction of a "citizen" by the nation-state through analysis of 20th-century legal procedures, court rulings, and public policies.

Websites

"Toyota v. United States 268 U.S. 402 (1925)." JUSTIA U.S. Supreme Court. This site contains the full text for *Toyota v. United Sates*. https://supreme.justia.com/cases/federal/us/268/402/case.html. Accessed November 10, 2016.

Wetherall, William. Nationality in the United States: The Convolutions of Jurisdiction and Race. 2014. This site contains comprehensive summaries and experts of legislation and court rulings that directly defined and constructed shifting notions of "race" in U.S. jurisprudence. http://www.yoshabunko.com/nationality/US_nationality_law.html. Accessed November 10, 2016.

Also Noteworthy

1925

The U.S. Supreme Court in *Chang Chan et al. v. John D. Nagle* rules that Chinese wives of American citizens are not entitled to residence and therefore not allowed to enter the United States in accordance with the Immigration Act of 1924.

May 26

1873

On this day, the San Francisco Board of Supervisors passes the "Queue" and "Laundry" ordinances. The Queue Ordinance requires that all Chinese prisoners in jail have their hair cut or clipped to a uniform length of an inch from the scalp. The Laundry Ordinance stipulates that laundries using one vehicle with a horse pay a license of $1 per quarter; those that use two vehicles pay $4 per quarter; and those that use more than two vehicles or that use no vehicle, $15 per quarter.

On May 26, 1873, two other anti-Chinese measures were brought before the San Francisco Board of Supervisors. They were known as the "Queue" and the "Laundry" ordinances. Many of the Chinese, when arrested by the San Francisco police and found guilty by the local courts, had refused to pay their fines, preferring instead to serve their sentences in the county jail. This proved costly to the community. After some discussion an ordinance was adopted requiring the sheriff to cut to the length of one inch the hair of all persons committed to his care. To a white person the regulation meant merely a free haircut, but to a Chinese it meant the loss of his queue, and consequent disgrace in the eyes of his countrymen.

Source: Cross, Ira Brown. *A History of the Labor Movement in California*. Berkeley: University of California Press, 1935, p. 82.

Books

Hu, Sen, and Jielin Dong, eds. *The Rocky Road to Liberty: A Documented History of Chinese Immigration and Exclusion.* Saratoga, CA: Javvin Press, 2010. A well-researched volume that includes primary documents is related to the history of Chinese exclusion.

Spickard, Paul. *Almost All Aliens: Immigration, Race, and Colonialism in American History and Identity.* New York: Routledge, 2009. Historian Paul Spickard rejects the melting-pot model of U.S. immigration history, and offers a critical interpretation base on case studies from 1600 to the present.

Websites

"A History of Chinese Americans in California: Racial Violence." National Park Service. 2004. This site discusses the early history of the Chinese in California and focuses on racial discrimination and violence. https://www.nps.gov/parkhistory/online_books/5views/5views3d.htm. Accessed October 8, 2016.

Wherever There's a Fight. California Civil Liberties Public Education Program. 2013. This site provides information on laws in early California and immigrants' rights. http://www.wherevertheresafight.com/timeline/issue/immigrants_rights. Accessed October 8, 2016.

Also Noteworthy

2000

President William Clinton signs a bipartisan bill, the Hmong Veterans' Naturalization Act, which grants Hmong and Laotian veterans who fought for the United States against the communist Lao government during the Vietnam War, an exemption from the English language requirement of the naturalization exam.

May 27

1895

In *Lem Moon Sing v. U.S.*, the U.S. Supreme Court rules that district courts can no longer review Chinese *habeas corpus* petitions for landing in the United States.

US Supreme Court

Lem Moon Sing v. United States

No. 946

Argued April 18–19, 1895

Decided May 27, 1895

158 U.S. 538

Syllabus

The power of Congress to exclude aliens altogether from the United States, or to prescribe the terms and conditions upon which they may come to this country, and to have its declared policy in that respect enforced exclusively through executive officers without judicial intervention, having been settled by previous adjudications, it is now decided that a statute passed in execution of that power is applicable to an alien who has acquired a commercial domicil within the United States but who, having voluntarily left the country, although for a temporary purpose, claims the right under some law or treaty to reenter it.

Lau Ow Bew v. United States, *144 U. S. 47, distinguished from this case. No opinion is expressed upon the question whether, under the facts stated in the application for the writ of habeas corpus, Lem Moon Sing was entitled, of right, under some law or treaty to reenter the United States.*

The case is stated in the opinion.

MR. JUSTICE HARLAN delivered the opinion of the Court.

. . . To avoid misapprehension, it is proper to say that the court does not now express any opinion upon the question whether, under the facts stated in the application for the writ of habeas corpus, Lem Moon Sing was entitled of right under some law or treaty to reenter the United States. We mean only to decide that that question has been constitutionally committed by Congress to named officers of the executive department of the government for final determination.

The judgment of the court below denying the application for the writ of habeas corpus is affirmed.

Source: Lem Moon Sing v. United States. 158 U.S. 538 (1895). JUSTIA U.S. Supreme Court.

Books

Kim, Hyung-chan, ed. *Asian Americans and the Supreme Court: A Documentary History*. Westport, CT: Greenwood Press, 1992. *Asian Americans and the Supreme Court* offers critiques of major U.S. Supreme Court cases related to Asian Americans.

McClain, Charles. *In Search of Equality. The Chinese Struggle against Inequality in Nineteenth-Century America*. Berkeley: University of California Press, 1996. For discussion of *Lem Moon Sing v. U.S.* see part 3, chapter 8.

Websites

Lem Moon Sing v. United States. 158 U.S. 538 (1895). JUSTIA U.S. Supreme Court. This site contains the full text for this U.S. Supreme court decision. https://supreme.justia.com/cases/federal/us/158/538/case.html. Accessed October 9, 2016.

Lewis, Thomas Tandy. "Chinese Exclusion Cases." Immigration to the United States. This site provides historical background to cases dealing with Chinese exclusion. http://immigrationtounitedstates.org/422-chinese-exclusion-cases.html. Accessed October 9, 2016.

Also Noteworthy

1994

Tak Kimura sells first packaged edamame at Whole Foods Market in Berkeley, California.

May 28

1992

The Korean Federation of Los Angeles organizes a meeting of Korean American community leaders to address the April 29, 1992, Los Angeles riots and mobilize the Korean Americans together postriots.

Held less than a month after the nation's largest civil unrest, the meeting grew increasingly heated over competing visions and strategies of how to organize the community's political response to the event that left the community in an unprecedented crisis. Frustrated with the increasingly divisive discussion, a representative of the Korean consulate pleaded with the activists: "I beg you to put aside your political differences. In this time of crisis, we cannot afford to be a Republican or a Democrat, or a conservative or a liberal. We must all be Koreans first and pursue a singular Korean interest." Two days later, his call for political unity was echoed in an editorial in the Korea Times*, the largest Korean language daily in the United States: "Although there has been a lot of political differences in the community, we should establish or choose a single Korean American political organization to represent all interests of Korean Americans. In engaging the mainstream society, we must speak with a singular, united voice." Korean Americans in Los Angeles, however, disregarded the pleas of the consulate and the* Korea Times*. Within six months of the civil unrest, they established two political organizations in response to the event—the Korean American Republican Association (KARA) and the Korean American Democratic Committee (KADC).*

Source: Park, Edward. "The Impact of Mainstream Political Mobilization on Asian American Communities: The Case of Korean Americans in Los Angeles, 1992–1998." In *Asian Americans and Politics: Perspectives, Experiences, Prospects*, edited by Gordon Chang, p. 286. Stanford, CA: Stanford University Press, 2001.

Books

Chon-Smith, Chong. *East Meets Black: Asian and Black Masculinities in the Post-Civil Rights Era*. Jackson: University Press of Mississippi, 2015. *East Meets Black* is a study that examines black and Asian masculinity vis-à-vis race and how it is representative in the media and pop culture.

Park, Carol. *Memoir of a Cashier: Korean Americans, Racism, and Riots*. Riverside, CA: The Young Oak Kim Center for Korean American Studies, 2017. *Memoir of a Cashier* is a Korean American woman's experience of the Los Angeles riots and reflection on race and racism and growing up in an environment riddled with violence.

Websites

Korean American Democratic Committee (KADC). Official web page. This web page is in English and Korean and provides a history and mission of the KADC. http://www.kadems.org/. Accessed February 6, 2018.

Lim, John. Legacy Project: SaIGu LA Riots. 2014. This site provides oral histories and video documentaries to tell the stories of Korean American lives. http://koreanamericanstory.org. Accessed February 6, 2018.

Also Noteworthy

2002

In Parish, New York, Cassie J. Hudson, a 19-year-old, is sentenced to three months in prison for vandalizing and setting fire to a Sikh Temple. Hudson received five years' probation, was fined $1,000, and was ordered to perform 200 hours of community service.

In Ken, Washington, John Bathel, a 45-year-old, is sentenced to two years in prison for assaulting a man of Indian descent after 9/11.

May 29

1970

Japanese American author and civil rights and antiwar activist Kiyoshi Kuromiya and fellow activists found the Gay Liberation Front (GLF) chapter in Philadelphia. The GLF as a whole sought the sexual liberation of all people. In addition, the GLF expressed solidarity with the ongoing black power, feminist, and antiwar movements at the time.

In June 1969, police raided the New York bar the Stonewall Inn. Instead of dispersing quietly and shamefully, as usual, the bar's patrons reacted to police repression with anger and self-defense efforts. The three-day Stonewall Riot opened the door to a nationwide Gay Pride movement, in which thousands of young people (and some not so young) came out of the closet. Within weeks, a new political group, the Gay Liberation Front (GLF), had been organized, modeling itself after the black power and other minority pride movements. Kiyoshi threw himself into the movement, and helped found the GLF's Philadelphia branch. . . . Throughout the 1970s, he worked on behalf of LGBT causes. He remained interested in justice for Japanese Americans as well. In the early 1980s, Kiyoshi discovered that he was HIV-positive. He soon became absorbed with treatment issues and improving the quality of life for people with AIDS. He helped found a Philadelphia chapter of the AIDS activist group ACT UP in 1987. Two years later, he created the Critical Path Project. Critical Path served as both newsletter and website for information on AIDS treatment options and as a space for people with AIDS to express themselves.

Source: Robinson, Greg. *The Great Unknown: Japanese American Sketches*. Boulder: University of Colorado, 2016, p. 244.

Books

Brick, Howard, and Christopher Phelps. *Radicals in America: The U.S. Left since the Second World War*. Cambridge: Cambridge University Press, 2015. See Chapter 4, "The Revolution Will Be Live, 1965–1973," for a discussion related to LGBT civil rights activists, including Kiyoshi Kuromiya.

Mecca, Tommi, ed. *The Early Years of Gay Liberation*. San Francisco, CA: City Lights Books, 2009. See Jason Serinus's "From the Closets of New Haven to the Collectives of New York GLF."

Websites

Martin, Douglas. "Kiyoshi Kuromiya, 57, Fighter for the Rights of AIDS Patients." *New York Times*, May 28, 2000. This is the obituary of Kiyoshi Kuromiya, highlighting his activism and impact. http://www.nytimes.com/2000/05/28/us/kiyoshi-kuromiya-57-fighter-for-the-rights-of-aids-patients.html?scp=1&sq=kiyoshi%20 kuromiya&st=cse. Accessed January 15, 2018.

Stein, Marc. Kiyoshi Kuromiya. June 17, 1997. OutHistory.org. Philadelphia LGBT History Project. 2009. This is transcript of an interview with Kiyoshi Kuromiya, with photographs. http://outhistory.org/exhibits/show/philadelphia-lgbt-interviews/interviews/kiyoshi-kuromiya. Accessed January 15, 2018.

May 30

1942

Fred Korematsu challenges the exclusion of Japanese Americans from the West Coast. Korematsu refused to obey the relocation order and was arrested for violating the Civilian Exclusion Order Number 34. He was found guilty in federal court on September 8, 1942. His conviction was upheld on January 7, 1944, by the Ninth Circuit Court of Appeals. Korematsu then appealed to the U.S. Supreme Court. His case completed Gordon Hirabayashi's case by forcing the court to address the constitutionality of forced relocation and exclusion.

On December 18, 1944, the court issued its ruling, with five justices affirming the lower court's ruling. Justice Hugo Black wrote the majority opinion and said that national security concerns outweighed Korematsu's constitutional rights. Three justices—Owen Roberts, Frank Murphy, and Robert Jackson—wrote dissenting opinions. Justice Roberts argued that relocation was akin to imprisonment. Furthermore, without evidence of disloyalty, and because there were no trails, Japanese Americans' Fifth Amendment rights had been violated. Justice Murphy concurred with Justice Roberts, but went on to add that the policies were acts of racism against Japanese Americans. Justice Jackson dissented on the grounds that since the relocation orders targeted only Japanese Americans whose parents were born in Japan, the order was unconstitutional because it was based on "inherited guilt."

Source: Lee, Jonathan H. X. *History of Asian Americans: Exploring Diverse Roots*. Santa Barbara, CA: Greenwood, 2015, pp. 44–45.

Books

Alonso, Karen. *Korematsu v. United States: Japanese American Internment Camps*. Berkeley Heights, NJ: Enslow Publishers, 1998. *Korematsu v. United States* offers a complete legal and historical profile of *Korematsu v. United States*.

Bannai, Lorraine. *Enduring Conviction: Fred Korematsu and His Quest for Justice*. Seattle: University of Washington Press, 2015. *Enduring Conviction* is a rich biography of Fred Korematsu that is based on archival research, personal letters, and interviews to Korematsu, his family, and close friends.

Websites

Fred T. Korematsu Institute. This site is dedicated to Fred Korematsu's life and legacy: it provides his biography, news stories, and educational materials for students and teachers. http://www.korematsuinstitute.org/homepage/. Accessed January 13, 2017.

Imai, Shiho. "Fred Korematsu." *Densho Encyclopedia*, March 19, 2013. This site discusses Fred Korematsu's life, dissent during World War II, and legacy. http://encyclopedia.densho.org/Fred_Korematsu/. Accessed January 13, 2017.

May 31

1893

On this day, Swami Vivekananda (1863–1902) boards a ship at Mumbai, India, to attend the Parliament of the World's Religions in Chicago, Illinois. At a chance meeting with Harvard professor John Henry Wright (1852–1908), who was impressed by the Indian monk's spiritual knowledge and charisma, Wright arranged for him to speak. Thus, on September 11, 1893, the 30-year-old Swami opened his address with "Sisters and Brothers of America . . ." to which the 7,000 attendees inexplicably offered applause lasting for more than three minutes.

Sisters and Brothers of America,

It fills my heart with joy unspeakable to rise in response to the warm and cordial welcome which you have given us. I thank you in the name of the most ancient order of monks in the world; I thank you in the name of the mother of religions; I thank you in the name of millions and millions of Hindu people of all classes and sects.

My thanks, also, to some of the speakers on this platform who, referring to the delegates from Orient, have told you that these men from far-off nations may well claim the honor of bearing to different lands the idea of toleration.

I am proud to belong to a religion which has taught the world both tolerance and universal acceptance. We believe not only in universal toleration, but we accept all religions as true. I am proud to belong to a nation which has sheltered the persecuted and the refugees of all religions and nations of the earth. I am proud to tell you that we have gathered in our bosom the purest remnant of the Israelites, who came to Southern India and took refuge with us in the very year in which their holy temple was shattered to pieces by Roman tyranny. I am proud to belong to the religion which has sheltered and is still fostering the remnant of the grand Zoroastrian nation.

I will quote to you, brethren, a few lines from a hymn which I remember to have repeated from my earliest boyhood, which is every day repeated by millions of human beings:

"As the different streams having their sources in different places all mingle their water in the sea, sources in different tendencies, various though they appear, crooked or straight, all lead to Thee."

The present convention, which is one of the most august assemblies ever held, is in itself a vindication, a declaration to the world of wonderful doctrine preached in the Gita: "Whosoever comes to Me, through whatsoever form, I reach him; all men are struggling through paths which in the end lead to Me."

Sectarianism, bigotry, and its horrible descendant, fanaticism, have long possessed this beautiful earth. They have filled the earth with violence, drenched it often and often with human blood, destroyed civilization and sent whole nations to despair. Had it not been for these horrible demons, human society would be far more advanced than it is now.

But their time is come; and I fervently hope that the bell that tolled this morning in honor of this convention may be the death-knell of all fanaticism, of all persecutions with the sword or with the pen, and of all uncharitable feelings between persons wending their way to the same goal.

—Swami Vivekananda

Source: Paranjape, Makarand, ed. *Swami Vivekananda: A Contemporary Reader*. London: Routledge, 2015, pp. 3–4.

Books

Adiswarananda, Swami, ed. *Vivekananda World Teacher: His Teachings on the Spiritual Unity of Humankind*. Woodstock, VT: SkyLight Paths Publishing, 2006. *Vivekananda World Teacher* discusses the Swami's teaching and influence in India and the United States and includes experts of his writings.

Vivekananda, Swami. *Complete Works of Swami Vivekananda*. 9 Vols. India: Advaita Ashrama, 2001.

Websites

Swami Vivekananda: Ramakrishna Math and Ramakrishna Mission. 2006. This site provides a detailed history of Vivekananda with links to his complete works in digital format. http://www.belurmath.org/swamivivekananda.htm. Accessed January 15, 2018.

Vivekananda: Vedanta Network. Ramakrishna Vedanta Society of Boston. 2003. This site provides a historical biography of Vivekananda, photos, and links to selected writings of the Swami, including his addresses at the Parliament of Religion. http://vivekananda.org/index2.asp. Accessed January 15, 2018.

Also Noteworthy

2017

U.S. Pan Asian American Chamber of Commerce holds its annual CelebrAsian Procurement Conference organized by Asian American businesses to connect with small, medium, and large enterprises. U.S. Pan Asian American Chamber of Commerce was founded in 1984 in Washington, D.C., by Susan Au Allen to represent the interests and future of Pan Asian American business and professional community.

June

June 1

1933

Mexican berry pickers in El Monte, California, strike against the largely Japanese growers for higher wages. Within a week, up to 7,000 Mexican workers walk off Japanese farms along the coast as well.

In the 1930s El Monte was a small community in the San Gabriel Valley with a population of approximately 16,000. El Monte proper had a population of about 12,000 and the remaining 4,000 lived in the agricultural center. The population was a mixed one comprised of Mexican, Japanese and Anglos. Mexicans accounted for approximately 20 per cent of the population, Japanese about 5 per cent and the remainder were Anglos. Most of the Japanese lived on farms and most of the Mexicans lived in three barrios. The largest of these barrios was Hick's Camp. Hick's Camp was a veritable shack town, located across a gulch from El Monte. It had a population of over 1,000 people most of whom were migratory laborers.... Towards the end of May a mixed group of about twenty people, Anglos, Mexicans, and Japanese (the group included two women) approached S. Fukami, secretary of the Japanese association and demanded higher wages. The group got no satisfaction from the secretary so they returned to Hick's Camp and began to call meetings to organize a strike. On the first of June, with some 500 to 600 present, the workers voted to strike. That day an estimated 1,500 workers went out on strike.... The growers reacted quickly to the strike. A long strike would have had a severe impact since the berries had to be picked within three days after ripening.... Finally on July 6, after a series of conferences that included the strike committee, the growers, the consuls of Mexico and Japan, and representatives of the State Division of Labor Statistics and Law Enforcement, a settlement was reached. The settlement called for a wage of $1.50 for a nine hour day.... The final agreement constituted a gain for the workers in the sense that the new wages were higher than those the growers had offered prior to the strike.

Source: Lopez, Ronald. "The El Monte Berry Strike of 1933." *Aztlan: A Journal of Chicano Studies* 1, no. 1 (October 1970): pp. 103–109.

Books

Daniel, Cletus. *Bitter Harvest: A History of California Farmworkers, 1870–1941*. Berkeley: University of California Press, 1981.

McWilliams, Carey. *Factories in the Field: The Story of Migratory Farm Labor in California*. Boston, MA: Little, Brown, 1939.

Website

"The El Monte Berry Strike." UFCW324: A Voice for Working California. This essay is a history of the strike. https://ufcw324.org/the-el-monte-berry-strike/. Accessed February 6, 2018.

1993

Constance (Connie) Yu-Hwa Chung Povich becomes permanent coanchor with Dan Rather on the *CBS Evening News*. This marked the second time (the first was Barbara Walters with ABC in 1976) a woman worked as coanchor for a major network's national news weekday broadcast.

On June 1, 1993, when Connie Chung took her seat next to Dan Rather as co-anchor of the CBS Evening News, she became the second woman to be named the full-time anchor of a weekly newscast at ABC, NBC, or CBS. Once again the move to elevate a woman into what is acknowledged to be one of the last bastions of male dominance in the news profession created controversy, criticism, and intense scrutiny. The pairing was described by some as a cosmetic change needed to bolster the demographics and ratings of the CBS newscast. The choice was also said to be less a result of journalistic accomplishment than due to Connie's high Q rating, a television industry measurement of a person's likability and recognizability among viewers. Twelve days shy of her second-year anniversary as co-anchor of the CBS Evening News, *Connie Chung was dropped from this position. The failure of this on-air dual-anchor team became one of the biggest media stories in 1995 and raised heatedly debated issues relating both to gender and to journalistic integrity and ability.*

Source: Marlane, Judith. *Women in Television News Revisited: Into the Twenty-First Century.* Austin: University of Texas Press, 1999, p. 78.

Books

Gutgold, Nichola. *Seen and Heard: The Women of Television News.* Lanham, MD: Lexington Books, 2008. See Chapter 3, "Anchors Away: Connie Chung and Elizabeth Vargas."

Signorielli, Nancy, ed. *Women in Communication: A Biographical Sourcebook.* Westport, CT: Greenwood Press, 1996. See Susan Kahlenberg's "Constance (Connie) Yu-Hwa Chung (1946–)" for a detailed history of Chung's life and work as a journalist.

Websites

Carter, Bill. "Chung to Join Rather as CBS News Anchor." *New York Times,* May 18, 1993. This article details why and how Chung was selected to be coanchor of *CBS Evening News.* http://www.nytimes.com/1993/05/18/arts/chung-to-join-rather-as-cbs-news-anchor.html. Accessed January 15, 2018.

Shales, Tom. "Connie Chung at the Top of the News." *Washington Post,* June 1, 1993. This article discusses Chung's performance as coanchor with Dan Rather. https://www.washingtonpost.com/archive/lifestyle/1993/06/01/connie-chung-at-the-top-of-the-news/17c4099f-9a3e-4046-b3dc-0a6f874f64ed/?utm_term=.5313f924fc97. Accessed January 15, 2018.

Also Noteworthy

1968

The Japanese American Religious Federation (JARF) is incorporated as a nonprofit organization.

1994

The Council of American-Islamic Relations, a nonprofit in Washington, D.C., is dedicated to grassroots civil rights and advocacy for American Muslims, and promotion of positive image of Islam and Muslims in America is established.

June 2

1952

The U.S. Supreme Court issues a ruling in *On Lee v. United States*: a case that questioned the legality of search and seizure techniques, wiretapping, and Fourth Amendment protection.

On Lee was suspected of selling opium. A federal undercover agent and former acquaintance of On Lee entered On Lee's laundry wearing a radio transmitter while engaging him in conversation, all of which was being monitored by offsite federal agents. The conversations played a significant role at trial in winning a conviction of On Lee for selling opium. The Court held that there was no trespass onto On Lee's premises, in that it was open to the public and entry was invited. No trespass occurred, but was there a breach of On Lee's reasonable expectation of privacy? The Court felt that as long as the police have the permission of one of the parties to the conversation, eavesdropping on or recording the conversation is not a Fourth Amendment issue. Because a person assumes the risk that whatever is said to another person may be reported to the police, it follows that if the police are invited to share in that conversation, there is no violation of the suspect's constitutional rights.

Source: Becker, Ronald, and Aric Dutelle. *Criminal Investigation*. 4th ed. Burlington, MA: Jones & Bartlett Learning, 2013, p. 168.

Book

Champion, Dean. *Dictionary of American Criminal Justice: Key Terms and Major Supreme Court Cases*. Chicago, IL: Fitzroy Dearborn Publishers, 1998. See section on "Electronic Surveillance, Wiretapping."

Website

On Lee v. United States, 343 U.S. 747 (1952). JUSTIA U.S. Supreme Court. 2018. The full text of the syllabus and case is available. https://supreme.justia.com/cases/federal/us/343/747/case.html. Accessed February 6, 2018.

Also Noteworthy

1989

Ten thousand Chinese soldiers are blocked by 100,000 citizens protecting students demonstrating for democracy in Tiananmen Square, Beijing.

1993

U.S. negotiating team assembles at the U.S. UN Mission in New York to open negotiations meant to resolve a crisis caused by North Korea's announcement of its withdrawal from the nuclear Non-Proliferation Treaty.

June 3

2003

On a radio show, ninth-term Republican congressman Howard Coble of North Carolina asserts that President Franklin Roosevelt's 1942 decision to relocate and intern Japanese Americans from the West Coast was appropriate, in response to a question about his thoughts on interning Middle Eastern Americans after the 9/11 attack. Immediately after, major newspapers, Arab and Muslim social justice organizations, and the Japanese American Citizens League, all publicly denounced Coble. To that end, the California state legislator passed an Assembly Joint Resolution No. 30 Relative to the Japanese American World War II Internment, to critique statements made by Coble regarding support for internment of Japanese Americans during World War II.

WHEREAS, President Franklin Roosevelt signed Executive Order 9066, which ordered the incarceration of more than 120,000 American citizens of Japanese ancestry and resident aliens in the internment camps during World War II; and

WHEREAS, The Commission on Wartime Relocation and Internment of Civilians (CWRIC) was established by Congress and signed into Public Law 96–317 by President Jimmy Carter on July 31, 1980; and

WHEREAS, The CWRIC was established to review and analyze the official government contention, historically accepted, that the exclusion, forced removal, and detention of Americans of Japanese ancestry were justified by military necessity; and

WHEREAS, Between July and December 1981, the CWRIC held 20 days of hearings and took testimony from more than 750 witnesses; and

WHEREAS, The CWRIC declared in its summary that "Executive Order 9066 was not justified by military necessity, and the decisions that followed from it—exclusion, detention, the ending of detention and the ending of exclusion—were not founded upon military considerations. The broad historical causes that shaped these decisions were race prejudice, war hysteria, and a failure of political leadership"; and

WHEREAS, In response to this finding, Congress adopted the Civil Liberties Act of 1988 (P.L. 100–383), which was signed into law by President Ronald Reagan; and

WHEREAS, The Civil Liberties Act of 1988 states that Congress, on behalf of the nation, apologizes to Americans of Japanese ancestry for their wrongful incarceration; and

WHEREAS, President George Bush wrote in his 1990 letter of apology to each Japanese American, "A monetary sum and words alone cannot restore lost years or erase painful memories; neither can they fully convey our Nation's resolve to rectify injustice and to uphold the rights of individuals. We can never fully right the wrongs of the past. But we can take a clear stand for justice and recognize that serious injustices were done to Japanese Americans during World War II"; and

WHEREAS, Representative Howard Coble of North Carolina, who chairs the Subcommittee on Crime, Terrorism, and Homeland Security of the Judiciary Committee of the United States House of Representatives, had made comments on a radio call-in program indicating that the internment of Japanese Americans was in their best interests; and

WHEREAS, Congressman Coble, stated, "We were at war," and called Japanese Americans "an endangered species." He added that, "For many of these Japanese Americans, it wasn't safe for them to be on the street"; and

WHEREAS, Congressman Coble said some Japanese Americans "probably were intent on doing harm to us . . . just as some of these Arab Americans are probably intent on doing harm to us"; and

WHEREAS, Congressman Coble's comments are insulting, inflammatory, and inconsistent with the findings of the CWRIC, inconsistent with the federal Civil Liberties Act of 1988, and inconsistent with the letter of apology issued by President George Bush; now, therefore, be it

Resolved by the Assembly and Senate of the State of California, jointly, That the Legislature of the State of California hereby condemns the statements made by Congressman Howard Coble as insulting, inflammatory, inaccurate, and inconsistent with the findings of the CWRIC, inconsistent with the letter of apology issued by President George Bush, and inconsistent with the laws passed by Congress; and be it further

Resolved, That the Legislature of the State of California urges Congressman Coble to apologize for his inaccurate statements regarding the incarceration of Japanese Americans during World War II; and be it further

Resolved, That the Legislature of the State of California encourages Congressman Coble to submit his resignation as Chairman of the Subcommittee on Crime, Terrorism, and Homeland Security of the Judiciary Committee of the United States House of Representatives; and be it further

Resolved, That the Chief Clerk of the Assembly provide a copy of this resolution to Congressman Coble and to every other member of the United States Congress and to the President of the United States; and be it further

Resolved, That the Chief Clerk of the Assembly provide a copy of this resolution to each member of the State Legislature of North Carolina and to the Governor of North Carolina to encourage them to take actions similar to those described in this resolution.

Source: Assembly Joint Resolution No. 30. California Legislative Information. http://leginfo.legislature.ca.gov/faces/billTextClient.xhtml?bill_id=200320040AJR30. Accessed February 6, 2018.

Books

Brysk, Alison. *Speaking Rights to Power: Constructing Political Will.* Oxford: Oxford University Press, 2013. *Speaking Rights to Power* illustrates the ways in which communication politics can address human rights violations worldwide.

Malkin, Michelle. *In Defense of Internment: The Case of "Racial Profiling" in World War II and the War on Terror.* Washington, DC: Regnery Publishing, 2013. *In Defense of Internment* is a problematic conservative argument for internment of Japanese Americans during World War II.

Websites

Betsch, Michael. "Free Speech No Excuse for Republican's 'Racist' Remarks, Critics Say." CNSnews.com, July 7, 2008. This essay discusses the public backlash on Coble's pro-Japanese American internment remarks. https://www.cnsnews.com/news/article/free-speech-no-excuse-republicans-racist-remarks-critics-say. Accessed February 6, 2018.

"U.S. Rep. Howard Coble, R-6th, about Japanese Internment during World War II." Media

Action Network for Asian Americans. February 7, 2003. This essay discusses Coble's "apology" for his comments, but without admitting that his comments about Japanese internment was wrong. http://manaa.org/?p=684. Accessed February 6, 2018.

June 4

1976

Sichan Siv (b. March 1, 1948) arrives to the United States as a refugee from Cambodia. Siv found a job picking apples and then worked in a Friendly's ice-cream store. He moved to New York City in January 1977 where he worked as an assistant cashier in a restaurant and then as a taxi driver, quickly memorizing the names and locations of streets in New York City. As refugees from Cambodia, Vietnam, and Laos landed in the United States in increasing numbers, Siv became a social worker first at the Lutheran Immigration and Refugee Service and then in the office of the Episcopalian Church's Presiding Bishops' Fund for World Relief. He later served the U.S. government in several capacities, rising to the rank of ambassador when he was the U.S. representative to the UN Economic and Social Council from 2001 to 2006.

Books

Siv, Sichan. *Golden Bones: An Extraordinary Journey from Hell in Cambodia to a New Life in America*. New York: HarperCollins, 2008. *Golden Bones* is Siv's memoir that narrates his journey from Cambodia due to war and genocide to becoming the U.S. ambassador to the United Nations and deputy assistant to President George H. W. Bush.

Smith-Hefner, Nancy. *Khmer American: Identity and Moral Education in a Diasporic Community*. Berkeley: University of California Press, 1999. *Khmer American: Identity and Moral Education* provides a comprehensive discussion of Cambodian refugee resettlement in the United States that critically contrasts Siv's extraordinary achievements.

Websites

Siv, Sichan. "From the Killing Fields to the White House." TEDxSanAntonio. December 29, 2011. This is a video of Siv's TEDx talk that details his experience as a refugee and life in America. https://www.youtube.com/watch?v=YX_9k6puvzY. Accessed January 15, 2018.

Siv, Sichan. Official web page. "Former United States Ambassador to the United Nations." 2017. This site provides detailed information on Siv, including links to articles, interviews, books, and photographs. http://sichansiv.com/. Accessed January 15, 2018.

Also Noteworthy

1982

Wayne Wang's *Chan Is Missing* (1982) is released.

1985

The Los Angeles Board of Zoning Appeals votes 4–1 to grant Wat Thai Buddhist Temple on Coldwater Canyon Avenue a permit to construct a Sunday school to serve the Thai Americans in Southern California.

2003

At the University of California, San Diego, hundreds of copies of a publication portraying Muslim women as sexual objects and ridiculing Jews, Jesus, and Palestinians are distributed on campus.

June 5

1984

Federal prosecutors charge Ronald Ebens and Michael Nitz with violating the civil rights of Vincent Jen Chin, whom they bludgeoned to death with a baseball bat on June 19, 1982. Although Ebens and Nitz were acquitted in the courts, the desire to seek justice for Vincent Chin sparked a pan-Asian American political movement.

In March 1983 Ebens and Nitz received three years' probation, and were fined $3,780. Chinese Americans were outraged, and the small community began to seek allies. As awareness of the Vincent Chin case grew throughout the country, other groups offered their support. There was a wide range of Chinese American groups, but also the Japanese American Citizens League (JACL), the Korean American Associations of Illinois, and, in the Detroit area, the Korean Society of Greater Detroit and the Korean American Women's Association. Although there was initially skepticism from some established civil rights groups, support eventually also came from many organizations with roots outside Asian American communities. For the Chin family, the effort ended unhappily. Ebens and Nitz were tried in a federal court in 1984, charged with violating Chin's civil rights, and Ebens was found guilty while Nitz was acquitted. However, a retrial was ordered on the grounds that there had been excessive pretrial publicity, and also that there were legal errors with some of the evidence. The retrial was held in Cincinnati in 1987, where Ebens was acquitted by a largely male, blue-collar jury. Ebens never apologized. Although Asian American activists lost the important legal battles of the Vincent Chin murder, they gained a great deal. Out of it came a determination to continue to fight against anti-Asian violence, and the case had a galvanizing effect on many Asian Americans. Perhaps most importantly, it helped to build alliances between different Asian American groups, and between Asian Americans and others, laying the groundwork for a much more effective politics in the years to come. Vincent Chin did not die in vain, and his legacy can be seen in the pan-Asian American coalitions that were inspired by his cause.

Source: Zia, Helen. *Asian American Dreams: The Emergence of an American People.* New York: Farrar, Straus, and Giroux, 2000, p. 30.

Books

Darden, Joe, and Richard Thomas. *Detroit: Race Riots, Racial Conflicts, and Efforts to Bridge the Racial Divide.* East Lansing: Michigan State University Press, 2013. Chapter 7 "The Declining Auto Industry and Anti-Asian Racism: The Murder of Vincent Chin" reflects on the murder of Vincent Chin, anti-Asian racism, and the decline of the Detroit auto industry.

Ma, Sheng-Mei. *The Deathly Embrace: Orientalism and Asian American Identity.* Minneapolis: University of Minnesota Press, 2000. See Chapter 4, "Vincent Chin and Baseball: Law, Racial Violence, and Masculinity."

Websites

Wu, Frank. "Why Vincent Chin Matters." *New York Times*, June 22, 2012. This newspaper opinion essay is written by legal scholar Frank Wu and discusses the Vincent Chin murder, details of the trial, its outcome, and its impact and significance for Asian Americans. http://www.nytimes.com/2012/06/23/opinion/why-vincent-chin-matters.html. Accessed February 7, 2018.

Zia, Helen. "Vincent Chin's Story/Lily Chin: The Courage to Speak." Asian Americans Advancing Justice. This article is written by an Asian American journalist and activist and discusses the Vincent Chin killing and Lily Chin's courage to speak out in her search for justice for her son. https://advancingjustice-la.org/sites/default/files/UCRS%205_Vincent_Chin_Lily_Chin_story%20r2.pdf. Accessed February 7, 2018.

Also Noteworthy

1953

The U.S. Senate rejects People's Republic of China's membership to the United Nations.

1976

In the predawn hours in an Arab immigrant neighborhood of Dearborn, Michigan, 22-year-old Ali Shebrin Eleshemmam, a Yemeni American, is brutally killed by two white gunmen.

June 6

1927

The U.S. Supreme Court in *Weedin v. Chin Bow* rules that a person born abroad of an American parent or parents who has never lived in the United States cannot be a citizen of the United States. It states, "All children heretofore born or hereafter born out of the limits and jurisdiction of the United States, whose fathers were or may be at the time of their birth citizens thereof are declared to be citizens of the United States, but the rights of citizenship shall not descend to children whose fathers never resided in the United States"; citizenship attaches only where the father has resided in the United States before the birth of the child.

The Supreme Court's decision in Weedin v. Chin Bow *(1927) showed another way to block racially undesirable segments. Chin Bow's grandfather, Chin Tong, was born in the United States and considered a citizen. His father, Chin Dun, was born in China and had never visited the United States until after his 10-year-old-son, the respondent, was born. The Taft court ruled that children of American parents who never resided in the United States were not of American nationality, thus not eligible for entry. This principle drew on common law, just as* Wong Kim Ark *had, but unlike the English precedent, it set the limit to children, not grandchildren. Citizenship was not perpetually inheritable. This would not matter for white people, who could naturalize, but for aliens ineligible for citizenship, a father could forfeit his son's citizenship by never visiting the United States. These cases may look like narrow decisions, but they worked to solidify Asians in general as alien. So legislation against Chinese could lead to restrictions against Japanese, and then set a general standard for nonwhites. For example, dispossession of Mexicans made California's Alien Land Laws, which prohibited aliens ineligible for citizenship more sensible, later that made Japanese internment more acceptable.*

Source, Carter, Gregory. "Race and Citizenship." *The Oxford Handbook of American Immigration and Ethnicity*, edited by Ronald Bayor, p. 175. Oxford: Oxford University Press, 2016.

Books

McWhirter, Robert. *The Citizenship Flowchart.* Chicago, IL: American Bar Association, 2007. *The Citizenship Flowchart* is a question-and-answer-style book related to American citizenship. Question 33 discusses *Weedin v. Chin Bow* and key words in the decision.

Odo, Franklin, ed. *The Columbia Documentary History of the Asian American Experience.* New York: Columbia University Press, 2002. See Chapter 65, "Supreme Court: Weedin v. Chin Bow, June 6, 1927."

Websites

Weedin, Com'r of Immigration, v. Chin Bow, No. 442. Circuit Court of Appeals, Ninth Circuit. August 3, 1925. Casetext. 2018. This is the full text of the case. https://casetext.com/case/weedin-v-chin-bow-2Accessed June 15, 2018.

Weedin v. Chin Bow 274 U.S. 657 (1927). JUSTIA U.S. Supreme Court. This is the full text of the *Weedin v. Chin Bow* decision. https://supreme.justia.com/cases/federal/us/274/657/case.html. Accessed January 15, 2018.

Also Noteworthy

1995

The Al-Baqi Mosque in Springfield, Illinois, is burned down.

June 7

1972

Hsuan Hua, Chan Buddhist monk, conducts first ordination ceremony at Gold Mountain Dhyana Monastery in San Francisco, California. Hsuan Hua founded several

Buddhist institutions in the United States. The Dharma Realm Buddhist Association is a global Buddhist organization with chapters in the United States, Canada, Australia, and Asia. The City of Ten Thousand Buddhas located in Ukiah, California, is the first Chan Buddhist monastery in America: it is also home of the Dharma Realm Buddhist University.

In 1959, Hsuan Hua's students established in the United States what would become the Dharma Realm Buddhist Association. After a brief visit to Australia in 1962, Hsuan Hua traveled to America where he would make his permanent home. Centering his teaching in San Francisco's Chinatown, he then moved into the Fillmore district and later to Japantown. Finally he settled back in Chinatown, where he established his center in the Tianhou Temple, the oldest Chinese temple in the United States. Although very much in traditional Chinese style, his teachings were a synthesis of Zen and Pure Land. They also provided a less rational perspective than Westerners had come to expect of Zen teachers. Once, early on, admirers in Seattle invited Hsuan Hua to come and teach there. He responded that if he were to leave San Francisco, the city would be ravaged by an earthquake and suggested they visit him instead. Emphasizing as he did the miraculous element in his teachings, Hsuan Hua attracted many interested primarily in psychic phenomena. In response, he strongly underscored how such things were secondary to real understanding of the Dharma.

Source: Ford, James. *Zen Master Who? A Guide to the People and Stories of Zen.* Boston, MA: Wisdom Publication, 2006, pp. 83–84.

Books

Fields, Rick. *How the Swans Came to the Lake: A Narrative History of Buddhism in America.* Boston, MA: Shambhala, 1981. *How the Swans Came to the Lake* is a comprehensive history of Buddhism in the United States.

Hua, Hsuan. *The Chan Handbook.* Ukiah, CA: The Buddhist Text Translation Society, 2004. *The Chan Handbook* is an accessible introduction to Chan Buddhism, and includes a biography of Hsuan Hua.

Websites

City of Ten Thousand Buddhas' official web page provides useful information about Hsuan Hua and history of Dharma Realm Buddhist Association in the United States. 2017. http://www.cttbusa.org/cttb/drba.asp. Accessed January 15, 2018.

Dharma Realm Buddhist Association's official web page provides a link to its history, locations around the world, teachings, and translations in English, Chinese, Vietnamese, and Spanish. 2017. http://www.drba.org/history.html. Accessed January 15, 2018.

Also Noteworthy

1948

The U.S. Supreme Court rules in *Takahashi v. Fish and Game Commission* (1948) that a California statute barring issuance of commercial fishing licenses to persons "ineligible to citizenship" is unconstitutional. Takahashi's victory stopped California's discrimination of Japanese Americans, and it is one of the rulings that would lead to the overturning of race-based discrimination six years later in *Brown v. Board of Education* school segregation case.

June 8

1938

On this day, the Chinese Ladies Garment Workers Union established by more than 100 Chinese women sewing for Joe Shoong's San Francisco-based National Dollar sewing factory ends their successful strike that started in February 26 that demanded wages closer to \$19–\$30 a week received by other unionized workers.

The garment sector was one of the first large-scale manufacturing industries in the United States. The word "sweatshop" was first coined in the sector because workers "sweated" long hours in cramped conditions. The industry was susceptible to a high degree of exploitation since it was labor intensive; "vertically dis-integrated," which meant it was outsourced by retailers and "jobbers" (the brands of today); and compounded by gender and racial oppression because it was both highly feminized and had a predominantly immigrant workforce.

Chinese American women, mostly in San Francisco's Chinatowns, began to work as seamstresses in small family-run shops or in their homes in the late 19th and early 20th centuries. By the 1930s these shops had become larger garment factories and were often used as a cheaper alternative to undermine the mostly white unionized garment contractors. In 1938, after years of failed attempts to unionize the Chinatown garment shops, workers formed the independent local Chapter 341 of the International Ladies' Garment Workers Union (ILGWU), known as the Chinese Ladies Garments Workers Union. The Chinese garment workers of San Francisco organizing themselves into an autonomous local in recognition that they might be disadvantaged in the largely white ILGWU San Francisco local.

The first target was the retailer National Dollar Stores. After a 108-day strike and picketing of its retail shop, the company capitulated, agreeing to become a "closed shop," 5 percent wage increase (to $14 per week), time-and-half for overtime, 40-hour work week, improved working conditions, and paid holiday for Labor Day. For many workers the terms did not go far enough, but in the end workers narrowly accepted the agreement. Almost all 100 union members lost their jobs within two years of the agreement and the union local shrunk to less than 40 members. Nonetheless, labor historians concur that the adversarial approach, collective class consciousness, and links with workers outside the community that were emblematic of the campaign changed the course of history for Chinese American women. Crucially, the strike and subsequent factory closure led the Chinese American women, with the assistance of ILGWU organizers, to break the racial barrier and be permitted to work in white-owned union shops.

With the outset of World War II, the ILGWU all but dissipated in Chinatown; nonetheless, Chinese American garment workers would become central to San Francisco and New York's labor movement. Forty years later the ILGWU organized its next large strike in Chinatown, now the center of New York's dwindling garment sector. In June of 1982, 15,000 Chinese American garment workers in New York City would walk out. The final agreement increased workers' wages, holidays, and employer healthcare contributions, and improved the cost of living adjustment. Through the ILGWU, Chinese American garment workers had organized across the sector to become outspoken union leaders, agitating strikes and work stoppages and directly confronting the stereotype of Asian passivity and subservience.

Source: Kumar, Ashok. "International Ladies' Garment Workers' Union." In *Chinese Americans: The History and Culture of a People*, edited by Jonathan H.X. Lee, pp. 206–207. Santa Barbara, CA: ABC-CLIO, 2016.

Books

Bao, Xiaolan. *Holding Up More Than Half the Sky: Chinese Women Garment Workers in New York City, 1948–92*. Urbana: University of Illinois Press, 2001. *Holding Up More Than Half the Sky* details the Chinese Women Garment Workers strike in New York City in 1982.

Ling, Huping. *Surviving on the Gold Mountain: A History of Chinese American Women and Their Lives*. New York: State University of New York Press, 1998. *Surviving on the Gold Mountain* is a comprehensive labor history of Chinese American women.

Websites

"The Chinatown Struggles of 1982." Cornell University ILR School. 2015. This site provides an overview history of the International Ladies' Garment Workers Union and the Chinese women workers' strike of 1982 with photographs and links to archival primary source materials. http://ilgwu.ilr.cornell.edu/announcements/oneLongAnnouncementFromDB.html?announcementID=5. Accessed January 15, 2018.

"Sue Ko Lee and the National Dollar Stores Strike of 1938." City College of San Francisco Library Exhibitions. March 24, 2010. This site documents one of the striker's oral history and provides photographs and archival documents. https://ccsfexhib.wordpress.com/2010/03/24/sue-ko-lee-and-the-national-dollar-stores-strike-of-1938/. Accessed January 15, 2018.

Also Noteworthy

2002

In Gainesville, Florida, Robert Rowland, a 53-year-old, is charged with two hate crimes after threatening three people of Indian descent while spraying them with bug spray.

June 9

1973

On this day, the Organization of Chinese Americans (now known as OCA—Asian Pacific American Advocates) is established in Washington, D.C. OCA identifies as a nonpartisan, nonprofit national organization dedicated to advancing the political, social, and economic well-being of Asian Pacific Americans. In 2013 the OCA renamed itself OCA—Asian Pacific American Advocates to reflect its pan-Asian American constituents. Currently, there are more than 100 chapters of OCA in the United States.

Open Letter to Rob Manfred, Commissioner of Baseball, Major League Baseball (MLB)

October 31, 2017

Dear Mr. Rob Manfred:

We are extremely disappointed in Yuli Gurriel's show of bad sportsmanship when he made a racist gesture and uttered a racial slur against LA Dodgers' Yu Darvish. Not only was this offensive to Mr. Darvish, but also to the many Asian baseball fans watching across the nation and worldwide. The MLB should have suspended Mr. Gurriel immediately for Game Five during the World Series. As such, the MLB should place a heavier fine on Mr. Gurriel and the Astros, as well as future immediate suspension for any racial slur or gesture against a player.

Although Mr. Gurriel publicly apologized after the game, it took 18 hours before there was an announcement that he would be suspended for five games without pay in the 2018 season. This sentence seems cosmetic and further insults the Asian and Asian American community.

The gesture of slanted eyes has historically been used to demonize and ostracize Asians, and it is the responsibility of an individual player, a team, and the MLB to make sure that this is understood—just as it is understood that it is, under any circumstances, appropriate to use the "n" word. Though we understand that Mr. Gurriel may not have thought the word he uttered, "chinito," was a racial slur due to cultural differences, he knew that his hand gesture was wrong.

The MLB punishes players for sins against baseball and sins against the greater society, and racism should not be exempt. The MLB must show that it will not tolerate discrimination, racism and slurs by both members of the MLB and baseball fans alike.

Many members of the Asian American community agree that the MLB has not done enough in reprimanding Mr. Gurriel and the Astros. We believe that can begin with stronger discipline such as an additional fine to the Astros next season and thorough diversity training. . . .

Sincerely,

OCA—Asian Pacific American Advocates

Source: OCA Asian Pacific American Advocates—New York Chapter. http://www.oca-ny.org/. 2018.

Books

Lee, Jonathan H. X. *Chinese Americans: The History and Culture of a People*. Santa Barbara, CA: ABC-CLIO, 2016. *Chinese Americans* provides comprehensive coverage of the Chinese American history: part II focuses on political and economic organizations, movements, and individuals.

Thomas, Clive, ed. *Research Guide to U.S. and International Interest Groups.* Westport, CT: Praeger, 2004. See Chapter 9 "Interests and Interest Groups in the Public Policy Process: (I) Strategies and Tactics" for discussion related to Asian American interest groups.

Websites

OCA—Asian Pacific American Advocates' official web page. 2017. https://www.ocanational.org/. Accessed January 16, 2018.

"Organizations of Chinese Americans—New York Chapter." Asian/Pacific American Archives Survey Project. January 28, 2015. This site provides an overview history of OCA, in particular the New York chapter and the content of its archive. http://apa.nyu.edu/survey/?p=189. Accessed January 16, 2018.

June 10

1854

The first Asian language newspaper is the Chinese weekly *Golden Hills News*, published by Howard and Hudson in San Francisco on April 22, 1854. It was established by American Methodist missionaries in San Francisco. Later on, the name was changed to *Gold Mountain News*. It was mostly a Chinese-language newspaper with an English editorial on the front page of each issue.

"The Chinese and the Times." Golden Hills News. *June 10, 1854.*

In this editorial the author wanted to place the Chinese higher in the racial hierarchy than African Americans, Irish, and Germans. The Golden Hills' News *wanted to ease the hostility towards the Chinese in America, but also to convert them to Christianity.*

To maximise the area of liberty and minimize that of tyranny has become essentially the principle of the Times. Every effort, of the really liberal, has professedly for its object the improvement of the moral, religious, and legal code of nations and races, but in doing so it is found, that sacred bigotries must be broken into, and vested prejudices be exposed. For instance, a Chinese Mission Chapel, with attached library and school-room, has been opened for the preaching of the gospel to the Chinese race, and for instructing them in the English language in all its branches. The spirit of philanthropy has hailed with unfeigned pleasure the benevolent enterprise. We, too, believing that Civil and Political knowledge is of infinite importance to the Chinese, both in their individual, social, and relative state, have established "The Golden Hills' News" for that special Mission. The influence of Chapel and Press intended to relieve the pressure of religious ignorance settle and explain our laws, assist the Chinese provide their wants, and soften, dignify, and improve their general character.

And what race of people more deserving of our efforts? They claim a national existence coeval with the most remote antiquity. We read of their virtuous sovereigns Fuh-he, and Yaou, reigning in the affection of this people some 2000 years before Christ—of their great philosopher Confucius, who was born 550 before Christ. The doctrines or philosophy of Confucius have obtained a reputation only national, but have been long celebrated among the literati of Europe, as evidencing a high state of intellectual and moral progress; and in fact, the precept of "Do unto others as you would be done unto" has been traced to the Confucian school of Philosophy. Indeed the doctrines of the Chinese sage contain a complete body of rules for the government of one's self, the regulation of social intercourse, the education of a community, the government of an empire, and the management of a complex social machinery.

Yet our Conductors of the Press describe them as "Apes," "Brutes," "social lice"! lower than the Negro-race. Did ever one of these Conductors or Editors see the Negroes as just imported from Africa! If they ever did, and should then compare them with Chinamen, we should consider than [sic] mentality—insanity. The Chinese is also said, to be "unfitted for Caucasian Civilization." Give them a fair trial before condemnation. Why, the Celtic-race have never fairly amalgamated with republican Institutions. In the last papers from the East we read that in every City of America of any size is to be found an "Ireland" and a "Germany." The London Times, and a New York paper say, that in every country the Celtic race wage a war of extermination upon each other and upon Protestantism! While the Germans of Louisville have published a series of resolutions against our present Institutions! We protest against making targets of the poor Chinese, and say, it is only fair, that Republicans should warmly encourage, cherish and protect every effort to diffuse the spirit of Christianity and Republicanism amongst this interesting race.

Source: Golden Hills News, San Francisco, June 10, 1854.

Books

Chen, Yong. *Chinese San Francisco, 1850–1943: A Trans-Pacific Community*. Stanford, CA: Stanford University Press, 2000. *Chinese San Francisco* documents the history of Chinese in San Francisco: see Chapter 3 "The Social Landscape of Chinese San Francisco" for discussion related to *Golden Hills News*.

Wilson, Clint, Felix Gutierrez, and Lena Chao. *Racism, Sexism, and the Media: The Rise of Class Communication in Multicultural America*. Thousand Oaks, CA: Sage Publications, 2003. See Chapter 11 "Alternatives: Colorful Firsts in Class Communication: Communication before the Europeans" for discussion of first Asian American newspapers and detailed discussion of the *Golden Hills News*.

Websites

Chinese in California Virtual Collection. CALISPHERE. University of California. 2018. This site provides digital images of archival *Golden Hills News* issues. https://calisphere.org/item/ark:/13030/hb3j49n625/. Accessed January 16, 2018.

Chiu, Kuei. "Asian Language Newspaper in the United States: History Revisited." Chinese American Librarians Association. November 13, 2008. This essay provides a detailed history of Asian language newspapers in the United States that includes a significant discussion on the *Golden Hills News* history. https://www.cala-web.org/cala-ej/no-09/chiu. Accessed January 16, 2018.

Also Noteworthy

1905

The first Korean American newspaper, the *Korean Times*, is published in Hawaii.

1942

The 100th Battalion, an all-Nisei (second-generation Japanese American) battalion, is activated in Hawaii.

June 11

1963

To protest the South Vietnamese government's persecution of Buddhism and other discriminatory policies, 66-year-old Vietnamese Mahayana Buddhist monk Thich Quang Duc (1897–1963) sets himself on fire while sitting in the full lotus meditation position. Duc's self-immolation was captured in a photograph in *Life* magazine. This image shocked President John F. Kennedy, who ordered a review of his administration's Vietnam policy: the review resulted in more troops deployed to Vietnam.

The Kennedy administration saw no alternative to protect its vision of a prosperous, stable, anticommunist state in Southeast Asia. "Nation-building" in Vietnam became a symbol of America's redoubled energy, ingenuity, and determination. Washington's intervention in the region promised to make the new frontier a reality at limited cost. The United States would not "take over" in Southeast Asia, but would instead provide the necessary assistance to foster economic and political "take-off." In the early 1960s this became a process of destroying villages in order to save them. Thousands of South Vietnamese citizens condemned the brutality of American-sponsored "nation-building." In June 1963 a Buddhist monk, Thich Quang Duc, burned himself in public as a protest against Diem's repression of religious dissidents. Duc's self-immolation shocked viewers around the world. It displayed the depth of popular indignation toward the Saigon regime. Diem did not respond with a series of needed reforms, as Americans hoped. Instead, he increased the use of police-force—including persecutions, arrests, and even public shootings. Under these circumstances, popular support for the communist insurgency grew throughout South Vietnam. American officials reported that urban professionals, intellectuals, and students "blamed" the United States for the corruption and repression under Diem. This observation frustrated the Kennedy administration. Why hadn't America's counterinsurgency programs produced favorable results? One could blame either the programs or their implementers. Almost unanimously, the president and his closest advisers condemned the latter. American attempts to foster development in South Vietnam could not possibly be flawed. After all, the assumptions about modernization and economic growth that underpinned the administration's policies had "scientific" support. They reflected the accumulated wisdom of extensive American thought and experience.

Source: Suri, Jeremi. *Power and Protest: Global Revolution and the Rise of Détente.* Cambridge, MA: Harvard University Press, p. 142.

Books

Jones, Howard. *Death of a Generation: How the Assassinations of Diem and JFK Prolonged the Vietnam War.* Oxford: Oxford University Press, 2003. See Chapter 2 "Democracy at Bay: Diem as Mandarin" and Chapter 3 "Counteraction to Counterinsurgency: The Military Solution" for discussion related to Thich Quang Duc and the United States' Vietnam policy.

Nguyen, Tai Thu, ed. *History of Buddhism in Vietnam.* Hanoi, Vietnam: Social Sciences, 1992. *History of Buddhism in Vietnam* provides comprehensive information on the historical development of Buddhism in Vietnam, in addition to its tenants and practices.

Websites

"50th Anniversary: The Burning Monk: A Defining Moment Photographed by AP's Malcolm Browne." Associated Press. 2013. This site offers historic photographs and step-by-step details of how Malcolm Browne was able to capture the photograph of the self-immolation of Thich Quang Duc. It includes a discussion of the impact of the historic photograph on shifting public sentiment on the war in Vietnam. https://www.ap.org/explore/the-burning-monk/. Accessed January 18, 2018.

Venerable Thich Tam Phuong. "The Self-Immolation of a Buddhist Monk." Buddhist Information. 2018. This essay provides a Buddhist perspective on Thich Quang Duc's self-immolation protest during the Vietnam War. http://www.buddhistinformation.com/self_immolation.htm. Accessed January 18, 2018.

Also Noteworthy

2010

In Sunnyvale, California, a Muslim man holding a Koran is attacked by two men who called him a terrorist.

June 12

1967

The U.S. Supreme Court rules that anti-miscegenation laws were unconstitutional in *Loving v. Virginia.* That ruling invalidated laws in 16 states that prevented whites from marrying "colored" spouses, including Asians. Until then many Asians had been forced to move to more liberal states in order to marry.

Landmark Supreme Court decisions declared racially restrictive housing covenants (1948) and school segregation (1954) illegal. Bans on racial intermarriages had also begun to be lifted in California (1959) and other western states; in 1967, the Loving v. Virginia *ruling rendered them all unconstitutional. The United States was unquestionably more open to peoples of Asian ancestry by the 1960s. Together, this conglomeration of decisions facilitated major demographic shifts in the nation's Japanese and Chinese communities. Between 1952 and 1961, Japanese Americans filed the most applications for naturalization among all Asian ethnic groups. As they became citizens, they were able to petition for their spouses to come on a non-quota basis. Men of all races who served in the post-war occupation of Japan, moreover, sought to bring their Japanese wives back to the United States.*

Source: Wu, Ellen. *The Color of Success: Asian Americans and the Origins of the Model Minority*. Princeton, NJ: Princeton University Press, 2014, p. 145.

Books

Liu, William Ming, Derek Kenji Iwamoto, and Mark H. Chae, eds. *Culturally Responsive Counseling with Asian American Men*. New York: Routledge, 2010. See Yong Park's Chapter 12, "Interracial and Interethnic Relationships."

Wallenstein, Peter. *Race, Sex, and the Freedom to Marry*. Lawrence: University Press of Kansas, 2014. *Race, Sex, and the Freedom to Marry* is a detailed study of the history of *Loving v. Virginia* apropos the social-political context, personalities, legal arguments, and marriage and law in America.

Websites

Loving v. Virginia, 388 U.S. 1 (1967). JUSTIA U.S. Supreme Court. 2018. This site provides the full text of the *Loving v. Virginia* ruling. https://supreme.justia.com/cases/federal/us/388/1/case.html. Accessed January 18, 2018.

Muto, David. "An Unsung Hero in the Story of Interracial Marriage." *New Yorker*, November 17, 2016. This essay reflects on *Loving v. Virginia* and discusses the role of the Japanese American Citizens League who were allowed to speak in support of the Lovings. https://www.newyorker.com/culture/cultural-comment/an-unsung-hero-in-the-story-of-interracial-marriage. Accessed January 18, 2018.

Also Noteworthy

1942

Fred Korematsu is charged with violating Exclusion Order No. 34, and a case against him is filed in the U.S. District Court for Northern California.

June 13

1989

On this day, Chinese American tennis player, Michael Chang, becomes the youngest male to win a Grand Slam (17 years) and the first American man in 34 years to win the French Open. The grueling five-set final against third-ranked Stefan Edberg lasted 3 hours and 41 minutes. When it was over, Chang had pulled off the year's second biggest upset by a score of 6–1, 3–6, 4–6, 6–4, 6–2. Chang's 1989 French Open exploits made him the first Asian American to attain the status of a global sports superstar. The Hoboken, New Jersey, native began his pro career at the age of 15 and went on to win 34 ATP career titles with earnings totaling over $18 million before retiring on September 4, 2003.

Michael was born in New Jersey, and the family later moved to Minnesota. There, he began playing Ping-Pong in the basement. He says, "I hope kids think about beating me while they're down in their basement, just like I thought of beating Borg and McEnroe." When Michael was 7, the Chang family moved to California so he could play year round against better competition. But soon he had beaten everybody his age. Years passed, and Michael eventually started college early so he could enter the National Collegiate Athletic Association Championships. Even that was too small a challenge. So Chang decided to turn pro, accepting a contract from Reebok shoes for more than $500,000. He was 15.

Source: "Michael Chang and Andre Agassi Are So Good That Fans May Soon Forget about Jimmy Connors and John McEnroe." *Boys' Life*, April 1989, p. 38.

Books

Chang, Michael. With Mike Yorkey. *Holding Serve: Persevering On and Off the Court*. Nashville,

TN: Thomas Nelson Publishers, 2002. *Holding Serve* is Chang's autobiography that narrates his career as a professional tennis player.

King, Richard, ed. *Asian American Athletes in Sport and Society*. New York: Routledge, 2015. See Nancy Spencer's Chapter 8, "The Spring of 1989: Michael Chang, Roland Garros, and Tiananmen Square."

Websites

Chang Family Foundation. 2018. This site provides a biography of Michael Chang with photographs. http://mchang.com/. Accessed January 20, 2018.

"Michael Chang." International Tennis Hall of Fame. 2016. This site provides a detailed history of Chang's career as a pro tennis player. https://www.tennisfame.com/hall-of-famers/inductees/michael-chang/. Accessed January 20, 2018.

Also Noteworthy

1972

The Taoist Temple at No. 12 China Alley in Hanford, California, that dates from 1893 is registered as a historic landmark and is listed on the U.S. National Register of Historic Places.

1999

Wat Buddharatanaram, locally referred to as Wat Keller, a Thai Buddhist temple, opens in Keller, Texas.

June 14

1900

The Hawaiian Islands officially become a U.S. territory, and all islanders become American citizens. President William McKinley appointed Sanford B. Dole the first governor. This also ended recruitment of contract laborers. It also gave native Hawaiians the right to vote but specifically excluded persons of Asian origin.

The United States emerged as a colonial power with insular colonies and territories in the wake of the Spanish-American War in 1898. Hawai'i was the only overseas territory to become a U.S. state. Guam, Puerto Rico, Samoa, and the Philippines remained unincorporated territories and Cuba a semi-independent protectorate, all lacking the legal possibility of incorporation. Yet it was by no means a foregone conclusion that Hawai'i would achieve annexation in 1898, status as an incorporated territory in 1900, and statehood in 1959. Annexation was fiercely debated in the U.S. Senate and popular press after the U.S.-backed overthrow of the Hawaiian kingdom. The debate largely centered on whether the islands and their racially suspect inhabitants were worthy of the privileges of American citizenship. Who and what were Hawaiians? Stoked by fears of racially suspect "mongrel" and "Asiatic" populations, Americans were deeply divided about whether to admit Hawai'i to the United States. Those who opposed and those who favored annexation issued opinions that took on a decidedly racist valence. A Chicago newspaper advocating annexation wanted universal suffrage withheld from Hawai'i on account of its racial character. The newspaper editorialized, "It would not do to admit Hawaii as a State, unless the character of the population underwent radical change." These suspicions erupted throughout the twentieth century; in the 1930s questions arose about whether Hawai'i even deserved territorial status, and after World War II, Southern senators argued that Hawai'i harbored too many Asians.

Source: Imada, *Adria. Aloha America: Hula Circuits through the U.S. Empire*. Durham, NC: Duke University Press, 2012, p. 5.

Books

Kinzer, Stephen. *Overthrow: America's Century of Regime Change from Hawaii to Iraq*. New York: Times Books, 2006. *Overthrow* is a history of U.S. imperialism in 14 countries.

Skwiot, Christine. *The Purposes of Paradise: U.S. Tourism and Empire in Cuba and Hawai'i*. Philadelphia: University of Pennsylvania Press, 2010. *The Purposes of Paradise* investigates U.S. imperialism from the 19th to 20th centuries and the ways travel and tourism informed U.S. imperialism in Cuba and Hawaii.

Websites

"CLEAR Timeline of Hawai'i Labor History." Center for Labor Education & Research. University of Hawai'i—West O'ahu. 2018. This site provides a useful annotated chronology of labor history in Hawaii. https://www.hawaii.edu/uhwo/clear/home/Timeline.html. Accessed January 20, 2018.

Walden, Andrew. "June 14, 1900: The Abolition of Slavery in Hawaii." Hawaii Free Press. June 14, 2017. This article provides a history of the contract labor in Hawaii with links to primary documents. http://www.hawaiifreepress.com/ArticlesMain/tabid/56/ID/4473/June-14-1900-The-Abolition-of-Slavery-in-Hawaii.aspx. Accessed January 20, 2018.

June 15

1884

South Asian American Taraknath Das is born on this day. Das arrived in the United States on June 18, 1906. Das published the *Free Hindusthan* while working for the U.S. Immigration Service in Vancouver, Canada. The *Free Hindusthan* is the only publication of its kind in North America that advanced India's independence.

Taraknath Das, a life member of the Association, long a familiar figure at its meetings, and instrumental in establishing two of the prizes it offers—the Watumull and the Schuyler—died in New York City on December 22, 1958, at the age of seventy-five. Dr. Das was an early fighter for the independence of India and an international figure in political science. Born in Bengal, he came to the United States in 1906 and soon afterward became an American citizen. After receiving his doctorate from Georgetown University in 1924 he was special lecturer for Catholic University of American, the University of Maryland, the City College of New York, Queens College (Flushing), and Columbia University. His principal interests were in the history of India, on various aspects of which he published a number of books, and in international relations as affecting the Far and Middle East. His greatest interest was in the promotion of better understanding among the peoples of the world, especially between East and West, and to this end he and his wife established the Taraknath Das Foundation (incorporated in 1935), which has been active in furthering Indian studies in a number of American universities.

Source: "Obituary for Taraknath Das." *American Historical Review* 64, no. 3 (April 1959): p. 831.

Books

Mukherjee, Tapan. *Taraknath Das: Life and Letters of a Revolutionary in Exile*. Kolkata, India: National Council of Education, Bengal, Jadavpur University, 1998. *Taraknath Das is a* comprehensive study of Das's life as a revolutionary freedom fighter with primary documents.

Ramnath, Maia. *Haj to Utopia: How the Ghadar Movement Charted Global Radicalism and Attempted to Overthrow the British Empire*. Berkeley: University of California Press, 2011. *Haj to Utopia* is a study of Ghadar, the Indian anticolonial movement to gain independence from colonial Great Britain.

Websites

Pusey, Grace. "Today in History: Taraknath Das Born June 15, 1884." SAADA: South Asian American Digital Archive. June 15, 2014. This essay is a biography of Taraknath Das with photographs and links to other historical primary documents. https://www.saada.org/news/20140615-3594. Accessed January 20, 2018.

"Taraknath Das." University of Washington Libraries. Special Collections. 2018. This site contains a detailed biography of Das, with links to further resources. http://www.lib.washington.edu/specialcollections/collections/exhibits/southasianstudents/das. Accessed January 20, 2018.

Also Noteworthy

1898

The Anti-Imperialist League is founded in Boston to oppose American imperialism, including U.S. colonization of the Philippines.

June 16

2012

The city of Long Beach, California, inaugurates the sign "Cambodia Town" at Watt Samaki, "Unity Temple." Cambodia Town is the official name of one-mile stretch of Anaheim Street between Atlantic and Junipero avenues in the eastside of Long Beach. It is most known for its numerous Cambodian American–owned businesses, including religious institutions and community organizations.

Using their experience from political practices at the national level in the Republican Party and locally, Cambodians built grassroots community support for the notion of Cambodia Town among neighbourhood residents. Cambodia Town representatives attended political fundraisers and various political action groups. They volunteered in community activities including the Martin Luther King Day Parade and Cinco de Mayo events to mobilise support for Cambodia Town. Through these grassroots efforts, city officials took notice and began to embrace the idea that having a Cambodia Town could be good for the city economically. Long Beach competes for tourists with the better-known City of Los Angeles and nearby Anaheim, home to Disneyland. Long Beach, a city reliant on the vagaries of the aerospace industry and the Port, often suffers longer during economic recessions. Also, the self-proclaimed "International City" had few, if any, viable examples of how Long Beach as a tourist destination lived up to this name. Cambodians, in the wake of the successful banner project and the other cultural events they sponsor during Cambodian New Year every April offered a potentially unique cultural experience and identity for the City. For these reasons, the City supported the pro-business model of the Cambodia Town leadership and urged them to seek a Business Improvement District (BID) designation. However, a BID meant that Cambodian Town, Inc., the official name of the non-profit organisation formed from the task force, needed business owners on Anaheim Street to sign and approve the designation and agree to an annual fee to fund improvement activities. The Cambodian Town, Inc. Board members began the lengthy process of obtaining a BID, but also continued to pressure the City Council for a cultural designation apart from the BID.

Source: Quintiliani, Karen, and Susan Needham. "Three Decades of Cambodian American Political Activism in Long Beach, California." In *The Age of Asian Migration: Continuity, Diversity, and Susceptibility*, edited by Yuk Wah Chan, David Haines, and Jonathan H.X. Lee, vol. I, pp. 276–277. Cambridge, England: Cambridge Scholars Publishing, 2014.

Books

Lee, Jonathan H.X. ed. *Cambodian American Experiences: Histories, Communities, Cultures, and Identities*. Dubuque, IA: Kendall and Hunt Publishing Company, 2010. *Cambodian American Experiences* is a comprehensive study of Cambodian American history, community formation, and resettlement-related issues.

Needham, Susan, and Quintiliani, Karen. *Cambodians in Long Beach*. Charleston, SC: Arcadia Publishing, 2008. *Cambodians in Long Beach* is a visual documentation of the resettlement of Cambodians in Long Beach, California.

Websites

Cambodia Town: Long Beach CA Cambodian Community. 2015. This is the web page of Cambodia Town Inc., a nonpartisan, nonprofit organization. http://www.cambodiatown.com/. Accessed January 20, 2018.

Shyong, Frank. "In Cambodia Town, A Community Moves from Survival to Success." *Los Angeles Times*, November 5, 2017. This essay documents the success of Cambodia Town with photographs and a video. http://www.latimes.com/local/lanow/la-me-cambodiatown-future-generation-20170629-htmlstory.html. Accessed January 20, 2018.

June 17

2003

Asian Americans, African Americans, Latino Americans, and women file a class action lawsuit against Abercrombie & Fitch (A&F) in the U.S. District Court of San Francisco, California, alleging discrimination in its hiring practices. The lawsuit *Eduardo Gonzalez, et al. v. Abercrombie & Fitch Stores, Inc., et al.* (No. C03–2817) claims that the retailer violated Title VII of the Civil Rights Act of 1964 by maintaining hiring and business practices that discriminated against minorities and women of color and maintained a nationwide corporate policy of preferring white employees. In a settlement, A&F agreed to pay $40 million to the class of Asian American, African American, Latino American, and female applicants and employees who charged the retailer with discrimination.

. . . [T]complaint alleges that A&F discriminates against people of color, including Latinos, Asian Americans, and African Americans, in its hiring, job assignment, compensation, termination, and other terms and conditions of employment. There are nine named litigants in the complaint who filed on behalf of the class they represent: Eduardo Gonzalez, Anthony Ocampo, Encarnacion Gutierrez, Johan Montoya, Juan Carlos Gomez-Montejano, Jennifer Lu, Austin Chu, Ivy Nguyen, and Angeline Wu. These litigants are represented by counsel from the Mexican American Legal Defense and Educational Fund; the Asian Pacific American Legal Center; the NAACP Legal Defense and Education Fund; and the law firm of Lieff, Cabraser, Heimann & Bernstein.

Source: McBride, Dwight. *Why I Hate Abercrombie & Fitch: Essays on Race and Sexuality*. New York: New York University Press, 2005, p. 77.

Books

Beachler, Donald, and Thomas Shevory. *When Good Companies Go Bad: 100 Corporate Miscalculations and Misdeeds*. Santa Barbara, CA: ABC-CLIO, 2014. See Chapter 3, "Abercrombie & Fitch: Employment-Related Race Discrimination (2004)."

Gallagher, Charles, and Cameron Lippard, eds. *Race and Racism in the United States: An Encyclopedia of the American Mosaic*. Santa Barbara, CA: Greenwood, 2014. See "*Gonzalez, et al. v. Abercrombie & Fitch Stores*" entry.

Websites

Gonzalez, et al. v. Abercrombie & Fitch Stores, Inc., et al. Cornell University ILR School. April 14, 2005. This is the consent decree of this case with details of the settlement. https://digitalcommons.ilr.cornell.edu/cgi/viewcontent.cgi?referer=https://www.google.com/&httpsredir=1&article=1022&context=condec. Accessed February 7, 2018.

Greenhouse, Steven. "Clothing Chain Accused of Discrimination." *New York Times*, June 17, 2003. This article provides background on the class action lawsuit. http://www.nytimes.com/2003/06/17/us/clothing-chain-accused-of-discrimination.html. Accessed February 7, 2018.

Also Noteworthy

1885

The second group of Japanese laborers arrives in Hawaii on the *Yamashiro Maru* along with Japanese special commissioner Katsunosuke Inoue.

1942

Milton Eisenhower resigns as director of the War Relocation Authority and is succeeded by Dillon S. Myer.

June 18

2002

Crystal Ali-Khan, an American Muslim who wears a hijab, is assaulted by a woman in a drug store in Houston, Texas.

Crystal Ali-Khan, a 24-year-old mother of three, was attacked by an enraged Anglo woman. Immediately prior to the assault, Ali-Khan had gotten out of her car to buy hay fever medicine at a pharmacy near her Southwest Houston home. Ali-Khan told the Houston Chronicle *that she had just left her vehicle when the Anglo woman abruptly body-slammed her, twisting her hijab into a strangulation hold and limiting her ability to breathe. Ali-Khan told her attacker that she would be facing a lawsuit if she didn't release her immediately. The Anglo woman responded that she would not be prosecuted for the crime because she was a Christian. During the assault, the Anglo woman compared Ali-Khan to the 9/11 terrorists. The police eventually arrived and took an incident report. Area Muslims were frightened by the attack and concerned that Ali-Khan might lose her children to state custody because she had momentarily left them unattended. Judy Hay, a spokeswoman for Children's Protective Services, confirmed that her agency was investigating Ali-Khan since Texas state law prohibits leaving children under seven unsupervised in a motor vehicle.*

Source: Karam, Nicoletta. *The 9/11 Backlash: A Decade of U.S. Hate Crimes Targeting the Innocent.* Berkeley, CA: Beatitude Press, 2012, p. 49.

Books

Bakalian, Anny, and Mehdi Bozorgmehr. *Backlash 9/11: Middle Eastern and Muslim Americans Respond*. Berkeley: University of California Press, 2009. *Backlash 9/11* examines the post–9/11 backlash against Arab, Muslim, and Sikh Americans anchored in historical comparative perspectives and their organized response and resistance.

Welch, Michael. *Scapegoats of September 11th: Hate Crimes & State Crimes in the War on Terror*. New Brunswick, NJ: Rutgers University Press, 2006. *Scapegoats of September 11th* covers various aspects of post–9/11 crimes.

Website

Human Rights Watch. "'We Are Not the Enemy': Hate Crimes against Arabs, Muslims, and Those Perceived to Be Arab or Muslim after September 11." Vol. 14, No. 6 (G)—November 2002. A report that summarizes Islamophobia and Arabphobia in the United States post–9/11 and documents hate crime cases up to date of publication. https://www.hrw.org/reports/2002/usahate/usa1102.pdf. Accessed January 24, 2018.

June 19

1868

Japan-based American businessman, Eugene M. Van Reed, illegally ships a group of approximately 150 Japanese to Hawaii to work on sugar plantations and another 40 people to Guam. This unauthorized recruitment and shipment of laborers, known as the *gannen-mono*, meaning "first year (of Meiji era) people," marked the beginning of Japanese labor migration overseas. However, for the next two decades, the Meiji government prohibited the departure of immigrant laborers due to the slave-like treatment that the first Japanese migrants received in Hawaii and Guam.

Van Reed got permission from the Tokugawa government to recruit some 300 people. Before preparations for their emigration were made, however, Japan's civil war ended. The new Meiji government denied permission to emigrate, revoking the permission that the Tokugawa government had issued. As a result, Van Reed could take only 149 Japanese (141 men, 6 women, and 2 children)—without government permission—to Hawaii. . . . Later that year, another 42 Japanese left for Guam to work in the sugar plantations. In both locations, the migrants were treated little better than slaves, so many ran away before their contracts ended.

Source: Adachi, Nobuko. "Emigrants from Japan." In *Japan at War: An Encyclopedia*, edited by Louis Perez, p. 79. Santa Barbara, CA: ABC-CLIO, 2013.

Books

Perez, Louis, ed. *Japan at War: An Encyclopedia*. Santa Barbara, CA: ABC-CLIO, 2013. This book covers many aspects of Japanese migration history. See Nobuko Adachi's entry "Emigrants from Japan," pp. 77–83.

Sant, John E. Van. *Pacific Pioneers: Japanese Journeys to America and Hawaii, 1850–80*. Urbana: University of Illinois Press, 2000. This book covers the early history of Japanese migration to the United States.

Websites

Japanese Emigration to Brazil. "Chapter 1 before the Beginning: Early History of Japanese Emigration." National Diet Library. Japan. 2014. This site, offered in English, Japanese, or Portuguese, offers historical background on early Japanese migration history, with images of archival documents. http://www.ndl.go.jp/brasil/e/s1/s1_1.html. Accessed October 8, 2016.

O, Hosok. "Cultural Analysis of the Early Japanese Immigration to the United States during Meiji to Taisho Era (1868–1926)." Unpublished dissertation. Oklahoma State University. 2010. Chapter 4 "Early Japanese Immigration to Hawaii" discusses early history of Japanese immigration to Hawaii. http://digital.library.okstate.edu/etd/O_okstate_0664D_11126.pdf. Accessed October 8, 2016.

1982

Vincent Chin, a 27-year-old Chinese American, is brutally murdered in Detroit by two white men, Ronald Ebens and Michael Nitz, who mistook him for a "Japanese." Ebens and Nitz blamed Chin for losing their jobs in the auto industry. Chin was struck repeatedly with a bat, including blows to the head. Chin was taken to the Henry Ford Hospital, where he was unconscious and died after four days in a coma on June 23, 1982.

Vincent Jen Chin was born on May 18, 1955 in Guangdong, China. Chin was the only child of Bing Hing Chin and Lily Chin. Bing Hing Chin brought his bride from China through his service in World War II. After Lily suffered a miscarriage in 1949, they adopted Vincent from a Chinese orphanage in 1961. Chin grew up in Highland Park and, later, Oak Park, Michigan.

*On June 19, 1982, Vincent Jen Chin, 27 years old, went to the Fancy Pants strip club in Highland Park with friends for his bachelor's party. There, Chin encountered two autoworkers, Ronald Ebens—a Chrysler plant supervisor—and his stepson, Michael Nitz, who racialized Chin for "Japanese." As many during this period did, they blamed the Japanese for the woes of the American auto industry. Ebens and Nitz harassed Chin with racial epithets and a fight broke out. Although Chin was not Japanese, and worked in the auto industry himself as a draftsman, Ebens was heard saying, "It's because of you little mother-****ers that we're out of work," as well as other anti-Chinese racial epithets. They were all thrown out of the strip club, but the fight continued in the parking, until Chin ran off. Ebens and Nitz pursued him and found Chin at a nearby McDonald's restaurant. There, Ebens and Nitz bludgeoned Chin with a baseball bat until his head cracked open. On June 23, 1982, Chin died.*

On March 18, 1983, Ebens and Nitz pleaded guilty to killing Chin. In an agreement with prosecutors, they pleaded to manslaughter (down from second-degree murder). Judge Charles Kaufman sentenced them to three years' probation and fined them $3,780 each. Explaining the light sentence, Judge Kaufman stated, "These aren't the kind of men you send to jail. You fit the punishment to the criminal, not the crime." To the dismay of the Asian American community, neither man spent a single day in jail for murdering Chin.

The brutal murder and light sentence outraged the Asian American community. In Detroit on March 31, 1983, Asian Americans founded the American Citizens for Justice to lobby for a federal trial for Chin's murderers. The campaign was spearheaded by journalist Helen Zia, lawyer Liza Chan, and Lily Chin—Chin's mother. Rallies in Detroit, San Francisco, and Los Angeles galvanized the Asian American communities and attracted national media attention. On June 5, 1984, federal prosecutors charged Ebens and Nitz with violating Chin's civil rights. After 23 days of deliberation, a Detroit federal jury acquitted Nitz but found Ebens guilty of violating Chin's civil rights: Ebens, was convicted and sentenced to 25 years in prison. Although it seemed a measure of justice has prevailed for Chin, but the conviction was overturned on appeal.

In 1987, Lily Chin left the United States and returned to her hometown of Guangzhou, China. She returned to the United States in 2001 for medical treatment and died on June 9, 2002. The violent killing of Vincent Chin in 1982, again, fueled many Chinese Americans to become politically active, especially with regard to civil rights struggles.

Source: Lee, Jonathan H. X., ed. *Chinese Americans: The History and Culture of a People*. Santa Barbara, CA: ABC-CLIO, 2016, pp. 26–28.

Books

Darden, Joe, and Richard Thomas. *Detroit: Race Riots, Racial Conflicts, and Efforts to Bridge the Racial Divide*. East Lansing: Michigan State University Press, 2013. Chapter 7 "The Declining Auto Industry and Anti-Asian Racism: The Murder of Vincent Chin" reflects on the murder of Vincent Chin, anti-Asian racism, and the decline of the Detroit auto industry.

Zia, Helen. *Asian American Dreams: The Emergence of an American People*. New York: Farrar, Straus, and Giroux, 2000. Chapter 3, "Detroit Blues: 'Because of You Motherfuckers,'" is a critical discussion of the murder of Vincent Chin.

Websites

Wu, Frank. "Why Vincent Chin Matters." *New York Times*, June 22, 2012. This newspaper opinion essay is written by legal scholar Frank Wu and discusses the Vincent Chin murder, details of the trial, its outcome, and its impact and significance for Asian Americans. http://www.nytimes.com/2012/06/23/opinion/why-vincent-chin-matters.html. Accessed January 17, 2017.

Zia, Helen. "Vincent Chin's Story/Lily Chin: The Courage to Speak." Asian Americans Advancing Justice. This article is written by an Asian American journalist and activist and discusses the Vincent Chin killing and Lily Chin's courage to speak out in her search for justice for her son. http://advancingjustice-la.org/sites/default/files/UCRS%205_Vincent_Chin_Lily_Chin_story%20r2.pdf. Accessed January 17, 2017.

2012

The U.S. House of Representatives unanimously passes a bipartisan resolution introduced by Congresswoman Judy Chu of California, who represents the 27th Congressional District (which includes Pasadena and the west San Gabriel Valley of southern California), which formally expresses the regret of the House of Representatives for the Chinese Exclusion Act of 1882 and other anti-Chinese legislations that discriminated against people of Chinese heritage in the United States.

H.Res.683—Expressing the regret of the House of Representatives for the passage of laws that adversely affected the Chinese in the United States, including the Chinese Exclusion Act.

In the House of Representatives, U. S.,

Whereas many Chinese came to the United States in the 19th and 20th centuries, as did people from other countries, in search of the opportunity to create a better life;

Whereas the United States ratified the Burlingame Treaty on October 19, 1868, which permitted the free movement of the Chinese people to, from, and within the United States and made China a "most favored nation";

Whereas in 1878, the House of Representatives passed a resolution requesting that President Rutherford B. Hayes renegotiate the Burlingame Treaty so Congress could limit Chinese immigration to the United States;

Whereas, on February 22, 1879, the House of Representatives passed the Fifteen Passenger Bill, which only permitted 15 Chinese passengers on any ship coming to the United States;

Whereas, on March 1, 1879, President Hayes vetoed the Fifteen Passenger Bill as being incompatible with the Burlingame Treaty;

Whereas, on May 9, 1881, the United States ratified the Angell Treaty, which allowed the United States to suspend, but not prohibit, immigration of Chinese laborers, declared that "Chinese laborers who are now in the United States shall be allowed to go and come of their own free will," and reaffirmed that Chinese persons possessed "all the rights, privileges, immunities, and exemptions which are accorded to the citizens and subjects of the most favored nation";

Whereas the House of Representatives passed legislation that adversely affected Chinese persons in the United States and limited their civil rights, Including. . . .

Whereas Chinese-Americans continue to play a significant role in the success of the United States; and

Whereas the United States was founded on the principle that all persons are created equal: Now, therefore, be it

Resolved,

SECTION 1. ACKNOWLEDGEMENT.

That the House of Representatives regrets the passage of legislation that adversely affected people of Chinese origin in the United States because of their ethnicity. . . .

Source: H. Res. 683 (2011–2012). Available at https://www.congress.gov/bill/112th-congress/house-resolution/683/text. Accessed June 16, 2018.

Books

Freedman, Amy. *Political Participation and Ethnic Minorities: Chinese Overseas in Malaysia, Indonesia, and the United States*. New York: Routledge, 2000. See Chapter 5, "Chinese in the United States," for background on Chinese American political participation, and Chapter 6, "Suburanization: Chinese in Monterey Park, California," for discussion related to Chu and her congressional district.

Horton, John. *The Politics of Diversity: Immigration, Resistance, and Change in Monterey Park, California*. Philadelphia, PA: Temple University Press, 1995. *The Politics of Diversity* discusses Chu's congressional district; see Chapter 7, "Dilemmas of Diversity," for discussion related to Chu.

Websites

Representative Judy Chu. Congress.gov. This site has a biography of Chu, in addition to legislation she sponsored. https://www.congress.gov/member/judy-chu/C001080. Accessed February 8, 2018.

U.S. Congresswoman Judy Chu 27th District of California. Office web page. https://chu.house.gov/. Accessed February 8, 2018.

June 20

1973

Bruce Lee (1940–1973) dies six days before *Enter the Dragon*'s (1973) release. Lee was born in Chinatown, San Francisco, on November 27, 1940. At the age of three months, his family moved back to Hong Kong, where Lee was frequently cast in films as a juvenile delinquent. While in Hong Kong, Lee received training in Wing Chun. At 18, Lee was sent to live in the United States. He finished high school in Seattle and studied philosophy and drama at the University of Washington. In 1959, Lee opened his first martial arts school, and in 1964, he relocated to Oakland, cofounding a second school. This is when he developed his own technique called Jeet Kune Do, or "Way of the Intercepting First"—a blend of kung fu and philosophy. Lee attracted attention from Hollywood when he appeared in the International Karate Championships; he was soon cast as the sidekick Kato in the television series *The Green Hornet* (1966–1967). Lee attributed his failure in Hollywood to racism. For instance, Lee's ideas for a show called *The Warrior* only became the TV series *Kung Fu* when white American actor David Carradine was casted to play the Chinese lead.

No other figure in Hong Kong cinema has done as much to bring East and West together in a common sharing of culture as Bruce Lee in his short lifetime. In him, Hong Kong cinema found its most forceful ambassador; an Asian role model espousing aspects of an Eastern culture who found receptive minds in the West. The only other examples of such a phenomenon that come to mind are figures from Japanese cinema such as Sessue Hayakawa or Toshiro Mifune, but they never enjoyed popular success on Lee's scale. Lee's success was based on the action choreography of his unique kung fu style—which he dubbed Jeet Kune Do *or "The Art of the Intercepting Fist". However, his international success harboured aspects other than the purely physical dimensions of his art which cannot so readily be adopted by other cultures. His death in 1973 spawned a legend and the world-wide scale of the cult which developed suggests that there was something universal about his figure.*

Source: Teo, Stepehn. "Bruce Lee: Narcissus and the Little Dragon." In *Asian Cinemas: A Reader and Guide*, edited by Dimitris Eleftheriotis and Gary Needham, p. 414. Honolulu: University of Hawaii Press, 2006.

Books

Bowman, Paul. *Beyond Bruce Lee: Chasing the Dragon through Film, Philosophy and Popular Culture*. New York: Columbia University Press, 2013. *Beyond Bruce* Lee explores Lee's legacy in popular culture and argues he is best understood in terms of "cultural translation."

Chan, Jachinson. *Chinese American Masculinities: From Fu Manchu to Bruce Lee*. New York: Routledge, 2001. See Chapter 4 "Bruce Lee: A Sexualized Object of Desire" for a focused discussion on Bruce Lee.

Websites

Bruce Lee. Bruce Lee Enterprises. 2016. This site contains historical essays on Lee, images, his form of martial arts, entertainment career history, and more. https://www.brucelee.com/. Accessed January 20, 2018.

Bruce Lee Foundation. 2018. This site contains information on Bruce Lee and includes videos and images of people impacted by his legacy. https://bruceleefoundation.org/. Accessed January 20, 2018.

June 21

1943

The Supreme Court issues a unanimous ruling in *Minoru Yasui v. United States* and declares that the curfew order applied to Japanese Americans and later removal to detention centers is constitutional. Yasui's challenge of the curfew was the first text by Japanese Americans of wartime restrictions against them. On August 19, 1943, Yasui was "released" from prison and escorted by a U.S. marshal back to the American internment camp at Minidoka.

Yasui v. United States (1943)

Argued May 11, 1943

Decided June 21, 1943

Syllabus

MR. CHIEF JUSTICE STONE delivered the opinion of the Court.

This is a companion case to Hirabayashi v. United States, ante . . . *decided this day.*

The case comes here on certificate of the Court of Appeals for the Ninth Circuit, certifying to us questions of law upon which it desires instructions for the decision of the case. § 239 of the Judicial Code as amended, 28 U.S.C. § 346. Acting under that section, we ordered the entire record to be certified to this Court so that we might proceed to a decision as if the case had been brought here by appeal.

Appellant, an American-born person of Japanese ancestry, was convicted in the district court of an offense defined by the Act of March 21, 1942. The indictment charged him with violation, on March 28, 1942, of a curfew order made applicable to Portland, Oregon, by Public Proclamation No. 3, issued by Lt. General J. L. DeWitt on March 24, 1942. 7 Federal Register 2543. The validity of the curfew was considered in the Hirabayashi *case, and this case presents the same issues as the conviction on Count 2 of the indictment in that case. From the evidence, it appeared that appellant was born in Oregon in 1916 of alien parents; that, when he was eight years old, he spent a summer in Japan; that he attended the public schools in Oregon, and also, for about three years, a Japanese language school; that he later attended the University of Oregon, from which he received A.B. and LL.B degrees; that he was a member of the bar of Oregon, and a second lieutenant in the Army of the United States, Infantry Reserve; that he had been employed by the Japanese Consulate in Chicago, but had resigned on December 8, 1941, and immediately offered his services to the military authorities; that he had discussed with an agent of the Federal Bureau of Investigation the advisability of testing the constitutionality of the curfew, and that, when he violated the curfew order, he requested that he be arrested so that he could test its constitutionality.*

The district court ruled that the Act of March 21, 1942, was unconstitutional as applied to American citizens, but held that appellant, by reason of his course of conduct, must be deemed to have renounced his American citizenship. 48 F.Supp. 40. The Government does not undertake to support the conviction on that ground, since no such issue was tendered by the Government, although appellant testified at the trial that he had not renounced his citizenship. Since we hold, as in the Hirabayashi *case, that the curfew order was valid as applied to citizens, it follows that appellant's citizenship was not relevant to the issue tendered by the Government, and the conviction must be sustained for the reasons stated in the* Hirabayashi *case.*

But as the sentence of one year's imprisonment—the maximum permitted by the statute—was imposed after the finding that appellant was not a citizen, and as the Government states that it has not and does not now controvert his citizenship, the case is an appropriate one for resentence in the light of these circumstances. See Husty v. United States, *282 U. S. 694, 282 U. S. 703. The conviction will be sustained, but the judgment will be vacated and the cause remanded to the district court for resentence of appellant, and to afford that court opportunity to strike its findings as to appellant's loss of United States citizenship.*

So ordered.

Source: Yasui v. United States (1943). JUSTIA U.S. Supreme Court. https://supreme.justia.com/cases/federal/us/320/115/case.html. Accessed January 13, 2017.

Books

Kim, Hyung-chan, ed. *Distinguished Asian Americans: A Biographical Dictionary*. Westport, CT: Greenwood Press, 1999. See entry on "Minoru Yasui" by Steven Fugita.

Maki, Mitchell, Harry Kitano, and Sarah Berthold. *Achieving the Impossible Dream: How Japanese Americans Obtained Redress*. Urbana: University of Illinois Press, 1999. *Achieving the Impossible Dream* covers many aspects of Japanese Americans who worked to get an apology from the U.S. government and achieve compensation for the unlawful internment of their community during World War II.

Websites

Asakawa, Gil. "Minoru Yasui." *Densho Encyclopedia*, 2017. This site provides an essay on the life and legacy of Minoru Yasui, with images and links to archival documents. http://encyclopedia.densho.org/Minoru_Yasui/. Accessed January 13, 2017.

Minoru Yasui v. United States (1943). U.S. Supreme Court. FindLaw. 2017. This site provides the text to the ruling in *Minoru Yasui v. United States*. http://caselaw.findlaw.com/us-supreme-court/320/115.html. Accessed January 13, 2017.

Also Noteworthy

1900

In an edict issued by China's Empress Dowager Cixi, China formally declares war on the United States, Britain, Germany, France, and Japan.

1943

The U.S. Supreme Court rules in *Hirabayashi v. U.S.* that the curfew law imposed on persons of Japanese ancestry is constitutional.

June 22

1999

On this day, Japanese American General Eric K. Shinseki becomes the U.S. Army's highest-ranking officer as he takes over as the 34th chief of staff (1999–2003). He also served as the seventh U.S. secretary of veterans affairs (2009–2014). Shinseki served two tours in the Vietnam War, and considered one of the most distinguished of any Vietnam veteran. He was wounded three times during those tours. On one occasion Shinseki's injuries were so severe that even his own sergeant assumed he had died in the hospital. Shinseki's valorous leadership under fire won him two Distinguished Service Medals, the Bronze Star, and several Purple Hearts. Shinseki publicly disagreed with the Bush administration regarding troop numbers needed for the war in Iraq.

Former General Eric Shinseki Chief of Staff of the United States Army was punished and undermined for contradicting Donald Rumsfeld's pre-war assessment of troop needs in Iraq. In February 2003, General Shinseki presciently testified before the Senate Armed Services Committee that the Defense Department's troop estimate for occupying Iraq was too low and that "something on the order of several hundred thousand soldiers" would be needed. He further stated, "We're talking about post-hostilities control over a piece of geography that's fairly significant, with the kinds of ethnic tensions that could lead to other problems." He continued: "It takes a significant ground force presence to maintain a safe and secure environment, to ensure that people are fed, that water is distributed all the normal responsibilities that go along with administering a situation like this." This, however, was very different from what the Defense Department had been telling Congress and the American public, as it had put the figure for occupation troop needs closer to 100,000 troops. Deputy Defense Secretary Paul Wolfowitz called General Shinseki's estimate "wildly off the mark" and Defense Secretary Rumsfeld, similarly stated that "[t]he idea that it would take several hundred thousand U.S. forces I think is far off the mark." It was also reported that in a semi-private meeting, the Pentagon's civilian leadership told the Village Voice newspaper that General Shinseki's remark was "bullshit from a Clintonite enamored of using the army for peacekeeping and not winning wars." General Shinseki refused to back down from his honest—and, ultimately correct—estimate.

Source: "Reining in the Imperial Presidency: Lessons and Recommendations Relating to the Presidency of George W. Bush." House Committee on the Judiciary Majority Staff Report to Chairman John Conyers Jr. Washington, DC (January 13, 2009), p. 225.

Books

Brown, John. *Kevlar Legions: The Transformation of the United States Army 1989–2005*. Washington, DC: Center of Military History U.S. Army, 2012. See Chapter 5, "The Shinseki Years, 1999–2003."

Farrell, Theo, Sten Rynning, and Terry Terriff. *Transforming Military Power since the Cold War: Britain, France, and the United States, 1991–2012*. Cambridge: Cambridge University Press, 2013. See Chapter 2, "Transformation from the Top Down: The United States Army, 1991–2012," for discussion related to Shinseki's term as 34th army chief of staff.

Websites

"General Eric K. Shinseki Exhibit." Hawaii Army Museum Society. 2016. This essay details General Shinseki's military career that includes photographs and links for other resources. http://www.hiarmymuseumsoc.org/exhibits/General_Eric_K_Shinseki.html. Accessed January 20, 2018.

Shinseki, Eric K. Collection. U.S. Army Military History Institute. U.S. Army Heritage and Education Center. 2018. This site contains documents related to General Eric K. Shinseki's career in the army. http://cdm16635.contentdm.oclc.org/cdm/ref/collection/p16635coll16/id/1150. Accessed January 20, 2018.

Also Noteworthy

2003

In Boston, Massachusetts, three men are arrested for hog-tying, beating, and stabbing a pizza deliveryman because they mistakenly identified him as a Muslim.

June 23

1899

Emilio Aguinaldo declares Philippines independent from Spain and establishes a revolutionary government with himself as president. Shortly afterward, Aguinaldo was against the United States in the Philippine-American War (1899–1901).

On January 23, 1899, Emilio Aguinaldo *was officially inaugurated as the first president of the Philippine Republic with Apolinario Mabini as prime minister. However, the United States did not recognize the new independent Philippine state. On February 4–5, 1899,* Emilio Aguinaldo's *troops fought for the first time against U.S. forces (Battle of Manila), and on June 2, 1899, the Philippine American War was declared. For two years,* Emilio Aguinaldo *and his followers were able to resist U.S. forces. But they faced internal dissent that was often violently resolved. For example, Emilio Aguinaldo was suspected in the assassination of General Antonio Luna (June 5, 1899), commander of the Philippine Revolutionary Army. On March 23, 1901, U.S. efforts to capture the Filipino leader were successful. The American military infiltrated Emilio Aguinaldo's headquarters at Palanan on the northeast coast of Luzon and seized the president. On April 1, 1901, the First Philippine Republic ended with Emilio Aguinaldo's formal surrender and his swearing allegiance to the United States. By July 4, the Philippine-American War officially came to a conclusion, even if hostilities continued until 1913.*

Source: Ricordeau, Gwenola. "Aguinaldo, Emilio (1869–1964)." In *Imperialism and Expansionism in American History: A Social, Political, and Cultural Encyclopedia and Document Collection*, edited by Chris Magoc and David Bernstein, p. 731. Santa Barbara, CA: ABC-CLIO, 2015.

Books

Aguinaldo, Emilio. *My Memoirs*. Manila, Philippines: C.A. Suntay, 1967. *My Memoirs* is an autobiography of Aguinaldo.

Saulo, Alfredo. *Emilio Aguinaldo: Generalissimo and President of the First Philippine Republic—First Republic in Asia*. Quezon City, Philippines: Phoenix Publishing House, 1983. *Emilio Aguinaldo* is a concise history of Emilio Aguinaldo.

Websites

Aguinaldo, Emilio. "Letter to the American People (1899)." America's History in the Making. Annenberg Learner: Teacher Resources and Professional Development across the Curriculum. Annenberg Foundation. 2017. This site provides the full text of Aguinaldo's letter critiquing U.S. imperialism in the Philippines. https://www.learner.org/courses/amerhistory/resource_archive/resource.php?unitChoice=16&ThemeNum=1&resourceType=2&resourceID=10144. Accessed January 20, 2018.

Dumindin, Arnaldo. "Philippine-American War, 1899–1902." http://www.filipinoamericanwar.com/. 2006. This site provides full coverage of the Philippine-American War, with photographs and links to historical documents. http://www.filipinoamericanwar.com/emilioaguinaldoreturns.htm. Accessed January 20, 2018.

Also Noteworthy

2003

In Salem, Oregon, a 12-year-old Israeli Arab boy playing outside his house is called a terrorist and punched in the face by another 12-year-old boy.

2007

In St. Cloud, Minnesota, Philip Joseph Massa, a 33-year-old, is charged with obstructing the legal process and fourth-degree misdemeanor for assaulting a man of Muslim descent.

June 24

1867

Several thousand Chinese railroad workers have gone on strike for a week demanding an end to beatings, increased wages from $35 to $40 per month, and eight hours workday. During the strike, management cut off their food supply and starved the workers back to work. As it turns out, the strike was not successful. The Chinese railroad workers were first hired in January 1864. The Central Pacific Railroad Company hired foreman Ah Toy and headman Hung Wah to lead a crew of 21 Chinese workers to clear Dutch Flat Donner Lake Wagon Road. They hired more during that year. In January 1865, assured that the Chinese workers were capable, the railroad hired 50 Chinese workers and then, shortly after, another 50. In 1865, Leland Stanford reported to Congress that the majority of the railroad workers were Chinese, and without them, it would be impossible to complete the western portion required by the congressional deadline. By July 1865, the Chinese workforce was nearly 4,000 strong; by February 1867, roughly 8,000 worked on the construction of the tunnels, while 3,000 laid tracks. In total, it was nearly 90 percent of the workforce. It is estimated that as many as 10,000–15,000 Chinese laborers worked on the railroad.

Excerpt from Sam S. Montague, Chief Engineer's Progress Report of the Central Pacific Railroad of California. November 25, 1865.

To the President and Directors of the Central Pacific Railroad of California: . . . It became apparent early in the season, that the amount of labor likely to be required during the summer could only be supplied by the employment of the Chinese element, of our population. Some distrust was at first felt regarding the capacity of this class for the service required, but the experiment has proved eminently successful. They are faithful and industrious, and under proper supervision, soon become skillful in the performance of their duties. Many of them are becoming very expert in drilling, blasting, and other departments of rock work.

Source: Sam S. Montague, Chief Engineer's "Report of the Chief Engineer upon Recent Surveys and Progress of Construction of the Central Pacific Railroad of California." December 1865. Central Pacific Railroad Photographic History Museum. CPRR.org. 2005. http://cprr.org/Museum/CPRR_1865_Engineering.pdf.

Books

Ambrose, Stephen. *Nothing Like It in the World: The Men Who Built the Transcontinental Railroad 1863–1869.* New York: Simon & Schuster, 2000. Historian Stephen Ambrose provides a sweeping narrative of the men who built the transcontinental railroad, from the engineers to the politicians and Irish and Chinese laborers.

Annian, Huang, ed. *The Silent Spikes: Chinese Laborers and the Construction of North American Railroads.* Translated by Zhang Juguo. Beijing: China Intercontinental Press, 2006. This is one of the books that specifically focused on the history and contribution of the Chinese laborers who built the *transcontinental* railroad.

Websites

"Chinese-American Contribution to Transcontinental Railroad." Central Pacific Railroad Photographic History Museum. This site provides historic photos, in addition to historical quotes from primary sources and links to multimedia materials. http://cprr.org/Museum/Chinese.html. Accessed January 29, 2018.

"Chinese Railroad Workers in North American Project." Stanford University. This site provides comprehensive historical information on the history of Chinese railroad workers. It contains a digital archive, oral histories, photographs, and much more useful information for anyone interested in this topic. http://web.stanford.edu/group/chineserailroad/cgi-bin/wordpress/. Accessed January 29, 2018.

1935

On this day, the U.S. Congress passes the Nye-Lea Bill that would make it possible for "alien veterans" and "veterans ineligible for citizenship" to naturalize and become citizens of the United States. The legislation was introduced into Congress by Clarence F. Lea of California and Gerald P. Nye of North Dakota. Congress now corrected an injustice committed by the courts that denied Asian veterans of World War I the right to citizenship. The original legislation granted any alien who served honorably the right to apply for citizenship. The courts held that other laws, as well as the *Ozawa* (1922) and *Thind* (1923) decisions, precluded that right for aliens otherwise ineligible for citizenship. Following a long campaign conducted by Asian veterans, in particular, Tokutaro Slocum, a Japanese American veteran of World War I, who was denied citizenship based on his race in 1923, he worked as a lobbyist for the Japanese American Citizens League (JACL) to get support for the Lea-Nye Bill. As a result, the United States granted citizenship to 500 World War I veterans of Asian descent. Many of them were Japanese Americans.

Roosevelt's attitude toward naturalization of Japanese immigrants is unclear. In 1935, following a long personal campaign by Tokie Slocum, a Japanese-American veteran of World War I, Congress approved by an overwhelming margin the Lea-Nye Bill, which granted citizenship to some 500 U.S. Army veterans from "oriental" countries. The bill's chief sponsors were pro-New Deal California Congressman Clarence Lea (who would, ironically, later become one of the chief instigators of the internment of Japanese Americans) and Senator Gerald Nye, a leading isolationist. Roosevelt signed the measure into law on June 25, 1935.

Despite his willingness to act on popular measures, Roosevelt had no interest in upsetting politically powerful nativist and anti-Asian forces by granting citizenship to more than a handful of Issei. During the same period, he refused, evidently on racial grounds, to grant citizenship rights to other Asian peoples. In 1933, after indigenous leaders in Guam heard reports that Roosevelt had expressed support during a private conversation for extending American citizenship to the colony's mixed-race Chamorro population, they organized a petition for citizenship which received almost 2,000 signatures. However, the secretary of the navy secured the President's agreement to oppose any citizenship bill based on the petition on the ground that the Chamorros "are Orientals."

Source: Robinson, Greg. *By Order of the President: FDR and the Internment of Japanese Americans*. Cambridge, MA: Harvard University Press, 2001, pp. 53–54.

Books

Hosokawa, Bill. *JACL in Quest of Justice: The History of the Japanese American Citizens League*. New York: William Morrow, 1982. *JACL in Quest of Justice* discusses the work of the JACL in advancing civil rights for Japanese Americans and Asian Americans.

Muller, Eric. *Free to Die for Their Country: The Story of the Japanese American Draft Resisters in World War II*. Chicago, IL: University of Chicago Press, 2001. *Free to Die for Their Country* discusses various forms of resistance to the internment of Japanese Americans during World War II.

Websites

Niiya, Brian. "Tokutaro Slocum." *Densho Encyclopedia*, November 15, 2017. This site provides a biographical and historical essay on Tokutaro Slocum, in addition to the significance of work to get the Nye-Lea Act of 1935 passed. http://encyclopedia.densho.org/Tokutaro%20Slocum/. Accessed March 2, 2018.

"The Nye-Lea Act (1935)." Rice on History: A (Mostly) Documentary Journey into the Past. This site provides a digital image of the Nye-Lea Act. https://riceonhistory.wordpress.com/2012/01/12/the-nye-lea-act-1935/. Accessed January 13, 2017.

Also Noteworthy

2005

Alice Wu's film *Saving Face* (2004) is released.

June 25

1948

President Harry S. Truman signs the Displaced Persons Act into law. This act helped individuals who were deemed to be victims of persecution by the Nazi government or who were fleeing persecution, or who could not return to their country because of fear of persecution based on race, religion, or political opinions. This act focused on individuals from Germany, Austria, and Italy; the French sector of either Berlin or Vienna; or the American or British zone and individuals from Czechoslovakia after World War II. This act will influence subsequent policies on refugees, especially those fleeing communist countries, including refugees from Hungary, Cuba, China, Vietnam, Laos, and Cambodia.

In a remarkable turnaround after World War II, the United States adopted new immigration policies to make possible a whole new wave of mass immigration. Foreign policy considerations combined with a booming economy, at least until the 1970s; ethnic lobbying and growing toleration in postwar America to bring out these changes. The process of reopening the door began cautiously in 1943 when, at the prodding of the Citizens Committee to Repeal the Chinese Exclusion acts, Congress gave China an annual immigration quota of 105. The law also permitted Chinese resident aliens to become naturalized American citizens. Legislation passed for other Asians in 1946 was also modest, permitting immigration annually of only 100 and naturalization rights for Indians and Filipinos. The problem for those reformers who wanted to accept European refugees after the war was the small national origins quota for many countries, which were kept in check by the McCarran-Walter Immigration Act of 1952. Congress had to enact special legislation for displaced persons and refugees. The legislators admitted about 600,000 European refugees when they passed the Displaced Persons acts of 1948 and 1950 and the Refugee Relief Act of 1953. Three years later President Dwight Eisenhower established a precedent when he used the parole power to admit Hungarian refugees fleeing the abortive Hungarian Revolution of 1956.

Source: Reimers, David. *Unwelcome Strangers: American Identity and the Turn against Immigration*. New York: Columbia University Press, 1998, pp. 25–26.

Books

Francis, Angus, and Rowena Maguire, eds. *Protection of Refugees and Displaced Persons in the Asia Pacific Region*. New York: Routledge, 2013. See Chapter 1 "Shifting Powers: Protection of Refugees and Displaced Persons in the Asia Pacific Region" for a historical discussion of the shifting view of "displaced persons" and "refugees" from the Asia Pacific region.

Qasmiyeh, Elena, Gil Loescher, Katy Long, and Nando Sigona, eds. *The Oxford Handbook of Refugee and Forced Migration Studies*. Oxford: Oxford University Press, 2014. This handbook is a complete reference for issues related to refugees and migration.

Websites

1948 Displaced Persons Act. HeinOnline. The University of Washington-Bothell Library. 2018. This site provides the full text of the Displaced Persons Act, along with a summary of the legislation. http://library.uwb.edu/Static/USimmigration/1948_displaced_persons_act.html. Accessed January 20, 2018.

Truman, Harry S. "Statement by the President upon Signing the Displaced Persons Act." June 25, 1948.The American Presidency Project. University of California, Santa Barbara. 2018. President Truman explains and defends signing the Displaced Persons Act into law. http://www.presidency.ucsb.edu/ws/?pid=12942. Accessed January 20, 2018.

Also Noteworthy

1950

The Korean War begins.

June 26

1913

On this day, 15 Korean fruit pickers are driven out of Hemet, California, by angry, unemployed, white workers. Similar to Chinese laborers, Korean laborers were scapegoated by white laborers and blamed for low wages and joblessness. This incident reflects the growing anti-Asian sentiment of the time and the expanding definition of who and what an "Asiatic" is.

Officials of Hemet were worried today as to the probable outcome of the incident yesterday when a party of Korean apricot pickers from Riverside were driven out of town by white field laborers and sympathizers who resented the competition of the Asiatics. Informed that the episode might become the basis for the diplomatic exchange between Japan and the United States, Mayor H. G. Shaw conferred with attorneys, and was informed that the city of Hemet could not be held responsible for the expulsion of the Koreans.

The Asiatics were imported, it is said, by fruit growers because they offered to pick fruit at rates from 2 to 3 cents per box less than white laborers demanded. The fruit growers asserted that they were forced to seek Asiatic labor because of the scarcity of white workmen. But it was denied that there was any scarcity of white labor in this section.

Deferring to the attitude of the citizens who participated in the expulsion of . . . Korean fruit pickers, ranchers . . . announced today that they were in favor of "a white man's valley," and would make no further efforts to procure Asiatic labor of any sort.

Source: "Hemet Mayor Worried: Disclaims Responsibility." *Los Angeles Times*, June 28, 1913, p. II.

Books

Chi, Tsung. *East Asian Americans and Political Participation: A Reference Handbook*. Santa Barbara, CA: ABC-CLIO, 2005. *East Asian Americans and Political Participation* discusses Chinese, Japanese, and Korean political activism and participation in America.

Hurh, Won Moo. *The Korean Americans*. Westport, CT: Greenwood Press, 1998. *The Korean Americans* covers the history of Korean migration and their experiences in the United States and community formation and demographics.

Websites

"A Brief History of Korean Americans." National Association of Korean Americans. This site provides a historical overview of the Korean American experience. http://www.naka.org/resources/history.asp. Accessed January 28, 2018.

The Ogden Standard. June 26, 1913. The Library of Congress. This site provides an archival newspaper that published an article on the Korean laborers being forced out of Hemet, California. However, this account had mistaken Koreans for Japanese. http://chroniclingamerica.loc.gov/lccn/sn85058396/1913-06-26/ed-1/seq-1/. Accessed October 20, 2016.

Also Noteworthy

1999

Cambodia Theravada Buddhist monk, Samdach Vira Dharmawara Bellong Mahathera (1889–1999), who was known simply as Bhante Dharma, dies in Stockton, California. At the age of 90, he established Wat Dhammararam in Stockton, California. During the next 20 years, Bhante Dharmawara was deeply involved in the refugee community.

June 27

1894

Shebata Saito, a Japanese man, applies for U.S. citizenship, but U.S. circuit courts refuse because it concluded that a native of Japan is not eligible for naturalization because it is restricted to only "aliens being free white persons." This case predates the *Takao Ozawa* case (1922) by nearly three decades.

In re Saito.

(Circuit Court, D. Massachusetts. June 27, 1849.)

Aliens—Naturalization of Japanese

A native of Japan, of the Mongolian race, is not entitled to naturalization, not being included within the term "white persons" in Rev. St. § 2169.

Application by Shebata Saito for naturalization.

J. Henry Taylor, for applicant.

Colt, Circuit Judge. This is an application by a native of Japan for naturalization.

The act relating to naturalization declares that "the provisions of this title shall apply to aliens being free white persons, and to aliens of African nativity and to persons of African descent." Rev. St. § 2169. The Japanese, like the Chinese, belong to the Mongolian race, and the question presented is whether they are included within the term "white persons."

These words were incorporated in the naturalization laws as early as 1802. . . . At that time the country was inhabited by three races, the Caucasian or white race, the Negro or black race, and the American or red race. It is reasonable, therefore, to infer that when congress, in designating the class of persons who could be naturalized, inserted the qualifying word "white," it intended to exclude from the privilege of citizenship all alien races except the Caucasian. . . .

Whether this question is viewed in the light of congressional intent, or of the popular or scientific meaning of "white persons," or of the authority of adjudicated cases, the only conclusion I am able to reach, after careful consideration, is that the present application must be denied.

Application denied.

Source: The Federal Report, Volume 61. Cases Argued and Determined in the Circuit Courts of Appeals and Circuit and District Courts of the United States. (June–August 1894). St. Paul, MN: West Publishing Co., 1894.

Books

Chuman, Frank. *The Bamboo People: The Law and Japanese-Americans*. Del Mar, CA: Publisher's Inc., 1976. *The Bamboo People* discusses the history and various core legal principles of the law and Japanese Americans.

Fukuda, Moritoshi. *Legal Problems of Japanese-Americans: Their History and Development in the United States*. Tokyo: Keio Tsushin Company, 1980. *Legal Problems of Japanese-Americans* examines the history of legal problems encountered by Japanese Americans from the late 19th century to the first half of the 20th century.

Websites

Randall, Vernellia. "Race, Racism and the Law." This site is created by law professor Vernellia Randall and provides information on domestic and international legal cases surrounding issues of race. http://racism.org/. Accessed October 10, 2016.

Thorndike, Jonathan. "Anti-Japanese Movement." Immigration to the United States. 2015. This site provides an overview history of the anti-Japanese movement in the United States. http://immigrationtounitedstates.org/348-anti-japanese-movement.html. Accessed October 10, 2016.

1952

McCarran-Walter Act, also known as the Immigration and Nationality Act, revises and consolidates all previous laws regarding immigration and naturalization. The 1952 Immigration and Nationality Act upheld the national origins quota system, which limited the number of immigrants allowed to enter the United States annually by country. It ended the Asian exclusion from immigrating to the United States and created a preference system, which determined eligibility by skill sets and family ties in the United States. The act eliminated laws preventing Asians from naturalizing, got rid of the Asiatic Barred Zone, and allotted each Asian country a minimum of 100 visas annually. However, the law allotted Asian quotas based on race rather than nationality. This allowed persons of Asian parentage and any nationality to receive visas under the generic quota for the "Asian Pacific Triangle," which ended up limiting Asian immigration.

The racial status quo of the nation was reinforced in the 1952 bill. Approximately 85% of the visas available annually were allotted to individuals from Northern and Western European lineage. The 1952 Act created symbolic opportunities for Asian immigration by allotting each Asian nation a minimum quota of 100 visas each year. The Act allotted Asian quotas based on race, not nationality. Under the 1952 law, an individual with one or more Asian parents, born anywhere in the world, and possessing the citizenship of any nation, was counted under the national quota of the Asian nation of his parent or parents. Low quota numbers ensured limited immigration from Asian nations.

Source: Koven, Steven, and Frank Götzke. *American Immigration Policy: Confronting the Nation's Challenges*. New York: Springer, 2010, p. 135.

Books

Divine, Robert. *American Immigration Policy, 1924–1952*. New Haven, CT: Yale University Press, 1957. *American Immigration Policy* covers various aspects of U.S. immigration policy up to post–World War II period.

Tichenor, Daniel. *Dividing Lines: The Politics of Immigration Control*. Princeton, NJ: Princeton University Press, 2002. *Dividing Lines* is a comprehensive study of U.S. immigration policy and history.

Websites

"The Immigration and Nationality Act of 1952 (The McCarran-Walter Act)." Office of the Historian, Bureau of Public Affairs. U.S. Department of State. This site contains a photograph of Patrick McCarran and general overview of the history of the act and its legacy and impact on U.S. immigration policy. https://history.state.gov/milestones/1945-1952/immigration-act. Accessed January 14, 2017.

"1952 Immigration and Nationality Act, a.k.a. the McCarran-Walter Act." HeinOnline. The University of Washington-Bothell Library. This site provides a summary of the act's historical background, discussion of its significance, and the full text of the act. http://library.uwb.edu/Static/USimmigration/1952_immigration_and_nationality_act.html. Accessed January 14, 2017.

Also Noteworthy

2009

In Yermo, California, Ali Abdelhadi Mohd, a 51-year-old Jordanian American, is found burned to death in his family's vacant house that had been set on fire.

June 28

1932

Noriyuki "Pat" Morita, a Japanese American actor, is born. Morita started his career as a stand-up comic and appeared in the TV sitcom *Happy Days* (1975–1983) but is best known as Mr. Kesuke Miyagi in *The Karate Kid* movie series. He is the first Asian American actor to be nominated for the Oscar for Best Supporting Actor for his performance in *The Karate Kid.*

Although almost always cast in the role of the alien Asian on television, Pat Morita is an American-born entertainer who began his career as a stand-up comedian. During the late 1960s appearance on The Tonight Show *(1954–present) with guest host Flip Wilson, Morita, billed as the "Hip Nip," jokes about the common perception among whites that people of Asian heritage in the United States are not truly Americans. Like only the best comedians, Morita reaches deep into existential issues and mines them as source material for humor. Still, it is not certain whether the audience "gets it," as a fidgety Morita puffs nervously on a cigarette while tossing off one-liners to a not-quite-comprehending studio audience. On the basis of his starring role in the popular feature film* The Karate Kid *(1984) and its sequels* The Karate Kid, Part II *(1986) and* The Karate Kid, Part III *(1989), Pat Morita began appearing in both TV and print media ads as the "Colgate Wisdom Tooth" in early 1989. In the course of his career as a performer, Morita had graduated from being the self-professed "Hip Nip" to an "Oriental" wise man who fights tooth decay by recommending liberal applications of Colgate Tartar Control Formula. Pioneering Asian American performers such as Pat Morita set the stage for new talent, including stand-up comedian Henry Cho, a second-generation Korean American born and raised in Knoxville, Tennessee.*

Source: Hamamoto, Darrell. *Monitored Peril: Asian Americans and the Politics of TV Representation*. Minneapolis: University of Minnesota Press, 1994, pp. 12–13.

Books

Bernardi, Daniel, and Michael Green, eds. *Race in American Film: Voices and Visions That Shaped a Nation*. Santa Barbara, CA: ABC-CLIO, 2017. See entry on "Asians in American Film."

Lee, Jonathan H.X. ed. *Japanese Americans: The History and Culture of a People*. Santa Barbara, CA: ABC-CLIO, 2017. See entry on "Japanese American Actors and Actresses."

Websites

Mok, Harry. "Aly Morita Calls for a Boycott of Karate Kid." *Hyphen: Asian American Unabridged*. June 11, 2010. This essay discusses Aly Morita's reason for boycotting the remake of *The Karate Kid*, citing that it perpetuates negative stereotypes of Asian Americans. https://hyphenmagazine.com/blog/2010/6/11/aly-morita-calls-boycott-karate-kid. Accessed January 20, 2018.

"Pat Morita." The Biography.com. A&E Television Network. June 7, 2014. This is a detailed biography of Morita's career. https://www.biography.com/people/pat-morita-20973585. Accessed January 20, 2018.

Also Noteworthy

1949

The last U.S. combat troops in Korea are ordered to leave.

1978

The U.S. Supreme Court upholds affirmative action in *Regents of the University of California v. Bakke* by allowing race to be one of several factors in college admission policy. However, it also rules that racial quotas, such as the one used by UC Davis School of Medicine, are impermissible.

June 29

1946

Congress enacts the Alien Fiancées Act, also known as the G.I. Fiancées Act, that grants fiancées of American servicemen during World War II a special exemption from immigration quotas to enter the United States. Amendments such as the 1945 War Bride Act and the 1946 Alien Fiancées Act allowed a larger number of Chinese women to immigrate to the United States. As a result, upward of 6,000 women immigrated as wives of Chinese American servicemen. One of the most noteworthy results of the period between 1846 and 1953 was that, due to the various exceptions for female immigration, almost 10,000 Chinese women immigrated, an important factor in allowing the Chinese American society to stabilize. The 1945 War Bride Act and the 1946 Alien Fiancées Act had a direct impact on Korean, Filipino, Japanese, and South Asian American communities as well.

Family reunification provisions—which had begun for the Chinese wives of American citizens under the terms of a 1946 act—made the close relatives of United States citizens nonquota immigrants. In consequence, wives, children, parents, brothers, and sisters of citizens were able to come in as nonquota entrants. In addition, some Asians came in under the provisions of the War Brides Act of 1945, the Alien Fiancées or Fiancés Act of 1946, and the Refugee Relief Act of 1953. These immigrants, too, were not chargeable to the tiny Asian quotas. As a result, in the 1950s some 45,000 Japanese and some 32,000 Chinese were able to enter legally as immigrants despite a quota system that ostensibly limited immigration to a total of about two thousand for each group for the entire decade. As has been the case with immigration legislation so many times before and since, the legislators and the bureaucrats who advised them had no accurate conception of even the short-term impact of their lawmaking.

Source: Daniels, Roger. *Asian America: Chinese and Japanese in the United States since 1850*. Seattle: University of Washington Press, 1988, p. 306.

Books

Lee, Jonathan H. X., ed. *Chinese Americans: The History and Culture of a People*. Santa Barbara, CA: ABC-CLIO, 2015. *Chinese Americans* contains several entries related to immigration history and policy and Chinese American women's issues.

Zinzius, Birgit. *Chinese America: Stereotype and Reality—History, Present, and Future of the Chinese Americans*. New York: Peter Lang, 2005. See Chapter 2 "Between 1924 and 1965" for discussion related to the development and impact of immigration policies related to Chinese women, and by extension, the development of Chinese American communities.

Websites

Lyon, Cherstin. "War Brides Act." *Densho Encyclopedia*, July 17, 2015. This essay discusses the impact of the War Brides Act among Japanese Americans. http://encyclopedia.densho.org/War%20Brides%20Act/. Accessed January 13, 2017.

Mabalon, Dawn. "The Significance of 1946 for Filipina/o Americans." Filipino American National Historical Society. 2017. This essay includes a discussion of the impact of the Alien Fiancées Act among Filipino Americans. http://fanhs-national.org/filam/about-fanhs/the-significance-of-1946-for-filipinao-americans/. Accessed January 13, 2017.

Also Noteworthy

1869

The *Colorado Tribune* documents the first person of Chinese ancestry in Denver, Colorado.

2007

In Nutley, New Jersey, Kerri A. Livesay, a 34-year-old, is charged with assault and bias crime for screaming curses and assaulting a teenager wearing traditional Muslim clothes at a store.

2010

Daniel Choi (b. February 22, 1981), a former American infantry officer in the U.S. Army, is discharged. Choi served in combat during the Iraq War in 2006–2007 and received a discharge letter after coming out on *The Rachel Maddow Show* in March 2009 to publicly critique the Don't Ask, Don't Tell policy, which prohibits openly gay, lesbian, and bisexual Americans from serving in the U.S. military.

June 30

1946

The War Relocation Authority (WRA) program officially ends after President Harry S. Truman signed Executive Order 9742, which officially terminated the WRA's mission. On February 19, 1942, President Franklin D. Roosevelt issued Executive Order 9066 that granted the secretary of war and his commanders the power "to prescribe military areas in such places and of such extent as he or the appropriate Military Commander may determine, from which any or all persons may be excluded." While no specific group or area was mentioned in the order, it was applied virtually to all Japanese Americans on the West Coast. On March 18, 1942, President Roosevelt signed Executive Order 9102 creating the WRA, a civilian agency charged with expediting the relocation of Japanese Americans from the West Coast.

Excerpt from *Relocation of Japanese-Americans*, published by the War Relocation Authority, Washington, D.C. (May 1943) as propaganda to gain support for their unjust policies against Japanese Americans.

The United States Government having called upon these people to move from their homes, also assumed a responsibility for helping them to become established. To carry out this responsibility, the President on March 18, 1942, created a civilian agency known as the War Relocation Authority.

The job of this agency, briefly, is to assist in the relocation of any persons who may be required by the Army to move from their homes in the interest of military security. So far, the work of the WRA has been concerned almost exclusively with people of Japanese descent who formerly lived close to the Pacific Rim of the country.

At first, plans were made by the Western Defense Command and the WRA to build accommodations only for a portion of the 110,000 evacuated people. A considerable percentage of them, it was hoped, would move out of the restricted area and resettle inland on their own initiative. During March of 1942, some 8,000 actually did move, but the great majority were held back by limited resources, general uncertainty, and mounting signs of community hostility in the intermountain region. By the latter part of March, it had become apparent that such a large-scale exodus could be handled effectively on a planned and systematic basis. Accordingly, all further voluntary evacuation was halted by the Western Defense Command on March 29 and plans were initiated by the WRA for establishing relocation centers with sufficient capacity and facilities to handle the entire evacuated population for as long as might be necessary.

The relocation centers, however, are NOT and ever were intended to be internment camps or places of confinement. They were established for two primary purposes: (1) To provide communities where evacuees might live and contribute, through their work, to their own support pending their gradual reabsorption into private employment and normal American life; and (2) to serve as wartime homes for those evacuees who might be unable or unfit to relocate in ordinary American communities. Under regulations adopted in September of 1942, the War Relocation Authority is now working toward a steady depopulation of the centers by urging all able-bodied residents with good records of behavior to reenter private employment in agriculture or industry.

Source: *Relocation of Japanese Americans*. Washington, DC: War Relocation Authority, 1943.

Books

Murray, Alice. *Historical Memories of the Japanese American Internment and the Struggle for Redress.* Stanford, CA: Stanford University Press, 2008. *Historical Memories* documents the shifting representation of Japanese relocation and redress over a span of six decades.

Robinson, Greg. *By Order of the President: FDR and the Internment of Japanese Americans.* Cambridge, MA: Harvard University Press, 2001. *By Order of the President* investigates the great contradiction of this period, when Franklin D. Roosevelt and his advisers were fighting to preserve democracy yet implanting unjust and undemocratic policies at home.

Websites

"Relocation of Japanese Americans." The Virtual Museum of the City of San Francisco. 2018. This essay is a detailed history of the War Relocation Authority and its legacy and impact on Japanese Americans. http://www.sfmuseum.org/hist10/relocbook.html. Accessed January 20, 2018.

"The War Relocation Authority & the Incarceration of Japanese-Americans during World War II." Harry S. Truman Presidential Library & Museum. 2017. This site provides detailed historical background to the Japanese American internment, along with photographs, lesson plans, and primary documents. https://www.trumanlibrary.org/whistlestop/study_collections/japanese_internment/. Accessed January 20, 2018.

July

July 1

1910

The United States seeks review of the decision of the Circuit Court of the United States for the Southern District of New York, which granted Bhicaji Framji Balsara (appellee) citizenship under section 2169 of the U.S. Revised Statutes. The United States contended that Balsara was not within that statute. Balsara was from India and had applied for citizenship. The United States contended that the appellee was not entitled to naturalization because he was not from England, Ireland, Scotland, Wales, Germany, Sweden, France, and Holland because Congress intended that statute for aliens coming from those countries only. The court argued that because the words in the statute referred to race, it included all persons of the white race only, as distinguished from the black, red, yellow, or brown races. Prior to Bhagat Singh Thind's attempt, Indians applying for citizenship yielded mixed results as some courts classified them as "white" while others did not. For instance, in the 1910 *United States v. Balsara* and in 1913 *Ajkoy Kumar Mazumdar* decisions, the courts held that Indians from India were "Caucasians" and therefore entitled to be legally considered as "white persons" eligible for citizenship under the 1790 law.

Opinion by Ward

WARD, Circuit Judge. The Parsees emigrated some 1,200 years ago from Persia into India, and now live in the neighborhood of Bombay, to the number of about 100,000. They constitute a settlement by themselves of intelligent and well-to-do persons, principally engaged in commerce, and are as distinct from the Hindus as are the English who dwell in India. Balsara himself is a merchant of this city, entirely qualified for citizenship but for the fact, as the government contends, that he is not within section 2169 of the United States Revised Statutes (U.S. Comp. St. 1901, p. 1333), which provides as to naturalization:

"The provisions of this title shall apply to aliens being free white persons and to aliens of African nativity and to persons of African descent."

. . . On the other hand, counsel for Balsara insist that Congress intended by the words "free white persons" to confer the privilege of naturalization upon members of the white or Caucasian race only. This we think the right conclusion and the one supported by the great weight of authority. In re Ah Yup, 5 Sawy. 155, Fed. Cas. No. 104; In re Saito (C.C.) 62 Fed. 126; In re Camille (C.C.) 6 Fed. 256; Matter of San C. Po., 7 Misc. Rep. 471, 28 N.Y. Supp. 383; In re Buntaro Kumagai (D.C.) 163 Fed. 922; In re Knight (D.C.) 171 Fed. 297; In re Najour (C.C.) 174 Fed. 735; In re Halladjian (C.C.) 174 Fed. 834. Doubtless Congressmen in 1790 were not conversant with ethnological distinctions and had never heard of the term "Caucasian race" mentioned in some of the foregoing decisions. They probably had principally in mind the exclusion of Africans, whether slave or free, and Indians, both of which races were and had been objects of serious public consideration. The adjective "free" need not have been used, because the words "white persons" alone would have excluded Africans, whether slave or free, and Indians. Still effect must be given to the words "white persons." The Congressmen certainly knew that there were white, yellow, black, red, and brown races. If a Hebrew, a native of Jerusalem, had applied for naturalization in 1790, we cannot believe he would have been excluded on the ground that he was not a white person, and, if a Parsee had applied, the court would have had to determine then just as the Circuit Court did in this case, whether the words used in the act did or did not cover him.

We think that the words refer to race and include all persons of the white race, as distinguished from the black, red, yellow, or brown races, which differ in so many respects from it. Whether there is any pure white race and what peoples belong to it may involve nice discriminations, but for practical purposes there is no difficulty in saying that the

Chinese, Japanese, and Malays and the American Indians do not belong to the white race. Difficult questions may arise and Congress may have to settle them by more specific legislation, but in our opinion the Parsees do belong to the white race and the Circuit Court properly admitted Balsara to citizenship.

Source: Federal & State Cases, Combined. Document: 180 F. 694, *1910 U.S. App. LEXIS 4794.

Books

Bald, Vivek. *Bengali Harlem and the Lost Histories of South Asian America*. Cambridge, MA: Harvard University Press, 2013. See Chapter 1 "Out of the East and into the South" for general history and Chapter 2 "Between Hindoo and Negro" for discussion of South Asian American historical racialization.

Lopez, Ian Haney. *White by Law: The Legal Construction of Race*. New York: New York University Press, 1996. *White by Law* details the social and legal construction of race in the United States.

Websites

Harpalani, Vinay. "To Be White, Black, or Brown? South Asian Americans and the Race-Color Distinction." *Washington University Global Studies Law Review* 14, no. 4 (2015): 609–636. This article discusses the history and issues surrounding the racialization of South Asian Americans in the United States. http://openscholarship.wustl.edu/cgi/viewcontent.cgi?article=1548&context=law_globalstudies. Accessed October 14, 2016.

Lopez, Ian Haney. "How the U.S. Courts Established the White Race." ModelMinority. This site provides a historical discussion of how U.S. court decisions have defined and redefined the "white race" and, by extension, other "races." http://moor4igws.org/uploads/3/4/4/2/34429976/how_the_u.s._courts_established_the_white_race.pdf. Accessed October 14, 2016.

Also Noteworthy

1872

Seventy Chinese laborers are brought to Beaver Falls, Pennsylvania, to work at Beaver Falls Cutlery Company as strikebreakers. They were recruited from San Francisco.

1902

The Philippines is officially made an American territory by the Philippine Organic Act. William Howard Taft, U.S. solicitor-general, is appointed governor.

1997

At midnight on this day, Hong Kong is returned to China and becomes a special administrative region.

2010

The Asian American Association of Boston, a nonprofit, is formed to advance culture and arts.

July 2

1635

The earliest documentation of an "East Indian" residing in the United States is July 2, 1635. An unconfirmed "East Indian" is listed in colonial Jamestown, Virginia. He is listed as "Tony a Turk" and "Tony East Indian." Later runaway slave advertisements prove early South Asians resided in America as either slaves or indentured servants.

Virginia Gazette, *August 4, 1768*

Richmond county, July 14. RUN away about the 20th of May last, an East-India Indian, named Thomas Greenwich; he is a well made fellow, about 5 feet 4 inches high, wears his own hair, which is long and black, has a thin visage, a very sly look, and a remarkable set of fine white teeth. A reward of 40s. will be paid the person who delivers him to the subscriber, besides what the law allows. WILLIAM COLSTON.

Source: The Geography of Slavery. Explore Advertisements. http://www2.vcdh.virginia.edu/gos/. Accessed January 29, 2018.

Books

Leonard, Karen Isaksen. *The South Asian Americans*. Westport, CT: Greenwood Press, 1997. This volume provides general historical background to South Asians in the United States, which includes Indians, Pakistanis, Bangladeshis, Sri Lankans, Nepalis, and Afghans.

Takaki, Ronald. *Strangers from a Different Shore: A History of Asian Americans*. Boston, MA: Back Bay Books, 1989. See Chapter 8, "The Tide of Turbans," for an overview of South Asian migration history to the United States.

Websites

Assisi, Francis. "Indian Slaves in Colonial America." *India Currents: The Complete Indian American Magazine*, May 16, 2007. This article provides a board narrative of early Indian migration to the United States. https://indiacurrents.com/indian-slaves-in-colonial-america/. Accessed January 29, 2018.

Costa, Tom. The Rector and Visitors of the University of Virginia. Virtual Jamestown's the Geography of Slavery in Virginia digital archive. 2005. http://www2.vcdh.virginia.edu/gos/. Accessed January 29, 2018.

1902

The U.S. Senate passes the Philippine Organic Act, which set up terms for the civil government established in 1901 under the governorship of William Howard Taft. The act allows for "self-government" while maintaining U.S. control.

Organic Act

An Act Temporarily to Provide For the Administration of the Affairs of Civil Government in the Philippine Islands, and for Other Purposes.

57th Congress of the United States of America, First Session, 1902

Be it enacted by the Senate and House of Representatives of the United States of America in Congress assembled, That the action of the President of the United States in creating the Philippine Commission and authorising said Commission to exercise the powers of government to the extent and in the manner and form and subject to the regulation and control set forth in the instructions of the President to the Philippine Commission, dated April seventh, nineteen hundred, and in creating the offices of Civil Governor and Vice-Governor of the Philippine Islands, and authorising said Civil Governor and Vice-Governor to exercise the powers of government to the extent and in the manner and form set forth in the Executive order dated June twenty-first, nineteen hundred and one, and is establishing four Executive Departments of government in said Islands as set forth in the Act of the Philippine Commission entitled "An Act providing an organisation for the Departments of the Interior, of Commerce and Police, of Finance and Justice, and of Public Instruction," enacted September sixth, nineteen hundred and one, is hereby approved, ratified, and confirmed, and until otherwise provided by law the said Islands shall continue to be governed as thereby and herein provided, and all laws passed hereafter by the Philippine Commission shall have an enacting clause as follows. "By authority of the United States, be it enacted by the Philippine Commission." The provisions of section eighteen hundred and ninety-one of the Revised Statutes of eighteen hundred and seventy eight shall not apply to the Philippine Islands.

Future appointments of Civil Governor, Vice-Governor, members of said Commission and heads of Executive Departments shall be made by the President, by and with the advice and consent of the Senate.

Source: A Compilation of the Acts of the Philippine Commission. The Organic Laws of the Philippine Islands. Manila, Philippines: Bureau of Printing, 1908, p. 22.

Books

Jones, Gregg. *Honor in the Dust: Theodore Roosevelt, War in the Philippines, and the Rise and Fall of America's Imperial Dream*. New York: New American Library, 2012. *Honor in the Dust* is a history of U.S. imperialism and colonialism in the Philippines and U.S.-Philippines relation.

McCoy, Alfred. *Policing America's Empire: The United States, the Philippines, and the Rise of the Surveillance State*. Madison: University of Wisconsin Press, 2009. Historian Alfred McCoy provides a critical history of U.S. intervention and domination in the Philippines that resulted in unstable undemocratic forces that remain today.

Websites

"History of Philippines." One World Nations Online. This site provides a complete history of the Philippines with discussions on notable figures. http://www.nationsonline.org/oneworld/History/Philippines-history.htm. Accessed October 12, 2016.

"The Philippine Organic Act of 1902." Official Gazette. Government of the Philippine. This site provides the full digital text of the Organic Act. http://www.officialgazette.gov.ph/constitutions/the-philippine-organic-act-of-1902/. Accessed October 12, 2016.

Also Noteworthy

1776

Slave owner William Brown reports a runaway "Asiatic Indian by birth" servant named John Newton. He offers a reward of $8 for the return of his slave.

1946

President Harry S. Truman signs the Luce–Celler Act into law, which grants naturalization rights to Filipinos and South Asians.

1948

President Harry S. Truman signs into law the Japanese Americans Evacuation Claims Act enabling World War II Japanese American internees to file claims for their financial losses.

July 3

1844

Treaty of Wanghia (also spelled Wang-hsia or Wangxia) is the first formal treaty signed between the United States and China. One important key to China-U.S. relations was that, after the mid-1840s, China had grown weak through repeated defeats in wars with Western colonial powers. In 1842, China and Britain signed the Treaty of Nanjing after the First Opium War. Importantly, China opened five treaty ports to Britain. The United States also wanted to negotiate a treaty with China and expand its trade with China. In 1844, the two countries signed the Treaty of Wanghia, which gave the United States most-favored-nation treatment in trade and extraterritoriality (exemption from Chinese laws) for American nationals in China, and the right to be tried by the U.S. consular court.

Excerpt from Treaty of Peace, Amity, and Commerce, with Tariff of Duties, signed at Wang Hiya, July 3, 1844

Desiring to establish firm, lasting, and sincere friendship between the two Nations, have resolved to fix, in a manner clear and positive, by means of a treaty or general convention of peace, amity, and commerce, the rules which shall in future be mutually observed in the intercourse of their respective countries; for which most desirable object, the President of the United States has conferred full powers on their Commissioner Caleb Cushing, Envoy Extraordinary and Minister Plenipotentiary of the

United States to China; and the August Sovereign of the Ta Tsing Empire on his Minister and Commissioner Extraordinary Tsiyeng, of the Imperial House, a Vice-Guardian of the Heir Apparent, Governor-general of the Two Kwang, and Superintendent-General of the trade and foreign intercourse of the five ports.

And the said Commissioners, after haying exchanged their said full powers, and duly considered the premises, have agreed to the following articles.

Article I

There shall be a perfect, permanent, universal peace, and a sincere and cordial amity, between the United States of America on the one part, and the Ta Tsing Empire on the other part, and between their people respectively, without exception of persons or places. . . .

Article III

The citizens of the United States are permitted to frequent the five ports of Kwangchow, Amoy, Fuchow, Ningpo and Shanghai, and to reside with their families and trade there, and to proceed at pleasure with their vessels and merchandize to and from any foreign port and either of the said five ports, and from either of the said five ports to any other of them. But said vessels shall not unlawfully enter the other ports of China, nor carry on a clandestine and fraudulent trade along the coasts thereof. And any vessel belonging to a citizen of the United States, which violates this provision, shall, with her cargo, be subject to confiscation to the Chinese government. . . .

Article XXXIV

When the present convention shall have been definitively concluded, it shall be obligatory on both Powers, and its provisions shall not be altered without grave cause; but, inasmuch as the circumstances of the several ports of China open to foreign commerce are different, experience may show that inconsiderable modifications are requisite in those parts which relate to commerce and navigation: in which case, the two Governments will, at the expiration of twelve years from the date of said convention, treat amicably concerning the same, by the means of suitable persons appointed to conduct such negotiation.

Source: Treaty of Wanghia. U.S. Statutes at Large, Volume 8: 1778–1845. Boston, MA: Little, Brown, and Company, 1867, p. 592.

Books

Mao, Haijian. *The Qing Empire and the Opium War: The Collapse of the Heavenly Dynasty*. Cambridge: Cambridge University Press, 2005. See Chapter 7, "Equal" and "Unequal," for an analysis of the treaty's article, in particular 34, that paved the way for the United States and other Western colonial powers to change the terms of past treaties with China.

Ruskola, Teemu. *Legal Orientalism: China, the United States, and Modern Law*. Cambridge, MA: Harvard University Press, 2013. Law professor Teemu Ruskola provides a theoretical analysis of U.S. "legal imperialism" and "legal orientalism" and how it continues to inform global politics.

Websites

"Opening the Door (1844–1911)." The Gerald R. Ford Presidential Library and Museum. This site discusses the impact of the Treaty of Wanghia in U.S.-China relations and policies. https://www.fordlibrarymuseum.gov/museum/exhibits/China_exhibit/opening%20the%20door.htm. Accessed January 29, 2018.

"The Opening to China Part 1: The First Opium War, the United States, and the Treaty of Wangxia, 1839–1844." Office of the Historian. U.S. Department of State. This article provides background that led to the treaty. https://history.state.gov/milestones/1830-1860/china-1. Accessed January 29, 2018.

Also Noteworthy

2008

In Seattle, Washington, Edward Campbell, a 42-year-old, is charged with harassment after he called a store clerk, he assumed to be Muslim, a terrorist and struck him on his head with a can of beer.

July 4

1898

The U.S. Congress passes the Newlands Resolution, which annexes Hawaii. President William McKinley signed it on July 7, 1898. Under this act further immigration of Chinese into the Hawaiian Islands is prohibited.

To Provide for Annexing the Hawaiian Islands to the United States

Whereas, the Government of the Republic of Hawaii having, in due form, signified its consent, in the manner provided by its constitution, to cede absolutely and without reserve to the United States of America, all rights of sovereignty of whatsoever kind in and over the Hawaiian Islands and their dependencies, and also to cede and transfer to the United States, the absolute fee and ownership of all public, Government, or Crown lands, public buildings or edifices, ports, harbors, military equipment, and all other public property of every kind and description belonging to the Government of the Hawaiian Islands, together with every right and appurtenance thereunto appertaining: Therefore,

Resolved by the Senate and House of Representatives of the United States of America in Congress assembled, That said cession is accepted, ratified, and confirmed, and that the said Hawaiian Islands and their dependencies be, and they are hereby, annexed as a part of the territory of the United States and are subject to the sovereign dominion thereof, and that all and singular the property and rights hereinbefore mentioned are vested in the United States of America.

The existing laws of the United States relative to public lands shall not apply to such lands in the Hawaiian Islands; but the Congress of the United States shall enact special laws for their management and disposition: Provided, That all revenue from or proceeds of the same, except as regards such part thereof as may be used or occupied for the civil, military, or naval purposes of the United States, or may be assigned for the use of the local government, shall be used solely for the benefit of the inhabitants of the Hawaiian Islands for educational and other public purposes.

Until Congress shall provide for the government of such islands all the civil, judicial, and military powers exercised by the officers of the existing government in said islands shall be vested in such person or persons and shall be exercised in such manner as the President of the United states shall direct; and the President shall have power to remove said officers and fill the vacancies so occasioned.

The existing treaties of the Hawaiian Islands with foreign nations shall forthwith cease and determine, being replaced by such treaties as may exist, or as may be hereafter concluded, between the United States and such foreign nations. The municipal legislation of the Hawaiian Islands, not enacted for the fulfillment of the treaties so extinguished, and not inconsistent with this joint resolution nor contrary to the Constitution of the United States nor to any existing treaty of the United States, shall remain in force until the Congress of the United States shall otherwise determine.

Until legislation shall be enacted extending the United States customs laws and regulations to the Hawaiian Islands the existing customs relations of the Hawaiian Islands with the United States and other countries shall remain unchanged.

The public debt of the Republic of Hawaii, lawfully existing at the date of the passage of this joint resolution, including the amounts due to depositors in the Hawaiian Postal Savings Bank, is hereby assumed by the Government of the United States; but the liability of the United States in this regard shall in no case exceed four million dollars. So long, however, as the existing Government and the present commercial relations of the Hawaiian Islands are continued as hereinbefore, provided said Government shall continue to pay the interest on said debt.

There shall be no further immigration of Chinese into the Hawaiian Islands, except upon such conditions as are now or may hereafter be allowed by the laws of the United States; and no Chinese, by reason of anything herein contained, shall be allowed to enter the United States from the Hawaiian Islands.

Sec. 1. The President shall appoint five commissioners, at least two of whom shall be residents of the Hawaiian Islands, who shall, as soon as reasonably practicable, recommend to Congress such legislation concerning the Hawaiian Islands as they shall deem necessary or proper.

Sec. 2. That the commissioners hereinbefore provided for shall be appointed by the President, by and with the advice and consent of the Senate.

Sec. 3. That the sum of one hundred thousand dollars, or so much thereof as may be necessary, is hereby appropriated, out of any money in the Treasury not otherwise appropriated, and to be immediately available, to be expended at the discretion of the President of the United States of America, for the purpose of carrying this joint resolution into effect.

SEREXO E. PAYNE,

Speaker of the House of Representatives Pro Tempore.

GARRETT A. HOBART,

Vice-President of the United States and President of the Senate.

Approved July 7th, 1898.

WILLIAM McKINLEY.

Source: Joint Resolution to Provide for Annexing the Hawaiian Islands to the United States, July 7, 1898; Enrolled Acts and Resolutions of Congress; General Records of the United States Government, 1778–1992; Record Group 11; National Archives.

Books

Kinzer, Stephen. *Overthrow: America's Century of Regime Change from Hawaii to Iraq*. New York: Times Books, 2006. Journalist Stephen Kinzer provides a comparative historical discussion of U.S. intervention and "regime change" as a cornerstone of U.S. foreign policy for over a century.

Silva, Noenoe. *Aloha Betrayed: Native Hawaiian Resistance to American Colonialism*. Durham, NC: Duke University Press, 2004. Political scientist Noenoe Silva provides a critical reassessment of U.S. colonial history in Hawaii with a discussion of native Hawaiian resistance to American imperialism.

Websites

Legal Foundation for Hawaiian Independence, Law Library, Historical Documents, and Research Material. In addition to the full text of the Newlands Resolution, this site provides other archival documents dealing with Hawaiian independence, annexation, and other legal documents. http://www.hawaii-nation.org/legal.html. Accessed January 29, 2018.

"Teaching with Documents: The 1897 Petition against the Annexation of Hawaii." The U.S. National Archives and Records Administration. This site provides an essay on the history and debate of Hawaii's annexation. In addition, there are archival documents against annexation. https://www.archives.gov/education/lessons/hawaii-petition/. Accessed January 29, 2018.

Also Noteworthy

1901

William Howard Taft becomes the first civil governor of the Philippines.

1902

President Theodore Roosevelt declares end to the Philippine-American War.

1946

The Philippines gains independence from the United States. This had been promised by the passage of the Tydings-McDuffie Act of 1934.

1947

The Filipino American Citizens Society of Michigan is established. By 1949, they published the Filipino American Citizens News of Michigan.

2017

The Radha Krishna Temple of Dallas, Texas, completes construction.

July 5

2015

Yoichiro Nambu (January 18, 1921–July 5, 2015) passes away at age 94. He was a Japanese-born American physicist and professor at the University of Chicago. In 2008, he was awarded one-half the Nobel Prize in Physics "for the discovery of the mechanism of spontaneous broken symmetry in subatomic physics."

Excerpt from Yoichiro Nambu's Nobel Lecture on December 8, 2008

I will begin with a short story about my background. I studied physics at the University of Tokyo. I was attracted to particle physics because of three famous names, Nishina, Tomonaga and Yukawa, who were the founders of particle physics in Japan. But these people were at different institutions than mine. On the other hand, condensed matter physics was pretty good at Tokyo. I got into particle physics only when I came back to Tokyo after the war. In hindsight, though, I must say that my early exposure to condensed matter physics has been quite beneficial to me. Particle physics is an outgrowth of nuclear physics, which began in the early 1930s with the discovery of the neutron by Chadwick, the invention of the cyclotron by Lawrence, and the "invention" of meson theory by Yukawa. . . . The appearance of an ever increasing array of new particles in the subsequent decades and advances in quantum field theory gradually led to our understanding of the basic laws of nature, culminating in the present standard model. When we faced those new particles, our first attempts were to make sense out of them by finding some regularities in their properties. Researchers invoked the symmetry principle to classify them. A symmetry in physics leads to a conservation law. Some conservation laws are exact, like energy and electric charge, but these attempts were based on approximate similarities of masses and interactions.

Source: Nambu, Yoichiro. "Spontaneous Symmetry Breaking in Particle Physics: A Case of Cross Fertilization." Nobel Lecture, December 8, 2008. https://www.nobelprize.org/nobel_prizes/physics/laureates/2008/nambu_lecture.pdf. Accessed June 17, 2018.

Book

Brink, Lars, Lay Nam Chang, Moo-Young Han, and Kok Khoo Phua, eds. *Memorial Volume for Y. Nambu*. Hackensack, NJ: World Scientific, 2016. *Memorial Volume for Y. Nambu* celebrates the life and work of Yoichiro Nambu, detailing his contributions and legacy in the field of physics.

Websites

Mukerjee, Madhusree. "Profile: Yoichiro Nambu in 1995." *Scientific American*, October 7, 2008. This is a revised profile of Nambu in *Scientific American* first published in 1995, but updated after he received the Nobel Prize. https://www.scientificamerican.com/article/profile-yoichiro-nambu/. Accessed January 20, 2018.

Obituary. "Yoichiro Nambu, Nobel-Winning Theoretical Physicist, 1921–2015." *UChicago News*, July 17, 2015. This essay focuses on Nambu's career and time at the University of Chicago and celebrates his legacy in the field of physics. https://news.uchicago.edu/article/2015/07/17/yoichiro-nambu-nobel-winning-theoretical-physicist-1921-2015. Accessed January 20, 2018.

July 6

1990

The Tibetan Association of Northern California is founded by 11 Tibetan Americans and 1 non-Tibetan spouse to preserve Tibetan culture and promote Tibetan independence in Tibet. This reflects the growing Tibetan diasporic community in America.

Happily, an estimated 2,000 Tibetans have settled safely in Northern California. Many participate in the community center established by the nonprofit Tibetan Association of Northern California (TANC). The community center provides Tibetan-language classes, instruction in traditional Tibetan music and dance, teachings on Tibetan Buddhism, and assistance with social-service programs, such as healthcare and employment. In January 2014, TANC hosted His Holiness the Dalai Lama, who blessed the community center and grave a public talk in Berkeley. The community center is located at 5200 Huntington Avenue, Suite 200, Richmond, CA 94804.

Source: Schinske, Marian. *Ani's Asylum*. Bloomington, IN: Xlibris LLC, 2010, p. 67.

Books

Lee, Jonathan H.X. *History of Asian Americans: Exploring Diverse Roots*. Santa Barbara, CA: Greenwood, 2015. See Chapter 8, "New Asians in America": in particular, section on Tibetan Americans.

Woeser, Tsering, and Wang Lixong. *Voices from Tibet: Selected Essays and Reportage*. Translated by Violet Law. Hong Kong: Hong Kong University Press, 2014. *Voices from Tibet* examines various aspects of the Chinese occupation of Tibet.

Websites

Tibetan Association of Northern California. Official web page. http://tanc.org/. Accessed February 6, 2018.

Tibetan Association of Northern California Facebook page. This site provides updates of events at TANC. https://www.facebook.com/tibetanassoc.norcal. Accessed February 8, 2018.

Also Noteworthy

1887

The Bayonet Constitution is forced on King Kalakaua of Hawaii by haole rebels. Among the results of this action is the abolition of citizenship for Asian migrants, abrogating one of the key provisions of the Immigration Convention of 1886.

2007

In Sarasota, Florida, anti-Islamic epithets are spray-painted on a Bosnian family's residence.

July 7

1879

Ho Ah Kow v. Nunan (1879) is an early example of civil rights litigation among Chinese Americans. Ho Ah Kow was a laborer living in San Francisco. At that time, San Francisco had a municipal ordinance call the "Cubic Air Ordinance" that forbid sleeping in a room with less than 500 cubic feet of air space per person. Ho Ah Kow was convicted under this statute and sent to prison. Owing to the "Queue Ordinance" his *queue* was cut off. Ho Ah Kow protested the discriminatory treatment and sued Sheriff Matthew Nunan for damages. U.S. Supreme Court justice Stephen J. Field ruled that the Queue Ordinance violated the Equal Protection Clause of the Fourteenth Amendment. Ho Ah Kow was awarded $10,000 for his damages and the law was overturned.

Ho Ah Kow v. Nunan *involved a Chinese attempt to strike down two obnoxious statutes—one, a San Francisco municipal ordinance that made it a crime to sleep in a room with less than 500 cubic feet of air space per person, and the other, a California state law based on an earlier San Francisco municipal ordinance that allowed jail wardens to cut off the hair of prisoners to within an inch of the scalp. Chinatown was indeed overcrowded, but so were other residential quarters in the poorer neighborhoods. What made the "cubic air ordinance" discriminatory was that it was enforced only against Chinese. As for the "queue ordinance," authorities knew that Qing-dynasty Chinese men were required to keep their hair long and wear it in a braid. Thus, cutting off their hair was a way to harass and punish them.* Ho Ah Kow v. Nunan, *decided in 1879 in the Circuit Court for the District of California, declared both statutes unconstitutional. Its historical significance lies in the fact that it was the first federal case to state clearly that the "equal protection" clause of the Fourteenth Amendment and Section 16 of the 1870 Civil Rights Act were applicable to Chinese as persons. This decision was crucial because just a year earlier Chinese had been denied the right to acquire naturalized citizenship in the* In re Ah Yup *case—a denial that would be reiterated in the 1882 Chinese Exclusion Law.*

Source: Chan, Sucheng, "Asian American Struggles for Civil, Political, Economic, and Social Rights." Originally published in *Chinese America: History & Perspectives*, 2002. Reprinted at the Free Library by Farlex. https://www.thefreelibrary.com/Asian+American+struggles+for+civil,+political,+economic,+and+social . . . -a0105160300.

Books

FitzGerald, David, and David Cook-Martin. *Culling the Masses: The Democratic Origins of Racist Immigration Policy in the Americas*. Cambridge, MA: Harvard University Press, 2014. *Culling the Masses* is a sociological investigation of the correlation between racism and democracy.

McClain, Charles, ed. *Chinese Immigrants and American Law*. New York: Garland Publishing, Inc., 1991. See Charles McClain's Chapter 7, "The Chinese Struggle for Civil Rights in Nineteenth-Century America: The First Phase, 1850–1870."

Websites

Chionsini, James. "Ho Ah Kow v. Nunan." James Chionsini provides a summary of the *Ho Ah Kow v. Nunan* case, and the full text of the decision, along with an article published in the *New York Times* on July 16, 1879, "The Tale of a Chinaman," that covers the case. http://www.foundsf.org/index.php?title=Ho_Ah_Kow_v._Nunan. Accessed October 8, 2016.

"Ho Ah Kow v. Nunan Case Brief Summary." lawschoolcasebriefs.net. This site provides the legal brief for *Ho Ah Kow v. Nunan*. http://www.lawschoolcasebriefs.net/2014/05/ho-ah-kow-v-nunan-case-brief-summary.html. Accessed October 8, 2016.

Also Noteworthy

1898

With support of President William McKinley, a joint resolution in Congress to annex the Hawaiian Islands is passed. As a result, thousands of Asian laborers migrated to the continental United States.

1937

Japan invades China.

1940

The *China Daily News* (*Meizhou Huaqiao Ribao*) is founded by a group of Chinese Americans to report on "ordinary Chinese Americans" and their opinions and to get objective information about China's domestic situation and news on the global overseas Chinese communities.

2002

In Nassau, New York, John Yang, a 25-year-old, is charged with second-degree criminal mischief and criminal possession of a dangerous weapon for threatening to shoot two Muslim brothers while yelling racial slurs. Yang also sprayed anti-Muslim epithets on the family's property.

July 8

1872

Polly Bemis (Lalu Nathoy) (1853–1933) arrives in Idaho Territory. She became famous in her lifetime because of her unusual circumstances: she was a Chinese woman married to a Caucasian man; she continued to live on the remote Salmon River even after his death. Several myths and legends grew up around her, both in her lifetime and afterward. A 1921 interview reported that her parents sold her as a slave girl because they had no food. An old woman smuggled her into Portland, Oregon, and sold her for $2,500 to an unnamed old Chinese man who took her to the gold-mining town of Warren, Idaho, in a pack train. She died in Idaho in 1933.

Polly Bemis came to the United States as part of a vast movement of Chinese people, mostly men, who began coming to the western United States during the mid-nineteenth century. The earliest arrivals came in response to employment opportunities made possible by the California gold discoveries in 1848. . . . Polly's arrival in Idaho in 1872 was part of a dispersion of Chinese people within the United States. Beginning in the mid-1850s, new gold rushes encouraged Chinese miners and businessmen to relocate to other areas of the West. After settling in remote mining regions, such as Idaho Territory, some brought women into their new communities. Chinese immigrant women were uncommon. They, including Polly, amounted to fewer than 4,000 in 1890, when the total population of Chinese in the United States was more than 107,000. Although some women accompanied husbands, were family servants, or became concubines for wealthy Chinese men, most arrived unwillingly and unlawfully, as prostitutes. Whereas respectable Chinese women were usually secluded from public view, Chinese prostitutes were not. As a result, Polly and other visible Chinese women were stereotyped by mistaken assumptions. For Polly, the myth is further exaggerated by the prevalent belief that she was "won in a poker game."

Source: Wegars, Priscilla. "Polly Bemis: Lurid Life or Literary Legend?" In *Wild Women of the Old West*, edited by Glenda Riley and Richard Etulain, pp. 46–47. Golden, CO: Fulcrum Publishing, 2003.

Books

Rutter, Michael. *Boudoirs to Brothels: The Intimate World of Wild West Women*. Helena, MT: Farcounty Press, 2015. See Chapter 4 "Polly Bemis: The Chinese Poker Bride."

Wegars, Priscilla. *Polly Bemis: A Chinese American Pioneer*. Cambridge, ID: Backeddy Books, 2003. *Polly Bemis* is a history of a historical figure that is wrapped around myths: this volume separates fact from fiction in the life story of Polly Bemis.

Websites

Fry, Katy. "Polly Bemis, Pedagogy, and Multiculturalism in the Classroom." *CLCWeb: Comparative Literature and Culture* (Purdue University Press) 10, no. 2 (2008), article 6. This article explores gaps in grade school instruction on the topic of the American West and critiques the multicultural narratives and perspectives of Polly Bemis's history. https://docs.lib.purdue.edu/cgi/viewcontent.cgi?article=1352&context=clcweb. Accessed January 20, 2018.

McCunn, Ruthanne. "Photos of Polly and Her Ranch." 2018. This site provides photographs of Polly Bemis, with a short essay that details her background and short introduction to author's McCunn's book *Thousand Pieces of Gold* that is based on the life of Polly Bemis. http://www.mccunn.com/PollyPic.html. Accessed January 20, 2018.

Also Noteworthy

2004

In Edmonds, Washington, a cross is burned on the front lawn of a Middle Eastern American family.

July 9

1952

The California Supreme Court upholds a lower court decision overturning the Alien Land Law in *Haruye Masaoka, et al., v. People.*

Following three months after the Fujii case *was* Haruye Masaoka et al. v. People, *which stands as the latest word to date on the issue of alien land ownership. In that case five American brothers agreed to build a home for their widowed mother, a Japanese alien ineligible to citizenship. The mother and her sons brought an action against the People of the State of California to determine whether the residential property had escheated to the State by operation of the Alien Land Law. The court's decision in the* Fujii case *was controlling and the Alien Land Law was held unconstitutional because [it was a] violation of the Fourteenth Amendment to the Federal Constitution.*

Source: Flanagan, Fintan, George Lorinczi, and Frank Schlax. "Constitutional Problems under the Alien Land Laws." *Marquette Law Review* 36, no. 3 (Winter 1952–1953), p. 272.

Books

Daniels, Roger. *The Politics of Prejudice: The Anti-Japanese Movement in California and the Struggle for Japanese Exclusion.* Berkeley: University of California Press, 1962 (2nd edition, 1977). *The Politics of Prejudice* covers the history of anti-Japanese movements in California.

Lee, Jonathan H.X. ed. *Japanese Americans: The History and Culture of a People.* Santa Barbara, CA: ABC-CLIO, 2017. See entries related to Alien Land Laws.

Websites

Haruye Masaoka v. People. FindLaw for Legal Professionals. 2018. The full text of the case is available. http://caselaw.findlaw.com/ca-supreme-court/1800631.html. Accessed February 8, 2018.

Lyon, Cherstin. "Alien Land Laws." *Densho Encyclopedia*, May 23, 2014. This essay discusses the history of Alien Land Laws in the United States. http://encyclopedia.densho.org/Alien_land_laws/. Accessed February 8, 2018.

July 10

1935

On this day, the U.S. Congress passes the Welch Repatriation Act and finances it with $300,000 to repatriate Filipinos. The Department of Labor even charted a train leaving New York for San Francisco, making stops at Cleveland, Chicago, and St. Louis, to deliver a trainload of Filipinos to the passenger ship President Coolidge for transportation to Manila. In 1936 the allocation was reduced to $100,000. The majority of Filipino men residing in the U.S. declined the offer of aid because Section 4 of the act stipulates that "no Filipino who receives the benefits of this act shall be entitled to return to the continental United States." Others declined the offer because by the late 1930s, the economy in California began to improve. The program lasted five years, and the government's goal was to lure some 45,000 Filipinos back to the Philippines, but only 2,190 Filipinos returned.

Excerpt from 1935 Filipino Repatriation Act

To provide means by which certain Filipinos can emigrate from the United States.

Be it enacted by the Senate and House of Representatives of the United States of America in Congress assembled, That any native Filipino residing in any State or the District of Columbia on the effective date of this Act, who desires to return to the Philippine Islands, may apply to the Secretary of Labor, upon such form as the Secretary may prescribe, through any officer of the Immigration Service for the benefits of this Act. Upon approval of such application, the Secretary of Labor shall notify such Filipino forthwith, and shall certify to the Secretary of the Navy and the Secretary of War that such Filipino is eligible to be returned to the Philippine Islands under the terms of this Act. Every Filipino who is so certified shall be entitled, at the expense of the United States, to transports is available, or on any ship of United States registry operated by a commercial steamship company which has a contract with the Secretary of Labor as provided in section 2. . . .

SEC. 4. No Filipino who receives the benefits of this Act shall be entitled to return to the continental United States except as a quota immigrant under the provisions of section 8 (a) (1) of the Philippine

Independence Act of March 24, 1934, during the period such section 8 (a) (1) is applicable.

Source: The Statutes at Large of the United States of America. Vol. XLIX, Part 1. Washington, DC: Government Printing Office, 1936.

Books

Hing, Bill Ong. *Making and Remaking Asian America through Immigration Policy: 1850–1990.* Stanford, CA: Stanford University Press, 1993. *Making and Remaking Asian America through Immigration Policy* is a comprehensive discussion of how U.S. immigration policies have influenced the demographic, economic, and social development of six Asian American communities in the United States.

Stern, Jennifer. *The Filipino Americans.* New York: Chelsea House, 1989. *The Filipino Americans* covers various aspects of Filipino American history, community development, immigration policies, economic development, and culture and identity.

Websites

Baldoz, Richard. "The Nativist Origins of Philippines Independence." *Truthout,* April 1, 2014. http://www.truth-out.org/news/item/22826-the-nativist-origins-of-philippines-independence. Accessed January 12, 2017.

Johansen, Bruce. "Filipino Repatriation Act of 1935." Immigration in America. November 28, 2011. This essay discusses the history and significance of the Filipino Repatriation Act of 1935. https://web.archive.org/web/20141006083819/http://immigrationinamerica.org/498-filipino-repatriation-act-of-1935.html. Accessed January 12, 2017.

July 11

1995

On this day, the United States officially normalizes diplomatic relations with Vietnam. Following President Clinton's *normalization* announcement, both nations upgraded their Liaison Offices opened during January 1995 to embassy status. As diplomatic ties between the nations developed, the United States opened a Consulate General in Ho Chi Minh City, and Vietnam opened a Consulate in San Francisco.

Thank you very much. I welcome you all here, those who have been introduced and distinguished Members of Congress and military leaders, veterans, others who are in the audience.

Today I am announcing the normalization of diplomatic relationships with Vietnam.

From the beginning of this administration, any improvement in relationships between America and Vietnam has depended upon making progress on the issue of Americans who were missing in action or held as prisoners of war. Last year, I lifted the trade embargo on Vietnam in response to their cooperation and to enhance our efforts to secure the remains of lost Americans and to determine the fate of those whose remains have not been found.

It has worked. In 17 months, Hanoi has taken important steps to help us resolve many cases. Twenty-nine families have received the remains of their loved ones and at last have been able to give them a proper burial. Hanoi has delivered to us hundreds of pages of documents shedding light on what happened to Americans in Vietnam. And Hanoi has stepped up its cooperation with Laos, where many Americans were lost. We have reduced the number of so-called discrepancy cases, in which we have had reason to believe that Americans were still alive after they were lost, to 55. And we will continue to work to resolve more cases.

Hundreds of dedicated men and women are working on all these cases, often under extreme hardship and real danger in the mountains and jungles of Indochina. On behalf of all Americans, I want to thank them. And I want to pay a special tribute to General John Vessey, who has worked so tirelessly on this issue for Presidents Reagan and Bush and for our administration. He has made a great difference to a great many families. And we as a nation are grateful for his dedication and for his service. Thank you, sir.

I also want to thank the Presidential delegation, led by Deputy Secretary of Veterans Affairs Hershel Gober, Winston Lord, James Wold, who have helped us to make so much progress on this issue. And I am especially grateful to the leaders of the families and the veterans organizations who have worked with the delegation and maintained their extraordinary commitment to finding the answers we seek.

Never before in the history of warfare has such an extensive effort been made to resolve the fate of soldiers who did not return. Let me emphasize, normalization of our relations with Vietnam is not the end of our effort. From the early days of this administration I have said to the families and veterans groups what I say again here: We will keep working until we get all the answers we can. Our strategy is working. Normalization of relations is the next appropriate step. With this new relationship we will be able to make more progress. To that end, I will send another delegation to Vietnam this year. And Vietnam has pledged it will continue to help us find answers. We will hold them to that pledge.

By helping to bring Vietnam into the community of nations, normalization also serves our interest in working for a free and peaceful Vietnam in a stable and peaceful Asia. We will begin to normalize our trade relations with Vietnam, whose economy is now liberalizing and integrating into the economy of the Asia-Pacific region. Our policy will be to implement the appropriate United States Government programs to develop trade with Vietnam consistent with U.S. law.

As you know, many of these programs require certifications regarding human rights and labor rights before they can proceed. We have already begun discussing human rights issues with Vietnam, especially issues regarding religious freedom. Now we can expand and strengthen that dialog. The Secretary of State will go to Vietnam in August where he will discuss all of these issues, beginning with our POW and MIA concerns.

I believe normalization and increased contact between Americans and Vietnamese will advance the cause of freedom in Vietnam, just as it did in Eastern Europe and the former Soviet Union. I strongly believe that engaging the Vietnamese on the broad economic front of economic reform and the broad front of democratic reform will help to honor the sacrifice of those who fought for freedom's sake in Vietnam.

I am proud to be joined in this view by distinguished veterans of the Vietnam War. They served their country bravely. They are of different parties. A generation ago they had different judgments about the war which divided us so deeply. But today they are of a single mind. They agree that the time has come for America to move forward on Vietnam. All Americans should be grateful especially that Senators John McCain, John Kerry, Bob Kerrey, Chuck Robb, and Representative Pete Peterson, along with other Vietnam veterans in the Congress, including Senator Harkin, Congressman Kolbe, and Congressman Gilchrest, who just left, and others who are out here in the audience have kept up their passionate interest in Vietnam but were able to move beyond the haunting and painful past toward finding common ground for the future. Today they and many other veterans support the normalization of relations, giving the opportunity to Vietnam to fully join the community of nations and being true to what they fought for so many years ago.

Whatever we may think about the political decisions of the Vietnam era, the brave Americans who fought and died there had noble motives. They fought for the freedom and the independence of the Vietnamese people. Today the Vietnamese are independent, and we believe this step will help to extend the reach of freedom in Vietnam and, in so doing, to enable these fine veterans of Vietnam to keep working for that freedom.

This step will also help our own country to move forward on an issue that has separated Americans from one another for too long now. Let the future be our destination. We have so much work ahead of us. This moment offers us the opportunity to bind up our own wounds. They have resisted time for too long. We can now move on to common ground. Whatever divided us before let us consign to the past. Let this moment, in the words of the Scripture, be a time to heal and a time to build.

Thank you all, and God bless America.

Source: President William J. Clinton. "Remarks Announcing the Normalization of Diplomatic Relations with Vietnam." The American Presidency Project. University of California, Santa Barbara. 2018. http://www.presidency.ucsb.edu/ws/?pid=51605. Accessed March 7, 2018.

Books

Hiebert, Murray, Phuong Nguyen, and Gregory Poling. *A New Era in U.S.-Vietnam Relations: Deepening Ties Two Decades after Normalization*. Lanham, MD: Rowman & Littlefield, 2014. *A New Era in U.S.-Vietnam Relations* is a report of the Center for Strategic & International Studies that offers recommendation to improve U.S.-Vietnam relations after normalization in the areas of security, trade, and migration.

Mather, Paul. M.I.A.: *Accounting for the Missing in Southeast Asia*. Washington, DC: National Defense University Press, 1994. See Chapter 2, "A Winding Down," for a discussion related to early development in U.S.-Vietnam normalization vis-à-vis M.I.A. (missing in action) and POWs (prisoners of war) from the Vietnam War.

Websites

Hays, Jeffrey. "Vietnamese Relations with the United States." Facts and Details. May 2014. This site provides detailed information related to U.S.-Vietnam foreign relations before and during the Vietnam War and postwar normalization development. http://factsanddetails.com/southeast-asia/Vietnam/sub5_9f/entry-3456.html. Accessed January 20, 2018.

Manyin, Mark. The Vietnam-U.S. Normalization Process. CRS Issue Brief for Congress. Library of Congress. June 17, 2005. This report includes a discussion of the history of U.S. efforts to normalize relations with Vietnam after the Vietnam War. https://fas.org/sgp/crs/row/IB98033.pdf. Accessed January 20, 2018.

July 12

1980

The National Coalition for Redress/Reparations (NCRR) is formed at a Los Angeles meeting. It includes the Little Tokyo People's Rights Organization, the Asian Pacific Student Union, Japanese American Citizens League-San Jose, National Council for Japanese American Redress, New England Nisei, Nihonmachi (San Jose) Outreach Committee, and the Tule Lake Committee, among others.

On July 12, 1980, individuals and organizations from Japanese communities from throughout the nation met and formed the National Coalition for Redress and Reparations (NCRR). The NCRR is an active coalition coordinating a nationwide campaign for justice. The NCRR has two major aims: (1) To seek restitution for losses and injuries suffered by Nikkei (persons of Japanese ancestry) and others who were unjustly evacuated and incarcerated by the U.S. government during World War II, and (2) to seek preventive steps to insure that similar racist acts and violations of constitutional rights will never occur again.

Source: National Coalition for Redress & Reparations poster/brochure. http://www.ncrr-la.org/NCRR_archives/foundingconf/1980postConfNCRRbrochurencrr.PDF. Accessed February 8, 2018.

Books

Maki, Mitchell, Harry Kitano, and Sarah Berthold. *Achieving the Impossible Dream: How Japanese Americans Obtained Redress*. Urbana: University of Illinois Press, 1999. *Achieving the Impossible Dream* covers many aspects of Japanese Americans who worked to get an apology from the U.S. government and achieve compensation for the unlawful internment of their community during World War II.

Murray, Alice. *Historical Memories of the Japanese American Internment and the Struggle for Redress*. Stanford, CA: Stanford University Press, 2008. *Historical Memories* documents the shifting representation of Japanese relocation and redress over a span of six decades.

Websites

NCRR Nikkei for Civil Rights & Redress, formerly known as National Coalition for Redress/Reparations. Official web page. http://www.ncrr-la.org/about.html. Accessed February 8, 2018.

Niiya, Brian. "National Coalition for Redress/Reparations." *Densho Encyclopedia*, June 29, 2015. This article documents the history of the NCRR. http://encyclopedia.densho.org/National_Coalition_for_Redress/Reparations/. Accessed February 10, 2018.

July 13

2013

Timothy LeRoy Lincecum (b. June 15, 1984) is son of Rebecca Asis, who is a daughter of Filipino immigrants. His father is Chris Lincecum. He was raised in a Filipino enclave in Renton, a Seattle suburb. Lincecum pitched for the San Francisco Giants from 2007 to 2015. He helped the Giants win the World Series in 2010. On Saturday, July 13, 2013, Lincecum throws his first no-hitter against the San Diego Padres. He repeated this feat the following year on June 25 and became the first pitcher in Major League Baseball history to secure the first no-hit repeat against the same team in consecutive seasons.

Pinoy fans said they've never seen Lincecum more confident, more in control of the game.

The year 2008 seemed like a long time ago when Lincecum was unsure of his skills. During the first FilAm Heritage Night of the Giants, Lincecum was the starting pitcher against the Colorado Rockies. The Giants lost.

After the game in 2008, "Balitang America" asked him what his message was to his Filipino fans. Instead of addressing the community, he talked about his performance during the game. Lincecum said, "That was a garbage start, a bad game. I just need to make improvements, bounce back from it."

At that time, Lincecum seemed a bit evasive to talk about his Filipino heritage. But he told "Balitang America" he valued diversity within professional baseball.

It does not bother Filipino fans that Lincecum was not as open to talk about his roots.

There's been talk within the Giants camp that it's Lincecum's strained relationship with his Filipino mother that's behind this. Nonetheless, Filipino fans have someone to emulate.

Parents of 10-year-old Demani Abalos have brought him to Giants games since he was a baby.

He said Lincecum inspires him to excel in sports. He said, "It means a lot to me that he's Filipino."

Daniel Magdael said it's about time a Filipino-American gets noticed in professional baseball.

Magdael said, "It's the best feeling in the world, to have a Pinoy on the biggest stage in the world, pitching the best that he could."

Source: Espinosa, Henni. "Pinoy Fans Applaud Giants Fil-Am Pitcher." *Filipino Reporter*, November 5, 2010, p. 33.

Books

Elias, Robert. *The Empire Strikes Out: How Baseball Sold U.S. Foreign Policy and Promoted the American Way Abroad*. New York: The New Press, 2010. *The Empire Strikes Out* is a political history of baseball that weaves together U.S. military, foreign policy, and baseball since the 18th century.

Franks, Joel. *Asian Pacific Americans and Baseball: A History*. Jefferson, N.C.: McFarland & Company Inc., Publishers, 2008. *Asian Pacific Americans and Baseball* is a history of baseball among Hawaiians in particular, but Asian Pacific Americans in general.

Websites

"Giants' World Series-winning pitcher has Pinoy Roots." GMA News Online, November 2, 2010. This article provides the history of Lincecum and his Filipino American ancestry. http://www.gmanetwork.com/news/sports/content/204955/giants-world-series-winning-pitcher-has-pinoy-roots/story/. Accessed January 21, 2018.

Guillermo, Emil. "Linceblog: Tim Lincecum Speaks Candidly about His Filipino Roots." AMOK! April 23, 2013. This essay details Lincecum's Filipino heritage with a link to video. http://www.amok.com/blog/tim-lincecum-speaks-candidly-about-his-filipino-roots-sf-giants-filipino-heritage-night-at-att-tonight/. Accessed January 21, 2018.

Also Noteworthy

1869

The Chinese Labor Convention in Memphis, Tennessee, is held to figure out a way to get cheap Chinese laborers to work on cotton plantations and railroad construction in Alabama, Georgia, Kentucky, Mississippi, South Carolina, Louisiana, Arkansas, Tennessee, and Missouri.

1942

A writ of habeas corpus is filed in the name of Mitsuye Endo by James Purcell.

2007

In San Antonio, Texas, a Muslim American family's vehicles are vandalized with messages telling them to move.

July 14

1870

On this day, the Naturalization Act of 1870 is signed into law by President Ulysses S. Grant. The act limits immigration and naturalization to "aliens of African nativity and to persons of African descent" and "whites," thus excluding all Chinese from receiving citizenship. The act also bans the entry laborers' wives. Economically, a nationwide recession fueled anti-Chinese sentiments on the West Coast as white labor scapegoat "Cheap Chinese labor" as their problem. Mobs of white labor attacked and destroyed Chinese communities in many areas of California and other states.

Still, the 1870 Naturalization Act continued to exclude from citizenship others considered to be non-white, such as Asians and Native Americans. Though Native Americans were granted the right to naturalize in 1890, Asian immigrants were largely prohibited from the naturalization process for several decades more.

Source: Conley, Meghan. "Naturalization and Citizenship Process." In *Race and Racism in the United States: An Encyclopedia of the American Mosaic*, edited by Charles Gallagher and Cameron D. Lippard, p. 867. Santa Barbara, CA: Greenwood, 2014.

Books

Gallagher, Charles, and Cameron D. Lippard, eds. *Race and Racism in the United States: An Encyclopedia of the American Mosaic*. Santa Barbara, CA: Greenwood, 2014. See entry by Meghan Conley, "Naturalization and Citizenship Process," pp. 865–868.

LeMay, Michael, and Elliott Robert Barkan, eds. *U.S. Immigration and Naturalization Laws and Issues: A Documentary History*. Westport, CT: Greenwood Press, 1999. This book provides over 100 primary documents dealing with the controversial history of U.S. immigration law.

Websites

Smith, Marian. "Race, Nationality, and Reality: INS Administration of Racial Provisions in U.S. Immigration and Nationality Law since 1898." *Prologue Magazine* 34, no. 2 (Summer 2002): pp. 91–104. In Part 1, historian Marian Smith of the U.S. Immigration and Naturalization Service discusses early naturalization policies. http://www.archives.gov/publications/prologue/2002/summer/immigration-law-1.html. Accessed October 8, 2016.

University of Pennsylvania's Computing and Humanities, Asian American History. This site provides a timeline of major U.S. legislation related to citizenship and naturalization. http://www.sas.upenn.edu/~rle/History.html. Accessed October 8, 2016.

Also Noteworthy

1985

Jeannette Chan is crowned Queen of the first annual Miss Asian America Pageant at the

Santa Clara County Fairgrounds in California. The pageant is founded by Rose Chung.

July 15

1943

The War Relocation Authority designates Tule Lake, California, as a segregation center for Japanese American detainees who would not sign the loyalty oath. Many renounced their U.S. citizenship and were slated for deportation. Later on, however, they regretted their decision and fought to remain in the United States with the help of civil rights attorney Wayne M. Collins. Tule Lake closed on March 20, 1946.

Isolated in northern California, the Tule Lake area is remote and self-sustained by farming, which made the area fit the War Relocation Authority's (WRA) ideal model for a relocation camp. Set on over 7,400 acres, the Tule Lake complex included the typical infrastructure of a normal American town with a post office, high school, hospital, cemetery, several factory and warehouse buildings, two sewage treatment plants, and over 3,500 acres of irrigated farmland made available by the efforts of the CCC. During the Tule Lake Segregation Center's tenure, roughly four years, nearly 1,500 babies were born and over 300 people died. At its peak capacity, Tule Lake was the temporary home to more than 18,000 internees and 1,200 soldiers. To accommodate these individuals the camp had 1,036 barrack dorms, 518 latrines, and 144 administrative and support buildings. Today, over 50 of these buildings still stand, including the original Stockade (or "prison within a prison"), the WRA Motor Pool, the Post Engineer's Yard and Motor Pool, over 1800 feet of the chain link, barbwire-topped "man-proof" fence, and a small part of the Military Police Compound.

In the summer of 1943, Tule Lake Relocation Center received a designation from the War Relocation Authority that set it apart from the other nine Japanese American internment camps in a dramatic fashion. The WRA determined that it needed a specific location for those deemed "disloyals," otherwise known as a segregation camp.

Source: "Tule Lake Unit, Part of WWII Valor in the Pacific National Monument California." National Park Service, U.S. Department of Interior. https://www.nps.gov/nr/travel/cultural_diversity/tule_lake_unit_wwii_valor_in_the_pacific_national_monument.html. Accessed June 15, 2018.

Books

Burton, Jeffery, Mary Farrell, Florence Lord, and Richard Lord. *Confinement and Ethnicity: An Overview of World War II Japanese American Relocation Sites*. Seattle: University of Washington Press, 2002. *Confinement and Ethnicity* was first published by the U.S. Department of the Interior in 1999. It is a report on the history of all the relocation sites used during World War II to intern Japanese Americans.

Smith, Page. *Democracy on Trial: The Japanese American Evacuation and Relocation in World War II*. New York: Simon & Schuster, 1995. *Democracy on Trial* documents the experiences of Japanese Americans who were interned in relocation campus during World War II through interviews and archival research.

Websites

U.S. War Relocation Authority. "A Challenge to Democracy." 1944. Archive.org. This site provides the documentary *A Challenge to Democracy* produced by the War Relocation Authority to defend the mass unjust internment and relocation of Japanese Americans during World War II. https://archive.org/details/Challeng1944. Accessed January 21, 2018.

U.S. War Relocation Authority. "Relocation of Japanese-Americans." Washington, D.C. 1943. Digital Public Library of America. This site provides the full document "Relocation of Japanese-Americans" produced by the War Relocation Authority to defend the mass unjust internment and relocation of Japanese Americans during World War II. https://dp.la/search?q=%E2%80%9CRelocation+of+Japanese-Americans.%E2%80%9D+. Accessed January 21, 2018.

Also Noteworthy

1946

The 100th Battalion and 442nd Regimental Combat Team are honored with the Presidential Unit Citation, presented by President Harry S. Truman.

2002

In Detroit, Michigan, Brent D. Seever, a 38-year-old, is sentenced to life in prison for killing an Arab American man after 9/11.

July 16

2009

Judy May Chu (b. July 7, 1953) wins the seat for U.S. House Representative from California's 27th District that includes Pasadena and the West San Gabriel Valley of Southern California. Chu won reelection for a full term in 2010. Chu is the first Chinese American woman to be elected to Congress in history.

Judy Chu began her political career in 1985 by getting elected to the School Board. In 1988 she ran for City Council. She ran at a time of extreme racial tension, and her opponent was Barry Hatch, a longtime Monterey Park resident who was at the forefront of several contentious campaigns for "English only" ordinances. Chu ran as part of a moderate, multiethnic coalition. She reached out to a broad spectrum of Democratic voters in Monterey Park and had the backing of the Monterey Park Democratic Club. Traditionally, presidents of the Monterey Park Democratic Club became candidates for City Council. George Ige, Al Song, and other club activists had been instrumental in assisting Lily Chen with her successful bid for City Council in 1982. In yet another departure from tradition, Chinese candidates have now formed their own networks for political success. For example, the Asian Pacific Democratic Club was formed in 1986 to mobilize Asian-American voters. In 1988 they became involved in Judy Chu's campaign. The club canvassed neighborhoods and worked to get out the vote. They also worked on local, state, and federal issues of interest to the Asian-American community. For instance, they worked to expand immigration under the fifth preference category, family sponsorship, and developed good working relations with other immigrant community leaders with whom they had common cause.

Source: Freedman, Amy. *Political Participation and Ethnic Minorities: Chinese Overseas in Malaysia, Indonesia, and the United States*. New York: Routledge, 2000, p. 148.

Books

Horton, John. *The Politics of Diversity: Immigration, Resistance, and Change in Monterey Park, California*. Philadelphia, PA: Temple University Press, 1995. *The Politics of Diversity* documents the raise of women, minorities, and immigrants in the political landscape of Monterey Park that is anchored in transnational ethnic and American identities.

Wei, William. *The Asian American Movement*. Philadelphia, PA: Temple University Press, 1993. See Chapter 3, "Race versus Gender: The Asian American Women's Movement," and Chapter 8, "From Radical to Electoral Politics: The Asian American Odyssey for Empowerment," for discussions related to Judy Chu and Asian Americans in politics.

Websites

Chu, Judy. 1953. Biographical directory of the U.S. Congress. This site provides a biography of Chu that highlights her education and career background. http://bioguide.congress.gov/scripts/biodisplay.pl?index=C001080. Accessed January 21, 2018.

U.S. Congresswoman Judy Chu. 27th District of California. This site is Congresswoman Judy Chu's official web page, and it provides a biography of Chu, her platform, and photographs. https://chu.house.gov/. Accessed January 21, 2018.

Also Noteworthy

1989

Christine Choy and Renee Tajima-Pena's documentary about the murder of Vincent Chin, *Who Killed Vincent Chin?* (1987), is released.

1995

Vandals severely damage a mosque in Huntsville, Alabama.

July 17

1942

President Franklin Roosevelt authorizes the resettlement of up to 15,000 persons from Hawaii "considered as potentially dangerous to national security" and their family members. Fewer than 2,000 Japanese Americans from Hawaii would actually be interned on the mainland.

Of particular concern to both military and government officials alike was Hawai'i community of nearly 158,000 residents of Japanese ancestry (including some 37,000 aliens who, by law, could not become citizens). Constituting approximately 37 percent of the population of the islands, the Nikkei *were regarded as a potential security threat—as to both sabotage and espionage, and as to the possibility of their undermining defense in the event of a Japanese invasion. However, in stark contrast to the mainland, where the notorious policy of mass removal and internment was pursued in early 1942, in Hawai'i the army instituted only selective arrests and internments or other categories of incarceration. Approximately 10,000 Nikkei residents in the islands, including all* Kibei, *were identified and investigated, and hundreds of them were then picked up for interrogation and loyalty assessments by the military authorities. Since nearly 50,000 of the Nikkei were children under sixteen years of age, more than one in eleven ethnic Japanese adults were involved as subjects of security operations. Of the 10,000 so affected, approximately 2,000 were incarcerated, although not all were formally designated as internees.*

Source: Scheiber, Harry, and Jane Scheiber. "Hawaii's Kibei under Martial Law: A Hidden Chapter in the History of World War II Internments." *Western Legal History* 22, no. 1 and 2 (2009): pp. 2–4.

Books

Robinson, Greg. *By Order of the President: FDR and the Internment of Japanese Americans*. Cambridge, MA: Harvard University Press, 2001. *By Order of the President* addresses history of various policies related to Japanese Americans during World War II.

Scheiber, Harry, and Jane Scheiber. *Bayonets in Paradise: Martial Law in Hawai'i during World War II*. Honolulu: University of Hawaii Press, 2016. *Bayonets in Paradise* details the history of Japanese Americans in Hawaii during World War II, struggles for constitutional rights, and the exercise of emergency power and martial law.

Websites

"Chronology of World War II Hawai'i Internees." The Untold Story: Internment of Japanese Americans in Hawai'i. Presented by the Japanese Cultural Center of Hawai'i. http://hawaiiinternment.org/untold-story/chronology-world-war-ii-hawai%CA%BBi-internees. Accessed February 8, 2018.

"Civil Rights: Japanese Americans." www.pbs.org. September 2007. This site provides background to the internment of Japanese Americans during World War II with photographs and links to videos. http://www.pbs.org/thewar/at_home_civil_rights_japanese_american.htm. Accessed February 8, 2018.

July 18

1992

The Filipino American Community Action Group (FIL-AM CAG) was established in

1991 to provide educational activities that promote civic engagement and positive social, economic, and political transformations in the Filipino American community at Hampton Roads (Tidewaters, Virginia). One main issue they currently work to address is the growing problem with youth gangs. On this day, the FIL-AM CAG sponsors a "Truce Dance" for Filipino youths, particularly gang members and their friends, to bring gang violence and other criminal activity among Filipino youths under control.

In Virginia, state police reports do not provide information on crime or arrest rates by specific ethnic groups. However, in the past few years, the Filipino community in the Hampton Roads metropolitan area has become concerned about the development of street gangs composed of Filipino youths. Several articles have appeared in local newspapers on die subject of Filipino gangs (Waltz 1991, Watson 1992). On July 18, 1992, the Filipino-American Community Action Group (FIL-AM CAG) sponsored a "Truce Dance" for Filipino youths, particularly gang members and their friends, in order to help control gang violence and other criminal activity among Filipino youths. The development of Filipino street gangs in the Hampton Roads metropolitan area appears to be recent. Admittedly, not all the problems of Filipino youths are connected with gangs. Nonetheless, there definitely seems to be an active interest within the Filipino community in the Hampton Roads area concerning delinquent activity of their youths, and this interest has spread to the larger community, as indicated by recent news accounts.

Source: Shoemaker, Donald. "Ethnic Identity and Delinquency American Filipino-American Youth: A Theoretical View." *Philippine Sociological Society* 43, no. 1/4 (January–December 1995): pp. 102–103.

Books

Covey, Herbert. *Street Gangs throughout the World.* Springfield, IL: Charles C. Thomas Publisher, 2010. See Chapter 2, "Street Gangs in the United States": in particular, the section on Asian American gangs.

Posadas, Barbara. *The Filipino Americans.* Westport, CT: Greenwood Press, 1999. See Chapter 7, "Filipino Americans Entering the Twenty-First Century": in particular, section on youth and gangs.

Websites

FIL-AM CAG Facebook page. This site provides updates and events organized by FIL-AM CAG. https://www.facebook.com/pg/Fil-Am-CAG-114686005265841/about/?ref=page_internal. Accessed February 8, 2018.

Fisher, Joe. "Special Report: Stopping the Growth of Gangs in Hampton Roads." WAVY.com. February 25, 2016. This is a television news report on the gang issue in Hampton Roads. http://wavy.com/2016/02/25/special-report-stopping-the-growth-of-gangs-in-hampton-roads/. Accessed February 8, 2018.

July 19

1921

A group of white vigilantes forcibly remove upward of 58 Japanese laborers from Turlock, California. They were driven roughly five miles out of town and ordered to never return.

"Oriental Laborers Chased from Town: Turlock Fruit Pickers Take Law into Own Hands and Deport Cheap Jap Labor; Other Japs Immediately Leave"

By the Associated Press

A general exodus of Japanese field laborers and their families from this district is taking place today, following the deportation to Keys, five miles north, of 58 Japanese male workers by white men, members of a union of fruit and melon pickers. The authorities announce the union is composed principally of itinerants, Japanese here who witnessed the encorced [sic] departure of their countrymen, complained to the police that they were roughly handled and in some instances were robbed. The authorities said that the members of the mob which numbered about 75, threatened to burn one Japanese hotel and two Japanese bunk houses to hasten the departure of their occupants. Fifteen Japanese were taken from the Gerard ranch near town and the remainder from various other properties. The police expect to arrest some of the mob leaders today. The Japanese leaving today are going in all directions, but the greater number are heading for Stockton, Keys and Modesto. The police were notified that a number of Japanese taken to Keys by the mob were placed aboard a freight train, which was flagged. The Japanese submitted in most instances without even protesting. The Japanese had been brought into the district under contract to pick the fruit and melon crops. They are being paid 16 cents a crate, whereas, the whites were given 25 cents and 26 cents, and this is given as the principal cause of the trouble.

Source: "Oriental Laborers Chased from Town." *Healdsburg Tribune*, July 20, 1921.

Books

Matsumoto, Valerie. *Farming the Home Place: A Japanese American Community in California, 1919–1982*. Ithaca, NY: Cornell University Press, 1993. *Farming the Home Place* is a history of the formation of a Japanese community in the San Joaquin Valley.

Treat, Payson. *Japan and the United States 1853–1921*. Stanford, CA: Stanford University Press, 1928. *Japan and the United States* focuses on Japan-U.S. relations and discusses how domestic events influence public opinion and Japan-U.S. relations and policies.

Websites

Blair, Doug. "The 1920 Anti-Japanese Crusade and Congressional Hearings." Seattle Civil Rights & Labor History Project. University of Washington. This article provides an overview of anti-Japanese movements, with a particular focus on the Japanese American community in Seattle, Washington. http://depts.washington.edu/civilr/Japanese_restriction.htm. Accessed October 26, 2016.

McAndrews, James. "Competition for Turlock Farm Jobs Once Led to 'Boneheaded' Move against Japanese Immigrants." *Modesto Bee*, September 20, 2014. This site provides a historical overview of the anti-Japanese movement in Turlock, California. http://www.modbee.com/news/local/article3172673.html#storylink=cpy. Accessed October 26, 2016.

July 20

1979

At a two-day (July 20 and 21) international conference in Geneva, Switzerland, the Orderly Departure Program (ODP) is established under the auspices of the UN High Commissioner for Refugees (UNHCR). The goal was to encourage refugees to leave their country safely, instead of the dangerous voyage by boat. On September 14, 1994, registration for the ODP was closed. Under the ODP from 1980 until 1997, 623,509 Vietnamese were resettled abroad of whom more than 450,000 went to the United States. Refugee camps opened in Thailand to house some 160,000 Cambodian and 105,000 Laotian refugees. UNHCR assisted another 350,000 Cambodian refugees who lived in Thailand outside of the camps, and some 100,000 Cambodians who fled to Vietnam.

With the Orderly Departure Program, Vietnam's proposal was adopted. The first agreement establishing the program was concluded between UNHCR and Vietnam during discussions in Hanoi on May 30, 1979. It entrusted UNHCR with the responsibility to "make effort to enlist support for this programme amongst potential receiving countries." No particular countries were mentioned. But the Geneva Conferences that followed in June and July 1979 made the Orderly Departure Program operational. British Prime Minister Margaret Thatcher pushed for the meeting, the first of its kind in the United Nations. Thatcher sought to alleviate Hong Kong's burden. Vice President Mondale headed the American delegation.

Mondale opened the conference in a celebratory note, citing Evian:

> *Forty-one years ago this very week, another international conference on Lake Geneva concluded its deliberations. Thirty-two "nations of asylum" convened at Evian to save the doomed Jews of Nazi Germany and Austria. . . . We have each heard similar arguments about the plight of the refugees in Indochina.*

The rhetoric generated legitimacy and sway for what was basically a large fundraising event. The idea was to redistribute Vietnamese population around the globe. And Vietnam, which the United States derided as persecutor of its own population, could for this purpose rise to become an equal member at the negotiating table. Instead of leaving by boat, people seeking to leave Vietnam could now enlist UNHCR offices in the country and obtain resettlement visas. They were encouraged to spread across numerous destinations around the globe.

Source: Mann, Itamar. *Humanity at Sea: Maritime Migration and the Foundations of International Law*. Cambridge: Cambridge University Press, 2016, pp. 74–75.

Books

Do, Hien Duc. *The Vietnamese Americans*. Westport, CT: Greenwood Press, 1999. *The Vietnamese Americans* covers various aspects of Vietnamese immigration experience and history in the United States.

Rutledge, Paul. *The Vietnamese Experience in America*. Bloomington: Indiana University Press, 1992. *The Vietnamese Experience in America* covers the history and policies that regulated Vietnamese refugee migration after the Vietnam War and includes discussions on various aspects of Vietnamese refugee resettlement.

Websites

"Flight from Indochina." UNHCR. The UN Refugee Agency. This article is a publication of the UNHCR that discusses the history and international policies of the refugee migration from Vietnam, Laos, and Cambodia after the Vietnam War. http://www.unhcr.org/3ebf9bad0.pdf. Accessed January 17, 2017.

Zhou, Min, and Carl Bankston III. "Vietnamese Americans: Lessons in American History." Teaching Tolerance: A Project of the Southern Poverty Law Center. This article provides a discussion of the history of Vietnamese refugee migration and the experiences of refugee children adapting to life in America. http://www.tolerance.org/sites/default/files/kits/vac_brief_history.pdf. Accessed January 17, 2017.

1999

The Chinese Communist Party begins a persecution campaign against Falun Gong, a new Buddhist movement, arresting thousands nationwide. As a result, many left China and resettled in the United States, including the founder Li Hongzhi. Falun Gong's presence in the United States changes the religious landscapes of the American religious mosaic.

Falun Gong would find itself outlawed in China, a move apparently inspired by a fear of the group's ability to rapidly mobilize such prominent groups of protesters and its certainly exaggerated claims of 100 million followers in China. However, the ban on Falun Gong was officially reasoned as due to the group's and its leader's overstepping the boundaries of religious freedom by engaging in illegal religious activities. Li Hongzhi, however, had left China in 1995, ultimately relocating to New York in the United States, where he remains in exile from his homeland to this day. From New York, in the intervening years, Falun Gong has built up an impressive headquarters for global media outreach, including the newspaper and website The Epoch Times *and the New Tang Dynasty Television station. While both organizations deliver a wide fare of news stories from around the world, each also gives extensive attention to mainland China's anti-Falun Gong campaigns since 1999, just as each is generally critical of the Chinese government.* The Epoch Times *has even issued a small book entitled* Nine Commentaries on the Chinese Communist

Party [CCP], which likens the CCP to a "giant, evil possessing spirit" that is destined to soon perish due to its persecution of Falun Gong. The New York-based television station, New Tang Dynasty TV, is related to Falun Gong in a fashion similar to the Epoch Times. *Falun Dafa has never operated as an institution in which individuals can be said to have "membership," and no records of "members" are kept. Since early on in China, however, Falun Dafa has proclaimed 100 million practitioners, a number that it now touts as being a "worldwide" tally, but this claim is surely an immense exaggeration, to say the least. Still, in large American cities, such as San Francisco, Los Angeles, or New York, as well as others around the world, there may be hundreds and even thousands of practitioners, while the movement may also have at least a presence in smaller towns where one might never suspect them. In those places where they have a significant presence, like major American cities, one often finds members in front of the Chinese embassy, both proselytizing for Falun Dafa and protesting the Chinese Communist Party over the continued outlawing of Falun Gong in mainland China and what practitioners understand to be an ongoing "persecution" of adherents in that country.*

Source: Adams, Ryan. "Falun Dafa/Falun Gong." In *Asian American Religious Cultures*, edited by Jonathan H. X. Lee, Fumitaka Matsuoka, Edmond Yee, and Ronald Y. Nakasone, pp. 367–368. Santa Barbara, CA: ABC-CLIO, 2015.

Books

Ownby, David. *Falun Gong and the Future of China*. Oxford: Oxford University Press, 2008. *Falun Gong and the Future of China* is a study based on fieldwork with Falun Gong practitioners in North America.

Penny, Benjamin. *The Religion of Falun Gong*. Chicago, IL: University of Chicago Press, 2012. *The Religion of Falun Gong* offers a history of Falun Gong's development, beliefs, and founder.

Websites

Falun Dafa. FalunDafa.org. 2018. This is the official web page of Falun Gong. http://en.falundafa.org/. Accessed January 21, 2018.

Porter, Noah. "Falun Gong in the United States: An Ethnographic Study." Master thesis. University of South Florida. 2003. Scholar Common. This is a master thesis that examines various aspects of Falun Gong in the United States. http://scholarcommons.usf.edu/cgi/viewcontent.cgi?article=2450&context=etd. Accessed January 21, 2018.

Also Noteworthy

1942

The War Relocation Authority adopts the first policy permitting indefinite leave from war relocation centers.

1954

The Geneva Conference on Indochina declares a demilitarized zone at the 17th parallel with South under the leadership of Prime Minister Ngo Dinh Diem and the North under Communist rule. Over in Laos, France finally surrenders all claims to Laos.

July 21

1997

Asian Avenue, or AsianAve, a social networking company launches its website to promote and advocate Asian American issues, such as protesting MSNBC headline for the 1998 Winter Olympics that read "American Beats Out [Michelle] Kwan." Kwan is an American of Chinese ancestry and represented the United States during the Olympics. AsianAve was also used during President Barack Obama's 2008 campaign to engage Asian American voters.

Senator Obama's campaign approached CCI's [Community Connect Inc.] niche social networking communities to facilitate compelling dialogues among passionate constituents. His presence across BlackPlanet.com, MiGente.com, AsianAve.com, GLEE.com [gay, lesbian, and everyone else] and Faithbase.com allows his messages to disseminate and circulate among highly targeted niche groups, and in turn, gives those audiences a voice on the issues that concern them.

Source: "Barack Obama Campaign Reaches Out to America's Niche Audiences through Online Social Networks." *PR Newswire*, October 15, 2007.

Books

Albarran, Alan, ed. *The Social Media Industries*. New York: Routledge, 2013. See Maria Williams-Hawkins's Chapter 12, "Bridging the Great Divide: African American and Asian American Use of Social Media."

Head, Tom. *It's Your World, So Change It: Using the Power of the Internet to Create Social Change*. San Francisco, CA: Pearson Education, 2010. *It's Your World, So Change It* is a study of the power of social media and social networking as tools for social change and political mobilization and includes a discussion on AsianAve and other ethnic social media networks.

Websites

AsianAve.com. Official web page. Membership is required to log in. http://www.asianave.com/. Accessed February 8, 2018.

Zhao, Qilan. "Ethnic Social Networking Sites." Masters of Media. New Media & Digital Culture M.A., University of Amsterdam. November 4, 2007. This article discusses three ethnic social media networking sites, including AsianAve. https://mastersofmedia.hum.uva.nl/blog/2007/11/04/the-surplus-of-ethnic-social-networking-sites/. Accessed February 8, 2018.

Also Noteworthy

1954

The First Indochina War, fought between France and Vietnamese forces, ends after seven years.

2006

In Naperville, Illinois, an Islamic center is burglarized.

July 22

1930

Carlos Bulosan (1911–1956) arrives in Seattle, Washington. Bulosan was 18 years old at the time. Bulosan arrived during the early years of the Great Depression, a time when there were very few jobs and anti-immigrant sentiments were on the rise. He soon left for California and became involved with the labor union movement instigated by left-wing political groups fighting to protect workers from wage cuts, unemployment, and adverse working conditions. Union organizers also challenged discriminatory legislation that sought to specifically exclude Filipinos from working in fish canneries, an occupation they heavily employed.

Excerpt from Carlos Bulosan's *America Is in the Heart.*

America is not a land of one race or one class of men. We are all Americans that have toiled and suffered and known oppression and defeat, from the first Indian that offered peace in Manhattan to the last Filipino pea pickers. America is not bound by geographical latitudes. America is not merely a land or an institution. America is in the hearts of men that died for freedom; it is also in the eyes of men that are building a new world. America is a prophecy of a new society of men: of a system that knows no sorrow or strife or suffering. America is a warning to those who would try to falsify the ideas of free men.

America is also the nameless foreigner, the homeless refugee, the hungry boy begging for a job and the black body dangling from a tree. America is the illiterate immigrant who is ashamed that the world of books and intellectual opportunities is closed to him. We are that nameless foreigner, that homeless refugee, that hungry boy, that illiterate immigrant and that lynched black body. All of us, from the first Adams to the last Filipino, native born or alien, educated or illiterate—We are America!

Source: Bulosan, Carlos. *America Is in the Heart: A Personal History*. Seattle: University of Washington Press, 1973, p. 189.

Books

Espiritu, Augusto. *Five Faces of Exile: The Nation and Filipino American Intellectuals*. Stanford, CA: Stanford University Press, 2005. See Chapter 2, "Suffering and Passion: Carlos Bulosan."

Rody, Caroline. *The Interethnic Imagination: Roots and Passages in Contemporary Asian American Fiction*. Oxford: Oxford University Press, 2009. See "Interchapter: Asian/African: Black Presences in Asian American Fiction" for analytical discussion that includes Bulosan's *America Is in the Heart*.

Websites

"Author, Poet, and Worker: The World of Carlos Bulosan." Digital Collections. University Libraries. University of Washington. This site provides an overview biography of Carlos Bulosan, in addition to links to some of his writings. https://content.lib.washington.edu/exhibits/bulosan/index.html. Accessed January 21, 2018.

Gurtiza, Richard. "The Legend of Carlos Bulosan." International Longshore and Warehouse Union. 2018. This essay details Carlos Bulosan's life and legacy. https://www.ilwu.org/the-legend-of-carlos-bulosan/. Accessed January 21, 2018.

Also Noteworthy

1943

The Women's Auxiliary Army Corps (WAAC) begins accepting Japanese Americans. On December 13, Iris Watanabe from Amache War Relocation Center became the first Japanese American internee to join the WAAC.

July 23

1969

A group of Thai Buddhist monks are sent to Los Angeles, which developed into the formation of a Thai Buddhist temple and by extension Thai community in America.

In 1969, the group [Thai American Buddhist Association] wrote a letter to the Supreme Patriarch in Thailand (who was appointed by King Bhumipol as the Head of the Buddhist Order) requesting that monks be assigned to Los Angeles. The Supreme Patriarch obliged, and on July 23, 1969, he sent six monks to Los Angeles. The monks immediately developed a relationship with the community by conducting Buddhist rituals in Thai homes and attending events. On August 2, 1969, the Thai American Buddhist Association and the monks organized a Buddhist ceremony festival at Lynwood High School to celebrate the birth of Gautama Buddha. The celebration, known as Asalah Boucha, *was the first held on U.S. soil. It attracted over one thousand participants and observers and raised nearly $4,000 in donations for a temple. More importantly, it demonstrated to Thai monastic elite that Los Angeles had enough commitment for Thais to make a temple a reality.*

Source: Padoongpatt, Mark. *Flavors of Empire: Food and the Making of Thai America*. Berkeley: University of California Press, 2017, pp. 122–123.

Books

Bao, Jiemin. *Creating a Buddhist Community: A Thai Temple in Silicon Valley*. Philadelphia, PA: Temple University Press, 2015. *Creating a Buddhist Community* is a case study of Thai American Buddhists and the formation of their temple and community.

Cadge, Wendy. *Heartwood: The First Generation of Theravada Buddhism in America*. Chicago, IL: University of Chicago Press, 2004. *Heartwood* studies the growth and history of Theravada Buddhist communities in the United States, which includes Thai Buddhists.

Websites

"Thai Temples in North America: Wat Thai in the USA." The Buddha Garden, 2018. This site provides a list of Thai Buddhist temples in the United States. https://www.thebuddhagarden.com/thai-temples-america.html. Accessed June 14, 2018.

Wat Thai of Los Angeles. Official web page. This site provides a detailed history of the Thai Buddhist temple in Los Angeles and history of Thai migration to the United States. http://www.watthailosangeles.com/history-of-wat-thai/. Accessed February 8, 2018.

Also Noteworthy

1850

A group of Chinese are invited to march in President Zachary Taylor's "grand funeral pageant" in New York.

1932

Two hundred white workers harass 58 Filipinos in a town near Canal Point, Florida, demanding that they leave the town.

1953

A truce ending the Korean War is signed.

2002

In Heber City, Utah, a Muslim American–owned hotel is set on fire.

July 24

2003

Korea Peace Forum is held in Washington, D.C., on U.S.-North Korea relations. North Korea started to publicly develop their nuclear program in 1993, prompting serious diplomatic talks among the United States, China, Japan, South Korea, and North Korea.

When the progress made in U.S.-DPRK relations from 1993 to 2000 was reversed beginning in late 2002, mutual suspicion reverted to a level equaling that of the worst days of the Cold War. Most important for the current talks, the United States and Japan strongly suspect that the current North Korean regime has no intention of abandoning its nuclear arsenal. In turn, this suspicion reinforces Pyongyang's conviction that what Washington really wants is regime change. Such a deeply held belief, with its origins in the Korean War and years of military confrontation, has compelled the North to pursue its policy of "nuclear deterrence" and the buildup of a nuclear arsenal.

Source: Carlin, Robert, and John Lewis. *Negotiating with North Korea: 1992–2007*. Center for International Security and Cooperation. Freeman Spogli Institute for International Studies. Stanford University. January 2008, p. 19.

Books

Chinoy, Mike. *Meltdown: The Inside Story of the North Korean Nuclear Crisis*. New York: St. Martin's Griffin, 2008. *Meltdown* investigates North Korea's nuclear program and weapons, documenting the shifts in U.S.-North Korea diplomacy.

Lee, Chae-Jin. *A Troubled Peace: U.S. Policy and the Two Koreas*. Baltimore, MD: Johns Hopkins University Press, 2006. *A Troubled Peace* is a study of U.S. foreign relations, policies, and history with North and South Korea.

Websites

National Association of Korean Americans (NAKA). 2018. This site is NAKA's official web page, and it provides a list of their conferences, documents, and so on. http://www.naka.org/about/. Accessed February 8, 2018.

Wertz, Daniel, and Chelsea Gannon. "A History of U.S.-DPRK Relations." The National Committee on North Korea. November 2015. This report provides a detailed history of U.S.-North Korea foreign relations and policies. https://www.ncnk.org/sites/default/files/issue-briefs/US_DPRK_Relations.pdf. Accessed February 8, 2018.

Also Noteworthy

1870

Hispano-Filipino Benevolent Society of New Orleans is established and is the first

Filipino American social club in the United States.

2003

In College Park, Maryland, a wooden cross is burned at an Islamic school. Two 17-year-old boys are charged with harassment and damaging property.

2004

In Buffalo, New York, two women in a car chase and threaten two teenage sisters while yelling anti-Muslim slurs and making references to the sisters' Muslim heritage.

July 25

2000

Norman Yoshio Mineta (b. November 12, 1931) is confirmed by President William J. Clinton as U.S. secretary of commerce, becoming the first Asian American to be appointed to a cabinet-level post (2000–2001). Six months later, he was confirmed by President George W. Bush as the new U.S. transportation secretary (2001–2006), making him the first person ever to serve in the cabinets of both Republican and Democratic presidents. Mineta has enjoyed a distinguished political career that began in 1967 when he became the first minority to win a seat on the San Jose City Council. He set another milestone in 1971 when he was elected mayor, becoming the first Asian American mayor of a major city. After being elected to Congress in 1975, he led the push for the Japanese American reparations bill (H.R. 442).

Although Japanese Americans accomplished their legislative goals, the Civil Liberties Act and the redress movement behind it have come under criticism.... These critics fall at both ends of the political spectrum. Republican Rep. Daniel Lundgren, who adopted the CWRIC [Wartime Relocation and Internment of Civilians] report as a commissioner but dissented from recommendations that included monetary reparations, believes that nothing more than an apology is required. While Lundgren argues that the passage of time makes monetary redress inappropriate—and fears its extension to the African American and Native American redress movements—[Roger] Daniels counters that these arguments are irrelevant, because the bill provided money only for survivors or direct victims. Dissent against monetary reparations also arose in liberal newspapers, such as the New York Times, *which argued for a symbolic "gesture of atonement"—for example, a scholarship fund—as an alternative to monetary redress.*

The testimony of former Rep. Norman Y. Mineta (D-Calif.), who was himself interned during World War II, also addresses criticisms of monetary redress. Mineta concedes that liberty is priceless, but argues that this does not make payments inappropriate. Japanese Americans did not sell their civil and constitutional rights. These rights were "ripped away," and that fact entitles survivors to compensation—that is, to atonement money. Most importantly, Mineta reminds us that "at issue here is the wholesale violation, based on race, of those very legal principles we were fighting to defend."

Source: Brooks, Roy. "Japanese American Redress and the American Political Process: A Unique Achievement?" In *When Sorry Isn't Enough: The Controversy over Apologies and Reparations for Human Injustice*, edited by Roy Brooks, p. 161. New York: New York University Press, 1999.

Books

Hatamiya, Leslie. *Righting a Wrong: Japanese Americans and the Passage of the Civil Liberties Act of 1988*. Stanford, CA: Stanford University Press, 1993. *Righting a Wrong* documents the history of Japanese American reparations that includes details of Mineta's contribution to its success.

Robinson, Greg. *A Tragedy of Democracy: Japanese Confinement in North America*. New York: Columbia University Press, 2009. *A Tragedy of Democracy* is a history of U.S. surveillance of Japanese Americans leading up to their relocation and internment during World War II. It examines the aftermath of confinement for postwar Japanese Americans.

Websites

Mineta, Norman. Biographical directory of the U.S. Congress. This site provides a short biography of Mineta that highlights his education and career. http://bioguide.congress.gov/scripts/biodisplay.pl?index=M000794. Accessed January 21, 2018.

"President's Statement on Transportation Secretary Norman Mineta." The White House, President George W. Bush. June 23, 2006. This is the press lease that acknowledges Mineta's contribution as U.S. transportation secretary. https://georgewbush-whitehouse.archives.gov/news/releases/2006/06/20060623-9.html. Accessed January 21, 2018.

July 26

1891

Prominent missionary Augustus Ward Loomis dies on this day in San Francisco. Loomis and his wife, Mary Ann Luce, served as Presbyterian missionaries in China (1844–1850), with Creek Indians in Oklahoma (1852), and the Chinese in San Francisco (1865–1867). During a period of anti-Chinese sentiments, Loomis is known for advocating fair treatment of the Chinese in America.

Excerpt from "Chinese Defenders: The Congressional Commission Resumes Its Inquiry: What Revs. Gibson and Loomis Think of the Moral Status of the Mood-Eyed Horde." *San Francisco Chronicle*, November 10, 1876.

Rev. Dr. Loomis, formerly a Presbyterian missionary in the Flowery Kingdom was next sworn. He had been in China for four years, and engaged in the good work of converting the heathen with fluctuating success on this coast. He said that in the early times the Chinese came here on their own responsibility, but in later days . . . they came here under labor contracts. No coolies had ever been brought to California, but many women . . . have been imported for the vilest purposes—either kidnapped, brought or contracted for. . . . As a people they compared favorably with any American community. As laborers the Chinese were desirable on account of their patience, perseverance and attention to business, and he was of the opinion that there are more families and more industries in California than there would have been without the Chinese.

Source: "CHINESE DEFENDERS." *San Francisco Chronicle* (1869–Current File), San Francisco, California, 1876. http://search.proquest.com/docview/571719596?accountid=13802. Accessed October 25, 2017.

Books

Chang, Derek. *Citizens of a Christian Nation: Evangelical Missions and the Problem of Race in the Nineteenth Century*. Philadelphia: University of Pennsylvania Press, 2010. Historian Derek Chang provides a discussion of African American and Chinese American religious history and shifting national discourse on citizenship and race.

Peffer, George Anthony. *If They Don't Bring Their Women Here: Chinese Female Immigration before Exclusion*. Urbana: University of Illinois Press, 1999. George Peffer documents the lives of Chinese American women seven years before the passage of the 1882 Chinese Exclusion Act.

Websites

"Guide to the Augusts Ward Loomis Papers, 1803–1897." Cornell University Library. This article provides information on the Loomis archive in the Division of Rare and Manuscript Collections. http://rmc.library.cornell.edu/EAD/htmldocs/RMM02474.html. Accessed October 6, 2016.

Waugh, Barry. "Augustus W. Loomis, 1816–1891." Presbyterians of the Past. 2016. This site contains a detailed biography of Loomis. http://www.presbyteriansofthepast.com/2015/03/26/augustus-w-loomis-1816-1891/. Accessed October 6, 2016.

Also Noteworthy

1894

On this day, Japanese immigrant Namyo Bessho, a U.S. Navy veteran of the Spanish-American War and World War I, petitions for naturalized U.S. citizenship under the act of July 26, 1894, which granted citizenship to "any alien" over 21 years of age who served five consecutive years in the navy or marine corps. On February 1, 1910, the Circuit Court of Appeals, Fourth Circuit, ruled against his appeal and denied his naturalization. Bessho finally became a U.S. citizen through a measure signed by President Franklin Roosevelt on June 24, 1935, granting Asian veterans citizenship rights.

1987

Jitsuo Morikawa (1912–1987) passes away. Morikawa was a leader who exercised tremendous influence on the American Baptist Churches USA (ABCUSA)—its predecessor bodies were known as the Northern Baptist Convention (NBC) from 1907 to 1950 and the American Baptist Convention (ABC) from 1950 to 1972, but in 1972 the convention changed its name to ABCUSA—to reflect the depth of its faith, the breadth of its witness, and its theological integrity. Morikawa was also a gigantic figure among the Asian American Baptists. He enabled them to discover their identity and their impact on the ABCUSA. He also helped the denomination to develop respect for and recognition of the dignity of the Asian American Baptists within the institution. And by enabling the Asian American Baptist churches to grow and to share their cultural, racial, and theological perspectives within the ABCUSA, he expanded the growth of the denomination.

2007

In Corvallis, Oregon, Jesse J. Mason, a 24-year-old, is arrested for throwing furniture and smashing a window at a residence of two men he identified as Middle Eastern while yelling "This is America—Arabs and al-Qaida out of the country."

July 27

1953

The United States, North Korea, and China sign an armistice, which ends the Korean War but fails to bring about a peace. To date, the Republic of Korea (South) and Democratic Peoples' Republic of Korea (North) have not signed a peace treaty. The Korean War (1950–1953) was the first "hot war" of the Cold War era. The war claimed an estimated 3.5 million Korean and over 54,000 U.S. lives only to end right where it began—divided along the 38th parallel.

The combat in Korea lasted thirty-seven months. The need to maintain a military alert and to defend the 38th Parallel continues today. The danger of hostile nations facing one another has lasted many years. Numerous nations fought under the aegis of the United Nations in this isolated and limited war, as did thousands of Chinese and millions of Koreans of varied political persuasion. The war in Korea took 54,200 American lives. More than a hundred thousand Americans were wounded in this war. Thousands were taken prisoner. Many persons identified as prisoners (POW) or missing in action (MIA) have never been identified or recovered. Both the Democratic People's Republic of Korea and the Republic of Korea suffered devastating economic breakdowns. Millions of refugees were uprooted from their homes, sometimes even their nations. The land was pocked by continual bombing and artillery. The nations suffered the loss of hydroelectric systems, the collapse of the infrastructure, and the failure of transportation and communication systems.

Source: Edwards, Paul. *To Acknowledge a War: The Korean War in American Memory*. Westport, CT: Greenwood Press, 2000, p. 3.

Books

Cumings, Bruce. *The Korean War: A History*. New York: Modern Library, 2011. *The Korean War: A History* reveals the origins of the war, U.S. involvement in Korea post World War II, and untold stories of bloody insurgencies, massacres, and rebellions committed by all involved.

Haruki, Wada. *The Korean War: An International History*. Translated by Frank Baldwin. Lanham, MD: Rowman & Littlefield, 2014. In this volume, Wada Haruki draws on archives and other primary sources from South Korea, Russia, China, Taiwan, Japan, and the United States that analyze the Korean War as an international conflict.

Websites

"Asian-Americans in the United States Military During the Korean War." This essay details Asian Americans who served in the U.S. military during the Korean War with photographs and further resources for investigation. The state of New Jersey website. http://www.nj.gov/military/korea/factsheets/asian.html. Accessed January 21, 2018.

"A Brief History of Korean Americans." National Association of Korean Americans. 2018. This essay provides an overview of Korean immigration history in the United States, with a section that focuses on the impact of the Korean War on Koran immigration. http://www.naka.org/resources/history.asp. Accessed January 21, 2018.

Also Noteworthy

1942

Hirota Isomura and Toshiro Kobata are killed by guards at Lordsburg Internment Camp in New Mexico because they are too sick to walk from the train station to the camp gate.

2011

Gary Locke is confirmed unanimously by the U.S. Senate as President Barack Obama's U.S. ambassador to China.

July 28

1868

The Burlingame Treaty of 1868 is an agreement between the United States and China facilitated by former Massachusetts congressman, Anson Burlingame. Two articles of the treaty addressed Chinese immigration to the United States. In exchange for privileges extended to American merchants and missionaries in China, the United States granted visiting or residing Chinese people the same privileges, immunities, and exemptions enjoyed by the citizens or subjects of the most-favored nations. The second article stated that both the United States and China should recognize the inalienable human right to mutual and free migration. These two provisions became a major political obstacle for the U.S. federal government as it sought to ban Chinese immigration. In 1880, the United States negotiated the second Burlingame Treaty with China that gave the former the unilateral right to limit, though not absolutely prohibit, Chinese immigration. This opened the way for the 1882 Chinese Exclusion Law, which suspended entry of Chinese laborers for a period of ten years.

Treaty signed at Washington July 28, 1868, supplementing treaty of June 18, 1858; Senate advice and consent to ratification, with amendments, July 24, 1868; Ratified by the President of the United States October 19, 1868.

Article II

The United States of America and his Majesty the Emperor of China, believing that the safety and prosperity of commerce will thereby best be promoted, agree that any privilege or immunity in respect to trade or navigation within the Chinese dominions which may not have been stipulated for by treaty, shall be subject to the discretion of the Chinese Government and may be regulated by it accordingly, but not in a manner or spirit incompatible with the treaty stipulations of the parties.

Article III

The Emperor of China shall have the right to appoint consuls at ports of the United States, who shall enjoy the same privileges and immunities as those enjoyed by public law and treaty in the United States by the consuls of Great Britain and Russia, or either of them. . . .

Article V

The United States of America and the Emperor of China cordially recognize the inherent and inalienable right of man to change his home and allegiance, and also the mutual advantage of the free migration and emigration of their citizens and subjects respectively from the one country to the other, for purposes of curiosity, of trade, or as permanent residents. The high contracting parties, therefore, join in reprobating any other than an entirely voluntary emigration for these purposes. They consequently agree to pass laws making it a penal offence for a citizen of the United States or Chinese subjects to take Chinese subjects either to the United States or to any other foreign country, or for a Chinese subject or citizen of the United States to take citizens of the United States to China or to any other foreign country, without their free and voluntary consent respectively.

Article VI

Citizens of the United States visiting or residing in China shall enjoy the same privileges, immunities or exemptions in respect to travel or residence as may there be enjoyed by the citizens or subjects of the most favored nation, and, reciprocally, Chinese subjects visiting or residing in the United States shall enjoy the same privileges, immunities and exemptions in respect to travel or residence as may there be enjoyed by the citizens or subjects of the most favored nation. But nothing herein contained shall be held to confer naturalization upon citizens of the United States in China, nor upon the subjects of China in the United States.

Source: Sanger, George P., ed. *The Statutes at Large, Treaties and Proclamations of the United States of America.* Boston, MA: Little, Brown and Company, 1871.

Books

Chen, Jack. *The Chinese of America.* San Francisco, CA: Harper & Row, 1980. This is a classic in the study of Chinese American history. It covers Chinese immigration history in the 19th-century United States.

Tsai, Shih-Shan Henry. *China and the Overseas Chinese in the United States, 1868–1911.* Fayetteville: University of Arkansas Press, 1983. This volume presents Chinese immigration history and experience from the perspective of the Chinese.

Websites

Brennan, Kevin. "Burlingame Treaty of 1868." Immigration to the United States. This essay focuses on the significance of the treaty and its impact on Chinese immigration to the United States. http://immigrationtounitedstates.org/395-burlingame-treaty-of-1868.html. Accessed January 13, 2017.

"The Burlingame-Seward Treaty, 1868." Office of the Historian, Bureau of Public Affairs, U.S. Department of State. This site provides historical background that led to the treaty, as well as its subsequent impact on China-U.S. relations. https://history.state.gov/milestones/1866-1898/burlingame-seward-treaty. Accessed January 13, 2017.

Also Noteworthy

1914

World War I begins. It lasted until November 11, 1918. In spite of racial discrimination against Asian Americans, many served in the war and were awarded naturalization for their military service granted by a May 1918 law.

2014

President Barack Obama presents the National Medal of Arts to writer Maxine Hong Kingston in a White House ceremony.

July 29

1918

Syngman Rhee establishes the New Church, a Korean Christian Church in Hawaii.

Rhee remained active in the Korean Christian Church in Hawaii. After leaving from the Methodist mission to form his own school, Rhee and eighty of his supporters also began in 1916 to worship separately from the Korean Methodist Church. They formed their own church in Honolulu in 1918, which led to the formation of several related churches in Hawaii and Los Angeles, which united as the Korean Christian Church. Although Rhee never served as a pastor, he wielded his influence to shape the denomination's polity, organizational structure, and church architecture. He told Bernice Kim that his driving vision for the denomination was independence from the Methodists so that his church members could say: "This is really our church which rests upon our land." During the construction of the Korean Christian Church in the Liliha Street neighborhood of Honolulu in 1935, Rhee instructed the architect to consult Korean art books and adopt Korean architectural styles. He gave instructions for the interior plan of the church, requesting two pulpits on the stage, one for public Bible reading and the other for the sermon, and he wanted the choir seating to be arranged so that the singers would face the preacher during the sermon. In 1938, the church was officially dedicated with a brightly colored and elaborate gateway to the main sanctuary that replicated an ancient palace entrance in Seoul. It was both a sacred place of worship and a national symbol evoking the rich culture and history of Korea.

Source: Yoo, William. *American Missionaries, Korean Protestants, and the Changing Shape of World Christianity, 1884–1965.* New York: Routledge, 2017, p. 127.

Books

Kwon, Ho-Youn, Kwang Chung Kim, and R. Stephen Warner, eds. *Korean Americans and Their Religions: Pilgrims and Missionaries from a Different Shore.* University Park: The Pennsylvania State University Press, 2001. *Korean Americans and Their Religions* examines multiple religious traditions, historical period, and generations of Korean Americans and their religious faiths.

Mulholland, John. *Hawaii's Religions.* Rutland, VT: Charles E. Tuttle Company, 1970. *Hawaii's Religions* examines the religious pluralism in Hawaii that includes a focused discussion of the Korean Christian Church.

Websites

"A Chronicle of the Last 100 Years." Koreans in Hawaii. HonoluluAdvertiser.com. 2003. This site provides a useful detailed chronology of Koreans in Hawaii with photos and links for oral histories of five families. http://the.honoluluadvertiser.com/specials/korean100/timeline/. Accessed January 21, 2018.

Gardner, Arthur. *The Koreans in Hawaii: An Annotated Bibliography.* Honolulu: University of Hawaii's Social Science Research Institute, 1970. This site provides the full text that includes an overview history of Korean immigration and settlement in Hawaii. http://hl-128-171-57-22.library.manoa.hawaii.edu/bitstream/10125/42153/1/The%20Koreans%20in%20Hawaii.pdf. Accessed January 21, 2018.

Also Noteworthy

1870

The Cubic Air Ordinance is passed by the San Francisco Board of Supervisors, requiring that every house or apartment within the city and county of San Francisco have within its walls at least 500 cubic feet for each adult dwelling or sleeping in the residence. Violation of the ordinance is a misdemeanor, and each offense carries a fine of $10–$500 and possible imprisonment of no more than three months. The ordinance targeted Chinese laborers.

July 30

2004

Harold & Kumar Go to White Castle, starring Kal Penn and John Cho, is released. The story follows Harold Lee (John Cho) and Kumar Patel (Kal Penn) who go on a comical odyssey to the fast-food chain White Castle after getting high from smoking marijuana. Many Asian American filmgoers and critics liked the way this film debunked traditional stereotypes of Asian Americans.

In Harold & Kumar Go to White Castle, *the cultural and national identity of Harold (John Cho) and Kumar (Kal Penn) is tied to their quest for the quintessential expression of American male consumption, the White Castle burger. In his review, film critic Roger Ebert says, "Many comedies have the same starting place: A hero who must obtain his dream, which should if possible be difficult, impractical, eccentric or immoral. As he marches toward his goal, scattering conventional citizens behind him, we laugh because of his selfishness, and because secretly that's how we'd like to behave, if we thought we could get away with it." To Ebert and the fans of the film, Harold and Kumar are heroes whose journey to obtain White Castle burgers exemplifies the American Dream. White Castle burgers are synonymous with American cultural identity because they are considered to be America's first ethnic food. Moreover, as one of the first fast-food restaurants in the United States, the White Castle brand is nationally known and a part of American history. The film redefines the concept of the "hero" and "conventional citizen" through the (comic) journey of two Asian American men and challenges American domestic racial stereotypes of Indian Americans and Korean Americans. The narrative journey shows the anxieties and pressures of young, educated, middle-class men trying to find their way in life. This film is an alternative to the immigrant journey often seen in American films in which the old country is full of hardships, and the new country of America offers freedom and opportunity.*

Source: Dave, Shilpa. *Indian Accents: Brown Voice and Racial Performance in American Television and Film*. Champaign: University of Illinois Press, 2013, pp. 112–113.

Books

Luther, Catherine, Carolyn Lepre, and Naeemah Clark. *Diversity in U.S. Mass Media*. West Sussex, England: Wiley-Blackwell, 2012. *Diversity in U.S. Mass Media* is a comparative study of racial/ethnic, gender, disability, age, and economic diversity in American mass media. Chapter 7 "Representations of Asians/Asian Americans" deals with Asian Americans.

Ono, Kent, and Vincent Pham. *Asian Americans and the Media*. Malden, MA: Polity Press, 2009. *Asian Americans and the Media* is a cultural critique of Asian American representation in the U.S. mass media.

Websites

Nguyen, Kevin. "How John Cho Defeated the Asian-American Actor Stereotypes." *GQ*, July 22, 2016. This essay reviews highlights in John Cho's film career to prove that he is breaking stereotypes of what type of roles Asian Americans can play. https://www.gq.com/story/john-cho-asian-american-actor-stereotypes. Accessed January 21, 2018.

Yi, Eugene. "November Cover Story: Harold, Kumar and the State of Asian American Media." *KoreAm*. This essay analyzes the Harold and Kumar film franchise and its impact of Asian American representation in the media. http://kore.am/november-cover-story-harold-kumar-and-the-state-of-asian-american-media-2/. Accessed January 21, 2018.

Also Noteworthy

1966

Mutual Trading Company, a Japanese importer, imports two cases of edamame (green soybean in the pod) from Japan. On July 1, 1970, edamame appears on Mutual Trading

Company's catalog. Sushi restaurants started to serve edamame as a side dish, which is now a trend in most sushi restaurants in the United States.

1976

The Oroville Chinese Temple built in 1863 in Oroville, California, is listed on the U.S. National Register of Historic Places.

2002

In Baltimore, Maryland, Dennis Odell Coe, a 32-year-old white man, is charged with three counts of committing a crime upon a person for ethnic reasons for attacking two men of Middle Eastern descent.

2007

In Shreveport, Louisiana, Russell Price, a 22-year-old, and a 16-year-old and 14-year-old are charged with spray-painting profanity and drug symbols on an Islamic Association building.

2011

The Bainbridge Island Japanese American Exclusion Memorial opens to the public. It is designed by local architect John Paul Jones.

July 31

1980

U.S. President Jimmy Carter signs the bill to create the Commission on Wartime Relocation and Internment of Civilians (CWRIC) with the purpose of reviewing Executive Order 9066 of February 19, 1942, and its consequences. E.O. 9066 set in motion the evacuation and detention of 120,000 Japanese and Japanese Americans living in the designated Military Areas 1 and 2 on the West Coast during World War II to 10 concentration camps located in isolated areas across the country. They were Manzanar in eastern California, Tule Lake (Newell) near the California–Oregon border, Minidoka (Hunt) in Idaho, Topaz in central Utah, Poston (Colorado River) and Gila River in Arizona, Amache in Colorado, Heart Mountain in Wyoming, Jerome (Denson) and Rohwer in Arkansas. Two-thirds of those interned were U.S. citizens and more than half were children. In late March 1942, a series of 108 "Civilian Evacuation Orders" began the removal initially to 16 hastily organized assembly centers located at fairgrounds, racetracks, and similar facilities where overcrowding, communal showers and outhouses, and former horse stables were the prevailing conditions while awaiting the construction of the 10 "relocation centers" or concentration camps. Limited to the standard two suitcases per person, only what they could carry, many lost what took a lifetime to build. By October 1942, the transfer to the 10 "camps" was completed, yet the dislocation was only beginning.

The Commission makes the following recommendation for remedies in several forms as an act of national apology.

1. *The Commission recommends that Congress pass a joint resolution, to be signed by the President, which recognizes that a grave injustice was done and offers the apologies of the nation for the acts of exclusion, removal and detention.*
2. *The Commission recommends that the President pardon those who were convicted of violating the statutes imposing a curfew on American citizens on the basis of their ethnicity and requiring the ethnic Japanese to leave designated areas of the West Coast or to report to assembly centers. The Commission further recommends that the Department of Justice review other wartime convictions of the ethnic Japanese and recommend to the President that he pardon those whose offenses were grounded in a refusal to accept treatment that discriminated among citizens on the basis of race or ethnicity.*

Both recommendations are made without prejudice to cases currently before the courts.

3. *The Commission recommends that Congress direct the Executive agencies to which Japanese Americans may apply for the restitution of positions, status or entitlements lost in whole or in part because of acts or events between December 1941 and 1945 to review such applications with liberality, giving full consideration to the historical findings of this Commission. For example, the responsible divisions of the Department of Defense should be instructed to review cases of less than honorable discharge of Japanese Americans from the armed services during World War II over which disputes remain, and the Secretary of Health and Human Services should be directed to instruct the Commissioner of Social Security to review any remaining complaints of inequity in entitlements due to the wartime detention.*
4. *The Commission recommends that Congress demonstrate official recognition of the injustice done to American citizens of Japanese ancestry and Japanese resident aliens during the Second World War, and that it recognize the nation's need to make redress for these events, by appropriating monies to establish a special foundation. The Commissioners all believe a fund for educational and humanitarian purposes related to the wartime events is appropriate, and all agree that no fund would be sufficient to make whole again the lives damaged by the exclusion and detention. The Commissioners agree that such a fund appropriately addresses an injustice suffered by an entire ethnic group, as distinguished from individual deprivations. Such a fund should sponsor research and public educational activities so that the events which were the subject of this inquiry will be remembered, and so that the causes and circumstances of this and similar events may be illuminated and understood. A nation which wishes to remain just to its citizens must not fort it lapses. The recommended foundation might appropriately fund comparative studies of similar civil liberties abuses or of the effect upon particular groups of racial prejudice embodied by government action in times of national stress; for example, the fund's public educational activity might include preparing and distributing the Commission's findings about these events to textbook publishers, educators and libraries.*
5. *The Commissioners, with the exception of Congressman Lungren, recommend that Congress establish a fund which will provide personal redress to those who were excluded, as well as serve the purposes set out in Recommendation 4. Appropriations of $1.5 billion should be made to the fund over a reasonable period to be determined by Congress. This fund should be used, first, to provide one-time per capita compensatory payment of $20,000 to each of the approximately 60,000 surviving persons excluded from their places of residence pursuant to Executive Order 9066. The burden should be on the government to locate survivors, without requiring any application for payment, and payments should be made to the oldest survivors first. After per capita payments, the remainder of the fund should be used for the public educational purposes discussed in Recommendation 4 as well as for the general welfare of the Japanese American community. This should be accomplished by grants for purposes such as aid to the elderly and scholarships for education, weighing, where appropriate, the effect of the exclusion and detention on the descendants of those who were detained. Individual payments in compensation for loss or damage should not be made. The fund should be administered by a Board, the majority of whose members are Americans of Japanese descent appointed by the President and confirmed by the Senate. The compensation of members of the Board should be limited to their expenses and per diem payments at accepted governmental rates.*

Source: Personal Justice Denied. Part 2: Recommendations. The Commission for Wartime Relocation and Internment of Civilians. Washington, DC. June 1983, pp. 8–10.

Books

Hatamiya, Leslie. *Righting a Wrong: Japanese Americans and the Passage of the Civil Liberties Act of 1988.* Stanford, CA: Stanford University Press, 1993. *Righting a Wrong* documents the history of Japanese American reparations.

Tateishi, John. *And Justice for All: An Oral History of the Japanese American Detention Camps.* New York: Random House, 1984. *And Justice for All* documents 30 oral histories of Japanese Americans who were imprisoned in detention centers during World War II.

Websites

Carter, Jimmy. "Commission on Wartime Relocation and Internment of Civilians Act Remarks on Signing S. 1647 into Law." July 31, 1980. The American Presidency Project. University of California, Santa Barbara. 2018. This site provides the full text of President Carter's remark after signing the commission into law. http://www.presidency.ucsb.edu/ws/?pid=44855. Accessed January 21, 2018.

Yamato, Sharon. "Commission on Wartime Relocation and Internment of Civilians." *Densho Encyclopedia*, 2018. This essay discusses the history of the commission, its findings, and impact. http://encyclopedia.densho.org/Commission_on_Wartime_Relocation_and_Internment_of_Civilians/. Accessed January 21, 2018.

Also Noteworthy

1943

Tule Lake War Relocation Center is designated a segregation center for "disloyal" internees.

2006

In Cliffside Park, New Jersey, William Brown, a 62-year-old, is charged with aggravated assault and bias intimidation after he yelled at a woman and her toddler—his neighbor—screaming "You Arabs, I'm going to get you back for September 11."

August

August 1

1952

Sammy Lee, Korean American army doctor, wins a second gold medal in the 10-meter platform diving competition at the Olympics in Helsinki, Finland. He won a gold medal in the same event four years earlier in the 1948 Olympics in London, England, which marked the first time an Asian American won Olympic gold medal for the United States.

On July 21, 2010, the Los Angeles City Council adopted a motion to dedicate "Dr. Sammy Lee Square."

Motion

Dr. Sammy Lee is the first American of Asian descent to win an Olympic gold medal for the United States. The diminutive diver, just 5-feet tall, had to overcome much discrimination before attainting his goals: to be an Olympic Champion and to be a Medical Doctor. In 1942, at the age of 22, Sammy competed in the National Diving Championships and became the first non-Caucasian to win. The 1940 and 1944 Olympic Games had been canceled due to the war. In 1948, at age 28, Sammy Lee won a gold medal in the International Olympic Men's platform and a bronze medal in the 3 meter springboard. In the 1952 Games, Sammy won his second gold medal in the International Olympic Men's platform. At 32, he was the oldest person to win a gold medal in diving, and the first male diver to win back-to-back diving gold medals. Dr. Lee, in addition to his medical practice served also as a very successful coach to future Olympic gold medal winners: he coached Bod Webster to gold medals in 1960 and 1964 and did the same with the great Greg Louganis, coaching him to a silver medal in 1976. In addition, Dr. Lee and his wife, Roz, discovered the PVA Shammy which was extremely convenient for practice dives—as regular towels became too wet. In recognition of the great contributions of Dr. Sammy Lee—for his life as a family man, a patriot, a physician, a coach and an Olympic champion, it is appropriate that the intersection of Olympic Boulevard and Normandie Avenue be named as "Dr. Sammy Lee Square." I THEREFORE MOVE that the intersection at Olympic Boulevard and Normandie Avenue Street be named as "Dr. Sammy Lee Square" and that the Department of Transportation be directed to erect permanent ceremonial sign(s) to this effect at this location.

Presented by Herb Wesson, Jr., Councilman, 10th District

Tom Labonge, Councilman, 4th District

Source: City of Los Angeles. http://clkrep.lacity.org/onlinedocs/2010/10-1231_CA_07-21-10.pdf.

Books

Fernbach, Erika. *Sammy Lee: Promises to Keep*. CreateSpace Independent Publishing, 2012. *Sammy Lee: Promises to Keep* is a biography of Lee that is based on interviews with Lee. It is a comprehensive narrative of Lee's life, his early childhood, career as diver and doctor, and legacy.

Wampler, Molly. *Not without Honor: The Story of Sammy Lee*. Santa Barbara, CA: Fithian Press, 1987. *Not without Honor* is a biography of Sammy Lee that covers various aspects of his life and career as athlete and doctor.

Websites

Samuel "Sammy" Lee. Sports Reference. 2016. This site provides a brief overview of Lee's biography and career medals. https://www.sports-reference.com/olympics/athletes/le/sammy-lee-1.html. Accessed January 22, 2018.

Yeomans, Patricia. "Sammy Lee: Oriental from Occidental." *Journal of Olympic History* 10, no. 2 (May 2002): 15–21. This article is a detailed biography of Sammy Lee and his Olympic career. http://library.la84.org/SportsLibrary/JOH/JOHv10n2/JOHv10n2f.pdf. Accessed January 22, 2018.

Also Noteworthy

1950

President Truman signs the federal law, Guam Organic Act of 1950, that had made several important changes such as designating Guam as an unincorporated territory, granting U.S. citizenship to Chamorros, the creation of a limited bill of rights, and establishment of executive, judicial, and legislative branches known as the Government of Guam.

August 2

2011

President Barack Obama nominates Attorney Miranda Mai Du to the U.S. district court bench for the district of Nevada. Du was born in Cá Mau, Vietnam. At the age of eight, she fled the country with her parents, two siblings, aunts, uncles, and cousins. Du and her family spent almost a year in a refugee camp before a U.S. family volunteered to sponsor their resettlement in Winfield, Alabama. Afterward, they relocated to Oakland, California, where Du attended junior high school and high school. She went on to the University of California, Davis for undergraduate studies and then the University of California Berkeley School of Law.

On August 2, 2011, President Barack Obama nominated Attorney Du to the United States District Court bench for the District of Nevada. Nevada Democratic Senator Harry Reid, who currently serves as Senate Majority Leader, originally presented Du's name to President Obama for consideration. Her candidacy was supported by a bipartisan coalition of Nevada public officials, a trend notably paralleled in October 2011, when Republican Senator Dean Heller joined Senator Reid in introducing Du at the Senate Judiciary Committee hearing. The Senate Judiciary Committee voted 10–8 in support of Du's appointment to the bench on November 3, 2011. Opposing votes were cast by Republican committee members who expressed concern over what they deemed to be Attorney Du's inexperience. A 2007 sanction by the federal court in Nevada also gave some committee members pause. Despite these concerns, Du's nomination was confirmed on March 28, 2013.

Source: Hua, Linh. "Du, Miranda (1969-)." In *Asian Americans: An Encyclopedia of Social, Cultural, Economic, and Political History*, edited by Xiaojian Zhao and Edward Park, p. 352. Santa Barbara, CA: ABC-CLIO, 2014.

Books

Nguyen, Phuong. *Becoming Refugee American: The Politics of Rescue in Little Saigon*. Urbana: University of Illinois Press, 2017. *Becoming Refugee American* provides historical and contemporary context for understanding the Vietnamese refugee migration history in the United States.

Zia, Helen. *Asian American Dreams: The Emergence of an American People*. New York: Farrar, Straus, and Giroux, 2000. See Part I "Beyond Our Shadows" for a discussion that includes the history and development of Asian Americans in the legal field.

Websites

"Miranda Du Appointed to U.S. District Court." Asian American Press. April 1, 2012. This article provides an overview of Miranda Du's life, education, and legal career. http://aapress.com/government/courts/miranda-du-appointed-to-u-s-district-court/. Accessed January 22, 2018.

"Senate Confirms Miranda Du as U.S. District Judge for District of Nevada." News Release. March 28, 2012. This document is a news release of Du's appointment that highlights her legal career. http://cdn.ca9.uscourts.gov/datastore/uploads/ce9/447-Du_Confirmed.pdf. Accessed January 22, 2018.

August 3

1977

Thousands of protestors form a human chain surrounding the International Hotel in San

Francisco's Manilatown at the height of a 10-year community battle resisting the eviction of elderly Filipino low-income residents. The largely Filipino American residents at the I-Hotel were evicted the next day.

Books

Brook, James, Chris Carlsson, and Nancy Peters, eds. *Reclaiming San Francisco: History, Politics, Culture*. San Francisco, CA: City Lights Publishers, 1998. See James Sobredo's chapter "From Manila Bay to Daly City: Filipinos in San Francisco" and Randy Shaw's "Tenant Power in San Francisco."

Habal, Estella. *San Francisco's International Hotel: Mobilizing the Filipino American Community in the Anti-Eviction Movement*. Philadelphia, PA: Temple University Press, 2007. *San Francisco's International Hotel* examines the antieviction protests apropos other movements and leftist politics of the period.

Websites

International Hotel Senior Housing Inc. *International Hotel's Final Victory*. San Francisco, CA. 2010. This is a booklet that details the history of the fall of the I-Hotel with a chronology and photographs. http://eslibrary.berkeley.edu/sites/default/files/ihotel_histbk_7.pdf. Accessed February 8, 2018.

Sobredo, James. "The Battle for the International Hotel." Shaping San Francisco's Digital Archive. http://www.foundsf.org. This site offers a history of the protest to fight eviction with photographs. http://www.foundsf.org/index.php?title=The_Battle_for_the_International_Hotel. Accessed February 8, 2018.

August 4

1961

Lauren Tom, American actress of Chinese descent, is born in Highland Park, Illinois, to parents Nancy and Chan Tom. She is known for her role as Lena St. Clair in *The Joy Luck Club* (1993) and as the voice actress for *Futurama*, as the voice of Amy Wong, and *King of the Hill*, where she voiced Minh and Connie Souphanousinphone.

Left with little choice, some Asian Americans try to make the best of a bad situation. Lauren Tom, who played one of the daughters in The Joy Luck Club, *said, "I don't want to be Pollyannaish about it, but my attitude is that you're aware of inequalities and the racism that goes on in the world of casting, but to just keep focusing on the positive has enabled me to get parts that are cross-over." Tom's latest role, in* Mr. Jones *(1993) with Richard Gere, was not originally written for an Asian American. It remains to be seen whether this practice is the rule or the exception.*

Source: Xing, Jun. "Cinematic Asian Representation in Hollywood." In *Performing Difference: Representation of "the Other" in Film and Theatre*, edited by Jonathan Friedman, p. 137. Lanham, MD: University Press of America, 2009.

Books

Hischak, Thomas. *American Literature on Stage and Screen: 525 Works and Their Adaptations*. Jefferson, NC: McFarland & Company, Inc., Publishers, 2012. See entry on "The Joy Luck Club."

Xing, Jun. *Asian America through the Lens: History, Representations, and Identity*. Walnut Creek, CA: AltaMira Press, 1998. *Asian America through the Lens* provides a historical survey of Asian Americans in film and television.

Websites

Lauren Tom. Behind the Voice Actors. 2018. This site provides a complete updated list of all the character roles that Lauren Tom is the voice actress for. http://www.behindthevoiceactors.com/Lauren-Tom/. Accessed January 22, 2018.

Lauren Tom. Official web page for Lauren Tom. 2018. This site is the official web page for actress Lauren Tom and includes her biography, reels, photos, latest news, and videos. http://laurentom.com/. Accessed January 22, 2018.

Also Noteworthy

1942

A riot breaks out at the Santa Anita Assembly Center in California.

1993

Ang Lee's *The Wedding Banquet* (1993) is released.

2009

North Korea releases two Asian American journalists, Laura G. Ling (b. December 1, 1976) and Euna Lee (b. 1972), after a visit from former U.S. president William J. Clinton.

August 5

1964

The United States enters Southeast Asia with the goal of preventing the spread of communism worldwide. American policy makers developed the "domino theory" as a justification for their involvement. This theory states that if South Vietnam falls to the communists, then Laos, Cambodia, Thailand, Burma, India, and Pakistan would also fall like dominos. The Pacific Islands and even Australia could be at risk. As such, the United States pledged unlimited support in the South's fight against the northern communists. On August 4, 1964, in response to American surveillance along its coast, North Vietnam launched an attack against the USS *C. Turner Joy* and the USS *Maddox*, two American destroyers on call in the Gulf of Tonkin. The first attack occurred on August 2, when three North Vietnamese boats charged the *Maddox* and fired torpedoes at it. On August 4, the *Maddox*, now joined by the *Turner Joy*, "allegedly" attacked during a stormy night. On August 5, President Lyndon B. Johnson ordered retaliatory attacks against North Vietnam and asked Congress to pass a resolution to give him broad powers to take "all necessary measures to repel any armed attacks against the forces of the United States and to prevent further aggression." Known as the Tonkin Gulf Resolution, it was passed by the Senate 88–2 and by the House of Representatives 466–0 on August 7, 1964. With this solution, the United States engaged in an undeclared war for nearly 11 years, popularly referred to as the Vietnam War (or the Second Indochina War). To date, there is no evidence that the second attack ever occurred, which many critics have argued is a conspiracy theory to escalate U.S. military actions in Southeast Asia that had steadily increased since 1961. President Johnson first authorized air war to destroy North Vietnam's ability to arm insurgency in South Vietnam. By 1965, the United States had 540,000 troops in Vietnam fighting against the communists. The United States began bombing in southern Vietnam, which forced thousands of peasants from the countryside into the southern cities. Instead of helping to free the South's people of communism, the U.S. presence drove the peasants closer to the Viet Cong.

President Lyndon B. Johnson's Message to Congress, August 5, 1964

To the Congress of the United States:

Last night I announced to the American people that the North Vietnamese regime had conducted further deliberate attacks against U.S. naval vessels operating in international waters, and therefore directed air action against gunboats and supporting facilities used in these hostile operations. This air action has now been carried out with substantial damage to the boats and facilities. Two U.S. aircraft were lost in the action.

After consultation with the leaders of both parties in the Congress, I further announced a decision to ask the Congress for a resolution expressing the unity and determination of the United States in supporting freedom and in protecting peace in southeast Asia.

These latest actions of the North Vietnamese regime have given a new and grave turn to the already serious situation in southeast Asia. Our commitments in that area are well known to the Congress. They were first made in 1954 by President Eisenhower. They were further defined in the Southeast Asia Collective Defense Treaty approved by the Senate in February 1955.

This treaty with its accompanying protocol obligates the United States and other members to act in accordance with their constitutional processes to meet Communist aggression against any of the parties or protocol states.

Our policy in southeast Asia has been consistent and unchanged since 1954. I summarized it on June 2 in four simple propositions:

1. America keeps her word. *Here as elsewhere, we must and shall honor our commitments.*
2. The issue is the future of southeast Asia as a whole. *A threat to any nation in that region is a threat to all, and a threat to us.*
3. Our purpose is peace. *We have no military, political, or territorial ambitions in the area.*
4. This is not just a jungle war, but a struggle for freedom on every front of human activity. *Our military and economic assistance to South Vietnam and Laos in particular has the purpose of helping these countries to repel aggression and strengthen their independence.*

The threat to the three nations of southeast Asia has long been clear. The North Vietnamese regime has constantly sought to take over South Vietnam and Laos. This Communist regime has violated the Geneva accords for Vietnam. It has systematically conducted a campaign of subversion, which includes the direction, training, and supply of personnel and arms for the conduct of guerrilla warfare in South Vietnamese territory. In Laos, the North Vietnamese regime has maintained military forces, used Laotian territory for infiltration into South Vietnam, and most recently carried out combat operations—all in direct violation of the Geneva agreements of 1962.

In recent months, the actions of the North Vietnamese regime have become steadily more threatening. In May, following new acts of Communist aggression in Laos, the United States undertook reconnaissance flights over Laotian territory, at the request of the Government of Laos. These flights had the essential mission of determining the situation in territory where Communist forces were preventing inspection by the International Control Commission. When the Communists attacked these aircraft, I responded by furnishing escort fighters with instructions to fire when fired upon. Thus, these latest North Vietnamese attacks on our naval vessels are not the first direct attack on armed forces of the United States.

As President of the United States I have concluded that I should now ask the Congress on its part, to join in affirming the national determination that all such attacks will be met, and that the United States will continue in its basic policy of assisting the free nations of the area to defend their freedom.

As I have repeatedly made clear, the United States intends no rashness, and seeks no wider war. We must make it clear to all that the United States is united in its determination to bring about the end of Communist subversion and aggression in the area. We seek the full and effective restoration of the international agreements signed in Geneva in 1954, with respect to South Vietnam, and again in Geneva in 1962, with respect to Laos.

I recommend a resolution expressing the support of the Congress for all necessary action to protect our Armed Forces and to assist nations covered by the SEATO Treaty. At the same time, I assure the Congress that we shall continue readily to explore any avenues of political solution that will effectively guarantee the removal of Communist subversion and the preservation of the independence of the nations of the area.

The resolution could well be based upon similar resolutions enacted by the Congress in the past—to meet the threat to Formosa in 1955, to meet the threat to the Middle East in 1957, and to meet the threat in Cuba in 1962. It could state in the simplest terms the resolve and support of the Congress for action to deal appropriately with attacks against our Armed Forces and to defend freedom and preserve peace in southeast Asia in accordance with the obligations of the United States under the Southeast Asia Treaty. I urge the Congress to enact such a resolution promptly and thus to give convincing evidence to the aggressive Communist nations, and to the world as a whole, that our policy in southeast Asia will be carried forward—and that the peace and security of the area will be preserved.

The events of this week would in any event have made the passage of a congressional resolution essential. But there is an additional reason for doing so at a time when we are entering on 3 months of political campaigning. Hostile nations must understand that in such a period the United States will continue to protect its national interests, and that in these matters there is no division among us.

Source: U.S. Congress, Senate, Committee on Foreign Relations, 90th Congress, 1st Session, Background Information Relating to Southeast Asia and Vietnam. 3rd Revised Edition. Washington, DC: U.S. Government Printing Office, July 1967, pp. 120–122.

Books

Moise, Edwin. *The A to Z of the Vietnam War.* Lanham, MD: Scarecrow Press, 2005. *The A to Z of the Vietnam War* is a reference that covers comprehensive aspects of the Vietnam War.

Moise, Edwin. *Tonkin Gulf and the Escalation of the Vietnam War.* Chapel Hill: University of North Carolina Press, 1996. Historian Edwin Moise reconstructs the events of the night of August 4, 1964, to argue that there were no North Vietnamese attack on the U.S. Navy destroyers *Maddox* and *Turner Joy*.

Websites

"Tonkin Gulf Resolution (1964)." www.ourdocuments.gov. This site provides links to the archival document, as well as summary of the history and implication of the Tonkin Gulf Resolution. https://ourdocuments.gov/doc.php?flash=true&doc=98. Accessed January 17, 2017.

"U.S. Involvement in the Vietnam War: The Gulf of Tonkin and Escalation, 1964." Office of the Historian, Bureau of Public Affairs. U.S. Department of State. This site provides an overview to the historical events leading up the Joint Resolution of the Gulf of Tonkin and discussion of its significance and impact with photographs and links to archival documents. https://history.state.gov/milestones/1961-1968/gulf-of-tonkin. Accessed January 17, 2017.

Also Noteworthy

1909

The Payne-Aldrich Tariff Act is signed into law, allowing free trade between the Philippines and the United States.

2012

A mass shooting takes place on this day at a Sikh temple in Oak Creek, Wisconsin, killing six people and wounding four more. The arrested suspect, Wade Michael Page, is a white neo-Nazi supremacist.

August 6

1945

The United States drops the atomic bomb on Hiroshima. The decision to employ the atomic bomb is a controversial issue that is still heatedly debated by historians and policy makers.

The attitudes of Americans toward the events of August 6, 1945, are a good deal more ambivalent than their attitudes toward those of December 7, 1941. One reason, perhaps, is that Americans were the actors in 1945—they dropped an atomic bomb on Hiroshima—whereas on Pearl Harbor Day they were acted upon. It is always easier to attach an unambiguous label to someone else's behavior than to one's own. President Roosevelt's characterization of December 7, 1941, as "a date which will live in infamy" may have faded somewhat, but it has certainly not disappeared from the national vocabulary; whereas attitudes toward Hiroshima have become hedged about with self-justification, feelings of guilt, and doubt. Was it necessary to drop the bomb? Could the war have been won without it? Should we have issued a warning or given a demonstration of the bomb's potential damage? Was it a racist act, something we would not have done in the war with Germany? Was the dropping of an A-bomb morally justifiable under any circumstances? Such nagging questions undoubtedly helped soften American attitudes towards Japanese wartime behavior: if they were beastly during the war, we were beastly too. But, paradoxically, American guilt feelings may also cause us to dislike the Japanese more. We not only tend to avoid people who make us feel guilty, we also tend to "project" our own feelings of guilt, so that the victim becomes transformed into an accuser whom we then hate for accusing us. It is a well-known psychological mechanism in unhappy marriages, and it can equally well color relationships between nations and peoples.

Source: Johnson, Sheila. *The Japanese through American Eyes*. Stanford, CA: Stanford University Press, 1988, pp. 39–40.

Books

Takaki, Ronald. *Hiroshima: Why America Dropped the Atomic Bomb*. Boston, MA: Little, Brown, 1996. *Hiroshima: Why America Dropped the Atomic Bomb* addresses why the bomb was dropped and factors in racism against the Japanese in his analysis.

Walker, J. Samuel. *Prompt and Utter Destruction: Truman and the Use of Atomic Bombs against Japan*. Chapel Hill: University of North Carolina Press, 2016. *Prompt and Utter Destruction* analyzes President Truman's decision to use the atomic bombs on Japan in 1945.

Websites

Myre, Greg. "A Survivor's Tale: How Hiroshima Shaped a Japanese-American Family." NPR. May 27, 2016. This essay documents Kikue Takagi's history of surviving Hiroshima and its impact on her life. https://www.npr.org/sections/parallels/2016/05/27/479464410/a-survivors-tale-how-hiroshima-shaped-a-japanese-american-family. Accessed January 22, 2018.

Wake, Naoko. "Japanese American Hibakusha." *Densho Encyclopedia*, 2018. This essay discusses Japanese Americans who survived the U.S. atomic bombings of Japan. http://encyclopedia.densho.org/Japanese%20American%20Hibakusha/. Accessed January 22, 2018.

Also Noteworthy

2002

In Reno, Nevada, David Nolette, a 15-year-old, and Scott Cannady, a 17-year-old, are sentenced to up to 40 years in prison for the baseball bat beatings of two Muslim men in March 2001.

2007

In Glendale, Arizona, a chemical bomb is thrown from a car at the Albanian American Islamic Center.

2012

Jujubee (b. June 21, 1984), an American drag queen of Lao ancestry, is selected as one of the 12 contestants from previous *Drag Race* seasons to be part of *RuPaul's Drag Race: All Stars*.

August 7

1903

On this day, Korean plantation workers in Oahu establish Sinminhoe (New People's Association) to unite all Koreans in America to defeat and defend Korea against Japanese colonialism.

The Sinminhoe was founded on August 7, 1903. One of the founders, Hyon Sun, recalled the circumstances: "All the outstanding young Koreans from all the islands were gathered in Honolulu under the leadership of Hong Sung Ha. . ." While its purpose was "to educate Koreans in Hawaii and to seek common interests through commercial activities," it is clear from Hyon's description of the first meeting that concerns about the decline of Korea were paramount: "After discussing the dangerous situation in Korea, we organized the Shin Min Hoi, or the new people's society." By the time the first branch of this organization was established on Kauai in December 1903, the purpose had become clearly political: "to rebuild Korea with regenerated people at home and abroad." Another source states, "Its purposes were to promote . . . reform of the home government." Almost immediately, however, factional problems arose to render the Sinminhoe ineffective. Hyon obliquely hints at that when he complained that the organization was begun only "after great difficulties."

First, factionalism within the Sinminhoe was driven in part by denominational disputes between Methodists and non-Methodists. Most of the Koreans who had been Christians before coming to Hawai'i were converted by American Presbyterian missionaries. But since the Presbyterian Church did not have a presence in Hawai'i, the majority of the Korean Christians chose the Methodist Church, while a smaller number affiliated themselves with the Episcopal Church. And still other Koreans considered themselves Buddhists. Several of the founders of the Sinminhoe, including Hyon Sun and Hong Sung-ha, were closely associated with the Methodist Church. Hong, for instance, had, since March 1903, collaborated with the Methodist minister George K. Pearson to publish the first Korean newspaper in Hawaii, the P'owa Hanin kyobo *(Hawaiian-Korean news), which was sold at churches on Sundays.*

Source: Patterson, Wayne. *The ILse: First-Generation Korean Immigrants in Hawaii, 1903–1973.* Honolulu: University of Hawaii Press, 2000, p. 49.

Books

Choe, Yong-ho, ed. *From the Land of Hibiscus: Koreans in Hawai'i, 1903–1950.* Honolulu: University of Hawaii Press, 2007. See Chapter 6, "Local Struggles and Diasporic Politics: The 1931 Court Cases of the Korean National Association of Hawai'i."

Hurh, Won Moo. *The Korean Americans: The New Americans.* Westport, CT: Greenwood Publishing Company, 1998. *The Korean Americans* covers various aspects of Korean immigration history to the United States and Hawaii.

Websites

Sik, Kim. "The Korean Americans in the War of Independence: The Left-Right Confrontation in Korea—Its Origin." Association for Asian Research. November 9, 2003. This essay details the history of Sinminhoe and Korean independence movement among Korean Americans. http://www.asianresearch.org/articles/1633.html. Accessed January 22, 2018.

"Sin Min Hoe—New Peoples Association." www.dosan.org. 2015. This site provides a historical overview of the Sinminhoe, in addition to photographs of key members. http://www.dosan.org/thejourney/1907backtokorea.html. Accessed January 22, 2018.

Also Noteworthy

1942

General DeWitt announces that the "evacuation" of all persons of Japanese ancestry from the West Coast is complete.

August 8

1988

From the late 1960s through the 1970s, the Japanese American Citizens League (JACL), National Coalition for Redress/Reparations, National Council for Japanese American Redress (NCJAR), and Japanese American politicians, such as Senator Daniel Inouye, Senator Spark Matsunaga, Congressman Norman Mineta, and Congressmen Robert Matsui, lawyers, and activists worked unstintingly to achieve redress for Japanese Americans interned during the war. Some, like the NCJAR, sought redress through the courts while others lobbied Congress. On April 20, 1988, after years of hard work, the U.S. Senate passed the Civil Liberties Act by a vote of 69–27. The act acknowledged that the U.S. government had committed a grave injustice against all those who were interned.

The Civil Liberties Act is signed into law by President Ronald Reagan. This act provides for individual payments of $20,000 to each surviving Japanese American internee and a $1.25 billion education fund among other provisions. Some people returned the checks out of protest, arguing that money could never repay them for all that they have suffered and lost. On October 9, 1990, the first nine redress payments were made at a Washington, D.C., ceremony. Rev. Mamoru Eto of Los Angeles, who at the time was 107 years old, was the first to receive his check.

By October 1993, reparation checks of $20,000 were issued to victims of World War II internment, along with a Presidential Letter of Apology by President William Clinton.

Over fifty years ago, the United States Government unjustly interned, evacuated, or relocated you and many other Japanese Americans. Today, on behalf of your fellow Americans, I offer a sincere apology to you for the actions that unfairly denied Japanese Americans and their families fundamental liberties during World War II.

In passing the Civil Liberties Act of 1988, we acknowledge the wrongs of the past and offered redress to those who endured such grave injustice. In retrospect, we understand that the nation's actions were rooted deeply in racial prejudice, wartime hysteria, and a lack of political leadership. We must learn from the past and dedicate ourselves as a nation to renewing the spirit of equality and our love of freedom. Together, we can guarantee a future with liberty and justice for all. You and your family have my best wishes for the future.

Bill Clinton

Source: The Children of the Camps Project. 1999. http://www.pbs.org/childofcamp/history/clinton.html.

Books

Hatamiya, Leslie. *Righting a Wrong: Japanese Americans and the Passage of the Civil Liberties Act of 1988*. Stanford, CA: Stanford University Press, 1993. *Righting a Wrong* studies the historical, legal, economic, political, social, and institutional variables that led to the passage of the Civil Liberties Act of 1988.

Maki, Mitchell, Harry Kitano, and Sarah Berthold. *Achieving the Impossible Dream: How Japanese Americans Obtained Redress*. Urbana: University of Illinois Press, 1999. *Achieving the Impossible Dream* covers many aspects of Japanese Americans who worked to get an apology from the U.S. government and achieve compensation for the unlawful internment of their community during World War II.

Websites

"Understanding the Civil Liberties Act of 1988." Anti-Defamation League. 2013. This report discusses the history, legacy, and significance of the Civil Liberties Act of 1988. http://www.adl.org/assets/pdf/education-outreach/Understanding-the-Civil-Liberties-Act-of-1988.pdf. Accessed January 17, 2017.

Yamato, Sharon. "Civil Liberties Act of 1988." *Densho Encyclopedia*, 2017. This essay covers the history of the Civil Liberties Act of 1988, its provisions, results, and impact on the Japanese American community. http://encyclopedia.densho.org/Civil_Liberties_Act_of_1988/. Accessed January 17, 2017.

Also Noteworthy

1974

President Richard M. Nixon resigns.

2002

In Palos Hills, Illinois, John Stewart, a 34-year-old, is sentenced to two years' probation and 20 hours of community service for threatening his Syrian American neighbors after 9/11.

2009

Amy Monmaly Chanthaphavong is crowned queen of the 24th Annual Miss Asian America Pageant at the Palace of Fine Arts Theater, San Francisco, California. Chanthaphavong is the first Miss Asian America of Laotian ancestry.

August 9

1785

The first recorded instance of the Chinese in the continental United States was of three Chinese seamen named Ashing, Achun, and Aceun who were left stranded, along with 32 "East Indian lascars, by Captain John O'Donnell who left on the *Pallas* after unloading his cargo at Baltimore. The "A" or "Ah" prefix indicates they were Cantonese.

There probably were other Chinese who came even earlier as crew members of ships trading between America and Asia, but no records of their presence have as yet come to light. There must also have been Chinese among the many "Filipinos" who served as crew on board the Manila Galleons that sailed each year between Mexico and the Philippines from the late 16th century onward. Again, however, no identifiably Chinese names have survived.

Source: Ho, Chuimei, and Bennet Bronson, eds. "History." *Chinese in Northwest America Research Committee*. May 19, 2013. http://www.cinarc.org/History.html#anchor_167.

Books

Snyder, James. *The Early American China Trade: A Maritime History of Its Establishment, 1783–1815*. New York: New York University, 1938. It covers many aspects of early U.S.-China maritime history.

Vexler, Robert. *Baltimore: A Chronological & Documentary History, 1632–1970*. New York: Oceana Publications, 1975. This book provides detailed chronology and useful archival documents on early American China trade in the city of Baltimore.

Websites

Chin, Philip. "The China Trade and the Mystery of the First Chinese in the United States." Chineseamericanheroes.org. March 11, 2015. This essay summarizes evidence through archival documents to the history of U.S.-China trade and the early Chinese who arrived on the shores of the United States because of it. http://chineseamericanheroes.org/wp-content/uploads/2015/03/The-China-Trade-and-the-Mystery-of-the-First-Chinese-in-the-United-States-2.pdf. Accessed December 12, 2017.

Ho, Chuimei, and Bennet Bronson, eds. "History." *Chinese in Northwest America Research Committee*. 2008. Chuimei Ho and Bennet Bronson are the editors and writers of this site. They are trained archeologists who have extensive research background on early Chinese American history. http://www.cinarc.org/History.html#anchor_167. Accessed January 25, 2018.

1853

People v. Hall (1854) made it illegal for Chinese to testify against a white person in court. On this day, George Hall, a white miner, accompanied by his brother and one other man, assaults and robs a Chinese placer miner on the Bear River in Nevada County, California. Ling Sing left his tent after hearing the sound of gunfire and was shot and killed by Hall. The sheriff arrested Hall and his companions. Hall was later tried and found guilty based on the testimony of three Chinese witnesses. The judge sentenced Hall to death by hanging. However, California Supreme Court chief justice Hugh Murray overturned the conviction on the basis that "Asiatics" were "Indians" and therefore unable to testify against a white man in court. Murray argued that "Asiatics" long ago traveled over the Bering Strait and "descended" into Indians. Indians were not allowed to testify in court against a white man, so since "Asiatics" (in this case, the Chinese eyewitnesses) were Indians, they too cannot testify in court against a white man.

Excerpt from *The People, Respondent, v. George W. Hall, Appellant*. Supreme Court of the State of California, October 1, 1854.

Mr. Ch. J. Murray delivered the opinion of the Court. Mr. J. Heydenfeldt concurred.

The appellant, a free white citizen of this State, was convicted of murder upon the testimony of Chinese witnesses.

The point involved in this case is the admissibility of such evidence.

The 394th section of the Act Concerning Civil Cases provides that no Indian or Negro shall be allowed to testify as a witness in any action or proceeding in which a white person is a party.

The 14th section of the Act of April 16th, 1850, regulating Criminal Proceedings, provides that "No black or mulatto person, or Indian, shall be allowed to give evidence in favor of, or against a white man."

The true point at which we are anxious to arrive is, the legal signification of the words, "black, mulatto, Indian, and white person," and whether the Legislature adopted them as generic terms, or intended to limit their application to specific types of the human species. . . .

The Act of Congress, in defining that description of aliens may become naturalized citizens, provides that every "free white citizen," etc. . . .

If the term "white," as used in the Constitution, was not understood in its generic sense as including the Caucasian race, and necessarily excluding all others, where was the necessary of providing for the admission of Indians to the privilege of voting, by special legislation?

We are of the opinion that the words "white," "Negro," "mulatto," "Indian," and "black person," wherever they occur in our Constitution and laws, must be taken in their generic sense, and that, even admitting the Indian of this continent is not of the Mongolian type, that the words "black person," in the 14th section, must be taken as contradistinguished from white, and necessary excludes all races other than the Caucasian.

We have carefully considered all the consequences resulting from a different rule of construction, and are satisfied that even in a doubtful case, we would be impelled to this decision on ground of public policy.

The same rule which would admit them to testify, would admit them to all the equal rights of citizenship, and we might soon see them at the polls, in the jury box, upon the bench, and in our legislative halls.

This is not a speculation which exists in the excited and overheated imagination of the patriot and statesman, but it is an actual and present danger.

The anomalous spectacle of a distinct people, living in our community, recognizing no laws of this State, except through necessity, bringing with them their prejudices and national feuds, in which they indulge in open violation of law; whose mendacity is proverbial; a race of people whom nature has marked as inferior, and who are incapable of progress or intellectual development beyond a certain point, as their history has shown; differing in language, opinions, color, and physical conformation; between whom and ourselves nature has placed an impassable difference, is now presented, and for them is claimed, not only the right to swear away the life of a citizen, but the further privilege of participating with us in administering the affairs of our Government.

These facts were before the Legislature that framed this Act, and have been known as matters of public history to every subsequent Legislature.

There can be no doubt as to the intention of Legislature, and that if it had ever been anticipated that this class of people were not embraced in the prohibition, then such specific words would have been employed as would have put the matter beyond any possible controversy.

For these reasons, we are of opinion that the testimony was inadmissible.

The judgment is reversed and the cause remanded.

Source: Reports of Cases Argued and Determined in the Supreme Court of the State of California. San Francisco: Marvin and Hitchcock, 1851–1860.

Books

Ancheta, Angelo. *Race, Rights, and the Asian American Experience*. New Brunswick, NJ: Rutgers University Press, 1998. Law professor Angelo Ancheta discusses the intersection of race and law in American history and widens the discourse from a binary "black v. white" model to include a critical analysis of the Asian American encounter with legal race-based policies.

McClain, Charles, ed. *Chinese Immigrants and American Law*. New York: Garland Publishing, Inc. 1991. See J.A.C. Grant's Chapter 3,

"Testimonial Exclusion Because of Race: A Chapter in the History of Intolerance in California."

Websites

Ancestors in the Americas. "The People vs. Hall, 1854." This site is maintained by the Center for Educational Telecommunications' the Loni Ding Legacy Project. Ding was an Asian American filmmaker who explores the Asian experience in America. Full text available here: http://www.cetel.org/1854_hall.html. Accessed October 6, 2016.

Zheng, Connie. "Chinese American Heroes—Attorneys." This article discusses the history and impact of *People v. Hall* and the history of Chinese American in the legal profession. http://www.chineseamericanheroes.org/history/CAH%20Attorneys%20-%20historic%20v3.pdf. Accessed October 6, 2016.

Also Noteworthy

1945

The United States drops the atomic bomb on Nagasaki.

2004

In Arlington, Virginia, three white men shout racial slurs at a pregnant black Muslim woman.

August 10

1988

House Resolution 442, the Civil Liberties Act of 1987, is signed into law by President Ronald Reagan. It provides for a payment of $20,000 to each surviving Japanese American internee and a $1.25 billion education fund, among other provisions. It sought to address the sense of betrayal felt by Japanese Americans when President Franklin D. Roosevelt signed Executive Order 9066 on February 19, 1942. It forced 110,000 Japanese Americans to liquidate their assets on three-day notice and relocate to remote internment camps. The campaign to seek reparations was begun on July 10, 1970, by the western branch of the Japanese American Citizens League. The campaign's emotional turning point came when 750 Japanese American witnesses recounted their experiences before the Commission on Wartime Relocation and Internment of Civilians. The first $20,000 redress payments were made on October 9, 1990, to 107-year-old Mamoru Eto and eight other elderly survivors. The success here fueled Japanese Canadians' movement for redress there.

The American action on redress triggered an almost immediate response in Canada. There the Mulroney government had been resisting redress payments although negotiations about them had been going on between the government and Japanese Canadian groups for years. Just forty-three days after the American redress bill was signed, the Canadian government and the community representatives reached a stunningly similar agreement, which was announced in Parliament with the support of all three political parties, on September 22, 1988. Canada agreed to pay, "as expeditiously as possible," $21,000 to each survivor (there were presumed to be from 12,000 to 14,000), which could amount to almost $300 million. Since the Canadian dollar was then worth about 85 percent of the American dollar, the Canadian per capita payment was actually smaller, although it seemed larger. All observers agreed that the American precedent was crucial in the volte-face of the Canadian government. It also did not hurt that a national election was approaching.

Source: Daniels, Roger. "Redress Achieved, 1983–1990." In *Japanese Americans: From Relocation to Redress*, edited by Roger Daniels, Sandra Taylor, and Harry Kitano, p. 222. Seattle: University of Washington Press, 1991.

Books

Hatamiya, Leslie. *Righting a Wrong: Japanese Americans and the Passage of the Civil Liberties Act of 1988.* Stanford, CA: Stanford University

Press, 1993. *Righting a Wrong* documents the history of Japanese American reparations.

Tateishi, John. *And Justice for All: An Oral History of the Japanese American Detention Camps.* New York: Random House, 1984. *And Justice for All* documents 30 oral histories of Japanese Americans who were imprisoned in detention centers during World War II.

Websites

Nikkei for Civil Rights & Redress. 2012. This site provides a video archive of members of the National Coalition for Redress/Reparations, annual newsletters, and a digital book that details their struggle for redress. http://www.ncrr-la.org/reader/index.html. Accessed January 22, 2018.

Yang, Alice. "Redress Movement." *Densho Encyclopedia*, 2018. This essay provides a historical overview of the Japanese American redress movement and includes a list of films that documents this movement, along with other academic and nonacademic resources. http://encyclopedia.densho.org/Redress_movement/. Accessed January 22, 2018.

Also Noteworthy

1996

The first two-day Los Angeles Tofu Festival is organized by Little Tokyo Service Center and House Foods Corporation.

1999

Joseph Santos Ileto, a Filipino American postal worker, is murdered by a self-proclaimed white supremacist in Chatsworth, California.

August 11

1997

Cambodian refugee Diameng Pa, a high school senior at Arlington's Wakefield High School in Virginia, testifies before the Senate Judiciary Committee's Subcommittee on Immigration on Ellis Island, New York, on his experience as an immigrant and becoming an American "thanks to my teachers and the miracle of TV." Pa fled Cambodia with his parents and sister in 1987.

Excerpt from Diameng Pa's speech before the Senate subcommittee.

America should continue to be a nation of immigrants. This institution is hope for those still seeking a new beginning similar to the one I received. I was born in Batdambang, Cambodia, on November 23, 1978 . . . a rural village . . . several miles from the Thai border. . . . This period produced a Cambodian Communist faction known as the Khmer Rouge, who killed more than 400,000 Cambodians and forced many more to flee. . . .

To acquire a better life for their family, my parents fled to a refugee camp in Thailand, fortunately able . . . then to escape to the United States. . . . By coming to the United States of America, we were traveling to a land that was foreign to us and whose language we did not speak. However . . . it is a land of opportunity.

My family initially settled in a minority neighborhood of South Arlington, Virginia, not far from Strayer College where my father, Mong Pa, pursued a degree in business administration. However, unfortunately, he abandoned his goals to support the family. My father would also mention the importance of education and its correlation with success. Though quiet young, I realized that my father sacrificed his opportunity to pursue his business degree so that the family was financially stable. He encouraged me to reach out and to appreciate one of the many precious gifts that America offered—formal education.

Source: Pa, Diameng. Speech before the Senate Judiciary Committee's Subcommittee on Immigration. Cited in Carol Berkin, Christopher Miller, Robert Cherny, and James Gormly. *Making America: A History of the United States*. 6th edition. Boston, MA: Wadsworth, 2014, p. 717.

Books

Lee, Jonathan H.X. ed. *Cambodian American Experiences: Histories, Communities, Cultures, and Identities*. Dubuque, IA: Kendall and Hunt

Publishing Company, 2010. *Cambodian American Experiences* covers the history and contemporary challenges of the Cambodian American community, including the issue related to education and the model minority stereotype.

Park, Clara, A. Lin Goodwin, and Stacey Lee, eds. *Asian American Identities, Families, and Schooling*. Greenwich, CT: Information Age Publishing, 2003. This collection of articles focuses on the intersections of race and schooling among Asian Americans; see Wayne Wright's Chapter 10, "The Success and Demise of a Khmer (Cambodian) Bilingual Education Program: A Case Study," for discussion focused on Cambodian Americans.

Websites

Hinojosa, Maria. (Anchor, Executive Producer, and Managing Editor). "Pass or Fail in Cambodia Town" (Television series episode). In *America by the Numbers with Maria Hinojosa*. Boston, MA: WGBH, November 6, 2014. This site provides the short video on the issues surrounding Cambodian American education. http://www.pbs.org/wgbh/america-by-the-numbers/episodes/episode-106/. Accessed February 9, 2018.

Rojas, Leslie. "For Younger Cambodian Americans, a Narrowing Education Gap." 89.3 KPCC. March 18, 2015. This essay discusses the historic problem of Cambodian American educational underachievement and efforts to correct it in Southern California. https://www.scpr.org/blogs/multiamerican/2015/03/18/17990/for-younger-cambodian-americans-a-narrowing-educat/. Accessed February 9, 2018.

Also Noteworthy

1957

David Henry Hwang, a playwright and screenwriter, is born in San Gabriel, California.

1972

Asian Americans Advancing Justice—Asian Law Caucus is founded.

August 12

2008

From August 12 to October 29, 2008, the National Asian American Survey (NAAS) collected information on the social and political attitudes and behaviors of 5,159 Asian American adults. The survey reveals the complexity and diversity within the Asian American communities.

Among Asian-American voters, a sizable portion remains undecided on a candidate for president—which could set the stage for Asian Americans to play a pivotal role in the outcome of the election, according to a recent national survey conducted by researchers at Rutgers; the University of California (UC), Berkeley; UC Riverside; and the University of Southern California (USC).

The "2008 National Asian American Survey" (NAAS) shows 41 percent of Asian Americans are likely to favor Barack Obama, while 24 percent support John McCain. In battleground states, where either candidate could win on Election Day, Obama leads with 43 percent of decided Asian-American voters supporting him and 22 percent favoring McCain.

Researchers say a key finding is the high proportion of undecided Asian-American potential voters—34 percent. Among the general population, national polls conducted since the major party conventions show undecided voters comprise approximately eight percent of the electorate. . . .

The multiethnic, multilingual survey of more than 4,000 Asian Americans likely to vote in the election was conducted from August 18 through September 26 and involved interviews conducted in English, Cantonese, Mandarin, Hindi, Japanese, Korean, Tagalog, and Vietnamese.

Janelle Wong, an associate professor of political science at USC, said "most national polls cannot report the preferences of these likely voters because they do not interview in multiple languages, and the number of interviews they conduct among Asian Americans is very small."

By drawing on the knowledge of political scientists with expertise in survey research and ethnic politics, and with support from several foundations, the NAAS data provide insight about Asian Americans as a whole, the researchers say, as well as about the six largest ethnic subgroups: Asian Indians, Chinese, Filipinos, Japanese, Koreans, and Vietnamese.

Source: "Asian Americans Could Be Key in Election Outcome." *Asian Reporter*, October 14, 2008, pp. 1–16.

Books

Shapiro, Robert, and Lawrence Jacobs, eds. *The Oxford Handbook of American Public Opinion and the Media*. Oxford: Oxford University Press, 2011. See Chapter 32, "Asian American Public Opinion," by Jane Junn, Taeku Lee, S. Karthick Ramakrishnan, and Janelle Wong.

Wong, Janelle, S. Karthick Ramakrishnan, Taeku Lee, and Jane Junn. *Asian American Political Participation: Emerging Constituents and Their Political Identities*. New York: Russell Sage Foundation, 2011. *Asian American Political Participation* analyzes data from the 2008 survey.

Websites

National Asian American Survey. 2008. Resource Center for Minority Data. University of Michigan. This site provides the data from the 2008 survey. https://www.icpsr.umich.edu/icpsrweb/RCMD/studies/31481. Accessed January 25, 2018.

National Asian American Survey. 2018. NAAS is a scientific and nonpartisan effort to poll the opinions of Asian Americans and Pacific Islanders. http://naasurvey.com/. Accessed January 25, 2018.

August 13

1898

Spain surrenders to the United States of America, but the Spanish-American War would not officially end until December 19, 1898, with the signing of the Treaty of Paris. This is a prelude to the Philippine-American War, Filipino migration to the United States, and American occupation of the Philippines.

Tensions between American and Filipino forces first began to mount in Manila in August 1898. Filipino revolutionaries had already wrested control of most of the Philippines from the Spanish except for a tiny walled section of Old Manila called the Intramuros. Some 12,000 Filipino soldiers had amassed around the perimeter of the Intramuros and were playing a waiting game, expecting the Spanish to surrender once their food supplies ran out. Meanwhile, the Spanish governor-general, Fermin Jaudenes y Alvarez, held secret discussions with Commodore George Dewey and Major General Wesley Merritt. Through these discussions, an agreement was reached whereby Spanish and American forces would stage a mock battle so that Spain could save face by surrendering to the Americans instead of to the Filipino rebels. After the staged First Battle of Manila, Spain handed over control of the Intramuros to the Americans on August 13, 1898. From there, U.S. forces set about occupying the rest of Manila, excluding Filipino troops beyond the line of demarcation. It was at this point that relations between the Americans and their former Filipino allies deteriorated rapidly.

Source: Hewitt, Marco. "Philippine-American War." In *Encyclopedia of the Spanish-American and Philippine-American Wars*, edited by Spencer Tucker, p. 476. Santa Barbara, CA: ABC-CLIO, 2009.

Books

Barnes, Mark. *The Spanish-American War and Philippines Insurrection, 1898–1902: An Annotated Bibliography*. New York: Routledge, 2011. *The Spanish-American War and Philippines Insurrection* provides a timeline and history of the Spanish-American War and Philippines Insurrection, along with an annotated bibliography of scholarship on this topic.

O'Toole, G.J.A. *The Spanish War: An American Epic 1898*. New York: W.W. Norton & Company, 1986. *The Spanish War* discusses various aspects of the Spanish-American War and its historical, cultural, ideological, and geopolitical impact.

Websites

"Battle of Manila Bay." History.com. This site provides a summary of the battle, along with videos. http://www.history.com/topics/battle-of-manila-bay. Accessed October 11, 2016.

"The Battle of Manila Bay, 1898." EyeWitness to History. 2011. This site provides an eyewitness account of the Battle of Manila Bay. www.eyewitnesstohistory.com. Accessed October 11, 2016.

August 14

1941

The Atlantic Charter is drafted by the leaders of the United Kingdom and the United States and issued on this day. The charter defined the Allied goals for postwar world that focused on mutual principles, peace, and policies they agreed to follow once the Nazis are defeated. Colonized countries in Southeast Asia and around the world will invoke the charter in their anticolonial struggles to decolonize their countries. The charter detailed eight principal points:

1. No territorial gains were to be sought by the United States or the United Kingdom.
2. Territorial adjustments must be in accord with the wishes of the peoples concerned.
3. All people had a right to self-determination.
4. Trade barriers were to be lowered.
5. There was to be global economic cooperation and advancement of social welfare.
6. The participants would work for a world free of want and fear.
7. The participants would work for freedom of the seas.
8. There was to be disarmament of aggressor nations and a postwar common disarmament.

The President of the United States of America and the Prime Minister, Mr. Churchill, representing His Majesty's Government in the United Kingdom, being met together, deem it right to make known certain common principles in the national policies of their respective countries on which they base their hopes for a better future for the world.

First, their countries seek no aggrandizement, territorial or other;

Second, they desire to see no territorial changes that do not accord with the freely expressed wishes of the peoples concerned;

Third, they respect the right of all peoples to choose the form of government under which they will live; and they wish to see sovereign rights and self-government restored to those who have been forcibly deprived of them;

Fourth, they will endeavor, with due respect for their existing obligations, to further the enjoyment by all States, great or small, victor or vanquished, of access, on equal terms, to the trade and to the raw materials of the world which are needed for their economic prosperity;

Fifth, they desire to bring about the fullest collaboration between all nations in the economic field with the object of securing, for all, improved labor standards, economic advancement and social security;

Sixth, after the final destruction of the Nazi tyranny, they hope to see established a peace which will afford to all nations the means of dwelling in safety within their own boundaries, and which will afford assurance that all the men in all lands may live out their lives in freedom from fear and want;

Seventh, such a peace should enable all men to traverse the high seas and oceans without hindrance;

Eighth, they believe that all of the nations of the world, for realistic as well as spiritual reasons must come to the abandonment of the use of force. Since no future peace can be maintained if land, sea or air armaments continue to be employed by nations which threaten, or may threaten, aggression outside of their frontiers, they believe, pending the establishment of a wider and permanent system of general security, that the disarmament of such nations is essential. They will likewise aid and encourage all other practicable measure which will lighten for peace-loving peoples the crushing burden of armaments.

Source: The Avalon Project. Documents in Law, History, and Diplomacy. http://avalon.law.yale.edu/wwii/atlantic.asp. Accessed January 13, 2017.

Books

Borgwardt, Elizabeth. *A New Deal for the World: America's Vision for Human Rights*. Cambridge, MA: Harvard University Press, 2005. *A New Deal for the World* discusses the history and legacy of the Atlantic Charter vis-à-vis American foreign policy, international human rights, trade, global security, and international law.

Brinkley, Doulgas, and David Facey-Crowther, eds. *The Atlantic Charter*. New York: St. Martin's Press, 1994. *The Atlantic Charter* provides a collection of critical essays that discusses the charter's formulation and significance during and after World War II.

Websites

"The Atlantic Conference and Charter, 1941." U.S. Office of the Historian, Bureau of Public Affairs, U.S. Department of State. https://history.state.gov/milestones/1937-1945/atlantic-conf. Accessed January 13, 2017.

"1941: The Atlantic Charter." United Nations. This site provides a history of the Atlantic Charter and its international significance and legacy. It includes historic images and full text of the UN document. http://www.un.org/en/sections/history-united-nations-charter/1941-atlantic-charter/. Accessed January 13, 2017.

August 15

1942

Toku Machida Shimomura kept a diary of her time in the Minidoka Relocation Center in southern Idaho. She was born on June 12, 1888, in Saitama Prefecture in central Japan near Tokyo. She graduated in 1905 from nursing school in Tokyo, where she trained as a nurse and midwife at the Japanese Red Cross Hospital. The diary she kept reveals little about her life before arriving to Seattle, Washington, where she worked as a nurse and midwife.

Excerpt from Toku Machida Shimomura's diary.

August 15

The heat was severe. The temperature was 107°.

I was concerned over Ayako and Roger who left early this morning. The whole day was difficult to bear because of the heat.

I went to bed with a feeling of relief after we sent out our baggage.

I was annoyed by the noise from the neighbors as well as all around.

Dawn came without sleep because of this.

When I think that tonight is the last night I will be here I somewhat regret leaving this barrack which was home to us.

Source: Shimomura, Toku Machida. Cited in Odo, Franklin, ed. *The Columbia Documentary History of the Asian American Experience*. New York: Columbia University Press, 2002, p. 277.

Books

Keene, Donald. *Modern Japanese Diaries: The Japanese at Home and Abroad as Revealed through Their Diaries*. New York: Columbia University Press, 1998. See *The Diary of Shimomura Toku*.

Smith, Susan. *Japanese American Midwives: Culture, Community, and Health Politics, 1880–1950*. Urbana: University of Illinois Press, 2005. See Chapter 3, "Seattle *Sanba* and the Creation of Issei Community," that discusses Toku Machida Shimomura.

Websites

Nakane, Kazuko, and Alan Lau. "Misrepresentation: or the Bittersweet Cartoon of Life. The Art of Roger Shimomura." Grantmakers in the Arts. *GIA Reader* vol. 22, no. 3 (Fall 2011). Roger Shimomura is Toku Machida Shimomura's grandson, whom she delivered. He is an acclaimed American painter, and this essay reflects on his paintings, including those inspired by his grandmother's diary. https://www.giarts.org/article/misrepresentation-or-bittersweet-cartoon-life. Accessed February 9, 2018.

Nickell, Joe. "Imprisoned in Minidoka: Grandmother's Diary Memorializes Life as an Interned Japanese American Following Attack on Pearl Harbor." *Missoulian*, October 4, 2009. This article details the paintings of Roger Shimomura, grandson of Toku Machida Shimomura, and includes excerpts from her diary. http://missoulian.com/lifestyles/territory/imprisoned-in-minidoka-grandmother-s-diary-memorializes-life-as-an/article_02cb6524-af96-11de-857e-001cc4c002e0.html. Accessed February 9, 2018.

Also Noteworthy

1971

The Amerasia bookstore opens in Little Tokyo, Los Angeles.

August 16

1829

Chang and Eng, the original Siamese twins, arrive in Boston on this day.

The first recorded Thai immigrants to the United States were Chang and Eng, the famous conjoined twins, who arrived in Boston on August 16, 1829. They were joined at the lower part of their chest by a strip of flesh "five to six inches long and eight inches in circumference." In Siam (as Thailand was known before 1939), Chang and Eng were called the "Chinese Twins" because they had a Chinese immigrant father and Chinese Siamese mother. In the United States, however, the twins coined the term "Siamese Twins," emphasizing where they came from instead of their ethnicity. Chang and Eng became successful performers, American citizens, gentlemen farmers, and slaveholders. Their achievements can, in part, be attributed to their having arrived in the United States before many of the discriminatory laws aimed at Asian immigrants were implemented.

Source: Bao, Jiemin. "The Thais." In *More Peoples of Las Vegas: One City, Many Faces*, edited by Jerry Simich and Thomas Wright, p. 184. Reno: University of Nevada Press, 2010.

Books

Orser, Joseph. *The Lives of Chang and Eng: Siam's Twins in Nineteenth-Century America.* Chapel Hill: University of North Carolina Press, 2014. Historian Joseph Orser's biography reflects on Chang and Eng's history through antebellum America, their family lives in North Carolina, their fame, and the shifting racial and cultural landscape of 19th-century American culture and society.

Wu, Cynthia. *Chang and Eng Reconnected: The Original Siamese Twins in American Culture.* Philadelphia, PA: Temple University Press, 2012. American studies professor Cynthia Wu traces the history of Chang and Eng through the terrain of American culture and representations of race, disability, and science vis-à-vis nation-building ideologies and narratives.

Websites

"Eng & Chang Bunker: Original Siamese Twins Exhibit, Mount Airy, North Carolina." This site provides a timeline of the twins' life, along with historical background, and images. Surry Arts Council. 2016. http://www.surryarts.org/siamesetwins/index.html. Accessed January 28, 2018.

Eng & Chang Bunker: The Siamese Twins collection. This site presents original primary source material on Chang and Eng Bunker from the special collections in Wilson Library at the University of North Carolina at Chapel Hill. http://dc.lib.unc.edu/cdm/compoundobject/collection/bunkers/id/504/rec/2. Accessed January 28, 2018.

August 17

1904

William Hang, a Union navy veteran of the American Civil War, is arrested for voting even though he is in a naturalized citizenship. On October 21, 1908, New York's Supreme Court stripped him of his citizenship.

. . . foreign-born Chinese veterans, having fought for the United States of America, sought to become its naturalized citizens. Congress had promised any honorably discharged foreign-born veteran citizenship upon petition. The 1790 Naturalization Law restricted naturalization to whites, however, and the Fourteenth Amendment, by which African Americans gained citizenship, did not apply to Chinese; then Congress passed the Exclusion Act in 1882 explicitly forbidding their naturalization. Yet these laws were applied so inconsistently that Hong Neok Woo was naturalized in Lancaster, Pennsylvania before the war, Thomas Sylvanus shortly after, Antonio Dardelle despite Exclusion, but Edward Day Cohota denied, and William Hang, a Navy veteran, thoroughly ensnared in the contradictions. Granted citizenship in New York on October 6, 1892, Hang voted until August 17, 1904, when he was arrested when exercising his franchise. Producing his naturalization papers, Hang was then subjected to a tirade by Joel M. Marx, assistant United States attorney, who accused the judge issuing the papers of inexcusable ignorance. Hang fought the ruling to no avail: On October 21, 1908, New York's Supreme Court vacated and set aside his citizenship. Thus Chinese veterans, however acculturated in language, religion, dress, and cultural practices, were relegated to permanent outsider status whereas European veterans found their service and citizenship accelerated their complete assimilation. For European veterans, then, their ethnicity could be "just one aspect of their character, not the burning core of their very being" (Melting Pot Soldiers). Chinese veterans, their ethnicity their sole definition by law, enjoyed no such luxury. And, after passage of the 1892 Geary Act, which extended exclusion and required all Chinese to carry identification proving their legal entry, Joseph Pierce changed his identity to Japanese; his children and those of Antonio Dardelle passed as white.

Source: McCunn, Ruthanne. "Chinese in the U.S. Civil War." In *Asian Americans: An Encyclopedia of Social, Cultural, Economic, and Political History*, edited by Xiaojian Zhao and Edward Park, p. 280. Santa Barbara, CA: ABC-CLIO, 2014.

Books

Eakman, Kate. *Discover the Story of Your Civil War Soldier Ancestor.* History & Heritage, 2013. *Discover the Story of Your Civil War Solider Ancestor* discusses ethnic minorities who served on both sides of the American Civil War.

Shively, Carol, ed., *Asians and Pacific Islanders and the Civil War.* Washington, DC: National Park Service, U.S. Department of the Interior, 2015. This book, part of a series, commemorates the 150th anniversary of the Civil War and documents the stories of Asian and the Pacific Islander Americans who fought for the Union or the Confederacy during the American Civil War.

Websites

Chin, Philip. "A Short History about Chinese American Military Veterans." Chinese American Heroes. This article documents Chinese American servicemen and women who have served in the U.S. military. http://www.chineseamericanheroes.org/history/111010%20Article%20on%20CA%20veterans%20-%20v%206.pdf. Accessed January 22, 2018.

Railton, Ben. "Veterans to Remember: Chinese Americans in the Civil War." We're History. November 7, 2014. This article provides information on Chinese Americans who served in the American Civil War based on the scholarship of Ruthanne McCunn. http://werehistory.org/veterans-to-remember/. Accessed January 22, 2018.

August 18

1941

In a letter to President Roosevelt, Representative John David Dingell of Michigan suggests incarcerating 10,000 Hawaiian Japanese Americans as hostages to ensure "good behavior" on the part of Japan. Many contend this is the inspiration for the internment of Japanese Americans during World War II.

The notion that the genesis of these events was solely due to the attack on Pearl Harbor and subsequent formal entry of the United States into World War II rarely has been questioned, yet the imprisonment camps were indeed a consequence of "anti-Japanese heritage." Moreover, U.S. corporate interests actively sought to curb Japanese economic success along the West Coast as early as the late nineteenth century, and their forcible removal served U.S. public and private sector interests. U.S. congressman John Dingell (D-MI) wrote President Roosevelt four months before the December 1941 attack suggesting the internment of some Japanese Americans. The predominant narrative consists of internees making lemonade out of proverbial lemons: quietly packing a few of their personal belongings, boarding trains headed to the camps, swearing allegiance to the United States, enlisting in the military, and earning Purple Hearts on the battle field (the super citizen). Conspicuously missing from the way most historians and journalists make sense of these events are the women and children who comprised the vast majority of internees, and the indigenous people whose sovereignty and freedom were trampled in the name of U.S. "national security." This hegemonic condition requires a critical analysis.

Source: Rodriguez, Pedro, and Pat Lauderdale. "Hegemony and Collective Memories: Japanese-American Relocation and Imprisonment on American Indian 'Land.'" In *Color behind Bars: Racism in the U.S. Prison System*, edited by Scott Bowman, p. 42. Santa Barbara, CA: Praeger, 2014.

Books

Daniels, Roger. *The Politics of Prejudice: The Anti-Japanese Movement in California and the Struggle for Japanese Exclusion*. Berkeley: University of California Press, 1962 (2nd edition, 1977). *The Politics of Prejudice* covers the history of anti-Japanese movements in California.

Robinson, Greg. *By Order of the President: FDR and the Internment of Japanese Americans*. Cambridge, MA: Harvard University Press, 2001. *By Order of the President* discusses the contradiction between Franklin D. Roosevelt's (FDR) image as humanitarian and preserver of democracy and the unjust internment of Japanese Americans during World War II.

Websites

Bos, Carole. "Japanese-American Internment." AwesomeStories.com. February 19, 2017. This essay discusses Dingell's letter and the motivation behind it. http://www.awesomestories.com/asset/view/Japanese-American-Internment. Accessed February 9, 2018.

Chronology of WWII Incarceration. Japanese American National Museum. 1998. This site provides a day-by-day chronology of Japanese American internment history. http://www.janm.org/projects/clasc/chronology.htm. Accessed February 9, 2018.

Also Noteworthy

2004

In New York City, New York, Brian Lydon, a 45-year-old, is charged with assault and harassment for attacking a man of Middle Eastern descent while yelling "You are Muslim."

August 19

1945

Edward "Eddie" Fung (June 20, 1922–March 25, 2018), a native of San Francisco, has the "dubious" distinction of being the only Chinese American soldier to be captured by the Japanese during World War II. During that time, he is forced to work on the Burma-Siam railroad (1942–1943), made famous by the film *The Bridge on the River Kwai*. He endured 42 months in captivity and suffered in brutal conditions in the Japanese prisoner of war (POW) camps.

Eddie is finally liberated on August 15, 1945, after the Japanese surrendered. He came home to a hero's welcome and finished his formal schooling on the G.I. Bill, earning a BA degree in chemistry from Stanford University.

Eddie Fung was born on June 20, 1922, in San Francisco. When he was sixteen he finished the tenth grade and ran away from home. He wanted to work with horses, so he went first to West Texas. He worked as a butcher and cowhand on ranches in Seminole, and in Tucumcari, New Mexico, before settling near Lubbock, Texas. He tried to join the cavalry but was too young, and his mother would not give her consent. Finally, in May 1940 he enlisted in Battery C, First Battalion, Texas National Guard. He was federalized with his unit in November and voluntarily transferred to Battery F, Second Battalion, just before it left Camp Bowie for the Orient. As an American artilleryman of Chinese descent in the Second Battalion, Fung was unique, but, according to him, his treatment did not differ because of his ethnic background. When the battalion surrendered in Java, he felt badly, later stating, "I think we all had the feeling that we hadn't done enough, even though we didn't have anything to do it with. But you still have a feeling that you didn't do a good job. Maybe that hurt as much as anything." Fung spent his years as a POW about as normally as could be expected for an American soldier in a Japanese prison camp during World War II. . . . When the Japanese announced the war had ended, he and his fellow prisoners stood in stunned silence for several minutes before reacting with some cheers. Each nationality constructed its national flag to fly in the camp. Fung followed the usual route of American POWs home, through the military hospital in Calcutta. Back in the States he had trouble getting used to eating. He also felt uneasy about his role in the war and the hero's welcome he received after it.

Source: La Forte, Robert, and Ronald Marcello, eds. *Building the Death Railway: The Ordeal of American POWs in Burma, 1942–1945*. Wilmington, DE: SR Books, 1993. See entry on "Edward Fung" pages 121 and 136.

Books

Yung, Judy, ed. *The Adventures of Eddie Fung: Chinatown Kid, Texas Cowboy, Prisoner of War.* Seattle: University of Washington Press, 2007. *The Adventures of Eddie Fung* is a historical memoir of Eddie Fung, edited by his wife, Judy Yung.

Yung, Judy, Gordon H. Chang, and H. Mark Lai, eds. *Chinese American Voices: From the Gold Rush to the Present.* Berkeley: University of California Press, 2006. See Eddie Fung's chapter "'There but for the Grace of God Go I': The Story of a POW Survivor in World War II (2002)."

Websites

Chin, Philip. "Eddie Fung: Part 4—Liberation and the Return Home 1944 to the Present." Chinese American Heroes. 2018. This essay details Eddie Fung's experience after being liberated from the Japanese POW camp and his life after returning home. http://chineseamericanheroes.org/wp-content/uploads/2015/04/Eddie-Fung-Part-4.pdf. Accessed January 22, 2018.

Kelly, Cathy. "Eddie Fung of Santa Cruz Survived Horrors of POW Camp in World War II." *Santa Cruz Sentinel*, February 17, 2013. This article covers his life and experience during World War II and includes photographs. http://www.santacruzsentinel.com/article/zz/20130217/NEWS/130217849. Accessed January 22, 2018.

Also Noteworthy

1945

The Viet Minh successfully seizes power in Hanoi, which they later declared the capital of the Democratic Republic of Vietnam.

August 20

1967

The Association of Indians in America is founded. It is the oldest national association of Asian Indians in America.

Many Indian political associations were created in the United States as early as the 1970s when members realized the need to get organized and to articulate their interests in a collective voice, like the Association of Indians in America, created in 1967, and the Indian League of America, founded in 1972. One exception is that by the end of the 1970s, the Association of Indians in America strongly and successfully lobbied in favour of a separate classification for Indians in the 1980 census.

Source: Alam, Mohammed. "Back to the Roots: Engagement of the Indian Diaspora in the United States and India." In *South Asian Migration: Remittances and Beyond*, edited by Md Mizanur Rahman and Zaara Zain Hussain, p. 157. Newcastle upon Tyne, England: Cambridge Scholars Publishing, 2015.

Books

Barkan, Elliott Robert, ed. *Immigrants in American History: Arrival, Adaptation, and Integration.* Santa Barbara, CA: ABC-CLIO, 2013. See Maritsa Poros's chapter "Asian Indians and Asian-Indian Americans, 1940–Present."

Leonard, Karen Isaksen. *The South Asian Americans.* Westport, CT: Greenwood Press, 1997. *The South Asian Americans* discusses various aspects of South Asian history, including discussions of economic development, political participation, and sociocultural adaptation.

Websites

The Association of Indians in America. Official web page. Information about its history and mission is available, in addition to its current leadership. http://aianational.com/?q=node/1. Accessed February 9, 2018.

The Association of Indians in America, NY Chapter. Official web page. Information about its history and mission is available. http://www.theaiany.org/. Accessed February 9, 2018.

Also Noteworthy

1989

Saved by the Bell, a television sitcom, begins to air on NBC, starring Mark-Paul Harry Gosselaar (b. March 1, 1974), an American actor of Dutch and Indonesian ancestry.

August 21

1959

Hiram Leong Fong (October 15, 1906–August 18, 2004) becomes the first Asian American to be elected to the U.S. Senate. At the time of his election, Fong was already one of Hawaii's most prominent citizens and successful businessmen. After graduating from McKinley High school and the University of Hawaii, he worked for several years to save money to attend Harvard Law School from which he graduated in 1935. After working as a Honolulu deputy city attorney and founding a law firm, Fong won a seat in the territorial House of Representatives in 1938 at the age of 31. He went on to become a Speaker of the House who was popular with both Democrats and Republicans. During World War II, Fong served as a judge advocate in the Seventh Fighter Command of the Seventh Air Force. When Hawaii won statehood in 1959, the 14-year veteran of the state legislature had little trouble winning election to the U.S. Senate as a Republican. In 1964, he became the first Asian American to seek the Republican Party's nomination as president of the United States. He retired from the Senate in 1977 to return to running his business interests.

Eulogy by Jon Miho.

"Remembering Senator Fong."

Now I know it isn't politically correct to talk about race in this day and age—but I'm not a politician. Sen. Fong was a son of immigrants who were illiterate. He formed a law partnership with my father, a Japanese American, in 1938. My father also had immigrant parents who were illiterate. So a second generation Chinese lawyer, the firs in his family to go to college-certainly the first to go to law school-and a second generation Japanese lawyer, who also was the first in his family to go to college and law school, formed a law partnership in 1938—both from poor families who could not pay for their education. So they both worked their way through college and law school. Both had faced insults and discrimination growing up in a Hawaii that was dominated by the Big Five. It is easy to see their pride in being one of the first Asian Americans to become lawyers in Hawaii. They wanted success, and to bring honor to their families, and pride and respect to their communities. They wanted to demonstrate their equality.

1938—Fong & Miho I believe that it became a real firm in 1942. My father was 4-F, he couldn't join the 442nd because of his age and because of his eyes—very poor eyesight. As I understand it, Sen. Fong was an officer in the Hawaii National Guard so, of course, was activated to serve in the Army after the outbreak of World War II. The Senator needed someone to service his clients to keep his practice going while he served full-time in the Army. He later told my father that his wife Ellyn told him to hire my father because he could be trusted and that he would be loyal. I believe that to be true of my father and I remember him telling me that he and Hiram had never had a fight. They treated each other with respect, courtesy and loyalty all their lives.

The Senator once told me that a bunch of his high school friends at McKinley High School got together and sent money every month when he was at Harvard Law School. They were his friends and they were investing in their future—the future of Hawaii. They all picked him to succeed—someone who would be able to help "the Chinese community" to a better life in Hawaii.

Source: Senator Hiram L. Fong. Official web page. http://senatorfong.com/. 2007. http://senatorfong.com/memorial_eulogy.html. Accessed January 22, 2018.

Books

Aoki, Andrew, and Okiyoshi Takeda. *Asian American Politics*. Malden, MA: Polity Press, 2008. See Chapter 5, "Elected Officials and Representation," for a comparative analysis and history of Asian Americans in elected politics.

Brown, Cleo, and Richard Ivory. *In Search of the Republican Party: A History of Minorities in the Republican Party*. Bloomington, IN: Xlibris LLC, 2012. See the chapter titled "Hiram L. Fung: Embodiment of the Puritan Work Ethic."

Websites

Crass, Scott. "Hiram Fong First Asian-American Senator, an R from Hawaii." Hawaii Free Press, June 7, 2013. This is an obituary of Hiram Fong that details his life, career, and legacy. http://www.hawaiifreepress.com/ArticlesMain/tabid/56/ID/9851/Hiram-Fong-First-Asian-American-Senator-An-R-From-Hawaii.aspx. Accessed January 22, 2018.

Senator Hiram L. Fong. Official web page. 2007. This site provides comprehensive information on Fong, which includes a biography and links to videos and publications on and about Fong, including tributes and memorials by leading Republican politicians. http://senatorfong.com/. Accessed January 22, 2018.

August 22

1910

Korea is formally annexed by Japan through the Japan-Korea Annexation Treaty. This mobilized the Korean communities in the United States to work toward Korea's independence that linked Koreans through their churches in Korea and America.

The creation of the protectorate in 1905 and annexation in 1910 triggered the rise of Korean nationalism. Within Korea, a "righteous army" unsuccessfully fought the Japanese in the hills. Overseas, Koreans in Manchuria and the United States assassinated Ito Hirobumi and D.W. Stevens in expressions of outrage. This nationalist movement, which called for the liberation of Korea from Japanese rule, looked toward the United States. One of the leading and controversial figures in this movement, Syngman Rhee, had become Woodrow Wilson's protégé at Princeton. Later, Wilson's Fourteen Points, which called for national self-determination, gave Korean nationalists hope. Unfortunately, the duality in the relationship interfered. Wilson meant self-determination for countries that had been colonized by the Germans, not for the colonies of allies like Japan. The Koreans discovered this to their dismay when they sent a delegation to the Versailles Peace Conference in 1919 hoping for independence.

Source: Patterson, Wayne, and Hilary Conroy. "Duality and Dominance: An Overview of Korean-American Relations, 1866–1997." In *Korean-American Relations: 1866–1997*, edited by Yur-Bok Lee and Wayne Patterson, pp. 4–5. Albany: State University of New York Press, 1999.

Books

Dudden, Alexis. *Japan's Colonization of Korea: Discourse and Power*. Honolulu: University of Hawaii Press, 2005. *Japan's Colonization of Korea* is a political intellectual history of Japan's work to legitimate its imperial ambition during the 20th century.

Duus, Peter. *The Abacus and the Sword: The Japanese Penetration of Korea, 1895–1910*. Berkeley: University of California Press, 1995. See Chapter 6, "The Politics of the Protectorate, 1905–1910," for discussion related to the history of Japan's annexation of Korea.

Websites

Kim, Ji-hyung. "The Japanese Annexation of Korea as Viewed from the British and American Press: Focus on the Times and the New York Times." *International Journal of Korean History* 16, no. 2 (August 2011): pp. 87–123. This article discusses international perceptions on Japan's colonization of Korea and argues that their own imperialist projects colored their presses' representation. https://ijkh.khistory.org/current/index.php?vol=16&no=2. Accessed January 22, 2018.

"Korea as a Colony of Japan, 1910–1945." *Asia for Educators*. 2009. This site provides key points on the topic of Japan's colonization of Korea. http://afe.easia.columbia.edu/main_pop/kpct/kp_koreaimperialism.htm. Accessed January 22, 2018.

Also Noteworthy

2002

In Seminole, Florida, Dr. Robert Goldstein, a 37-year-old, is charged with possessing destructive devices and attempting to damage and destroy buildings by means of explosive devices after police found his plans to attack an Islamic center and objectives to "Kill all 'rags.'"

August 23

1862

Antonio Dardelle (d. 1933) enlists in the 27th Connecticut Volunteer Infantry, Company A. Although a Chinese subject, he served in the American Civil War. Despite the strictures of exclusion, he secured naturalized citizenship and became politically active. Dardelle was brought to Connecticut at the age of seven, by Captain and Mrs. David White. He worked as a servant in their home, and therefore, had limited schooling. He passed away of pneumonia on January 18, 1933.

As a veteran, Dardelle joined the New Haven Grays. He also used his service to secure U.S. citizenship, the Court of Common Pleas in New Haven accepting his enlistment as the equivalent to "the taking out of first papers." "With his American citizenship, [Dardelle] embraced the Christian faith and became a member of the First Methodist Church." Moreover, he entered the Masonic Order in Guilford in 1865, changing his affiliation to the Wooster Lodge in 1882, and he was an active worker with the Young Men's Republican Club, as well as the organization of the party in the ward where he made his home. For several years after Dardelle mustered out, "home" continued to be Clinton. But on April 9, 1868, he married a Marcy C. Payne from Madison, and the following year, they moved to New Haven. All three of his daughters were born there—Minnie on November 7, 1873, Carrie on July 7, 1875, Alice on November 18, 1880—and he supported his family as a tinner and plumber. Dardelle worked well into old age, perhaps in part because for many years he could not secure the veteran's pension due him. Whether he had served was never in doubt. His exact age, however, was.

Source: McCunn, Ruthanne. "Chinese in the Civil War: Ten Who Served." *Chinese America: History and Perspectives* (1996): p. 159.

Books

McCunn, Ruthanne Lum. *Chinese Yankee: A True Story from the Civil War*. San Francisco, CA: Design Enterprises of San Francisco, 2014. *Chinese Yankee* documents the story of Chinese American Thomas Sylvanus (Ah Yee Way) who joined the Freedom Army during the American Civil War.

Shively, Carol, ed. *Asians and Pacific Islanders and the Civil War*. Washington, DC: National Park Service, U.S. Department of the Interior, 2015. This book, part of a series, commemorates the 150th anniversary of the Civil War and documents the stories of Asian and the Pacific Islander Americans who fought for the Union or the Confederacy during the American Civil War.

Websites

"Antonio Dardelle." Association to Commemorate the Chinese Serving in the American Civil War. April 10, 2008. This site provides a biography of Dardelle, photographs, and excerpts from scholarly sources that provide an overview for Chinese who served in the American Civil War. https://sites.google.com/site/accsacw/Home/dardelle. Accessed January 22, 2018.

"Antonio Dardelle." The Blue, the Gray and the Chinese: American Civil War Participants of Chinese Descent." March 28, 2014. This site provides detailed biographical information on Dardelle. http://bluegraychinese.blogspot.com/2014/03/antonio-dardelle.html. Accessed January 22, 2018.

August 24

1973

Bruce Lee becomes the first Asian American Hollywood action superstar and legend as *Enter the Dragon* (1973) premieres at Grauman's Chinese Theatre. Unfortunately, the star had died on July 20 of a mysterious swelling of the brain. Death didn't keep Lee from becoming a global icon of martial arts action and a hero to Asian Americans fed up with stereotypes of Asian men as subservient sidekicks or unsavory villains. Bruce Lee had enjoyed some success as Kato, the Green Lantern's sidekick, but left for Hong Kong after being rebuffed as being "too Chinese" to play the lead in the *Kung Fu* TV series. It didn't matter to Hollywood that Lee had conceived the series as a vehicle for his martial arts skills. Lee showed Hollywood that he can be successful with two low-budget Hong Kong–made features: *Fists of Fury* (1971) and *The Chinese Connection* (1972). Both were box-office smash hits with global audiences, laying the groundwork for Warner Brothers to produce *Enter the Dragon*.

In the 1960s, ABC aired an adventure series, Hong Kong, *which reinforced the Chinese stereotype of intrigue, sexy women, smuggling, and drug peddling. At least two Asian actors were cast as series regulars during its run from 1960 to 1961. The same network brought* The Green Hornet *to prime-time TV from 1966–1967. The significance of the series was the casting of Bruce Lee as the Green Hornet's sidekick, Kato. Lee's weekly demonstration of crime-fighting martial arts helped launch the popularity of Asian self-defense techniques in the United States. Interestingly,* The Green Hornet *was the creation of George Trendle, who also developed* The Lone Ranger. *In both shows, a trusty ethnic minority sidekick, perhaps for the purpose of adding fantasy appeal for the mass audience, supports the hero. Bruce Lee influenced another ABC series,* Kung Fu *(which ran from 1972 to 1975), which was a Western starring David Carradine and with supporting Asian actors including Keye Luke and Philip Ahn. Lee was a consultant to those who developed the* Kung Fu *show and labored under the impression that he was to be their choice for the lead role. When Carradine was selected for the part, Lee confided to friends that he had been the victim of racism.* Kung Fu's *producers told Lee that they didn't believe a Chinese actor could be seen as a hero in the eyes of the American television audience. The show revived the "mysterious" Asian stereotype. With racism standing as a barrier to Bruce Lee's achieving stardom in the United States, he went to Hong Kong and achieved superstardom throughout Asia as a film star. Lee, who died at 33, ultimately became a cult figure in the United States after the release of his final movie,* Enter the Dragon, *in 1973.*

Source: Wilson, Clint, Felix Gutierrez, and Lena Chao. *Racism, Sexism, and the Media: The Rise of Class Communication in Multicultural America*. Thousand Oaks, CA: Sage Publications, 2003, pp. 105–106.

Books

Bowman, Paul. *Beyond Bruce Lee: Chasing the Dragon through Film, Philosophy and Popular Culture*. New York: Columbia University Press, 2013. *Beyond Bruce Lee* explores Lee's legacy in popular culture and argues he is best understood in terms of "cultural translation."

Chan, Jachinson. *Chinese American Masculinities: From Fu Manchu to Bruce Lee*. New York: Routledge, 2001. See Chapter 4 "Bruce Lee: A Sexualized Object of Desire" for a focused discussion on Bruce Lee.

Websites

Bruce Lee. Bruce Lee Enterprises. 2016. This site contains historical essays on Lee, images, his form of martial arts, entertainment career history, and more. https://www.brucelee.com/. Accessed January 20, 2018.

Bruce Lee Foundation. 2018. This site contains information on Bruce Lee and includes videos and images of people impacted by his legacy. https://bruceleefoundation.org/. Accessed January 20, 2018.

Also Noteworthy

2010

In Madera, California, a sign reading "Wake Up America, the enemy is here," is left at an Islamic center. Over in New York City, Michael Enright, a 21-year-old, slashes a taxi driver's neck and face after he discovers the man is Muslim.

August 25

1934

White farmers in Salt River Valley in Arizona form the Farmers' Anti-Oriental Society in 1934 amid alarms over increasing Japanese migration from the Imperial Valley in California. The farmers viewed the Japanese as an economic threat, a condition made worse under the Great Depression, and as part of a racial conspiracy to take over farmland from whites. The Farmers' Anti-Oriental Society demanded the Japanese to leave by August 25, 1934. A gathering of over 600 white farmers and a parade of 150 cars were organized to ensure that the ultimatum was obeyed. On September 14, 1934, the first of several assaults was reported on the properties of the Salt River Valley Japanese farmers. Six days later, dynamite was used to blow up three dams on three separate Japanese farms, though again no one was hurt. The government of Japan pressured the United States to intervene. In return, federal officials pressed Arizona's governor and legislature to control the mob violence. The attacks, however, continued with neither the governor of Arizona stopping them nor the farmers signaling retreat. In fact, it became quite clear that the governor's silence was an act of tolerance of the attackers. The attacks continued through the year as anti-Japanese terrorism and harassment in Salt River Valley escalated and eventually waned. The threats, demonstrations, occasional violence, and political pressure persisted, at times becoming volatile, resulting in the decrease in size of the already small community by approximately 30 percent, as families and individuals moved elsewhere. The majority of the Japanese community, however, despite the attacks against themselves and their property, remained.

Little else was done until the summer of 1934, when a group of white farmers organized the agricultural community against the Japanese. Eight militant farmers, calling themselves the Anti-Alien Committee, headed the group. Although the members of the committee agreed not to make their names public, Mesa Farmer Fred Kruse gained much notoriety as its chairman. The committee planned to hold mass meetings, pressure public officials to enforce the alien land law, and consolidate valley-wide support for the movement. Significantly, the Anti-Alien Committee did not distinguish between Issei (Japanese foreign-born) and Nisei (American-born Japanese); to them such distinctions seemed irrelevant.

Source: August, Jack. "The Anti-Japanese Crusade in Arizona's Salt River Valley, 1934–35." *Arizona and the West* 21, no. 2 (Summer 1979): p. 115.

Books

Daniels, Roger. *The Politics of Prejudice: The Anti-Japanese Movement in California and the Struggle for Japanese Exclusion*. Berkeley: University of California Press, 1962 (2nd edition, 1977). *The Politics of Prejudice* covers the history of anti-Japanese movements in California.

Walz, Eric. *Nikkei in the Interior West: Japanese Immigration and Community Building, 1882–1945*. Tucson: University of Arizona Press, 2012. *Nikkei in the Interior West* is a history of the Japanese American experience in Arizona, Colorado, Idaho, Nebraska, and Utah.

Websites

Anderson, Emily. "Anti-Japanese Exclusion Movement." *Densho Encyclopedia*, March 20, 2014. This essay provides a historical overview of the anti-Japanese movements in the United States. http://encyclopedia.densho.org/Anti-Japanese_exclusion_movement/. Accessed January 23, 2018.

Bloch, Avital. "The Anti-Chinese and Anti-Japanese Movements in Cananea, Sonora, and Salt Lake River, Arizona, during the 1920 and 1930s." *Americana E-Journal of American Studies in Hungary* 6, no. 1 (Spring 2010). This article compares the history of anti-Chinese and anti-Japanese movements in Arizona. http://americanaejournal.hu/vol6no1/bloch-ortoll. Accessed January 23, 2018.

Also Noteworthy

1945

Emperor Bao Dai is forced to abdicate to Ho Chi Minh and the Viet Minh.

2007

The Viet Museum in Kelley Park, San Jose, California opens.

August 26

1903

Congress passes the Pensionado Act to train Filipino students in the U.S. institution of higher education. By November 3, 1903, 100 Filipino pensionados arrived in California. By 1912, 209 Filipino men and women had been educated through the Pensionado program.

Historically, the pensionados *(students) were the first group of Filipino immigrants. They constituted the first wave in a four-stage immigration process. The* pensionado *stage lasted from 1903 to 1924. . . . Regarding the first wave, in August 1903 the Pensionado Act passed by Congress provided support for selected young Filipino students to pursue college education in the United States. The* pensionados *were enrolled at elite institutions like Harvard, Cornell, Stanford, and the University of California at Berkeley. The goal was that they would absorb the principles of democracy and return to their homeland as representatives of the American way. These students were actively involved in student activities at their campuses. Initially, the Pensionado Act allowed 100 Filipino students to attend colleges and live with American families. In addition, some 14,000 "self-supporting students" entered the United States between 1910 and 1930. But only 10% of these actually enrolled in colleges. . . . After completion of their studies, they returned home to be social, political, and economic leaders. However, their pioneering efforts were continued as thousands of young Filipinos, inspired by the success stories of the* pensionados, *came to the United States in search of education.*

Source: Burgonio-Watson, Thelma. "Filipina Americans: Personal Reflections." In *Nurturing Success: Successful Women of Color and Their Daughters*, edited by Lee Essie, p. 96. Westport, CT: Praeger, 2000.

Books

Baldoz, Rick. *The Third Asiatic Invasion: Migration and Empire in Filipino America, 1898–1946*. New York: New York University Press, 2011. *The Third Asiatic Invasion* investigates the interplay between Filipinos and the United States through immigration policies, race, and struggle for citizenship.

Labrador, Roderick. *Building Filipino Hawai'i*. Urbana: University of Illinois Press, 2015. *Building Filipino Hawai'i* is based on ethnographic as well as archival research. It chronicles the history and formation of the Filipino community in Hawaii.

Websites

Orosa, Mario. The Philippine Pensionado Story. This site offers a history of the Pensionado Act, oral histories of some of the students and their experiences in the United States, photographs, and archival newspaper articles. http://www.orosa.org/The%20Philippine%20Pensionado%20Story3.pdf. Accessed October 13, 2016.

"The Pensionado Act of the Philippines." 2016. This site offers a discussion of the historical background of the Pensionado Act, in addition to listing the names of the pensionados and the institutions they graduated from. https://www.geni.com/projects/The-Pensionado-Act-of-the-Philippines/13372. Accessed October 13, 2016.

August 27

1951

Anna May Wong stars in a DuMont Television Network detective series *The Gallery of Madame Liu-Tsong*. The series, which was written specifically for her, ran from August 27 to November 21, 1951. Wong's character is an art gallery owner who becomes involved in detective work, mystery, and international intrigue. The 10 half-hour episodes aired during prime time, from 9:00 to 9:30 P.M. DuMont canceled the show in 1952, even though it initially planned for a second season. No copies of the show or its scripts are known to exist, except one.

Anna May Wong . . . was still a proven performer. Accepting the starring role in a series offered by Dumont, she became the first Asian-American entertainer to have her own television series. The title was The Egyptian Idol *. . .; Miss Wong played the owner of an art gallery who becomes involved in international intrigue in the art world.*

Dumont was the fourth network in those early days of live television, but the second to become part of this business, closely following NBC. In 1945, it established a link between its Washington, D.C. and New York stations, broadcasting over Channel 5 in both cities. Only those cities received Dumont's entire lineup of programs; WABC in New York and WTTG in Washington. Developed by Dumont Laboratories, which had been founded by the inventor Dr. Allen B. DuMont, it eventually folded in 1956, having failed to capture a large enough segment of the viewing audience to be profitable. Part of the problem was funds for decent production values, one of the factors which doomed Anna May's series. The story goes that all remaining Dumont kinescopes were dumped into one of New York's rivers in the 1970s after it was determined that it would be too expensive to preserve them. In the late 1990s one of the Gallery episodes on 16mm was advertised for sale, according to a noted early TV expert Ed Hurley. It is not known which one, however, but it is good to know at least one episode of this pioneering series has survived.

Source: Leibfried, Philip, and Chei Mi Lane. *Anna May Wong: A Complete Guide to Her Film, Stage, Radio and Television Work*. Jefferson, NC: McFarland & Company, Inc., Publishers, 2004, p. 163.

Books

Chan, Anthony. *Perpetually Cool: The Many Lives of Anna May Wong (1905–1961)*. Lanham, MD: Scarecrow Press, 2003. *Perpetually Cool* is a comprehensive study of Anna May Wong's life, cinematic career, identity, and legacy.

Hodges, Graham Russell Gao. *Anna May Wong: From Laundryman's Daughter to Hollywood Legend*. New York: Palgrave Macmillan, 2004. *Anna May Wong* examines the life of the most well-known Chinese American actress.

Websites

Chung, Nicole. "The Search for Madame Liu-Tsong." Vulture Devouring Culture. September 5, 2017. This article discusses Anna May Wong's *The Gallery of Madame Liu-Tsong*: its history and legacy. http://www.vulture.com/2017/09/the-search-for-the-gallery-of-madame-liu-tsong.html. Accessed February 9, 2018.

De Riggi, Nicola. "Anna May Wong." *Vogue Italia*, January 3, 2013. This essay discusses Anna May Wong's work and includes photographs. http://www.vogue.it/en/magazine/editor-s-blog/2013/01/january-3th#ad-image241226. Accessed February 9, 2018.

Also Noteworthy

1934

The Filipino Labor Union is established in Salinas, California, and calls a strike against the Central California Vegetable Growers and Shippers.

2002

In Boston, Massachusetts, Zachary J. Rolnik, a 40-year-old, is sentenced to two months in prison and fined $5,000 for threatening to kill an Arab American and his family.

August 28

1896

Li Hongzhang (also spelled Li Hong Chang), a special envoy of the Chinese emperor, arrives in New York City, his first stop of an 11-day tour of the United States. Reporters focused on Li's clothes and what he ate. Li met with President Cleveland, the next day. It is alleged that Li fancied eating chop suey during his visit, which journalists widely reported on, making it the best-known Chinese dish among Americans.

As the governor-general of Zhili (Chihli) and the Beiyang Tongshang Dachen (Minister-Superintendent of Trade of Beiyang [Northern China]), Li Hung Chang had been an important figure in handling China's foreign affairs since the 1870s. He had had extensive contacts with American politicians, diplomats, and missionaries. Just a few years before his visit to America, several articles appeared in American magazines introducing this important Chinese policymaker to the American people.

Under pressure from those businessmen who were interested in investing in China's railroads and mining and developing the China market, the Cleveland administration arranged sumptuous receptions for Li's visit. When Li's ship sailed into New York harbor on August 28, 1896, the North Atlantic Squadron paid him "naval honors." On August 29 Cleveland came up to New York from Washington D.C., to hold a presidential reception in ex-Secretary of the Navy William C. Whitney's palatial town houses at 57th Street and Fifth Avenue. Secretary of State Richard Olney took part in most of Li's activities in New York City. There was a grand military parade down Fifth Avenue with Li and Olney riding an open carriage. Li also took a trip up the Hudson River in Cleveland's own boat. The New York Times *inaccurately described Li as "the virtual ruler of more people than are governed by all the monarchs of the continent of Europe" and as "the greatest man the Chinese race has produced since Confucius." It further stated that he was an "absolutely unique figure in the history of the world that has stirred curiosity to its depths." The paper asserted that "no living man, save, possibly the Craz and the Kaiser, could arouse such popular enthusiasm."*

Source: Yu, Renqiu. "Chop Suey: From Chinese Food to Chinese American Food." *Chinese America: History and Perspectives* (1987): pp. 92–93.

Books

Chen, Yong. *Chop Suey, USA: The Story of Chinese Food in America.* New York: Columbia University Press, 2014. *Chop Suey, USA* is a story of chop suey and includes a discussion of Li Hongzhang eating chop suey during his visit to the United States.

Chu, Samuel, and Kwang-Ching Liu, eds. *Li Hung-Chang and China's Early Modernization.* Armonk, NY: M.E. Sharpe, 1994. This is a collection of articles that examines various aspects of Li's life, career, and legacy.

Websites

"Li Hung Chang's American Visit." *San Francisco Call* 80, no. 76 (August 15, 1896). California Digital Newspaper Collection. It's an archival newspaper article about Li's visit. https://cdnc.ucr.edu/cgi-bin/cdnc?a=d&d=SFC18960815.2.30. Accessed February 9, 2018.

Wang, Haixia. "From a Confucian Literati to a Military General: Li Hung Chang's Views of Western Technology (1885–1896)." *Asian Culture and History* 8, no. 2 (2016): 155–159. It's a concise essay that discusses Li's visit to England and the United States. https://mafiadoc.com/li-hung-changs-views-of-western-technology-canadian-center-of-_5a9e5b471723dd9a8448b6a2.html. Accessed August 1, 2018.

Also Noteworthy

1960

Leroy Chiao, astronaut and scientist, is born in Milwaukee, Wisconsin.

1963

Thirty-five members of the Japanese American Citizens League (JACL) participated in the civil rights "March on Washington" with Dr. Martin Luther King Jr. The JACL was the only known Asian American organization represented in this group of 200,000 demonstrators for jobs, freedom, peace, and justice for all Americans regardless of race or ethnic background.

2002

In Santa Barbara, California, Thomas W. Byrne, a 42-year-old, is charged with making terroristic threats, possessing a handgun, and committing a hate crime for attacking and threatening a man of Iranian descent while yelling racial slurs.

August 29

1842

On this day, the First Opium War (1839–1842) ends. China is defeated by the British Empire in the First Opium War, resulting in Treaty of Nanjing whereby China is forced to cede the island of Hong Kong and open ports to foreign commerce. Following China's First Opium War (1839–1842), Chinese migration to the United States began. Conditions in China for much of its population in the mid-19th century were difficult, with widespread flooding and famine between 1846 and 1848 increasing poverty and hunger. Disease and declining markets for Chinese-made products increased tension, and people rebelled against the Qing dynasty. Suppression of the rebellion resulted in an estimated 100 million lives lost between 1850 and 1875. Prosperity of the 18th century had clearly waned, and many in China looked abroad to improve their chances at a better life.

The wars waged in Asia would be responsible for bringing the largest numbers of Asian immigrants to these shores. The earliest major conflict to consider is the first Opium War (1839–1842) between China and Great Britain, which was the result of a trade imbalance between the two countries. The British bought a number of goods from the Chinese (tea, spices, porcelain products, silks, etc.), but the Chinese wanted little but silver from the British.

Source: Wong, Scott K. "War." In *Keywords for Asian American Studies*, edited by Cathy J. Schlund-Vials, K. Scott Wong, and Linda Trinh Vo, p. 239. New York: New York University Press, 2015.

Books

Lovell, Julia. *The Opium War: Drug, Dreams and the Making of China*. London: Picador, 2011. Julia Lovell uses both English and Chinese sources to examine the history and impact of the Opium Wars.

Polachek, James M. *The Inner Opium War*. Cambridge, MA: Council on East Asian Studies, Harvard University, 1992. This book uses archival documents, such as court records and diaries, to examine the debates among Chinese officials on how to deal with importation of opium into China.

Websites

Perdue, Peter. "The First Opium War: The Anglo-Chinese War of 1839–1842." Visualizing Cultures. Massachusetts Institute of Technology. 2011. This site provides a thorough historical account of the First Opium War, using visual art as data. https://ocw.mit.edu/ans7870/21f/21f.027/opium_wars_01/ow1_essay01.html. Accessed October 8, 2016.

Wilkes, Jonny. "In a Nutshell: The Opium Wars." History Revealed. June 14, 2018. This site provides a question-and-answer-style essay on the history and legacy of the Opium Wars. http://www.historyrevealed.com/facts/nutshell-opium-wars. Accessed June 14, 2018.

Also Noteworthy

1914

Under the leadership of Pak Yong-Man (1881–1928), all Korean military training programs are consolidated into the Korean National Brigade in Hawaii. The brigade had roughly 311 cadets who were all training to liberate Korea from Japanese occupation.

August 30

1944

Koreans in the United States organize the Post-War Assistance Society to send relief goods to Korea.

In anticipation of the war's end, Koreans in Hawai'i established the Post-war Assistance Society and collected seven hundred tons of relief supplies for Korea. On the continent, Koreans established another assistance society that operated until 1955. After Japan's surrender on August 15, 1945, the United Korean Committee met in Honolulu and sent a delegation to assist Korean in postwar reconstruction.

Source: Okihiro, Gary. *American History Unbound: Asians and Pacific Islanders*. Berkeley: University of California Press, 2015, p. 358.

Books

Azimi, Nassrine, Matt Fuller, and Hiroko Nakayama, eds. *Post-Conflict Reconstruction in Japan, Republic of Korea, Vietnam, Cambodia, East Timor and Afghanistan*. New York: United Nations, 2003. See section II for discussion of postwar reconstruction in Korea.

Koo, Hagen, ed. *State and Society in Contemporary Korea*. Ithaca, NY: Cornell University Press, 1993. See Stephan Haggard and Chung-in

Moon's Chapter 2, "The State, Politics, and Economic Development in Postwar South Korea."

Websites

Kwon, Tai-Hwan. "Population Change and Development in Korea." Center for Global Education. Asia Society. This essay provides an overview history of Korea's development from the early 20th century to early 21st century. https://asiasociety.org/education/population-change-and-development-korea. Accessed February 10, 2018.

Shen, Zhihua, and Yafeng Xia. "China and the Post-War Reconstruction of North Korea, 1953–1961." Woodrow Wilson International Center for Scholars. Working Paper #4. This report is a detailed analysis of postwar reconstruction in North Korea. https://www.wilsoncenter.org/sites/default/files/NKIDP_Working_Paper_4_China_and_the_Postwar_Reconstruction_of_North_Korea.pdf. Accessed February 10, 2018.

Also Noteworthy

2002

In Palo Alto, California, Sanjay Nair, an 18-year-old Hindu American, rapes a 15-year-old Muslim girl while making derogatory comments about her religion.

August 31

1987

Time magazine cover features a group of Asian American youth, with the headline "Asian American Whiz Kids."

Conservatives were quick to employ the model minority stereotype to argue against the progress of the civil rights movement, as it critiqued the demands of the black, brown, red, and yellow power movements by arguing that American society and institutions are in fact equal. The model minority stereotype was employed to fuel the flames of ethnic antagonism whereby minority groups fight each other instead of the structures and historical conditions that limit their access to resources. By the 1980s, the model minority image had spread to include Koreans, Asian Indians, and new refugees from Vietnam, Cambodia, and Laos. This period also witnessed an increasing number of publications documenting Asian Americans as a model minority, as seen in Scientific American's *"Indochinese Refugee Families and Academic Achievement" (February 1992), Dennis Williams's "Formula for Success" in* Newsweek *(April 23, 1984), and David Brand's article "The New Whiz Kids" in* Time *(August 31, 1987). These popular media accounts document young Asian Americans' academic drive and achievements from elementary school to college; all conclude that their cultural work ethics and value of schooling are key to their success.*

Source: Pham, Mary Thi, and Jonathan H.X. Lee. "Model Minority." In *Asian American Culture: From Anime to Tiger Moms*, edited by Lan Dong, pp. 531–532. Santa Barbara, CA: ABC-CLIO, 2016.

Books

Lee, Robert. *Orientals: Asian Americans in Popular Culture*. Philadelphia, PA: Temple University Press, 1999. *Orientals* examines various aspects of cultural stereotypes of Asian Americans vis-à-vis its origins, evolution, and consequences.

Wu, Ellen. *The Color of Success: Asian Americans and the Origins of the Model Minority*. Princeton, NJ: Princeton University Press, 2014. *The Color of Success* documents the transformation of the image of Asians in the United States from being the "yellow peril" to "model minorities."

Websites

Patel, Viraj. "Challenging the Monolithic Asian American Identity on Campus: A Context for Working with South Asian American Students." *Vermont Connection* 31 (2010): 72–81.

This article analyzes South Asian American students and the model minority stereotype. https://www.uvm.edu/~vtconn/v31/Patel.pdf. Accessed February 10, 2018.

Petersen, William. "Success Story, Japanese-American Style." *New York Times*, January 9, 1966, p. 180. San Francisco University High School. This site provides the full text of the article. http://inside.sfuhs.org/dept/history/US_History_reader/Chapter14/modelminority.pdf. Accessed January 28, 2018.

Also Noteworthy

2002

In Selden, New York, Richard Bossi, a 19-year-old, and Matthew Martin, a 18-year-old, are charged with second-degree aggravated harassment after they taunted and attacked a Pakistani American woman and her 15-year-old son.

September

September 1

1874

The Chinese Mission Home is founded in San Francisco's Chinatown. A California outgrowth of the Philadelphia-based Women's Foreign Missionary Society, the founding group had originally formed to establish an orphanage in Shanghai. However, when the board could not sustain support for the orphanage, they shifted their goals to helping the victims of "slavery" in San Francisco: Chinese women forced into prostitution. Although saving Chinese prostitutes was the main goal, even from its inception the Chinese Mission Home served a broader range of women and the burgeoning Chinese American community. The Home's most famous leader, Donaldina Cameron, persuaded authorities to pass laws allowing judges to grant her temporary custody of girls who could otherwise have been claimed by their exploiters. Additionally, before the establishment of Angel Island in 1909 (and after its abandonment in 1940), Chinese women seeking admission to the United States were often paroled to 920 Sacramento Street, the site of the Mission Home, while immigration authorities decided the cases. Moreover, testimony from Miss Cameron often helped secure favorable outcomes in legal cases, so Chinatown residents and prospective immigrants, as well as immigration officials, often sought the help of the Home.

The home at 920 Sacramento Street gave Cameron a base on the fringe of San Francisco's Chinatown from which she could pursue her prime objective, the destruction of the Chinese slave trade. Assisted by Chinese and American friends, she became a living legend as a crusader, and was credited with helping more than two thousand women and girls who had been smuggled into the United States from China. Cameron broke into brothels and gambling clubs in response to calls for help, brought the women and girls she rescued to "920," fought in court for their custody, and exposed the importers of slave girls. She also developed educational programs at the home, and found staff positions, schools, homes, and husbands for the women assigned by the courts to her as foster daughters. In 1925 she established in Oakland a second home, designed by Julia Morgan, as a refuge for young children. Donaldina Cameron's actions and her persistence corrected American and Chinese neglect of the slave trade and contributed to its demise. Although the last slave girl was admitted to the home as late as 1938, the trade had begun to weaken after the destruction of the old Chinatown in the San Francisco fire of 1906 and as a result of the reforms that followed the Chinese Revolution of 1911. The home continued to serve as a refuge, but by the 1920s its original function had been increasingly replaced by educational and community activities. In the early 1920s all the work of the Presbyterian church related to the Chinese on the west coast was transferred to the Board of National Missions, and the Mission Home became a social service center of the church in the 1930s.

Source: Barth, Gunther. "Cameron, Donaldina Mackenzie." In *Notable American Women: The Modern Period: A Biographical Dictionary*, edited by Barbara Sicherman and Carol Green, p. 131. Cambridge, MA: Harvard University Press, 1980.

Books

Gray, Dorothy. *Women of the West*. Lincoln: University of Nebraska Press, 1976. See Chapter 5, "Minority Women in the West," for discussion related to the work and history of Donaldina Cameron.

Martin, Mildred. *Chinatown's Angry Angel: The Story of Donaldina Cameron*. Palo Alto, CA: Pacific Books, 1977. *Chinatown's Angry Angel* is the biographical history of Donaldina Cameron's life and work as missionary in San Francisco.

Websites

Donaldina Cameron House. 2018. This is the official web page of Cameron House that includes an essay on its history and mission. https://cameronhouse.org/. Accessed January 23, 2018.

Peterson, Art. "Donaldina Cameron House." Shaping San Francisco's Digital Archive. http://www.foundsf.org. This article is a historical essay that details the history of Donaldina Cameron's work in Chinatown and includes photographs. http://www.foundsf.org/index.php?title=Donaldina_Cameron_House. Accessed January 23, 2018.

Also Noteworthy

2011

Viet Stories: Vietnamese American Oral History Project at the University of California, Irvine, is established.

September 2

1885

Rock Springs, Wyoming, witnesses one of the worst instances of anti-Chinese violence. White miners attack Chinese miners in Rock Springs on September 2. Twenty-eight Chinese miners were murdered, 15 wounded, 75 Chinese homes were burned, and hundreds were chased out of town.

On the 3d of September, a telegraph message was received in Boston to the effect that armed men to the number of a hundred or more had on the previous day driven all the Chinese miners employed by the company out of the coal-mines at Rock Springs, Wyoming: had killed and wounded a large number of them; had plundered and burned their quarters, including some fifty houses owned by the company; had stopped all work at the mines; had ordered certain officers of the company's mining department to leave town at an hour's notice; and now demanded, as the condition upon which they would permit the resumption of work in the mines, a pledge that the Chinese should be no longer employed. Later advices on that and the following day not only confirmed the first reports, but increased the number of killed and wounded, and the extent of the destruction of property. . . .

Naturally, an affair involving the killing of between thirty and forty men, the expulsion from their homes of five or six hundred human beings, and the burning and plundering of a hundred houses, attracted general attention. East of the Missouri River, the voice of the press was outspoken and unanimous in condemnation. The universal judgment was that such acts admitted neither of palliation nor excuse. The fact that the victims were of an alien race, not only unarmed with weapons of physical defense, but unprotected by the shield of citizenship—their only dependence being the good faith of the United States Government in the fulfillment of its treaty obligations—was commented upon as a national disgrace; nor did the somewhat deliberate action of the federal authorities in ordering troops to the scene of disturbance escape criticism and censure. Had it then been stated that not one of those concerned in the outrage would ever be brought to justice, and that although these things took place in the light of day, and in plain view of several hundred spectators, no grand jury would ever indict a single person concerned in them, it would have been pronounced a libel upon the administration of justice in any civilized country.

Source: Bromley, Isaac. *The Chinese Massacre at Rock Springs, Wyoming Territory, September 2, 1885*. Boston: Franklin Press, 1886. The full manuscript is available at archive.org. https://archive.org/details/chinesemassacrea00brom. Accessed October 8, 2016.

Books

Lyman, Stanford. *Roads to Dystopia: Sociological Essays on the Postmodern Condition.* Fayetteville: University of Arkansas Press, 2001. *Roads to Dystopia* examines contradictions of the "American Dilemma" in American discourses on race and community. One case study is on the Chinese workers, which includes a discussion of the Rock Springs Riot.

Yung, Judy, Gordon H. Chang, and H. Mark Lai, eds. *Chinese American Voices: From the Gold Rush to the Present*. Berkeley: University of California Press, 2006. This volume contains introductions to accompany primary historical documents. See "Memorial of Chinese Laborers at Rock Springs, Wyoming (1885)."

Websites

Alexander, Dave. "Wyoming Legends: Riot in Rock Springs Leads to Massacre." Legends of America. December 2015. Alexander presents a historical account of the riot citing historical newspaper accounts. It is also accompanied by visual depictions of the historic incident. http://www.legendsofamerica.com/wy-rockspringsriot.html. Accessed October 8, 2016.

Rea, Tom. "The Rock Springs Massacre." WyoHistory.org: A Project of the Wyoming State Historical Society. This site contains a detailed historical essay on the Rock Springs Massacre and links to primary and secondary sources and images. http://www.wyohistory.org/essays/rock-springs-massacre. Accessed October 8, 2016.

1945

Japan formally surrenders to the Allies on board the battleship USS *Missouri*. General Douglas MacArthur, Supreme Commander for the Allied Powers, accepts the formal surrender of Japanese forces in Tokyo Bay. After the surrender ceremony, General MacArthur broadcast a short speech. A Japanese representative reported to the emperor his relief at General MacArthur's generous speech. Signing for the Allied powers were representatives from the United States, China, the Netherlands, the United Kingdom, Union of Soviet Socialist Republics (USSR), Australia, Canada, France, and New Zealand: World War II officially ended.

Today the guns are silent. A great tragedy has ended. A great victory has been won. The skies no longer rain death—the seas bear only commerce men everywhere walk upright in the sunlight. The entire world is quietly at peace. The holy mission has been completed. And in reporting this to you, the people, I speak for the thousands of silent lips, forever stilled among the jungles and the beaches and in the deep waters of the Pacific which marked the way. I speak for the unnamed brave millions homeward bound to take up the challenge of that future which they did so much to salvage from the brink of disaster.

As I look back on the long, tortuous trail from those grim days of Bataan and Corregidor, when an entire world lived in fear, when democracy was on the defensive everywhere, when modern civilization trembled in the balance, I thank a merciful God that he has given us the faith, the courage and the power from which to mold victory. We have known the bitterness of defeat and the exultation of triumph, and from both we have learned there can be no turning back. We must go forward to preserve in peace what we won in war.

A new era is upon us. Even the lesson of victory itself brings with it profound concern, both for our future security and the survival of civilization. The destructiveness of the war potential, through progressive advances in scientific discovery, has in fact now reached a point which revises the traditional concepts of war.

Men since the beginning of time have sought peace. Various methods through the ages have attempted to devise an international process to prevent or settle disputes between nations. From the very start workable methods were found insofar as individual citizens were concerned, but the mechanics of an instrumentality of larger international scope have never been successful. Military alliances, balances of power, leagues of nations, all in turn failed, leaving the only path to be by way of the crucible of war. We have had our last chance. If we do not now devise some greater and more equitable system, Armageddon will be at our door. The problem basically is theological and involves a spiritual recrudescence and improvement of human character that will synchronize with our almost matchless advances in science, art, literature and all material and cultural developments of the past two thousand years. It must be of the spirit if we are to save the flesh.

We stand in Tokyo today reminiscent of our countryman, Commodore Perry, ninety-two years ago. His purpose was to bring to Japan an era of enlightenment and progress, by lifting the veil of isolation to the friendship, trade, and commerce of the world. But alas the knowledge thereby gained of western science was forged into an instrument of oppression and human enslavement. Freedom of expression, freedom of action, even freedom of thought were denied through appeal to superstition, and through the application of force. We are committed by the Potsdam Declaration of principles to see that the Japanese people are liberated from this condition of slavery. It is my purpose to implement this commitment just as rapidly as the armed forces are demobilized and other essential steps taken to neutralize the war potential.

The energy of the Japanese race, if properly directed, will enable expansion vertically rather than horizontally. If the talents of the race are turned into constructive channels, the country can lift itself from its present deplorable state into a position of dignity.

To the Pacific basin has come the vista of a new emancipated world. Today, freedom is on the offensive, democracy is on the march. Today, in Asia as well as in Europe, unshackled peoples are tasting the full sweetness of liberty, the relief from fear.

In the Philippines, America has evolved a model for this new free world of Asia. In the Philippines, America has demonstrated that peoples of the East and peoples of the West may walk side by side in mutual respect and with mutual benefit. The history of our sovereignty there has now the full confidence of the East.

And so, my fellow countrymen, today I report to you that your sons and daughters have served you well and faithfully with the calm, deliberated determined fighting spirit of the American soldier, based upon a tradition of historical truth as against the fanaticism of an enemy supported only by mythological fiction. Their spiritual strength and power has brought us through to victory. They are homeward bound—take care of them.

Source: "General MacArthur's Radio Address to the American People, September 2, 1945." Battleship Missouri Memorial, Pearl Harbor, Hawaii. https://ussmissouri.org/learn-the-history/surrender/general-macarthurs-radio-address#. Accessed January 13, 2017.

Books

Dower, John. *Embracing Defeat: Japan in the Wake of World War II.* New York: W.W. Norton & Company, 2000. *Embracing Defeat*'s main focus is the six years of U.S. occupation of Japan after World War II, but it includes a comprehensive historical discussion of Japan's surrender.

Duffy, Bernard, and Ronald Carpenter. *Douglas MacArthur: Warrior as Wordsmith.* Westport, CT: Greenwood Press, 1997. *Douglas MacArthur: Warrior as Wordsmith* analyzes MacArthur's speeches and how he balances avoiding extreme praise or blame, and his ability to capture audience's attention, with text of the speeches.

Websites

Chen, C. Peter. "Japan's Surrender (14 Aug 1945–2 Sep 1945)." World War II Database. 2017. This site provides historical details on Japan's surrender, documentary of the surrender ceremonies, as well as a detailed surrender timeline. http://ww2db.com/battle_spec.php?battle_id=13. Accessed January 13, 2017.

"1945: Japan Signs Unconditional Surrender." BBC. This site provides a historical overview of events leading the surrender of Japan that ended World War II and includes a timeline and photographs. http://news.bbc.co.uk/onthisday/hi/dates/stories/september/2/newsid_3582000/3582545.stm. Accessed January 13, 2017.

Also Noteworthy

1899

The Buddhist Churches of America is established in San Francisco.

1911

Sun Yat-sen begins his tour of the United States.

September 3

1908

On this day, the district court in Washington rules that Buntaro Kumagai, a Japanese alien who had served honorably in the U.S. Army, is ineligible for citizenship (*In re Buntaro Kumagai*) because people of Japanese ancestry are not "white."

Rather than address the question of whether military naturalization laws provided a challenge to the ideology of race-based citizenship, Judge Hanford shifted the legal issue to whether Congress had intended military naturalization to provide an exception to laws limiting naturalization to whites and blacks. In presenting the court's ruling, Judge Hanford held that because both the Act of July 17, 1862, which had authorized military naturalization, and the (Naturalization) Act of February 18, 1875, which limited naturalization to whites and blacks, had been incorporated into succeeding immigration and naturalization laws, Congress must have intended military naturalization to give away to the broader framework of race-based naturalization.

Source: Sohoni, Deenesh. "Fighting to Belong: Asian-American Military Service and American Citizenship." In *Inclusion in the American Military: A Force for Diversity*, edited by David Rohall, Morten Ender, and Michael Matthews, p. 66. Lanham, MD: Lexington Books, 2017.

Books

Lopez, Ian Haney. *White by Law: The Legal Construction of Race*. New York: New York University Press, 1996. *White by Law* is a legal history of the social-political-construction of "race."

Rohall, David, Morten Ender, and Michael Matthews, eds. *Inclusion in the American Military: A Force for Diversity*. Lanham, MD: Lexington Books, 2017. *Inclusion in the American Military* is a study of diversity in the U.S. military.

Websites

In Re Buntaro Kumagai. https://archive.org/. The full text of the district court ruling is available at https://archive.org/details/jstor-2186149. Accessed January 23, 2018.

Sohoni, Deenesh, and Amin Vafa. "The Fight to Be American: Military Naturalization and Asian Citizenship." *Asian American Law Journal* 17 (January 2010): 119–151. This article is a legal history of court cases that constructed the shifting parameters of citizenship for Asian Americans. https://scholarship.law.berkeley.edu/cgi/viewcontent.cgi?article=1164&context=aalj. Accessed January 23, 2018.

September 4

1907

A horde of 400–500 white working men in Bellingham, Washington, gather to drive a community of South Asians out of the city. By the end of the day, 125 South Asians had been driven out of town, 6 were hospitalized, and roughly 400 were held in jail for "protective custody." Since 1905, the *San Francisco Chronicle* launched an anti-Asian campaign to stop Asian migration to the United States. In this article, their opposition to Asian migration is to protect the Asian migrants.

This Hindoos employed in the mills about Bellingham, in Washington, have been forcibly expelled by the white laborers with the evident approval of a controlling majority of the community. It is unnecessary to say that the "Chronicle" is utterly opposed to violence of that kind, wherever it occurs, and no matter against whom directed. No one, however, who is familiar with conditions as they are in California, Iowa or Massachusetts can doubt that such outbreaks are certain to occur wherever the masses of white men and masses of Orientals compete in the same community for the same work. They may be punished, but they cannot be prevented.

It is for this reason that we strongly insist that before it is too late all immigration of Oriental labor shall be stopped—not by any "treaty," heaven forbid—but by an act of Congress, signed by the President and rigorously enforced. It is the only way to keep the friendship of Oriental nations. The "Chronicle" believes the presence of these people in this country wholly undesirable from all standpoints, but even if it were not so ordinary prudence and rational statesmanship demand that Oriental and Occidental labor shall keep each to its own continent.

Source: "Oriental Complications: British Subjects Driven Out of One of Our Sister States." *San Francisco Chronicle*, September 9, 1907.

Books

Bhatt, Amy, and Nalini Iyer. *Roots and Reflections: South Asians in the Pacific Northwest.* Seattle: University of Washington Press, 2013. *Roots and Reflections* employs oral histories to narrate the historical and contemporary South Asian migration experience in the Pacific Northwest.

Jensen, Joan. *Passage from India: Asian Indian Immigrants in North America.* New Haven, CT: Yale University Press, 1988. *Passage from India* is a general history of immigrants from India to the United States and Canada from the early 1900s to the 1920s.

Websites

Cahn, David. "The 1907 Bellingham Riots in Historical Context." Seattle Civil Rights & Labor History Project. University of Washington, 2008. This site provides a detailed history of this riot, historical photographs, and link to *Present in All That We Do*, a documentary film about this riot. http://depts.washington.edu/civilr/bham_history.htm. Accessed October 14, 2016.

South Asian American Digital Archive. This site provides primary documents and descriptions of them related to the Bellingham riot. https://www.saada.org/browse/subject/bellingham-riot. Accessed October 14, 2016.

1945

The Western Defense Command issues Public Proclamation No. 24 revoking exclusion orders and military restrictions against Japanese Americans.

Excerpt from poet Toyo Suyemoto's memoir.

The first week of September 1945, the Western Defense Command issued Public Proclamation No. 24, revoking all individual exclusion orders and all further military restrictions against persons of Japanese descent. So came the end to a peculiar, catastrophic experience, our American experience. What we now had before us was to decide how we would leave camp and resume a normal life.

Source: Suyemoto, Toyo. *I Call to Remembrance: Toyo Suyemoto's Years of Internment*. Edited by Susan Richardson. New Brunswick, NJ: Rutgers University Press, 2007, p. 194.

Books

Daniels, Roger. *Concentration Camps North America: Japanese in the United States and Canada during World War II.* Malabar, FL: Robert E. Krieger Publishing Co., 1993. *Concentration Camps* is the history of "our worst wartime mistake" that details the forced relocation and imprisonment of Japanese Americans from California, Oregon, and Washington.

Robinson, Greg. *A Tragedy of Democracy: Japanese Confinement in North America.* New York: Columbia University Press, 2009. *A Tragedy of Democracy* provides a comprehensive critical and transnational analysis of official government policy toward West Coast Japanese Americans in North America.

Websites

"Timeline: Japanese Americans during World War II." National Park Service. It is a detailed chronology of the Japanese American experience during World War II. https://www.nps.gov/tule/planyourvisit/upload/WWII_%20JA_timeline_2010.pdf. Accessed January 23, 2018.

"Western Defense Command." *Densho Encyclopedia*, January 21, 2014. This essay is a history of the Western Defense Command. http://encyclopedia.densho.org/Western_Defense_Command/. Accessed January 23, 2018.

Also Noteworthy

1885

Five hundred Chinese are driven out of Rock Springs, Wyoming, by coal miners; 28 Chinese are killed.

2001

In Chicago, Illinois, a man attacks a female Muslim student on a college campus.

2012

Maya Kasandra Soetoro-Ng (b. August 15, 1970), President Barack Obama's half sister, highlights his administration's accomplishments at the 2012 Democratic National Convention in Charlotte, North Carolina, with First Lady Michelle Obama's older brother, Craig Robinson.

September 5

1885

Five white men and 2 Indians attack a camp of 35 Chinese at the hopyard of the Wold brothers in Squak, or Issaquah Valley. The attackers fired into the tents, killing 3 Chinese and wounding 3 others.

The news of the Wyoming outrage, instead of being universally condemned, was loudly applauded by the masses, and the next day, September 5, 1885, an attack more cowardly and brutal was made upon a party of Chinese hop pickers in Issaquah Valley. The Wyoming mob set upon their victims in broad daylight and the latter had some show to defend themselves, but at Issaquah they were set upon as they slept in their tents and three of them shot to death by hidden assailants under the cover of darkness. The others escaped with their lives by plunging into the stream that ran past their camp and then hiding in the thick brush along its banks until they could get away in safety. It was a matter of current knowledge in the community where this murder was committed who were they guilty leaders and followers, but public sentiment was so strong that although they were brought to trail no conviction could be secured. These two widely separated outrages added fuel to the flames. Public meetings were held in almost every town and village west of the Cascades and north of the Columbia. Incendiary speeches were made, applauding the work of the murderers and exhorting the people to similar deeds. The determination was openly expressed to rid the country of the Chinamen at all hazards, peaceably if possible, otherwise by intimidation, assault and murder if need be.

Source: Bagley, Clarence. *History of Seattle from the Earliest Settlement to the Present Time*. Vol. II. Chicago, IL: The S. J. Clarke Publishing Company, 1916, p. 458

Books

Grant, Frederic, ed. *History of Seattle, Washington*. New York: American Publishing and Engraving Co., 1891. See Chapter 7, "The Anti-Chinese Agitation."

Pfaelzer, Jean. *Driven Out: The Forgotten War against Chinese Americans*. Berkeley: University of California Press, 2007. Jean Pfaelzer used primary documents, such as newspaper articles, to narrate the societal impact of the anti-Chinese movement from 1848 into the 20th century.

Websites

"Mapping Anti-Chinese Violence." The Tacoma Method. This site discusses the anti-Chinese movement in Washington. https://www.tacomamethod.com/mapping-antichinese-violence/. Accessed January 24, 2018.

"Violence." Chinese in Northwest American Research Committee. June 7, 2017. This site discusses upward of 50 cases of anti-Chinese violence in the Pacific Northwest. http://www.cinarc.org/Violence.html. Accessed January 24, 2018.

September 6

1899

The United States proposes the Open Door Policy for China, calling for maintaining free trade with the United States, Britain, Germany, Japan, and other major world powers.

The United States and Great Britain had been trading with China long before John Hay proposed the Open Door Policy. However, China's increasingly important markets were becoming a source of international tensions, and Hay wish to find a way to maintain the U.S.'s influence. Hay's inspiration came from British and American experts William R. Rockhill (1854–1914) and Alfred E. Hippisley (1842–1940), who held that Great Britain and the United States had to protect and advance their economic interests in China. Both men suggested drafting a formal statement of principles, which outlined the concept of maintaining an Open Door Policy for trade and commerce. It aimed to protect the equal privileges among countries trading with China and to support Chinese territorial and administrative integrity.

The statement was issued in the form of a circular Open Door Notes and sent by Hay on September 6, 1899, to other foreign nations interested in trade and commerce with China, including Great Britain, Germany, France, Russia, and Japan. These countries were all still protective over their own economic presence in China and other Asian countries. The 1899 Open Door Notes proposed three main points. First, they called for a free, open market between foreign merchants with a presence in China. This meant that each power needed to have free access to a treaty port or to any other vested interest within its sphere. Hay's argument was that the Open Door Policy would help reinforce U.S. economic capacities and decrease tensions between the great powers having a sphere in China. Second, taxes on trade should be collected only by China; Hay maintained that dissolving economic advantages between China and its foreign occupants was an effort to eliminate discriminatory treatment in trade and commerce. Third, the Notes declared that no great power already operating in China was to be granted exemptions from paying harbor dues or railroad charges.

Source: Nguyen, Hang. "Open Door Policy." In *Reforming America: A Thematic Encyclopedia and Document Collection on the Progressive Era*, edited by Jeffery Johnson, p. 92. Santa Barbara, CA: ABC-CLIO, 2017.

Books

Israel, Jerry. *Progressivism and the Open Door: America and China, 1905–1921*. Pittsburgh, PA: University of Pittsburgh Press, 1971. *Progressivism and the Open Door* studies the factors that developed into formal U.S. policy toward China.

Moore, Gregory. *Defining and Defending the Open Door Policy: Theodore Roosevelt and China, 1901–1909*. Lanham, MD: Lexington Books, 2015. *Defining and Defending the Open Door Policy* examines Roosevelt and his administration's policy on foreign relations between China and America and discusses Chinese exclusion.

Websites

Cheng, Dean. "The Complicated History of U.S. Relations with China." The Heritage Foundation. This essay provides an overview of the history of China and U.S. relations. https://www.heritage.org/asia/report/the-complicated-history-us-relations-china. Accessed February 10, 2018.

"Secretary of State John Hay and the Open Door in China, 1899–1900." Office of the Historian. Bureau of Public Affairs. U.S. Department of State. This essay discusses Secretary John Hay's role in developing the Open Door China policy. https://history.state.gov/milestones/1899-1913/hay-and-china. Accessed February 10, 2018.

September 7

1940

Korean nationalist Kilsoo Kenneth Haan, leader of the Sino-Korean People's League, urges Korean residents living in Hawaii to register as Koreans, and not as Japanese, since at that time, Korea was occupied by Japan.

> *At first, Haan showed no evidence of Yellow Peril ideas, and his background instead bred in him a racialist type of Korean nationalism. He was born in Changdan, Korea (near Seoul), arrived in Honolulu as a five-year-old in 1905, and received little formal education, completing only the eighth grade. But from his education at the Korean Compound, a boarding school established in 1906 for Hawai'i's Korean children, he learned Syngman Rhee's... Korean racialist nationalism: "You are Americans by birth, but you are Koreans by blood. Someday you will be builders of [a] new Korea. Mingle yourselves with Korean boys and girls. Study hard the Korean language and Korean history if you truly love your fatherland."*
>
> *Source*: Hayashi, Brian Masaru. "Kilsoo Haan, American Intelligence, and the Anticipated Japanese Invasion of California, 1931–1943." *Pacific Historical Review* 83, no. 2 (May 2014): p. 283.

Books

Kim, Richard. *The Quest for Statehood: Korean Immigrant Nationalism and U.S. Sovereignty, 1905–1945*. New York: Oxford University Press, 2011. *The Quest for Statehood* examines the role of Korean immigrants in Korea's independence movement, and their engagement with American civil and political activities, that ultimately assimilated them to America.

Thompson, Robert. *A Time for War: Franklin Delano Roosevelt and the Path to Pearl Harbor*. Upper Saddle River, NJ: Prentice Hall Press, 1991. *A Time for War* includes a discussion of Kilsoo Haan warning the U.S. government of Japan's planned attack on Pearl Harbor.

Websites

Kim, Richard. "Kilsoo Haan." *Densho Encyclopedia*, September 17, 2015. This essay provides a biography of Haan and his work before, during, and after World War II. http://encyclopedia.densho.org/Kilsoo%20Haan/. Accessed February 10, 2018.

Macmillan, Michael. "Unwanted Allies: Koreans as Enemy Aliens in World War II." *Hawaiian Journal of History* 19 (1985): 179–203. This article discusses Korean's vexing national identity during World War II as Korea was a colony of Japan and was considered "Japanese" although many considered themselves "stateless." https://evols.library.manoa.hawaii.edu/bitstream/handle/10524/571/JL19199.pdf?sequence=1. Accessed February 10, 2018.

Also Noteworthy

1907

A riot against Asians in the Chinese and Japanese sections of Vancouver, British Columbia, erupts.

September 8

1965

On this day, the Agricultural Workers Organizing Committee (AWOC) initiates the historic Delano Grape Strike. It is led by Larry Dulay Itliong, Pete Velasco, Andy Imutan, and Philip Vera Cruz. They went to Cesar Chavez and asked the mostly Latino members of the National Farm Workers Association to join them, which they voted to do on September 16, 1965. This strike is one of the most well-known strikes of modern U.S. labor history that blended labor and civil rights agendas and lasted five years.

Soon after the AWOC called the strike the primarily Mexican American National Farm Workers Association under Cesar E. Chavez joined and later merged to become the United Farm Workers Organizing Committee (UFWOC; now known as the United Farm Workers). Among the other issues the UFWOC engaged through the strike were the use of dangerous and toxic pesticides on fruits and vegetables, the differential wages between Mexican and Filipino farm workers and Braceros *(i.e., contract laborers from Mexico brought to the United States through a federal program designed to alleviate agricultural labor shortages during World War II), deplorable living conditions, the use of undocumented workers as strikebreakers and the general dignity of working-class people. In addition to the strike by workers themselves, the movement gained momentum through a highly publicized consumer secondary boycott of grocery stores that sold nonunionized California grapes that, due to the use of pesticides, also posed general public health risks. A dramatic 350-mile march by the united Filipino and Mexican farm workers from Delano to California's state capital, Sacramento, also brought the plight of agricultural labor to a national audience. After several long years, in 1970 the UFW finally signed contracts with major grape growers. Because of antimiscegenation laws the Filipino farm workers remained largely a bachelor society and by the end of the 1970s most had retired; however, the UFW now affiliated with the Change To Win Federation, continues to push for social and economic justice for farm workers today.*

Source: DeGuzman, Jean-Paul. "Filipino Farm Labor Union (FFLU)." In *Asian Americans: An Encyclopedia of Social, Cultural, Economic, and Political History*, edited by Xiaojian Zhao and Edward Park, p. 411. Santa Barbara, CA: ABC-CLIO, 2014.

Books

Dunne, John. *Delano: The Story of the California Grape Strike*. New York: Farrar, Straus & Giroux, 1967. *Delano: The Story of the California Grape Strike* is a memoir of Dunne's observations during the strike with analysis of Chavez's legacy.

Pawel, Miriam. *The Union of Their Dreams: Power, Hope, and Struggle in Cesar Chavez's Farm Worker's Movement*. New York: Bloomsbury Press, 2009. See Chapter 5, "Please Don't Eat Grapes."

Websites

Morehouse, Lisa. "The Forgotten Filipino-Americans Who Led the '65 Delano Grape Strike." KQED News, September 7, 2015. This essay documents the untold stories of Filipino Americans in the Delano Grape Strike that includes audio interviews, photographs, and links to new research on this topic. https://ww2.kqed.org/news/2015/09/07/50-years-later-the-forgotten-origins-of-the-historic-delano-grape-strike/. Accessed January 23, 2018.

"This Day in UFW history—September 8, 1965." United Farm Workers. March 21, 2017. This site provides a concise history of the strike's origins. http://ufw.org/day-ufw-history-september-8-1965/. Accessed January 23, 2018.

Also Noteworthy

1907

Fighting between South Asian and white workers erupts at West Mill, Aberdeen, Washington.

1993

The movie adaption of Amy Tan's *The Joy Luck Club* (1989) is released.

September 9

1924

On this day, violence erupts in Hanapepe on the island of Kauai as police fire on a mass of strikers, killing 16 and wounding others (4 policemen were killed as well). The incident became known as the Hanapepe Massacre. Over 160 strikers were jailed and 76 were indicted for rioting, with 57 others pleading guilty to assault and battery charges. Indicative of the collusion between the sugar industry and local authorities, a county attorney was assisted by two special deputy attorney generals hired and paid for by the Hawaiian Sugar Planters' Association in the ensuing legal proceedings.

The HSPA used the territorial legal system to punish strike participants jailed in the aftermath of the Hanapepe massacre. Planters subsidized the prosecution of activists, providing financial aid to county law enforcement and supplying extra legal counsel to the local district attorney's offices to assist with the trails. Public sentiment against the Hanapepe workers ran high, as local politicians and the press labeled them as violent troublemakers. Although there was little local sympathy for the Hanapepe strikers, they did receive some support from concerned political leaders back home. Members of the Philippine legislature passed a resolution demanding an official investigation of labor conditions in Hawaii in response to the Hanapepe massacre, but American colonial officials ultimately derailed these efforts. . . . Seventy-two Filipinos were charged with rioting for their role in the Hanapepe affair (another fifty-seven pleaded guilty to other charges before going to trial). The HSPA capitalized on the trails to make an example of the strikers, hoping to send a strong message to other potential partisans. The limitless resources, both financial and political, of the HSPA made the outcome of the trial a forgone conclusion. The strikers never had a chance for a fair hearing on Kauai, and in fact, they were not even granted legal counsel until after the trial had already begun. Sixty of the defendants were eventually found guilty of various charges (e.g., assault, vagrancy, rioting) in connection with the Hanapepe incident, receiving sentences ranging from four to ten years in prison. The trial judge, parroting the HSPA party line on the 1924 strike, blamed the massacre on the violent and "anti-American" ideology of Filipino labor leaders.

Source: Baldoz, Rick. *The Third Asiatic Invasion: Empire and Migration in Filipino America, 1898–1946*. New York: New York University Press, 2011, pp. 58–59.

Books

Chapin, Helen. *Shaping History: The Role of Newspapers in Hawai'i*. Honolulu: University of Hawaii Press, 1996. See Chapter 20, "Suppressing the News and Contributing to a Massacre."

Jung, Moon-Kie. *Reworking Race: The Making of Hawaii's Interracial Labor Movement*. New York: Columbia University Press, 2006. *Reworking Race* is a history of the development of the multiracial and multiethnic International Longshoremen's and Warehousemen's Union in Hawaii.

Websites

Alegado, Dean. "Blood in the Fields: The Hanapepe Massacre and the 1924 Filipino Strike." *Positively Filipino*, November 26, 2012. This essay is a historical account of the strike and massacre and its impact on Asian laborers in Hawaii. http://www.positivelyfilipino.com/magazine/2012/11/26/blood-in-the-fields-the-hanapepe-massacre-and-the-1942-filipino-strike. Accessed January 23, 2018.

Hill, Tiffany. "A Massacre Forgotten." *Honolulu* magazine, December 30, 2009. This essay discusses the history of the Hanapepe Massacre and its legacy. http://www.honolulumagazine.com/Honolulu-Magazine/January-2010/A-Massacre-Forgotten/. Accessed January 23, 2018.

Also Noteworthy

2008

Grace Meng (b. October 1, 1975) wins the general election with 86 percent of the vote for the member of the New York State Assembly in the 22nd Assembly District. She is the first Asian American to represent part of New York in Congress.

September 10

2003

Army Capt. James J. Yee is arrested "for suspicion of espionage and aiding captured Taliban and al-Qaida fighters."

Captain Yee was arrested while returning to the States for a two-week leave with his wife and daughter. Yee was arrested by the FBI at the Jacksonville, Florida, Naval Air Station and whisked away in shackles, blackened eye goggles, and soundproof earmuffs to an isolation cell in the U.S. Navy brig in Charleston, South Carolina, where he was kept for 76 days. Yee was charged with five offenses: sedition, spying, espionage, aiding the alleged Taliban and Al Qaeda prisoners, and failure to obey general orders. After months of government investigation, all criminal charges against Yee were dropped. Yee was then reinstated to full duty at Fort Lewis, Washington. Even though he was assured his record would be wiped clean, Yee sensed his superiors and his fellow chaplains maintained doubts about his loyalty. On January 7, 2005, Yee received an honorable discharge from the U.S. Army. Upon separation, Yee received an Army Commendation medal for "exceptionally meritorious service." Captain Yee's defense fund was organized by Justice for New Americans, first formed during the case of Wen Ho Lee, the Taiwan-born Los Alamos National Laboratory scientist who was arrested by the FBI in 1999 and found not guilty after 10 months in solitary confinement and the ruination of his career. The FBI had initially investigated Lee as a potential Chinese spy, but never had any evidence to back up the charge.

Source: Lee, Jonathan H. X. "Yee, James J. (1968–)." In *Asian American Religious Cultures*, edited by Jonathan H. X. Lee, Fumitaka Matsuoka, Edmond Yee, and Ronald Nakasone, pp. 975–976. Santa Barbara, CA: ABC-LIO, 2015.

Books

Kurashige, Lon, and Alice Yang, eds. *Major Problems in Asian American History: Documents and Essays*. 2nd ed. Boston, MA: Cengage Learning, 2017. See Chapter 15, "Asian Americans and National Security," Section 4, "Former Guantanamo Chaplain James Yee Is Exonerated after Being Imprisoned as a Terrorist."

Yee, James. *For God and Country: Faith and Patriotism under Fire*. New York: PublicAffairs Books, 2005. *For God and Country* is Yee's memoir.

Websites

"Justice for Yee." 2010. This is the official web page for James Yee. http://www.justiceforyee.com. Accessed January 23, 2018.

New York Times. 2018. This site contains an index of articles published in the *New York Times* related to James J. Yee. http://topics.nytimes.com/top/reference/timestopics/people/y/james_j_yee/index.html. Accessed January 23, 2018.

September 11

2001

The terrorist attacks on September 11, 2001, have had a big impact on South Asian Americans (i.e., Bangladeshi, Nepali, Pakistani, Sri Lankan, Indian), in particular Sikh Americans because they wear turban. The media treatment of the event from a religious standpoint, however, created anti-Muslim, Islamophobic sentiments and unprecedented fear. Asian Muslim Americans have experienced the most emotional and psychological stress. In the months following 9/11, there was an overwhelming fear of detention and deportation among Asian Muslim Americans. Due to Islamophobia and religious racialization, South Asian American, Sikh American, and Asian Muslim American citizens were afraid that they or their families could become victims of hate crimes. Women who wore hijab were targets for harassment on the street, and many also experienced workplace discrimination. The mass media, government policies, and restrictions all contributed to hate crimes and public paranoia against any Asian American who looked like or resembled a "Muslim."

Immediately after the attacks, individuals who appeared Middle Eastern or had Arabic- or Islamic-sounding names became the scapegoats of Americans' anger and vengeance. Balbir Singh Sodhi was the first murder victim of the backlash because his traditional Sikh looks—dastaar (turban) and kesh (unshorn hair)—were confused with Osama Bin Laden's kaffiyeh (male headdress) and beard. Ironically, Sikhs are neither Arab nor Muslim. Hate crimes and bias incidents spiked immediately. According to the organization South Asian American Leaders of Tomorrow (SAALT 2001), 645 bias incidents were reported in metropolitan newspaper across the country in the week after 9/11. The New York Times *put it most succinctly: "Since the attacks, people who look Middle Eastern and Muslim, whatever their religion or nation of origin, have been singled out for harassment, threats and assaults." More seriously, a few weeks after 9/11, the U.S. government generated a series of initiatives and policies that targeted Middle Eastern and Muslim immigrant populations, especially men. Ostensibly, these decrees, administrative rule changes, executive orders, and laws aimed to stop terrorism; however, they legitimized the backlash in the eyes of the American public. From the perspective of Middle Eastern and Muslim Americans, it seemed as if the government was condoning stereotyping and scapegoating.*

Source: Bakalian, Anny, and Mehdi Bozorgmehr. *Backlash 9/11: Middle Eastern and Muslim Americans Respond.* Berkeley: University of California Press, 2009, pp. 1–2.

Books

De, Aparajita, ed. *South Asian Racialization and Belonging after 9/11: Masks of Threat.* Lanham, MD: Lexington Books, 2016. In this anthology, essays examine the post–9/11 racialization of South Asian Americans that vexingly correlates South Asian Americans to terrorism and threats to national security.

Maira, Sunaina. *The 9/11 Generation: Youth, Rights, and Solidarity in the War on Terror.* New York: New York University Press, 2016. *The 9/11 Generation* is an ethnographic study of Arab, South Asian, and Afghan American youth resistance to and encounters with America's War on Terror.

Websites

Maniar, Sacha. "16 Years after 9/11, We Can't Be Silent Anymore." Asian Americans Advancing Justice. Asian Law Caucus. September 11, 2017. This essay discusses the continued racialization of Asian Americans as "terrorist" and hate crimes that result from Islamophobic beliefs. https://www.advancingjustice-alc.org/news_and_media/16-years-after-911-we-cant-be-silent-anymore/. Accessed January 23, 2018.

"Post 9–11 Backlash." South Asian Americans Leading Together. This is an Asian American civil rights organization that seeks to address hate crimes against South Asian, Sikh, Muslim, and Arab Americans since November 2015. http://saalt.org/policy-change/post-9-11-backlash/. Accessed January 23, 2018.

Also Noteworthy

1885

Chinese are attacked in Coal Creek, Washington.

2001

In Ronkonkoma, New York, Brian Harris, 29, is charged with a hate crime after he held an Arab American at gunpoint while making anti-Arab threats.

In Eugene, Oregon, Christopher Paul Younce, 33, is charged with a hate crime after making threatening anti-Muslim phone calls to the Islamic Cultural Center.

2007

On the sixth anniversary of the 9/11 terrorist attack, Michael Estes, 32, is charged with disorderly conduct after he cursed at an imam at an Islamic community center at Tempe, Arizona.

September 12

1934

Tadashi Tadano, a Japanese American farmer, is a victim of anti-Japanese hate crime that is part and parcel of a mass movement to drive out Japanese farmers from Arizona.

In the early hours of September 19, 1934, three separate dynamite explosions shattered the stillness in the vicinity of Japanese homes and farmland in Arizona's Salt River Valley. Two of the bombs landed approximately eight to a hundred feet away from the targeted residences of Fred Okuma and Ryemon Asano; and at Frank Sugino's farm near Mesa, a blast tore out a floodgate, inundated twenty acres of land, and slightly damaged his roof and a window screen. One week earlier another farmer, Tadashi Tadano, was tending a floodgate on his farm when fifteen masked men in six automobiles approached, pulled pistols, and ordered him to raise his hands. The men left only after firing two shots over Tadano's head and two into his truck, which they had shoved into an irrigation canal. According to historian Jack August, these and other acts of terrorism against Japanese farmers in the Salt River Valley were caused when local white farmers, suffering from depressed economic conditions and angered by alien agricultural excellence, organized a movement to oust all Japanese farmers from the valley in 1934 and 1935. Trying to capitalize on the "yellow menace" for the September 11 elections in 1935, politicians had also hurled accusations at Japanese farmers in an opportunistic effort to gain favor among white constituents. Soon after the September 19 incidents, an Arizona Republic editorial condemned the agitators: "The fools who have been recklessly tossing dynamite about are yet to learn that grievances cannot be adjusted by terrorism. They will learn before this incident is closed that dynamite possesses an even greater explosive quality than they had supposed. They will know that the detonation has been heard as far to the west as Tokyo, and . . . to the east as far as Washington. Dynamite is a weapon peculiarly, of cowards and criminals."

Source: Melton, Brad. "Prelude to War." In *Arizona Goes to War: The Home Front and the Front Lines during World War II*, edited by Brad Melton and Dean Smith, pp. 3–4. Tucson: University of Arizona Press, 2003.

Books

Daniels, Roger. *The Politics of Prejudice: The Anti-Japanese Movement in California and the Struggle for Japanese Exclusion*. Berkeley: University of California Press, 1977. *The Politics of Prejudice* covers the history of anti-Japanese movements in California.

Walz, Eric. *Nikkei in the Interior West: Japanese Immigration and Community Building, 1882–1945*. Tucson: University of Arizona Press, 2012. *Nikkei in the Interior West* is a history of the Japanese American experience in Arizona, Colorado, Idaho, Nebraska, and Utah.

Websites

Bloch, Avital. "The Anti-Chinese and Anti-Japanese Movements in Cananea, Sonora, and Salt Lake River, Arizona, during the 1920 and 1930s." *Americana E-Journal of American Studies in Hungary* 6, no. 1 (Spring 2010). This article compares the history of anti-Chinese and anti-Japanese movements in Arizona. http://americanaejournal.hu/vol6no1/bloch-ortoll. Accessed January 23, 2018.

Murray, Vince, and Scott Solliday. "City of Phoenix: Asian American Historic Property Survey." Arizona Historical Research. This report is a comprehensive historical survey of the

Asian American communities and properties in Phoenix, Arizona. See the section on Japanese Americans that discusses Japanese Americans in Arizona in general, and Phoenix in particular. http://azhistory.net/aahps/f_aahps.pdf. Accessed January 23, 2018.

Also Noteworthy

2001

Faiza Ejaz, a Pakistani American woman, is a victim of a hate crime outside a mall in Huntington, New York. While waiting for her husband to pick her up, Adam Lang, a 76-year-old man, sitting in his car started driving toward her. Ejaz jumped out of the way and ran into the mall. Lang got out and shouted he was "doing this for my country." He was arrested and charged with first-degree reckless endangerment.

In Salt Lake City, Utah, Michael Herrick, a 31-year-old white man, is charged with a hate crime after starting a fire in a Pakistani family restaurant.

September 13

1879

Harper's Weekly publishes an illustration titled "The Nigger Must Go" and "The Chinese Must Go." The caption read, "The poor barbarians can't understand our civilized Republican form of government." The illustrator, Thomas Nast, was showing a visual division and public debate regarding African and Chinese place in American society.

February 1871 saw the publication of one of Thomas Nast's most powerful "pro-Chinese" drawings, a direct and angry response to the Chinese labor protests at Tompkins Square and North Arlington. Titled "The Chinese Question," the drawing depicts Columbia standing at center stage defending a huddled, overwhelmed Chinese American man. She looks fiercely at a crowd of armed male rioters, shouting, "Hands off, gentlemen! America means fair play for all men." The rioters' faces are portrayed as threatening and animal-like, with deep-set beady eyes and menacing scowls. The leader is typical of Nast's anti-Irish caricatures; he holds a rock in one hand and a raised billy club in the other. The crowd has just burned down a "colored" orphan asylum during the New York City Draft Riots and are now ready to go after "John Chinaman." The wall of posters behind Columbia reproduces specific statements made about the Chinese; John Swinton's four objections to Chinese immigration are quoted verbatim, as is a racist statement by Wendell Phillips ("The Chinaman works cheap because he is a barbarian and seeks gratification of only the lowest, the most inevitable wants"). Democratic newspapers and trade unions are clearly represented as having stirred up hatred toward the poor "Chinaman." . . . Racial groups were portrayed in Nast's drawings as caught between the purity and ideals of Columbia's America and the America of the unruly Democratic Party, marked by prejudice and mob violence. Nast consistently tried to draw parallels between the Chinese Question and the injustice visited upon African Americans, American Indians, and European immigrants.

Source: Tchen, John. *New York before Chinatown: Orientalism and the Shaping of American Culture 1776–1882*. Baltimore, MD: Johns Hopkins University Press, 1999, p. 205.

Books

Halloran, Fiona. *Thomas Nast: The Father of Modern Political Cartoons*. Chapel Hill: University of North Carolina Press, 2012. *Thomas Nast* is a biography of the artist and history of his works.

Wong, Edlie. *Racial Reconstruction: Black Inclusion, Chinese Exclusion, and the Fictions of Citizenship*. New York: New York University Press, 2015. See Chapter 2, "From Emancipation to Exclusion: Racial Analogy in Afro-Asian Periodical Print Culture," which includes a discussion and analysis of Thomas Nast's anti-Chinese racist cartoons and illustrations.

Websites

Nast, Thomas. "The Nigger Must Go" and "The Chinese Must Go." Library of Congress Digital Repository. The digital version of the image is available, as well as background information on the illustration. https://www.loc.gov/item/2010644337/. Accessed January 23, 2018.

"The Nigger Must Go" and "The Chinese Must Go." 1879. These are illustrations on Chinese Exclusion. This site contains cartoons and illustrations by Thomas Nast with explanations. https://thomasnastcartoons.com/2014/04/01/the-nigger-must-go-and-the-chinese-must-go/. Accessed January 23, 2018.

Also Noteworthy

2001

Partick Cunningham attempts to burn Issa Qandeel's car at the Idris Mosque in Seattle, Washington. Police later discovered that he planned to burn cars around the mosque's driveway because of the anger as a result of the attack on 9/11.

Sikh American taxi driver Kulwinder Singh is a victim of a hate crime committed by Raymond Isais Jr. around the SeaTac, Washington, area. Isais pulled out tufts of his beard and told Singh, "You have not right to attack our country!"

In Somerset, California, three teenagers—Craig Jennings, 18; Jeffrey Lizotte, 17; and a 16-year-old—are all charged with a hate crime after throwing a Molotov cocktail onto the roof of a convenience store owned by an Arab American.

In Chicago, Illinois, Andrew Holden, a 49-year-old white man, is charged with a hate crime after threatening to bomb a food store owned by an Arab American family.

In Bloomington, Indiana, a Muslim student is assaulted and verbally harassed by a white student.

September 14

1994

Comedian Margaret Cho's *All-American Girl* premieres. The show is canceled, and the last episode airs on March 15, 1995.

Perhaps initially, All-American Girl *may have had potential for positive advancements in minority representation on television. But rather than focus on a specific comedic form, the show focused on the ideas they had regarding ethnic authenticity. The show seemed to overemphasize the characters' Asianness marking the Asian face, body, and family structure as decidedly uncanny. When the show was in a decline and receiving harsh criticism from all sides, the remedy was to repackage the product in efforts to normalize the Asian ethnic identity and appease viewers. At the age of 23, Cho was cast as the main character of the show. The hook was that she would be playing herself—a twenty-something college student named Margaret Kim—and the show would be based on her standup routines. Almost immediately, Cho's life/family/comedy routine model was displaced in favor more formulaic sitcom structure.* All-American Girl *focuses on familial drama and conflict, similar to many sitcom families before them. The nuclear unit serves as the stage for comedic television. However, the Kim family is also identifiable as the central site for the presentation of racial and cultural identity. The character Margaret Kim is a placeholder between the old Asian culture and the new Asian American culture. Whereas her family (especially her mother and brother) maintain traditional Asian mannerisms, Margaret Kim embodies her Americanization. Cho has repeatedly commented on the "adversarial relationship" she had to maintain with the mother character since most of the show's jokes stem from the clashing of mother and daughter. Ultimately, these adversarial jokes between the two characters are generational conflicts of culture and assimilation.*

Source: Cassinelli, Sarah Moon. "'If We Are Asian, Then Are We Funny?': Margaret Cho's

'All-American Girl' as the First (and Last?) Asian American Sitcom." *Studies in American Humor* 3, no. 17 (2008): pp. 131–132.

Books

Cho, Margaret. *I Have Chosen to Stay and Fight.* New York: Riverhead Trade, 2006. This is a collection of essays that reflects on Cho's fighting sexism, racism, and homophobia.

Cho, Margaret. *I'm the One That I Want.* New York: Ballantine Books, 2001. *I'm the One That I Want* is Cho's memoir that reflects on the failure of *All-American Girl.*

Websites

Lim, Pam. "From *All American Girl* to *Fresh Off the Boat*: Exploring the Relationship between Media Representations and Identity Formation." Master of Arts thesis. Carleton University. Ottawa, Ontario, Canada. 2017. This thesis explores the history of Asian Canadian and Asian American media presentation. https://curve.carleton.ca/system/files/etd/106ac38a-8b57-4935-b7a5-dd6fb32a331d/etd_pdf/e19fb361ff1b3584df949662fcc0db77/lim-fromallamericangirltofreshofftheboatexploring.pdf. Accessed June 14, 2018.

Woo, Michelle. "20 Years Later, Margaret Cho Looks Back on 'All-American Girl.'" Kore Asian Media. September 15, 2014. This is an interview in which Cho addresses questions about her show, Asian Americans and American pop culture, and Eddie Huang's *Fresh off the Boat*, that premiered in 2015. http://kore.am/20-years-later-margaret-cho-looks-back-on-all-american-girl/. Accessed February 10, 2018.

Also Noteworthy

2002

In Sterling, Virginia, swastikas and racial slurs are spray-painted on a Muslim community center.

September 15

2001

Balbir Singh Sodhi, a Sikh American gas station owner in Mesa, Arizona, is shot to death by a man who told witnesses that he planned to kill "Arabs."

Particularly horrifying for Sikh Americans was the 15 September 2001 murder of Balbir Singh Sodhi, in Mesa, Arizona. The first person to die from domestic terrorism after 9/11, Mr Sodhi was a Sikh American gas station owner who was killed on his business property by a vigilante racist. . . . But Mr Sodhi's murder, a hateful act of racist vengeance, was largely lost in the broader narrative of our national tragedy, much like that of the Sikh American community itself. While we can debate the reasons for this, his murder made little long-term national impact, except in Sikh and progressive South Asian American communities. Mr Sodhi's marginalization is evidenced by the scarcity of his name in public discourse around discussions of such topics as contemporary hate crimes, religious intolerance, or the grass roots impact of the nation's increasingly vicious political discourse demonizing immigrants, racialized minorities, and the followers of Islam. Despite the direct linkage of his murder to 9/11, and the fact that he was killed because of the way he looked, news reports about his death rarely presented the public with a photo of Mr Sodhi. The impact of that omission by the news media in this country is now evident. Balbir Singh Sodhi has never become a symbol of contemporary hate violence in this country, and neither have Sikh Americans. Mr Sodhi is a non-entity to the vast majority of Americans—forgotten like so many true American heroes of color who emerged in the wake of the national trauma of 9/11. The dearth of visually impactful depictions of Mr Sodhi after his murder reinforced the pervasive western media trope that still represents bearded, turbaned men as religious fundamentalists, misogynists, movie villains, foreigners who seek to harm the country, and terrorists. These vicious stereotypes contrast sharply with the reality of Mr Sodhi being a model immigrant, who came to the USA not only for economic opportunity but to find religious freedom unavailable in his homeland. The immigrant business-owner had just emptied his wallet to donate to the victims of 9/11 at a local store, before returning to his business and being gunned down by a man claiming: "I'm a patriot . . . I'm a damn American all the way."

Source: Singh, Jaideep. "Memory, Invisibility, and the Oak Creek Gurdwara Massacre: A Sikh American Perspective of the 'Post-Racial' US." *Sikh Formations* 9, no. 2 (2013): pp. 216–217.

Books

Iyer, Deepa. *We Too Sing America: South Asian, Arab, Muslim, and Sikh Immigrants Shape Our Multiracial Future*. New York: The New Press, 2015. *We Too Sing America* explores various aspects of anti-Muslim and anti-Asian racial hatred and crimes in the United States.

Karam, Nicoletta. *The 9/11 Backlash: A Decade of U.S. Hate Crimes Targeting the Innocent*. Berkeley, CA: Beatitude Press, 2012. *The 9/11 Backlash* examines a decade of Islamophobia and Hinduphobia that fueled hate crimes against South Asians, Muslims, Arabs, Sikhs, and other Asian Americans.

Websites

"The First 9/11 Backlash Fatality: The Murder of Balbir Singh Sodhi." Sikh American Legal Defense and Education Fund. August 30, 2011. This essay includes a biography of Balbir Singh Sodhi, his murder, and the Sikh American community response. http://saldef.org/issues/balbir-singh-sodhi/#.WmmKVKinGUk. Accessed January 24, 2018.

Khalsa, Ek Ong Kaar K. "Balbir Singh Sodhi Honored." SikhNet. September 21, 2001. This is the memorial web page for Balbir Singh Sodhi. http://fateh.sikhnet.com/s/BalbirSodhi. Accessed January 24, 2018.

Also Noteworthy

2001

On September 15, 2001, James Herrick sets fire to the Curry in a Hurry restaurant in Salt Lake City, Utah, causing minimal damage. Herrick admitted to setting the fire because he was angry over the September 11 attacks and knew that the restaurant owners were from Pakistan. A federal district court in Utah sentenced him on January 7, 2001, to 51 months in jail.

2007

In Matinecock, New York, an Iranian American nail salon owner is beaten by two robbers who call her a "terrorist" and scrawl anti-Muslim messages on a mirror in her shop.

September 16

1912

The Korean Youth Corps (KYC) graduates its first class of 13 students. The KYC was established as a voluntary military training program in Hastings, Nebraska, under the leadership of Park Yong-man (July 2, 1881–October 17, 1928) to fight for Korean independence from Japanese occupation.

Park Yong-man . . . thought that military means were necessary to liberate Korea. He had served a prison term before coming to the United States in 1904. According to one source, there were about 700 ex-soldiers among the immigrants, and Park became their leader. After graduating from the University of Nebraska in 1909, he set up the Korean Youth Military Academy in Nebraska, where he trained some two dozen cadets. He next established four other military academics in California, Kansas, and Wyoming, as well as an airplane-pilot training program in Willows, California—the last endeavor financed by Kim Chong-lim, the Korean Rice King. In 1912 the different groups of cadets were consolidated into a single Korean National Brigade, with over three hundred members commanded by Park and headquartered at the Ahumanu Plantation on the island of Oahu in Hawaii.

Source: Lee, Mary Paik, ed., "Introduction." In *Quiet Odyssey: A Pioneer Korean Woman in America*, edited by Sucheng Chan, pp. LII–LIII. Seattle: University of Washington Press, 1990.

Books

Lee, Chong-Sik. *The Politics of Korean Nationalism*. Berkeley: University of California Press, 1965. *The Politics of Korean Nationalism* explores various aspects of Korean nationalism.

Park, Young. *Korea and the Imperialists: In Search of a National Identity*. Bloomington, IN: AuthorHouse, 2009. See Chapter 6, "Revolutionaries in Exile," for discussion of Korean nationalists in the United States.

Websites

Choe, Yong-Ho, Ilpyong Kim, and Moon-Young Han. "Chronology of the Korean Immigration to the United States: 1882 to 1940." This site provides a detailed chronology of Korean immigration history in the United States. http://www.phy.duke.edu/~myhan/kaf1601.pdf. Accessed February 10, 2018.

Kim, Jake. "Nebraska, A Portal to Korean Pride." *Antelope*, the weekly news publication of the University of Nebraska at Kearney. November 4, 2015. This essay details Korean nationalists who studied at the University of Nebraska with photographs. http://unkantelope.com/wordpress_antelope/2015/11/04/nebraska-a-portal-to-korean-pride/. Accessed February 10, 2018.

Also Noteworthy

2001

On this day, someone allegedly sets fire to Prime Tires, a Pakistani-owned auto mechanic shop located in an enclave of Pakistani businesses in Houston, Texas. The fire destroyed the store. The store had received threats immediately after September 11. Thus far, police have been unable to determine who started the blaze or what was their motivation.

2003

In the Bronx, New York, a 14-year-old teenage boy is charged with assault and harassment for attacking a Muslim American girl while yelling racial slurs at her.

2004

In Berkeley, California, three men use racial slurs and throw water bottles at eight Muslim students at University of California, Berkeley, campus.

September 17

1942

The first volunteers from Heart Mountain, Wyoming, leave to work in the beet fields in the surrounding area, but only on the condition that they be returned to Heart Mountain by December 1, as demanded by Wyoming governor Nels Smith. Roughly, 1,100 internees participated in the 1942 beet harvest in Wyoming and Montana.

During 1942, approximately 10,000 incarcerees left centers for seasonal farm work in eastern Oregon, Idaho, Utah, Montana, and Colorado. Late that year, the U.S. Department of Agriculture declared the sugar beet crop had been saved, with significant contributions made by Japanese American laborers.[Oregon governor Charles A.] Sprague sent a letter to the editor of the Minidoka Irrigator commending the incarcerees, particularly those from Oregon, for their work in harvesting crops. The WRA later estimated that nearly a quarter billion pounds of sugar had been saved.

Source: Young, Morgen. "Russell Lee in the Northwest: Documenting Japanese American Farm Labor Camps in Oregon and Idaho." *Oregon Historical Quarterly* 114, no. 3 (Fall 2013): pp. 361–362.

Books

Mackey, Mike, ed. *Remembering Heart Mountain: Essays on Japanese American Internment in Wyoming*. Powell, WY: Western History Publications, 1998. *Remembering Heart Mountain* is a collection of 16 essays written by archivists, former internees, War Relocation Authority staff members at Heart Mountain internment camp, and scholars who covered various aspects of life at the camp.

Walz, Eric. *Nikkei in the Interior West: Japanese Immigration and Community Building, 1882–1945*. Tucson: University of Arizona Press, 2012. *Nikkei in the Interior West* is a history of the Japanese American experience in Arizona, Colorado, Idaho, Nebraska, and Utah.

Websites

Heart Mountain. WWII Japanese American Confinement Site. Heart Mountain Interpretive Center. 2013. This site includes a history of Heart Mountain internment camp and archival photographs from the period. http://www.heartmountain.org/history.html. Accessed February 10, 2018.

Matsumoto, Mieko. "Heart Mountain." *Densho Encyclopedia*, April 1, 2016. This essay is a detailed history of Heart Mountain internment camp. http://encyclopedia.densho.org/Heart_Mountain/. Accessed February 10, 2018.

September 18

1976

Rev. Sun Myung Moon holds "God Bless America" festival. Moon immigrated to the United States in 1971. Speaking at America's Bicentennial at Washington, D.C., Moon said:

Honorable Citizens of the United States and world delegates: I would like to express my heartfelt thanks and appreciation to all of you for "Meeting us at the Monument." Tonight we are celebrating America's Bicentennial in the Name of God. For you and me, this is an historical moment. Tonight I would like to speak on the subject "America and God's Will." . . . Today, America and Christianity together must take up the sacred task of world restoration. America must unite the cultures of the West and the East, as well as the Middle East, and create one great unified culture, ultimately fulfilling the mission of establishing the Kingdom of God on Earth. . . .

Ladies and gentlemen, at this crossroads of human history, we must listen to the calling of God. God prepared America for 200 years. This is the time for awakening. America must accept her global responsibility. Armed with Godism, she must free the Communist world, and at last, build the Kingdom of God here on earth. God has chosen America as the flag bearer. America must rise up. Today. Tomorrow may be too late. I not only respect America but truly love this nation. I respect and love her as a great nation, as a godly nation, and as the central nation in God's Providence. She is now at the threshold of her third century. She must not disappoint God. Today let us pledge to God Almighty that we shall do His will. . . . Today in this holy place, let us together lay the cornerstone of the Kingdom of God on earth. . . . We know we can build the Kingdom of God here on earth, in His power, and with our own hands. May God bless you and your families, and forever more, God bless America.

Source: Moon, Sun Myung. "America and God's Will." *40 Years in America*. HDH Study, pp. 136–139. http://hdhstudy.com/wp-content/uploads/Testimonials/40-Years-in-America-Complete.pdf. Accessed January 24, 2018.

Books

Pak, Bo Hi. *Messiah: My Testimony to Rev. Sun Myung Moon*. Vol. I. Lanham, MD: University Press of America, 2000. *Messiah* is a complete biography of Sun Myung Moon.

Pak, Bo Hi. *Messiah: My Testimony to Rev. Sun Myung Moon*. Vol. II. Lanham, MD: University

Press of America, 2002. *Messiah* is a complete biography of Sun Myung Moon.

Websites

"Biography of Rev. Sun Myung Moon." https://www.tparents.org. 2007. This chronological biography includes photographs and links for other multimedia resources related to Moon. https://www.tparents.org/Library/Unification/Publications/Smm-Org/life_biography.html. Accessed January 24, 2018.

HDH Study. 2014. This website is an archive of all things related to Moon and includes publications on and by Moon. http://hdhstudy.com/. Accessed January 24, 2018.

Also Noteworthy

2001

In Fort Worth, Texas, three middle school students are charged with making threats and harassing a peer of Indian descent.

2003

In Tempe, Arizona, a swastika, a thunderbolt-shaped "SS," and other Nazi symbols are spray-painted on a mosque.

September 19

2011

Republican governor Terry Brandstad appoints Swati A. Dandekar (b. March 6, 1951) to the Iowa Utilities Board and cites her science training and experience with the utility industry and the energy needs of Iowa as factors in her appointment. She became the first Asian American elected to the Iowa state legislature in 2002 and served in the House of Representatives until 2008. Dandekar then served in the Iowa State Senate from 2009 until her appointment to the Iowa Utilities Board.

The re-election of Democrat Swati Dandekar for a second term from District 36 to the Iowa House of Representatives is significant because, apart from the fact that she won again in a majority Republican district, this time she had to reckon with the powerful political machinery of Republican Senator Charles Grassley, chairman of the Senate Finance Committee.

Grassley put his political action committee and his wife at the disposal of Dandekar's opponent Cory Crowley. Grassley's political machinery not only funded Crowley's campaign, but it financed a barrage of negative advertisements against Dandekar, accusing her of being anti-small business and anti-education.

Dandekar prevailed by more than eight percentage points, winning with 54.4 percent or 9,772 votes.

In an exclusive interview with India Abroad a day after a grueling campaign, Dandekar said she remained positive and focused throughout the campaign and had enough money to respond quickly to the allegations against her even though she said, "It's very stressful to have a positive campaign."

Dandekar, who was Iowa co-chair of Senator John Kerry's campaign and had promised to deliver Iowa to Kerry, lamented his loss to President George W Bush and her failure to help him carry Iowa. She said the overriding factor that apparently gave Bush the popular vote was that Americans thought it unwise to change a leader when the country is at war.

Source: Haniffa, Aziz. "Swati Dandekar." *India Abroad*, November 12, 2004.

Books

Lien, Pei-te, M. Margaret Conway, and Janelle Wong. *The Politics of Asian Americans: Diversity and Community*. New York: Routledge, 2004. *The Politics of Asian Americans* is a survey of Asian American participation in American politics.

Raghuram, Parvati, Ajaya Sahoo, Brij Maharaj, and Dave Sangha, eds. *Tracing an Indian Diaspora: Contexts, Memories, Representations.* Los Angeles: Sage, 2008. See Pierre Gottschlich's Chapter 7, "The Indian Diaspora in the United States of America: An Emerging Political Force?"

Websites

"Swati Dandekar." Ballotpedia. This site provides statistics and data related to Dandekar's political career. https://ballotpedia.org/Swati_Dandekar. Accessed January 24, 2018.

"Swati Dandekar's Biography." Vote Smart. 2018. This site provides Dandekar's education background, career experience, and political history. https://votesmart.org/candidate/biography/32466/swati-dandekar#.WmjL4ainGUk. Accessed January 24, 2018.

Also Noteworthy

1885

White miners drive out Chinese from Black Diamond, injuring nine Chinese men.

2001

Satpreet Singh, a Sikh American who wears a turban, is a victim of a hate crime in Frederick County, Maryland.

In San Francisco, California, anti-Arab graffiti is spray-painted on an Iraqi American grocery store.

2005

Kappa Lambda Delta, an Asian/Asian American interest sorority, is founded at Texas Christian University.

September 20

1885

Anti-Chinese sentiments motivate racist-nativists to drive Chinese miners out of Washington Territory.

On 20 September 1885, the presence of over 3,200 Chinese miners, concentrated along the Tacoma-Seattle corridor bordering Puget Sound, led to a meeting of disgruntled workers in Tacoma. Rallying to the slogan "The Chinese must go," these workers considered exerting legislative and social pressures to harass the Chinese and deny them jobs. Many, however, favored more direct action—forcible expulsion, as at Rock Springs.

Under the auspices of the Knights of Labor, a second meeting, now including workers from Seattle as well as Tacoma, was held on 28 September. R. Jacob Weisbach, Tacoma's mayor, presided as the participants resolved to rid the territory of all "Chinese slave labor" by asking employers to discharge the Chinese and by having local committees order them to leave Tacoma and Seattle by 1 November. If necessary, the white workers would use force. . . .

The proposed ultimatum for the Chinese to depart Seattle alarmed the Imperial Chinese vice consul in San Francisco and the Washington territorial chief justice in Seattle. Having visited Rock Springs, Consul Frederick Bee knew what a racist mob could do. On 4 October he asked Governor Squire whether he could protect the Chinese and, if not, whether he would arrange for federal military protection. . . .

Violence erupted first in Tacoma on 2 November. Unopposed by local authorities, a mob of nearly 300 whites, many of them armed, forced some 200 Chinese to leave in wagons. During a drive in pouring rain to Lake View Station, where the Chinese were to board a train for Portland, several Chinese suffered ill effects from exposure and died soon after.

Source: Laurie, Clayton, and Ronald Cole. *The Role of Federal Military Forces in Domestic Disorders, 1877–1945*. Washington, DC: Center for Military History, U.S. Army, 1997, pp. 99–101.

Books

Lutz, J. Brenda, and James M. Lutz. *Terrorism in America*. New York: Palgrave Macmillan, 2007. *Terrorism in America* argues that since the birth of the nation, terrorism has existed in America. It provides examples of instances when Americans acted as terrorists or were victims of it.

White, Richard. *"It's Your Misfortune and None of My Own": A New History of the American West*. Norman: University of Oklahoma Press, 1991. Historian Richard White draws on critical scholarship and perspective to present a new history of the creation of the Western region. See Chapter 13, "Social Conflict," for coverage of the anti-Chinese riots.

Websites

Lee, Jennifer H. "Anti-Chinese Riots in Washington State." It is a detailed history of the anti-Chinese riots in Washington State with photographs and links to other riots or massacres. http://www.dartmouth.edu/~hist32/History/S01%20-%20Wash%20State%20riots.htm. Accessed January 29, 2018.

"Lesson Fifteen: Industrialization, Class, and Race; Chinese and Anti-Chinese Movement in the Late 19th-Century Northwest." Center for the Study of the Pacific Northwest, University of Washington. This site provides a rich history of the Chinese and anti-Chinese movement in the Pacific Northwest. Data come from archival materials, the Pacific Northwest Quarterly. There are photographs as well from the Special Collections, University of Washington. http://www.washington.edu/uwired/outreach/cspn/Website/Classroom%20Materials/Pacific%20Northwest%20History/Lessons/Lesson%2015/15.html. Accessed January 29, 2018.

Also Noteworthy

2004

In El Paso, Texas, Antonio Flores, a 57-year-old, is charged with arson and possession of weapons for throwing a makeshift firebomb at children playing outside an Islamic daycare center.

2005

Built in the 1870s, the Kam Wah Chung Company Building is designated as a National Historic Landmark. It is a state park in John Day, Oregon.

2011

Unforgettable, a crime drama, premieres on CBS, with Daya Vivian Vaidya (b. May 20, 1980), an American actress of mixed-Nepali ancestry, as a regular cast member in the role of Nina Inara.

September 21

2008

Sugar Pie DeSanto, birth name Peylia Marsema Balinton (b. October 16, 1935), receives the Pioneer Award at the 20th Rhythm and Blues Foundation Award Show.

The diminutive Sugar Pie DeSanto was born Umpeylia Balinton on October 16, 1935, in Brooklyn, New York. Her mother was an African American concert pianist, and her father was Filipino. The family moved across the country to San Francisco when Umpeylia was a child. She befriended Etta James in her youth while a member of the Johnny Otis Revue, and a short time later, she joined the James Brown Revue. Johnny Otis came up with her stage name, Sugar Pie DeSanto. Her first recording sessions were for Cincinnati's Federal Records label with Henry Houston as Hand and Sugar Pie (Federal #12217—"I'm So Lonely"). She also teamed up with Pee Wee Kingsley as Sugar Pie and Pee Wee for the Aladdin and Rhythm record labels. While in the Bay Area, she recorded a doo-woop single for a small Jody Records label (#11) as Paliya DeSantos ("Wishing Well" backed with "Darling Be Mine"). However, in 1960 as Sugar Pie DeSanto (no s), she scored her first big hit—a Top Five smash on the R&B charts (on which she harmonizes with herself) titled "I Want to Know" (Veltone #103). It took her a while to follow up that hit, but upon signing with Chicago's Checker Records label in 1964, she scored on the R&B charts with an answer to Tommy Tucker's "High Heel Sneakers" titled "Slip-in Mules" (Checker #1073), and yet another 1964 release titled "Soulful Dress" (Checker #1082). She scored one more time in a duet with her longtime friend Etta James titled "In the Basement" (Cadet $5539) in 1966. . . . Unfortunately, DeSanto didn't score any other big hits, but continued her high energy/athletic performances. She was given *the Bay Area Music Award for best female blues singer in 1999.*

Source: Leszczak, Bob. *Encyclopedia of Pop Music Aliases, 1950–2000*. Lanham, MD: Rowman & Littlefield, 2015, p. 98.

Books

Komara, Edward, ed. *Encyclopedia of the Blues*. New York: Routledge, 2006. See Edward Komara's entry on "Sugar Pie DeSanto."

Pepin, Elizabeth, and Lewis Watts. *Harlem of the West: The San Francisco Fillmore Jazz Era*. San Francisco, CA: Chronicle Books, 2006. *Harlem of the West* is an illustrated history of San Francisco's Fillmore District in the 1940s through 1960s.

Websites

Burlison, Dani. "Celebrating Sugar Pie DeSanto, Oakland's Soul Survivor." KQED Arts. January 6, 2015. This article discusses DeSanto's six decades' musical career. https://ww2.kqed.org/arts/2015/01/06/celebrating-sugar-pie-desanto-oaklands-soul-survivor/. Accessed February 10, 2018.

Sugar Pie DeSanto. This site is Sugar Pie DeSanto's official web page that contains a biography, photographs, videos, and up-to-date news and events. http://www.sugarpiedesanto.com/. Accessed February 10, 2018.

Also Noteworthy

1969

The first national Asian American Studies conference is held at Berkeley, California. It was sponsored by the University of California campuses at Davis, Los Angeles, and Berkeley. The conference was held during September 20–21.

1996

The *Los Angeles Times* publishes an article that alleges President William F. Clinton's reelection campaign and the Democratic National Committee fundraising linked to Chinese lobbying groups. Asian American critics expressed concern and protested the negative and racist coverage of the scandal.

September 22

1903

Chinmokhoe (Friendship Association) is established by Ahn Chang Ho in San Francisco to assist Koreans assimilate to Western culture. It is the first Korean organization in the United States.

The three best-known U.S.-based Korean expatriate leaders were Ahn Chang-ho (1878–1938), Park Yong-man (1881–1928), and Syngman Rhee (1875–1965). Ahn, who believed in salvation through cultural renewal, had arrived in San Francisco in 1899, before Korean laborers started going to Hawaii and California. Four years later, he established the first social organization among Koreans in California, the Chin'mok-hoe (Friendship Society). He visited the homes of Koreans in the city and urged them to cleanse and beautify their dwellings because he thought cleanliness was a manifestation of moral rectitude; he also set up an employment agency to supply Korean laborers to Americans. Returning to Korea in 1907, he set up schools and organized secret societies, but he fled the country in 1910 when the Japanese fully took it over. Back in California, while earning a living as a general construction worker and a cleaner of hotel rooms—an unheard of occupation for an educated, upper-class Korean—Ahn formed the Hung Sa Dan (Young Korean Academy) in 1913 in San Francisco. He believed that the first step toward regaining Korean independence involved the "regeneration" of the Korean people through the development of their character.

Source: Chan, Sucheng. "European and Asian Immigration into the United States in Comparative Perspective, 1820s to 1920s." In *Immigration Reconsidered: History, Sociology, and Politics*, edited by Virginia Yans-McLaughlin, p. 50. Oxford: Oxford University Press, 1990.

Books

Cha, Marn. *Koreans in Central California (1903–1957): A Study of Settlement and Transnational Politics.* Lanham, MD: University Press of America, 2010. *Koreans in Central California* provides a historical overview of the Korean American experience in California.

Hurh, Won Moo. *The Korean Americans: The New Americans.* Westport, CT: Greenwood Publishing Company, 1998. *The Korean Americans* covers many dimensions of Korean immigration history and community development.

Websites

"Dosan the Global Sojourner: Life in America—San Francisco 1920." www.dosan.org. This site contains a digital archive of Ahn Chang Ho that includes a detailed biography, his writings, photographs, and much more. http://www.dosan.org/thejourney.html. Accessed January 24, 2018.

Kim, Han-kyo. "The Korean Independence Movement in the United States: Syngman Rhee, An Ch'ang-Ho, and Pak Yong-Man." *International Journal of Korean Studies* (Spring/Summer 2002): 1–27. This article details three of the leaders in Korea's independence movement. http://icks.org/data/ijks/1482456493_add_file_1.pdf. Accessed January 24, 2018.

Also Noteworthy

1922

The U.S. Congress passes the Cable Act, which stripped any women of European or African ancestry of their citizenship if they married an "alien ineligible to citizenship." They could regain their citizenship through the naturalization process if they divorced their alien husbands or if he died. The act was repealed in 1936.

1940

Japan is granted rights to station troops in Indochina from the Vichy French government. By 1941, Japan extended its control over the whole of French Indochina.

September 23

1950

The McCarran Internal Security Act is passed by Congress, overturning President Harry S. Truman's veto. This reflects the fear of communism in the United States, which foretold wars in Korea and Vietnam (Cambodia and Laos) as a means to stop the spread of communism.

In response to the Cold War, and the fears that Communists would try to take over the country, the United States experienced a second period of hysteria against any sort of radical threat, real or perceived. The first took place just after the end of World War I and carried through the early years of the 1920s in the first Red Scare. With the atomic age in full swing, many wondered if the Communist threat was not only real again, but possible from both internal and external characters. In 1950, Congress passed the Internal Security Act, which is usually referred to as the McCarran Act after Senator Pat McCarran of Nevada. Besides calling for the investigation of radicals, it also prescribed the denial of passports, citizenship, or entrance to the country, as well as detainment of potentially dangerous individuals. President Harry Truman vetoed the bill on civil rights grounds but Congress overrode the veto. Only portions of the act have actually been repealed.

Source: Newton-Matza, Mitchell. *Disasters and Tragic Events: An Encyclopedia of Catastrophes in American History*. Santa Barbara, CA: ABC-CLIO, 2014, p. 700.

Books

Bogle, Lori, ed. *Cold War Espionage and Spying.* Vol. IV, *The Cold War.* New York: Routledge, 2001. See Christopher Gerard's chapter "On the Road to Vietnam: 'The Loss of China Syndrome,' Pat McCarran and J. Edgar Hoover."

Thompson, Francis. *Frustration of Politics: Truman, Congress, and the Loyalty Issue, 1945–1953.*

Rutherford, NJ: Fairleigh Dickinson University Press, 1979. *Frustration of Politics* is a study of the struggle between President Truman and Congress regarding claims that the Democratic Party was home to communists and communist sympathizers.

Websites

Internal Security Act of 1950. The Gilder Lehrman Institute of American History. 2018. This site provides a history of the act, along with links on essays with related topics that include the Korean War, links to primary sources, and other scholarly resources. https://new.gilderlehrman.org/history-by-era/postwar-politics-and-origins-cold-war/timeline-terms/internal-security-act-1950. Accessed February 10, 2018.

Truman, Harry S. "Speech on the Veto of the McCarran Internal Security Act." TeachingAmericanHistory.org. Truman's full speech is available. http://teachingamericanhistory.org/library/document/speech-on-the-veto-of-the-mccarran-internal-security-act/. Accessed February 10, 2018.

Also Noteworthy

2001

In a case of mistaken identity, St. John's Assyrian American Church is set on fire in Chicago, Illinois, causing approximately $150,000 worth of damage. According to the church's pastor, Reverend Charles Klutz, the person whom he believed set the fire had asked a local resident whether the church was a mosque. Reverend Klutz also stated that local police initially asked whether the church was a mosque when they first arrived even though many crosses were located prominently on the church premise.

September 24

1987

San-J International, the American subsidiary of San Jirushi Company in Japan, opens the first tamari brewery out of Japan in Henrico, Virginia.

"San-J has been a corporate staple on Virginia's roster of international companies for nearly 30 years and continues to invest in its Henrico County operation," said Maurice Jones, Virginia Secretary of Commerce and Trade. "The Henrico plant was the first Tamari brewing facility built in the U.S., and product demand continues to grow. An expansion of this size ensures the company's future longevity in the Commonwealth and is a great testament to San-J's success in our first-class business environment."

San-Jirushi was founded by the Sato family as a tamari and miso company in 1804 in Mie, Japan. Current San-J President, Takashi Sato, is an eighth-generation member of the founding family. The company began brewing the first tamari from its Henrico, Virginia facility in 1987, continuing the 200-year tradition of Japanese brewing mastery. The existing Henrico County plant employs 55.

"We have long appreciated the commitment of the Commonwealth and Henrico County to our company's continued prosperity," noted Takashi Sato, President of San-J International, Inc. "Governor McAuliffe's personal visit with our corporate leadership during his recent trade mission to Japan, along with the many years of support from Henrico, assured us that making such a large investment to serve the growing U.S. market from right here was the best choice for us."

The Virginia Economic Development Partnership worked with the Henrico County Economic Development Authority to secure the project for Virginia. Governor McAuliffe approved a $300,000 performance-based grant from the Virginia Investment Partnership program, an incentive available to existing Virginia companies. Funding and services to support the company's employee training and retraining activities will be provided through the Virginia Jobs Investment Program.

Source: "Press Release: San-J International to Invest $38 Million in Henrico Expansion." HenricoNow. February 2015. http://news.henrico.com/news/press-release-san-j-international-to-invest-38-million-in-henrico-expansion. Accessed January 24, 2018.

Books

Shurtleff, William, and Akiko Aoyagi, compilers. *History of Soybeans and Soyfoods in Japan, and in Japanese Cookbooks and Restaurants outside Japan (701 CE to 2014)*. Lafayette, CA: Soyinfo Center, 2014.

Shurtleff, William, and Akiko Aoyagi, compilers. *How Japanese and Japanese-Americans Brought Soyfoods to the United States and the Hawaiian Islands—A History (1851–2011)*. Lafayette, CA: Soyinfo Center, 2011.

Websites

"San-J Introduces Hoisin Sauce—A Tradition Ingredient in Asian Artisanal Cooking." Specialty Food Association. June 6, 2017. This is a brief essay that details the history of San-J and their contributions in introducing Asian foods into the American homes. https://www.specialtyfood.com/news/article/san-j-introduces-hoisin-sauce-a-traditional-ingredient-in-asian-artisanal-cooking-124351/. Accessed January 24, 2018.

"The Story behind San-J." San-J. 2018. This site provides a chronological history of San-J with photos and annotations. https://san-j.com/about-us/our-story/. Accessed January 24, 2018.

September 25

1953

California governor Earl Warren appoints John F. Aiso a judge in Los Angeles: he is the first Nisei (second-generation Japanese American) to be appointed a judge in the continental United States.

Judge John Fugue Aiso was born in Burbank, California, on December 14, 1909. He attended LeConte Junior High School in Hollywood, where he ran for—and won by a margin of 600 votes—the office of student body president. However, pressure from angry parents, local newspapers, and an anti-Asian student petition resulted in the school administration's suspension of student government until after Aiso graduated. Aiso attended Hollywood High School, where he applied for but was rejected from the Junior ROTC program. When he tried out for cheerleader, the principal "advised" him to drop out. He did join the debate team and eventually became its captain. Aiso led the Hollywood High School debate team to a Southern California High Schools championship in 1926. He was the first Japanese American to be elected to the honorary Ephebian Society. Aiso was also selected by faculty members to be the valedictorian of his class.

Source: Fugita, Steve. "John Fugue Aiso (1909–1987)." In *Distinguished Asian Americans: A Biographical Dictionary*, edited by Hyung-chan Kim, p. 15. Westport, CT: Greenwood Press, 1999.

Books

Daniels, Roger. *Asian America: Chinese and Japanese in the United States since 1850*. Seattle: University of Washington Press, 1988. See Chapter 5, "Japanese America, 1920–1941," for discussion that includes John F. Aiso's biography.

McNaughton, James. *Nisei Linguists: Japanese Americans in the Military Intelligence Service during World War II*. Washington, DC: Department of the Army, 2007. Chapter 4, "Camp Savage, 1942–1943," includes a detailed discussion of John F. Aiso's military service during World War II.

Websites

California Courts. "John F. Aiso, Biography." http://www.courts.ca.gov/documents/AisoJ.pdf. Accessed February 10, 2018.

Nakamura, Kelli. "John Aiso." *Densho Encyclopedia*, June 10, 2015. This essay is a biography of Aiso's life, career, and legacy. http://encyclopedia.densho.org/John_Aiso/. Accessed February 10, 2018.

Also Noteworthy

2008

In Joplin, Missouri, a sign at the Islamic Society is set on fire.

September 26

2001

President George W. Bush meets with Sikh American leaders at the White House after Balbir Singh Sodhi is killed in the post–9/11 backlash.

It's my honor to welcome citizens from all across our country here to the Roosevelt Room and the White House to discuss our common commitment to make sure that every American is treated with respect and dignity during this period of—during any period, for that matter, of American history, but particularly during this time.

An American Sikh has been killed, unjustly so. These citizens bring their hearts with them, and I can assure them that our Government will do everything we can to not only bring those people to justice but also to treat every human life as dear and to respect the values that made our country so different and so unique. We're all Americans, bound together by common ideals and common values.

So I want to welcome you all here. We're honored that you're here in the White House, and I look forward to a good, frank discussion.

Thank you for coming.

Source: Bush, George W. "Remarks Prior to a Meeting with Sikh Community Leaders." The American Presidency Project. University of California, Santa Barbara. http://www.presidency.ucsb.edu/ws/index.php?pid=62916. Accessed February 10, 2018.

Books

Iyer, Deepa. *We Too Sing America: South Asian, Arab, Muslim, and Sikh Immigrants Shape Our Multiracial Future*. New York: The New Press, 2015. *We Too Sing America* explores various aspects of anti-Muslim and anti-Asian racial hatred and crimes in the United States.

Karam, Nicoletta. *The 9/11 Backlash: A Decade of U.S. Hate Crimes Targeting the Innocent*. Berkeley, CA: Beatitude Press, 2012. *The 9/11 Backlash* examines a decade of Islamophobia and Hinduphobia that fueled hate crimes against South Asians, Muslims, Arabs, Sikhs, and other Asian Americans.

Websites

"The First 9/11 Backlash Fatality: The Murder of Balbir Singh Sodhi." Sikh American Legal Defense and Education Fund. August 30, 2011. This essay includes a biography of Balbir Singh Sodhi, his murder, and the Sikh American community response. http://saldef.org/issues/balbir-singh-sodhi/#.WmmKVKinGUk. Accessed February 10, 2018.

Khalsa, Ek Ong Kaar K. "Balbir Singh Sodhi Honored." SikhNet. September 21, 2001. This is the memorial web page for Balbir Singh Sodhi. http://fateh.sikhnet.com/s/BalbirSodhi. Accessed February 10, 2018.

September 27

1942

Dith Pran, a Cambodian-born translator and photojournalist who worked for the *New York Times* in Cambodia, is born in Siem Reap. Pran was captured by the Khmer Rouge when they took over. His journalistic account of the Khmer Rouge genocide is the central theme of the film *The Killing Fields* (1984). Haing S. Ngor, a Cambodian physician, portrayed Pran and won the Academy Award for Best Supporting Actor.

It is important for me that the new generation of Cambodians and Cambodian Americans become active and tell the world what happened to them and their families under the Khmer Rouge. I want them never to forget the faces of their relatives and friends who were killed during that time. The dead are crying out for justice. Their voices must be heard. It is the responsibility of the survivors to speak out for those who are unable to speak, in order that the genocide and holocaust will never happen again in this world. The ghosts of the innocent will be on my mind forever. This is why I have compiled these stories. I want future generations to learn about what these survivors, these heroes have gone through and be moved enough to do their part in helping to make the world a better place.

Source: Pran, Dith. "Compiler's Note." In *Children of Cambodia's Killing Fields: Memoirs by Survivors*, edited by Kim DePaul, p. x, New Haven, CT: Yale University Press, 2002.

Books

DePaul, Kim, ed. *Children of Cambodia's Killing Fields: Memoirs by Survivors*. Compiled by Dith Pran. New Haven, CT: Yale University Press, 2002. *Children of Cambodia's Killing Fields* is a compilation of testimonies from survivors of the Khmer Rouge genocide from 1975 to 1979.

Schanberg, Sydney. *The Death and Life of Dith Pran*. New York: RosettaBooks, 2013. Sydney Schanberg worked with Dith Pran in Cambodia. *The Death and Life of Dith Pran* recounts the days before the fall of Phnom Penh to Khmer Rouge forces.

Websites

Dith Pran. *New York Times*. This site is a *New York Times*' archive of articles related to Dith Pran. https://www.nytimes.com/topic/person/dith-pran. Accessed February 10, 2018.

"Dith Pran Biography." *Encyclopedia of World Biography*, 2018. This is a concise biographical history of Dith Pran. http://www.notablebiographies.com/Pe-Pu/Pran-Dith.html. Accessed February 10, 2018.

Also Noteworthy

1935

In the California district court ruling of *Abe v. Fish and Game Commission of California*, Section 990 of the Fish and Game Code—which had prevented those who hadn't resided in the state for one year from selling fish—is struck down. The state supreme court upheld this decision on November 25.

1940

Germany, Italy, and Japan sign the Tripartite Pact, which is known as the Axis alliance.

September 28

1885

Anti-Chinese groups hold the "Anti-Chinese Congress" in Seattle, Washington. Mayor Weisbach of Tacoma presided over the meeting. They concluded their meeting with a resolution that the Chinese must leave western Washington by November 1, 1885.

The radical element desired immediate action and were disposed to get this by any method available, lawful or otherwise. This group met in Seattle at the so called "Anti-Chinese Congress" on September 28th. The Mayor of Tacoma presided over this meeting. Delegates from all directions were in attendance. All the labor organizations and several fraternal orders were well represented. "Every socialist and anarchist who could walk or steal a ride was a self-elected but none the less welcome delegate. Long-haired men and short-haired women were noticeable by their numbers and their noise." This body, after hearing a number of speeches, put forth a series of resolutions on the Chinese situation and proclaimed that the Chinese must leave Western Washington by November 1st 1885. It condemned the employment of the Chinese in households and factories. They planned that "ouster Committees" should be selected in mass meetings in Tacoma and Seattle to notify the Chinese of these cities that they were to leave by the date set. These committees were to be fifteen in number in each case.

Source: Wilcox, W. P. "Anti-Chinese Riots in Washington." *Washington Historical Quarterly* 20, no. 3 (1929): p. 206.

Books

Grant, Frederic, ed. *History of Seattle, Washington*. New York: American Publishing and Engraving Co., 1891. See Chapter 7, "The Anti-Chinese Agitation."

Pfaelzer, Jean. *Driven Out: The Forgotten War against Chinese Americans*. Berkeley: University of California Press, 2007. Jean Pfaelzer used primary documents, such as newspaper articles, to narrate the societal impact of the anti-Chinese movement from 1848 into the 20th century.

Websites

A Troubling Legacy: Anti-Asian Sentiment in America. Japanese American Citizens League, 2015. The full text of this report is available at https://jacl.org/wordpress/wp-content/uploads/2015/01/A-Troubling-Legacy.pdf. Accessed January 24, 2018.

"Violence." Chinese in Northwest American Research Committee. June 7, 2017. This site discusses upward of 50 cases of anti-Chinese violence in the Pacific Northwest. http://www.cinarc.org/Violence.html. Accessed January 24, 2018.

Also Noteworthy

2007

Asian American Film Lab is incorporated. It is a nonprofit dedicated to the support and promotion of gender and ethnic diversity in film and television that started in 1998.

September 29

1973

Beginning on September 29 to October 11, at the 64th General Convention of the Episcopal Church, at Louisville, Kentucky, a resolution is passed to establish the Episcopal Asiamerica Ministry "to deepen and strengthen the existing ministries of the Episcopal Church involved with Asian and Pacific Island peoples as well as to establish new ones."

The word "Asiamerica" was invented to include both American-born as well as foreign-born (immigrant) persons of Asian ancestry. . . . The establishment of the national Episcopal Asiamerica Ministries enabled more intentional church planting among the Asian diaspora. With the mandate from the General Convention and funding received, Episcopal Asiamerica Ministries began to establish structures and networks to further the work of the Asiamerica ministry. With Episcopal Asiamerica Ministries, the Episcopal Church in the provinces, dioceses, and parishes became more aware of the increasing Asian immigrant populations in their localities. Serving as an advocate for existing Asian congregations and as a resource for dioceses within Asian communities, Episcopal Asiamerica Ministries made inroads to Asian ministries throughout the country, developing and supporting new ministries and strengthening older ones.

Source: Vergara, Winfred. "Asiamericans in the Episcopal Church." In *Asian American Religious Cultures*, edited by Jonathan H. X. Lee, Fumitaka Matsuoka, Edmond Yee, and Ronald Y. Nakasone, pp. 195–196. Santa Barbara, CA: ABC-CLIO, 2015.

Books

Vergara, Winfred. *Mainstreaming: Asian Americans in the Episcopal Church*. New York: Office of Asian American Ministries, 2005.

Vergara, Winfred. *Milkfish in Brackish Water: Filipino Christian Ministry in American Context*. Manila, Philippines: Filipino American Ministry Institute, 1992.

Websites

Asiamerica Ministries. The Episcopal Church. 2018. This is the official web page for the Episcopal Asiamerica Ministry. https://www.episcopalchurch.org/asiamerica-ministries. Accessed January 24, 2018.

Asiamerica Ministries in the Episcopal Church. This is the brochure for Episcopal Asiamerica

Ministry that includes its history and purpose. https://www.episcopalchurch.org/files/asiameria_ministries_brochure.pdf. Accessed January 24, 2018.

Also Noteworthy

2001

In Reedley, California, Abdo Ali Ahmed, a 51-year-old Yemeni man, is shot to death outside his convenience store. Two days earlier a note reading, "We're going to kill all fucking Arabs," was left on his car's windshield.

September 30

2001

A Sikh American woman, Swaran Kaur Bhullar, is attacked by two men who stabbed her in the head twice as she was sitting in her car waiting at a red light in San Diego, California. Law enforcement has not been able to identify her attackers.

Swaran Kaur Bhullar, 52, emigrated from Kenya in 1988 after falling in love with the San Diego area during an earlier visit to her husband's relatives. She now is an owner of a video store in Del Mar. Bhullar, a mother of three, is one of an estimated 100,000 Sikhs in California. Her middle name, Kaur, is carried by many Sikh women as a reminder that all people are created equal. She has never been to the Middle East and is a U.S. citizen. But she is, as she puts it, "a brown woman." She was one of dozens of people of foreign ancestry who were victims of hate crimes in the weeks after Sept. 11. Two men ripped open her car door, slashed her in the head with a knife and shouted: "This is what you get for what you've done to us!" She has recovered from her wounds, but she locks the door now when she drives.

Source: "Swaran Kaur Bhullar." *Los Angeles Times*, September 11, 2002, p. S-14.

Books

Karam, Nicoletta. *The 9/11 Backlash: A Decade of U.S. Hate Crimes Targeting the Innocent*. Berkeley, CA: Beatitude Press, 2012. *The 9/11 Backlash* examines a decade of Islamophobia and Hinduphobia that fueled hate crimes against South Asians, Muslims, Arabs, Sikhs, and other Asian Americans.

Welch, Michael. *Scapegoats of September 11th: Hate Crimes & State Crimes in the War on Terror*. New Brunswick, NJ: Rutgers University Press, 2006. *Scapegoats of September 11th* covers various aspects of post–9/11 crimes.

Websites

Human Rights Watch. "'We Are Not the Enemy': Hate Crimes against Arabs, Muslims, and Those Perceived to Be Arab or Muslim after September 11." Vol. 14, No. 6 (G)—November 2002. This report summarizes Islamophobia and Arabphobia in the United States post–9/11 and documents hate crime cases up to date of publication. https://www.hrw.org/reports/2002/usahate/usa1102.pdf. Accessed January 24, 2018.

Kaur, Valarie. "Swaran Bhullar in San Diego." This site provides an interview with Bhullar that details her attack, in addition to photographs of her and her daughter in her video store. http://valariekaur.com/2005/07/swaran-bhullar-in-san-diego/. Accessed January 24, 2018.

Also Noteworthy

2002

In Boise, Idaho, a mosque is vandalized after receiving a series of threatening phone calls.

October

October 1

1888

Six years after the passage of the 1882 Chinese Exclusion Act, the Scott Act is passed by the U.S. Congress and signed into law by President Grover Cleveland to prohibit the return of Chinese laborers who temporarily returned to China. It was introduced by Representative William Lawrence Scott of Pennsylvania. At the time of its effective date, over 20,000 Chinese laborers possessed reentry certificates, and 600 of them were in transit back to the United States: none were allowed reentry. However, the Scott Act did allow teachers and merchants to reenter if they had proper documentation. As a result of this loophole, the "paper" family relations industry developed, whereby Chinese created fake identities to reenter. The constitutionality of the Scott Act of 1888 was upheld in *Chae Chan Ping v. United States* (1989).

Is the Scott Act Constitutional?

The Supreme Court will take up to-day the case of Chae Chan Ping, appellant, vs. The United States. This case involves the constitutionality of the Scott Exclusion Act, approved October 1, 1888. Chae Chan Ping was a laborer who on his departure from the United States June 2, 1887, received from the Collector at San Francisco a return certificate, as provided for in the law of June 2, 1887. On his return October 2, 1888, he was refused admittance to the country on the ground that under the Scott law his certificate had become void. Ex-Governor Hoadley, of Ohio, and James O. Carter, of New York, will appear for the appellant tomorrow and Solicitor General Jenks for the United States, while Hon. John F. Swift, S. M. White and Attorney General Johnson, of the State of Colorado, will appear to guard the interest of that State.

Source: "Is the Scott Act Constitutional?" *Washington Post (1877–1922), March 28, 1889, p. 6. ProQuest Historical Newspapers: The Washington Post.* https://search-proquest-com.jpllnet.sfsu.edu/docview/138410451?accountid=13802. Accessed October 9, 2016.

Books

Gold, Martin. *Forbidden Citizens: Chinese Exclusion and the U.S. Congress: A Legislative History*. Alexandria, VA: TheCapitol.Net, Inc., 2012. *Forbidden Citizens* is a comprehensive work that covers the history of anti-Chinese politics, debates, and legislation from the U.S. Congress. See Chapter 7, "The Scott Act of 1888."

Hall, Kermit, James Ely, and Joel Grossman, eds. *The Oxford Companion to the Supreme Court of the United States*. Oxford: Oxford University Press, 2005. This book is an essential guide for judges, lawyers, academics, journalists, and anyone interested in the impact of the Court's decisions on American society.

Websites

Chin, Philip. "Enforcing Chinese Exclusion: The Scott Act of 1888, Part 1." http://www.chineseamericanheroes.org. This essay discusses the history of the Scott Act, as well as the social-political milieu of the period. http://www.chineseamericanheroes.org/history/Enforcing%20Chinese%20Exclusion%20Part%202%20-%20The%20Scott%20Act%201.pdf. Accessed January 29, 2018.

"Scott Act (1888)." The Chinese American Experience: 1857–1892. *HarpWeek*, 1998–1999. It provides historical overview and impact of the Scott Act. http://immigrants.harpweek.com/ChineseAmericans/2KeyIssues/ScottAct.htm. Accessed October 9, 2016.

Also Noteworthy

1949

Chinese Communist leader Mao Zedong declares the creation of the People's Republic of China.

2005

In Coralville, Iowa, Troy Carter Anderson, a 24-year-old, is charged with a hate crime for punching a Middle Eastern woman outside a bar and yelling racial slurs at her.

October 2

1903

Wong Yak Chong, a 30-year-old Chinese laundryman, is shot and killed in Chinatown by two men, identified as Wong Ching and Charlie Chinn. This event led to the infamous police raid in Boston's Chinatown on October 11.

By the evening of October 7, the murder case had taken on a new twist, one which would have a direct relation to the eventual raid, Captain Cain stated that the friction between the two associations was not a gambling feud, but was the result of the On Leung Tong being angry because the Hip Sing Tong was collecting more than their share of the organized backmail [sic] that was allegedly taking place in Chinatown as a result of the Geary Act of 1892. According to the Globe, "It is an open secret that both societies have been bleeding the more ignorant of their countrymen by promising them immunity from police interference. They have also been levying blackmail upon the Chinese who are in the city without having complied with the requirements of the Chinese registration law." An unidentified police official claimed that when the Geary Act was passed, "Some of the more intelligent of the Chinese went to their ignorant compatriots and advised them they had better not be registered." When the time limit for registration expired, those who had advised them to not register are said to have returned demanding a fee in exchange for not turning them into the authorities. The police, thus, implied that the Hip Sing Tong was making more money on this system of protection than the On Leung Tong, a situation that precipitated the murder of Wong Yak Chong.

Source: Wong, K. Scott. "'The Eagle Seeks a Helpless Quarry': Chinatown, the Police, and the Press—The 1903 Boston Chinatown Raid Revisited." *Amerasia Journal* 22, no. 3 (1996): pp. 84–85.

Books

Seligman, Scott. *Tong Wars: The Untold Story of Vice, Money, and Murder in New York's Chinatown*. New York: Viking, 2016. *Tong Wars* details New York's Chinatown gangs.

To, Wing-Kai, and the Chinese Historical Society of New England. *Chinese in Boston: 1870–1965*. Charleston, SC: Arcadia Publishing, 2008. *Chinese in Boston* is a pictorial history of the Chinese community in Boston.

Websites

"Chinatown Tong Wars of the 1920s." Virtual Museum of the City of San Francisco. This essay details the history of Chinatown Tong Wars in San Francisco. http://www.sfmuseum.org/sfpd/sfpd4.html. Accessed January 25, 2018.

Chinese in Northwest America Research Committee. January 12, 2018. This site provides information on various aspects of early Chinese American history: related to this topic is the resources on "Secret Societies." http://www.cinarc.org/. Accessed January 25, 2018.

Also Noteworthy

2015

Sundar Pichai assumes the position of Google's CEO. Pichai is an American business executive of Indian ancestry.

October 3

1965

On October 3, 1965, the U.S. Congress passes the Immigration and Nationality Act, also known as the Hart-Celler Act, which eliminated national origins quota that was America's immigration policy since the 1920s. A preference system replaced the quota system that focused on immigrants' skills and family relationships with citizens and residents. Twenty thousand people per country are allowed entry annually, which does not include immediate relatives of citizens. Priority is given to those with skills and or family in the United States. There are seven preferences:

1. Adults, unmarried children under 21 years of age of U.S. citizens
2. Spouses and unmarried children of permanent residents (green card holders)
3. Members of the professions who possess exceptional ability in the sciences or the arts, who can benefit the economy, cultural interests, or welfare of the United States
4. Married children over 21 years of age and their spouses and children of U.S. citizens
5. Siblings of U.S. citizens
6. Skilled or unskilled workers in occupations with labor shortages
7. Political refugees, persons fleeing the Middle East, uprooted by natural calamity, and because of persecution due to race, religion, or political opinion from Communist or Communist-dominated countries.

The act was proposed by Representative Emanuel Celler of New York, cosponsored by Senator Philip Hart of Michigan, and promoted by Senator Ted Kennedy of Massachusetts.

President Lyndon B. Johnson's Remarks at the Signing of the Immigration Bill at Liberty Island, New York (October 3, 1965).

Mr. Vice President, Mr. Speaker, Mr. Ambassador Goldberg, distinguished Members of the leadership of the Congress, distinguished Governors and mayors, my fellow countrymen:

We have called the Congress here this afternoon not only to mark a very historic occasion, but to settle a very old issue that is in dispute. That issue is, to what congressional district does Liberty Island really belong—Congressman Farbstein or Congressman Gallagher? It will be settled by whoever of the two can walk first to the top of the Statue of Liberty.

This bill that we will sign today is not a revolutionary bill. It does not affect the lives of millions. It will not reshape the structure of our daily lives, or really add importantly to either our wealth or our power.

Yet it is still one of the most important acts of this Congress and of this administration.

For it does repair a very deep and painful flaw in the fabric of American justice. It corrects a cruel and enduring wrong in the conduct of the American Nation.

Speaker McCormack and Congressman Celler almost 40 years ago first pointed that out in their maiden speeches in the Congress. And this measure that we will sign today will really make us truer to ourselves both as a country and as a people. It will strengthen us in a hundred unseen ways.

I have come here to thank personally each Member of the Congress who labored so long and so valiantly to make this occasion come true today, and to make this bill a reality. I cannot mention all their names, for it would take much too long, but my gratitude—and that of this Nation—belongs to the 89th Congress.

We are indebted, too, to the vision of the late beloved President John Fitzgerald Kennedy, and to the support given to this measure by the then Attorney General and now Senator, Robert F. Kennedy.

In the final days of consideration, this bill had no more able champion than the present Attorney General, Nicholas Katzenbach, who, with New York's own "Manny" Celler, and Senator Ted Kennedy of Massachusetts, and Congressman Feighan of Ohio, and Senator Mansfield and Senator Dirksen constituting the leadership of the Senate, and

Senator Javits, helped to guide this bill to passage, along with the help of the Members sitting in front of me today.

This bill says simply that from this day forth those wishing to immigrate to America shall be admitted on the basis of their skills and their close relationship to those already here.

This is a simple test, and it is a fair test. Those who can contribute most to this country—to its growth, to its strength, to its spirit—will be the first that are admitted to this land.

The fairness of this standard is so self-evident that we may well wonder that it has not always been applied. Yet the fact is that for over four decades the immigration policy of the United States has been twisted and has been distorted by the harsh injustice of the national origins quota system.

Under that system the ability of new immigrants to come to America depended upon the country of their birth. Only 3 countries were allowed to supply 70 percent of all the immigrants.

Families were kept apart because a husband or a wife or a child had been born in the wrong place.

Men of needed skill and talent were denied entrance because they came from southern or eastern Europe or from one of the developing continents.

This system violated the basic principle of American democracy—the principle that values and rewards each man on the basis of his merit as a man.

It has been un-American in the highest sense, because it has been untrue to the faith that brought thousands to these shores even before we were a country.

Today, with my signature, this system is abolished.

We can now believe that it will never again shadow the gate to the American Nation with the twin barriers of prejudice and privilege.

Our beautiful America was built by a nation of strangers. From a hundred different places or more they have poured forth into an empty land, joining and blending in one mighty and irresistible tide.

The land flourished because it was fed from so many sources—because it was nourished by so many cultures and traditions and peoples.

And from this experience, almost unique in the history of nations, has come America's attitude toward the rest of the world. We, because of what we are, feel safer and stronger in a world as varied as the people who make it up—a world where no country rules another and all countries can deal with the basic problems of human dignity and deal with those problems in their own way.

Now, under the monument which has welcomed so many to our shores, the American Nation returns to the finest of its traditions today.

The days of unlimited immigration are past.

But those who do come will come because of what they are, and not because of the land from which they sprung.

When the earliest settlers poured into a wild continent there was no one to ask them where they came from. The only question was: Were they sturdy enough to make the journey, were they strong enough to clear the land, were they enduring enough to make a home for freedom, and were they brave enough to die for liberty if it became necessary to do so?

And so it has been through all the great and testing moments of American history. Our history this year we see in Viet-Nam. Men there are dying—men named Fernandez and Zajac and Zelinko and Mariano and McCormick.

Neither the enemy who killed them nor the people whose independence they have fought to save ever asked them where they or their parents came from. They were all Americans. It was for free men and for America that they gave their all, they gave their lives and selves.

By eliminating that same question as a test for immigration the Congress proves ourselves worthy of those men and worthy of our own traditions as a Nation.

ASYLUM FOR CUBAN REFUGEES

So it is in that spirit that I declare this afternoon to the people of Cuba that those who seek refuge here in America will find it. The dedication of America to our traditions as an asylum for the oppressed is going to be upheld.

I have directed the Departments of State and Justice and Health, Education, and Welfare to immediately make all the necessary arrangements to permit those in Cuba who seek freedom to make an orderly entry into the United States of America.

Our first concern will be with those Cubans who have been separated from their children and their parents and their husbands and their wives and that are now in this country. Our next concern is with those who are imprisoned for political reasons.

And I will send to the Congress tomorrow a request for supplementary funds of $12,600,000 to carry forth the commitment that I am making today.

I am asking the Department of State to seek through the Swiss Government immediately the agreement of the Cuban Government in a request to the President of the International Red Cross Committee. The request is for the assistance of the Committee in processing the movement of refugees from Cuba to Miami. Miami will serve as a port of entry and a temporary stopping place for refugees as they settle in other parts of this country.

And to all the voluntary agencies in the United States, I appeal for their continuation and expansion of their magnificent work. Their help is needed in the reception and the settlement of those who choose to leave Cuba. The Federal Government will work closely with these agencies in their tasks of charity and brotherhood.

I want all the people of this great land of ours to know of the really enormous contribution which the compassionate citizens of Florida have made to humanity and to decency. And all States in this Union can join with Florida now in extending the hand of helpfulness and humanity to our Cuban brothers.

The lesson of our times is sharp and clear in this movement of people from one land to another. Once again, it stamps the mark of failure on a regime when many of its citizens voluntarily choose to leave the land of their birth for a more hopeful home in America. The future holds little hope for any government where the present holds no hope for the people.

And so we Americans will welcome these Cuban people. For the tides of history run strong, and in another day they can return to their homeland to find it cleansed of terror and free from fear.

Over my shoulders here you can see Ellis Island, whose vacant corridors echo today the joyous sound of long ago voices.

And today we can all believe that the lamp of this grand old lady is brighter today—and the golden door that she guards gleams more brilliantly in the light of an increased liberty for the people from all the countries of the globe.

Thank you very much.

Source: Public Papers of the Presidents of the United States: Lyndon B. Johnson, 1965. Vol. II, entry 546. Washington, DC: Government Printing Office, 1966, pp. 1037–1040.

Books

Chin, Gabriel, and Rose Villazor, eds. *The Immigration and Nationality Act of 1965: Legislating a New America*. Cambridge: Cambridge University Press, 2015. *The Immigration and Nationality Act of 1965* is a collection of critical essays by legal scholars on the history, legacy, significance, and impact of the landmark 1965 Immigration and Nationality Act.

Orchowski, Margaret. *The Law That Changed the Face of America: The Immigration and Nationality Act of 1965*. Lanham, MD: Rowman & Littlefield, 2015. *The Law That Changed the Face of America* covers the history of the 1965 act, in addition to critical issues of globalization, war on terrorism, and other 21st-century issues related to the U.S. immigration.

Websites

Chishti, Muzaffar, Faye Hipsman, and Isabel Ball. "Fifty Years On, the 1965 Immigration and Nationality Act Continues to Reshape the United States." Migration Policy Institute. October 15, 2015. This site contains an analytical essay on the impact and significance of the 1965 Immigration and Nationality Act with graphs and charts of immigration statistical data. http://www.migrationpolicy.org/article/fifty-years-1965-immigration-and-nationality-act-continues-reshape-united-states. Accessed January 17, 2017.

Roberts, Sam. "Minorities in the U.S. Set to Become Majority by 2042." *New York Times*, August 14, 2008. This newspaper article discusses the impact of the 1965 Immigration and Nationality Act on U.S. racial demographics. http://www.nytimes.com/2008/08/14/world/americas/14iht-census.1.15284537.html?_r=0. Accessed January 17, 2017.

October 4

2001

In a post–9/11 hate crime, Vasudev Patel is shot behind the counter of his gas station in Mesquite, Texas. His killer, a white supremacist, Mark Anthony Stroman, walked into Patel's gas station and fired a .44-calibre round into the victim's chest and said, "God bless America." Patel is survived by his wife and son. During Stroman's racist rampage, he also killed Pakistani American Waqar Hasan, and Bangladeshi American Rais Bhuiyan was seriously wounded and left blind in one eye.

Patel, a 49-year-old immigrant from India, had a family. I visited Patel's family a year after his death and here's what I found: his wife, Alka Patel, behind the counter of their station selling cigarettes and lottery tickets. Her teenage son was crowded under the counter at her feet, doing his homework. The sadness and sense of loss was palpable. For her, her loss was directly linked to those killed at the World Trade Center and the Pentagon and . . . those hijacked jetliners.

"If it wasn't for September 11, my husband would still be here," Alka Patel told me at the time. "Why shouldn't our families be treated the same? I feel like we all have the same story."

Her sentiment is one that I have heard over and over again from Muslims—and those mistaken for "looking" Muslim—throughout the country over the past decade. They scream silently: It wasn't me. I didn't do it. Please don't look at me that way. Please, don't hurt my family.

Since Sept. 11, as the country sought to crack down on terrorism, people like Anya Cordell have ramped up their efforts to remind the people of the nation not to take out their frustrations on innocent Muslims, Sikhs, Hindus, Arabs, South Asians and others. Patel's killing was one of more than 80 hate crimes against people who became targets after the terrorist attacks that authorities prosecuted in the year after the terrorist attacks.

Source: Pierre, Robert. "Hate in the Wake of 9/11." *News India—Times*, September 23, 2011, p. 2.

Books

Iyer, Deepa. *We Too Sing America: South Asian, Arab, Muslim, and Sikh Immigrants Shape Our Multiracial Future*. New York: The New Press, 2015. *We Too Sing America* explores various aspects of anti-Muslim and anti-Asian racial hatred and crimes in the United States.

Karam, Nicoletta. *The 9/11 Backlash: A Decade of U.S. Hate Crimes Targeting the Innocent*. Berkeley, CA: Beatitude Press, 2012. *The 9/11 Backlash* examines a decade of Islamophobia and Hinduphobia that fueled hate crimes against South Asians, Muslims, Arabs, Sikhs, and other Asian Americans.

Websites

Human Rights Watch. "'We Are Not the Enemy': Hate Crimes against Arabs, Muslims, and Those Perceived to Be Arab or Muslim after September 11." Vol. 14, No. 6 (G)—November 2002. This report summarizes Islamophobia and Arabphobia in the United States post–9/11 and documents hate crime cases up to date of publication. https://www.hrw.org/reports/2002/usahate/usa1102.pdf. Accessed January 24, 2018.

Mears, Bill. "Texas Man Executed for Post-9/11 Murder." CNN, July 20, 2011. This article is about Vasudev Patel's killer's execution. http://www.cnn.com/2011/CRIME/07/20/texas.execution/index.html. Accessed January 24, 2018.

Also Noteworthy

1914

The First Japanese Presbyterian Church begins to worship together with the Japanese Congregational Church. The churches formed the Federated Japanese Church of Christ of San Francisco, an arrangement that continued through the war years, the period of incarceration in the "relocation camps," until the return of the Japanese Americans to San Francisco and the rebuilding of their lives, at which point the federation dissolved.

1983

The Federal District Court of San Francisco reverses Fred Korematsu's original conviction and rules that the U.S. government had no justification for issuing the internment orders.

2001

A Pakistani restaurant in Salt Lake City, Utah, is burned down.

2002

In Queens, New York, two men attack a 17-year-old Middle Eastern teenager because of his ethnicity and accuse him of being a Taliban, blaming him for the 9/11 terrorist attack.

October 5

1978

On this day, President Carter signs Public Law 95–419 designating Asian Pacific Heritage Week to occur from May 4 to 10, 1979. Through Presidential Proclamation 4650 issued March 28, 1979, Carter designated the first Asian Pacific Heritage Week in 1979. For the next 10 years through annual presidential proclamations, Presidents Carter, Reagan, and Bush renewed the designation. Not until 1990 did Congress ask the president to expand the week to the month of May with Public Law 101–283 (amending Public Law 95–419).

By the President of the United States of America

A Proclamation

America's greatness: its ideals, its system of government, its economy, its people—derives from the contribution of peoples of many origins who come to our land seeking human liberties or economic opportunity. Asian-Americans have played a significant role in the creation of a dynamic and pluralistic America, with their enormous contributions to our science, arts, industry, government and commerce.

Unfortunately, we have not always fully appreciated the talents and the contributions which Asian-Americans have brought to the United States. Until recently, our immigration and naturalization laws discriminated against them. They were also subjected to discrimination in education, housing, and employment. And during World War II our Japanese-American citizens were treated with suspicion and fear.

Yet, Asians of diverse origins: from China, Japan, Korea, the Philippines, and Southeast Asia, continued to look to America as a land of hope, opportunity, and freedom.

At last their confidence in the United States has been justified. We have succeeded in removing the barriers to full participation in American life, and we welcome the newest Asian immigrants to our shores, refugees from Indochina displaced by political and social upheavals. Their successful integration into American society and their positive and active participation in our national life demonstrates the soundness of America's policy of continued openness to peoples from Asia and the Pacific.

The Ninety-Fifth Congress has requested the President by House Joint Resolution 1007, approved October 5, 1978, to designate the seven-day period beginning on May 4, 1979, as "Asian/Pacific American Heritage Week."

Now, Therefore, I, Jimmy Carter, *President of the United States of America, declare the week beginning on May 4, 1979, as Asian/Pacific American Heritage Week. I call upon the people of the United States, especially the educational community, to observe this week with appropriate ceremonies and activities.*

In Witness Whereof, *I have hereunto set my hand this twenty-eighth day of March, in the year of our Lord nineteen hundred seventy-nine, and of the Independence of the United States of America the two hundred and third.*

JIMMY CARTER

Source: Carter, Jimmy. "Proclamation 4650—Asian/Pacific American Heritage Week, 1979." March 28, 1979. The American Presidency Project. University of California, Santa Barbara. http://www.presidency.ucsb.edu/ws/index.php?pid=32111. Accessed January 22, 2018.

Books

Lee, Jonathan H. X., and Kathleen Nadeau, eds. *Asian American Identities and Practices: Folkloric Expressions in Everyday Life*. Lanham, MD: Lexington Books, 2014. See Dawn Lee Tu's Chapter 3, "The 'Movement' as Folklore: Asian American College Youth and Vernacular Expressions of Asian Pacific American Heritage."

Lee, Jonathan H. X., and Kathleen Nadeau, eds. *Encyclopedia of Asian American Folklore and Folklife*. Santa Barbara, CA: ABC-CLIO, 2011. See entries related to Asian Pacific American Heritage Month.

Websites

"Asian/Pacific American Heritage Month." Library of Congress. May 5, 2017. This site provides an overview of Asian Pacific American Heritage Month and links to primary documents, such as the proclamations. https://www.loc.gov/law/help/commemorative-observations/asian.php. Accessed January 25, 2018.

Asian Pacific American Heritage Month. Library of Congress. 2018. This site is the official web page for Asian Pacific American Heritage Month that contains useful resources for teaching. https://asianpacificheritage.gov/. Accessed January 25, 2018.

October 6

1877

Several Japanese Christian students residing in San Francisco assemble and organize the Fukuinkai, or Gospel Society for Bible study, that also encourages mutual support for one another. This is the first immigrant association formed by the Japanese.

The Fukuinkai was the first organization formed by Japanese living in America and can be considered "a cradle society for Japanese students." It responded to the needs of migrant working students and provided a supportive environment that enabled them to continue their studies in American society. The organization's activities and services included night classes, dormitories, meals, assistance in finding employment, and support for studying abroad. These programs were not just beneficial to Fukuinkai members. The various activities also nurtured a vision and concern for the welfare of others outside the organization. While the educational and missionary work by American Protestant churches among Japanese students during this time is often noted, it needs to be recognized that the Fukuinkai also played a major role in the initial formation of the Japanese community.

Source: Ryo, Yoshida. 2007. "Japanese Immigrants and Their Christian Communities in North America: A Case Study of the Fukuinkai, 1877–1896." *Japanese Journal of Religious Studies* 34, no. 1: pp. 229–244, 230–231.

Books

Ichioka, Yuji. *The Issei: The World of the First Generation Japanese Immigrants, 1885–1924*. New York: Free Press, 1988. *The Issei* covers the history of the first generation of Japanese immigrants, using both English and Japanese primary sources.

Niiya, Brian, ed. *Japanese American History: An A-to-Z Reference from 1868 to the Present*. New York: Facts on File, 1993. See entry on the "Gospel Society (Fukuinkai)."

Websites

"Asiamerica Ministries in the Episcopal Church." The Episcopal Church. The Domestic and Foreign Missionary Society. New York: Asiamerica Ministries Office. This brochure provides the history of the Episcopal missionary among Asian American communities. http://www.episcopalchurch.org/files/asiameria_ministries_brochure.pdf. Accessed January 29, 2018.

Japantown History. "Nihonmachi, Historical Background." This is the official site for Japantown in San Francisco; it provides a historical essay on the early Japanese Americans in San Francisco. http://www.jtowntaskforce.org/jtown_history01.htm. Accessed January 29, 2018.

Also Noteworthy

2007

In Bakersfield, California, two men enter the women's section of a mosque and yell anti-Muslim, anti-Arab slurs, such as "terrorist go home." Later on, windows of the mosque and cars are damaged by a group of people.

October 7

1955

Yo-Yo Ma, an internationally acclaimed cellist and musician, is born in Paris, France.

His father, Hiao-Tsiun, also a musician, taught him to concentrate intensively. Through his father's pedagogical techniques, he developed a feeling for musical structure. Yo, which in Chinese means friendship, is the generational character for Ma. Ma tells of how he had to deal with 2 contradictory worlds. At home he spoke only Chinese & was expected to adhere to Chinese values, but he was also an American growing up with American values. At 17 he decided to go to Harvard rather than pursue a full-time musical career. At Harvard he learned a new vocabulary for understanding music, one that made him consider a work's overall musical architecture. During his Harvard years, he also made his London debut with the Royal Philharmonic Orchestra. Ma met his wife, Jill Hornor, during one of the 4 summers he spent at the Marlboro Festival in Vermont. Ma's playing can't be judged by traditional standards. Even though his movements appear awkward & impetuous, there's no loss of tonal beauty or accuracy of intonation. Bach's solo suites stand at the pinnacle of Ma's repertoire. Still, he's set on expanding his repertoire to include 20th century music. Since he was 16 Ma has played on 3 superb cellos: 2 are Venetian dating from 1722 & 1733 & the third is a 1712 Stradivari.

Source: Blum, David. "A Process Larger Than Oneself." *New Yorker*, May 1, 1989, p. 41.

Books

Kenneson, Claude. *Musical Prodigies: Perilous Journeys, Remarkable Lives.* Portland, OR: Amadeus Press, 1998. See Chapter 16, "Born for the Cello: Jacqueline de Pre and Yo-Yo Ma."

Whiting, Jim. *Yo-Yo Ma: A Biography.* Westport, CT: Greenwood Press, 2008. *Yo-Yo Ma* covers various aspects of Ma's personal and professional life.

Websites

"A Musician of Many Cultures." NPR, March 10, 2008. This essay discusses Ma's diverse cultural experiences and influences with links to other resources available through NPR. https://www.npr.org/templates/story/story.php?storyId=87960790. Accessed January 25, 2018.

Tassel, Janet. "Yo-Yo Ma's Journeys." *Harvard Magazine*, March 1, 2000. This essay is based on interviews with Ma's professors and music teachers. https://www.harvardmagazine.com/2000/03/yo-yo-mas-journeys-html. Accessed January 25, 2018.

October 8

1888

On this day, Chae Chan Ping, a Chinese unskilled laborer working in San Francisco, attempts to return to the United States after visiting China: he had the proper reentry certificate. He left the United States to visit China before the passage of the Scott Act. He was stopped at the port of entry and denied entry. Under the Scott Act, reentry certificates were abolished. Ping challenged the denial, and his case reached the U.S. Supreme Court. *Chae Chan Ping v. United States* was decided on May 13, 1889, in favor of the United States. The Supreme Court's decision was an important precedent both for establishing the federal government's discretionary power over immigration and for upholding the government's authority to pass and enforce legislation contradictory to the terms of past international treaties (the treaty in question being the Burlingame Treaty of 1868).

The Chinese Exclusion Case, 130 U.S. 581 (1889)

No. 1448

Argued March 28–29, 1889

Decided May 13, 1889

130 U.S. 581

APPEAL FROM THE CIRCUIT COURT OF THE UNITED

STATES FOR THE NORTHERN DISTRICT OF CALIFORNIA

Syllabus

In their relations with foreign governments and their subjects or citizens, the United States are a nation, invested with the powers which belong to independent nations.

So far as a treaty made by the United States with any foreign power can become the subject of judicial cognizance in the courts of this country, it is subject to such acts as Congress may pass for its enforcement, modification, or appeal. The Head Money Cases, *112 U. S. 580, and* Whitney v. Robertson, *124 U. S. 190, followed.*

The abrogation of a treaty, like the repeal of a law, operates only on future transactions, leaving unaffected those executed under it previous to the abrogation.

The rights and interests created by a treaty, which have become so vested that its expiration or abrogation will not destroy or impair them, are such as are connected with and lie in property, capable of sale and transfer or other disposition, and not such as are personal and untransferable in their character.

The power of the legislative department of the government to exclude aliens from the United States is an incident of sovereignty which cannot be surrendered by the treaty making power.

The Act of October 1, 1888, 25 Stat. 504, c. 1064, excluding Chinese laborers from the United States, was a constitutional exercise of legislative power, and, so far as it conflicted with existing treaties between the United States and China, it operated to that extent to abrogate them as part of the municipal law of the United States.

A certificate issued to a Chinese laborer under the fourth and fifth sections of the Act of May 6, 1882, 22 Stat. 58, c. 126, as amended July 5, 1884, 23 Stat. 115, c. 220, conferred upon him no right to return to the United States of which he could not be deprived by a subsequent act of Congress.

The history of Chinese immigration into the United States stated, together with a review of the treaties and legislation affecting it.

The Court stated the case as follows in its opinion:

This case comes before us on appeal from an order of the Circuit Court of the United States for the Northern District of California refusing to release the appellant, on a writ of habeas corpus, from his alleged unlawful detention by Capt. Walker, master of the steamship Belgic, *lying within the harbor of San Francisco. The appellant is a subject of the Emperor of China, and a laborer by occupation. He resided at San Francisco, California, following his occupation, from sometime in 1875 until June 2, 1887, when he left for China on the steamship* Gaelic, *having in his possession a certificate in terms entitling him to return to the United States, bearing date on that day, duly issued to him by the collector of customs of the port of San Francisco, pursuant to the provisions of § 4 of the Restriction Act of May 6, 1882, as amended by the Act of July 5, 1884, 22 Stat. 59, c. 126; 23 Stat. 115, c. 220.*

On the 7th of September, 1888, the appellant, on his return to California, sailed from Hong Kong in the steamship Belgic, *which arrived within the port of San Francisco on the 8th of October following. On his arrival, he presented to the proper custom house officers his certificate and demanded permission to land. The collector of the port refused the permit solely on the ground that under the Act of Congress approved October 1, 1888, supplementary to the Restriction Acts of 1882 and 1884, the certificate had been annulled and his right to land abrogated, and he had been thereby forbidden again to enter the United States. 25 Stat. 504, c. 1064. The captain of the steamship therefore detained the appellant on board the steamer. Thereupon a petition on his behalf was presented to the Circuit Court of the United States for the Northern District of California, alleging that he was unlawfully restrained of his liberty and praying that a writ of habeas corpus might be issued directed to the master of the steamship commanding him to have the body of the appellant, with the cause of his detention, before the court at a time and place designated, to do and receive what might there be considered in the premises. A writ was accordingly issued, and in obedience to it the body of the appellant was produced before the court. Upon the hearing which followed, the court, after finding the facts substantially as stated, held as conclusions of law that the appellant was not entitled to enter the United States and was not unlawfully restrained of his liberty, and ordered that he be remanded to the custody of the master of the steamship from which he had been taken under the writ. From this order an appeal was taken to this Court.*

Source: "The Chinese Exclusion Case, 130 U.S. 581 (1889)." JUSTIA U.S. Supreme Court. 2016. https://supreme.justia.com/cases/federal/us/130/581/case.html. Accessed October 9, 2016.

Books

Hall, Kermit, ed. *The Oxford Guide to United States Supreme Court Decisions*. Oxford: Oxford University Press, 1999. See John R. Wunder's entry "Chinese Exclusion Cases" (pp. 53–54) for historical discussion of the development of Chinese exclusion legislation.

Scott, David. *China and the International System, 1840–1949: Power, Presence, and Perceptions in a Century of Humiliation*. Albany: State University of New York Press, 2008. *China and the International System* discusses various aspects of U.S.-China relations' history and its impact on China. See Chapter 3, "Humiliations Maintained," for discussion on U.S.-China relations and political restrictions in California.

Websites

"The Chinese Exclusion Case, 130 U.S. 581 (1889)." JUSTIA U.S. Supreme Court. 2016. The full text of *Chae Chan Ping v. United States* is available at https://supreme.justia.com/cases/federal/us/130/581/case.html. Accessed October 9, 2016.

Lewis, Thomas Tandy. "Chinese Exclusion Cases." Immigration to the United States. Lewis discusses the significance of *Chae Chan Ping v. United States*. http://immigrationtounitedstates.org/422-chinese-exclusion-cases.html. Accessed October 9, 2016.

October 9

1949

Political conflict between supporters of the new People's Republic of China, founded on October 1, 1949, and the exiled Kuomintang, Chinese Nationalist Party, erupts in San Francisco, Chinatown.

Despite the apparent growing support for the PRC [People's Republic of China] in the Chinese community, developments in international and domestic events soon applied brakes to its further progress. In 1948 the cold war had begun with the Soviet Union's Berlin blockade. The same year, the anti-Communist hysteria in the United States was launched by the Alger Hiss investigation of the House Un-American Activities Committee. These developments were creating an atmosphere favorable to the continued existence of the KMT [Kuomintang, Chinese Nationalist Party] in this country despite their imminent debacle on the China mainland. Thus on October 9, 1949, when San Francisco's Chinese workers Mutual-Aid Association celebrated the founding of the People's Republic of China in Chinatown, the local KMT leadership was emboldened to hire hoodlums to break up the meeting and seize the five-starred flag of the new government. The next evening on Double Ten KMT partisans passed out leaflets calling for the eradication of fifteen progressives from the Chinese community.

Source: Lai, Him Mark. "China and the Chinese American Community: The Political Dimension—The Huangling Du Community in Northern California." *Chinese America: History and Perspectives* (1999): p. 9.

Books

Brooks, Charlotte. *Between Mao and McCarthy: Chinese American Politics in the Cold War Years*. Chicago, IL: University of Chicago Press, 2015. *Between Mao and McCarthy* examines the complex and vexing political climate within Chinese American communities during the Cold War era.

Lai, Him Mark. *Chinese American Transnational Politics*. Urbana: University of Illinois Press, 2010. See Chapter 1, "China and the Chinese American Community: The Political Dimension," for a discussion related to the October 9 incident.

Websites

Lai, Him Mark. "A Historical Survey of Organizations of the Left among the Chinese in America." History Is a Weapon. 1972. This site provides a reprint of Him Mark Lai's article that discusses the political organization and history of Chinese in America. http://www.historyisaweapon.com/defcon1/leftchineseamerica.html. Accessed January 25, 2018.

"Meanwhile, Back in Chinatown . . ." *San Francisco Bay Guardian* 6, no. 2 (March 28, 1972): 3–7. https://archive.org/. This site provides the archival newspaper and the article that discusses the political history of the Chinese American community in San Francisco. https://archive.org/stream/Iss06.02#page/n0/mode/2up. Accessed January 25, 2018.

October 10

1911

After the revolutionary uprising of October 10, 1911 (known as Double Ten Day), which led to the establishment of a republic in China, many Chinese Americans go back to China with hopes of a bright future, free of racism, but many others remained in the United States.

As the Reform Movement waned, failing in its efforts to modernize China, popular support turned to Sun Yat-sen's Tongmenghui, or Revolutionary Party, which advocated the overthrow of the Qing dynasty and the establishment of a republic. With the support of overseas Chinese money, underground rebels at home attempted eight armed rebellions between 1907 and 1911 in the southern provinces of Guangdong and Guangxi. Victory was not won until the Wuchang uprising of October 10, 1911. The participation of women in this revolutionary movement in both China and the United States is well documented in CSYP *[Chung Sai Yat Po, a Chinese language newspaper]. Revolutionary activities on the part of women in China ranged from organizing benefit performances to enlisting in the army. . . . There was reportedly a revolutionary unit in Shanghai consisting of five hundred patriotic women, armed and ready to do battle under the leadership of a female commander. . . . Stories on women engaged in dangerous undercover work also appeared in the newspaper—for example, the assassination of Anhui's provincial governor by a female student and the Revolutionary Party's use of women as ammunition smugglers and spies. . . . Meanwhile Chinese American women were doing their part in support of the revolutionary cause. According to CSYP, female orators of the Young China Society were speaking up for the revolution as well as for women's rights. They had also made two-sided flag, one bearing the Chinese flag and the other, the flag of the Revolutionary Army. . . . When Dr. Sun Yat-sen, leader of the revolution, spoke to over six hundred people in Chinatown, the newspaper noted that there were at least fifty women in attendance. Chinese American women also donated money and jewelry and helped with Red Cross work—fund-raising, preparing bandages and medicines, and sewing garments for the war effort.*

Source: Yung, Judy. "The Social Awakening of Chinese American Women as Reported in *Chung Sai Yat Po*, 1900–1911." *Chinese American: History and Perspectives* (1988): pp. 95–96.

Books

Chang, Iris. *The Chinese in America: A Narrative History*. New York: Penguin Books, 2004. *The Chinese in America* covers 150-year history of the Chinese experience in the United States.

Wey, Nancy. *A History of Chinese Americans in California*. Sacramento: State of California, Department of Parks and Recreation, 1988. *A History of Chinese Americans in California* covers many aspects of the Chinese experience in California.

Websites

"A Century of Change: China 1911–2011." Hoover Institution. April 12, 2011. This site provides a history of the 1911 revolution in both English and Chinese. https://www.hoover.org/events/century-change-china-1911-2011. Accessed January 25, 2018.

Chie, Ho. "100 Years of History behind 'Double Ten' Day of the R.O.C." TaiwaneseAmerican.org. October 10, 2011. It provides a historical overview of the October 10, 1911, uprising from a Taiwanese American perspective. http://www.taiwaneseamerican.org/2011/10/100-years-of-history-behind-double-ten-day-of-the-r-o-c/. Accessed January 25, 2018.

Also Noteworthy

2010

In Staten Island, New York, three 14-year-old Latino youths and one 15-year-old black youth are charged with assault and aggravated harassment for bullying and harassing a peer of Muslim faith. And at Florence, South Carolina, the words "Pig Chump" are spelled out with bacon placed outside an Islamic center.

October 11

1903

Federal immigration officials and the police raid Boston's Chinatown without search warrants and arrest 234 Chinese, including American-born citizens who allegedly had no registration certificates on their persons. Only 50 were found to be in the country without proper documentation. This incident is directly related to the passage of the Geary Act of 1892, which required that all Chinese in the United States carry identification cards.

At Boston in 1903 the whole Chinese colony of several thousand persons was surrounded in the evening by police and immigration officers and 234 of them who could not at once produce certificates were taken to the Federal building, of whom 45 only were afterward deported [other sources document 50]. They were put in two small rooms where they could not lie down; although a few were released during the night the greater part were kept till the next day when friends or legal proceedings brought relief. The citizens of Boston held an indignation meeting and the Press attacked the Immigration department, which defended itself with the excuse that the arrest was necessary to rid the Chinese quarter of Highbinders and pointed to the deportation of 45 of those arrested and the escape of a few more released on bonds. But the Department apparently did not consider the outrage inflicted upon the whole colony of peaceful Chinese holding certificates of lawful residence and entitled by treaty to the protection of the laws.

Source: Coolidge, Mary Roberts. *Chinese Immigration*. New York: Henry Holt and Company, 1909, p. 323.

Books

Coben, Stanley. *A. Mitchell Palmer: Politician*. New York: Columbia University Press, 1963. *A. Mitchell Palmer* is a historical biography of an American politician, who as attorney general authorized immigration raids in 33 cities. For a detailed discussion of the Boston Chinatown raid, see pp. 217–245.

Coolidge, Mary Roberts. *Chinese Immigration*. New York: Henry Holt and Company, 1909. *Chinese Immigration* covers the early history of Chinese immigration to the United States.

Websites

Keith, Zak. "Anti-Chinese USA: Racism and Discrimination from the Onset." 2009. This site provides a chronological and historical discussion of anti-Chinese history in the United States with photographs and links to resources. http://www.zakkeith.com/articles,blogs,forums/anti-Chinese-persecution-in-the-USA-history-time line.htm. Accessed October 13, 2016.

Onion, Rebecca. "The papers Late-19th-Century Chinese Immigrants Had to Carry to Prove Their Legal Status." *Slate*. January 30, 2015. This article discusses the history and impact of the Geary Act of 1892. http://www.slate.com/blogs/the_vault/2015/01/30/history_of_chinese_exclusion_certificates_required_by_the_geary_act.html. Accessed June 14, 2018.

Also Noteworthy

1906

San Francisco Board of Education passes a resolution that orders all Chinese, Japanese, and Korean children to be placed in a segregated Oriental Public School situated on the south side of Clay Street, between Powell and Mason Streets.

October 12

1839

The Thai Chinese Siamese twins Chang and Eng become naturalized U.S. citizens.

After a decade of tours, the twins retired from show business to settle in Wilkesboro, North Carolina. Welcomed by a resolution passed by the state legislature declaring them honorary citizens, the twins officially became naturalized U.S. citizens on October 12, 1839. They were the first known Asians to do so in American history. As citizens, they exercised their right to participate in all elections, becoming the first Asian Americans to cast votes.

Source: Perreira, Todd LeRoy. "Bunker, Chang and Eng (1811–1874)." In *Asian American History and Culture: An Encyclopedia*, edited by Huping Ling and Allan Austin, p. 569. Armonk, NY: M. E. Sharpe, Inc., 2010.

Books

Orser, Joseph. *The Lives of Chang and Eng: Siam's Twins in Nineteenth-Century America*. Chapel Hill: University of North Carolina Press, 2014. Historian Joseph Orser's biography of Chang and Eng focuses on their history through antebellum America, their family lives in North Carolina, their fame, and the shifting racial and cultural landscape of 19th-century American culture and society.

Wu, Cynthia. *Chang and Eng Reconnected: The Original Siamese Twins in American Culture*. Philadelphia, PA: Temple University Press, 2012. American studies professor Cynthia Wu traces the history of Chang and Eng through the terrain of American culture and representations of race, disability, and science vis-à-vis nation-building ideologies and narratives.

Websites

"Eng & Chang Bunker: Original Siamese Twins Exhibit, Mount Airy, North Carolina." This site provides a timeline of the twins' life, along with their historical background, and images. Surry Arts Council. 2016. http://www.surryarts.org/siamesetwins/index.html. Accessed January 28, 2018.

Eng & Chang Bunker: The Siamese Twins collection. This site presents original primary source material on Chang and Eng Bunker from the special collections in Wilson Library at the University of North Carolina at Chapel Hill. http://dc.lib.unc.edu/cdm/compoundobject/collection/bunkers/id/504/rec/2. Accessed January 28, 2018.

2000

Delta Chi Lambda, an Asian American interest sorority, is founded at the University of Arizona.

October 13

1942

Tanforan, California, Assembly Center is in operation from April 28 to October 13. Assembly centers were makeshift internment camps that provided temporary housing for roughly 92,000 Japanese Americans who were displaced by Executive Order 9066. Those residing in the San Francisco Bay Area were assigned to Tanforan, a racetrack located in San Bruno.

As the Tanforan racetrack was situated just thirty kilometers south of San Francisco, the transfer was a relatively short one for the Bay Area residents. The first group of evacuees arrived on April 27, a volunteer contingent of 421 workers to handle the primary needs of transforming the racetrack into an Assembly Center. In the following days, numerous buses unloaded their human cargo from the Bay Area. By May 10, Tanforan housed 7,496 people, and by May 20, with the arrival of the last group of evacuees, the population had risen to 7,796 and remained at that level for almost four months.

As the Greyhound buses approached the compound, the arrivals first noticed the grandstand, the dominating feature of the former racetrack, capable of seating 10,000 people. Then, a high barbed wire fence, pierced at regular intervals by tall guard towers, came into view. Scattered over the compound, which measured 118 acres (0.5 km2), were rows of barracks and horse stalls in near-perfect symmetry. Everywhere construction was taking place. . . . The baleful contrast of grandstand and barbed wire fence prefigured the many paradoxes and incongruities that the evacuees were about to endure.

Source: Linke, Konard. "Dominance, Resistance, and Cooperation in the Tanforan Assembly Center." *Amerikastudien/American Studies* 54, no. 4 (2009): pp. 630–631.

Books

Ng, Wendy. *Japanese American Internment during World War II: A History and Reference Guide.* Westport, CT: Greenwood Press, 2002. Ng's volume covers various aspects of Japanese American internment, along with primary documents, photographic essays, and biographies of personalities behind the internment program.

Okihiro, Gary, ed. *Encyclopedia of Japanese American Internment.* Santa Barbara, CA: Greenwood, 2013. See section on Camps, Centers, and Prisons.

Websites

Kawahara, Lewis. "Tanforan (detention facility)." *Densho Encyclopedia*, July 14, 2015. It provides the history of Tanforan Assembly Center. http://encyclopedia.densho.org/Tanforan_%28detention_facility%29/. Accessed January 25, 2018.

Linke, Konrad. "Assembly Centers." *Densho Encyclopedia*, July 31, 2015. It provides a historical overview of assembly centers. http://encyclopedia.densho.org/Assembly_centers/. Accessed January 25, 2018.

October 14

2009

President Barack Obama signs Executive Order 13515 to increase participation of Asian Americans and Pacific Islanders in federal programs.

Increasing Participation of Asian Americans and Pacific Islanders in Federal Programs

(a) Mission and Function of the Initiative. The Initiative shall work to improve the quality of life of AAPIs through increased participation in Federal programs in which AAPIs may be underserved. The Initiative shall advise the Co-Chairs on the implementation and coordination of Federal programs as they relate to AAPIs across executive departments and agencies. . . .

(d) Federal Agency Plans and Interagency Plan. Each executive department and agency designated by the Initiative shall prepare a plan (agency plan) for, and shall document, its efforts to improve the quality of life of Asian Americans and Pacific Islanders through increased participation in Federal programs in which Asian Americans and Pacific Islanders may be underserved.

Source: Executive Order 13515. U.S. Government Publishing Office. https://www.gpo.gov/fdsys/pkg/CFR-2010-title3-vol1/pdf/CFR-2010-title3-vol1-eo13515.pdf. Accessed January 25, 2018.

Books

Lien, Pei-te. *The Making of Asian America through Political Participation*. Philadelphia, PA: Temple University Press, 2001.

Wong, Janelle, S. Karthick Ramakrishnan, Taeku Lee, and Jane Junn. *Asian American Political Participation: Emerging Constituents and Their Political Identities.* New York: Russell Sage Foundation, 2011. *Asian American Political Participation* analyzes data from the 2008 survey.

Websites

Ahuja, Kiran. "Celebrating Four Years: Opening the Government's Doors to the AAPI Community." *HuffPost*, December 3, 2013. This essay reflects on the significance of President Obama's Executive Order 13515. https://www.huffingtonpost.com/kiran-ahuja/celebrating-four-years-op_b_4454128.html. Accessed January 25, 2018.

"Opening Doors for the Asian American and Pacific Islander Community." Asian Americans/Pacific Islanders in Philanthropy (AAPIP). 2017. AAPIP's report reflects on the impact of President Obama's Executive Order 13515 on Asian Pacific American communities. https://aapip.org/publications/opening-doors-for-the-asian-american-and-pacific-islander-community. Accessed January 25, 2018.

Also Noteworthy

1940

The U.S. Nationality Act of 1940 requires that resident aliens annually register at post offices and keep the government apprised of any change in residency: 91,858 Japanese aliens registered.

October 15

1933

Nitobe Inazo (1862–1933), a Japanese Quaker, educator, and writer, dies.

Nitobe Inazo was Japan's best known twentieth-century internationalist. Born in Morioka in northern Japan, he studied at the most prestigious institutions: Sapporo Agricultural College and the University of Tokyo in Japan, Johns Hopkins University in the United States, and several German universities. While abroad, he married Mary Elkington, a Quaker from Philadelphia, and for the rest of his life he remained a steadfast Quaker.

Source: Huffman, James. "Nitobe Inazo." In *Encyclopedia of Modern Asia*, edited by David Levinson and Karen Christensen, p. 334. New York: Thomson Gale, 2002.

Books

Howes, John. *Nitobe Inazo: Japan's Bridge across the Pacific.* Boulder, CO: Westview Press, 1995. *Nitobe Inazo* is a collection of essays that details the life of Inazo.

Nitobe, Inazo. *Bushido: The Soul of Japan.* Rutland, VT: Charles E. Tuttle, 1969. In *Bushido: The Soul of Japan*, Nitobe discusses samurai ethics and Japanese culture.

Websites

"Nitobe Inazo." Quakers in the World. This biography of Nitobe includes discussion of his time in the United States and Canada. http://www.quakersintheworld.org/quakers-in-action/191/Nitobe-Inazo. Accessed January 25, 2018.

Snipes, Samuel. "The Life of Japanese Quaker Inazo Nitobe." *Friends Journal*, August 1, 2011. This is a biography of Nitobe's life, his educational background, and his career. https://www.friendsjournal.org/life-japanese-quaker-inazo-nitobe-1862-1933/. Accessed January 25, 2018.

October 16

1991

Chinese American veterans of the 14th Air Service Group raise funds and commission a monument in Taishan county, China. The 14th Air Service Group was the only all–Chinese American military unit to serve during World War II.

Some unit members have even returned to China, on a recent Fourteenth Air Service Group tour or on their own, and visited the places they first saw nearly fifty years ago. During the past decade, the Chinese American veterans of the Fourteenth Air Service Group raised funds and commissioned a monument to be built in Taishan county in order to commemorate the men and women who served in the unit. The site was chosen because most of the Chinese American soldiers had roots in the Taishan region. Designed by Frank Leong (who was with the Headquarters Squadron), the monument was dedicated on October 6, 1991 in the new Air Force Memorial Park. Many veterans including 407th members Thomas Fong, Paul Lee, and William Lim attended the ceremony. Other veteran groups are planning monuments that will be placed in Kunming, Kweilin, and Nanking. A memorial was also dedicated in Dayton, Ohio, during the summer of 1991.

Source: Lim, Christina, and Sheldon Lim. "In the Shadow of the Tiger, the 407th Air Service Squadron, Fourteenth Air Service Group, Fourteenth Air Force, World War II." *Chinese America: History and Perspectives* (1993): pp. 66–67.

Books

Lim, Christina. *In the Shadow of the Tiger, the 407th Air Service Squadron, Fourteenth Air Service Group, Fourteenth Air Force, World War II.* Sacramento, CA: Griffin Print, 1993. *In the Shadow of the Tiger* focuses on Chinese Americans who served in the U.S. military during World War II.

Wong, K. Scott. *Americans First: Chinese Americans and the Second World War.* Cambridge, MA: Harvard University Press, 2005. See Chapter 5, "The Fourteenth Air Service Group."

Websites

14th Air Service Group. CBI Order of Battle: Lineages and History. This provides historical data on the 14th ASG. http://www.cbi-history.com/part_vi_14th_asg.html. Accessed January 25, 2018.

McNaughton, James. "Chinese-Americans in World War II." U.S. Army Center of Military History. May 16, 2000. This reflects on short treatment of Chinese American service in the U.S. military during World War II. https://history.army.mil/html/topics/apam/chinese-americans.html. Accessed January 25, 2018.

Also Noteworthy

2001

In Racine, Wisconsin, Andrew E. Savage, a 40-year-old, is charged with a hate crime after yelling at an Indian American store owner whom he believed to be of Middle Eastern descent.

October 17

1834

Afong May, the first Chinese immigrant, arrives in New York from Canton, China, on the cargo vessel, the *Washington.*

When the Washington *sailed into New York Harbor on October 17, 1834, New Yorkers reading the shipping news could see that the cargo included some tea and the expected assortment of fancy non-necessities that had become the Carnes' stock-in-trade. But what made this ship's arrival extraordinary was one of the passengers, who received special mention in the* New York Daily Advertiser: *"The ship Washington, Capt. Obear, has brought out a beautiful Chinese Lady, called* Julia Foochee ching-chang king, *daughter of* Hong wang-tzang tzee king. *As she will see all who are disposed to pay twenty five cents. She will no doubt have many admirers." A short article in another paper, the* Commercial Advertiser, *printed her name as "Miss Ching-Chang-foo" and provided a detailed description of the practice of foot binding, which caused a Chinese woman "to twaddle about all her life." Though the young woman had yet to appear in public, the press was already beginning to circle her.*

Source: Haddad, John. "The Chinese Lady and China for the Ladies: Race, Gender, and Public Exhibition in Jacksonian America." *Chinese America: History and Perspectives* (2011): p. 9.

Books

Ling, Huping. *Surviving on the Gold Mountain: A History of Chinese American Women and Their Lives*. Albany: State University of New York Press, 1998. Historian Huping Ling provides a historical overview and analysis of the history of Chinese women in America that spans 150 years.

Yung, Judy. *Unbound Feet: A Social History of Chinese Women in San Francisco*. Berkeley: University of California Press, 1995. Historian Judy Yung employs oral histories to document the history of Chinese women in the United States.

Websites

Gandhi, Lakshmi. "Four Asian-American Women You Didn't Learn about in School." NBC News, March 1, 2017. This article provides brief historical sketches of four Asian American women—Afong Moy is the first. https://www.nbcnews.com/news/asian-america/four-asian-american-women-you-didn-t-learn-about-school-n727841. Accessed February 11, 2018.

Sun, Derek. "The First Chinese Woman in America." *Headstuff* weekly newsletter, March 12, 2016. Blogger Derek Sun provides a general history of Afong May. https://www.headstuff.org/history/first-chinese-woman-america/. Accessed February 11, 2018.

Also Noteworthy

1928

Park Yong-man is assassinated in Beijing, China.

1973

George Ariyoshi becomes acting governor of Hawaii, when Governor John A. Burns falls ill.

1982

Wat Thai of Los Angeles becomes a full-fledged monastery of the Sangha according to the Thai ecclesiastical legal tradition.

October 18

1587

Filipinos arrive at Morro Bay, San Luis Obispo, California, on board the Manila-built galleon ship *Nuestra Senora de Esperanza* under the command of Spanish captain Pedro de Unamuno. This site is now a historic Filipino American landmark at Coleman Park at Morro Bay, California.

Inscription on the historical marker at Moro Bay Historic Site Dedication at Coleman Park, Morro Bay, California

During the Manila, Acapulco Galleon Trade era from 1565 to 1815, Spanish Galleons crossed the Pacific between the Philippines and Mexico. On October 18, 1587, the Manila Galleon, Nuestra Senora de Esperanza commanded by Pedro de Unamuno, entered Morro Bay near here. A landing party was sent to shore which included Luzon Indios, marking the first landing of Filipinos in the continental United States. The landing party took official possession of the area for Spain by putting up a cross made of branches. The group was attacked by Native Indians two days later, and one of the Filipinos was killed. Unamuno and his crew gave up further exploration of the part of the coast.

Historical Landmark declared by the Filipino American National Historical Society. California Central Coast Chapter. Dedicated October 21, 1995.

Source: Filipino American National Historical Society's historic marker at Coleman Park, Morro Bay, California.

Books

Mercene, Floro L. *Manila Men in the New World: Filipino Migration to Mexico and the Americas from the Sixteenth Century*. Quezon City: University of the Philippines Press, 2007. This is a comprehensive volume on Filipino migration. See Chapter 5 "The First Filipinos in America" for a discussion on the first Filipinos in America.

Wagner, Henry R. *Spanish Voyages to the Northwest Coast of America in the Sixteenth Century*.

San Francisco: California Historical Society, 1929. Wagner is a noted California historian and offers the first documented account of the landing of Filipino sailors in America.

Websites

Filipino American National Historical Society. 2011. The Filipino American National Historical Society is comprised of 10 chapters: the Central Coast of California chapter is one of them. http://fanhs10.com/history.html. Accessed September 30, 2016.

Santos, Hector. "Did Philippine Indios Really Land in Morro Bay?" *Sulat sa Tansô*, April 9, 1997. Santos is author and editor of the site and provides a summary analysis of the evidence used to document the first Filipino landing in Morro Bay. http://bibingka.baybayin.com/sst/esperanza/morrobay.htm. Accessed September 30, 2016.

Also Noteworthy

1952

Hong Fook Tong, also called Tong Hook Tong or Hong Took Tong, is the first legitimate Chinese theatrical troupe to stage full-scale Chinese opera performances—Cantonese opera, in particular—in the United States. The troupe, from the Guangdong Province in China, premiered at the American Theater on Sansome Street.

2011

In Detroit, Michigan, Douglas Snyder, a 46-year-old, is charged with five counts of felony ethnic intimidation for using the Internet to threaten Arab and Muslim Americans.

October 19

2006

Alia Ansari, an Afghan American Muslim woman, is shot in the face while walking with her three-year-old daughter through the Glenmoor neighborhood of Fremont to pick up three other children from elementary school. Witnesses saw a man get out of the car and shoot her at point-blank range. Ansari's surviving husband and children moved back to Afghanistan after the murder.

Alia Ansari always wore her traditional Muslim headscarf in public. She was a doting wife and mother who spent most of her time in the Afghan neighborhood of Fremont known as "Little Kabul." She typically drove her six children to and from school and cricket practice, but on the afternoon of October 19, 2006, she had no choice but to walk.

The family minivan had recently overheated, and her husband, Ahmad, an auto mechanic, was too busy to fix it. So the 37-year-old woman set out on foot to pick up her children from the nearby elementary school. Before she got far, a car stopped and a man jumped out. He walked straight up to Alia and shot her in the head. She died clutching her three-year-old daughter's hand.

The brazen murder stunned Fremont's Afghan community and Muslims throughout the Bay Area. Muslim women, in particular, suddenly were afraid to wear their headscarves. . . .

Shortly after Ansari's murder, Melanie Gadener and Anu Natarajan proposed "Wear a Hijab Day" to honor the immigrant's life and celebrate Fremont's multiculturalism.

The women came up with the idea after visiting Fremont's Muslim mosque, the Islamic Society of East Bay, during an open house. "We had heard from the women there—especially after 9/11—that wearing a hijab drew attention that made them feel uncomfortable," explained Natarajan, the first South Asian immigrant on the Fremont City Council. "They feel like they don't belong, and we felt that we should show them that they do belong." The event eventually morphed into "Wear a Hijab/Turban Day," expanding to incorporate local Sikh men who also had felt wrongly conspicuous in the wake of September 11.

Source: Gammon, Robert. "Who's Killing the Immigrant Mothers of Fremont?" *East Bay Express*, January 10, 2007. https://www.eastbayexpress.com/oakland/whos-killing-the-immigrant-mothers-of-fremont/Content?oid=1082568. Accessed February 11, 2018.

Books

Haddad, Yvonne, Jane Smith, and Kathleen Moore. *Muslim Women in America: The Challenge of Islamic Identity Today*. Oxford: University of Oxford Press, 2006. *Muslim Women in America* covers critical issues confronting Muslim American women in America that include identity, conversion, discrimination, marriage, dress, parenting, and post–9/11 anti-Muslim sentiments.

Karam, Nicoletta. *The 9/11 Backlash: A Decade of U.S. Hate Crimes Targeting the Innocent*. Berkeley, CA: Beatitude Press, 2012. *The 9/11 Backlash* examines a decade of Islamophobia and Hinduphobia that fueled hate crimes against South Asians, Muslims, Arabs, Sikhs, and other Asian Americans.

Websites

"Anti-Muslim Incidents since Sept. 11, 2001." Southern Poverty Law Center. March 29, 2011. This site provides a list of anti-Muslim hate crimes post-9/11. https://www.splcenter.org/news/2011/03/29/anti-muslim-incidents-sept-11-2001. Accessed February 11, 2018.

Kuruvila, Matthai, and Henry K. Lee. "Religious Hate Seen as Motive in Killing/Fremont Slaying: Muslim Leaders and Relatives of Afghan American Mother Shot at Point-Blank Range Say Only Motive They Can Imagine for Anyone Wanting Her Dead Was the Garment of Her Faith, Her Head Scarf." *SFGate*, October 21, 2006. This article discusses Alia Ansari's murder shortly after it happened. http://www.sfgate.com/bayarea/article/Religious-hate-seen-as-motive-in-killing-2485506.php. Accessed February 11, 2018.

Also Noteworthy

1944

Martial law is terminated in Hawaii.

1984

The Hindu Temple of Atlanta is incorporated.

2004

Jin Au-Yeung (b. June 4, 1982), known as MC Jin, an American rapper, songwriter, and actor of Hakka Chinese ancestry, releases his debut album *The Rest Is History*. He is the first Asian American rapper to be signed to a major record label.

October 20

1979

The John F. Kennedy Presidential Library and Museum is dedicated. The Kennedy Library was designed by acclaimed Chinese American architect, Ieoh Ming Pei (b. April 26, 1917).

After an unremarkable early career, much of which he would like to disown, Pei's first break came with his commission for the National Center for Atmospheric Research at Boulder, Colorado. Pei's solution, using independent tower blocks inter-linked by lower rise buildings and circulation elements, faced with sandstone-colored concrete, was a response to striking singularity of the surrounding landscape, the sandstone mesa above Boulder. The success of this venture would garner Pei his next, and significantly more historically important, project, namely the John F. Kennedy Memorial Library. This was a critical project, given the collective grief embodied in any edifice dedicated to this much-loved assassinated president. Although the building was not finally dedicated until 1979, its design established key signature elements of Pei's distinct language. These include the use of opaque or transparent prismatic solids, a tautness of exterior surface that augments the sense of monumental solidity, and the use of 45-degree angles in plan that enable him to dissemble complexity in the arrangement of programmatic volumes.

Source: Dutta, Arindam. "Pei, I.M." In *Encyclopedia of Postmodernism*, edited by Victor Taylor and Charles Winquist, pp. 275–276. New York: Routledge, 2001.

Books

Rubalcaba, Jill. *I.M. Pei: Architect of Time, Place and Purpose*. Singapore: Marshall Cavendish, 2011. *I.M. Pei: Architect of Time, Place and Purpose* examines six of I. M. Pei's buildings.

Von Boehm, Gero. *Conversations with I.M. Pei: Light Is the Key*. New York: Prestel Publishing, 2000. *Conversations with I.M. Pei* is a collection of interviews with the architect that explores his inspiration, ideas, motivations, and architectural style.

Websites

"I. M. Pei, Architect." John F. Kennedy Presidential Library and Museum. This essay discusses the reasons why I. M. Pei was selected to be the architect of Kennedy's presidential library. https://www.jfklibrary.org/About-Us/About-the-JFK-Library/History/IM-Pei--Architect.aspx. Accessed February 11, 2018.

LeMaire, Greg. "AD Classics: JFK Presidential Library/I.M. Pei." *ArchDaily*, August 7, 2011. This essay discusses I. M. Pei's architectural design with photographs of the architecture of JFK Presidential Library. https://www.archdaily.com/153285/ad-classics-jfk-presidential-library-i-m-pei. Accessed February 11, 2018.

Also Noteworthy

1942

The Gordon Hirabayashi's trial begins in Seattle, Washington. He is charged with violating exclusion orders and curfew.

October 21

2001

In Anaheim, California, several Asian men shout ethnic slurs and allegedly assault a man of South Asian descent who they thought was a Middle Eastern Arab Muslim. In New York City, New York, three men attack a Pakistani American store owner.

Attacks on Hindu Americans have encompassed a wide range of incidents and involved a variety of motivations. In many instances, especially after 9/11, bias crimes against Hindus have been based on the perpetrator's mistaken belief that the victim is Muslim or Arab. For example, in April 2012, two Asian individuals allegedly assaulted an Indian man in New York, while using an anti-Arab slur. . . .

Furthermore, in the immediate aftermath of 9/11, there were several reported hate-crimes against Indian Americans, many of whom were also Hindu. The following provide a few representative examples:

- *A man leaving a Hindu temple in Queens, New York was shot in the forehead with a BB gun.*
- *An Indian Hindu man told police he was assaulted by a group of men in Richardson, Texas, who called him an Arab.*
- *A man called in a bomb threat to a hotel in Augusta, Georgia owned by Indians, whom he insisted were Muslim.*
- *In Salem, Oregon a hate sign, "Towell [sic] Heads Go-Home!" was left outside a convenience store owned by an Indian American.*
- *An Indian owned gas station in Kalamazoo, Michigan was vandalized and spray painted with ethnic slurs on its windows and walls, including "White Power," "Arab" and derogatory epithets about Arabs.*
- *An Indian man was cut by a knife-wielding assailant at a Broken Arrow, Oklahoma convenience store.*
- *Andrew E. Savagae was charged with a hate crime in Racine, Wisconsin for allegedly yelling at an Indian store owner thought to be of Middle Eastern descent.*
- *Several Asian men in Anaheim, California shouted ethnic slurs and allegedly assaulted a man of Indian descent who they thought was Middle Eastern.*
- *John Bethel was sentenced to nearly two years in prison for assaulting a man of Indian descent in Kent, Washington.*
- *Robert Rowland was charged with two hate crimes after allegedly threatening three people of Indian descent while spraying them with bug spray in Gainesville, Florida.*

- *A Indian-owned convenience store was firebombed by three teenagers in Somerset, Massachusetts. The teens reportedly told police officers that "they wanted to get back at the Arabs for what they did in New York."*

Source: Hindu American Foundation. "Formal Comments on the Expansion of the FBI Hate Crime's Anti-Religious Bias Motivation Categories." December 13, 2012. https://www.hafsite.org/sites/default/files/FBI_Policy_Advisory_Board_Submission_HateCrimes_HAF12.13.12.pdf. Accessed February 11, 2018.

Books

Karam, Nicoletta. *The 9/11 Backlash: A Decade of U.S. Hate Crimes Targeting the Innocent*. Berkeley, CA: Beatitude Press, 2012. *The 9/11 Backlash* examines a decade of Islamophobia and Hinduphobia that fueled hate crimes against South Asians, Muslims, Arabs, Sikhs, and other Asian Americans.

Welch, Michael. *Scapegoats of September 11th: Hate Crimes & State Crimes in the War on Terror*. New Brunswick, NJ: Rutgers University Press, 2006. *Scapegoats of September 11th* covers various aspects of post–9/11 crimes.

Websites

Human Rights Watch. "'We Are Not the Enemy': Hate Crimes against Arabs, Muslims, and Those Perceived to Be Arab or Muslim after September 11." Vol. 14, No. 6 (G)—November 2002. This report summarizes Islamophobia and Arabphobia in the United States post–9/11 and documents hate crime cases up to date of publication. https://www.hrw.org/reports/2002/usahate/usa1102.pdf. Accessed January 24, 2018.

South Asian American Leaders of Tomorrow (SAALT). "American Backlash: Terrorists Bring War Home in More Ways Than One." Washington, DC: SAALT, 2001. This report documents the post–9/11 backlash against Sikh Americans and their efforts to combat anti-Sikh racialization and Islamophobia. http://saalt.org/wp-content/uploads/2012/09/American-Backlash-report.pdf. Accessed February 11, 2018.

Also Noteworthy

1937

Kilsoo Haan, a Korean resident of Hawaii, testifies before a congressional state committee that the Japanese government was attempting to unite Asians in Hawaii in opposition to the whites.

October 22

1907

The United Korean Society, headquartered in Honolulu, begins publishing its newspaper, the *United Korean News*, a nationalist newspaper.

Other early newspapers for Korean immigrants, which all eventually folded, were United Korean News, *which was published from 1907 to 1968 in various forms, the* United Korean Weekly, New Korean News, Korean Review *and* Great United Information.

Source: Mansfield-Richardson, Virginia. *Asian Americans and the Mass Media: A Content Analysis of Twenty United States Newspapers and a Survey of Asian American Journalists.* New York: Routledge, 2000, p. 54.

Books

Park, Heui-Yung. *Korean and Korean American Life Writing in Hawai'i: From the Land of Morning Calm to Hawai'i Nei*. Lanham, MD: Lexington Books, 2016. *Korean and Korean American Life Writing in Hawai'i* discusses poems, oral histories, autobiography, and memories published in Korean American newspapers, among them, the *United Korean News*.

Yoo, David. *Contentious Spirits: Religion in Korean American History, 1903–1945*. Stanford, CA: Stanford University Press, 2010. See Chapter 5, "Enduring Faith," for discussion of *Korean Independence*, another nationalist Korean American newspaper.

Website

Korean American Digital Archive. USC Digital Library. This digital archive includes Korean American newspapers, oral history, and photographs. http://digitallibrary.usc.edu/cdm/landingpage/collection/p15799coll126. Accessed February 11, 2018.

Also Noteworthy

1953

Laos gains independence from French rule, but as an independent state within the French Union.

October 23

1992

President George H.W. Bush signs legislation, Public Law 102–450, to finally designate May of each year as "Asian Pacific American Heritage Month." This month focuses on the contribution of Asian Americans to the development and history of the United States, in addition to the diverse cultural riches of Asian American cultures in the American mosaic.

In 1978, a joint congressional resolution established Asian/Pacific American Heritage Week. The first 10 days of May were chosen to coincide with two important milestones in Asian/Pacific American history: the arrival in the United States of the first Japanese immigrants (May 7, 1843) and contributions of Chinese workers to the building of the transcontinental railroad, completed May 10, 1869.

Source: "May Is Asian/Pacific American Heritage Month." *Curriculum Review* 51, no. 8 (2012): p. 11.

Books

Lee, Jonathan H.X., and Kathleen Nadeau, eds. *Encyclopedia of Asian American Folklore and Folklife*. Santa Barbara, CA: ABC-CLIO, 2011. In this three-volume reference, Dawn Lee Tu's entry on Asian/Pacific American Heritage Week discusses Asian Pacific Heritage Month from a folklore studies perspective: see pp. 63–64.

Zhao, Xiaojian, and Edward Park, eds. *Asian Americans: An Encyclopedia of Social, Cultural, Economic, and Political History*. Santa Barbara, CA: Greenwood, 2013. The entry on Asian/Pacific American Heritage Week is authored by Dawn Lee Tu, an expert on this topic: see pp. 118–119.

Websites

"About Asian/Pacific American Heritage Month." The Library of Congress. This site explains history and purpose of Asian Pacific American Heritage Month. https://www.loc.gov/law/help/commemorative-observations/asian.php. Accessed January 25, 2018.

"Public Law 102–450." The Law Library of the Library of Congress. Full text of the legislation is available here. https://www.loc.gov/law/help/commemorative-observations/pdf/106%20stat%202251.pdf. Accessed January 25, 2018.

Also Noteworthy

2001

Fashion designer Vera Ellen Wang releases her book, *Vera Wang on Weddings*.

October 24

1871

Chinese residents at Los Angeles's Chinatown are attacked, robbed, and killed by a mob of white men, over 500 strong. The riots happened on Calle de los Negros "Nigger Alley" (now part of Los Angeles Street). Historian C. P. Dorland noted that the trouble began with the Chinese themselves. Dorland wrote, "Yo Hing as the leader of one faction and Sam Yeun of another. The cause of the outbreak in the beginning was the possession of a Chinese woman named Ya Hit, young and attractive, and from a Chinese estimate of female worth, of the financial value of $2500. This woman was stolen, or had run away, from her owner and had come into the possession of the rival company." In their conflict, an old resident of the city, Robert Thompson, was hit by a bullet fired through the door of a Chinese store. Shortly thereafter, in retaliation of Thompson's death, a mob began hunting down and assaulting every Chinese they could find. After five hours, the mobs had killed 19 Chinese men and boys. Chinese homes and businesses had also been looted.

Excerpt from a report of the Grand Jury Report of the Los Angeles Massacre.

Eight Chinamen Indicted.

The Grand Jury find that for some considerable time past a deadly feud has existed between different Chinese companies engaged in business in this city; that on the afternoon of October 24th, 1871, members of the inimical companies, having previously provided themselves with a large number of firearms, met in a public street of this city and commenced a rapid and deadly fire upon one another, by which at least one life was taken; that their shots were instantly turned upon two policemen and their assistants, who hurried to the place and attempted to quell the tumult and arrest the offenders. That in this effort one citizen was killed, and one police officer and our citizen was shot and wounded; that the great number of shots fired indiscriminately by the Chinese upon the streets and from the doors of the houses occupied by them, at the officers and those citizens who hastily repaired to the scene of disturbance, to lend their aid to the officers, created an alarm reaching almost if not quite to a panic.

Source: "The Los Angeles Massacre." *Daily Alta California* 28, no. 7922 (December 3, 1871).

Books

Faragher, John Mack. *Eternity Street: Violence and Justice in Frontier Los Angeles*. New York: W.W. Norton & Company, 2016. *Eternity Street* documents violent places and violent times in mid-nineteenth-century history of Los Angeles as it relates to conquest and ethnic suppression.

Zesch, Scott. *The Chinatown War: Chinese Los Angeles and the Massacre of 1871*. New York: Oxford University Press, 2012. Scott Zesch reexamines the history of the massacre and provides an authoritative account of this little known historical event.

Websites

C.P. Dorland's full text "Chinese Massacre at Los Angeles in 1871" is available at Archive.org. https://archive.org/stream/jstor-41167579/41167579_djvu.txt. Accessed January 29, 2018.

KCET. "Chinese Massacre of 1871: A Polarized Los Angeles." July 1, 2010. This site provides a brief synopsis of the history of the massacre, along with videos that discuss the massacre and its historic impact. https://www.kcet.org/shows/departures/chinese-massacre-of-1871-a-polarized-los-angeles. Accessed January 29, 2018.

1929

On this day, an anti-Filipino riot erupts in the rural farming community of Exeter, in California's San Joaquin Valley. Similar to earlier incidents of anti-Filipino violence, this episode was a racially motivated attack by white laborers. This incident precipitated a larger attack in Watsonville, California, several months later. Filipino farm laborers were seen as economic competitors to white farm laborers. Moreover, Filipino men were seen as a sexual threat to white women. Filipino farm laborers inherited the anti-Asian animus that Chinese and Japanese immigrants before them experience. The event that led to the development of this riot occurred on this day, when Filipino men escorted white women to the street carnival and were subsequently pelted with rubber bands by white men. A fight between the Filipino men and white men erupted that resulted in the stabbing of a white man, which then escalated into a riot. The local police joined a group of 300 white vigilantes and attacked the Filipino laborers in the fields. In total, it is estimated that roughly 50 Filipino laborers were injured, and more than 200 were driven out of their camp.

Asian labor was indispensable to the ranchers and farmers of California, but white workers blamed the Chinese and Japanese for undermining their wages. So the Immigration Act of 1924 was passed to exclude Asians from the United States. However, Filipinos could not be excluded because they were from an American territory, and they were recruited to fill the void left by the excluded Chinese and Japanese. By 1929 Filipinos were the major migrant labor group in the fields of the Central Valley. They had also become the new target of white hostility, even though many white workers often refused to do the work for which Filipinos were hired.

In Exeter, townspeople prepared for an autumn festival in October 1929 to celebrate the successful harvest of Thompson grapes and other crops. Weeks before the festivities, the 200 Filipino farm workers in town had been harassed by white youths who shoved them off the sidewalks, threw stones at them and in general tried to make them leave. The Filipinos in town were blamed for keeping wages low or taking jobs away from whites.

There were several versions of what precipitated the major outbreak of violence on October 24. One version blames a white truck driver for teasing a Filipino man who responded violently to the insult. Another version has locals getting incensed over the attention Filipinos were giving white women. In any case, an unidentified Filipino felt that his "honor" had been injured and he attacked Adolph Borgman and Harry Latham with a knife. Although the wounds were minor, the two appeared more seriously injured at the time of the incident.

A mob of more than 300 men quickly formed, pursued the Filipino attacker to the E. J. Firebaugh ranch and set fire to the barn where the Filipinos workers were living.

Source: Pabros, Alex. "In the Heat of the Night: The Exeter and Watsonville Riots 1929–1930." *Filipino Express*, October 3, 2014, p. 15.

Books

DeWitt, Howard. *Anti-Filipino Movements in California: A History, Bibliography and Study Guide.* San Francisco, CA: R and E Research Associates, 1976. *Anti-Filipino Movements in California* covers various aspects of the history of Filipino laborers in California and anti-Filipino history with a comprehensive bibliography.

DeWitt, Howard. *Violence in the Fields: California Filipino Farm Labor Unionization during the Great Depression.* Saratoga, CA: Century Twenty One Publishing, 1980. *Violence in the Fields* offers a comprehensive history of Filipino laborers in California.

Websites

Erskine, Thomas. "Exeter Incident." Immigration to the United States. 2015. This essay discusses the historical background of the anti-Filipino riot in Exeter, California, in addition to its impact and significance. http://immigrationtounitedstates.org/395-burlingame-treaty-of-1868.html. Accessed January 12, 2017.

"Racial Riots." The Philippine History Site. This is an online project funded by the Hawai'i Committee for the Humanities, the Filipino-American Society of Hawai'i, and the University of Hawai'i's Office of Multicultural Student Services. This article discusses the history of anti-Filipino race riots in the United States. http://opmanong.ssc.hawaii.edu/filipino/riots.html. Accessed January 12, 2017.

Also Noteworthy

1885

Seattle's Chinatown is burned due to anti-Chinese rioters.

1954

President Dwight D. Eisenhower pledges support to Prime Minister Ngo Dinh Diem and military forces.

1998

The Immigration and Naturalization Service reports that an estimated 100,000 Chinese have been arriving illegally in the United States annually for several years, despite increased border security.

2007

In Philadelphia, Pennsylvania, Kia Reid, a 35-year-old former employee at a hotel, sends her Arab American boss an anonymous note threatening her children and referring to 9/11.

October 25

1906

Japanese ambassador to the United States, Viscount Aoki, meets with Secretary of State Elihu Root to discuss the segregation of Japanese American school children into the Oriental Public School in San Francisco.

Aoki claimed that "the fact that Japanese children, because of their nationality, are segregated in special schools and not permitted to attend the ordinary public schools constitutes an act of discrimination carrying with it a stigma and odium which it is impossible to overlook." "After all the years of friendship between the two nations," Aoki lamented, "it seems too bad that the poor innocent Japanese school children should be subjected to such indignities." The attitude of the Japanese government was duly noted by Japanese-language newspaper in San Francisco. . . . The Soko Shimpo bitterly criticized "the most unjustifiable treatment at the hands of the unscrupulous elements in California." On the evening of October 25, San Francisco's Japanese community held a protest meeting at Jefferson Square Hall. More than 1,200 people crowded the auditorium "to suffocation" and heard speeches by leaders of the Japanese Association, Japanese businessmen and Protestant clergymen. Misuji Miyakawa, the only Japanese lawyer eligible to appear before federal courts in the United States, announced that he and a well-known San Francisco attorney, Charles Fickert, had brought suit against the board action earlier that afternoon and asked for moral and financial support. Both were granted, and the meeting voted to "emphatically oppose" the segregation order and delegate the Japanese Association as spokesman for the community.

Source: Wollenberg, Charles. "'Yellow Peril' in the Schools (II)." In *The Asian American Educational Experience: A Source Book for Teachers and Students*, edited by Don Nakanishi and Tina Nishida, pp. 16–17. New York: Routledge, 1995.

Books

Noguera, Pedro, Jill Pierce, and Roey Ahram, eds. *Race, Equity, and Education: Sixty Years from Brown*. New York: Springer, 2016. See Evelyn Hu-DeHart's chapter "An Asian American Perspective on Segregated Schooling, *Brown v. Board*, and Affirmative Action."

Wollenberg, Charles. *All Deliberate Speed: Segregation and Exclusion in California Schools, 1855–1975*. Berkeley: University of California Press, 1976. *All Deliberate Speed* is a history of segregation in California schools: see Chapters 2 and 3 for specific discussion of the "Yellow Peril."

Websites

"Asian Americans and Pacific Islanders: Beyond Black and White: API Students and School Desegregation." Focus On. National Educational Association. May 2008. This report chronicles the history of school segregation and desegregation among Asian Pacific Islander American students. http://www.nea.org/assets/docs/HE/mf_apifocus08.pdf. Accessed January 25, 2018.

"Keikichi Aoki—Japanese Boy Who Figures in International Episode." *Red Bluff Daily News*, no. 165 (April 2, 1907). California Digital Newspaper Collection. This is a newspaper article about Keikichi Aoki. https://cdnc.ucr.edu/cgi-bin/cdnc?a=d&d=RBDN19070402.2.24. Accessed January 25, 2018.

October 26

2000

Swastikas are tagged on the Islamic center of Southern California.

For the third time in two weeks, the Islamic Center of Southern California has been vandalized; police are investigating the incidents as hate crimes.

Salam Al-Marayati, national director of the Muslim Public Affairs Council, said that, in the past, similar acts have been triggered by tensions between Palestinians and Israelis in the Mideast. But he could not recall three other incidents in such a short time span.

In response, officials have heightened security at the Vermont Avenue center, which houses a school for 105 students from preschool to sixth grade. The Los Angeles Police Department is also providing extra officers for the thousands of Muslims who attend Friday prayers at the center.

"We're disturbed that it's three incidents, and we're worried that the Mideast conflict is being exploited by some local political group," Al-Marayati said. "Our immediate concern is the safety and security of the Muslim community and the children who attend the school."

Source: Ramirez, Margaret. "Security Tightened after Repeated Vandalism at Islamic Center." *Los Angeles Times*, November 9, 2000.

Books

Bakalian, Anny, and Mehdi Bozorgmehr. *Backlash 9/11: Middle Eastern and Muslim Americans Respond*. Berkeley: University of California Press, 2009. *Backlash 9/11* examines the post–9/11 backlash against Arab, Muslim, and Sikh Americans anchored in historical comparative perspectives and their organized response and resistance.

Welch, Michael. *Scapegoats of September 11th: Hate Crimes & State Crimes in the War on Terror*. New Brunswick, NJ: Rutgers University Press, 2006. *Scapegoats of September 11th* covers various aspects of post–9/11 crimes.

Websites

Human Rights Watch. "'We Are Not the Enemy': Hate Crimes against Arabs, Muslims, and Those Perceived to Be Arab or Muslim after September 11." Vol. 14, No. 6 (G)—November 2002. This report summarizes Islamophobia and Arabphobia in the United States post–9/11 and documents hate crime cases up to date of publication. https://www.hrw.org/reports/2002/usahate/usa1102.pdf. Accessed January 24, 2018.

"Nationwide Anti-Mosque Activity." ACLU. January 2018. This essay provides an overview of anti-mosque activities throughout the United States with an interactive map. https://www.aclu.org/issues/national-security/discriminatory-profiling/nationwide-anti-mosque-activity. Accessed February 11, 2018.

Also Noteworthy

1962

The Japanese American Citizens League begins a letter drive to ABC Studios protesting the use of the word "Japs" in the October 11 (debut episode) and October 25 broadcasts of *McHale's Navy*. Later shows do not use the derogatory racial slur.

2010

In Oxford, North Carolina, a white man is charged with ethnic intimidation after he shouted racial slurs and spit on a black woman whom he discovered as Muslim.

October 27

1921

Valentine Stuart McClatchy (1857–1938), publisher of the *Sacramento Bee* and a leading anti-Japanese agitator in California, delivers a speech to the Honolulu Rotary Club, arguing that Japanese residents cannot be molded into "good, dependable American citizens."

Compounding the problem in the eyes of Californians was the fact that Japanese laborers had a much different work philosophy than their Chinese predecessors. They formed cooperatives, pooled their resources, bought land, and ended up competing with their former employers. As Japanese immigrants became farm owners, California passed the Alien Land Law of 1913. This prohibited aliens who were ineligible for citizenship from owning real property. This land law also did not solve the "problems," and as far as the California nativists were concerned, the situation only continued to worsen. It was during this period, in 1919, that V. S. McClatchy became a public figure in the debates, focusing on economic rather than racial issues. . . . McClatchy argued that California organizations opposed the admission of Japanese immigrants "on the ground that they were undesirable economically rather than racially." . . . McClatchy later appeared before the House Immigration Committee and urged the members to consider deportation of Asians already in the United States. McClatchy argued that open immigration would result in the "United States being made a Japanese province." He later gave a similar testimony before the Senate Immigration Committee. . . . Apparently, McClatchy had been doing such a good job of arguing the anti-Japanese case that late in 1920 the Japanese Exclusion League of California named McClatchy as its official spokesman. As that spokesman, McClatchy then went about briefing local branches of the Asian exclusion movement and California politicians.

Source: Lukens, Patrick. *A Quiet Victory for Latino Rights: FDR and the Controversy over "Whiteness."* Tucson: University of Arizona Press, 2012, pp. 26–27.

Books

Duus, Masayo Umezawa. *The Japanese Conspiracy: The Oahu Sugar Strike of 1920.* Translated by Beth Cary and adapted by Peter Duus. Berkeley: University of California Press, 1999. *The Japanese Conspiracy* provides a historical discussion of labor strikes in Hawaii, with particular focus on the strike of 1920.

Okihiro, Gary. *Cane Fires: The Anti-Japanese Movement in Hawai'i, 1865–1945.* Philadelphia, PA: Temple University Press, 1991. *Cane Fires* is a well-researched history of anti-Japanese movements in the United States, with an emphasis on Hawaii.

Websites

McClatchy, V. S. *Japanese Immigration and Colonization.* Washington, DC: Government Printing Office, 1921. This book contains anti-Japanese communications that McClatchy submitted to the secretary of state as a representative of the Japanese Exclusion League of California. Archive.org. April 26, 2009. https://archive.org/details/japaneseimmigra00caligoog. Accessed January 26, 2018.

Niiya, Brian. "V.S. McClatchy." *Densho Encyclopedia,* March 19, 2013. http://encyclopedia.densho.org/V.S._McClatchy/. Accessed January 26, 2018.

Also Noteworthy

1994

On this day, the Berkeley Buddhist Monastery, a branch of the Dharma Realm Buddhist Association, opens. It is located at a former historic Nazarene church building. The monastery maintains a full daily monastic schedule including morning and evening ceremonies and the noon meal offering. There are also regular Buddhist events throughout the week and open daily meditation in the morning and afternoon. In the evenings, there are lectures on the Buddhist scriptures as well as meditation classes. Ceremonies and lectures are in English and Chinese, with Vietnamese translation sometimes also available.

1999

The Los Angeles City Council votes unanimously to designate a six-block area of East Hollywood "Thai Town."

October 28

1889

Katsu Goto is lynched in Hawaii. Goto was a prominent merchant and interpreter who was murdered for his advocacy work on behalf of Japanese plantation workers.

Goto arrived to Hawaii on February 8, 1885, along with the first group of Japanese contract laborers. He was blamed for a fire on the Overend's Camp in Honokaa on October 19, 1889, and was lynched as a result.

On October 28, 1889, the trussed-up body of Katsu Goto, a storekeeper and an out-spoken advocate of Japanese workers in the Honoka'a area of the island of Hawai'i, was found hanging from a telephone pole. Five white lunas on a nearby plantation and a Hawaiian were charged with the killing, but many believed that Goto's lynching was instigated by the planters to make an example of him because of his defense of Japanese laborers. The five whites were found guilty of the lesser charge of manslaughter and were released on bail pending an appeal, before which they vanished from the islands.

Source: Okihiro, Gary. *American History Unbound: Asians and Pacific Islanders*. Berkeley: University of California Press, 2015, p. 131.

Books

Daniels, Roger. *The Politics of Prejudice: The Anti-Japanese Movement in California and the Struggle for Japanese Exclusion*. Berkeley: University of California Press, 1962. The *Politics of Prejudice* discusses various aspects of anti-Japanese racism in California history.

Okihiro, Gary. *Cane Fires: The Anti-Japanese Movement in Hawaii, 1865–1945*. Philadelphia, PA: Temple University Press, 1991. *Cane Fires* is a well-researched history of anti-Japanese movements in the United States, with an emphasis on Hawaii.

Websites

Iwasaki, Patsy. "The Legacy of Katsu Goto." Historic Honokaa Town Project. 2016. This essay provides a history of Goto's lynching and memorial to him. http://www.historichonokaaproject.com/katsu_goto.html. Accessed January 26, 2018.

Kubota, Gaylord. "The Lynching of Katsu Goto." Center for Labor Education & Research. University of Hawai'i—West O'ahu. This essay provides a historical overview of Japanese immigration to Hawaii and the lynching of Goto. https://www.hawaii.edu/uhwo/clear/home/KatsuGoto.html. Accessed January 26, 2018.

Also Noteworthy

1977

Public Law 95-145 is passed by the U.S. Congress authorizing Indochinese refugees from Vietnam, Cambodia, and Laos to become permanent residents upon request. Refugees are able to apply for U.S. citizenship after five years of residence in the United States from the date of their arrival.

2005

George Takei, American actor of Japanese ancestry, publicly comes out of the closet as gay. Takei is most known for his role as Lt. Hikaru Sulu in the *Star Trek* series.

2009

The U.S. House of Representatives overwhelmingly passes a resolution (H. Res. 784) honoring the 2560th anniversary of the birth of Confucius and recognizing the invaluable contributions he made to philosophy and social and political thought. It was further pointed out that Confucianism has had a tremendous influence on Japan, Korea, Vietnam, and the cultures of a number of Southeast Asian nations. Moreover, it has likewise made quite an impact on numerous American scholars as well as contributed to the multicultural reality of America.

October 29

2017

Islamic center of Southern California organizes Open Mosque Day Festival to address anti-Muslim, anti-Arab, anti-Islam bigotry.

On Sunday, Oct. 29, the Islamic Center of Southern California opened its doors for our annual Open Mosque Day Festival. Energy was buzzing hours before guests began arriving as volunteers and organizers met early Sunday morning to discuss the setup and day's plans. This year, the ICSC Interfaith Council decided to take a somewhat new approach on this well-known event—adding in new fun and educational activities for everyone.

In the main lobby, a registration table was setup for guests to sign-in. Throughout the day, volunteers greeted visitors with a smile before leading them on guided tours of our Center. Many of our guests were new—some had never met Muslims or stepped inside of a mosque before. These tours gave visitors an opportunity to learn about the history of the ICSC along with our programs and services.

While tours were going on, some visitors chose to sit-in on Storytelling in the Lecture Hall. During these short sessions, Religious Director, Asim Buoksoy, emceed a presentation of personal stories shared by community members about the mosque and its impact on each person. The stories ranged from funny and insightful anecdotes from elders, to origin stories from converts, to coming of age stories of our youth. This part of the day offered an inspiring, humanizing element—giving people the chance to connect on basic principles that relate across faith lines.

The day was fun and educational for all. Our interfaith community expressed gratitude for our hospitality and for the opportunity to join us in our spiritual home. Thank you to all of our volunteers and organizers who made the day possible. We look forward to hosting more enriching events like this in the future.

Source: "Open Mosque Day Festival." Islamic Center of Southern California. November 3, 2017. http://www.islamiccenter.com/open-mosque-day-festival/. Accessed February 11, 2018.

Books

Klausen, Jytte. *The Islamic Challenge: Politics and Religion in Western Europe*. Oxford: Oxford University Press, 2005. Based on interviews with nearly 300 Muslim leaders in Europe, *The Islamic Challenge* explores the struggles with Europe's Muslim communities and Muslim leaders' attempts to resolve them.

Niebuhr, Gustav. *Beyond Tolerance: Searching for Interfaith Understanding in America*. New York: Viking, 2008. *Beyond Tolerance* is a critical exploration of interfaith dialogue and bridge building among different faith traditions across the United States.

Websites

Islamic Center of South California. Official web page. http://www.islamiccenter.com/. Accessed February 11, 2018.

Visit My Mosque. #VisitMyMosque day is a national initiative organized by the Muslim Council of Britain to encourage mosques throughout the United Kingdom to hold Open Mosque Day. http://www.visitmymosque.org/. Accessed February 11, 2018.

Also Noteworthy

1929

Stock market crash, known as "Black Thursday," triggers the Great Depression.

1942

Mary Oyama Mittwer's "Heart Mountain Breezes" column begins to appear in the *Powell Tribune*, a weekly paper in a local Wyoming community. In her column, she extolls the American nature of the incarcerated Japanese Americans.

2002

Chang-lin Tien (1935–2002), chancellor of the University of California, dies: he is remembered as the first Asian American to become the leader of a major research university.

October 30

1942

The Fresno Assembly Center is located at the Fresno County Fairgrounds, operated for a total of 177 days, and is the last of the assembly centers to close.

This memorial is dedicated to over 5,000 Americans of Japanese ancestry who were confined at the Fresno Fairgrounds from May to October 1942. This was an early phase of the mass incarceration of over 120,000 Japanese Americans during World War II pursuant to Executive Order 9066. They were detained without charges, trial or establishment of guilt. May such injustice and suffering never recur.

Source: Fresno Assembly Center Marker. Erected in 1992 by the State Department of Parks and Recreation. Marker No. 934. It is located at the Fresno District Fairgrounds, front of Commerce Building, Chance Avenue entrance, Fresno, California.

Books

Burton, Jeffery, Mary Farrell, Florence Lord, and Richard Lord. *Confinement and Ethnicity: An Overview of World War II Japanese American Relocation Sites.* Seattle: University of Washington Press, 2002. *Confinement and Ethnicity* is an archeological overview of all the assembly centers and internment camps.

Masumoto, David Mas. *Gathering before the Storm: Fresno Assembly Center, 1942.* Del Rey, CA: Inaka Countryside Publications, 1991. *Gathering before the Storm* covers various aspects of the Fresno Assembly Center.

Websites

The California State Military Museum. "Fresno Army Air Forces Training Center." March 26, 2016. This site provides a history of the assembly center with photographs and maps. http://www.militarymuseum.org/FresnoAssyCtr.html. Accessed January 26, 2018.

"Fresno (detention facility)." *Densho Encyclopedia*, July 31, 2015. This essay provides historical data and overview of the Fresno Assembly Center and includes links to oral histories of survivors. http://encyclopedia.densho.org/Fresno_%28detention_facility%29/. Accessed January 26, 2018.

Also Noteworthy

1942

The U.S. Army completes its transfer of all Japanese American detainees from 15 temporary assembly centers to 10 permanent War Relocation Authority internment camps: Manzanar, Poston, Gila River, Topaz, Granada, Heart Mountain, Minidoka, Tule Lake, Jerome, and Rohwer.

2001

In Los Angeles, California, a swastika and the phrase "Go home Arab" is spray-painted on a business owned by an Arab American man.

In Elgin, Illinois, Jose Ares-Torres, a 27-year-old, is charged with committing a felony hate crime for threatening to kill Muslim Americans.

October 31

1880

On this day, an anti-Chinese riot erupts at "Hop Alley" in Denver, Colorado. While at the John Asmussen's salon at 16th Street and Wazee, two Chinese men and one white were playing pool, a conflict between them and a group of three to four intoxicated whites that escalated into a fight. As a result of the mass anti-Chinese hysteria, it quickly enveloped the entire city. Although the majority of the 2000 Chinese residents were not involved, they were targets of violence by the white mob. Most of Chinatown was destroyed as the mob plundered Chinese businesses. A Chinese laundryman named Sing Lee was beaten and kicked to death, and later accounts suggested that he was lynched; those indicted for his murder were later acquitted. David Cook was appointed acting police chief in an emergency city council meeting. He, along with 15 men, and 10 others whom he knew were good with their guns were able to suppress the riot late that night.

> Excerpt from Roy T. Wortman's "Denver's Anti-Chinese Riot, 1880," published in the *Colorado* magazine (1965).
>
> *George Hickey, a printer, gave this account:*
>
> *I saw Sing Lee on his knees, and when he saw me he came and dropped down in front of me for protection, and I endeavered* [sic] *to shield him and prevent them from putting the rope around his neck. The crowd then commenced kicking him, and said I was a damned Chinaman, and they would hang me if I did not get away, and attempted to put the rope over my neck.*
>
> *Source*: Wortman, Roy T. "Denver's Anti-Chinese Riot, 1880." *Colorado Magazine* 42 (1965): p. 285.

Books

Wei, William. *Asians in Colorado: A History of Persecution and Perseverance in the Centennial State.* Seattle: University of Washington Press, 2016. Historian William Wei provides a comprehensive history of Asians in Colorado, from the 19th century through the 20th century. See Chapter 2, "Chinese Pioneers: Looking for Work, Finding Violence Instead," and Chapter 5, "The Denver Race Riot and Its Aftermath."

Zhu, Liping. *The Road to Chinese Exclusion: The Denver Riot, 1880 Election, and Rise of the West.* Lawrence: University Press of Kansas, 2013. Historian Liping Zhu argues that 19th-century anti-Chinese nativism developed from a regional political concern to become a pressing national issue. The Denver Chinese riot reveals this complicated interplay between anti-Chinese racial politics and the rise of the West.

Websites

Ellis, Mark. "Denver's Anti-Chinese Riot." In *Encyclopedia of the Great Plains*, edited by David Wishart. University of Nebraska–Lincoln. 2011. http://plainshumanities.unl.edu/encyclopedia/doc/egp.asam.011. Accessed December 15, 2017.

"Hop Alley/Chinese Riot of 1880, Denver, Co." Groundspeak, Inc. 2016. This site contains an image of the historic marker at Lower Downtown Denver and other historical photographs. In addition, it contains a historical account of the Hop Alley Chinese riot. http://www.waymarking.com/waymarks/WM2YYY. Accessed December 15, 2017.

Also Noteworthy

2001

In Grand Forks, North Dakota, Kevin Dvorak, a 22-year-old, is charged with assault for attacking a Saudi Arabian student.

2006

In St. Peters, Missouri, the letters "KKK" and the words "Kill Muslim" are spray-painted on a Pakistani American man's garage door.

November

November 1

1913

The Hindu Association's weekly paper the *Ghadar* is published.

Lala Har Dayal, a political exile from India, arrived in California in April 1911. He taught briefly at Stanford University and soon involved himself in political activity. The bomb attack on Lord Hardinge, the Viceroy of India, in Delhi on December 23, 1912 excited his imagination. In May 1913 he set up the Hindi Association in Portland. Har Dayal set forth his plan of action: "The root cause of Indian poverty and degradation is British rule and it must be overthrown, not by petitions but by armed revolt; carry this message to the masses and to the soldiers in the Indian Army; go to India in large numbers and enlist their support." A Weekly paper The Ghadar, *was started for free circulation. The party also set up a headquarters called* Yugantar Ashram *in San Francisco. On November 1, 1913, the first issue of* Ghadar *in Urdu, was published and on 9 December the Gurumukhi edition.* Ghadar *meant Revolt. The paper exposed the evils of British rule, including the drain of wealth, the low per capita income of Indians, the high land tax, the high expenditure on the military, the recurrence of famines and plague that killed millions of Indians, the discriminatory treatment meted out to Englishmen who were guilty of killing Indians, the effort to foment discord between Hindus and Muslims. It suggested solution. While the Indian population numbered 31 crores, there were only 79,614 British officers and soldiers and the time had come for a second Revolt after 1857.* The Ghadar *was widely circulated among Indians in North America. Within a few months, it reached a large section of people in the Philippines, Hong Kong, China, Malay States, Singapore, Trinidad, Honduras and of course India. Har Dayal was surprised by the intensity of the response.*

Source: Sen, S. N. *History Modern India*. New Delhi: New Age International Limited Publishers, 2006, p. 165.

Books

Puri, Harish. *Ghadar Movement to Bhagat Singh: A Collection of Essays*. Ludhiana, India: Unistar Books, 2012. *Ghadar Movement to Bhagat Singh* is a history of the Ghadar movement in the United States.

Read, Anthony, and David Fisher. *The Proudest Day: India's Long Road to Independence*. New York: W.W. Norton & Company, 1997. *The Proudest Day* is a history of India's independence movement. See Chapter 8, "A Spontaneous Loyalty," for discussion of Dayal's role.

Websites

Bhatia, Nishtha. "India's Ghadar Party Born in San Francisco." FoundSF.org. This essay discusses the history of the Ghadar Party in San Francisco with historic photographs. http://www.foundsf.org/index.php?title=India%27s_Ghadar_Party_Born_in_San_Francisco. Accessed January 26, 2018.

"Lala Har Dayal—Revolutionary of the Gadar Movement." *IndiaWest*, May 14, 2014. This essay details Dayal's life and legacy. http://www.indiawest.com/online_features/lala-har-dayal---revolutionary-of-the-gadar-movement/article_35cd856c-dbb8-11e3-b730-0019bb2963f4.html. Accessed January 26, 2018.

Also Noteworthy

2001

In Prince William County, Virginia, Stanley Elburn Smith III, a 27-year-old, and James M. Terrell, a 25-year-old, are charged with assault and battery for attacking a Pakistani American man.

2008

At Gaithersburg, Maryland, an Islamic center is vandalized with 30 paintball blasts to its building.

November 2

1907

"Demonstration" intended to scare the "Hindus" drives out South Asians from Everett, Washington.

Several days following the riot in Bellingham, a larger race riot broke out in Vancouver in which a mob attacked Chinese, Japanese, and East Indian residents that seemed to have been triggered by the Bellingham events and agitation by the Asiatic Exclusion League. In the months following the riots in Bellingham and Vancouver, anti-Punjabi hostilities occurred in other locations in the Puget Sound region of Washington State, including Everett and Aberdeen, which caused many more South Asian immigrants to flee the region.

Source: Englesberg, Pual. "Bellingham 'Anti-Hindu Riot' (1907)." In *Asian Americans: An Encyclopedia of Social, Cultural, Economic, and Political History*, edited by Xiaojian Zhao and Edward Park, p. 143. Santa Barbara, CA: ABC-CLIO, 2014.

Books

Jensen, Joan. *Passage from India: Asian Indian Immigrants in North America.* New Haven, CT: Yale University Press, 1988. *Passage from India* is a complete history of the Indian experience in the United States.

Sohi, Seema. *Echoes of Mutiny: Race, Surveillance, and Indian Anticolonialism in North America.* Oxford: Oxford University Press, 2014. See Chapter 3, "Anarchy, Surveillance, and Repressing the 'Hindu' Menace."

Websites

Englesberg, Paul. "The 1907 Anti-Punjabi Hostilities in Washington State: Prelude to the Ghadar Movement." Interpreting Ghadar: Echoes of Voices Past—Ghadar Centennial Conference Proceedings. Satwinder Kaur Bains, ed. Abbotsford, Canada: Centre for Indo-Canadian Studies, University of the Fraser Valley, 2013. This article, among other articles, is available at http://scholarworks.waldenu.edu/cgi/viewcontent.cgi?article=1063&context=cel_pubs. Accessed January 26, 2018.

"Pioneer Asian Indian Immigration to the Pacific Cost." http://legacy.sikhpioneers.org. This is a chronology of South Asian immigration in the United States. http://legacy.sikhpioneers.org/chrono.html. Accessed January 26, 2018.

Also Noteworthy

2001

In Seattle, Washington, a 36-year-old man and two teenage boys are charged with suspicion of second-degree arson and malicious harassment after setting fire to a local mosque. Nearby in Tacoma, Washington, a bomb is detonated outside the home of a family of Middle Eastern descent.

2010

Nikki Haley (1972–), an Indian American politician, wins the gubernatorial election in South Carolina and becomes the first minority governor in the history of the state. She assumed office as governor on January 12, 2011.

November 3

1964

Patsy Takemoto Mink becomes the first Japanese American woman to serve in Congress as House of Representative from Hawaii. She started her political career in 1956 when she was elected to the state of Hawaii's House of Representatives. During her four decades' tenure, she championed the rights of immigrants, minorities, women, and children. She is best known for her role in passing Title IX, the legislation that transformed academic and athletic equity in American institutions of higher education.

Patsy T. Mink, the first woman of color elected to Congress, participated in the passage of much of the 1960s Great Society legislation during the first phase of her congressional career. After a long hiatus, Mink returned to the House in the 1990s as an ardent defender of the social welfare state at a time when much of the legislation she had helped establish was being rolled back. As a veteran politician who had a significant impact on the nation during both stints in the House of Representatives, Mink's legislative approach was premised on the belief, "You were not elected to Congress, in my interpretation of things, to represent your district, period. You are national legislators." . . .

Throughout her political career, Mink remained true to her liberal ideals. Previously in the majority, both in her party affiliation and her political ideology, she often found herself in the minority during her second stretch in the House. . . . An outspoken critic of the welfare overhaul legislation that the Republican Congress and the William J. Clinton administration agreed upon in 1996, Mink exclaimed, "Throwing people off welfare and forcing them to take the lowest-paying jobs in the community has created a misery index for millions." She also raised concerns about the establishment of the Department of Homeland Security (DHS) in 2002. Created in response to the terrorist attacks against the United States on September 11, 2001, the DHS was charged with preventing further domestic terrorist strikes. Mink feared the DHS might undermine civil liberties by violating the privacy of American citizens in the name of national security.

Source: "Mink, Patsy Takemoto." History, Art & Archives. U.S. House of Representatives. Office of the Historian. Office of the Clerk. http://history.house.gov/People/detail/18329. Accessed January 17, 2017.

Books

Davidson, Sue. *A Heart in Politics: Jeannette Rankin and Patsy T. Mink*. Seattle, WA: Seal Press, 1994. *A Heart in Politics* examines the life, legacy, and contribution of two women politicians.

Mayhead, Molly, and Brenda Marshall. *Women's Political Discourse: A 21st-Century Perspective*. Lanham, MD: Rowman & Littlefield Publishers, 2005. *Women's Political Discourse* covers critical aspects of women and politics. See Chapter 2 "Echoes from the Pioneers: Women's Political Voices in the Twentieth Century" that discusses Pasty Mink.

Websites

"Mink, Patsy Takemoto." History, Art & Archives. U.S. House of Representatives. Office of the Historian. Office of the Clerk. This site provides a detailed biography of Patsy Takemoto Mink. http://history.house.gov/People/detail/18329. Accessed January 17, 2017.

"Pasty T. Mink Papers at the Library of Congress." The Library of Congress. October 14, 2010. This site is an archive dedicated to Pasty Mink. It contains links to images, archival documents, and a comprehensive biography of Mink. http://www.loc.gov/rr/mss/mink/mink-about.html. Accessed January 17, 2017.

Also Noteworthy

1885

A mob of hundreds forces every Chinese resident in Tacoma, Washington, to a train station outside of town in an attempt to expel them. Several Chinese died from exposure, and Chinatown was burned shortly after to ensure the Chinese would not return.

1964

Lyndon B. Johnson wins the presidential election in a landslide victory over Republican Barry Goldwater of Arizona.

1969

President Richard M. Nixon gives public speech on the policy of "Vietnamization." The goal of the policy is to transfer the burden of defeating the Communists onto the South Vietnamese army and away from the United States.

1998

David Wu is elected to the U.S. House of Representatives for Oregon's First Congressional District. Wu is a member of the Democratic Party. He was reelected in 2000, 2004, 2006, and 2008.

November 4

1904

Syngman Rhee, cofounder of the Independence Club in Korea, moves to the United States after six years in prison for protesting as a student in the Korean reform movement. Upon his arrival, Rhee enrolled at George Washington University where he earned his bachelor's degree, at Harvard for his master's degree, and then finally at Princeton for his doctorate. He would later become the first president of South Korea.

In 1896 he [Philip Jaisohn or Jae-pil] formed the Independence Club, with Syngman Rhee as one of his lieutenants.

The alleged purpose of the club was "to discuss matters concerning official improvements, customs, laws, religion, and various pertinent affairs in modern lands." In practice, Jaisohn sought to American the Korean government by making it responsive to public opinion. But before tackling the task of creating public opinion, the Independence Club sought to bolster the independence of the feeble monarchy. To the king, they petitioned:

"We, Your Majesty's humble servants, desire to state that two important factors constitute an independent and sovereign state, namely: first, it must not lean upon another nation nor tolerate foreign intervention in the national administration; secondly, it must help itself by adopting a wise policy and enforcing justice throughout the realm. The power of establishing these two great principles has been invested to Your Gracious Majesty by Heaven above. Whenever this power is destroyed there is no sovereignty."

Source: Allen, Richard. *Korea's Syngman Rhee: An Unauthorized Portrait.* Clarendon, VT: Charles E. Tuttle Company, 1960, pp. 27–28.

Books

Lew, Yong Ick. *The Making of the First Korean President: Syngman Rhee's Quest for Independence.* Honolulu: University of Hawaii Press, 2013. *The Making of the First Korean President* is a full historical biography of Rhee's political life.

Rhee, Syngman. *The Spirit of Independence: A Primer for Korean Modernization and Reform.* Translated by Han-Kyo Kim. Honolulu: University of Hawaii Press, 2001. *The Spirit of Independence* is Rhee's memoir that provides insights into his thoughts during key moments in his and his country's history.

Websites

Choe, Yong-Ho, IIpyong Kim, and Moon-Young Han. "Chronology of the Korean Immigration to the United States: 1882–1940." This site provides a detailed chronology of Korean immigration history in the United States. http://www.phy.duke.edu/~myhan/kaf1601.pdf. Accessed October 13, 2016.

Kim, Han-kyo. "The Korean Independence Movement in the United States: Syngman Rhee, An Ch'ang-Ho, and Pak Yong-Man." *International Journal of Korean Studies* (Spring/Summer 2002): 1–27. This article details three of the leaders in Korea's independence movement. http://www.icks.org/pdf/2002-SPRING-SUMMER/2002.pdf. Accessed October 13, 2016.

Also Noteworthy

1882

The Temple of Kwan Tai in Mendocino, California, holds an opening ceremony.

1924

Nevada passes an Alien Land Law.

November 5

1974

March Kong Fong Eu is elected California's secretary of state. She was born in 1922 in Oakdale, California, and attended the University of California, Berkeley, as an undergraduate and completed graduate schooling first at Mills College and then a doctorate at Stanford University. Her career as a politician began when she was elected to the Alameda County Board of Education in 1956. Eu is known for being the first Asian American woman elected to California state office.

March Fong Eu was born on March 29, 1922. She is a third-generation Californian, born in the small Central Valley city of Oakdale, the daughter of Chinese immigrants, Yuen Kong and Shiu Shee Kong. In 1943, Eu earned a bachelor of science degree in dentistry from the University of California at Berkeley; in 1951, she earned a master of education degree from Mills College; and in 1954, she earned a doctorate in education from Stanford University. During World War II, Eu worked as a dental hygienist at the Presidio in San Francisco. She also served as chairperson of the Division of Dental Hygiene and professor of health education at the University of California at San Francisco. Eu has been awarded many honors, including honorary doctor of law degrees from Western State University (1975), the University of San Diego (1977), and Lincoln University (1984). In her successful career, she has achieved acclaim as an American politician of the Democratic Party.

Eu was the first Asian American, and first woman, to serve on the Alameda County Board of Education, where she served three terms; in her last term, she served as the first woman president. Eu was elected to represent Oakland and parts of Castro Valley in the California State Assembly, becoming the first Asian American woman to serve in that body. In 1974, Eu was selected by three million votes as California's first woman Secretary of State, and first Asian American in statewide office. Eu's accomplishments and contributions as California Secretary of State includes implementing voter registration by mail; including candidate statements in the state ballot pamphlet; making the mail-ballot available to all who want to use it; and pioneered reporting of election results on the Internet. In addition, Eu expanded voter outreach efforts, forging partnerships between government and the private sector to create programs to encourage citizens to register and to vote.

In 1994, Eu accepted President Clinton's appointment as the U.S. Ambassador to the Federated States of Micronesia, where she worked to promote cultural exchange and understanding. In total, Eu served 19 years as California Secretary of State (1975–1993), 8 years as State Assemblywoman representing District 15 (1967–1974), 10 years as school board member, and a term as U.S. Ambassador (1994–1996).

In 2002, Eu lost the Democratic nomination for California Secretary of State during the primaries; in 2003, she expressed interest in running for governor of California in the recall special election of Governor Gray Davis, but then withdrew her intention. Eu's life and career as a public servant is groundbreaking, making history for not just Chinese Americans, but for Asian Americans and women as well.

Source: Lee, Jonathan H.X., ed. *Chinese Americans: The History and Culture of a People*. Santa Barbara, CA: ABC-CLIO, 2016, pp. 195–196.

Books

Kim, Hyung-chan, ed. *Distinguished Asian Americans: A Biographical Dictionary*. Westport, CT: Greenwood Press, 1999. *Distinguished Asian Americans* contains general biographical essays on notable Asian Americans.

Weatherford, Doris. *Women in American Politics: History and Milestones*. Los Angeles, CA: Sage, 2012. *Women in American Politics* is a comprehensive study of the history on women in American politics. Chapter 3, pages 74–75, focuses on March Fong Eu's history and legacy.

Websites

"Full Biography of March Fong Eu." League of Women Voters of California. This site contains an essay with a biography of Eu's background, political career, and legacy. http://www.smartvoter.org/2002/03/05/ca/state/vote/eu_m/bio.html. Accessed January 17, 2017.

"March Fong Eu: In the News." *Los Angeles Times*. This site provides links to all *Los Angeles Times* newspaper articles that cover March Fong Eu. http://articles.latimes.com/keyword/march-fong-eu. Accessed January 17, 2017.

Also Noteworthy

1976

Dr. Samuel Ichiye (S.I.) Hayakawa is the first American of Asian descent to be elected to the U.S. Senate from a mainland state.

1996

Gary Locke becomes the first and only Asian American elected governor of a mainland state as he wins the Washington State governorship by a wide margin.

November 6

1595

Filipinos aboard a Spanish galleon, the *San Agustin*, which was commanded by Captain Sebastian Rodriguez Cermeno, arrive on the shores of Point Reyes, Marin County, across the bay from San Francisco. The ship was on a trip to Acapulco before it was shipwrecked off Point Reyes. The Marin History Museum describes the fate of the *San Agustin* as follows: "More than 70 men were stranded in an unfamiliar land with little more than the clothes on their back when the San Agustin went down off Point Reyes in 1595. The Captain, Sebastian Rodriguez Cermeno, would pilot the surviving crew more than 1500 miles back to New Spain (Mexico), using only a small craft the galleon had carried with her for exploration, saving all but their dog."

Probably the first explorer to see Monterey Bay itself was Sebastian Rodriguez Cermeno, a Portuguese in command of the Spanish galleon San Agustin, *in 1595. Cermeno had been sent out to discover a port on the California coast where the Manila ships might find protection and supplies and receive warning of enemies. On November 30, the* San Agustin *was wrecked at Drakes Bay, but Cermeno continued his voyage in the* San Buenaventura, *a little launch or open sailboat that he had constructed. In this frail craft he saw Monterey Bay on December 10, 1595, and called it San Pedro Bay.*

Source: Kyle, Douglas, Hero Rensch, Ethel Rensch, Mildred Hoover, and William Abeloe. *Historic Spots in California*. 5th ed. Palo Alto, CA: Stanford University Press, 2002, p. 225.

Books

Bolton, Herbert E. *Spanish Exploration in the Southwest, 1542–1706*. New York: Charles Scribner's Sons, 1916.

Schurz, William L. *The Manila Galleon*. New York: E. P. Dutton & Co., Inc., 1939.

Websites

For more background on Captain Sebastian Rodriguez Cermeno and the shipwreck, see Meniketti, Marco, "Searching for a Safe

Harbor on a Treacherous Coast: The Wreck of the Manila Galleon San Agustin." 1997. http://www.caribbeanarchaeology.com/SanAgustin.htm. Accessed January 26, 2018.

National Park Service. U.S. Department of the Interior. Point Reyes National Seashore California's online Archeology Program shares images and evidence of the *San Agustin* shipwreck. https://www.nps.gov/archeology/sites/npSites/pointReyes.htm. Accessed January 26, 2018.

1853

Missionary Rev. Dr. William Speer (1822–1904) spent five years in China as a medical missionary in Canton (Guangdong). He arrived in San Francisco in 1852 and worked with Cantonese-speaking Chinese residents. He asked the Presbyterian Board of Foreign Missions to evangelize to the city's Chinese community. Under his lead, they open the Presbyterian mission for Chinese in San Francisco, which is the oldest Asian American Christian congregation in North America.

Speer was sent by the Presbyterian Board of Foreign Mission in New York to open a mission in San Francisco's Chinese community in 1852. A talented writer and an eloquent lecturer, he published extensively on China and Chinese, frequently spoke out to defend Chinese immigrants, set up the first Sunday school for the Chinese in San Francisco in 1854, and helped found The Oriental in 1855. In fact, missionaries remained friendly and supportive of Chinese immigrants throughout the years and were often the sole public defenders of the Chinese in California, although their motives were subject to controversy.

Source: Yin, Xiao-huang. *Chinese American Literature since the 1850s.* Urbana: University of Illinois Press, 2000, p. 20.

Books

Pierson, Arthur, ed. *The Missionary Review of the World.* Volume 17. New York: Funk & Wagnalls Company, 1904. This book contains the obituary for William Speers that details his life and accomplishments.

Tiedemann, R. G. ed. *Handbook of Christianity in China, Volume 2, 1800 to the Present.* Leiden, the Netherlands: Brill, 2010. This reference volume provides an entry that covers William Speer's time working as a missionary in China.

Websites

Presbyterian Church in Chinatown. 2016. This site provides a history of the church as well as historic photos. http://www.pccsf.org/ourstory/timeline/oldestAsianChurch.html. Accessed December 17, 2017.

Presbyterian Heritage Center. http://www.phcmontreat.org. 2015. This site provides information on the history of the church throughout the world, in addition to biographies of its early pioneers. http://www.phcmontreat.org/bios/Bios-Missionaries-China.htm. Accessed December 17, 2017.

1956

Dalip Singh Saund from the Imperial Valley, California, is the first Sikh/Punjabi American elected to the U.S. Congress from the California's 29th Congressional District, which then comprised Riverside and Imperial counties.

Saund campaigned for an end to the restrictions prohibiting the naturalization of India natives as U.S. citizens. His campaign organization became the India Association of America with Saund as its national head. It became successful in 1946 when the bill was signed by President Harry Truman. One of the earliest applicants under the revised law was Saund himself. He took the oath as a citizen on December 16, 1949. In 1950 he ran for justice of peace for Westmorland Township. He won in the balloting but a lawsuit by Westmorland business men resulted in a count decision voiding the election on the ground that he hadn't been a citizen for the required year. (He was a citizen by the beginning of the term for which he was elected.)

Source: Patterson, Tom. "Triumph and Tragedy of Dalip Saund." Published originally in *California Historian*, June 1992. The full text of this article is available at http://www-tc.pbs.org/rootsinthesand/dalip.pdf. Accessed January 14, 2017.

Books

Leonard, Karen Isaksen. *The South Asian Americans*. Westport, CT: Greenwood Press, 1997. *The South Asian Americans* discusses various aspects of South Asian history, including discussions of economic development, political participation, and socio-cultural adaptation.

Saund, Dalip Singh. *Congressman from India*. New York: E. P. Dutton and Company, 1960. *Congressman from India* is Dalip Singh Saund's memoir. The full text is available online at http://www.saund.org/dalipsaund/cfi/cfi.html. Accessed January 14, 2017.

Websites

Dalip Singh Saund Collection. South Asian American Digital Archive. This site is an online archive collection on Dalip Singh Saund that contains a biography and archival documents. https://www.saada.org/collection/dalip-singh-saund-collection. Accessed January 14, 2017.

Tisdale, Sara. "Breaking Barriers: Congressman Dalip Singh Saund." Pew Research Center. Religion & Public Life, December 19, 2008. This site gives a biographical summary of Dalip Sing Saund's life, career, and the role of his faith in public life. http://www.pewforum.org/2008/12/19/breaking-barriers-congressman-dalip-singh-saund/. Accessed January 14, 2017.

1968

The Black Student Union and the coalition of other student groups known as the Third World Liberation Front lead a strike at San Francisco State University to demand establishment of ethnic studies programs and classes.

On November 6, the Black Student Union and Third World Liberation Front called for a general strike at San Francisco State, and over a two-month period, from December 1968 to January 1969, police arrested about 600 strikers, more than 50 of whom suffered Mace burns, fractured skulls and other head injuries, ruptured spleens, and broken ribs, hands, arms, and legs. In January, the strike spread across the bay to the University of California, Berkeley, where students demanded, like their San Francisco State counterparts, a Third World College that would study domestic and international dimensions of repression and resistance. "The Third World movement," wrote members of Berkeley's Third World Liberation Front, "was and continues to be a demand of colonized peoples for freedom and self-determination—for the right to control and develop their own economic, political, and social institutions."

Source: Okihiro, Gary. *Margins and Mainstreams: Asians in American History and Culture*. Seattle: University of Washington Press, 1994, p. 163.

Books

At 40: Asian American Studies @ San Francisco State: Self-Determination, Community, Student Service. San Francisco, CA: Asian American Studies Department, San Francisco State University, 2009. *At 40* is an anniversary issue of the 1968 student strike that discusses the history and development of Asian American studies at San Francisco State University.

Yang, Philip. *Ethnic Studies: Issues and Approaches*. New York: State University of New York Press, 2000. *Ethnic Studies: Issues and Approaches* discusses the history and development of ethnic studies as an academic discipline and its transdisciplinary methodological and theoretical approaches.

Websites

Springer, Denize. "Campus Commemorates 1968 Student-Led Strike." SF State News. This essay discusses the history and legacy of the 1968 student strike at San Francisco

State University that led to the development of ethnic studies. http://www.sfsu.edu/news/2008/fall/8.html. Accessed January 17, 2017.

Whitson, Helene. "S.F. State Strike 1968–69 Chronology." FoundSF. This site provides a detailed chronology of the San Francisco State University student strike with archival photographs. http://www.foundsf.org/index.php?title=S.F._STATE_STRIKE_1968-69_CHRONOLOGY. Accessed January 17, 2017.

Also Noteworthy

1937

Japan and Nazi Germany sign Anti-Comintern Pact directed at the Soviet Union.

1956

California Proposition 13 is repealed in California's 1913 Alien Land Law by popular vote.

1962

Daniel K. Inouye becomes U.S. senator, and Spark Matsunaga becomes U.S. congressman from Hawaii.

1968

Republican Richard M. Nixon is elected president of the United States. President Nixon promises to achieve "Peace with Honor" in Vietnam.

1979

The Southeast Asia Resource Action Center (SEARAC), a national organization that advances the interests of Cambodian, Laotian, and Vietnamese Americans, is established to empower communities through advocacy, leadership development, and capacity building. They are located in Sacramento, California, and Washington, D.C.

1986

The U.S. Congress enacts the Immigration Reform and Control Act, which includes civil and criminal penalties on employers who knowingly hire undocumented "aliens."

2001

In Madison, Wisconsin, Jeremy A. Giese, a 21-year-old, is charged with a hate crime for smashing a window at a bar after sighting two men who appeared to be of Middle Eastern descent.

November 7

1927

The influx of Filipinos to the United States mainland during the 1920s incensed xenophobic nativist leaders who viewed the newcomers' special status as "U.S. nationals" as an affront to the restrictive spirit of the 1917 Asiatic Barred Zone Act (also known as the Immigration Act of 1917) and 1924 National Origins Quota Act. Section 4 of the Philippine Bill of 1902 (also known as the Cooper Act) defined Filipinos as "citizens of the Philippine Islands and, as such, entitled to the protection of the United States.". . . Filipinos claimed that their compulsory allegiance to the United States entitled them to civic recognition from their political sovereignty and exploited loopholes in statutory language to claim rights creating headaches for authorities. Filipinos did not fit neatly into the preexisting racial hierarchy and social-political order, which generated a good deal of confusion for authorities tasked with enforcing a patchwork structure of racial regulations enacted at the federal, state, and local governments. One example of this problem was evident in early disputes over whether Filipinos were eligible for citizenship in the United States. Clear resolution of this issue proved elusive because American naturalization law only applied to "aliens" and contained no procedure for naturalizing the newly invented class of persons known as "nationals." The U.S. Congress in 1906 did not help xenophobic nativists by allowing, under certain circumstances, persons who hold allegiance to the United States to petition for citizenship. The Naturalization Act of 1906 also required immigrants to learn English in order to become naturalized citizens, which was not difficult for Filipinos since many learned English. In 1918, the U.S. Congress stipulated that Filipinos (and Puerto Ricans) who served three years in the U.S. Navy, Army, Marine Corps, Coast Guard, or merchant marines could petition for citizenship. Javier, a native-born Filipino who entered the United States in 1907, filed for naturalization but did not serve in America's armed forces. At first, he was successful in his bid for naturalization, but the U.S. government appealed it and filed to have his naturalization canceled on the premise that he was not "free white person nor a person of African nativity or descent." His case is known as *United States v. Javier*. 22 F. 2d 879 (D.C. Cir. 1927).

Excerpt from Court of Appeals District of Columbia. 22 F.2D 879 (D.C. CIR. 1927). Decided November 7, 1927. *United States v. Javier*. 22 F. 2d 879 (D.C. Cir. 1927).

ROBB, Associate Justice.

Appeal from a decree in the Supreme Court of the District of Columbia dismissing appellant's bill for the cancellation of appellee's certificate of naturalization. No brief was filed in this court by the appellee, nor was there any appearance on his behalf, presumably because every question involved has been determined by the Supreme Court of the United States.

Javier is a native-born Filipino. He came to the United States in 1907, and on November 30, 1921, filed his declaration of intention to become a citizen of this country. On April 8, 1924, he filed his petition for naturalization in the Supreme Court of the District of Columbia. It does not appear that he had served in the United States Navy, Marine Corps, or Naval Auxiliary Service, as provided in the seventh subdivision of section 4 of the Act of June 29, 1906, 34 Stat. 596, as amended by the Act of May 9, 1918, § 1, 40 Stat. 542 (8 USCA § 388 et seq.).

At the hearing on the petition for naturalization a representative of the government, from the Bureau of Naturalization, appeared and objected to the granting of the petition on the ground that Javier was not a free white person, nor a person of African nativity or descent, as provided by section 2169 of the Revised Statutes (8 USCA § 359); but the court, on December 4, 1924, issued the certificate of naturalization. On February 27, 1925, the United States filed in the court below the petition now before us, for the cancellation of the certificate on the ground that it was illegally issued; Javier not being a free white person nor a person of African nativity or descent...

It has been determined that, in a suit under section 15 of the act of 1906, to set aside a certificate issued in disregard of an essential requirement of the statute, the United States is not estopped [sic] by an order of naturalization, although pursuant to section 11 of the same act (8 USCA § 399) it had entered its appearance in the naturalization proceeding and there unsuccessfully raised the same objection. Johannessen v. United States, 225 U.S. 227, 32 S. Ct. 613, 56 L. Ed. 1066; United States v. Ginsberg, 243 U.S. 472, 37 S. Ct. 422, 61 L. Ed. 853; United States v. Ness, 245 U.S. 319, 38 S. Ct. 118, 62 L. Ed. 321.

In Toyota v. United States, 268 U.S. 402, 45 S. Ct. 563, 69 L. Ed. 1016, it was held that prior to the act of 1906, to which reference has been made, citizens of the Philippine Islands were not eligible to naturalization under section 2169 of the Revised Statutes, because not aliens, and therefore not within its terms; that section 30 of the act of 1906 (8 USCA § 360), extending the naturalization laws, with modifications, to "persons not citizens who owe permanent allegiance to the United States, and who may become residents of any state or organized territory of the United States," did not affect the distinction based on race or color in section 2169; that prior to the act of 1918, already referred to, Filipinos, not being "free white persons" or "of African nativity," were not eligible to citizenship of the United States, but an effect of that act was to authorize the naturalization of native-born Filipinos, of whatever race or color, having the qualifications specified in section 4 of the seventh subdivision, to which reference has been made.

It is clear, therefore, that Javier, not having the qualifications specified in section 4, was not entitled to naturalization; that his certificate was illegally obtained and should have been canceled.

The decree is reversed, and cause remanded for further proceedings.

Reversed and remanded.

Source: United States *v.* Javier. 22 F. 2d 879 (D.C. Cir. 1927). https://casetext.com/case/united-states-v-javier. Accessed November 20, 2017.

Books

Baldoz, Rick. *The Third Asiatic Invasion: Empire and Migration in Filipino America, 1898–1946.* New York: New York University Press, 2011. *The Third Asiatic Invasion* looks at the vexing and complex relationship between Filipinos and the United States through immigration policies, discourses on race, and citizenship.

Gates, E. Nathaniel, ed. *Racial Classification and History*. New York: Garland Publishing, 1997. *Racial Classification and History* is a collection of essays that explores the social and historical construction of race.

Websites

Bankston, Carl. "Filipino Immigrants." Immigration to the United States. 2015. This site provides a general history of Filipino migration to the United States. http://immigrationtounitedstates.org/497-filipino-immigrants.html. Accessed November 10, 2016.

Sohoni, Deenesh, and Amin Vafa. "The Fight to Be American: Military Naturalization and Asian Citizenship." *Asian American Law Journal* 17, no. 119 (2010): 119–151. This article provides a historical analysis of competing legal definitions and eligibility of naturalization between military law and existing law. Available at http://scholarship.law.berkeley.edu/aalj/vol17/iss1/4. Accessed November 10, 2016.

2001

In Tulelake, California, three white men fire gunshots while yelling racial slurs at a Latino man whom they thought was Arab Middle Eastern descent.

November 8

2016

Ladda Tammy Duckworth (b. March 12, 1968) is elected as senator of Illinois. Duckworth was born in Bangkok, Thailand, to an American father and Thai mother. Duckworth lost both her legs in 2004 when her helicopter was shot down in Iraq.

An Iraq War veteran, Duckworth achieved the rank of Major in the Illinois National Guard, and is a former Army Aviator whose Black Hawk helicopter was hit by an Iraqi rocket propelled grenade in 2004. As a result of that insurgent attack, she is a double amputee who lost both legs and sustained severe injury to her right arm.

Duckworth was born in Bangkok, Thailand, in 1968. She comes from a military family. Her father was a U.S. Marine who fought in Vietnam. Her spouse Army National Guard Major Bryan Bowlsbey is a signal officer and an Iraq War veteran. During her formative years, Duckworth's father's career at the United Nations and in international companies meant a series of family moves including a move to Hawaii when Duckworth was 16. After high school, she earned a bachelor's degree from the University of Hawaii and a master's degree in international affairs from George Washington University. Duckworth was working on a Ph.D. in political science at Northern Illinois University when she was deployed to Iraq in 2004.

After a yearlong recovery from her war injuries in the Walter Reed Army Medical Center and acclimation to prosthetic limbs, Duckworth continued her life of public service. In 2006, she ran for an open U.S. House of Representatives seat in the 6th District of Illinois. Her issue positions included support for healthcare reform, immigration reform, gun control, and abortion rights. She expressed opposition to the entry and conduct of the Iraq War, and was critical of the No Child Left Behind Act. After winning a competitive Democratic primary and a wide range of endorsements, Duckworth lost a close general election race to her Republican opponent, Peter Roskam. In 2006, Duckworth was appointed Director of the Illinois Department of Veteran Affairs.

Source: Thomas, Sue. "Duckworth, Tammy." In *The Multimedia Encyclopedia of Women in Today's World*, edited by Mary Stange, Carol Oyster, and Jane Sloan, p. 431. Los Angeles, CA: Sage, 2011.

Books

Cross, Robin, and Rosalind Miles. *Warrior Women: 3000 Years of Courage and Heroism*. New York: Quercus, 2011. *Warrior Women* highlights heroic women throughout history, and it includes a chapter on Tammy Duckworth.

Kinder, John. *Paying with Their Bodies: American War and the Problem of the Disabled Veteran*. Chicago, IL: University of Chicago Press, 2015. See Tammy Duckworth's Chapter 8, "'The Shiny Plate of Prestige': Disabled Veterans in the American Century."

Websites

"Tammy Duckworth Biography." Biography.com website. A&E Television Networks. This essay highlights Duckworth's activism, military service, and leadership and her career in the U.S. Congress, the House of Representatives, and the Senate. https://www.biography.com/people/tammy-duckworth-21129571. Accessed February 13, 2018.

Weinstein, Adam. "Nobody Puts Tammy Duckworth in a Corner." *Mother Jones*, September/October 2012. This article discusses Duckworth's 2012 election campaign and includes photographs and one video link. https://www.motherjones.com/politics/2012/08/tammy-duckworth-versus-joe-walsh-congress/. Accessed February 13, 2018.

Also Noteworthy

1960

John F. Kennedy barely defeats Richard M. Nixon for the presidential election.

November 9

2004

Iris Chang (1968–2004) commits suicide with a revolver on a rural road in Los Gatos, California, and ends her painful struggle for historical truth, social justice, and human dignity. Chang, a Chinese American author and activist, had written three nonfictional works during her short lifetime and brought attention to important issues in Chinese and Chinese American histories.

As Chang was doing research on her fourth book concerning the Bataan Death March, the devastating nature of her subject matter finally took its toll on her body and mind. She suffered from severe depression and had to be admitted into Norton Psychiatric Hospital in Louisville, where she would be diagnosed with reactive psychosis and placed on medication for three days before her release. On the morning of November 9, 2004, Chang took her young life with a revolver on a rural road in Los Gatos, California, and ended her painful struggle for historical truth, social justice, and human dignity. In 2005, the Nanjing Massacre Memorial Hall in the city of Nanjing, China, dedicated a statue and a wing to Chang, whose love, courage, and integrity would be remembered by people of Chinese descent and people cherishing truth and justice.

Source: Shu, Yuan. "Chang, Iris (1968–2004)." In *Asian Americans: An Encyclopedia of Social, Cultural, Economic, and Political History*, edited by Xiaojian Zhao and Edward Park, p. 189. Santa Barbara, CA: ABC-CLIO, 2014.

Books

Chang, Ying-Ying. *The Woman Who Could Not Forget: Iris Chang before and beyond the Rape of Nanking*. New York: Pegasus Books, 2012. Ying-Ying Chang, mother of Iris Chang, tells her story in this memoir.

Kamen, Paula. *Finding Iris Chang: Friendship, Ambition, and the Loss of an Extraordinary Mind*. Philadelphia, PA: Da Capo Press, 2007. *Finding Iris Chang* attempts to understand the author's suicide at the age of 36.

Websites

Benson, Heidi. "Historian Iris Chang Won Many Battles/The War She Lost Ragged Within." *SF Gate*, April 17, 2005. This article discusses Iris Chang's suicide and body of work. http://www.sfgate.com/health/article/Historian-Iris-Chang-won-many-battles-The-war-2679354.php. Accessed January 27, 2018.

Chang, Iris. Chang's official web page. http://www.irischang.net/. Accessed January 26, 2018.

Also Noteworthy

1953

Cambodia gains independence from French rule.

1961

Flower Drum Song, the film adaptation of the 1958 Broadway musical by Richard Rodgers and Oscar Hammerstein, is released. It is based on a 1957 novel of the same name by C. Y. Lee.

November 10

1882

John Makini Kapena is sent by the Hawaiian government to Japan to press for the allowing of labor migration to Hawaii.

Despite the repeated requests for further Japanese immigration to Hawaii by the Hawaiian government, represented by such distinguished figures as King Kalakaua, who visited Japan in 1881 at the beginning of his celebrated world tour, and John Makini Kapena, sent to Japan in 1882 as Special Ambassador to negotiate Japanese immigration to Hawaii, the Japanese government continued to be reluctant about emigration of its subjects to Hawaii. However, by the time Colonel Curtis P. Iaukea went to Japan as Special Envoy from Hawaii's foreign minister, Walter Murray Gibson, in December 1883, the Japanese government had become more disposed to consider the subject. After successful negotiations, Iaukea came back to Hawaii with Robert W. Irwin, Hawaiian consul to Tokyo, to prepare for resumption of Japanese immigration. As part of the preparations, they interviewed two Gannen Mono, who described their problems as the poor living conditions, the lack of understanding on the part of the overseers and employers, the inadequate subsistence pay they received, and their inferior status compared to that of other ethnic groups.

Source: Kimura, Yukiko. *Issei: Japanese Immigrants in Hawai'i*. Honolulu: University of Hawaii Press, 1988, pp. 3–4.

Books

Kuykendall, Ralph. *The Hawaiian Kingdom 1874–1893: The Kalakaua Dynasty*. Vol. III. Honolulu: University of Hawaii Press, 1967.

The Hawaiian Kingdom is a seminal work by a leading historian of Hawaii. This volume covers the history of Hawaii before Cook to the death of Kamehameha III.

Lueras, Leonard, ed. *Kanyaku Imin: A Hundred Years of Japanese Life in Hawaii*. Honolulu, HI: International Savings and Loan Association Ltd., 1985. *Kanyaku Imin* provides a pictorial history of Japanese historical life in Hawaii.

Websites

Japanese Overseas Migration Museum. Japan International Cooperation Agency. 2015. This website provides historical overview of Japanese migration around the world. http://www.jomm.jp/. Accessed February 13, 2018.

Ono, Philbert. "Robert Walker Irwin." Updated January 9, 2017. This site provides a general biography of Irwin, along with photos of his life, family, and career. http://photoguide.jp/txt/Robert_Walker_Irwin. Accessed February 13, 2018.

Also Noteworthy

1954

U.S. Marines raises the U.S. flag atop Mount Suribachi, during the Battle of Iwo Jima.

1971

In Cambodia, the Khmer Rouge attacks the city of Phnom Penh.

November 11

1927

Anti-Filipino sentiment and violence were strong in the state of Washington. Politicians invoked anti-Filipino rhetoric in their appeal for votes, and this fueled eruptions of actual anti-Filipino violence and riots, such as the one that kicked out Filipino farm laborers from Yakima Valley, Washington. The intense anti-Filipino racist sentiments were also exacerbated by economic competition during the Great Depression. As such, mobs of white laborers raided, beat, and kicked out Filipinos. Additionally, a fear that Filipino farm laborers were wooing white women strengthened the white anxiety that transformed into anti-Filipino violence.

Books

Lott, Juanita Tamayo. *Common Destiny: Filipino American Generations*. Lanham, MD: Rowman & Littlefield Publishers, 2006. In Chapter 2 "Crossing Waters: The Pioneer Generation of Filipino Americans," *Common Destiny* provides a historical discussion of anti-Filipino violence in the United States.

Tiongson, Antonio, Ricardo Gutierrez, and Edgardo Gutierrez, eds. *Positively No Filipinos Allowed: Building Communities and Discourse*. Philadelphia, PA: Temple University Press, 2006. *Positively No Filipinos Allowed* discusses the colonial history and legacy of the Filipino American experience, identity, culture, and community formations.

Websites

Griffey, Trevor. "The Ku Klux Klan and Vigilante Culture in Yakima Valley." Seattle Civil Rights & Labor History Project. University of Washington. This article provides a history of the white supremacy and anti-Asian violence in the state of Washington and includes primary documents and historical images. http://depts.washington.edu/civilr/kkk_yakima.htm. Accessed January 12, 2017.

"Racial Riots." The Philippine History Site. An online project funded by the Hawai'i Committee for the Humanities, the Filipino-American Society of Hawai'i, and the University of Hawai'i's Office of Multicultural Student Services. This article discusses the history of anti-Filipino race riots in the United States. http://opmanong.ssc.hawaii.edu/filipino/riots.html. Accessed January 12, 2017.

Also Noteworthy

1918

The armistice treaty formally ends World War I.

November 12

1923

The U.S. Supreme Court in *Terrace v. Thompson* upholds constitutionality of Washington's Alien Land Law.

Like many other western states, Washington passed laws targeting Japanese and other Asian immigrant farmers during the early 20th century. In 1921, Washington passed its first Alien Land Law restricting land leasing to U.S. citizens. This was in addition to the state constitution's already-existing provision banning aliens ineligible for citizenship from owning land. This made it virtually impossible for Asian immigrants, banned from naturalizing by federal law, to own land.

Source: Chi, Sang, and Emily Robinson, eds. *Voices of the Asian American and Pacific Islander Experience*. Vol. II. Santa Barbara, CA: Greenwood, 2012, p. 405.

Books

Allerfeldt, Kristofer. *Race, Radicalism, Religion, and Restriction: Immigration in the Pacific Northwest, 1890–1924*. Westport, CT: Praeger, 2003. Kristofer Allerfeldt researches the development of anti-Asian policies in the Pacific Northwest from 1890 to 1924.

Goldstein, Leslie. *The U.S. Supreme Court and Racial Minorities: Two Centuries of Judicial Review on Trial*. Northampton, MA: Edward Elgar Publishing, 2017. *The U.S. Supreme Court and Racial Minorities* provides general historical overview, in chronological order, of court rulings on racial minorities.

Websites

Stefancic, Jean. "*Terrace v. Thompson* and the Legacy of Manifest Destiny." *Nevada Law Journal* 12, no. 532 (2012): 532–548. This article offers an analysis of *Terrace v. Thompson* through the doctrine of Manifest Destiny. It's available at Seattle University School of Law Digital Commons. https://digitalcommons.law.seattleu.edu/cgi/viewcontent.cgi?referer=https://www.google.com/&httpsredir=1&article=1103&context=faculty. Accessed January 27, 2018.

Terrace v. Thompson, 263 U.S. 197 (1923). JUSTIA U.S. Supreme Court. 2018. The syllabus for the case is available. https://supreme.justia.com/cases/federal/us/263/197/case.html. Accessed January 27, 2018.

Also Noteworthy

1923

The U.S. Supreme Court in *Porterfield v. Webb* upholds constitutionality of California's Alien Land Law.

2001

In Trenton, Michigan, Rob Moran, a 20-year-old, is charged with ethnic intimidation for harassing a woman of Palestinian Muslim descent.

November 13

1922

Takao Ozawa v. United States was a landmark Supreme Court case that denied the right to naturalization for all Issei (first-generation Japanese immigrants). Under the Nationality Acts of 1790 and 1870, federal law had restricted the right of naturalization to aliens who were either "free white" or of "African nativity and descent." Ozawa's argument rested in the ambiguity of the term "white," which he claimed could apply to Japanese immigrants who were physically "whiter" than many Southern and Eastern Europeans who had become naturalized citizens.

Takao Ozawa himself was a Japanese immigrant who had come to the United States as a minor in 1894. He attended the University of California before moving to the territory of Hawaii in 1906 when the Great Earthquake in San Francisco disrupted his studies.

By the time he applied to become a naturalized citizen, Ozawa had lived in the United States for 20 years. He was the model of an assimilated immigrant: he spoke English at home with his wife and children, belonged to a Christian church, worked for an American company, and did not drink, smoke, or gamble. When he applied for naturalization, Ozawa did not ask for the support of the Japanese American Citizens League or Japanese immigrant organizations.

When the U.S. District Court in Northern California denied Ozawa's application, he took his case to the U.S. District Court in Hawaii, where he again was rebuffed. Ozawa appealed and his case was referred to the U.S. Supreme Court in 1917. Justice George Sutherland wrote the unanimous opinion upholding the lower court ruling that Ozawa was racially "ineligible for citizenship" because he was "not Caucasian." In other words, in 1922 the Court determined that racial origins, rather than skin color, was what mattered in defining who was eligible for naturalization.

Excerpt from *Takao Ozawa v. United States*. Decided November 13, 1922.

Mr. Justice SUTHERLAND delivered the opinion of the Court.

The appellant is a person of the Japanese race born in Japan. He applied, on October 16, 1914, to the United States District Court for the Territory of Hawai'i to be admitted as a citizen of the United States. His petition was opposed by the United States District Attorney for the District of Hawai'i. Including the period of his residence in Hawai'i appellant had continuously resided in the United States for 20 years. He was a graduate of the Berkeley, Cal., high school, had been nearly three years a student in the University of California, had educated his children in American schools, his family had attended American churches and he had maintained the use of the English language in his home. That he was well qualified by character and education for citizenship is conceded. . . .

The question then is: Who are comprehended within the phrase "free white persons"? Undoubtedly the word "free" was originally used in recognition of the fact that slavery then existed and that some white persons occupied that status. The word, however, has long since ceased to have any practical significance and may now be disregarded. . . .

The determination that the words "white person" are synonymous with the words "a person of the Caucasian race" simplifies the problem, although it does not entirely dispose of it. Controversies have arisen and will no doubt arise again in respect of the proper classification of individuals in border line cases. The effect of the conclusion that the words "white person" means a Caucasian is not to establish a sharp line of demarcation between those who are entitled and those who are not entitled to naturalization, but rather a zone of more or less debatable ground outside of which, upon the one hand, are those clearly eligible, and outside of which, upon the other hand, are those clearly ineligible for citizenship. . . .

The appellant, in the case now under consideration, however, is clearly of a race which is not Caucasian and therefore belongs entirely outside the zone on the negative side. A large number of the federal and state courts have so decided and we find no reported case definitely to the contrary. These decisions are sustained by numerous scientific authorities, which we do not deem it necessary to review. We think these decisions are right and so hold.

Source: Cases Argued and Decided in the Supreme Court of the United States. Book 67. Rochester, NY: The Lawyers Co-operative Publishing Company, 1924.

Books

McKenzie, Roderick. *Oriental Exclusion: The Effect of American Immigration Laws, Regulations and Judicial Decisions upon the Chinese and Japanese on the American Pacific Coast.* New York: J. S. Ozer, 1971. *Oriental Exclusion* discusses various aspects of anti-Asian exclusion policies and anti-Asian legal decisions in U.S. history.

Parker, Kunal. *Making Foreigners: Immigration and Citizenship Law in America, 1600–2000.* Cambridge: Cambridge University Press, 2015. Law professor Kunal Parker conceptualizes the history of U.S. immigration and citizenship law from the colonial period to the beginning of the 21st century through comparative analysis of minority communities, women, and the poor.

Websites

Imai, Shiho. "Ozawa v. United States." *Densho Encyclopedia*, April 16, 2014. This article discusses the history and impact of the Ozawa decision for Japanese Americans and other Asian Americans. http://encyclopedia.densho.org/Ozawa_v._United_States/. Accessed October 26, 2016.

"Takao Ozawa v. US." FindLaw.com. This site provides the full text of the *Ozawa* decision. http://caselaw.findlaw.com/us-supreme-court/260/178.html. Accessed October 26, 2016.

Also Noteworthy

1982

Maya Lin's Vietnam Veterans Memorial is dedicated.

November 14

1984

As a token of esteem for this overlooked Asian American screen icon, the city of Los Angeles under Mayor Tom Bradley proclaims November 14, 1984, as "Philip Ahn Day" or "Korean Day" and posthumously honors the actor with a star on the Hollywood Walk of Fame. Among his contemporary actors of Asian descent, only Anna May Wong and Keye Luke have received similar honors.

Although Ahn was promoted as an ethnic star at various points in his prolific career (especially during his early years at Paramount), he never achieved the status of a top-billed star, which was a "whites only" club in classical Hollywood cinema. In this article, I hope to recuperate Ahn for the pioneering role he played in the U.S. and South Korean film industries. Ahn was once called the "Oriental Clark Gable" in Hollywood, where he played leading roles opposite Anna May Wong and was a distinguished character actor until his death in 1978. His career should be recuperated as part of Korean film and cultural history on two grounds: first, Ahn endeavored time and again to enter the South Korean film industry as a leader, actor, and producer, although he lost many opportunities because of political and economic conditions; and, second, Ahn's direct and indirect manifestations in American film and television of Korean diasporic identities deserve critical attention in the broader context of transnational Korean media. By foregrounding his biography, which intersects two different national and film histories, I hope to demonstrate not only the interdisciplinary scope of my project but also the intricate relationship between diasporic screen identities and the homeland (both real and imaginary).

Source: Chung, Hye Seung. "Portrait of a Patriot's Son: Philip Ahn and Korean Diasporic Identities in Hollywood." *Cinema Journal* 45, no. 2 (2006): pp. 43–44.

Books

Chung, Hye Seung. *Hollywood Asian: Philip Ahn and the Politics of Cross-Ethnic Performance.* Philadelphia, PA: Temple University Press, 2006. *Hollywood Asian* examines Ahn's career in Hollywood before World War II.

Hodges, Graham Russell Gao. *Anna May Wong: From Laundryman's Daughter to Hollywood Legend*. New York: Palgrave Macmillan, 2004. *Anna May Wong* examines the life of the most well-known Chinese American actress, who is Philip Ahn's contemporary.

Websites

Chung, J. "Philip Ahn, the First Asian Actor in Hollywood." *KCrush Magazine*, 2015. This essay discusses Ahn's legacy and biography. https://www.kcrush.com/philip-ahn-the-first-asian-actor-in-hollywood/. Accessed January 27, 2018.

"Philip Ahn (1905–1978)" IMDb. 2018. This site provides a complete list of Philip Ahn's works, including photographs and videos. https://www.imdb.com/name/nm0014217/. Accessed June 15, 2018.

November 15

1919

The Los Angeles County Anti-Asiatic Society is formed and includes the American Legion and organized labor. The society's specific target were Japanese residents, to protect the alien land policies and to protect the racial purity of California. The society also supported James D. Phelan, who was up for reelection as senator in 1920, who ran on a platform to "Keep California White."

In October 1919, a Los Angeles "joint Anti-Asiatic Committee" was convened by the Native Sons, in order to hold weekly meetings and to encourage other like-minded groups. On November 15, 1919, the committee formally reorganized itself as the Los Angeles County Anti-Asiatic Society. Chief components of the Society were the Native Sons, the American Legion, and (briefly) organized labor. Chairman, both at its organizational meeting and subsequently, was Sheriff William I. Traeger, a potentate in the Native Sons. The other officers were either Native Sons or persons professionally involved in law enforcement. By August, 1920, the Society, now attached to the statewide Asiatic Exclusion League, had a working alliance with the senatorial campaign of James D. Phelan, himself a leading Native Son.

Source: Modell, John. *The Economics and Politics of Racial Accommodation: The Japanese of Los Angeles 1900–1942*. Urbana: University of Illinois Press, 1977, pp. 39–40.

Books

Brooks, Charlotte. *Alien Neighbors, Foreign Friends: Asian Americans, Housing, and the Transformation of Urban California*. Chicago, IL: University of Chicago Press, 2009. *Alien Neighbors, Foreign Friends* explores the shift in perception—from anti-Asian to relative acceptance—of Asians in Southern California between 1900 and the 1950s.

Daniels, Roger. *The Politics of Prejudice: The Anti-Japanese Movement in California and the Struggle for Japanese Exclusion*. Berkeley: University of California Press, 1962. *The Politics of Prejudice* is a historical study of the anti-Japanese prejudice in California from the late 19th century to 1924.

Websites

"Asiatic Coolie Invasion." Virtual Museum of the City of San Francisco. This site provides a history of the Asiatic Exclusion League, established in San Francisco, and contains primary documents, images, and other useful archival materials. http://www.sfmuseum.org/1906.2/invasion.html. Accessed February 13, 2018.

"Finding Aid to the Asiatic Exclusion League Records." Labor Archives and Research Center. San Francisco State University. Online Archive of California. This site contains information on the Asiatic Exclusion League's archival, with a historical description. http://www.oac.cdlib.org/findaid/ark:/13030/c89k4c1p/entire_text/. Accessed February 13, 2018.

Also Noteworthy

1969

The Anti-Vietnam War Peace March takes place in San Francisco and is attended by upward of 275,000 marchers.

2017

Nineteen Asian American activists are arrested outside Speaker Paul Ryan's office demanding that Congress pass a clean DREAM Act.

November 16

1942

Minoru Yasui challenged the U.S. government's curfew against people of Japanese descent on March 28, 1942, and became the first Japanese American to challenge the military orders of Gen. John L. DeWitt. On this day, Oregon federal district judge James Alger Fee rules that a curfew order against U.S. citizens is unconstitutional but that because Yasui had worked for the Japanese consulate, he had forfeited his U.S. citizenship and became an enemy alien. Fee disregarded Yasui's birth in Oregon, his membership in the Bar in both Oregon and Illinois, and his service in the U.S. Army Reserve. In 1943, in *Yasui v. United States*, the Supreme Court upheld the evacuation order and denied Yasui's appeal. Yasui spent nine months in jail and was then shipped to the Minidoka War Relocation Authority camp.

Japanese Americans . . . fought against the removal order. Those who were removed to the campus resisted through strikes and disobedience, refusal to take loyalty oaths, even riots. . . . Some of those who were arrested took their cases to the Supreme Court. Gordon Hirabayashi, Minoru Yasui, and Fred Korematsu all challenged the constitutionality of the executive order. "The thing that struck me immediately," Minoru Yasuri said about the evacuation order, "was that the military was ordering the civilian to do something. In my opinion, that's the way dictatorships are formed. And if I, as an American citizen stood still for this, I would be derogating the rights of all citizens. By God, I had to stand up and say, 'That's wrong.' I refused to report for evacuation." As a result, he was arrested and served nine months in solitary confinement. Yasui, who had received a law degree from the University of Oregon in 1939, appealed his case to the Supreme Court. In November 1942, while in jail, he wrote his sister. "The insidious dander of creating a precedent of confining American citizens behind barbed wire fences and machine guns when they have committed no crime seemed reprehensible to me. . . . But surely as the attack on Pearl Harbor endangered our democracy, . . . [the] evacuation of American citizens on the basis of race is just as dangerous a threat to democracy!" Thus it was clear to Yasui that it was his patriotic *duty, as a loyal American, to fight the internment policy. "Caucasian Americans are no better nor worse than I, for we are all human beings. It is only the principles of liberty, democracy and justice, and the adherence to these principles that made America great, and as a loyal American who can suffer his native land to do no wrong, I must hold true to those principles."*

Source: Young, Ralph. *Dissent: The History of an American Idea*. New York: New York University Press, 2015, p. 398.

Books

Bangarth, Stephanie. *Voices Raised in Protest: Defending Citizens of Japanese Ancestry in North America, 1942–49*. Vancouver: University of British Columbia Press, 2008. *Voices Raised in Protest* is a comparative analysis of history and impact of internment of Japanese Americans and Japanese Canadians during World War II.

Irons, Peter. *Justice at War: The Story of the Japanese American Internment Cases*. Berkeley: University of California Press, 1993. *Justice at War* reveals the U.S. government's attempt to suppress, alter, and destroy critical evidence that could have persuaded the U.S. Supreme Court to strike down World War II internment order.

Websites

Asakawa, Gil. "Minoru Yasui." *Densho Encyclopedia*, March 21, 2016. This essay discusses Yasui's personal background, his act of civil disobedience, and his experience during and after World War II. http://encyclopedia.densho.org/Minoru_Yasui/. Accessed January 27, 2018.

Minoru Yasui Tribute Project. 2014. This web page pays tribute to Minoru Yasui and includes a biography, resources, photographs, and videos related to Yasui. https://www.minoruyasuitribute.org/. Accessed January 27, 2018.

Also Noteworthy

2001

On this day, during an evening Ramadan prayer service, rocks are thrown through two windows of the United Muslim Masjid in Waterbury, Connecticut. Approximately 35–40 people were in the mosque at the time. Local police investigated the incident as a possible hate crime. Dr. Magdy Adbelhady, a member of the mosque, said that local police were responsive to mosque member concerns and seemed to be taking the matter seriously. He said that immediately after the attack on the mosque, mosque attendance had dropped but was now back to normal.

November 17

1904

Isamu Noguchi, American artist of Japanese heritage, is born on this day in Los Angeles, California.

An innovative and exceptionally versatile sculptor, Noguchi is often credited with having resurrected the lost art of designing great public spaces. His sculptured gardens—such as the marble court for the rare book library at Yale University, the sunken water garden for Chase-Manhattan Plaza in New York, the fountain and plaza in Detroit, the Japanese-style garden at UNESCO headquarters in Paris, and the remarkable sculpture garden and terraces carved from a mountain at the Jerusalem Museum—established new environmental practices that have instructed artists and architects throughout the world.

Noguchi's aesthetics were influenced by the unusual circumstances of his birth. His father, Yone Noguchi, was an ambitious Japanese poet who visited America before the turn of the century, and his mother was an aspiring American writer. Noguchi, born in Los Angeles, spent his childhood in Japan, but was sent to America when he was thirteen where he completed high school in a small Indiana town. His mixed parentage and early displacements contributed to his pronounced internationalism. The recognition he received at the age of twenty as an academic sculptor in New York encouraged his restless spirit of research.

Source: Ashton, Dore. "Noguchi, Isamu." In *The Reader's Companion to American History*, edited by Eric Foner and John Arthur Garraty, 1st ed. Boston: Houghton Mifflin, 2014.

Books

Hart, Dakin. *Isamu Noguchi, Archaic/Modern*. London: Giles and the Smithsonian American Art Museum, 2017. This volume represents more than 80 works by Noguchi that span six decades.

Herrera, Hayden. *Listening to the Stone: The Art and Life of Isamu Noguchi*. New York: Farrar, Straus and Giroux, 2015. *Listening to the Stone* is a biography that chronicles Noguchi's life as an artist.

Websites

Isamu Noguchi. Guggenheim. Collection Online. The Solomon R. Guggenheim Foundation. 2018. This site highlights Noguchi's art education and career along with images of his works. https://www.guggenheim.org/artwork/artist/Isamu-Noguchi. Accessed January 27, 2018.

The Noguchi Museum. This is an online museum dedicated to Isamu Noguchi's work, with images, photographs, and detailed biography and chronology of his life and works. http://www.noguchi.org/. Accessed January 27, 2018.

Also Noteworthy

1880

The United States and China sign treaty giving the United States the right to limit but "not absolutely prohibit" Chinese immigration.

1905

With the Japan–Korea Treaty, Japan declares Korea its virtual protectorate.

1985

Lon Nol, former President of Cambodia, dies in Fullerton, California.

November 18

1942

Japanese American detainees protest at the Poston War Relocation Center in Arizona. The "Poston Strike" was one of the largest acts of resistance to the War Relocation Authority. The strikers were successful in gaining changes that they demanded. Poston was also known as one of the camps with the largest number of draft resisters. Poston was closed down in 1945.

Misao Yamano was born on July 14, 1919, in San Jose, California. She was the eldest of four children of Shige and Teiichi Yamano. She attended schools in Gilroy, California and graduated from high school in 1937. She went to Japan and studied sewing, music, and traditional Japanese cultural arts. Following the signing of Executive Order 9066, she was evacuated with her parents and siblings to the Salinas Assembly Center. On July 5, 1942, they were transferred to the Poston, Arizona concentration camp and lived at camp 2 block 215.

In March of 1943 at Poston, Arizona, Misao married Pvt. Sam Shiotsuka, who was training with the 442nd Regimental Combat Team in Hattisburg, Mississippi. He had sent an engagement ring which was sized with a piece of string that he had sent earlier to camp. Tec/ 4 Sam Shiotsuka served with the famed 442 Regimental Combat Team 2nd Battalion E Company in the European Theatre. The following year, baby Barbara was born at the Poston General Hospital. On February 22, 1945, she departed with her daughter and headed for Fruita, Colorado. After the war, they settled in the Gilroy-Hollister area. Misao became a seamstress and homemaker, and raised three children. Misao Yamano Shiotsuka passed away June 17, 2016 at the age of 96. She is predeceased by her husband Sam Shiotsuka in 2000; and survived by daughters Barbara Sakakihara (Phil), Wanda Shiotsuka (Bob Center) and son, Edwin Shiotsuka (Arline); grandsons, and four great grandchildren.

Source: "Biographies of People at Poston—One of America's Concentration Camps." Poston Community Alliance. http://postoninterneeobituaries.blogspot.com/. Accessed January 13, 2017.

Books

Bailey, Paul. *City in the Sun: The Japanese Concentration Camp at Poston, Arizona.* Los Angeles, CA: Westernlore Press, 1971. *City in the Sun* covers general aspects of the history and events at Poston.

Tajiri, Vincent, ed. *Through Innocent Eyes: Writings and Art from the Japanese American Internment by Poston I Schoolchildren.* Los Angeles, CA: Keiro Services Press and the Generation

Fund, 1990. *Through Innocent Eyes* offers first-hand accounts and artworks of children who were interned at Poston camp.

Websites

Fujita-Rony, Thomas. "Poston (Colorado River)." *Densho Encyclopedia*, July 14, 2015. This site provides a detailed history of Poston, Arizona, and the "Poston Strike" of November 1942 with links to archival documents, historical photographs, and video clips. http://encyclopedia.densho.org/Poston_(Colorado_River)/. Accessed January 27, 2018.

Poston Community Alliance. This site provides comprehensive material related to the Poston internment camp that includes historical photographs, archival documents, demographic and vital statistics of internees, oral histories, and essays that document the history of Japanese internment at Poston. http://postoncamp.blogspot.com/. Accessed January 27, 2018.

Also Noteworthy

1904

Hawaii Sugar Planters' Association's trustees adopt a resolution stating that all skilled positions on the plantations will be filled by "American citizens, or those eligible for citizenship."

November 19

1923

The U.S. Supreme Court in *Frick v. Webb* forbids aliens "ineligible to citizenship" in California from owning stocks in corporations formed for farming.

Justice Butler delivered opinions in the other two cases, Webb v. O'Brien *and* Frick v. Webb. *J.J. O'Brien owned 10 acres in Santa Clara County, California and wanted to sign a cropping contract for four years with an Issei named J. Inouye, "a capable farmer." The land litigation committee that the Japanese Agricultural Association and the Japanese Association of America had established jointly in the fall of 1920 acted on behalf of O'Brien and Inouye and applied for an interlocutory injunction to enjoin Santa Clara County's district attorney from taking action against them. The Santa Clara County Superior Court granted the petition but Attorney General Webb appealed and took the case to the U.S. District Court for the Northern District of California located in San Francisco, which reversed the earlier decision. O'Brien, Inouye, and their lawyers filed an appeal and took the case to the U.S. Supreme Court. Attorney Marshall argued that "a contract is necessary so that the owner may receive the largest return from the land, and that the alien may receive compensation therefrom." If O'Brien and Inouye were to be prosecuted, he said, they would "be deprived of their property without due process of law and denied the equal protection." Justice Butler declared that "the state has power to deny to aliens the right to own land within its borders" and the 1920 law did not violate the due process and equal protection clauses of the Fourteenth Amendment nor did it contravene the 1911 treaty with Japan. The justice reasoned that sharecropping violated the 1920 Alien Land Law because "the cropper has use, control, and benefit of land for agricultural purposes substantially similar to that granted to a lessee." In this case, too, the U.S. Supreme Court upheld the constitutionality of California's 1920 Alien Land Law and its 1923 amendment, making cropping contracts illegal from then on. The last case,* Frick v. Webb, *involved Raymond Frick who wished to sell 28 shares of stock in the Merced Farm Company, which owned 2,200 acres of land, to Satow Nobutada. Frick and Satow sought an interlocutory injunction from the U.S. District Court in San Francisco, which refused to grant them the injunction they asked for. Upon appeal, the case moved to the U.S. Supreme Court. Justice Butler opined that a state may "forbid indirect [emphasis added] as well as direct ownership and control of agricultural land by ineligible aliens. The right to carry on trade given by the treaty does not give the privilege to acquire the stock." Declaring that Section 3 of the 1920 alien land did not "conflict with the Fourteen Amendment or with the treaty," the U.S. Supreme Court once more upheld the constitutionality of California's 1920 Alien Land Law, making Issei ownership of stocks in a landholding company henceforth illegal.*

Souce: Chan, Sucheng. "Alien Land Laws." In *Asian Americans: An Encyclopedia of Social, Cultural, Economic, and Political History*, edited by Xiaojian Zhao and Edward Park, p. 29. Santa Barbara, CA: ABC-CLIO, 2014.

Books

Kim, Hyung-chan, ed. *Asian Americans and the Supreme Court: A Documentary History*. Westport, CT: Greenwood Press, 1992. *Asian Americans and the Supreme Court* offers critiques of major U.S. Supreme Court cases related to Asian Americans.

Yamamoto, Eric, Margaret Chon, Carol Izumi, Jerry Kang, and Frank Wu. *Race, Rights, and Reparation: Law and the Japanese American Internment*. New York: Wolters Kluwer Law & Business, 2013. See Chapter 1 "Context" for discussion of anti-Japanese policies in American history.

Websites

Frick v. Webb, 263 U.S. 326 (1923). JUSTIA U.S. Supreme Court. 2018. This site provides the syllabus for *Frick v. Webb*. https://supreme.justia.com/cases/federal/us/263/326/. Accessed January 27, 2018.

Powell, Thomas. "Alien Land Cases in United States Supreme Court." *California Law Review* 12, no. 4 (May 1924): 259–282. This article provides a legal history and overview of U.S. Supreme Court cases regarding Alien Land Law. https://scholarship.law.berkeley.edu/cgi/viewcontent.cgi?referer=https://www.google.com/&httpsredir=1&article=3965&context=californialawreview. Accessed January 27, 2018.

Also Noteworthy

2002

In Boston, Massachusetts, Phea Meas, a 24-year-old; Jamie Roldan, a 23-year-old; and another man are charged with a hate crime for beating a Pakistani American convenience store clerk.

November 20

2007

Nada Nadim Prouty, an Arab American Central Intelligence Agency (CIA) agent, is described as "Jihad Jane" in the *New York Post*. Prouty was an American intelligence officer of Lebanese descent who worked in counterterrorism with the Federal Bureau of Investigation (FBI) and CIA. Prouty reassigned after a government investigation of her brother-in-law, Talal Khali Chahin, led to her investigation that exposed her involvement in immigration-related marriage fraud. In addition, the government alleged that she accessed information about Hezbollah and her relatives on the FBI's computer system, which is a misdemeanor violation of the Computer Fraud and Abuse Act. Prouty denied it and claimed that she informed the FBI of the fake marriage when she applied to be a counterterrorism agent. In 2007, Prouty pleaded guilty to two felonies related to the fake marriage and to one misdemeanor count of unauthorized uses of the FBI computer. Prouty contends that she pleaded guilty to protect and care for her young daughter; she served no jail time, but her citizenship was revoked, and he was allowed to stay in the United States because there is a greater threat to her life and safety in Lebanon due to her former work with the FBI and CIA.

Prouty grew up during the civil war in Lebanon before she came to the United States for college. Once in the United States, she did not wish to return, so she engaged in a fake marriage to secure US citizenship. Then, American by nationality, she joined the FBI and later the CIA, serving in Iraq, Yemen, and Pakistan. From 2005 to 2010, Prouty faced investigations for illegally accessing the FBI computer databases and providing information to her brother-in-law, Talal Chachine, a Lebanese national who fled the United States after he was accused of transferring money to Hezbollah in Lebanon. In 2007 Prouty pled guilty to counts of criminal conspiracy, unauthorized computer access, and naturalization fraud. Press releases from the DOJ US Attorney's Office in Detroit kept the media informed about her case, fueling panic about the infiltration by Hezbollah in Detroit and the United States. A 2007 press release claimed, "It's hard to imagine a greater threat than someone like Nada Prouty." . . . Because she had been a CIA agent, in 2008 the US Senate held a closed-door hearing about her case. The outcome of the hearing is not available, but an internal CIA investigation cleared Prouty of any wrongdoing or breach of national security. . . .

In 2010 and 2011, Prouty chose to break her silence and publicly comment on her own case, countering the moniker "Jihad Jane." . . . She sold her side of the story, and her autobiography made the best-seller lists as a hardback book in 2011 and appeared in paperback two years later. She convinced CBS to do a segment on her case by taking on the narrative of an Arab American woman and immigrant who suffered both patriarchal and anti-immigrant oppression. Prouty tapped into a mass appeal by reminding audiences that she fought in support of the United States.

Source: Kayyali, Randa. "'Jihad Jane' as Good American Patriot and Bad Arab Girl: The Case of Nada Prouty after 9/11." In *Bad Girls of the Arab World*, edited by Nadia Yaqub and Rula Quawas, pp. 65–66. Austin: University of Texas Press, 2017.

Book

Prouty, Nada. *Uncompromised: The Rise, Fall, and Redemption of an Arab American Patriot in the CIA*. New York: Palgrave Macmillan, 2011. *Uncompromised* is Prouty's autobiography that covers her work with the FBI and CIA, her background, and the investigation, trial, her plea deal, and her life after being portrayed as a traitor-spy.

Website

"The Case against Nada Prouty." *60 Minutes*. CBS News. March 26, 2010. The full text and segments of the episode investigating Prouty's case are available. https://www.cbsnews.com/news/the-case-against-nada-prouty-26-03-2010/. Accessed February 13, 2018.

November 21

1927

Gong Lum was a resident of Rosedale, Mississippi, and father of nine-year-old Martha Lum, an American-born U.S. citizen, in Mississippi. In 1924, Martha Lum attended the Rosedale Consolidated School in the morning but by noon recess was informed by the superintendent that she would not be allowed to return to school on the grounds that she was of "Chinese descent" and not a member of the "white or Caucasian race." In a state trial, the court entered a writ of mandamus in favor of Gong Lum, which ordered the members of the board of trustees to readmit Martha Lum. However, on appeal, the Mississippi Supreme Court reversed the order in favor of the board of trustees to exclude Martha Lum from attending school with white children. Gong Lum appealed to the U.S. Supreme Court. In an unanimous decision, written by Chief Justice William Howard Taft, the Court affirmed the Mississippi Supreme Court decision, arguing that the petitioner had not illustrated that there were no segregated schools that she could not attend. In addition, the Supreme Court affirmed that Martha Lum was "not White" and therefore was "colored." Gong Lum argued that classifying Martha Lum as a member of the "colored race" (i.e., black race) denied her equal protection under the laws under the Fourteenth Amendment, but in referencing *Cumming v. Richmond County Board of Education* (1899), Chief Justice Taft argued in favor of state rights to manage and provide public education to its youth. As such, the Supreme Court cited a long list of federal and state court decisions that reach back as far as *Roberts v. City of Boston* (1849), apparently the first case to introduce the doctrine of "separate but equal," and *Plessy v. Ferguson* (1896), which brought "separate but equal" to the national level—which all upheld segregation in the public sphere, especially with regard to public education. *Gong Lum v. Rice* was overturned following *Brown v. Board of Education of Topeka I* (1954) and *Brown v. Board of Education of Topeka II* (1955). In 1971, the San Francisco Unified School District attempted to desegregate its schools and reassign Chinese and other Asian American students to other public schools, but Chinese parents objected because at the Asian schools, their children were able to learn about their cultural heritage, which other public schools did not offer. In *Guey Heung Lee v. Johnson* (1971), the U.S. Supreme Court declined to issue a stay on a federal district court's order to desegregate public schools in San Francisco.

Gong Lum v. Rice *(1927) stands out as the case within which the U.S. Supreme Court explicitly extended the pernicious doctrine of "separate but equal" that it introduced at the national level to public education in* Plessy v. Ferguson (1896). *At issue in* Gong Lum, *which was decided 27 years prior to* Brown v. Board of Education of Topeka (1954), *were two related issues. The first issue was whether the state of Mississippi was required to provide a Chinese citizen equal protection of the law under the Fourteenth Amendment when he was taxed to pay for public education but was forced to send his daughter to a school for children of color. The second question that the Court addressed was whether the state denied a Chinese citizen of the United States equal protection of the law in classifying her among the "colored" races, and provided facilities for education that, although separate, were equal to those offered to all children, regardless of their race.*

Source: Gooden, Mark. "Gong Lum v. Rice." In *Encyclopedia of Education Law*, edited by Charles Russo, p. 387. Los Angeles, CA: Sage, 2008.

Books

Patterson, James. *Brown v. Board of Education: A Civil Rights Milestone and Its Troubled Legacy*. Oxford: Oxford University Press, 2001. *Brown v. Board of Education* is a concise historical narrative of *Brown v. Board of Education*, its historical development, and legacy. *Gong Lum v. Rice* is an essential part of this history.

Zirkel, Alan, Sharon Nalbone Richarson, and Steven Goldberg. *A Digest of Supreme Court Decisions Affecting Education*. Bloomington, IN: Phi Delta Kappa Educational Foundation, 2001. *A Digest of Supreme Court Decisions Affecting Education* provides summaries and discussion of significance of U.S. Supreme Court decisions related to and affecting education in the United States.

Websites

"Gong Lum v. Rice 275 U.S. 78 (1927)." JUSTIA U.S. Supreme Court. This site contains the full text of *Gong Lum v. Rice*. https://supreme.justia.com/cases/federal/us/275/78/case.html. Accessed November 10, 2016.

Simba, Malik. "Gong Lum v. Rice (1927)." BlackPast.org: Remembered & Reclaimed. 2015. This site contains a background discussion on *Gong Lum v. Rice* and its impact of African American History. http://www.blackpast.org/aah/rice-gong-lum-v-1927. Accessed November 10, 2016.

November 22

2005

Musician Mike Kenji Shinoda (b. February 11, 1977) releases *The Rising Tied*, his debut solo album for Fort Minor. There is a track "Kenji" that describes his family's internment camp experience during World War II.

Michael Kenji "Mike" Shinoda is a Japanese American multi-instrumentalist, record producer, and rapper for the alternative rock group Linkin Park.

Shinoda was born in Agoura Hills, California, in 1977, and established a musical side project from 2003–2006 called Fort Minor. The Fort Minor project was primarily formed to highlight his rap and hip-hop creative energies that were rather limited within the Linkin Park framework. Consequently, he does not incorporate musical elements, including melodies, instruments, and vocals indicative of traditional or contemporary Japanese music. Still, Fort Minor includes one vestige of Japanese American history involving cultural ties with World War II.

Shinoda's Japanese American ancestry is poignantly illustrated in the song "Kenji," from Fort Minor's 2005 The Rising Tied *album. The song details the life of his family before, during, and after internment at Manzanar during World War II. Manzanar was a large Japanese American internment camp located in Owens Valley near Lone Pine, California, that housed over 100,000 individuals in 1942. "Kenji" is an anthem or a voice for Japanese Americans everywhere. It encapsulates the racial tensions, violence, and paranoia between Japanese and Americans before, during, and after World War II.*

"Kenji," which is Shinoda's middle name, is also a Japanese word for "wise" or "healthy." In the song, Kenji serves as a symbol of hope for survival in the midst of impossible living conditions. The authenticity of the song is highlighted by soundbites from an interview with actual Shinoda family members. The cross generational lyrics help bridge the gap between elders and youth across social, historical, and cultural spectrums. The crossroads of Japanese ancestry and American hip-hop music provide an inspirational and nostalgic examination of early American history, international relations, music, and war.

Source: Forss, Matthew. "Shinoda, Michael Kenji 'Mike' (1977–)." In *Japanese Americans: The History and Culture of a People*, edited by Jonathan H.X. Lee, pp. 399–400. Santa Barbara, CA: ABC-CLIO, 2018.

Books

Dancer, Billy. *Linkin Park: The Unauthorised Biography in Words and Pictures*. New Malden, United Kingdom: Chrome Dreams, 2002. *Linkin Park* is a chronological documentation of Linkin Park and biographies of its members, including Shinoda.

Lee, Jonathan H.X. ed. *Japanese Americans: The History and Culture of a People*. Santa Barbara, CA: ABC-CLIO, 2018. See entries on Japanese American music and hip-hop.

Websites

"Kenji Lyrics." Genius.com. The full lyrics to Kenji is available. https://genius.com/Fort-minor-kenji-lyrics. Accessed February 13, 2018.

"Mike Shinoda." Discover Nikkei: Japanese Migrants and Their Descendants. This site provides a short biography and video interview with Shinoda. http://www.discovernikkei.org/en/interviews/profiles/55/. Accessed February 13, 2018.

Also Noteworthy

1894

A Treaty of Commerce and Navigation between Japan and the United States is signed and later proclaimed on March 21, 1895. The treaty guarantees Japanese in the United States "full and perfect protection for their persons and property."

2009

In Kinsman, Illinois, Scott Finch and Luke Harty, both 32 years old, are charged with aggravated battery for attacking a Muslim man outside a pub.

November 23

1962

Maxine Hong (b. October 27, 1940) marries Earll Kingston, thereby acquiring the surname Kingston.

Excerpt is of an interview between Kingston and Nicoleta Zagni.

Maxine Hong Kingston: -When I'm writing, I imagine a large audience, that is people from throughout space and time. I feel that I am addressing people of the future, and also people of the world. Every once in a while I will horn in on Chinese Americans? "This part I address to you!" Or I will say, "Father . . .", and I'll speak to my father or I'll speak to my mother, and so there are individuals that I talk to. . . . Then when I finished, when I was ready to send The Woman Warrior *to publishers, I was thinking that I had written a book that was so unusual, different from anything else that was done before that I probably could not get it published in the United States. I thought the American publishers would not understand, and that I would send it to Hong Kong and London and see whether they could understand me better there. I was thinking, in a way, that I would find an audience through the UK, or I could find an audience through Hong Kong? I guess I was thinking that Hong Kong being a place that's between East and West, surely they would understand. . . . However, before I sent it to them, the American publishers did pick up the book! I think that my sense of audience was . . . always trying to get to the largest audience and also to as many individuals as I possibly could; I feel that I'm able to do this. Even the question of not being translated well in other languages? I feel alright about that, because I see that English is becoming the lingua franca of the world and so, I am using a language that people throughout the world are trying to learn.*

Source: Alexoae-Zagni, Nicoleta. "An Interview with Maxine Hong Kingston." *Revue française d'études américaines*, no. 110 (December 2006): p. 98.

Books

Ludwig, Sämi, and Nicoleta Alexoae-Zagni, eds. *On the Legacy of Maxine Hong Kingston*. Zurich: LIT Verlag, 2014. *On the Legacy of Maxine Hong Kingston* is a collection of recent scholarship that examines Maxine Hong Kingston's literary works, including less discussed publications, and examines her legacy in American and Asian American literature.

Trombley, Laura. *Critical Essays on Maxine Hong Kingston*. New York: Twayne Publishers, 1998. *Critical Essays on Maxine Hong Kingston* is a collection of essays that critically analyzes various aspects of her literary works.

Websites

Martin, Michel. "Maxine Hong Kingston Takes Pride in Mixed Heritage." NPR.org. KQED. July 4, 2007. This is an interview transcript of an interview with Kingston that explores her identities and includes a link to radio broadcast. https://www.npr.org/templates/story/story.php?storyId=11732740. Accessed February 14, 2018.

"Maxine Hong Kingston Biography." Biography.com. A&E Television Network. October 27, 2016. This essay provides a complete biography of Kingston. https://www.biography.com/people/maxine-hong-kingston-37925. Accessed February 14, 2018.

Also Noteworthy

1894

More than 200 Japanese laborers march from Kahuku to Honolulu to protest the beating of a worker by a brutal luna. It took a full day for them to march 38 miles, and upon reaching Honolulu, they expressed their grievance to Goro Narita, the Japanese charge d'affaires to Hawaii, but were punished, fined, arrested, and forced to walk back to the plantation.

November 24

1894

After a failed attempt at revolution in Guangdong, China, the father of modern China, Sun Yat-sen, goes to Hawaii and founds his first revolutionary organization, the Xingzhonghui (Revive China Society) in Honolulu to "promote the interest and uphold the dignity of China."

Sun Yat-sen founded his first revolutionary organization, the Xingzhonghui, in Honolulu in 1894 "to promote the interest and uphold the dignity of China." It attracted about fifty young men, a good portion of whom were Hakkas and Christians or had been classmates of Sun during his days at the Iolani School. Many of them had also been involved in the 1889 Wilcox uprising. The association collected six thousand dollars for Sun to instigate an uprising in China that year and held military drills in the yard of the Reverend Frank Damon (who later claimed that the overthrow of the Qing in 911 was "God-ordained for the advancement of humanity," and even took some credit for it, claiming that "I had the honor to place in Sun Yat Sen's hands a copy of a volume on American democracy which I believe has been the foundation for his propaganda for the constitutional government in China.") In 1896, in the wake of his failed uprising, Sun returned to Hawaii to find that the military training had been discontinued, and the former Xingzhonghui members received him with somewhat less enthusiasm. Although the impact of the Xingzhonghui at the time of its founding was minimal, it attained much greater significance later as some Chinese in Hawaii sought to claim a revolutionary heritage.

Source: McKeown, Adam. *Chinese Migrant Networks and Cultural Change: Peru, Chicago, and Hawaii 1900–1936*. Chicago, IL: University of Chicago Press, 2001, pp. 240–241.

Books

Lai, Him Mark. *Chinese American Transnational Politics*. Edited and with an Introduction by Madeline Y. Hsu. Urbana: University of Illinois Press, 2010. In this volume, Lai documents how Chinese politics, China-U.S. relations, and immigration are shaped by transnational Chinese and Chinese American organizations.

To, Lee Lai, and Lee Hock Guan, eds. *Sun Yan-Sen, Nanyang and the 1911 Revolution*. Singapore: Chinese Heritage Center Singapore, and the Institute of Southeast Asian Studies, 2011. This volume provides background information on Sun Yat-sen's political ideology and inspiration, as well as his influence among the Chinese communities in Southeast Asia.

Websites

Chen, Zhongping. "Sun Yat-sen: Father of Republican China." Victoria's Chinatown: A Gateway to the Past and Present of Chinese Canadians. This site provides a biography of Sun Yat-sen and information on other historic aspects of Victoria's Chinatown. http://chinatown.library.uvic.ca/sun_yat-sen. Accessed January 27, 2018.

Dr. Sun Yat-Sen Hawaii Foundation: His Hawaii Roots—A Virtual Library. 2009–2010. This site provides information about Sun Yat-sen, with specific focus on his time in Hawaii and links to research and photographs. http://sunyatsenhawaii.org/index.php?limitstart=10&lang=en. Accessed January 27, 2018.

Also Noteworthy

2015

Minoru Yasui is posthumously awarded the Medal of Freedom by President Barack Obama.

November 25

1957

Chinese language newspaper *Chinese World* (*Sai Gai Yat Po*) was a major Chinese American newspaper published in San Francisco from 1891 to 1969. The paper became a Chinese English bilingual daily in 1949. On November 25, 1957, the *Chinese World* launches an East Coast edition in New York. Every day printing mats were sent from San Francisco to New York by air. However, because of unreliable flight schedules and insufficient personnel in New York, the experiment failed. The Atlantic Coast edition was discontinued on January 17, 1959.

A very interesting Chinese daily is the Sai Gai Yat Bo *or* Chinese World, *edited by a young, California-born Chinese named Robert L. Park. The* World *is probably the most thoroughly Americanized of San Francisco's Oriental papers. It has a staff-photographer, a corps of reporters who can write a news-story in English as well as in Chinese, and who cover the police courts, city hall, incoming and outgoing steamers with remarkable thoroughness. The* World *publishes daily, half-tones of news events, and will soon install an engraving plant—a dignity to which no Oriental paper in America has yet attained. The* World *is an afternoon paper and, while having no telegraphic service, prints a very complete line of cable news, translated and "boiled down" from the American morning papers. It has correspondents all over the Pacific Coast and a representative at Pekin who occasionally wires some news items of importance in addition to his regular mail service. The circulation, though small, not exceeding five thousand copies, is almost unlimited geographically. The* World *goes to a score of different American cities, and has subscribers in Asia, Africa, Europe, Australia and Hawaii. Its policy is that of the Reform party which wished to depose the Empress Dowager and to seat the Emperor on the throne. Though not as aggressive as the* Free Press, *its editorials are vigorous enough to excite considerable attention both at home and abroad, and its clientele is to a marked extent among the more enlightened and progressive of the Chinese in all parts of the world.*

Source: Stellmann, Louis. "Yellow Journals: San Francisco's Oriental Newspapers." *Sunset: The Magazine of the Pacific and of All the Far West* XXIV, no. 2 (February 1910): p. 199.

Books

Chen, Shehong. *Being Chinese, Becoming Chinese American*. Urbana: University of Illinois Press, 2002. *Being Chinese, Becoming Chinese American* explores the role of Chinese language newspapers in transforming Chinese immigrants in the United States to Chinese Americans between 1911 and 1927.

Danky, James, and Wayne Wiegand, eds. *Print Culture in a Diverse America*. Urbana: University of Illinois Press, 1998. See Yumei Sun's Chapter 4, "San Francisco's *Chung Sai Yat Po* and the Transformation of Chinese Consciousness, 1900–1920."

Websites

Lai, Him Mark. "A Brief History of the Chinese World." The Him Mark Lai Digital Archive. Chinese Historical of America. 2018. This article is a history of *Chinese World* (*Sai Gai Yat Po*). https://himmarklai.org/wordpress/wp-content/uploads/A-Brief-History-of-the-Chinese-World-December-1976.pdf?x42697. Accessed January 27, 2018.

Yang, Tao. "Press, Community, and Library: A Study of the Chinese-Language Newspaper Published in North America." *Chinese Librarianship: An International Electronic Journal* 29 (2009): 1–17. This article discusses the history of Chinese newspaper in America. http://www.white-clouds.com/iclc/cliej/cl27yang.pdf. Accessed January 27, 2018.

Also Noteworthy

1941

The Japanse naval fleet sails toward Hawaii.

November 26

1982

Dorothy Laigo Cordova and Frederic A. Cordova found the Filipino American National Historical Society in Seattle, Washington.

. . . [T]he Filipino American National Historical Society (FANHS), was established in 1982 in Seattle, Washington, by Dorothy Laigo Cordova and Fred Cordova. The Cordovas wanted to have a centralized location where historical documents and achievements of Filipino Americans could be housed for future generations. This organization collects, verifies, and preserves historical information about the Filipino experience in America. Its mission is to promote the historical education of Filipino Americans and to preserve their cultural heritage. Today, the FANHS has over 30 chapters across the United States and sponsors numerous national conferences.

Source: Henry, Candy. "Filipino American Community Organizations." *Asian American Culture: From Anime to Tiger Moms*, edited by Lan Dong, p. 284. Santa Barbara, CA: Greenwood, 2016.

Books

Cordova, Fred. *Filipinos, Forgotten Asian Americans: A Pictorial Essay, 1763–Circa 1963.* Dubuque, IA: Kendall and Hunt Publishing Company, 1983. *Filipinos, Forgotten Asian Americans* contains 250 photographs and 22 essays that illustrate the Filipino experience in America from 1763 to 1963.

Pang, Valerie, and Li-Rong Cheng, eds. *Struggling to Be Heard: The Unmet Needs of Asian Pacific American Children.* Albany: State University of New York Press, 1998. See Fred Cordova's Chapter 10, "The Legacy: Creating a Knowledge Base on Filipino Americans."

Websites

Filipino American National Historical Society. Official web page. 2017. http://fanhs-national.org/filam/. Accessed January 27, 2018.

"Fred and Dorothy Cordova." Seattle Civil Rights & Labor History Project. University of Washington. This site provides videos of Fred and Dorothy as they share their memories and work as activists for civil rights. http://depts.washington.edu/civilr/cordovas.htm. Accessed January 27, 2018.

Also Noteworthy

1988

Fo Guang Shan Hsi Lai Temple completes construction in Puente Hills, Hacienda Heights, Los Angeles, California. It is the largest Buddhist temple in the United States.

November 27

1912

Journalist James Matsumoto Omura, journalist, is born in Winslow on Bainbridge Island, Washington. Omura is also known for supporting the Heart Mountain draft resisters.

Jimmie Omura was born Utaka Matsumoto on 27 November 1912, in Winslow, the largest town on Bainbridge Island, just off the coast of Seattle, Washington. His father had emigrated illegally from the Japanese prefecture of Nagasaki during the 1880s in order to avoid conscription in the Japanese army. Because a sawmill at Port Blakely on Bainbridge Island commonly employed Issei, he went there to work and launched a career in carpentry construction. He was the person other Japanese turned to when they wanted to deal with the white community. Whenever any of the older Issei contacted him, they called him Omura, not Matsumoto. His son, Utaka, reasoning that his father had assumed a new name in America to avoid detection and deportation by the Japanese authorities, realized that his surname was actually Omura. Later, he made this name a part of his identity (along with the first name of James—and its diminutive form of Jimmie—which he adopted as a concession to Americanization). About 1908, the senior Omura returned to Japan, entered into an arranged marriage, and brought his bride back with him to Bainbridge Island. She became sick after having given birth to six children. In 1919, his father took her back to Japan with their three youngest children. The three older children, including Jimmie, were given a choice of whether to remain in America or to go live, permanently, in Japan with their mother, an option they all declined. Seeking adventure as well as employment, Jimmie decided in the spring of 1926 to drop out of school at age thirteen to get a job. . . . Labor contractors signed him up in Seattle and ticketed him for the cannery in Alaska where he became part of a work crew that consisted only of Issei men, along with some Koreans and Filipinos.

Source: Hansen, Arthur. "James Matsumoto Omura: An Interview." *Amerasia Journal* 13, no. 2 (1986): pp. 100–101.

Books

Mackey, Mike. *Remembering Heart Mountain: Essays on Japanese American Internment in Wyoming.* Powell, WY: Western History Publications, 1998. *Remembering Heart Mountain* is a collection of essays that explores various aspects of Japanese American internment at Heart Mountain Camp.

Nelson, Douglas. *Heart Mountain: The History of an American Concentration Camp*. Madison: State Historical Society of Wisconsin for the Department of History, University of Wisconsin, 1976. *Heart Mountain* examines the history and impact of the evacuation and internment of Japanese Americans from the West Coast to Wyoming.

Websites

Hansen, Arthur. "James Omura." *Densho Encyclopedia*, January 4, 2014. This essay is a historical biography of Omura before, during, and after World War II, his involvement in postwar civil rights activism, and his legacy. http://encyclopedia.densho.org/James_Omura/. Accessed January 27, 2018.

Hansen, Arthur. "Peculiar Odyssey: Newsman Jimmie Omura's Removal from the Regeneration within Nikkei Society, History, and Memory—Part 1 of 7." Discover Nikkei: Japanese Migrants and Their Descendants. August 17, 2012. This is a critical essay that analyzes Omura's complex relationship with the Japanese American Citizen League. http://www.discovernikkei.org/en/journal/2012/8/17/peculiar-odyssey-1/. Accessed January 27, 2018.

Also Noteworthy

1940

Bruce Lee, American actor and kung fu expert, is born at Chinese Hospital in San Francisco, California.

2006

In Detroit, Michigan, a group of 10 white men assault a Muslim American man outside his home.

November 28

1910

Sara Choe is the first picture bride to come from Korea. She came to Hawaii and married someone named Yi Nae-su. Yi Nae-su had picked her from a catalog and mailed her $200 for the journey. The way picture brides worked out was that a matchmaker would receive photographs and pair couples together solely based on these photographs and family advice. While this is just an extension from the traditional matchmaking that was the standard in Korea, it was completely different. The majority of picture brides that came to the United States were from Japan and Korea. Sara Choe was only the first of 950 picture brides who would eventually arrive in America during the early 20th century. This was a way for immigrant workers to marry. The concept also closely links to the origins of the mail-order bride.

I came to Hawaii and was so surprised and very disappointed, because my husband sent his twenty-five-year-old handsome-looking picture. . . . He came to the pier, but I see he's really old, old-looking. He was forty-five years old, twenty-five years more old than I am. My heart stuck. I was so disappointed, I don't look at him again. So, I don't eat and only cry for eight days. I don't eat nothing, but at midnight when everybody sleeps I sneak out to drink water, so I don't die. I was so angry at my cousin because she arranged the marriage. If I don't marry, immigration law send me back to Korea free. Oh, I was thinking, thinking . . . better I marry and stay here. . . . My parents would be very shame, so I can't go back. So, after eight days, I made up my mind, I told my cousin to help me get married. I better marry and live in Hawaii.

Then, I didn't talk to him for three months, living together in the same house. Morning time early, I got up, cooked for him. . . . After three months, well . . . I cooled down . . . thirty-four years we lived together before he died.

Source: Chai, Alice. "'Mrs. K.': Oral History of a Korean Picture Bride." The Feminist Press at the City University of New York. *Women's Studies Newsletter* 7, no. 4 (Fall 1979): p. 11.

Books

Hune, Shirley, and Gail Nomura, eds. *Asian/Pacific Islander American Women: A Historical Anthology*. New York: New York University Press, 2003. *Asian/Pacific Islander American Women* explores diverse issues in Asian/Pacific Islander American women history. See Lili Kim's Chapter 6, "Redefining the Boundaries of Traditional Gender Roles: Korean Picture Brides, Pioneer Korean Immigrant Women, and Their Benevolent Nationalism in Hawai'i."

Patterson, Wayne. *The Ilse: First-Generation Korean Immigrants in Hawai'i, 1903–1973*. Honolulu: University of Hawaii Press, 2000. *The Ilse* covers many aspects of the history and issues of Korean immigration to Hawaii. See Chapter 6, "The Picture-Bride System."

Websites

Kang, Hyun-kyung. "'Picture Brides' in Hawaii Backed Korea's Independence." *Korea Times*, September 19, 2011. This newspaper article chronicles the life of several Korean picture brides from Hawaii. http://www.koreatimes.co.kr/www/news/nation/2011/09/116_95014.html. Accessed October 14, 2016.

"Picture Brides." Hawaii Digital Newspaper Project. This site provides a history of picture brides in Hawaii along with links to archival newspaper articles related to picture brides. https://sites.google.com/a/hawaii.edu/ndnp-hawaii/Home/historical-feature-articles/picture-brides. Accessed October 14, 2016.

Also Noteworthy

1983

Lily Lee Chen is inaugurated as the nation's first Chinese American woman elected as mayor in Monterey Park, California.

November 29

1944

The local American Legion at Hood River, Oregon, removes the names of 16 Nisei servicemen from a commemorative plaque located in front of city hall. One of the names was that of Frank Hachiya, a military intelligence service staffer who had been killed while on duty in the Philippines. Public outrage and protest followed, resulting in the restoration of their names by April 1945.

On 30 December the 32rd Infantry captured a prisoner and called for an interpreter. Frank Hachiya, acting team chief for the 7th Infantry Division, was slated to return to Hawaii but volunteered for one last combat mission. He had been born and raised in the farming community of Hood River, Oregon. Before the war his parents had sent him to Japan to attend Keio University in Tokyo. He returned to Oregon in 1941 for college but was drafted shortly after the war broke out. Even though his father was interned in the United States and his mother had remained in Japan, Hachiya volunteered for the language school. Earnest and articulate, he believed fervently in America and was eager to prove himself. Hachiya hurried to the 32rd Infantry's command post and interrogated the prisoner; but on the return trip, even though he was escorted by an American patrol, he was shot in the abdomen. The New York Times *described what happened next:*

Private Hachiya, mortally wounded though he was, could not lie there. The battalion wanted the information he had gathered. He must get back. So he crawled, bleeding and in agony, out of the valley and up the hill, through the grass and the scrub and around the merciful protection of little hillocks. He was dying when he finally reached his lines. He made his report while they bound his wound.

The field surgeons operated at once, but the bullet had torn through his liver. Most of the men in his regiment volunteered to give him blood transfusions, but he expired on 3 January 1945. Hachiya's death came to national attention at a critical moment for Americans of Japanese ancestry. On 17 December 1944, the War Department rescinded the exclusion orders that had kept Americans of Japanese ancestry away from the West Coast for over two years. The War Relocation Authority began to allow them to leave the camps for their homes, but the decision was not universally popular on the West Coast. Vigilante incidents were staged by people who did not want to see Japanese Americans return. On 29 November the American Legion post in Hood River, Hachiya's hometown, removed sixteen Nisei names from the county "roll of honor." When Hachiya's death was announced, readers across the country immediately linked him to the Hood River Incident. Americans of all races were outraged. The Portland Oregonian *took up the cause, and the national press gave the story wide circulation. Even the national headquarters of the American Legion applied pressure on the local post. The* New York Times *editorial, titled "Private Hachiya, American," concluded: "Perhaps Private Hachiya never knew that the Legion post had dishonored him back home. Perhaps some day what is left of him may be brought back to this country for reburial among the honored dead." In April 1945 the American Legion post reversed its stand and stored all names of Nisei servicemen from Hood River to the sign, this time including Frank Hachiya.*

Source: McNaughton, James. *Nisei Linguists: Japanese Americans in the Military Intelligence Service during World War II*. Washington, DC: Department of the Army, 2007, pp. 296–297.

Books

Tamura, Linda. *The Hood River Issei: An Oral History of Japanese Settlers in Oregon's Hood River Valley*. Urbana: University of Illinois Press, 1993. *The Hood River Issei* provides detailed history of the first-generation Japanese Americans in Hood River.

Tamura, Linda. *Nisei Soldiers Break Their Silence: Coming Home to Hood River*. Seattle: University of Washington Press, 2012. *Nisei Soldiers Break Their Silence* documents Japanese American servicemen from Hood River who served during World War II.

Websites

Katagiri, George. "Japanese Americans in Oregon." *The Oregon Encyclopedia*, October 4, 2017. This essay is a history of the Japanese experience in Oregon with photographs and videos. https://oregonencyclopedia.org/articles/japanese_americans_in_oregon_immigrants_from_the_west/#.Wm09b6inGUk. Accessed January 27, 2018.

Tamura, Linda. "Hood River Incident." *Densho Encyclopedia*, March 20, 2015. This essay covers the background, the national response, and the legacy of Hood River incident. http://encyclopedia.densho.org/Hood_River_incident/. Accessed January 27, 2018.

Also Noteworthy

1990

The Immigration Act is enacted, and it has increased the annual visa cap to 700,000 annually. The act also created the Diversity Immigrant Visa program.

November 30

2001

The U.S. Senate passes a resolution to recognize the historical significance of the 100th anniversary of Korean immigration to the United States beginning in 2003.

The Centennial of Korean Immigration to the United States

A Proclamation by the President of the United States

Released by the White House, Office of the Press Secretary

Washington, DC

January 13, 2003

From every corner of the world, immigrants have come to America to discover the promise of our Nation. On January 13, 1903, the first Korean immigrants to the United States arrived in Honolulu, Hawaii, on the SS Gaelic. *Today, Korean Americans live throughout the United States, representing one of our largest Asian-American populations. As we commemorate the centennial anniversary of Korean immigration to the United States, we recognize the invaluable contributions of Korean Americans to our Nation's rich cultural diversity, economic strength, and proud heritage.*

For the past century, Korean immigrants and their descendants have helped build America's prosperity, strengthened America's communities, and defended America's freedoms. Through their service in World War I, World War II, the Korean Conflict, the Vietnam War, and other wars, Korean Americans have served our Nation with honor and courage, upholding the values that make our country strong.

The American and Korean people share a love of freedom and a dedication to peace. The United States was the first Western country to sign a treaty of commerce and amity with Korea in 1882, promising "perpetual peace and friendship" between our nations. Since that time, the United States has built a strong friendship with Korea—a friendship based on our common commitment to human dignity, prosperity, and democracy. In the coming months, more than 1 million Korean Americans throughout our Nation will celebrate the 100th anniversary of the arrival of the first Korean immigrants to the United States. During this time, we acknowledge and commend Korean Americans for their distinguished achievements in all sectors of life and for their important role in building, defending, and sustaining the United States of America.

NOW, THEREFORE, I, GEORGE W. BUSH, President of the United States of America, by virtue of the authority vested in me by the Constitution and laws of the United States, do hereby proclaim January 13, 2003, as the Centennial of Korean Immigration to the United States. I call upon all Americans to observe the anniversary with appropriate programs, ceremonies, and activities honoring Korean immigrants and their descendants for their countless contributions to America.

IN WITNESS WHEREOF, I have hereunto set my hand this thirteenth day of January, in the year of our Lord two thousand three, and of the Independence of the United States of America the two hundred and twenty-seventh.

GEORGE W. BUSH

Source: The Code of Federal Regulations of the United States of America. The President. 2003 Compilation and Parts 100–102. Washington, DC: Office of the Federal Register National Archives and Records Administration, 2004, p. 7.

Books

Choy, Bong Youn. *Koreans in America*. Chicago, IL: Nelson-Hall, 1979. *Koreans in America* covers various aspects of Korean immigration history and resettlement in the United States.

Kim, Hyung-Chan, and Wayne Patterson, eds. *The Koreans in America, 1882–1974: A Chronology and Fact Book*. Dobbs Ferry, NY: Oceana Publications, 1974. *The Koreans in America* is a chronological history of the Korean experience in Hawaii and the continental United States.

Websites

"In Observance of Centennial of Korean Immigration to the U.S." National Association of Korean Americans. 2003. This essay discusses 100 years of Korean American history. http://www.naka.org/resources/history.asp. Accessed January 27, 2018.

National Association of Korean Americans. This site provides the full text of the Senate resolution. 2018. http://www.naka.org/news/news.asp?prmid=1. Accessed January 27, 2018.

December

December 1

1936

The Filipino Cannery Workers' and Farm Laborers' Union's (CWFLU) president, Virgil Duyungan, and its secretary, Aurelio Simon, are murdered at a restaurant by Placido Patron, an agent of a labor contractor. Their murder unified members who rallied for support.

In pool halls and cafes, dormitories and flophouses, Trinidad Rojo, Tony Rodrigo, Aurelio Simon, Joe Mislang, Frank Alonzo, and Virgil Duyungan . . . met to discuss what they could do as laborers to address the wretched working conditions and blatant racism of the canning industry. With the help of other members (including Victorio Velasco) who spent many cold days during the winter of 1932 drumming up support for the organization on the streets of Seattle, the American Federation of Labor (AFL) officially granted a charter to the CWFLU in June 1933 at the beginning of the season. The 120 mostly Filipino union members voted Duyungan and Simon as their leaders and attacked their first major problem: the corrupt and dangerous labor contractors. . . .

Amid a struggle against the powerful contractors and the failure to create solidarity, the CWFLU faced an unthinkable tragedy in 1936, just three short years after its beginning. On December 1, the nephew of a noted labor contractor invited Duyungan and Simon to dinner at a Japanese café in Seattle, claiming he wanted to discuss the CWFLU's plans for abolishing the contracting system. As soon as Duyungan and Simon arrived, the nephew shot and killed both men, leaving the CWFLU leaderless and its members stunned and deeply saddened. Those two fatal shots could have destroyed whatever existed of a labor-based Filipino rights movement, but the CWFLU members picked themselves up after the funeral for the slain leaders and installed former University of Washington student and FSCM (Filipino Students' Christian Movement) member Irineo Cabatit as president. Instead of dwelling solely on the issue of demolishing the contractor system, Cabatit and Conrad Espe (a white member of the union) encouraged members to focus on broader goals, including promoting interracial cooperation and ending discrimination of the shop floor and in communities.

Source: Hinnershitz, Stephaine. *Race, Religion, and Civil Rights: Asian Students on the West Coast, 1900–1968*. New Brunswick, NJ: Rutgers University Press, 2015, pp. 90–92.

Books

Buchholdt, Thelma. *Filipinos in Alaska: 1788–1958*. Anchorage, AK: Aboriginal Press, 1996. *Filipinos in Alaska* is a history of Filipinos in Alaska.

Friday, Chris. *Organizing Asian American Labor: The Pacific Coast Canned-Salmon Industry, 1870–1942*. Philadelphia, PA: Temple University Press, 1994. *Organizing Asian American Labor* traces the historical shifts in the ethnic and gender composition of the cannery labor market.

Websites

Dade, Nicole. "The Murders of Virgil Duyungan and Aurelio Simon and the Filipino Cannery Workers' Union." The Great Depression in Washington State Pacific Northwest Labor & Civil Rights Projects. University of Washington. 2009. This essay examines the murder of union leaders Virgil Duyungan and Aurelio Simon, and the impact it had on the Filipino community and the CWFLU. http://depts.washington.edu/depress/cannery_workers_union_murders.shtml. Accessed January 27, 2018.

Fresco, Crystal. "Cannery Workers' and Farm Laborers' Union 1933–39: Their Strength in Unity." Seattle Civil Rights & Labor History Project. University of Washington. 1999. This essay is a history of the CWFLU. http://depts.washington.edu/civilr/cwflu.htm. Accessed January 27, 2018.

December 2

1968

American actress and artist of Chinese ancestry Lucy Alexis Liu is born in Jackson Heights, Queens, New York. Since 2004, Liu has been UNICEF ambassador advocating for children's health and protection, and has traveled on missions to Lesotho, Pakistan, the Democratic Republic of Congo, Russia, Cote d'Ivoire, Egypt, Peru, and Lebanon.

Known for her repertoire of cool, competent women, particularly sharp-tongued attorney Ling Woo on TV's Ally McBeal *('98–'01; one Emmy nod). The role was originally a guest spot crafted for her by creator David E. Kelley, but soon became permanent. Unfortunately, TV audiences had a hard time differentiating between the character and the actress in real life. Walking down the street, Liu recalled, "They run to the other side . . . as soon as they see me."*

Born December 2, 1968, in the New York borough of Queens, Liu was the youngest of three kids. Mom and dad were immigrants from China and Liu spoke Mandarin until entering kindergarten. While studying Chinese language and culture at the University of Michigan, she discovered acting in her senior year. Small screen debut: serving burgers to Beverly Hills teens as a waitress on an episode of 90210. Made a play for the movies as one of sports manager Jerry Maguire's ex-girlfriends ('96).

Source: "Lucy Liu." *Biography* 7, no. 11 (November 2003): p. 18.

Books

Shea, Therese. *Lucy Liu: Actress, Artist, and Activist*. New York: Enslow Publishing, 2016. *Lucy Liu* is a biography that covers various aspects of the actor's life and career.

Shimizu, Celine Parreñas. *The Hypersexuality of Race: Performing Asian/American Women on Screen and Scene*. Durham, NC: Duke University Press, 2007. See Chapter 3 "The Sexual Bonds of Racial Stardom: Asian American Femme Fatales in Hollywood" for discussion that includes Lucy Liu as Asian American femme fatale in Hollywood.

Websites

Lucy Liu. Emmys. This site contains a profile of Liu, along with photographs. http://www.emmys.com/bios/lucy-liu. Accessed January 27, 2018.

Lucy Liu: Actress/Artist/Advocate. Official website. 2018. http://lucyliu.net/. Accessed January 27, 2018.

Also Noteworthy

1975

The Pathet Lao establishes the Lao People's Democratic Republic after forcing King Savang Vatthana to abdication and capturing Vientiane.

1989

Texas Tech University formally establishes the Vietnam Center and Archive.

2002

In Annapolis, Maryland, Ray C. Bailey, a 21-year-old; David J. Grobani, a 19-year-old; and Robert J. Canter, a 20-year-old are charged with assault and committing a hate crime for making ethnic slurs and attacking a cab driver of Middle Eastern descent.

December 3

2004

Chinese American mathematician Shiing-Shen Chern (1911–2004) dies in his home in Tianjin. Born on October 26, 1911, in Jiaxing, China, Chern became a naturalized citizen in 1961.

Shiing-Shen Chern was one of the most prominent mathematicians in the world in the twentieth century, a pioneer especially in the field of differential geometry, and an influential leader of the Chinese American scientific community. He made major contributions to the development of mathematics and science in China and the United States as well as strengthening the scientific relations between the two countries before his death in 2004. . . .

Chern's coming to the United States in 1949 fostered a renaissance of differential geometry in the country. After a half-year stay at Princeton, he took up a professorship in mathematics at the University of Chicago and helped make it into a new center of mathematics in the world. During this period Chern also had a chance to work with the Chinese American physicist Chen Ning Yang, one of his former students at Kunming, with whom he would later share the Nobel Prize in Physics in 1957.

Source: Wang, Zuoyue. "Chern, Shiing-Shen (1911–2004)." In *Asian Americans: An Encyclopedia of Social, Cultural, Economic, and Political History*, edited by Xiaojian Zhao and Edward Park, pp. 206–207. Santa Barbara, CA: ABC-CLIO, 2014.

Books

Cheng, S.Y., P. Li, and G. Tian, eds. *A Mathematician and His Mathematical Work: Selected Papers of S. S. Chern*. Singapore: World Scientific Publishing Company, 1996. The first six chapters provide a biographical sketch of Chern and his mathematic education and contributions to the field.

Yau, S.T., ed. *S. S. Chern: A Great Geometer of the Twentieth Century*. Cambridge, MA: International Press, 1998. *S. S. Chern* is a collection of essays that chronicles his life and career as a mathematician from people who worked with him and his students at several prestigious universities.

Websites

Jackson, Allyn. "Interview with Shiing Shen Chern." *Notices of the American Mathematical Society* 45, no. 7 (August 1998): pp. 860–865. This interview documents Chern's education, love of math, and transnational lifestyle . http://www.ams.org/notices/199807/chern.pdf. Accessed January 27, 2018.

Sanders, Robert. "Renowned Mathematician Shiing-Shen Chern, Who Revitalized the Study of Geometry, Has Died at 93 in Tianjin, China." *UCBerkeleyNews*, December 6, 2004. This essay profiles his life, career, and contributions to the field of mathematics. http://www.berkeley.edu/news/media/releases/2004/12/06_chern.shtml. Accessed January 27, 2018.

Also Noteworthy

1967

The Wing Luke Museum, located in the Chinatown-International District of Seattle, Washington, opens its doors to the public to document and exhibit the Asian Pacific American historical experience, culture, art, and history.

2009

In Coeur d'Alene, Idaho, swastikas and racial slurs are spray-painted on a pickup truck belonging to a Muslim American man of Jordanian descent.

December 4

1943

During World War II, General Order No. 45 is issued, which exempted Koreans in the United States from "enemy alien" status. Koreans in America possessed a vexing subjectivity as they were considered "Japanese nationals" because Korea was colonized by Japan, and were thus treated as such, but they themselves possessed a strong nationalism in their efforts to free Korea and regain its sovereignty, thereby expressing a strong sense of "anti-Japanese" sentiments.

The enforcement of enemy-alien curfew regulations on Korean—which had come to symbolize enemy-alien status itself—was finally dropped with little fanfare on December 4, 1943, when the military government promulgated General Order 45. This order amended earlier orders relating to curfew restrictions and enemy aliens, adding a specific exemption for Koreans. The change coincided with the publication on December 1 of the Cairo Declaration, in which the United States, Great Britain, and China declared their determination "that in due course Korea shall become free and independent." The official army history states that this was in keeping with the declaration that the curfew restriction was lifted. However, in view of the oft-expressed concern about internal security, in all likelihood the Cairo Declaration was found to be a convenient pretext for dropping a policy that could no longer be rationally defended in a way that involved minimum embarrassment. Six months later, on May 6, 1944, General Order 59, issued by Lieutenant General Robert C. Richardson, military governor of Hawai'i, formally removed the stigma of enemy aliens from Koreans. And five months later, in October 1944, martial law was revoked.

Source: Patterson, Wayne. *The Ilse: First-Generation Korean Immigrants in Hawai'i, 1903–1973*. Honolulu: University of Hawaii Press, 2000, p. 203.

Books

Kim, Hyung-chan, and Wayne Patterson, eds. *The Koreans in America, 1882–1974*. Dobbs Ferry, NY: Oceana Publications, 1974. *The Koreans in America* is a detailed, extensive chronology of Korean American history from 1882 to 1974.

Ryang, Sonia, and John Lie, eds. *Diaspora without Homeland: Being Korean in Japan*. Berkeley: University of California Press, 2009. See Erin Chung's Chapter 7, "The Politics of Contingent Citizenship: Korean Political Engagement in Japan and the United States."

Websites

Elsea, Jennifer. "Detention of U.S. Persons as Enemy Belligerents." Congressional Research Service. December 4, 2012. This report provides a legal historical comparison of U.S. policy and detention of "enemy combatants" that includes a discussion of enemy aliens during World War II. http://www.refworld.org/pdfid/50d1f11d2.pdf. Accessed February 14, 2018.

Macmillan, Michael. "Unwanted Allies: Koreans as Enemy Aliens in World War II." *Hawaiian Journal of History* 19 (1985): pp. 179–203. This article analyzes the complex subjectivity of Koreans in America during World War II. https://evols.library.manoa.hawaii.edu/bitstream/handle/10524/571/JL19199.pdf?sequence=1. Accessed February 14, 2018.

December 5

1942

The Manzanar riot is triggered by the beating of Fred Tayama, a Japanese American Citizens League leader, and arrest of Harry Ueno for the beating. It revealed a divide within the interned Japanese Americans and camp administration.

The Manzanar "Riot" or "Resistance" occurred on December 5–6, 1942, when Japanese American prisoners incarcerated at the Manzanar War Relocation camp openly resisted the policies of the War Relocation Authority (WRA). This violence was a culmination of an intergenerational struggle predating incarceration. After Pearl Harbor, in an attempt to curry favor with authorities and secure power, Nisei (second generation) members of the Los Angeles branch of the Japanese American Citizens League (JACL) began reporting to federal agents on alleged activities in the camp. During incarceration, some felt deeply betrayed by the JACL calling them inu *(literally translated as dog). On the night of December 5, 1942, six masked assailants attacked Fred Tayama, a JACL leader, in his barracks sending him to the hospital. The next morning, the WRA arrested Hawaiian Kibei (Nisei educated in Japan), Harry Ueno, who was perceived as a dissident because of early challenges to WRA policies. He organized kitchen workers into the Mess Hall Union to protect their rights and accused Assistant Project Director Ned Campbell of stealing rationed sugar and meat from Japanese inmates to sell on the black market. Despite the lack of physical evidence or proof of involvement,*

Ueno was removed from Manzanar and jailed in nearby Independence, California.

Source: Rafferty-Osaki, Terumi. "Manzanar Riot (1942)." In *Japanese Americans: The History and Culture of a People*, edited by Jonathan H. X. Lee, p. 85. Santa Barbara, CA: ABC-CLIO, 2018.

Books

Alinder, Jasmine. *Moving Images: Photography and the Japanese American Incarceration*. Urbana: University of Illinois Press, 2009. *Moving Images* examines the importance of photographers in the process of Japanese American relocation and internment; Chapter 3 focuses on Toyo Miyatake's photographs of Manzanar.

Cooper, Michael. *Remembering Manzanar: Life in a Japanese Relocation Camp*. New York: Clarion Books, 2002. *Remembering Manzanar* is a social history, based on oral histories, diaries, journals, memoirs, and other personal writings of Manzanar internees.

Websites

Niiya, Brian. "Manzanar Riot/Uprising." *Densho Encyclopedia*, December 5, 2017. This essay discusses the historical background and aftermath of the Manzanar riot. http://encyclopedia.densho.org/Manzanar_riot/uprising/. Accessed January 27, 2018.

Tanaka, Togo. "A Report on the Manzanar Riot of Sunday December 6, 1942." The Japanese American Evacuation and Resettlement: A Digital Archive, Bancroft Library, University of California, call number BANC MSS 67/14 c, folder O10.12 (2/2). This report provides profiles of the parties involved. http://digitalassets.lib.berkeley.edu/jarda/ucb/text/cubanc6714_b211o10_0012_2.pdf. Accessed January 27, 2018.

Also Noteworthy

1941

Korean nationalist and spy against Japan Kilsoo Kenneth Haan warns U.S. officials that Japan is planning to attack Pearl Harbor that weekend. He was ignored.

December 6

1933

Dear Wing Jung (also known as Dear Kai Gay) arrives in San Francisco in December 1933, at the age of 10. He entered the United States as a paper son of Dear Bing Quong (also known as Dear Nay Lim), an alleged native-born U.S. citizen. On December 6, 1933, Dear Wing Jung was successful in his application for his Certificate of Identity that served as proof that he was an American citizen. The U.S. government discovered the paper family system that undermined Chinese exclusion policies and implemented a Chinese Confession Program (1956–1966) that offered legal status for confession of illegal entry. At this time, the U.S. government, fueled by the anticommunist fervor and the McCarthy era, was also looking to people who had affiliations with leftist organizations. Dear Wing Jung was a member of Min Qing, which made him a target for arrest and deportation.

Dear Wing Jung's lawyer, Lloyd E. McMurray, was well aware of the government's actions. So, when the San Francisco Grand Jury indicted Dear Wing Jung on March 30, 1961, on three counts of fraud and conspiracy, his lawyer motioned to dismiss the indictment. McMurray argued that the only reason Dear Wing Jung was prosecuted was because of his affiliation with a leftist organization. By singling him out, it was discriminatory and a violation of Dear Wing Jung's freedom of speech and assembly under the First Amendment as well as a violation of his due process rights under the Fourteenth Amendment to the United States Constitution. McMurray asserted that the Chinese Confession Program was in reality a pretext to punish those who were members of leftist organizations. The motion was denied. . . .

On appeal, Dear Wing Jung made many arguments, but the Ninth Circuit agreed with the Attorney General on every argument except for one. The Ninth Circuit found the sentence too harsh. Because the government argued that Dear Wing Jung was not a United States citizen, his departure from the United States would leave him with no means of returning. Judge Magruder of the Ninth Circuit wrote, the sentence is ". . . equivalent to a 'banishment' from this country and from his wife and children, who will presumably remain here. This is either a 'cruel and unusual' punishment or a denial of due process of law. Be it one or the other, the condition is unconstitutional." On December 27, 1962, the case was remanded back to the District Court for resentencing. On April 15, 1963, the District Court sentenced Dear Wing Jung to five years probation and a fine of $500.

Source: Lee, Jennifer. "Dear Wing Jung v. United States of America (1962)." In *Asian Americans: An Encyclopedia of Social, Cultural, Economic, and Political History*, edited by Xiaojian Zhao and Edward Park, pp. 341–342. Santa Barbara, CA: ABC-CLIO, 2014.

Books

Lau, Estelle. *Paper Families: Identity, Immigration Administration, and Chinese Exclusion*. Durham, NC: Duke University Press, 2006. *Paper Families* documents the history and legacy of the Chinese paper family in the United States.

Lee, Shelley. *A New History of Asian America*. New York: Routledge, 2014. See Chapter 9, "Asian America in the Early Cold War Years," for discussion that includes the Chinese Confession Program.

Websites

Dear Wing Jung, Appellant, v. United States of America, Appellee 312 F.2d 73 (9th Cir. 1963). JUSTIA U.S. Law. https://law.justia.com/cases/federal/appellate-courts/F2/312/73/53975/. Accessed January 27, 2018.

Kwok, Steve. "My Father Was a Paper Son." Angel Island Immigration Station Foundation. 2018. This is an oral history of a paper son: there are other oral histories of Chinese Americans who were detained at Angel Island Immigration Station during the Chinese Exclusion year. https://www.aiisf.org/immigrant-voices/stories-by-author/737-my-father-was-a-paper-son/. Accessed January 28, 2018.

Also Noteworthy

1865

The United States adopts the Thirteenth Amendment, which states that neither slavery nor involuntary servitude shall exist within the United States or its jurisdictions.

1942

Mass demonstrations erupt at the Manzanar detention camp in California. James Ito and James Kanagawa were killed when military police fired into a crowd.

December 7

1941

The bombing of Pearl Harbor by Japanese forces on the morning of December 7, 1941, marks a bitter turning point in Japanese American history. Around 8 A.M. that morning, hundreds of Japanese fighter planes attacked the American naval base at Pearl Harbor. The attack lasted just two hours, but it was devastating. Japan managed to destroy 20 American naval vessels, 8 battleships, and more than 300 airplanes. Over 2,000 U.S. service men and civilians were killed, and another 1,000 plus were wounded as a result of the attack. President Franklin D. Roosevelt asked the U.S. Congress to declare war on Japan the very next day. It was approved with one dissenting vote. Three days later, Japan's allies, Germany and Italy, declared war on the United States. America was officially a part of World War II, which had been raging for over two years.

On that terrible Sunday, December 7, 1941, eighteen-year-old Daniel Inouye heard of the Pearl Harbor attack on the radio, stepped outside his Honolulu house, and saw three planes as they flew over, gray planes with red circles on their wings. "I knew they were Japanese," he remembered. Inouye later became a United States senator representing Hawaii, but at the time he had just been accepted as a premedical student at the University of Hawaii. "I felt that the world I had known, and had dreams about and planned for, had come to a shattering end." Already trained in first aid, the teenager bicycled to the harbor to help medical personnel. More than twenty-four hundred sailors, soldiers, and civilians were killed in the attack. He helped doctors there for five days before returning home.

Source: Reeves, Richard. *Infamy: The Shocking Story of the Japanese American Internment in World War II*. New York: Henry Holt and Company, 2015, p. 1.

Books

Mawdsley, Evan. *December 1941: Twelve Days That Began a World War*. New Haven, CT: Yale University Press, 2011. *December 1941* provides a day-by-day history of the events that led to the attack on Pearl Harbor. See Chapter 10 "7 December. Date of Infamy: Japan's Undeclared Wars in Malaya and Hawaii" for details on the attack on Pearl Harbor.

Odo, Franklin. *No Sword to Bury: Japanese Americans in Hawaii during World War II*. Philadelphia, PA: Temple University Press, 2004. *No Sword to Bury* tells the story of Japanese American college students who picked up the call to defend Hawaii and America. See Chapter 4 "Pearl Harbor" for a full discussion of events during the attack on Pearl Harbor and after.

Websites

"Civil Rights: Japanese Americans." PBS.org. September 2007. This site provides a history of the attack on Pearl Harbor, as well as a discussion of the subsequent internment of Japanese Americans and their struggles for civil rights, during and after World War II. It includes videos, historical images, and oral histories of Japanese Americans. https://www.pbs.org/thewar/at_home_civil_rights_japanese_american.htm. Accessed January 13, 2017.

The Official Pearl Harbor Tour Site. This site is the official site for the Pearl Harbor memorial and includes a discussion on the history of the attack on Pearl Harbor, with historical and aerial images. https://pearlharboroahu.com/. Accessed January 13, 2017.

December 8

1941

On December 8, 1941, one day after the bombing of Pearl Harbor by a Japanese air force, Congress declares war against Japan.

President Franklin D. Roosevelt: *Yesterday, December 7, 1941—a date which will live in infamy—the United States of America was suddenly and deliberately attacked by naval and air forces of the Empire of Japan.*

The United States was at peace with that nation, and, at the solicitation of Japan, was still in conversation with its government and its emperor looking toward the maintenance of peace in the Pacific. Indeed, one hour after Japanese air squadrons had commenced bombing in the American island of Oahu, the Japanese ambassador to the United States and his colleague delivered to our secretary of state a formal reply to a recent American message. While this reply stated that it seemed useless to continue the existing diplomatic negotiations, it contained no threat or hint of war or armed attack.

It will be recorded that the distance of Hawaii from Japan makes it obvious that the attack was deliberately planned many days or even weeks ago. During the intervening time the Japanese government has deliberately sought to deceive the United States by false statements and expressions of hope for continued peace.

The attack yesterday on the Hawaiian Islands has caused severe damage to American naval and military forces. I regret to tell you that very many American lives have been lost. In addition, American ships have been reported torpedoed on the high seas between San Francisco and Honolulu.

Yesterday the Japanese government also launched as attack against Malaya.

Last night Japanese forces attacked Hong Kong.

Last night Japanese forces attacked Guam.

Last night Japanese forces attacked the Philippine Islands.

Last night Japanese forces attacked Wake Island.

And this morning the Japanese attacked Midway Island.

Japan has, therefore, undertaken a surprise offensive extending throughout the Pacific area. The facts of yesterday and today speak for themselves. The people of the United States have already formed their opinions and well understand the implications to the very life and safety of our nation.

As commander in chief of the Army and Navy I have directed that all measures be taken for our defense. But always will our whole nation remember the character of the onslaught against us. . . .

Source: "FDR's 'Day of Infamy' Speech." Our Heritage in Documents. National Archives. Vol. 33, no. 4 (Winter 2001). https://www.archives.gov/publications/prologue/2001/winter/crafting-day-of-infamy-speech.html. Accessed January 28, 2018.

Books

Gillon, Steven. *Pearl Harbor: FDR Leads the Nation into War*. New York: Basic Books, 2011. In this volume, historian Steven Gillon focuses on the first 24 hours after the attack on Pearl Harbor.

Otfinoski, Steven. *Day of Infamy: The Story of the Attack on Pearl Harbor*. North Mankato, MN: Capstone Press, 2016. *Day of Infamy* is a detailed history of the attack on Pearl Harbor with a minute-by-minute chronology.

Websites

Declaration of a State of War with Japan, Germany, and Italy. 77th Congress. 1st Session. U.S. Senate. This site provides the full text to the Senate's declaration of law. http://faculty.virginia.edu/setear/students/fdrneutr/WarDeclarations.htm#joint-1. Accessed January 28, 2018.

"'This Is No Joke: This Is War': A Live Radio Broadcast of the Attack on Pearl Harbor." History Matters. George Mason University. This site provides an audio of the NBC broadcast of the attack. http://historymatters.gmu.edu/d/5167. Accessed January 28, 2018.

Also Noteworthy

1930

A white man bombs a Filipino boarding house in the Imperial Valley, California. As a result, there was one casualty, and three persons were severely injured.

2016

Tenzin Dorjee, Tibetan American scholar, is appointed a commissioner of the U.S. Commission on International Religious Freedom by House Majority Leader Nancy Pelosi.

December 9

1941

Sand Island Detention Center, Honolulu, opens and soon becomes the camp that all Hawaii-based internees would pass through. Beginning in February 1942, Sand Island internees began to be transferred to internment camps in the continental United States. Later that same year, dependent family members of the interned men were given the "opportunity" to join their husbands/fathers/brothers in internment camps. Over 1,000 dependent family members entered internment camps through this process. On March 1, 1943, Sand Island Detention Center was closed, and the remaining internees were transferred to the Honouliuli Camp located in central Oahu.

The first stop for those arrested on suspicion of being sympathetic to Japan or Germany were county jails; the immigration station, which had a lockup section; or an internment camp hastily set up in Haiku, on Maui. After processing, the internees were usually transferred to the Sand Island Detention Center across Honolulu Harbor, and from there some were sent to camps on the mainland.... Each internee was given a hearing, but this procedure typically consisted of a summary of FBI evidence and questions about whether the internee had ever visited Japan or Germany or had ever donated money, food, or clothing to that country's war effort. The hearings were pretty much one-sided and rarely lasted more than fifteen or twenty minutes. Internees were not allowed to have lawyers, nor were they allowed to question government witnesses or present character witnesses.

Source: Dickerson, James. *Inside America's Concentration Camps: Two Centuries of Internment and Torture.* Chicago, IL: Lawrence Hill Books, 2010, p. 48.

Books

Kim, Heidi. *Taken from the Paradise Isle: The Hoshida Family Story*. Boulder: University Press of Colorado, 2015. *Taken from the Paradise Isle* is based on George Hoshida's diary and memoir and details his family's history in Hawaii, including their experience in the internment camp.

Soga, Yasutaro. *Life behind Barbed Wire: The World War II Internment Memoirs of a Hawai'i Issei*. Translated by Kihei Hirai. Honolulu: University of Hawaii Press, 2008. *Life behind Barbed Wire* is a firsthand account of life in Hawaii's internment camp during World War II.

Websites

"Internment Camps in Hawai'i." The Untold Story: Internment of Japanese Americans in Hawai'i. Japanese Cultural Center of Hawai'i. This site documents all internment camps in the Hawaiian Islands. http://hawaiiinternment.org/students/internment-camps-hawai%E2%80%98i. Accessed January 28, 2018.

Rosenfeld, Alan. "Sand Island (detention facility)." *Densho Encyclopedia*, July 15, 2015. This article discusses various aspects of the history and life in the camp and has links to oral histories of survivors from the camp. http://encyclopedia.densho.org/Sand_Island_%28detention_facility%29/. Accessed January 28, 2018.

Also Noteworthy

1974

Far East National Bank, a Chinese American bank, opens in Los Angeles.

December 10

1898

Spain cedes the Philippines and Guam to the United States with the Treaty of Paris, which ended the Spanish-American War. The United States paid Spain $20 million for the Philippines. This was the start of Filipino migration to the United States. Filipinos were "wards," "nationals," or "colonial subjects" and were exempt from anti-Asian immigration policies.

Concerned about the quality of the Philippines' human resources, the American colonial rulers introduced an English language-based educational system mirrored after their own. Although not meant as an inducement for Filipinos to work in America, this similar academic preparation gave Filipinos access to the basic skills needed to perform well and adjust easily to America's growing labour market. This comparative edge, however, did not prepare them for the abuse, discrimination, and bigotry they would face in America. Conversely, education and ability to speak English were not seen as pluses, and even cited as a disadvantage by the early labour migrants, since recruiters were interested in people with brawn and not brain to work in harsh conditions with very low pay. Given this dismal work-setting, those fluent in English and with a good educational background were the last persons enterprising American employers wanted. They were quite happy with workers who spoke less and did their work without complaining. Thus many who had the language proficiency and educational preparation but desperately wanted to go and try their luck in the New World pretended to be "uneducated and hard-working."

Source: Gonzalez, Joaquin. *Philippine Labour Migration: Critical Dimensions of Public Policy*. Singapore: Institute of Southeast Asian Studies, 1998, pp. 28–29.

Books

Baldoz, Rick. *The Third Asiatic Invasion: Empire and Migration in Filipino America, 1898–1946*. New York: New York University Press, 2011. *The Third Asiatic Invasion* is a sociological analysis of Filipino migration to the United States linked to the experiences of Puerto Ricans, Mexicans, Chinese, Native Americans, and other minorities to reveal how immigration policies and the politics of exclusion informed and impacted various ethnic communities.

Barnes, Mark. *The Spanish-American War and Philippine Insurrection, 1898–1902: An Annotated Bibliography*. New York: Routledge, 2011. Mark Barnes compiled a comprehensive annotated bibliography detailing the war, its impact and legacy, along with a chronology.

Websites

"The Spanish-American War, 1898." Office of the Historian. U.S. Department of State. This essay provides historical overview of the Spanish-American War. https://history.state.gov/milestones/1866-1898/spanish-american-war. Accessed January 28, 2018.

"Treaty of Paris between the United States and Spain; December 10, 1898." The Avalon Project Documents in Law, History and Diplomacy. Yale Law School, Lillian Goldman Law Library. 2018. Full text of the treaty is available. http://avalon.law.yale.edu/19th_century/sp1898.asp. Accessed January 28, 2018.

Also Noteworthy

1942

The War Relocation Authority establishes an isolation center at Moab, Utah, for "troublemakers" in the Japanese internment camps.

1999

Wen Ho Lee, American nuclear scientist of Taiwanese (Chinese) descent who worked at the University of California Los Alamos National Laboratory, is arrested and indicted on 59 counts related to espionage and jailed in solitary confinement without bail for 278 days until September 13, 2000. He was ultimately charged only with improper handling of restricted data. Lee contended that his Asian ethnicity was a primary factor behind his prosecution by the government. As evidence of such racial profiling, he cited cases of several scientists of non-Asian and non-Chinese ancestry who were responsible for similar security transgressions but were able to continue their careers.

December 11

1999

The Asian Pacific Islander Queer Women and Transgender Community (APIQWTC) holds its official public launch in San Francisco, California, to address the needs of Asian and Pacific Islander queer women and transgender people.

Historically, Asian Americans have been concentrated on the two coasts (California, New York, and New Jersey being key states). In recent years, their communities have become visible in other regions of the country. However, in more established urban areas, organizations and resources for LGBT Asian American youth are more likely to be found. "Pan-Asian" organizations, such as Gay Asian/

Pacific Islander Men of New York (GAPIMNY), provide general support and information to diverse Asian Americans[.] Other community LGBT support groups, such as Asian & Pacific Islander Queer Women and Transgender Coalition (APIQWTC) is a San Francisco area organization which facilitates networking and communication for Asian and Pacific Islander queer women and transgender people. It has a link to AQU25A (Asian and Pacific Islander, Queer and Questioning, Under 25 and Under, All Together)—a group for and run by young queer (lesbian, gay, bi, and trans) and questioning Asians and Pacific Islanders. AQU25A offers drop-in hours, workshops, individual counseling, a peer leadership program, youth scholarships, socials, and retreats throughout the year.

Source: Asher, Nina. "Asian American Youth." *Youth, Education, and Sexualities: An International Encyclopedia*, edited by James Sears, pp. 57–58. Westport, CT: Greenwood Press, 2005.

Books

Eng, David, and Alice Hom, eds. *Q & A: Queer in Asian America*. Philadelphia, PA: Temple University Press, 1998. *Q & A: Queer in Asian America* is a comparative critical analysis of issues of queer sexuality, identities, politics, subjectivities, expressions, and so on among Asian American queers.

Wilkinson, Willy. *Born on the Edge of Race and Gender: A Voice for Cultural Competency*. Oakland, CA: Hapa Papa Press, 2015. In this memoir, Wilkinson, an Asian American of mixed heritage, a writer, activist, and public health consultant, discusses issues of being Asian and transgender.

Websites

Asian Pacific Islander Queer Women and Transgender Community (APIQWTC). Official web page. http://www.apiqwtc.org/. Accessed February 14, 2018.

"Family and Coming Out Issues for Asian Pacific Americans." Human Rights Campaign. This essay discusses the cultural and social issues related to coming out as queer among Asian Americans. https://www.hrc.org/resources/family-and-coming-out-issues-for-asian-pacific-americans. Accessed February 14, 2018.

Also Noteworthy

1941

Germany and Italy declare war on the United States. The West Coast of the United States was declared a "theater of war" following the Japanese attack on Pearl Harbor, and Lieutenant General John L. DeWitt was appointed commander with the establishment of the Western Defense Command.

December 12

1897

On this day, noted Japanese interpreter, Joseph Heco, dies. Born Hikozō Hamada (1837–1897), later known as Joseph Heco, was the first Japanese national to be naturalized as a U.S. citizen on June 1858. He was also the first to publish a Japanese-language newspaper, and he was known in Japan as the father of Japanese journalism. Heco was a fisherman from the province of Harima, Japan, who was shipwrecked in the Pacific and rescued by the American freighter *Auckland*, and brought to California in February 1851, along with 16 other survivors. He was baptized as "Joseph" in 1854 while attending a Catholic school in Baltimore. In 1859, he returned to Japan as an interpreter-translator for American merchant and diplomat Townsend Harris and for E. M. Door.

Excerpt from Joseph Heco's *The Narrative of a Japanese*, Chapter 11.

While lying there, our friend the interpreter Thomas got tired of waiting for Commodore Perry's squadron. He wished to get back to California before the gold fever was over, to make money. One day he explained his purpose to me and asked me to accompany him, offering to pay all my expenses. He said that if I went with him I could learn the English language, and that in a few years Japan would surely be opened, and then I could go back without any fear. He pointed out that it was for my own interest as well as for the interest of the Government of Japan that I should return with a full knowledge of the foreigners' language.

Source: Heco, Joseph. *The Narrative of a Japanese: What He Has Seen and the People He Has Met in the Course of the Last Forty Years*. Vol. I. Printed by the Yokohama Printing & Publishing, Co., 1895. Both volumes are available at the HathiTrust's digital library. https://catalog.hathitrust.org/Record/001968369.

Books

Heco, Joseph. *The Narrative of a Japanese: What He Has Seen and the People He Has Met in the Course of the Last Forty Years*. Vol. I. Yokohama, Japan: Yokohama Printing & Publishing, Co., 1895.

Ling, Huping, and Allan Austin. *Asian American History and Culture: An Encyclopedia*. New York: M.E. Sharpe, 2010. See Todd Munson's entry on "Joseph Heco." There are limited secondary sources on Joseph Heco published in English, and this article provides an overview of his life and accomplishments.

Websites

Baxley, George. "Joseph Heco." *The Narrative of a Japanese*. Vols. I and II. 1895 Original/First Printing. This site contains images in the first printed volumes of this publication. http://www.baxleystamps.com/litho/meiji/heco_1895_vol2.shtml. Accessed August 18, 2017.

Joseph Heco Collection. Syracuse University Libraries. This site contains a biography and archival materials related to Heco. http://library.syr.edu/digital/guides/h/heco_j.htm. Accessed August 18, 2017.

Also Noteworthy

1916

On this day, Korean national Byuen H. Leem arrives in San Francisco and tells immigration officials that he was Filipino and that his name was Eduardo Sanchez, because they were considered "nationals" and not "aliens" and therefore not subject to the Asian exclusion laws. The immigration officer suspected that he was Japanese and sent him to Angel Island Immigration Station. He was detained on the island for 44 days, and when he confessed to being Korean, he was sent back to Hawaii due to Executive Order 589, which prohibited Japanese and Korean laborers in Hawaii from entering the continental United States. He was sent back to Hawaii on January 24, 1917.

1925

The Ming Quong Home for Young Chinese Girls opens in Oakland, California, to serve young Chinese girls from broken homes.

December 13

1910

Japanese "picture brides" arrive in the United States. The Gentlemen's Agreement of 1907 stopped the issuance of passports to Japanese laborers wanting to go to America or Hawaii. However, a loophole in the agreement allowed wives and children of Japanese laborers already residing in the United States to emigrate. As a result of the loophole, many Japanese picture brides were able to migrate to Hawaii and the United States.

San Francisco. Dec. 13.—Of the thirty Japanese "picture brides" who arrived on the Chiyo Maru on Friday, thirteen met disappointment on the eve of matrimony.

When they were taken to the hospital at Angel Island to undergo an examination for the hookworm disease the brides made no objection. It was afterward learned that they thought this ceremony was but a part of the American marriage service, as they had been instructed that the department required brides who had been wedded by the photograph method to be married here according to the local customs.

But when thirteen of them were informed that they were victims of the hookworm disease, which, according to the American law, would prevent their meeting their picture husbands and necessitates their departure, there was great lamentation.

Fortunately for the brides a section of the revised statues was discovered that permits aliens certified by medical examiners to be held for treatment when this course seems advisable "to meet the ends of justice and humanity."

So the picture brides will remain on Angel Island until they are cured, or pronounced incurable, paying $1.25 a day for the Government as a hospital fee. When Dr. Glover pronounces the happy word they will be allowed to join their waiting husbands.

Source: "Nippon Brides Have Hookworm." *Evening Bulletin*, December 20, 1910.

Books

Kawakami, Barbara. *Picture Bride Stories*. Honolulu: University of Hawaii Press, 2016. *Picture Bride Stories* recounts the lives of 16 picture brides in Hawaii.

Kimura, Yukiko. *Issei: Japanese Immigrants in Hawai'i*. Honolulu: University of Hawaii Press, 1988. *Issei: Japanese Immigrants in Hawai'i* provides a historical overview of Japanese immigration to Hawaii.

Websites

"Picture Brides." Hawaii Digital Newspaper Project. This site provides a history of picture brides in Hawaii along with links to archival newspaper articles related to picture brides. https://sites.google.com/a/hawaii.edu/ndnp-hawaii/Home/historical-feature-articles/picture-brides. Accessed October 14, 2016.

Simpson, Kelly. "Japanese Picture Brides: Building a Family through Photographs." KCET. August 1, 2012. This site provides a history of Japanese picture brides with historic photographs. https://www.kcet.org/shows/departures/japanese-picture-brides-building-a-family-through-photographs. Accessed October 14, 2016.

December 14

1916

On this day, the trial of *The People of the State of California v. Jukichi Harada, et al.* begins, and the case gains national notoriety because it is the first case to test the constitutionality of the Alien Land Law. The suit claimed that an immigrant, Jukichi Harada, was ineligible for citizenship and therefore was not allowed to possess, acquire, transfer, or enjoy any real property in the state of California. On September 17, 1918, Judge Hugh Craig of the Riverside County Superior Court ruled in favor of the Harada family. Because the three children were American citizens, he ruled that Mine, Sumi, and Yoshizo, who were born in the United States, were entitled to equal protection as any other U.S. citizen no matter their parents' background. Appeals to the decision were not pursued, and that allowed other immigrants who followed to acquire property under their children's name.

Jukichi purchased the house on Lemon Street in the names of his minor American-born children—Mine, Sumi, and Yoshizo—in December of 1915, with a loan from the First National Bank in Riverside. The Harada House became the center of the case The People of the State of California v. Jukichi Harada. A group of residents in the Haradas' new neighborhood organized a committee even before the sale was finalized to try to convince the family that they were not welcome on Lemon Street.... Riverside County Superior Court Judge Hugh Craig decided in favor of the Haradas based on the constitutional rights of their American-born children. Motions from the State to move for a new trial were met by a denial from Judge Craig, whose decision on the "internationally famous Japanese land case" was printed in the Riverside Daily Press *in January 1919. However, Judge Hugh Craig did not question the constitutionality of the Alien Land Law.*

Source: Gettis, Erin, Donna Graves, Catherine Gudis, Sue Hall, Kevin Hallaran, Krystal Marquez, and Lynn Voorheis. "Reading the Sites: The Japanese-American Community in Riverside." *Journal of the Riverside Historical Society*, no. 16 (February 2012): pp. 39–40.

Books

Rawitsch, Mark. *The House on Lemon Street: Japanese Pioneers and the American Dream*. Boulder: University Press of Colorado, 2012. *The House on Lemon Street* is a history of the Harada's family's experiences in Riverside, California.

Rawitsch, Mark. *No Other Place: Japanese American Pioneers in a Southern California Neighborhood*. Riverside, CA: Department of History, University of California, Riverside, 1983. *No Other Place* is a history of Japanese Americans in Riverside, California.

Websites

"The Harada House." Asian American Riverside. University of California, Riverside. 2006. This site provides photographs that document the Harada family's history in Riverside, California. http://www.asianamericanriverside.ucr.edu/sites/HaradaHouse/index.html. Accessed January 28, 2018.

"Harada House, Riverside, California." National Park Service. It discusses the Harada House at 3356 Lemon Street, Riverside, California, and details the family's history. https://www.nps.gov/nr/travel/asian_american_and_pacific_islander_heritage/Harada-House.htm. Accessed January 28, 2018.

Also Noteworthy

1992

President George H.W. Bush allows U.S. companies to open offices, sign contracts, and do feasibility studies in Vietnam.

December 15

1978

President Jimmy Carter declares that the United States will recognize the People's Republic of China (PRC) and cut diplomatic relations with Taiwan.

After Nixon's resignation, and several years of continued U.S.-PRC negotiations, on December 15, 1978, President Jimmy Carter revealed that the United States would formally recognize the PRC as the sole legal government of China and permit the expiration of the U.S.-ROC Mutual Defense Treaty. The United States would cease to recognize the ROC [Republic of China, Taiwan] government as of January 1, 1979. . . . Carter's announcement . . . marked the end of the United States alliance with the ROC that had existed since World War II. However, derecognition did not mean a complete severing of ties. The joint U.S.-China communique of 1978 which announced the establishment of diplomatic relations stated that the people of the United States would maintain cultural, commercial, and other unofficial relations with the people of Taiwan.

Source: Chen, Lung-chu. *The U.S.-Taiwan-China Relationship in International Law and Policy*. Oxford: Oxford University Press, 2016, p. 18.

Books

Myers, Ramon, ed. *A Unique Relationship: The United States and the Republic of China under the Taiwan Relations Act*. Stanford, CA: Hoover Institution Press, 1989. This collection of essays explores various dimensions of Taiwan-U.S. relations.

Ng, Franklin. *The Taiwanese Americans*. Westport, CT: Greenwood Press, 1998. Anthropologist Franklin Ng details Taiwanese American history and other aspects of Taiwanese American life, community, and culture in the United States.

Websites

Carter, Jimmy. "Address to the Nation on Diplomatic Relations between the United States and the People's Republic of China." The American Presidency Project. University of California, Santa Barbara. The full text of President Carter's speech is available. http://www.presidency.ucsb.edu/ws/?pid=30308. Accessed January 28, 2018.

"China Policy." Office of the Historian. U.S. Department of State. This essay provides an overview of U.S.-China-Taiwan relations. https://history.state.gov/milestones/1977-1980/china-policy. Accessed January 28, 2018.

Also Noteworthy

1946

Genny Lim, American poet, performance artist, and playwright of Chinese ancestry, is born in San Francisco, California.

December 16

2002

Pakistanis and Saudi Arabians are added to the Special Registration list and are given time until March 21, 2003, to register with Immigration and Naturalization Service, unless they would depart the United States before then.

By June 2002 the Department of Homeland Security (DHS) had also launched the National Security Entry-Exit Registration System (NSEERS) program. The early stages of NEERS, known as Special Registration, *launched in September 2002, specifically targeted noncitizen men 16 years of age and older who were present in the United States between September 2002 and January 2003 and who were from predominantly 25 Muslim-dominated countries, with the exception of North Korea—sites considered hostile to the United States. These men were required to meet with Immigration and Naturalization Service (INS) officials who would assess their potential criminality. For example, immigrants found to be in violation of their visa permits were immediately detained and incarcerated without notification to family or friends. Many were permanently deported ("removed"). Although* Special Registration *was officially halted in 2003, some of its aspects were continued to specifically police the US's immigrant community.*

Source: Rajan, Julie, and Jeannette Gabriel. "Redefining US 'Homeland Security' Post-9/11: Extra-Judicial Measures, Vigilantism and Xenophobia." *Security Journal* 28, no. 2 (April 2015): p. 109.

Books

Cainkar, Louise. *Homeland Insecurity: The Arab American and Muslim American Experience after 9/11*. New York: Russell Sage Foundation, 2009. *Homeland Insecurity* covers various aspects of what it means to be Arab or Muslim in the United States post–9/11.

Zureik, Elia, and Mark Salter, eds. *Global Surveillance and Policing: Borders, Security, Identity*. New York: Routledge, 2005. See Jonathan Finn's Chapter 9, "Potential Threats and Potential Criminals: Data Collection in the National Security Entry-Exit Registration System."

Websites

Jachimowicz, Maia, and Ramah McKay. "'Special Registration' Program." Migration Policy Institute. April 1, 2003. This article discusses the history of the U.S. "Special Registration" program. https://www.migrationpolicy.org/article/special-registration-program. Accessed February 14, 2018.

"National Security Entry-Exit Registration System." Arab American Institute. This essay discusses the development of the special registration system, criticizes it, and provides recommendations for its repeal. http://www.aaiusa.org/nseers. Accessed February 14, 2018.

December 17

1943

The Burlingame Treaty of 1868 recognizes the "free migration and emigration" of the Chinese to the United States as visitors, traders, and permanent residents. It also provides the Chinese with rights and privileges of movement and residency as subjects of the "most favored nation." The flow of immigration (encouraged by the Burlingame Treaty) was stopped by the 1882 Chinese Exclusion Act. The Chinese population declined until the act was repealed in 1943 by the Magnuson Act, also known as the Chinese Exclusion Repeal Act. The Magnuson Act repealed 61 years of official racial discrimination against the Chinese. This allowed for a modest increase in Chinese immigration and allowed Chinese nationals in the United States to become naturalized citizens. The act is passed on December 17, 1943, two years after China and the United States became officially allied nations during World War II. The act provided an annual quota of 105 new entry visas, which was disproportionately low in ratio compared to other nationalities. This act inspired the passage of the Luce-Celler Act of 1946, which established a quota of 100 Indians and 100 Filipinos to immigrate to the United States per year from each country. In addition, it permitted Indian nationals already living in the United States (roughly 2,500–3,000 at the time) to become naturalized citizens. It granted Filipinos who arrived before 1934 the right to become naturalized citizens as well.

Chapter 344. An Act to repeal the Chinese Exclusion Acts, to establish quotas, and for other purposes.

Be it enacted by the Senate and House of Representatives of the United States of America in Congress assembled, That the following Acts or parts of Acts relating to the exclusion or deportation of persons of the Chinese race are hereby repealed: May 6, 1882 (22 Stat. L. 58)*; July 5, 1884 (23 Stat. L. 115); September 13, 1888 (25 Stat. L. 476); October 1, 1888 (25 Stat. L. 504); May 5, 1892* (27 Stat. L. 25)*; November 3, 1893 (28 Stat. L. 7); that portion of section 1 of the Act of July 7, 1898 (30 Stat. L. 750, 751), which reads as follows: "There shall be no further immigration of Chinese into the Hawai'ian Islands except upon such conditions as are now or may hereafter be allowed by the laws of the United States; and no Chinese, by reason of anything herein contained, shall be allowed to enter the United States from the Hawai'ian Islands."; section 101 of the Act of April 30, 1900 (31 Stat. L. 141, 161); those portions of section 1 of the Act of June 6, 1900 (31 Stat. L. 588, 611), which read as follows: "And nothing in section four of the Act of August fifth, eighteen hundred and eighty-two (twenty-second Statutes at Large, page two hundred and twenty-five), shall be constructed to prevent the Secretary of the Treasury from hereafter detailing one officer employed in the enforcement of the Chinese Exclusion Acts for duty at the Treasury Department at Washington and hereafter the Commissioner General of Immigration, in addition to his other duties, shall have charge of the administration of the Chinese exclusion law, under the supervision and direction of the Secretary of the Treasury."; March 3, 1901 (31 Stat. L. 1093); April 29, 1902 (32 Stat. L. 176); April 27, 1904 (33 Stat. L. 428); section 25 of the Act of March 3, 1911 (36 Stat. L. 1087, 1094); that portion of the Act of August 24, 1912 (37 Stat. L. 417, 476), which reads as follows: "Provided, That all charges for maintenance or return of Chinese persons applying for admission to the United States shall hereafter be paid or reimbursed to the United States by the person, company, partnership, or corporation, bringing such Chinese to a port of the United States as applicants for admission."; that portion of the Act of June 23, 1913 (38 Stat. L. 4, 65), which reads as follows: "Provided, That from and after July first, nineteen hundred and thirteen, all Chinese persons ordered deported under judicial writs shall be delivered by the marshal of the district or his deputy into the custody of any officer designated for that purpose by the Secretary of Commerce and Labor, for conveyance to the frontier or seaboard for deportation in the same manner as aliens deported under the immigration laws."*

SEC. 2. With the exception of those coming under subsections (b), (d), (e), and (f) of section 4, Immigration Act of 1924 (43 Stat. 155; 44 Stat. 812; 45 Stat. 1009; 46 Stat. 854; 47 Stat. 656; 8 U.S.C. 204), all Chinese persons entering the United States annually as immigrants shall be allocated to the quota for the Chinese computed under the provisions of section 11 of the said Act. A preference up to 75 per centum of the quota shall be given to Chinese born and resident in China.

SEC. 3. Section 303 of the Nationality Act of 1940, as amended (54 Stat. 1140; 8 U.S.C. 703), is hereby amended by striking out the word "and" before the word "descendants", changing the colon after the word "Hemisphere" to a comma, and adding the following: "and Chinese persons or persons of Chinese descent."

Approved December 17, 1943.

Source: United States Statutes at Large Containing the Laws and Concurrent Resolutions Enacted during the First Session of the Seventy-Eighth Congress of the United States, 1943. Vol. LVII. Washington, DC: Government Printing Office, 1944.

Books

Lee, Erika. *At America's Gates: Chinese Immigration during the Exclusion Era, 1882–1943*. Chapel Hill: University of North Carolina Press, 2004. *At America's Gates* covers various aspects of Chinese immigration history and exclusion.

Lee, Jonathan H.X., ed. *Chinese Americans: The History and Culture of a People*. Santa Barbara, CA: ABC-CLIO, 2016. Part I of *Chinese Americans* provides comprehensive coverage of Chinese immigration history and policy in the United States.

Websites

Dewey, Joseph. "Immigration Act of 1943." Immigration to the United States. 2015. This essay provides historical context for the passage of the Magnuson Act. http://immigrationtounitedstates.org/591-immigration-act-of-1943.html. Accessed January 13, 2017.

"Repeal of the Chinese Exclusion Act, 1943." Office of the Historian, Bureau of Public Affairs. U.S. Department of State. This site provides historical background to the Magnuson Act and its impact on Asian immigration to the United States. https://history.state.gov/milestones/1937-1945/chinese-exclusion-act-repeal. Accessed January 13, 2017.

Also Noteworthy

1943

The Magnuson Act is signed into law. This act repealed Chinese Exclusion Act, allowed Chinese to become naturalized citizens, and gave China a quota of 105 immigrants per year.

December 18

1944

In *Ex Parte Endo*, the U.S. Supreme Court unanimously rules that the War Relocation Authority cannot continue to, and by extension, has no authority to detain a "concededly loyal" American citizen. Mitsuye Endo was born on May 10, 1920, in Sacramento, California. She graduated from Sacramento Senior High School and then attended secretarial school and later was hired in a clerical job with the state department of employment. Shortly after the attack on Pearl Harbor, the California State Personnel Board fired all Japanese American state employees. Endo was among 63 employees, out of hundreds who challenged their firings with the assistance of the Japanese American Citizens League (JACL). The JACL enlisted attorney James C. Purcell. As this unfolded, Endo and her family were sent to the Sacramento Assembly Center and then to the Tule Lake internment camp. Purcell filed the petition on July 12, 1942, in federal district court in San Francisco, beginning a chain of events that would end with the U.S. Supreme Court ruling in Endo's favor in December 1944. The army opened up the West Coast to "loyal" Japanese Americans just prior to the Supreme Court decision, which had been leaked to government officials.

The fourth challenger was Mitsuye Endo, a civil servant of the state of California with brothers serving overseas in the United States Army. She had obeyed all of DeWitt's orders but from the start intended to make a test case. She contacted a civil-liberties attorney, James Purcell, who visited her in the horse stall at Tanforan where the army had put her. The strategy they decided on was to wait until she was shipped to a relocation center and then apply for a writ of habeas corpus, which, if granted, would give her immediate freedom. Although she had to wait for more than two years before her case, Ex Parte Endo *. . . was decided, she was victorious. A unanimous court restored her freedom.*

Justice William O. Douglas's opinion, however, did not suggest that the President, the Congress, or even the army had done anything unconstitutional or improper when it ordered her to leave her home and incarcerated her. The villain, according to Douglas, was the civilian War Relocation Authority! "Whatever power the War Relocation Authority may have to detain other classes of citizens, it has no authority to [detain] citizens who are concededly loyal. . ." Both Murphy and Roberts, who agreed with the result, filed critical concurrences. Murphy again complained of "the unconstitutional resort to racism inherent in the entire evacuation program," while Roberts criticized the majority for ignoring the serious constitutional questions Endo's detention raised: "An admittedly loyal citizen has been deprived of her liberty for a period of years. Under the Constitution she should be free to come and go as she pleases."

Source: Daniels, Roger. *Prisoners without Trial: Japanese Americans in World War II*. New York: Hill and Wang, 2004, p. 63.

Books

Bangarth, Stephanie. *Voices Raised in Protest: Defending North American Citizens of Japanese Ancestry in North America, 1942–49*. Vancouver: University of British Columbia Press, 2008. *Voices Raised in Protest* is a comparative analysis of history and impact of internment of Japanese Americans and Japanese Canadians during World War II.

Irons, Peter. *Justice at War: The Story of the Japanese American Internment Cases*. Berkeley: University of California Press, 1993. *Justice at War* is a critical historical analysis of the U.S. government's suppression, alteration, and destruction of evidence that could have convinced the U.S. Supreme Court to strike down the internment order.

Websites

Ex Parte Endo (1944). JUSTIA U.S. Supreme Court. This site provides the full text for *Ex Parte Endo*. https://supreme.justia.com/cases/federal/us/323/283/case.html. Accessed January 13, 2017.

Niiya, Brian. "Mitsuye Endo: The Women behind the Landmark Supreme Court Case." *Densho Blog*, March 24, 2016. This site provides a historical essay on Mitsuye Endo and her landmark Supreme Court case. http://www.densho.org/mitsuye-endo/. Accessed January 13, 2017.

Also Noteworthy

1944

In *Korematsu v. United States*, the U.S. Supreme Court rules that, based solely on one's ancestry, one group of citizens may be singled out and relocated from their homes and imprisoned for several years without trial.

The War Relocation Authority announces that it would close all relocation centers before the end of 1945, and its program would be terminated on June 30, 1946.

December 19

1941

General Delos Emmons rejects a suggestion made by the Joint Chiefs of Staff in Washington to intern all persons of Japanese ancestry residing in Hawaii either at the former leper colony site of Molokai or in mainland detention campus. General Emmons replaced Lieutenant General John L. DeWitt as commander general of the

Western Defense Command 10 days after the attack on Pearl Harbor.

Books

Allen, Gwenfread. *Hawaii's War Years, 1941–1945.* Westport, CT: Greenwood Press, 1971. *Hawaii's War Years* is an official history that is based on the Hawaii War Records Depository. It covers, in detail, the attack on Pearl Harbor, military and civil reactions, violations of civil liberties and civil rights, martial law in Hawaii, and more.

Anthony, Garner. *Hawaii under Army Rule.* Honolulu: The University Press of Hawaii, 1955. *Hawaii under Army Rule* is a history of Hawaii under martial law during World War II, which General Emmon oversaw.

Websites

"Lt. Gen. Delos C. Emmons Biography." U.S. Army Pacific. This site provides a short biography of General Emmons and includes a photograph of him. http://www.usarpac.army.mil/history2/cg_emmons.asp. Accessed February 14, 2018.

Nakamura, Kelli. "Delos Emmons." *Densho Encyclopedia*, June 10, 2015. This article discusses Emmons's military career in Hawaii during World War II. http://encyclopedia.densho.org/Delos_Emmons/. Accessed February 14, 2018.

Also Noteworthy

1946

First Indochina War starts when Viet Minh forces attacked French forces at Hanoi.

December 20

1906

The first issue of *Kahumei* (*Revolution*), the official journal of the Shakai Kakumeito (Social Revolutionary Party), is published in Berkeley, California. Shakai Kakumeito was founded in Berkeley on June 1, 1906.

The party, consisting of more than fifty Japanese radicals described by Kotoku as "clever and devoted libertarians," called on its members to abolish private property and class inequality as well as to "eliminate national and racial prejudice" and "unite with the comrades of the world to carry out a great social revolution." The group founded a bilingual newspaper, Kakumei (Revolution), *that promoted the violent overthrow of the bourgeoisie and the Japanese emperor while exhorting American workers to unite with Japanese migrants, noting, "Rejection of one nation from our country will not put a stop to the capitalist class taking all and leaving you only what he [sic] must in order to keep you alive so that you produce more wealth for them." The paper also promoted the IWW, and members of the Shakai Kakumeito worked with local IWW [Industrial Workers of the World] organizers to translate the union's pamphlets into Japanese.*

Source: Zimmer, Kenyon. *Immigrants against the State: Yiddish and Italian Anarchism in America.* Urbana: University of Illinois Press, 2015, pp. 103–104.

Books

Buhle, Paul, and Dan Georgakas, eds. *The Immigrant Left in the United States.* Albany: State University of New York Press, 1996. See Robert Lee's Chapter 9, "The Hidden World of Asian Immigrant Radicalism."

Notehelfer, F. G. *Kotoku Shusui: Portrait of a Japanese Radical.* Cambridge: Cambridge University Press, 2010. *Kotoku Shusui* is a political biography of the left-wing thinker who opposed Japan's nationalism and militarism and predicted that it would lead to conflict with the United States.

Website

"Japanese American Activist Timeline: Five Generations of Community Activism." Legacy of Japanese American Activism Conference. It is a detailed chronology that includes various Japanese American left-wing organizations and their historical development. https://jalegacy2011.wordpress.com/about/japanese-american-activist-timeline-five-generations-of-community-activism/. Accessed February 14, 2018.

December 21

1898

President William McKinley issues "Benevolent Assimilation" Proclamation arguing that the U.S. occupation of the Philippines is an "altruistic" mission. As a result, the American colonial government sought to restructure the nature of life in the Philippines by modernizing its culture, environment, education, polity, and economy. McKinley's proclamation exemplified the ideology of "White Man's Burden."

Executive Order

December 21, 1898

The Secretary of War.

SIR: The destruction of the Spanish fleet in the harbor of Manila by the United States naval squadron commanded by Rear-Admiral Dewey, followed by the reduction of the city and the surrender of the Spanish forces, practically effected the conquest of the Philippine Islands and the suspension of Spanish sovereignty therein.

With the signature of the treaty of peace between the United States and Spain by their respective plenipotentiaries at Paris, on the 10th instant, and as the result of the victories of American arms, the future control, disposition, and government of the Philippine Islands are ceded to the United States. In fulfillment of the rights of sovereignty thus acquired and the responsible obligations of government thus assumed, the actual occupation and administration of the entire group of the Philippine Islands become immediately necessary, and the military government heretofore maintained by the United States in the city, harbor, and bay of Manila is to be extended with all possible dispatch to the whole of the ceded territory.

In performing this duty the military commander of the United States is enjoined to make known to the inhabitants of the Philippine Islands that in succeeding to the sovereignty of Spain, in severing the former political relations of the inhabitants, and in establishing a new political power the authority of the United States is to be exerted for the security of the persons and property of the people of the islands and for the confirmation of all their private rights and relations.

It will be the duty of the commander of the forces of occupation to announce and proclaim in the most public manner that we come, not as invaders or conquerors, but as friends, to protect the natives in their homes, in their employments, and in their personal and religious rights. All persons who, either by active aid or by honest submission, co-operate with the Government of the United States to give effect to these beneficent purposes will receive the reward of its support and protection. All others will be brought within the lawful rule we have assumed, with firmness if need be, but without severity so far as may be possible.

Within the absolute domain of military authority, which necessarily is and must remain supreme in the ceded territory until the legislation of the United States shall otherwise provide, the municipal laws of the territory in respect to private rights and property and the repression of crime are to be considered as continuing in force and to be administered by the ordinary tribunals so far as practicable. The operations of civil and municipal government are to be performed by such officers as may accept the supremacy of the United States by taking the oath of allegiance, or by officers chosen as far as may be practicable from the inhabitants of the islands.

While the control of all the public property and the revenues of the state passes with the cession, and while the use and management of all public means of transportation are necessarily reserved to the authority of the United States, private property, whether belonging to individuals or corporations, is to be respected, except for cause duly established. The taxes and duties heretofore payable by the inhabitants to the late government become payable to the authorities of the United States, unless it be seen fit to substitute for them other reasonable rates or modes of contribution to the expenses of government, whether general or local. If private property be taken for military use, it shall be paid for when possible in cash at a fair valuation, and when payment in cash is not practicable receipts are to be given.

All ports and places in the Philippine Islands in the actual possession of the land and naval forces of the United States will be opened to the commerce of all friendly nations. All goods and wares not prohibited for military reasons, by due announcement of the military authority, will be admitted upon payment of such duties and other charges as shall be in force at the time of their importation.

Finally, it should be the earnest and paramount aim of the military administration to win the confidence, respect, and affection of the inhabitants of the Philippines by assuring to them in every possible way that full measure of individual rights and liberties which is the heritage of free peoples, and by proving to them that the mission of the United States is one of benevolent assimilation, substituting the mild sway of justice and right for arbitrary rule. In the fulfillment of this high mission, supporting the temperate administration of affairs for the greatest good of the governed, there must be sedulously maintained the strong arm of authority to repress disturbance and to overcome all obstacles to the bestowal of the blessings of good and stable government upon the people of the Philippine Islands under the free flag of the United States.

WILLIAM MCKINLEY

Source: McKinley, William. "Executive Order." December 21, 1898. The American Presidency Project. University of California, Santa Barbara. http://www.presidency.ucsb.edu/ws/index.php?pid=69309. Accessed January 28, 2018.

Books

Miller, Stuart. *"Benevolent Assimilation": The American Conquest of the Philippines, 1899–1903.* New Haven, CT: Yale University Press, 1982. *"Benevolent Assimilation"* is a history of U.S. imperialism in the Philippines.

Tan, Samuel. *A History of the Philippines.* Quezon City: University of the Philippines Press, 1987. See Chapter 6, "Imperialism and Filipinism (1898–1946)."

Websites

"American Designs and the Benevolent Assimilation." The Philippine History Site. University of Hawaii. It provides historical overview of McKinley's proclamation and links to other topics related to the Philippine-American War. http://opmanong.ssc.hawaii.edu/filipino/benevolent.html. Accessed January 28, 2018.

Dumindin, Arnaldo. *Philippine-American War, 1899–1902.* http://www.filipinoamericanwar.com/. 2006. This digital book provides photographs and archival documents related to the Philippine-American War. http://www.filipinoamericanwar.com/benevolentassimilation.htm. Accessed January 28, 2018.

December 22

1902

On this day, the arrangements made by Allen and Deshler would result in the first shipload of 121 immigrants who left Incheon for Hawaii. They were inspected by Japanese physicians in Kobe and sailed for Honolulu on SS *Gaelic*.

As an agent of the Hawaii Sugar Planters Association . . ., David W. Deshler established the East-West Development Company . . . in Inchon to recruit Korean laborers. The first shipload of Koreans left Inchon harbor for Japan aboard a Japanese ship, Genkai-maru, *on December 22, 1902. There are, however, conflicting reports on the exact number of the first group. . . . Kim Won-yong . . . claims that 121 workers left Korea as the first group of Korean emigrants for Kobe, Japan, where they underwent a physical examination and that those who passed the physical (101 persons along with interpreters) boarded an American merchant ship,* Gaelic, *on a voyage to Hawaii. . . . To add to the confusion . . . a contemporary Korean newspaper published in Seoul, carried the following news article . . . "Hawaii Emigration" (Hawaii Imin) on December 27, 1902: "As previously reported, Deshler . . . was engaged in recruiting Korean emigrants to Hawaii. Fifty-four Koreans who responded to [Deshler's call for] recruitment left on the 22nd of this month for Hawaii via Japan." Because this news appeared only five days after the departure . . . this number . . . would seem to be the most reliable. This, however, is not the case. It may have referred only to the number of adult male workers, not including women and children who accompanied them.*

Source: Ch'oe, Yŏng-ho. "The Early Korean Immigration: An Overview." In *From the Land of Hibiscus: Koreans in Hawai'i, 1903–1950*, edited by Yŏng-ho Ch'oe, p. 12. Honolulu: University of Hawaii Press, 2007.

Books

Hurh, Won Moo. *The Korean Americans: The New Americans*. Westport, CT: Greenwood Press, 1998. *The Korean Americans* covers various historical and contemporary aspects of the Korean American community.

Patterson, Wayne. *The Korean Frontier in America: Immigration to Hawaii, 1896–1910*. Honolulu: University of Hawaii Press, 1988. *The Korean Frontier in America* covers the history of Korean emigration to Hawaii, in addition to U.S.-Korean relation. See Chapter 3, "Enter Horace Allen," for discussion related to David W. Deshler.

Websites

Kim, Young-sik. "A Brief History of the US-Korea Relations Prior to 1945." *Korea Web Weekly*, July 10, 2003. This site covers various aspects of U.S.-Korea relations and history before 1945. http://www.freerepublic.com/focus/news/943949/posts. Accessed October 12, 2016.

Kim, Young-sik. "Koreans in America in the late 1800s." Association for Asian Research. This site provides a historical overview of early Korean American history. http://www.asianresearch.org/articles/1506.html. Accessed October 12, 2016.

1987

The U.S. Congress enacts the Amerasian Homecoming Act that eases immigration of Amerasian children born, or war babies, during the Vietnam War—mostly the offspring of American fathers and Vietnamese mothers. According to U.S. Department of State statistics, between September 1982 and August 1988, Orderly Departure Program (ODP) brought approximately 4,500 Amerasian children and 7,000 accompanying relatives to the United States. They entered the United States under ODP and not the Amerasian Homecoming Act because the United States and Vietnam did not maintain diplomatic relations.

History of U.S. Response to Amerasians

The first U.S. legislative response to Amerasians was embodied in the 1982 "Amerasian Immigration Act." . . . This law offers top priority U.S. immigration to children not only in Vietnam, but also in Korea, Laos, Cambodia or Thailand who are known to have been fathered by U.S. citizens. Unfortunately, this landmark law grants immigration privileges only to the Amerasians; mothers and half-siblings are not permitted to immigrate, and the mothers of minor Amerasians must sign an irrevocable release in order for their children to emigrate. And the U.S. law places such stringent legal and financial obligations on potential sponsors that only a few Amerasians (most from Korea and Thailand) have benefited from it. Ironically, the law cannot be implemented where the need is greatest; since the U.S. and Vietnam do not have diplomatic relations, the Amerasian Immigration Act does not apply to Vietnamese Amerasians.

Since September 1982, however, Amerasians have been leaving Vietnam through the Orderly Departure Program (ODP). An emigration mechanism established in 1979 by the Vietnamese government and the United Nations High Commissioner for Refugees (UNHCR), the ODP provides a legal alternative to the desperate and dangerous exodus of Vietnamese Boat People. Persons emigrating via ODP must obtain exit permits from the Vietnamese government, and satisfy the receiving nation's eligibility criteria.

The first Amerasians to exit Vietnam in 1982 were children whose American fathers had filed visa applications for them and who thus arrived as U.S. citizens. Later, ODP was expanded to include Amerasians for whom firm documentation was not available, but who appeared to have been fathered by Americans. These children were admitted as refugees. They included a small number of Amerasians traveling alone ("unaccompanied minors," only a small percentage of whom are orphans), but mostly they were Amerasians traveling with immediate relatives.

Source: Migration and Refugee Services of the United States Conference of Catholic Bishops. *To Welcome the Amerasians: An MRS Staff Report*. Washington, DC: Migration and Refugee Services of the United States Conference of Catholic Bishops, 1988.

Books

DeBonis, Steven. *Children of the Enemy: Oral Histories of Vietnamese Amerasians and Their Mothers*. Jefferson, NC: McFarland & Co., 1994. *Children of the Enemy* documents 38 oral histories of Vietnamese Amerasians.

McKelvey, Robert. *The Dust of Life: America's Children Abandoned in Vietnam*. Seattle: University of Washington Press, 2000. *The Dust of Life* discusses various aspects of Vietnamese Amerasians, including their postwar migration out of Vietnam.

Websites

Chuong, Chung Hoang, and Le Van. *The Amerasians from Vietnam: A California Study*. Folsom, CA: Southeast Asia Community Resource Center, 1994. This report covers various aspects of Amerasian refugees from Vietnam in California. http://www.reninc.org/other-publications/handbooks/amerasn.pdf. Accessed January 17, 2017.

Phan, Shandon. "Vietnamese Amerasians in America." *Asian-Nation: The Landscape of Asian America*. 2003. This essay discusses the historical issues of Vietnam Amerasians, their unique struggles as biracial refugees, and their marginalization in Vietnam and the United States. http://www.asian-nation.org/amerasians.shtml. Accessed January 17, 2017.

December 23

1947

President Harry S. Truman grants full pardons to all Japanese American draft resisters who had violated the Selective Training and Service Act of 1940. The draft resisters were known for protesting their conscription while they remained excluded from the West Coast and confined without due process of law. In addition, they resisted being drafted to serve in segregated combat units in the army or being treated as "enemy aliens" by the government. Unlike the "No-No boys," draft resisters answered "Yes-Yes" to the loyalty questions. Draft resisters were punished and served time for their act of civil disobedience.

Gordon Hirabayashi, a social activist studying religion at the University of Washington; Minoru Yasui, a lawyer; Fred Korematsu, a welder; and Mitsuye Endo, a civil service stenographer, disagreed with Executive Order 9066 and individually challenged the constitutionality of the government's actions in the courts. Their initial efforts were unsuccessful. In the meantime, broader resistance to the notion of compliance developed in the concentration camps when the government—with the support of the JACL—established a loyalty review program which included a loyalty questionnaire. Based on their responses to the questionnaire, inmates would be allowed to leave the camps or be accepted for the draft. The JACL, therefore, encouraged inmates to respond affirmatively to loyalty questions and to indicate their acceptance of the draft. . . .

The questionnaire . . . was problematic because its creators had failed to take into consideration the ages, gender, and political status of the population it was designed to interrogate. The most serious concerns were raised by questions 27 and 28. Question 27 asked:

"Are you willing to serve in the armed forces of the United States on combat duty, whenever ordered?" Question 28 asked: "Will you swear unqualified allegiance to the United States and faithfully defend the United States of America from any and all attack by foreign or domestic forces, and forswear any form of allegiance or obedience to the Japanese emperor and to any other foreign government power or organization?"

The majority of the seventy eight thousand eligible Japanese American adults who filled out the questionnaire affirmed their allegiance to the United States; however, more than ten thousand Japanese Americans who felt betrayed by their government qualified their answers in some way. . . . Moreover, when replying to their draft notices, approximately 300 draft resisters stated that military service was unacceptable; they would not serve a country that had violated their constitutional rights.

Source: Castelnuovo, Shirley. *Soldiers of Conscience: Japanese American Military Resisters in World War II*. Westport, CT: Greenwood Press, 2008, pp. xi–xii.

Books

Lyon, Cherstin. *Prisons and Patriots: Japanese American Wartime Citizenship, Civil Disobedience, and Historical Memory*. Philadelphia, PA: Temple University Press, 2011. *Prisons and Patriots* examines Japanese American protest and dissent during World War II.

Muller, Eric. *Free to Die for Their Country: The Story of the Japanese American Draft Resisters in World War II*. Chicago, IL: University of Chicago Press, 2001. *Free to Die for Their Country* discusses various forms of resistance to the internment of Japanese Americans during World War II.

Websites

Muller, Eric. "Draft Resistance." *Densho Encyclopedia*, 2017. This site provides a detailed historical essay on the draft resisters. http://encyclopedia.densho.org/Draft_resistance/. Accessed January 14, 2017.

Wang, Frances Kai-hwa. "The Untold Stories of Internment Resisters." NBC News. This site provides stories of World War II Japanese American draft resisters with historical photographs. http://www.nbcnews.com/news/asian-america/uclas-suyama-project-document-japanese-american-resistance-internment-during-world-n321426. Accessed January 14, 2017.

Also Noteworthy

1952

Hong Fook Tong theatrical troupe moves to a theater of its own construction on Dupont Street, San Francisco, the New Chinese Theater.

December 24

1947

President Harry S. Truman issues a pardon for all Nisei resisters of conscience during World War II.

Not all acts of courage are recognized or rewarded. And some wrongs can never be fully righted. Nevertheless, in early 1947, the government attempted to address the wrongs committed against the Nisei draft resisters. A.L. Wirin, who had represented some of the resisters during their trials, submitted a petition for amnesty on their behalf. President Truman convened a board to review their cases, along with the cases of other World War II draft resisters. Upon the Board's advice, President Truman gave the draft resisters a Presidential Pardon with the restoration of all civil and political rights on December 24, 1947.

Source: Bannai, Lorraine. "Taking the Stand: The Lessons of the Three Men Who Took the Japanese American Internment to Court." *Seattle Journal of Social Justice* 4, no. 1 (2005): p. 30.

Books

Lyon, Cherstin. *Prisons and Patriots: Japanese American Wartime Citizenship, Civil Disobedience, and Historical Memory*. Philadelphia, PA: Temple University Press, 2011. *Prisons and Patriots* examines Japanese American protest and dissent during WWII.

Muller, Eric. *Free to Die for Their Country: The Story of the Japanese American Draft Resisters in*

World War II. Chicago, IL: University of Chicago Press, 2001. *Free to Die for Their Country* discusses various forms of resistance to the internment of Japanese Americans during World War II.

Websites

Abe, Frank. "Conscience and the Constitution: The Story Timeline." 2000. This is a detailed chronology of Japanese immigration, World War II experience, and postwar developments. http://resisters.com/conscience/the_story/timeline/index.html. Accessed January 28, 2018.

Muller, Eric. "Draft Resistance." *Densho Encyclopedia*, February 2, 2016. http://encyclopedia.densho.org/Draft_resistance/. Accessed January 28, 2018.

December 25

2003

The *Young Black Stallion*, a children's film, is released but is critiqued by activists as Islamophobic, anti-Arab, and anti-Muslim.

On occasion, Hollywood costume designers dressed movie villains in Middle Eastern garb, reinforcing the notion that Oriental attire is somehow evil. In the 2003 movie, Lord of the Rings: Return of the King, *nefarious Bedouin creatures appear in black headscarves before attacking the movies' protagonists. . . . Other children's movies also contained xenophobic messages. The movie,* Young Black Stallion, *uses Arab villains to create tension and suspense. In one scene, a lecherous Arab leers at Neera, the female child protagonist. In another scene, unscrupulous Middle Easterners take financial advantage of a senior citizen, teaching young American audiences that foreigners are not to be trusted. This movie was released in the U.S. on December 25, 2003, to entertain American family audiences at Christmas time. Some activists saw a connection between Islamophobic children's movies and anti-Muslim hate crimes taking place on American school campuses.*

Source: Karam, Nicoletta. *The 9/11 Backlash: A Decade of U.S. Hate Crimes Targeting the Innocent*. Berkeley, CA: Beatitude Press, 2012, p. 131.

Books

Esposito, John, ed. *Islamophobia: The Challenge of Pluralism in the 21st Century*. Oxford: Oxford University Press, 2011. *Islamophobia* is a collection of critical articles that explores various aspects of Islamophobia in the West vis-à-vis politics, racism, War on Terror, among other critical topics.

Shaheen, Jack. *Guilty: Hollywood's Verdict on Arabs after 9/11*. Northampton, MA: Olive Branch Press, 2008. *Guilty* argues that nearly all Hollywood films after 9/11 deploy an Orientalistic, racialized portrayal of Islam, Arabs, Muslims, and Middle Easterners as enemy and "Other."

Websites

"Islamophobia and Hollywood: A Brief History." Millennial Influx. This essay discusses the history of Islamophobic representation in Hollywood films. http://www.millennialinflux.com/islamophobia-and-hollywood-a-brief-history/. Accessed February 14, 2018.

Sardar, Nouri. "Why Hollywood Is to Blame for Islamophobia in America." TheMuslimVibe.com. March 21, 2017. This article is a critical analysis of Hollywood films and Islamophobic stereotyping and portrayals of Islam and Muslims. https://themuslimvibe.com/featured/why-hollywood-is-to-blame-for-islamophobia-in-america-long-read. Accessed February 14, 2018.

December 26

1972

The Chinese Progressive Association is founded in San Francisco, Chinatown. Its mission was to educate, organize, and empower low-income and working-class immigrant Chinese community to build collective power in solidarity with other oppressed communities.

For two decades, the Chinese Progressive Association (CPA), a nonprofit, grassroots organization based in San Francisco's Chinatown, has worked to serve and empower the Chinese community—immigrant and American-born—by providing educational and training programs and mobilizing citizens to pursue an agenda of freedom and equality for Asian Americans.

For a non-profit grassroots organization, surviving and growing for 20 years is no small feat, particularly with the wave of conservatism at the state and federal levels under the Reagan and Bush administrations which have been characterized by cutbacks in public education and social services, and eroding civil rights protections. . . .

From its first small office in the basement of what was then the International Hotel, to its current office on Waverly Place in Chinatown, CPA has been resolute in confronting issues head on and stimulating constructive dialogue and activism.

Inspired by the legacy of the Civil Rights Movement and the struggle of students of color on college campuses for equal access to higher education and the establishment of ethnic studies, CPA formed in response to the needs and concerns of both the immigrant and American-born Chinese community.

Some of CPA's early work involved consulting with Asian American lawyers to establish the first free bilingual legal clinic in Chinatown, helping immigrants qualify for legal status and fighting unfair deportation laws and practices, supporting Chinese workers in their attempt to unionize and fighting racial discrimination.

CPA became involved in the historic struggle to save from destruction what was then the International Hotel, which provided low-cost housing for primarily Pilipino and Chinese tenants, small shops and grassroots organizations.

In the early 1970s, CPA worked with other groups city-wide to demand that the United States normalize diplomatic relations with the People's Republic of China, which many within the Chinese community considered an act of self-respect and pride.

Source: Muto, Shelia. "20 Years of Empowering the Chinese American Community: The Chinese Progressive Association." *AsianWeek*, November 6, 1992, p. 16.

Books

Hall, Patricia Wong, and Victor Hwang, eds. *Anti-Asian Violence in North America*. Walnut Creek, CA: AltaMira Press, 2001. See Eric Mar's Chapter 4, "From Vincent Chin to Kuan Chung Kao: Restoring Dignity to Their Lives," which discusses Mar's membership and work with the Chinese Progressive Association in San Francisco.

Ho, Fred, ed. *Legacy to Liberation: Politics and Culture of Revolutionary Asian Pacific America*. San Francisco, CA: AK Press, 2000. *Legacy to Liberation* is a collection of essays that documents Asian American revolutionary movements from the 1960s to the 1990s.

Websites

Chinese Progressive Association. The association's official website includes its history and documents members' stories. http://www.cpasf.org/mission. Accessed January 28, 2018.

"History of I Wor Kuen." *Encyclopedia of Anti-Revisionism On-Line*. It discusses the history of I Wor Kuen, which later created the Chinese Progressive Association. https://www.marxists.org/history/erol/ncm-1a/iwk-history.htm. Accessed January 28, 2018.

December 27

1925

Hilario Camino Moncado establishes the Filipino Federation of America, a quasi-religious mutual aid society.

. . . [T]he Filipino Federation was an organization with Filipino-American roots and concerns. It was formed on December 27, 1925 in Los Angeles and

incorporated for fifty years in 1927 in the state of California. A factor that impressed those who joined the organization was this incorporation. It distinguished the Federation from other Filipino groups. The "Inc." after its name gave it an image of legitimacy, importance, status, power and connoted an organization that was serious about its business and purpose.

Source: Buenaventura, Steffi. "The Master and the Federation: A Filipino-American Social Movement in California and Hawaii." *Social Process in Hawaii* 33 (1991): p. 171.

Books

Gonzalez, Joaquin. *Filipino American Faith in Action: Immigration, Religion, and Civic Engagement.* New York: New York University Press, 2009. See Chapter 2, "Resurrecting Christian Faith," for discussion that includes the history and development of the Filipino Federation of America.

Yoo, David, ed. *New Spiritual Homes: Religion and Asian Americans.* Honolulu: University of Hawaii Press, 1999. See Steffi Buenaventura's Chapter 2, "Filipino Folk Spirituality and Immigration: From Mutual Aid to Religion."

Website

"Filipino Federation of America." Routes and Roots: Cultivating Filipino American History on the Central Coast. This site provides a history of the Filipino Federation of America, in addition to photographs. https://sites.google.com/site/centralcoastroutesandroots/roots/fraternal-organizations/frat-organization_front/filipino-federation-of-america. Accessed January 28, 2018.

Also Noteworthy

1992

Between December 27 and 29, 1992, a group of 500 Caodaists from different countries congregates in Anaheim to discuss visions and strategies for the development of the overseas Caodai community. The meeting ended with the formation of the Confederation of Overseas Caodaists, a nondenominational group. Moreover, plans were put in place to purchase a piece of land in Riverside to build a nondenominational Caodai temple. Members of the Caodai Temple of Westminster attended the meeting but did not want to participate in the new organization's projects, which could pose threats to their Tay Ninh base.

December 28

1945

An Act to Expedite the Admission to the United States of Alien Spouses and Alien Minor Children of Citizen Members of the United States Armed Forces (Public Law 271) is enacted, and many Chinese Americans and their allies viewed it as a positive step in righting the wrongs of 70 years of federal legislative enactments prohibiting Chinese immigration into the United States. However, it was soon evident that dismantling almost 75 years of anti-Chinese immigration law was a complicated process requiring a complete overhaul of decades of reactionary legislation directed at the Chinese. Like the December 17, 1943, Magnuson Act to Repeal the Chinese Exclusion Acts, to Establish Quotas, and for Other Purposes (Public Law 199), the 1945 War Brides Act reflected America's wartime and postwar commitment to eradicate racism and ethnocentrism from American law. By allowing "alien spouses or alien children of United States citizens serving in, or having an honorable discharge certificate from the armed forces of the United States during the Second World War" entry into the United States as nonquota aliens, the 1945 act supplanted the immigration quota barriers put in place under the Immigration Act of 1924 (An Act to Limit the Immigration of Aliens into the United States, and for Other Purposes—Public Law 139). Because the 1945 War Brides Act did not repeal the provisions delineated in Section 3 of the 1917 law, Chinese American servicemen with wives and children in China were met with a conflict in law that ostensibly barred the promise of family reunification granted to other American soldiers made in recognition and honor of their wartime service. On August 9, 1946, An Act to Place Chinese Wives of American Citizens on a Non Quota Basis modified both the 1924 Immigration Act and the 1943 Magnuson Act, allowing Chinese wives and children nonquota entry into the United States. The 1946 act did not repeal immigration prohibition from the entire geographic region delimited under the 1917 law; that change would come about on December 24, 1952, under the provisions of the McCarran-Walter Act.

To expedite the admission to the United States of alien spouses and alien minor children of citizen members of the United States armed forces.

Be it enacted by the Senate and House of Representatives of the United States of America in Congress assembled, That notwithstanding any of the several clauses of section 3 of the Act of February 5, 1917, excluding physically and mentally defective aliens, and notwithstanding the documentary requirements of any of the immigration laws or regulations, Executive orders, or Presidential proclamations issues thereunder, alien spouses or alien children of United States citizens serving in, or having an honorable discharge certificate from the armed forces of the United States during the Second World War shall, if otherwise admissible under the immigration laws and if application for admission is made within three years of the effective date of this Act, be admitted to the United States: Provided, That every alien of the foregoing description shall be medically examined at the time of arrival in accordance with the provisions of section 16 of the Act of February 5, 1917, and if found suffering from any disability which would be the basis for a ground of exclusion except for the provision of this Act, the Immigration and Naturalization Service shall forthwith notify the appropriate public medical officer of the local community to which the alien is destined: Provided further, That the provisions of the Act shall not affect the duties of the United States Public Health Service so far as they relate to quarantinable diseases.

SEC. 2. Regardless of section 9 of the Immigration Act of 1924, any alien admitted under section 1 of this Act shall be deemed to be a nonquota immigrant as defined in section 4 (a) of the Immigration Act of 1924.

SEC. 3. Any alien admitted under section 1 of this Act who at any time returns to the United States after a temporary absence abroad shall not be excluded because of the disability or disabilities that existed at the time of that admission.

SEC. 4. No fine or penalty shall be imposed under the Act of February 5, 1917 except those arising under section 14, because of the transportation to the United States of any alien admitted under this Act.

SEC. 5. For the purpose of this Act, the Second World War shall be deemed to have commenced on December 7, 1941, and to have ceased upon the termination of hostilities as declared by the President or by a joint resolution of Congress.

Approved December 28, 1945.

Source: *United States Statutes at Large Containing the Laws and Concurrent Resolutions Enacted during the First Session of the Seventy-Ninth Congress of the United States, 1945*. Volume LIX. Washington, DC: Government Printing Office, 1946.

Books

Glenn, Evelyn Nakano. *Issei, Nisei, War Bride: Three Generations of Japanese American Women in Domestic Service*. Philadelphia, PA: Temple University Press, 1986. See Chapter 3 for a discussion of Japanese American war brides.

Zeiger, Susan. *Entangling Alliances: Foreign War Brides and American Soldiers in the Twentieth Century*. New York: New York University Press, 2010. *Entangling Alliances* is a comprehensive and complex study of the history of war brides in 20th-century American history.

Websites

Lyon, Cherstin. "War Brides Act." *Densho Encyclopedia*, 2017. This site provides an essay that discusses the history and impact of the War Brides Act. http://encyclopedia.densho.org/War%20Brides%20Act/. Accessed January 13, 2017.

"1946 Chinese War Brides Act." Hein Online. The University of Washington-Bothell Library. This site provides the full text for the Chinese War Brides Act, in addition to a discussion of the impact of the legislation. http://library.uwb.edu/Static/USimmigration/1946_chinese_war_brides_act.html. Accessed January 13, 2017.

December 29

2001

Vandals break into the Islamic Foundation of Central Ohio in Columbus, Ohio, sometime during the evening, causing hundreds of thousands of dollars in damages.

The vandals broke a bathroom pipe and clogged the sink, forcing it to overflow for hours; tore frames encasing religious verses off a wall; destroyed a chandelier in the main prayer hall; flipped over the pulpit; cut the wires of high mounted speakers and amplifiers and threw them to the ground; tore posters off a mosque classroom wall; pulled down curtains and drapes; and tipped over bookcases and file cabinets in a classroom and threw approximately one hundred copies of the Quran onto the floor. Water from the stopped-up third-floor sink seeped into the second floor main prayer hall, causing plaster pieces from the main prayer hall ceiling to fall. A torn Quran and a smashed clock from the mosque were found in the mosque parking lot. The damage to the mosque was estimated at $379,000.

Source: Singh, Amardeep. "'We Are Not the Enemy': Hate Crimes against Arabs, Muslims, and Those Perceived to Be Arab or Muslim after September 11." *Human Rights Watch: United States* 14, no. 6 (G) (November 2002): p. 22.

Books

Altschiller, Donald. *Hate Crimes: A Reference Handbook*. 3rd ed. Santa Barbara, CA: ABC-CLIO, 2015. This book examines all aspects of hate crimes; see section on Arab and Muslim Americans.

Jalil, Mazhar, Norman Hosansky, and Pual Numrich, eds. *The Abrahamic Encounter: Local Initiatives, Large Implications*. Eugene, OR: Wipf & Stock, 2016. See Paul Numrich's Chapter 1, "The Central Ohio Abrahamic Encounter."

Websites

Islamic Foundation of Central Ohio. This official website has information and photograph of the center. https://www.ifco-columbus.org/. Accessed January 28, 2018.

"Mosque Vandalized in Columbus, Ohio." The Pluralism Project. Harvard University. 2018. This site provides links for newspaper coverage related to the incident. http://pluralism.org/news/mosque-vandalized-in-columbus-ohio/. Accessed January 28, 2018.

Also Noteworthy

1941

All "enemy aliens" (people of Japanese, German, and Italian ancestry) in California, Orgeon, Washington, Montana, Idaho, Utah, and Nevada are ordered to surrender all contraband, including shortwave radios, cameras, binoculars, and weapons.

December 30

1898

The first celebration of Rizal Day in Manila, Philippines, is held on this day. It is celebrated on December 30 of each year among Filipino American communities. Rizal Day marks the martyrdom of Jose Rizal, the national hero of the Philippines.

Since the 1920s each major center of Filipino residence in the United States has hosted a Rizal Day banquet and dance—sometimes more than one if sponsoring clubs and organizations were unable to agree on the site or the arrangements. In more recent years, the growing numbers of Filipino Americans within a metropolitan area can necessitate multiple locations in the city and its suburbs. Typically, the festivities have always included a lavish dinner, live music, the playing of national anthems, speeches by dignitaries, songs and performances, and without fail, a dramatic recitation of Rizal's farewell, his "Ultima Adios." The crowning of a Rizal Day queen from among the candidates of rival organizations has also long been an important tradition.

Source: Posadas, Barbara. *The Filipino Americans*. Westport, CT: Greenwood Press, 1999, p. 55.

Books

Lee, Jennifer, and Min Zhou, eds. *Asian American Youth: Culture, Identity, and Ethnicity*. New York: Routledge, 2004. See Arleen de Vera's Chapter 4, "Rizal Day Queen Contests, Filipino Nationalism, and Femininity."

Lee, Jonathan H. X., and Kathleen Nadeau, eds. *Encyclopedia of Asian American Folklore and Folklife*. Santa Barbara, CA: ABC-CLIO, 2011. See section on Filipino Americans.

Websites

"Filipino Community Honors Rizal in Los Angeles Ceremony." Inquirer.net. January 3, 2018. It documents the celebration of Rizal Day among Filipino Americans in Los Angeles. http://usa.inquirer.net/9128/filipino-community-honors-rizal-los-angeles-ceremony. Accessed January 28, 2018.

Palafox, Quennie. "Why We Celebrate Rizal Day Every 30th Day of December." National Historical Commission of the Philippines. September 19, 2012. It discusses the history and significance of Jose Rizal and Rizal Day. http://nhcp.gov.ph/why-we-celebrate-rizal-day-every-30th-day-of-december/. Accessed January 28, 2018.

Also Noteworthy

1975

Professional golfer Tiger Woods is born in Cypress, California, to Kultida Punsawad, originally from Thailand, and Earl Woods, who met her while on a tour of duty in 1968.

December 31

1899

In November 1899, two ships from Hong Kong carried bubonic plague victims into Honolulu. The SS *Nippon Maru* was one of the ships. It contained the corpses of two bodies and rats infected with the plague. Dr. George Herbert treated the first patient with the plague in December. On December 31, 1899, the Board of Health plans a controlled burn of a few targeted buildings in Honolulu's Chinatown, followed by several more buildings in the first week of January 1900. On January 20, 1900, while the wooden buildings between Smith Street and Nuuanu Avenue on Beretania Street were being burned, the fire got out of control and several unintended buildings caught on fire. Flames spread from the steeple of Kaumakapili Church to the surrounding buildings, and in the end, most of the buildings in Honolulu's Chinatown were destroyed and an estimated 4,000–4,500 people were left homeless.

In 1900, following a public health scare over bubonic plague spreading from Chinatown, Hawai'i's Board of Health ordered a controlled burn of some buildings. The fire spread into a conflagration that reduced all of Chinatown to ashes and rubble, destroying homes and businesses and leaving four thousand people homeless. "To a great extent," a white eyewitness at the scene remained, "these crowds [of the displaced] were in a state of panic, as well as anger at the whites, who, as they believed, had deliberately burned them out." Most of Chinatown's residents were Chinese, Japanese, and Hawaiian, and the businesses alone claimed losses totaling $3 million. Honolulu's example sent several West Coast cities inspecting their Chinatowns and Japantowns for similar contagions.

Source: Okihiro, Gary. *American History Unbound: Asians and Pacific Islanders*. Berkeley: University of California Press, 2015, p. 235.

Books

Echenberg, Myron. *Plague Ports: The Global Urban Impact of Bubonic Plague, 1894–1901.* New York: New York University Press, 2007. *Plague Ports* discusses the history of the plague. See Chapter 7, "Plague in Paradise: Honolulu, 1899/1900," for discussion of the bubonic plague in Honolulu.

Mohr, James. *Plague and Fire: Battling Black Death and the 1900 Burning of Honolulu's Chinatown.* Oxford: Oxford University Press, 2005. *Plague and Fire* details the history of the Hawaiian public health officers to control and contain the bubonic plague in Hawaii by burning down Chinatown.

Websites

"Chinatown Fire of 1900." HawaiiHistory.org. 2016. This site provides a historical account of the plague and fire in Chinatown with historical images. http://www.hawaiihistory.org/index.cfm?fuseaction=ig.page&PageID=548. Accessed October 11, 2016.

McClain, Charles. "Of Medicine, Race, and American Law: The Bubonic Plague Outbreak of 1900." *Law & Social Inquiry* 14 (1988): 447–513. This article discusses the impact of the plague on legislation in Asian American history. Available at http://scholarship.law.berkeley.edu/cgi/viewcontent.cgi?article=1135&context=facpubs. Accessed October 11, 2016.

Bibliography

Abe, David. *Rural Isolation & Dual Cultural Existence: The Japanese-American Kona Coffee Community*. New York: Palgrave Macmillan, 2017.

Adachi, Nobuko. "Emigrants from Japan." In *Japan at War: An Encyclopedia*, edited by Louis Perez. Santa Barbara, CA: ABC-CLIO, 2013.

Agger, Ben, and Timothy Luke, eds. *Tragedy and Terror at Virginia Tech: There Is a Gunman on Campus*. Lanham, MD: Rowman & Littlefield Publishers, 2008.

Aguilar-San Juan, Karin. *Little Saigons: Staying Vietnamese in America*. Minneapolis: University of Minnesota Press, 2009.

Ahuja, Kiran. "Celebrating Four Years: Opening the Government's Doors to the AAPI Community." *Huffpost*, December 3, 2013. https://www.huffingtonpost.com/kiran-ahuja/celebrating-four-years-op_b_4454128.html. Accessed January 25, 2018.

Alam, Mohammed. "Back to the Roots: Engagement of the Indian Diaspora in the United States and India." In *South Asian Migration: Remittances and Beyond*, edited by Md Mizanur Rahman and Zaara Zain Hussain. Newcastle upon Tyne, England: Cambridge Scholars Publishing, 2015.

Albarran, Alan, ed. *The Social Media Industries*. New York: Routledge, 2013.

Alinder, Jasmine. *Moving Images: Photography and the Japanese American Incarceration*. Urbana: University of Illinois Press, 2009.

Altschiller, Donald. *Hate Crimes: A Reference Handbook*. 3rd ed. Santa Barbara, CA: ABC-CLIO, 2015.

Anastacio, Leia Castañeda. *The Foundations of the Modern Philippine State: Imperial Rule and the American Constitutional Tradition, 1898–1935*. Cambridge: Cambridge University Press, 2016.

Arora, Anupama. "Mexican-Indian Marriages." In *Asian American History and Culture: An Encyclopedia*, edited by Huping Lig and Allan Austin. Armonk, NY: M.E. Sharpe Inc., 2010.

Ashton, Dore. "Noguchi, Isamu." In *The Reader's Companion to American History*, edited by Eric Foner and John Arthur Garraty, 1st ed. Boston: Houghton Mifflin, 2014.

At 40: Asian American Studies @ San Francisco State: Self-Determination, Community, Student Service. San Francisco, CA: Asian American Studies Department, San Francisco State University, 2009.

Bald, Vivek. *Bengali Harlem and the Lost Histories of South Asian America*. Cambridge, MA: Harvard University Press, 2013.

Baldoz, Rick. *The Third Asiatic Invasion: Empire and Migration in Filipino America, 1898–1946*. New York: New York University Press, 2011.

Bangarth, Stephanie. *Voices Raised in Protest: Defending Citizens of Japanese Ancestry in North America, 1942–49*. Vancouver: University of British Columbia Press, 2008.

Bannai, Lorraine. *Enduring Conviction: Fred Korematsu and His Quest for Justice*. Seattle: University of Washington Press, 2015.

Bao, Jiemin. *Creating a Buddhist Community: A Thai Temple in Silicon Valley*. Philadelphia, PA: Temple University Press, 2015.

Barajas, Frank. *Curious Unions: Mexican American Workers and Resistance in Oxnard, California, 1898–1961*. Lincoln: University of Nebraska Press, 2012.

Barde, Robert. *Immigration at the Golden Gate: Passenger, Ships, Exclusion, and Angel Island*. Westport, CT: Praeger, 2008.

Barkan, Elliott Robert, ed. *Immigrants in American History: Arrival, Adaptation, and Integration*. Santa Barbara, CA: ABC-CLIO, 2013.

Barnes, Mark. *The Spanish-American War and Philippines Insurrection, 1898–1902: An Annotated Bibliography*. New York: Routledge, 2011.

Beachler, Donald, and Thomas Shevory. *When Good Companies Go Bad: 100 Corporate Miscalculations and Misdeeds*. Santa Barbara, CA: ABC-CLIO, 2014.

Bergquist, Kathleen Ja Sook. "Operation Babylift or Babyabduction? Implications of the Hague Convention on the Humanitarian Evacuation and 'Rescue' of Children." *International Social Work* 52, no. 5 (August 24, 2009): 621–633.

Bernardi, Daniel, and Michael Green, eds. *Race in American Film: Voices and Visions That Shaped a Nation*. Santa Barbara, CA: ABC-CLIO, 2017.

Bhatia, Sunil. *American Karma: Race, Culture, and Identity in the Indian Diaspora*. New York: New York University Press, 2007.

Bhatt, Amy, and Nalini Iyer. *Roots and Reflections: South Asians in the Pacific Northwest*. Seattle: University of Washington Press, 2013.

Blussé, Leonard. *Visible Cities: Canton, Nagasaki, and Batavia and the Coming of the Americans*. Cambridge, MA: Harvard University Press, 2008.

Borah, Eloisa. "Chronology of Filipinos in America Pre-1898." 1997–2004. http://personal.anderson.ucla.edu/eloisa.borah/chronology.pdf. Accessed June 15, 2018.

Bowman, Paul. *Beyond Bruce Lee: Chasing the Dragon through Film, Philosophy and Popular Culture*. New York: Columbia University Press, 2013.

Brick, Howard, and Christopher Phelps. *Radicals in America: The U.S. Left since the Second World War*. Cambridge: Cambridge University Press, 2015.

Briggs, Vernon. *Mass Immigration and the National Interest: Policy Directions for the New Century*. Armonk, NY: M. E. Sharpe, 2003.

Brilliant, Mark. *The Color of America Has Changed: How Racial Diversity Shaped Civil Rights Reform in California, 1941–1978*. New York: Oxford University Press, 2012.

Brinkley, Joel. *Cambodia's Curse: The Modern History of a Troubled Land*. New York: PublicAffairs, 2011.

Bromley, Isaac. *The Chinese Massacre at Rock Springs, Wyoming Territory, September 2, 1885*. Boston, MA: Franklin Press, 1886.

Bronson, Bennet, and Chuimei Ho. *Coming Home in Gold Brocade: Chinese in Early Northwest America*. Bainbridge Island, WA: Chinese in Northwest America Research Committee, 2015.

Brooks, Charlotte. *Alien Neighbors, Foreign Friends: Asian Americans, Housing, and the Transformation of Urban California*. Chicago, IL: University of Chicago Press, 2009.

Brown, Cleo, and Richard Ivory. *In Search of the Republican Party: A History of Minorities in the Republican Party*. Bloomington, IN: Xlibris, 2012.

Brown, John. *Kevlar Legions: The Transformation of the United States Army 1989–2005*. Washington, DC: Center of Military History United States Army, 2012.

Brysk, Alison. *Speaking Rights to Power: Constructing Political Will*. Oxford: Oxford University Press, 2013.

Burdeos, Ray. *Pinoy Stewards in the U.S. Sea Services: Seizing Marginal Opportunity*. Bloomington, IN: AuthorHouse, 2010.

Cahn, David. "The 1907 Bellingham Riots in Historical Context." Seattle Civil Rights & Labor History Project. http://depts.washington.edu/civilr/bham_history.htm. Accessed June 15, 2018.

Cainkar, Louise. *Homeland Insecurity: The Arab American and Muslim American Experience after 9/11.* New York: Russell Sage Foundation, 2009.

Capozzola, Christopher. "Filipinas/os." In *Anti-Immigration in the United States: A Historical Encyclopedia*, edited by Kathleen R. Arnold. Santa Barbara, CA: ABC-CLIO, 2011.

Carlin, Robert, and John Lewis. *Negotiating with North Korea: 1992–2007.* Center for International Security and Cooperation. Freeman Spogli Institute for International Studies. Stanford University. January 2008.

Carter, Gregory. "Race and Citizenship." In *The Oxford Handbook of American Immigration and Ethnicity*, edited by Ronald Bayor. Oxford: Oxford University Press, 2016.

Cha, Marn. *Koreans in Central California (1903–1957): A Study of Settlement and Transnational Politics.* Lanham, MD: University Press of America, 2010.

Chacón, Jennifer. "The Security Myth: Punishing Immigrants in the Name of National Security." In *Governing Immigration through Crime: A Reader*, edited by Julie Dowling and Jonathan Xavier Inda. Palo Alto, CA: Stanford University Press, 2013.

Chan, Sucheng. "Alien Land Laws." In *Asian Americans: An Encyclopedia of Social, Cultural, Economic, and Political History*, edited by Xiaojian Zhao and Edward Park. Santa Barbara, CA: ABC-CLIO, 2014.

Chan, Yuk Wah, ed. *The Chinese/Vietnamese Diaspora: Revisiting the Boat People.* New York: Routledge, 2011.

Chang, Derek. *Citizens of a Christian Nation: Evangelical Missions and the Problem of Race in the Nineteenth Century.* Philadelphia: University of Pennsylvania Press, 2010.

Chang, Ying-Ying. *The Woman Who Could Not Forget: Iris Chang before and beyond the Rape of Nanking.* New York: Pegasus Books, 2012.

Cheah, Joseph. "The Function of Ethnicity in the Adaptation of Burmese Religious Practices." In *Emerging Voices: Experiences of Underrepresented Asian Americans*, edited by Huping Ling. New Brunswick, NJ: Rutgers University Press, 2008.

Chen, Lung-chu. *The U.S.-Taiwan-China Relationship in International Law and Policy.* Oxford: Oxford University Press, 2016.

Chen, Yong. *Chop Suey, USA: The Story of Chinese Food in America.* New York: Columbia University Press, 2014.

Cheng, Cindy I-Fen. *Citizens of Asian America: Democracy and Race during the Cold War.* New York: New York University Press, 2013.

Chiang, Ying, and Tzu-hsuan Chen. "Adopting the Diasporic Son: Jeremy Lin and Taiwan Sport Nationalism." *International Review for the Society of Sports* 50, no. 6 (2015): 705–721.

Chin, Gabriel, and Rose Villazor, eds. *The Immigration and Nationality Act of 1965: Legislating a New America.* Cambridge: Cambridge University Press, 2015.

Chinoy, Mike. *Meltdown: The Inside Story of the North Korean Nuclear Crisis.* New York: St. Martin's Griffin, 2008.

Cho, Grace. *Haunting the Korean Diaspora: Shame, Secrecy, and the Forgotten War.* Minneapolis: University of Minnesota, 2008.

Chon-Smith, Chong. *East Meets Black: Asian and Black Masculinities in the Post-Civil Rights Era.* Jackson: University Press of Mississippi, 2015.

Chu, Steven. "Letter from Secretary Steven Chu to Energy Department Employees." Department of Energy. February 1, 2013. https://www.energy.gov/articles/letter-secretary-steven-chu-energy-department-employees. Accessed September 4, 2017.

Chu Nomination. Hearing before the Committee on Energy and Natural Resources U.S. Senate. 111th Congress. First Session to Consider the Nomination of Steven Chu to Be Secretary of Energy. January 13, 2009. Washington, DC: U.S. Government Printing Office, 2009.

Ciment, James. "The Indian American Experience: History and Culture." In *Asian American History and Culture: An Encyclopedia*, edited by Huping Ling and Allan Austin. Armonk, NY: M.E. Sharpe Inc., 2010.

Cordova, Dorothy, and Filipino American National Historical Society. *Filipinos in Puget Sound.* Charleston, SC: Arcadia Publishing, 2009.

Corfield, Justin. *Historical Dictionary of Pyongyang.* London: Anthem Press, 2013.

Cornfield, Justin. *The History of Cambodia.* Santa Barbara, CA: ABC-CLIO, 2009.

Covey, Herbert. *Street Gangs throughout the World.* Springfield, IL: Charles C. Thomas Publisher, 2010.

Cross, Robin, and Rosalind Miles. *Warrior Women: 3000 Years of Courage and Heroism.* New York: Quercus, 2011.

Cruz, Adrian. "There Will Be No 'One Big Union': The Struggle for Interracial Labor Unionism in California Agriculture, 1933–1939." *Cultural Dynamics* 22, no. 1 (2010): 29–48.

Cuison Villazor, Rose. "Rediscovering Oyama v. California: At the Intersection of Property, Race, and Citizenship." *Washington University Law Review* 87, no. 5 (2010): 979–1042.

Cumings, Bruce. *The Korean War: A History.* New York: Modern Library, 2011.

Daems, Jim, ed. *The Makeup of RuPaul's Drag Race: Essays on the Queen of Reality Shows.* Jefferson, NC: McFarland & Company Inc., Publishers, 2014.

Dalrymple, Timothy. *Jeremy Lin: The Reason for the Linsanity.* New York: Center Street, 2012.

Daniels, Roger. *The Japanese American Cases: The Rule of Law in Time of War.* Lawrence: University of Kansas Press, 2013.

Darden, Joe, and Richard Thomas. *Detroit: Race Riots, Racial Conflicts, and Efforts to Bridge the Racial Divide.* East Lansing: Michigan State University Press, 2013.

Dawson, Toby, and Lena Dawson. *Twenty-Two Years for Twenty-Two Seconds.* Self-Published. Amazon.com, CreateSpace Independent Publishing, 2010.

Daynes, Byron, Glen Sussman, and Jonathan P. West. *American Politics and the Environment.* 2nd ed. Albany: State University of New York Press, 2016.

De, Aparajita, ed. *South Asian Racialization and Belonging after 9/11: Masks of Threat.* Lanham, MD: Lexington Books, 2016.

Demos, John. *The Heathen School: A Story of Hope and Betrayal in the Age of the Early Republic.* New York: Alfred A. Knopf, 2014.

Dere, Jean. "Born Lucky: The Story of Laura Lai." *Chinese America: History & Perspectives—The Journal of the Chinese Historical Society of America.* San Francisco, CA: Chinese Historical Society of America with UCLA Asian American Studies Center, 2011, 29–35.

Diamant, Neil. *Embattled Glory: Veterans, Military Families, and the Politics of Patriotism in China, 1949–2007.* Lanham, MD: Rowman & Littlefield Publishers, 2009.

Dickerson, James. *Inside America's Concentration Camps: Two Centuries of Internment and Torture.* Chicago, IL: Lawrence Hill Books, 2010.

Dickinson, Frederick. "Japanese Empire." In *Encyclopedia of the Age of Imperialism, 1800–1914*, edited by Carl C. Hodge. Westport, CT: Greenwood Press, 2008.

Dilley, Whitney. *The Cinema of Ang Lee: The Other Side of the Screen.* London: Wallflower Press, 2015.

Dillon, Michael. *Deng Xiaoping: The Man Who Made Modern China.* London: I.B. Tauris, 2015.

Doubek, Robert. *Creating the Vietnam Veterans Memorial: The Inside Story.* Jefferson, NC: McFarland & Company, 2015.

Dowling, Julie, and Jonathan Xavier Inda, ed. *Governing Immigration through Crime: A Reader.* Palo Alto, CA: Stanford University Press, 2013.

Duiker, William. *Ho Chi Minh: A Life.* New York: Hachette Books, 2012.

Duong, Van Nguyen. *The Tragedy of the Vietnam War: South Vietnamese Officer's Analysis.* Jefferson, NC: McFarland & Company, 2008.

Eakman, Kate. *Discover the Story of Your Civil War Soldier Ancestor.* History & Heritage, 2013.

Elias, Robert. *The Empire Strikes Out: How Baseball Sold U.S. Foreign Policy and Promoted the American Way Abroad.* New York: The New Press, 2010.

Elkind, Jessica. *Aid under Fire: Nation Building and the Vietnam War.* Lexington: The University Press of Kentucky, 2016.

Englesberg, Paul. "Bellingham 'Anti-Hindu Riot' (1907)." In *Asian Americans: An Encyclopedia of Social, Cultural, Economic, and Political History*, edited by Xiaojian Zhao and Edward Park. Santa Barbara, CA: ABC-CLIO, 2014.

Esguerra, Maria Paz Gutierrez. "Filipino Immigrants." In *Multicultural America: An Encyclopedia of the Newest Americans*, edited by Ronald H. Bayor. Santa Barbara, CA: ABC-CLIO, LLC, 2011.

Espinosa, Henni. "Pinoy Fans Applaud Giants Fil-Am Pitcher." *Filipino Reporter*, November 5, 2010, 33.

Esposito, John, ed. *Islamophobia: The Challenge of Pluralism in the 21st Century*. Oxford: Oxford University Press, 2011.

Farrell, Theo, Sten Rynning, and Terry Terriff. *Transforming Military Power since the Cold War: Britain, France, and the United States, 1991–2012*. Cambridge: Cambridge University Press, 2013.

Feifer, George. *The Battle of Okinawa: The Blood and the Bomb*. Guilford, CT: Lyons Press, 2012.

Fernbach, Erika. *Sammy Lee: Promises to Keep*. CreateSpace Independent Publishing, 2012.

Fijitani, Takashi. *Race for Empire: Koreans as Japanese and Japanese as Americans during World War II*. Berkeley: University of California Press, 2011.

FitzGerald, David, and David Cook-Martin. *Culling the Masses: The Democratic Origins of Racist Immigration Policy in the Americas*. Cambridge, MA: Harvard University Press, 2014.

Fleischauer, Stefan. "Perspectives on 228: The '28 February 1947 Uprising' in Contemporary Taiwan." In *Taiwanese Identity in the 21st Century: Domestic, Regional and Global Perspectives*, edited by Gunter Schubert and Jens Damm, 35–50. London: Routledge, 2011.

Francis, Angus, and Rowena Maguire, eds. *Protection of Refugees and Displaced Persons in the Asia Pacific Region*. New York: Routledge, 2013.

Franks, Joel. *Asian Pacific Americans and Baseball: A History*. Jefferson, NC: McFarland & Company Inc., Publishers, 2008.

Fredriksen, John. *Fighting Elites: A History of U.S. Special Forces*. Santa Barbara, CA: ABC-CLIO, 2012.

Fryer, Heather. "The Japanese American Experience: History and Culture." In *Asian American History and Culture: An Encyclopedia*, edited by Huping Ling and Allan Austin. Armonk, NY: M.E. Sharpe Inc., 2010.

Fujikane, Candance, and Jonathan Okamura, eds. *Asian Settler Colonialism: From Local Governance to the Habits of Everyday Life in Hawai'i*. Honolulu: University of Hawai'i Press, 2008.

Fujita-Rony, Dorothy. "1898, U.S. Militarism, and the Formation of Asian American." *Asian American Policy Review* 19 (January 1, 2010): 67–71.

Fuller, Karla, ed. *Ang Lee: Interviews*. Jackson: University Press of Mississippi, 2016.

Gallagher, Charles, and Cameron Lippard, eds. *Race and Racism in the United States: An Encyclopedia of the American Mosaic*. Santa Barbara, CA: Greenwood, 2014.

Gettis, Erin, Donna Graves, Catherine Gudis, Sue Hall, Kevin Hallaran, Krystal Marquez, and Lynn Voorheis. "Reading the Sites: The Japanese-American Community in Riverside." *Journal of the Riverside Historical Society*, no. 16 (February 2012): 33–52.

Gold, Martin. *Forbidden Citizens: Chinese Exclusion and the U.S. Congress: A Legislative History*. Alexandria, VA: TheCapitol.Net, Inc., 2012.

Goldstein, Leslie. *The U.S. Supreme Court and Racial Minorities: Two Centuries of Judicial Review on Trial*. Northampton, MA: Edward Elgar Publishing, 2017.

Gooden. Mark. "Gong Lum v. Rice." In *Encyclopedia of Education Law*, edited by Charles Russo. Los Angeles, CA: Sage, 2008.

Gradziuk, Artur, and Ernest Wyciszkiewicz, eds. *Energy Security and Climate Change: Double Challenge for Policymakers*. Warsaw, Poland: Polski Instytut Spraw Miedzynarodowych, 2009.

Grant, Larry. "Tydings-McDuffie Act of 1934." In *Anti-Immigration in the United States: A Historical Encyclopedia*, edited by Kathleen R. Arnold. Santa Barbara, CA: ABC-CLIO, 2011.

Griffin, Nicholas. *Ping-Pong Diplomacy: The Secret History behind the Game That Changed the World*. New York: Scribner, 2014.

Gross, Ariela. *What Blood Won't Tell: A History of Race on Trial in America.* Cambridge, MA: Harvard University Press, 2008.

Gumpert, Matthew. *The End of Meaning: Studies in Catastrophe.* Newcastle upon Tyne, England: Cambridge Scholars Publishing, 2012.

Gutgold, Nichola. *Seen and Heard: The Women of Television News.* Lanham, MD: Lexington Books, 2008.

Gutman, Bill. *Jeremy Lin: The Incredible Rise of the NBA's Most Unlikely Superstar.* New York: Sports Publishing, 2012.

Gwak, S. Sonya. *Be(com)ing Korean in the United States: Exploring Ethnic Identity Formation through Cultural Practices.* Amherst, MA: Cambria Press, 2008.

Haddad, John. "The Chinese Lady and China for the Ladies: Race, Gender, and Public Exhibition in Jacksonian America." *Chinese America: History & Perspectives*, 2011, 5–19.

Hagopian, Patrick. *The Vietnam War in American Memory: Veterans, Memorials, and the Politics of Healing.* Amherst: University of Massachusetts Press, 2009.

Haines, David. *Safe Haven? A History of Refugees in America.* Sterling, VA: Kumarian Press, 2010.

Halloran, Fiona. *Thomas Nash: The Father of Modern Political Cartoons.* Chapel Hill: University of North Carolina Press, 2012.

Han, C. Winter. *Geisha of a Different Kind: Race and Sexuality in Gaysian America.* New York: New York University Press, 2015.

Hart, Dakin. *Isamu Noguchi, Archaic/Modern.* London: Giles and the Smithsonian American Art Museum, 2017.

Haruki, Wada. *The Korean War: An International History.* Translated by Frank Baldwin. Lanham, MD: Rowman & Littlefield, 2014.

Hawley, Michael, ed. *Sikh Diaspora: Theory, Agency, and Experience.* Leiden, the Netherlands: Brill, 2013.

Hayashi, Brian Masaru. "Kilsoo Haan, American Intelligence, and the Anticipated Japanese Invasion of California, 1931–1943." *Pacific Historical Review* 83, no. 2 (May 2014): 277–293.

Head, Tom. *It's Your World, So Change It: Using the Power of the Internet to Create Social Change.* San Francisco, CA: Pearson Education, 2010.

Henry, Candy. "Filipino American Community Organizations." In *Asian American Culture: From Anime to Tiger Moms*, edited by Lan Dong. Santa Barbara, CA: Greenwood, 2016.

Herrera, Hayden. *Listening to the Stone: The Art and Life of Isamu Noguchi.* New York: Farrar, Straus and Giroux, 2015.

Hess, Julia. *Immigrant Ambassadors: Citizenship and Belonging in the Tibetan Diaspora.* Stanford, CA: Stanford University Press, 2009.

Hewitt, Marco. "Philippine-American War." In *The Encyclopedia of the Spanish-American and Philippine-American Wars*, edited by Spencer Tucker. Santa Barbara, CA: ABC-CLIO, 2009.

Hiebert, Murray, Phuong Nguyen, and Gregory Poling. *A New Era in U.S.-Vietnam Relations: Deepening Ties Two Decades after Normalization.* Lanham, MD: Rowman & Littlefield, 2014.

Hinnershitz, Stephanie. *Race, Religion, and Civil Rights: Asian Students on the West Coast, 1900–1968.* New Brunswick, NJ: Rutgers University Press, 2015.

Hirabayashi, Gordon, James Hirabayashi, and Lane Ryo Hirabayashi. *A Principled Stand: The Story of Hirabayashi v. United States.* Seattle: University of Washington Press. 2013.

Hischak, Thomas. *American Literature on Stage and Screen: 525 Works and Their Adaptations.* Jefferson, NC: McFarland &Company, Inc., Publishers, 2012.

Ho, Chuimei, and Bennet Bronson. *Three Chinese Temples in California: Weaverville, Oroville, Marysville.* Bainbridge Island, WA: Chinese in Northwest America Research Committee, 2016.

Hoang, Kimberly K. "Vietnamese and Vietnamese Americans, 1975-Present." In *Immigrants in American History: Arrival, Adaptation, and Integration*, edited by Elliott R. Barkan, vol. III, 1365–1374. Santa Barbara, CA: ABC-CLIO, 2013.

Hom, Laureen. "Early Chinese Immigrants Organizing for Healthcare: The Establishment of the Chinese Hospital in San Francisco." In *Handbook of Asian American Health*, edited by Grace Yoo, Mai-Nhung Le, and Alan Odo. New York: Springer, 2013.

Hu, Sen, and Jielin Dong, eds. *The Rocky Road to Liberty: A Documented History of Chinese Immigration and Exclusion*. Saratoga, CA: Javvin Press, 2010.

Huang, C.J. *Charisma and Compassion: Cheng Yen and the Buddhist Tzu Chi Movement*. Cambridge, MA: Harvard University Press, 2009.

Huang, Eddie. *Fresh off the Boat: A Memoir*. New York: Spiegel & Grau, 2013.

Humes, James, and Jarvis Ryals. *"Only Nixon": His Trip to China Revisited and Restudied*. Lanham, MD: University Press of America, 2009.

Hunt, Ira. *Losing Vietnam: How America Abandoned Southeast Asia*. Lexington: The University Press of Kentucky, 2013.

Hurh, Won Moo. "Korean Immigrants." In *Multicultural America: An Encyclopedia of the Newest Americans*, edited by Ronald H. Bayor. Santa Barbara, CA: ABC-CLIO, LLC, 2011.

Iaukea, Sydney. *The Queen and I: A Story of Dispossessions and Reconnections in Hawai'i*. Berkeley: University of California Press, 2012.

Itoh, Mayumi. *The Origin of Ping-Pong Diplomacy: The Forgotten Architect of Sino-U.S. Rapprochement*. New York: Palgrave Macmillan, 2011.

Iyer, Deepa. *We Too Sing America: South Asian, Arab, Muslim, and Sikh Immigrants Shape Our Multiracial Future*. New York: The New Press, 2015.

Jalil, Mazhar, Norman Hosansky, and Pual Numrich, eds. *The Abrahamic Encounter: Local Initiatives, Large Implications*. Eugene, OR: Wipf & Stock, 2016.

Janardhanan, Vinod. "Political Participation of the Indian Diaspora in the USA." *Journal of International and Global Studies* 5, no. 1 (2013): 16–34.

Jones, Gregg. *Honor in the Dust: Theodore Roosevelt, War in the Philippines, and the Rise and Fall of America's Imperial Dream*. New York: New American Library, 2012.

Jones, Howard. *Death of a Generation: How the Assassinations of Diem and JFK Prolonged the Vietnam War*. Oxford: Oxford University Press, 2003.

Jorae, Wendy. *The Children of Chinatown: Growing Up Chinese American in San Francisco, 1850–1920*. Chapel Hill: University of North Carolina Press, 2009.

Kamal, Rabia. "Pakistani Americans: History, People, and Culture." In *Encyclopedia of Asian American Folklore and Folklife*, edited by Jonathan H.X. Lee and Kathleen Nadeau. Santa Barbara, CA: ABC-CLIO, 2011, 955–960.

Karam, Nicoletta. *The 9/11 Backlash: A Decade of U.S. Hate Crimes Targeting the Innocent*. Berkeley, CA: Beatitude Press, 2012.

Kaufman, Burton, and Diane Kaufman. *Historical Dictionary of the Eisenhower Era*. Lanham, MD: Scarecrow Press, 2009.

Kawakami, Barbara. *Picture Bride Stores*. Honolulu: University of Hawaii Press, 2016.

Kawana, Lauren. "Long Live Raja." *Hyphen Magazine*, no. 27 (Summer 2013), 9.

Kayyali, Randa. "'Jihad Jane' as Good American Patriot and Bad Arab Girl: The Case of Nada Prouty after 9/11." In *Bad Girls of the Arab World*, edited by Nadia Yaqub and Rula Quawas. Austin: University of Texas Press, 2017.

Kim, Eleana. "Human Capital: Transnational Korean Adoptees and the Neoliberal Logic of Return." *Journal of Korean Studies* 17, no. 2 (Fall 2012): 299–328.

Kim, Heidi. *Taken from the Paradise Isle: The Hoshida Family Story*. Boulder: University Press of Colorado, 2015.

Kim, Richard. *The Quest for Statehood: Korean Immigrant Nationalism and U.S. Sovereignty, 1905–1945*. Oxford: Oxford University Press, 2011.

Kim, Youna, ed. *The Routledge Handbook of Korean Culture and Society*. London: Routledge, 2017.

Kinder, John. *Paying with Their Bodies: American War and the Problem of the Disabled Veteran*. Chicago, IL: University of Chicago Press, 2015.

King, Richard, ed. *Asian American Athletes in Sport and Society*. New York: Routledge, 2015.

King, Sallie. "A Buddhist Perspective." In *Sharing Wisdom: Benefits and Boundaries of Interreligious Learning*, edited by Alon Goshen-Gottstein. Lanham, MD: Lexington Books, 2017.

Koven, Steven, and Frank Götzke. American Immigration Policy: Confronting the Nation's Challenges. New York: Springer, 2010.

Kumar, Ashok. "International Ladies' Garment Workers' Union." In *Chinese Americans: The History and Culture of a People*, edited by Jonathan H.X. Lee. Santa Barbara, CA: ABC-CLIO, 2016.

Kurashige, Lon. *Two Faces of Exclusion: The Untold History of Anti-Asian Racism in the United States.* Chapel Hill: University of North Carolina Press, 2016.

Kurashige, Lon, and Alice Yang, eds. *Major Problems in Asian American History: Documents and Essays.* 2nd ed. Boston: Cengage Learning, 2017.

Kwon, Hyeyong, and Chanhaeng Lee. "Korean American History." Los Angeles: Korean Education Center in Los Angeles, 2009.

Labrador, Roderick. *Building Filipino Hawai'i.* Urbana: University of Illinois Press, 2015.

Lackey, Jill. *American Ethnic Practices in the Twenty-First Century: The Milwaukee Study.* Lanham, MD: Lexington Books, 2013.

Lai, Him Mark. *Chinese American Transnational Politics.* Urbana: University of Illinois Press, 2010.

Lau, Albert, ed. *Southeast Asia and the Cold War.* New York: Routledge, 2012.

Law, Anna. *The Immigration Battle in American Courts.* Cambridge: Cambridge University Press, 2010.

Le, Long S. "Vietnamese Americans: History, People, and Culture." In *Encyclopedia of Asian American Folklore and Folklife*, edited by Jonathan H.X. Lee and Kathleen Nadeau. Santa Barbara, CA: ABC-CLIO, 2011.

Lee, Anne. *The Hawaii State Constitution.* Oxford: University of Oxford Press, 2011.

Lee, Erika, and Judy Yung. *Angel Island: Immigrant Gateway to America.* Oxford: Oxford University Press, 2010.

Lee, Jennifer. "Dear Wing Jung v. United States of America (1962)." In *Asian Americans: An Encyclopedia of Social, Cultural, Economic, and Political History*, edited by Xiaojian Zhao and Edward Park. Santa Barbara, CA: ABC-CLIO, 2014.

Lee, Jennifer, and Min Zhou. *The Asian American Achievement Paradox.* New York: Russell Sage Foundation, 2015.

Lee, Jonathan H.X. *History of Asian Americans: Exploring Diverse Roots.* Santa Barbara, CA: Greenwood, 2015.

Lee, Jonathan H.X., ed. *Cambodian American Experiences: Histories, Communities, Cultures, and Identities*, Dubuque, IA: Kendall and Hunt Publishing Company, 2010.

Lee, Jonathan H.X., ed. *Chinese Americans: The History and Culture of a People.* Santa Barbara, CA: ABC-CLIO, 2016.

Lee, Jonathan H.X., ed. *Japanese Americans: The History and Culture of a People.* Santa Barbara, CA: ABC-CLIO, 2018.

Lee, Jonathan H.X., and Kathleen Nadeau, eds. *Asian American Identities and Practices: Folkloric Expressions in Everyday Life.* Lanham, MD: Lexington Books, 2014.

Lee, Jonathan H.X., and Kathleen Nadeau, eds. *Encyclopedia of Asian American Folklore and Folklife.* Santa Barbara, CA: ABC-CLIO, 2011.

Lee, Sabine. *Children Born of War in the Twentieth Century.* Manchester: Manchester University Press, 2017.

Lee, Shelley. *A New History of Asian America.* New York: Routledge, 2014.

Leibovitz, Liel, and Matthew Miller. *Fortunate Sons: The 120 Chinese Boys Who Came to America, Went to School, and Revolutionized an Ancient Civilization.* New York: W.W. Norton, 2011.

Leo, Mark S. "(In)Visible Within: Igorot Filipino Americans." MA Thesis, San Francisco State University, 2011.

Leonard, Karen Isaksen. "Indian (Asian Indian) Immigrants." In *Multicultural America: An Encyclopedia of the Newest Americans*, edited by Ronald H. Bayor. Santa Barbara, CA: Greenwood, 2011.

Leszcrak, Bob. *Encyclopedia of Pop Music Aliases, 1950–2000.* Lanham, MD: Rowman & Littlefield, 2015.

Lew, Yong Ick. *The Making of the First Korean President: Syngman Rhee's Quest for Independence.* Honolulu: University of Hawaii Press, 2013.

Lien, Pei-Te. *Making of Asian America through Political Participation.* Philadelphia, PA: Temple University Press, 2001.

Ling, Huping, and Allan Austin. *Asian American History and Culture: An Encyclopedia.* New York: M.E. Sharpe, 2010.

Linke, Konard. "Dominance, Resistance, and Cooperation in the Tanforan Assembly Center." *Amerikastudien/American Studies* 54, no. 4 (2009): 625–655.

Linn, Brian MacAllister. *The Philippine War, 1899–1902.* Lawrence: University Press of Kansas, 2000.

Liu, William Ming, Derek Kenji Iwamoto, and Mark H. Chae, eds. *Culturally Responsive Counseling with Asian American Men.* New York: Routledge, 2010.

Lovell, Julia. *The Opium War: Drug, Dreams and the Making of China.* London: Picador, 2011.

Loving v. Virginia, 388 U.S. 1 (1967). JUSTIA U.S. Supreme Court. 2018. https://supreme.justia.com/cases/federal/us/388/1/case.html. Accessed January 18, 2018.

Ludwig, Sämi, and Nicoleta Alexoae-Zagni, eds. *The Legacy of Maxine Hong Kingston.* Zurich: LIT Verglag, 2014.

Lukens, Patrick. *A Quiet Victory for Latino Rights: FDR and the Controversy over "Whiteness."* Tucson: University of Arizona Press, 2012.

Lurie, Jonathan. *William Howard Taft: The Travails of a Progressive Conservative.* Cambridge: Cambridge University Press, 2012.

Luther, Catherine, Carolyn Lepre, and Naeemah Clark. *Diversity in U.S. Mass Media.* West Sussex, England: Wiley-Blackwell, 2012.

Lyon, Cherstin. *Prisons and Patriots: Japanese American Wartime Citizenship, Civil Disobedience, and Historical Memory.* Philadelphia, PA: Temple University Press, 2011.

Maeda, Daryl. *Chains of Babylon: The Rise of Asian America.* Minneapolis: University of Minnesota Press, 2009.

Maeda, Daryl. *Rethinking the Asian American Movement.* London: Routledge, 2011.

Maira, Sunaina. *The 9/11 Generation: Youth, Rights, and Solidarity in the War on Terror.* New York: New York University Press, 2016.

Makana, Kale. *Queen Liliuokalani: The Hawaiian Kingdom's Last Monarch, Hawaii History: A Biography.* CreateSpace Independent Publishing, 2015.

Malkin, Michelle. *In Defense of Internment: The Case of "Racial Profiling" in World War II and the War on Terror.* Washington, DC: Regnery Publishing, 2013.

Mann, Itamar. *Humanity at Sea: Maritime Migration and the Foundations of International Law.* Cambridge: Cambridge University Press, 2016.

Mansfield-Richardson, Virginia. *Asian Americans and the Mass Media: A Content Analysis of Twenty United States Newspapers and a Survey of Asian American Journalists.* New York: Routledge, 2014.

Matthews, Frederick. *American Merchant Ships, 1850–1900.* Mineola, NY: Dover Publications, 2012.

Mawdsley, Evan. *December 1941: Twelve Days That Began a World War.* New Haven, CT: Yale University Press, 2011.

"May Is Asian/Pacific American Heritage Month." *Curriculum Review* 51, no. 8 (2012): 11.

McCoy, Alfred. *Policing America's Empire: The United States, the Philippines, and the Rise of the Surveillance State.* Madison: University of Wisconsin Press, 2009.

McCunn, Ruthanne. *Chinese Yankee: A True Story from the Civil War.* San Francisco, CA: Design Enterprises of San Francisco, 2014.

McLellan, Janet. *Cambodian Refugees in Ontario: Resettlement, Religion, and Identity.* Toronto: University of Toronto Press, 2009.

Mecca, Tommi, ed. *Smash the Church, Smash the Gate.* San Francisco, CA: City Lights Books, 2009.

Meyer, Evelene. *Wakamatsu Tea and Silk Farm Colony.* North Charleston, SC: CreateSpace Independent Publishing, 2016.

Moore, Gregory. *Defining and Defending the Open Door Policy: Theodore Roosevelt and China, 1901–1909.* Lanham, MD: Lexington Books, 2015.

Morley, Ian. "Manila." *Cities* 72 (February 2018): 17–33.

Morris, Charles, ed. *The 1906 San Francisco Earthquake and Fire as Told by Eyewitnesses*. Mineola, NY: Dover Publications, 2015.

Mortland, Carol. *Cambodian Buddhism in the United States*. Albany: State University of New York Press, 2017.

Mortland, Carol. "Cambodian Resettlement in America." In *Cambodian American Experiences: Histories, Communities, Cultures, and Identities*, edited by Jonathan H. X. Lee. Dubuque, IA: Kendall and Hunt Publishing Company, 2010.

Moss, George. *Vietnam: An American Ordeal*. 6th ed. London: Routledge, 2016.

Murchie, Scott, and Brett Williams, directors. *Nickel City Smiler: From the Jungle to the Streets*. Chance Encounter Productions, LLC, 2010. DVD.

Neuman, Gerald. *Strangers to the Constitution: Immigrants, Borders, and Fundamental Law*. Princeton, NJ: Princeton University Press, 2010.

Newton-Matza, Mitchell. *Disasters and Tragic Events: An Encyclopedia of Catastrophes in American History*. Santa Barbara, CA: ABC-CLIO, LLC, 2014.

Ngai, Mae. *The Lucky Ones: One Family and the Extraordinary Invention of Chinese America*. Princeton, NJ: Princeton University Press, 2012.

Nguyen, Hang. "Open Door Policy." In *Reforming America: A Thematic Encyclopedia and Document Collection on the Progressive Era*, edited by Jeffery Johnson. Santa Barbara, CA: ABC-CLIO, 2017.

Nguyen, Phuong. *Becoming Refugee American: The Politics of Rescue in Little Saigon*. Urbana: University of Illinois Press, 2017.

Nguyen, Vivian. "Fresh Off the Boat." *Northwest Asian Weekly*, February 14, 2015, 1, 15.

Noguera, Pedro, Jill Pierce, and Roey Ahram, eds. *Race, Equity, and Education: Sixty Years from Brown*. New York: Springer, 2016.

Nokes, Gregory. *Massacred for Gold: The Chinese in Hells Canyon*. Corvallis: Oregon State University Press, 2009.

Notehelfer, F. G. *Kotoku Shusui: Portrait of a Japanese Radical*. Cambridge: Cambridge University Press, 2010.

O, Hosok. "Cultural Analysis of the Early Japanese Immigration to the United States during Meiji to Taisho Era (1868–1926)." Unpublished dissertation. Oklahoma State University, 2010.

Ogden, Johanna. "Ghadar, Historical Silences and Notions of Belonging: Early 1900s Punjabis of the Columbia River." *Oregon Historical Quarterly* 113, no. 2 (Summer of 2012): 164–197.

Okihiro, Gary. *American History Unbound: Asians and Pacific Islanders*. Berkeley: University of California Press, 2015.

Okihiro, Gary. *Third World Studies: Theorizing Liberation*. Durham, NC: Duke University Press, 2016.

Okihiro, Gary, ed. *Encyclopedia of Japanese American Internment*. Santa Barbara, CA: Greenwood, 2013.

Olivas, Michael, and Ronna Schneider, eds. *Education Law Stories*. New York: Foundation Press, 2008.

Ono, Kent, and Vincent Pham. *Asian Americans and the Media*. Cambridge: Polity Press, 2009.

Orchowski, Margaret. *The Law That Changed the Face of America: The Immigration and Nationality Act of 1965*. Lanham, MD: Rowman & Littlefield, 2015.

O'Reilly, Shauna, and Brennan O'Reilly. *Alaska Yukon Pacific Exposition*. Charleston, SC: Arcadia Publishing, 2009.

Orser, Joseph. *The Lives of Chang and Eng: Siam's Twins in Nineteenth-Century America*. Chapel Hill: University of North Carolina Press, 2014.

Osborne, Thomas. *Pacific Eldorado: A History of Greater California*. Chichester, England: John Wiley & Sons, Ltd, 2013.

Osornprasop, Sutayut. "Thailand and the Secret War in Laos, 1960–74." In *Southeast Asia and the Cold War*, edited by Albert Lau. New York: Routledge, 2012.

Otfinoski, Steven. *Day of Infamy: The Story of the Attack on Pearl Harbor*. North Mankato, MN: Capstone Press, 2016.

Ownby, David. *Falun Gong and the Future of China.* Oxford: Oxford University Press, 2008.

Pa, Diameng. Speech before the Senate Judicial Committee's Subcommittee on Immigration. Cited in Berkin, Carol, Christopher Miller, Robert Chemy, and James Gormly, eds., *Making America: A History of the United States.* 6th ed. Bsoton, MA: Wadsworth, 2014.

Pabros, Alex. "In the Heat of the Night: The Exeter and Watsonville Riots 1929–1930." *Filipino Express*, October 3, 2014, 15.

Padoongpatt, Mark. *Flavors of Empire: Food and the Making of Thai America.* Berkeley: University of California Press, 2017.

Paranjape, Makarand, ed. *Swami Vivekananda: A Contemporary Reader.* London: Routledge, 2015.

Park, Carol. *Memoir of a Cashier: Korean Americans, Racism, and Riots.* Riverside, CA: The Young Oak Kim Center for Korean American Studies, 2017.

Park, Heui-Yung. *Korean and Korean American Life Writing in Hawai'i: From the Land of Morning Calm to Hawai'i Nei.* Lanham, MD: Lexington Books, 2016.

Park, Young. *Korea and the Imperialists: In Search of a National Identity.* Bloomington, IN: Author-House, 2009.

Parker, Kunal. *Making Foreigners: Immigration and Citizenship Law in America, 1600–2000.* Cambridge: Cambridge University Press, 2015.

Pawel, Miriam. *The Union of Their Dreams: Power, Hope, and Struggle in Cesar Chavez's Farm Worker's Movement.* New York: Bloomsbury Press, 2009.

Penny, Benjamin. *The Religion of Falun Gong.* Chicago, IL: University of Chicago Press, 2012.

Perez, Louis, ed. *Japan at War: An Encyclopedia.* Santa Barbara, CA: ABC-CLIO, 2013.

Perreira, Todd LeRoy. "Bunker, Chang and Eng (1811–1874)." In *Asian American History and Culture: An Encyclopedia*, edited by Huping Ling and Allan Austin, p. 569. Armonk, NY: M. E. Sharpe, Inc., 2010.

Perreira, Todd LeRoy. "The Gender of Practice: Some Findings among Thai Buddhist Women in Northern California." In *Emerging Voices: Experiences of Underrepresented Asian Americans*, edited by Huping Ling. New Brunswick, NJ: Rutgers University Press, 2008, 160–182.

Perreria, Todd LeRoy. "Thai Americans: Religion." In *Encyclopedia of Asian American Folklore and Folklife*, edited by Jonathan H.X. Lee and Kathleen Nadeau, 1109–1112. Santa Barbara, CA: ABC-CLIO, 2011.

Pham, Mary Thi, and Jonathan H.X. Lee. "Model Minority." In *Asian American Culture: From Anime to Tiger Moms*, edited by Lan Dong. Santa Barbara, CA: ABC-CLIO, 2016.

Philippines Country Study Guide: Volume 1. Strategic Information and Developments. Washington, DC: International Business Publications, USA, 2013.

Pierre, Robert. "Hate in the Wake of 9/11." *News India—Times*, September 23, 2011.

Pinder, Sherrow. *Whiteness and Racialized Ethnic Groups in the United States: The Politics of Remembering.* Lanham, MD: Lexington Books, 2012.

Poole, Peter. *Politics and Society in Southeast Asia.* Jefferson, NC: McFarland & Company, 2009.

Prouty, Nada. *Uncompromised: The Rise, Fall, and Redemption of an Arab American Patriot in the CIA.* New York: Macmillan, 2011.

Puri, Harish. *Ghadar Movement to Bhagat Singh: A Collection of Essays.* Ludhiana, India: Unistar Books, 2012.

Qasmiyeh, Elena, Gil Loescher, Katy Long, and Nando Sigona, eds. *The Oxford Handbook of Refugee and Forced Migration Studies.* Oxford: Oxford University Press, 2014.

Qiu, Lian. "First International Lao New Year Festival." *AsianWeek*, April 3, 2009.

Rafferty-Osaki, Terumi. "Manzanar Riot (1942)." In *Japanese Americans: The History and Culture of a People*, edited by Jonathan H.X. Lee. Santa Barbara, CA: ABC-CLIO, 2018.

Railton, Ben. *The Chinese Exclusion Act: What It Can Teach Us about America.* New York: Palgrave Macmillan, 2013.

Rajan, Julie, and Jeannette Gabriel. "Redefining US 'Homeland Security' Post-9/11: Extra-Judicial Measures, Vigilantism and Xenophobia." *Security Journal* 28, no. 2 (April 2015): pp. 109–149.

Ramnath, Maia. *Haj to Utopia: How the Ghadar Movement Charted Global Radicalism and Attempted to Overthrow the British Empire*. Berkeley: University of California Press, 2011.

Rawitsch, Mark. *The House on Lemon Street: Japanese Pioneers and the American Dream*. Boulder: University Press of Colorado, 2012.

Reeves, Richard. *Infamy: The Shocking Story of the Japanese American Internment in World War II*. New York: Henry Holt and Company, 2015.

"Reining in the Imperial Presidency: Lessons and Recommendations Relating to the Presidency of George W. Bush." House Committee on the Judiciary Majority Staff Report to Chairman John Conyers Jr. Washington, DC (January 13, 2009).

Rhoads, Edward. *Stepping Forth into the World: The Chinese Educational Mission to the United States*. Hong Kong: Hong Kong University Press, 2011.

Risse, Guenter. *Plague, Fear, and Politics in San Francisco's Chinatown*. Baltimore, MD: The Johns Hopkins University Press, 2012.

Roberts, Christopher. *The Contentious History of the International Bill of Human Rights*. Cambridge: Cambridge University Press, 2015.

Robinson, Greg. *After Camp: Portraits in Midcentury Japanese American Life and Politics*. Berkeley: University of California Press, 2012.

Robinson, Greg. *The Great Unknown: Japanese American Sketches*. Boulder: University of Colorado, 2016.

Robinson, Greg. *A Tragedy of Democracy: Japanese Confinement in North America*. New York: Columbia University Press, 2009.

Rody, Caroline. *The Interethnic Imagination: Roots and Passages in Contemporary Asian American Fiction*. Oxford: Oxford University Press, 2009.

Rogers, Robert. "Work at Richmond Tibetan Center Speeds Up Ahead of Dalai Lama Visit." *Contra Costa Times*, February 12, 2014.

Rohall, David, Morten Ender, and Michael Matthews, eds. *Inclusion in the American Military: A Force for Diversity*. Lanham, MD: Lexington Books, 2017.

Roy, Lucinda. *No Right to Remain Silent: What We've Learned from the Tragedy at Virginia Tech*. New York: Three Rivers Press, 2009.

Rubalcada, Jill. *I.M. Pei: Architect of Time, Place and Purpose*. Singapore: Marshall Cavendish, 2011.

Ruskola, Teemu. *Legal Orientalism: China, the United States, and Modern Law*. Cambridge, MA: Harvard University Press, 2013.

Rutter, Michael. *Boudoirs to Brothels: The Intimate World of Wild West Women*. Helena, MT: Farcounty Press, 2015.

Ryang, Sonia, and John Lie, eds. *Diaspora without Homeland: Being Korean in Japan*. Berkeley: University of California Press, 2009.

Sachs, Dana. *The Life We Were Given: Operation Babylift, International Adoption, and the Children of War in Vietnam*. Boston, MA: Beacon Press, 2010.

Schanberg, Sydney. *The Death and Life of Dith Pran*. New York: Rosettabooks, 2013.

Scheiber, Harry, and Jane Scheiber. *Bayonets in Paradise: Martial Law in Hawai'i during World War II*. Honolulu: University of Hawaii Press, 2016.

Schein, Louisa, Va-Megn Thoj, Bee Vang, and Ly Chong Thong Jalao. "Beyond *Gran Torino*'s Guns: Hmong Cultural Warriors Performing Genders." *positions: east asia cultures critique* 20, no. 3 (2012): 763–792.

Schinske, Marian. *Ani's Asylum*. Bloomington, IN: Xlibris LLC, 2010.

Schlund-Vials, Cathy J., K. Scott Wong, and Linda Trinh Vo, eds. *Keywords for Asian American Studies*. New York: New York University Press, 2015.

Scripter, Sami, and Sheng Yang. *Cooking from the Heart: The Hmong Kitchen in America*. Minneapolis: University of Minnesota Press, 2009.

Sederquist, Betty. *Coloma: Images of America*. Charleston, SC: Arcadia Publishing, 2012.

Seligman, Scott. *Tong Wars: The Untold Story of Vice, Money, and Murder in New York's Chinatown.* New York: Viking, 2016.

Senauth, Frank. *The Making of the Philippines.* Bloomington, IN: AuthorHouse, 2012.

Setiyawan, Dahlia. "Indonesian Americans: History, People, and Culture." In *Encyclopedia of Asian American Folklore and Folklife*, edited by Jonathan H. X. Lee and Kathleen Nadeau, 515–520. Santa Barbara, CA: ABC-CLIO, 2011.

Shah, Nyan. *Stranger Intimacy: Contesting Race, Sexuality, and the Law in the North American West.* Berkeley: University of California Press, 2011.

Shapiro, Robert, and Lawrence Jacobs, eds. *The Oxford Handbook of American Public Opinion and the Media.* Oxford: Oxford University Press, 2011.

Shea, Therese. *Lucy Liu: Actress, Artist, and Activist.* New York: Enslow Publishing, 2016.

Shively, Carol, ed. *Asians and Pacific Islanders and the Civil War.* Washington, DC: National Park Service, U.S. Department of the Interior, 2015.

Shu, Yuan. "Chang, Irs (1968–2004)." In *Asian Americans: An Encyclopedia of Social, Cultural, Economic, and Political History*, edited by Xiaojian Zhao and Edward Park. Santa Barbara, CA: ABC-CLIO, 2014.

Shurtleff, William, and Akiko Aoyagi, compiler. *History of Soybeans and Soyfoods in Japan, and in Japanese Cookbooks and Restaurants Outside Japan (701 CE to 2014).* Lafayette, LA: Soyinfo Center, 2014.

Shurtleff, William, and Akiko Aoyagi, compiler. *How Japanese and Japanese-Americans Brought Soyfoods to the United States and the Hawaiian Islands—A History (1851–2011): Extensively Annotated Bibliography and Sourcebook.* Lafayette, LA: Soyinfo Center, 2011.

Singh, Jaideep. "Jawala Singh (1859–1938)." In *Asian American History and Culture: An Encyclopedia*, edited by Huping Ling and Allan Austin. Armonk, NY: M.E. Sharpe Inc., 2010.

Singh, Jaideep. "Memory, Invisibility, and the Oak Creek Gurdwara Massacre: A Sikh American Perspective of the 'Post-racial' US." *Sikh Formations* 9, no. 2 (2013): 215–225.

Singh, Jaideep. "Punjabi Americans: History, People, and Culture." In *Encyclopedia of Asian American Folklore and Folklife*, edited by Jonathan H. X. Lee and Kathleen M. Nadeau. Santa Barbara, CA: ABC-CLIO, 2011.

Singh, Pashaura, and Louis Fenech, eds. *The Oxford Handbook of Sikh Studies.* Oxford: Oxford University Press, 2014.

Skwiot, Christine. *The Purposes of Paradise: U.S. Tourism and Empire in Cuba and Hawai'i.* Philadelphia: University of Pennsylvania Press, 2010.

Smith, T. O. *Vietnam and the Unravelling of Empire: General Gracey in Asia 1942–1951.* New York: Palgrave Macmillan, 2014.

Soennichsen, John. *The Chinese Exclusion Act of 1882.* Santa Barbara, CA: Greenwood, 2011.

Soh, Sarah. *The Comfort Women: Sexual Violence and Postcolonial Memory in Korea and Japan.* Chicago, IL: University of Chicago Press, 2009.

Sohi, Seema. *Echoes of Mutiny: Race, Surveillance, and Indian Anticolonialism in North America.* Oxford: Oxford University Press, 2014.

Sohoni, Deenesh. "Fighting to Belong: Asian-American Military Service and American Citizenship." In *Inclusion in the American Military: A Force for Diversity*, edited by David Rohall, Morten Ender, and Michael Matthews. Lanham, MD: Lexington Books, 2017.

Spickard, Paul. *Almost All Aliens: Immigration, Race, and Colonialism in American History and Identity.* New York: Routledge, 2009.

Springer, Paul, and Spencer Tucker. "Spanish-American and Philippine American Wars Battles." In *U.S. Leadership in Wartime: Clashes, Controversy, and Compromise*, edited by Spencer Tucker. Santa Barbara, CA: ABC-CLIO, 2009.

Starr, Kevin. *Golden Dreams: California in an Age of Abundance, 1950–1963.* Oxford: Oxford University Press, 2009.

Su, Christine. "Southeast Asians and Southeast Asian Americans, 1940-Present." In *Immigrants in American History: Arrival, Adaption, and Integration*, edited by Elliott Robert Barkan, 1295–1314. Santa Barbara, CA: ABC-CLIO, 2013.

Sugiyama, Al. "History Lessons." *International Examiner*, April 3, 1998, 3.

Sunoo, Sonia Shinn. *Korean Picture Brides: 1903–1920: A Collection of Oral Histories*. Bloomington, IN: Xlibris Corporation, 2002.

Suri, Jeremi. *American Foreign Relations since 1898: A Documentary Reader*. Oxford: Blackwell Publishing, 2010.

Szmanko, Klara. *Visions of Whiteness in Selected Works of Asian American Literature*. Jefferson, NC: McFarland & Company, 2015.

Tamura, Eileen. *In Defense of Justice: Joseph Kurihara and the Japanese American Struggle for Equality*. Urbana: University of Illinois Press, 2013.

Tamura, Linda. *Nisei Soldiers Break Their Silence: Coming Home to Hood River*. Seattle: University of Washington Press, 2012.

Thayer, Carlyle. "Cambodia-United States Relations." In *Cambodia: Progress and Challenges since 1991*, edited by Pou Sothirak, Geoff Wade, and Mark Hong. Singapore: Institute of Southeast Asian Studies, 2012.

Thomas, Sue. "Duckworth, Tammy." In *Encyclopedia of Women in Today's World*, edited by Mary Stange, Carol Oyster, and Jane Sloan. Los Angeles, CA: Sage, 2011.

Tiedemann, R. G., ed. *Handbook of Christianity in China, Volume 2, 1800 to the Present*. Leiden, the Netherlands: Brill, 2010.

To, Lee Lai, and Lee Hock Guan, eds. *Sun Yan-Sen, Nanyang and the 1911 Revolution*. Singapore: Chinese Heritage Center Singapore, and the Institute of Southeast Asian Studies, 2011.

Torbenson, Craig, and Gregory Parks, eds. *Brothers and Sisters: Diversity in College Fraternities and Sororities*. Madison, WI: Fairleigh Dickinson University Press, 2009.

Tsu, Cecilia. *Garden of the World: Asian Immigrants and the Making of Agriculture in California's Santa Clara Valley*. Oxford: Oxford University Press, 2013.

Tsui, Pauline, ed. *History of the Organization of Chinese American Women*. Honolulu: University of Hawaii Press, 2014.

Tuan, Mia, and Jiannbin Lee Shiao. *Choosing Ethnicity, Negotiating Race: Korean Adoptees in America*. New York: Russell Sage Foundation, 2011.

Tucker, Spencer, ed. *The Encyclopedia of the Vietnam War: A Political, Social, and Military History*. Santa Barbara, CA: ABC-CLIO, 2011.

Tudda, Chris. *A Cold War Turning Point: Nixon and China, 1969–1972*. Baton Rouge: Louisiana State University Press, 2012.

Vergara, Benito. *Pinoy Capital: The Filipino Nation in Daly City*. Philadelphia, PA: Temple University Press, 2009.

Vogel, Ezra. *Deng Xiaoping and the Transformation of China*. Cambridge, MA: Harvard University Press, 2011.

Walker, J. Samuel. *Prompt and Utter Destruction: Truman and the Use of Atomic Bombs against Japan*. Chapel Hill: University of North Carolina Press, 2016.

Wallenstein, Peter. *Race, Sex, and the Freedom to Marry*. Lawrence: University Press of Kansas, 2014.

Walz, Eric. *Nikkei in the Interior West: Japanese Immigration and Community Building, 1882–1945*. Tucson: University of Arizona Press, 2012.

Wang, Zuoyue. "Chern, Shiing-Shen (1911–2004)." In *Asian Americans: An Encyclopedia of Social, Cultural, Economic, and Political History*, edited by Xiaojian Zhao and Edward Park. Santa Barbara, CA: ABC-CLIO, 2014.

Watts, Tim J. "Acculturation and the Indian American Community." In *Asian American History and Culture: An Encyclopedia*, edited by Huping Ling and Allan Austin. Armonk, NY: M.E. Sharpe Inc., 2010.

Weatherford, Doris. *Women in American Politics: History and Milestones*. Los Angeles, CA: Sage, 2012.

Weil, Patrick. *The Sovereign Citizen: Denaturalization and the Origins of the American Republic*. Philadelphia: University of Pennsylvania Press, 2013.

Wilkinson, Willy. *Born on the Edge of Race and Gender: A Voice for Cultural Competency*. Oakland, CA: Hapa Papa Press, 2015.

Willbanks, James, ed. *Vietnam War: The Essential Reference Guide*. Santa Barbara, CA: ABC-CLIO, 2013.

Williams, Duncan Ryuken, and Tomoe Moriya. *Issei Buddhism in the Americas*. Urbana: University of Illinois Press, 2010.

Wilson, Flannery. *New Taiwanese Cinema in Focus: Moving within and beyond the Frame*. Edinburgh: Edinburgh University Press, 2014.

Woeser, Tsering, and Wang Lixong. *Voices from Tibet: Selected Essays and Reportage*. Translated by Violet Law. Hong Kong: Hong Kong University Press, 2014.

Wong, Edlie. *Racial Reconstruction: Black Inclusion, Chinese Exclusion, and the Fictions of Citizenship*. New York: New York University Press, 2015.

Wong, Janelle, S. Karthick Ramakrishnan, Taeku Lee, and Jane Junn. *Asian American Political Participation: Emerging Constituents and Their Political Identities*. New York: Russell Sage Foundation, 2011.

Wong, Patricia, and Victor Hwang, eds. *Anti-Asian Violence in North America*. Walnut Creek, CA: AltaMira Press, 2001.

Wu, Cynthia. *Chang and Eng Reconnected: The Original Siamese Twins in American Culture*. Philadelphia, PA: Temple University Press, 2012.

Wu, Ellen. *The Color of Success: Asian Americans and the Origins of the Model Minority*. Princeton, NJ: Princeton University Press, 2014.

Xing, Jun. "Cinematic Asian Representation in Hollywood." In *Performing Difference: Representation of "The Other" in Film and Theatre*, edited by Jonathan Friedman. Lanham, MD: University Press of America, 2009.

Xu, Wendy. *Historical Dictionary of Asian American Literature and Theater*. Lanham, MD: Scarecrow Press, 2012.

Yahirun, Jenjira. "Thai Immigrants." In *Multicultural America: An Encyclopedia of the Newest Americans*, edited by Ronald Bayor, 2097–2133. Santa Barbara, CA: ABC-CLIO, 2011.

Yamamoto, Eric, Margaret Chon, Carol Izumi, Jerry Kang, and Frank Wu. *Race, Rights, and Reparation: Law and the Japanese American Internment*. New York: Wolters Kluwer Law & Business, 2013.

Yeo, Andrew. *Activists, Alliances, and Anti-U.S. Base Protests*. Cambridge: Cambridge University Press, 2011.

Yoo, David. *Contentious Spirits: Religion in Korean American History, 1903–1945*. Stanford, CA: Stanford University Press, 2010.

Yoo, David, and Eiichiro Azuma, eds. *The Oxford Handbook on Asian American History*. Oxford: Oxford University Press, 2016.

Yoo, Grace, Mai-Nhung Le, and Alan Odo, eds. *Handbook of Asian American Health*. New York: Springer, 2013.

Young, Morgen. "Russell Lee in the Northwest: Documenting Japanese American Farm Labor Camps in Oregon and Idaho." *Oregon Historical Quarterly* 114, no. 3 (Fall 2013): 360–364.

Young, Ralph. *Dissent: The History of an American Idea*. New York: New York University Press, 2015.

Zeiger, Susan. *Entangling Alliances: Foreign War Brides and American Soldiers in the Twentieth Century*. New York: New York University Press, 2010.

Zesch, Scott. *The Chinatown War: Chinese Los Angeles and the Massacre of 1871*. Oxford: Oxford University Press, 2012.

Zhao, Xiaojian. *Asian American Chronology: Chronologies of the American Mosaic*. Santa Barbara, CA: ABC-CLIO, 2009.

Zhao, Xiaojian, and Edward Park, eds. *Asian Americans: An Encyclopedia of Social, Cultural, Economic, and Political History*. Santa Barbara, CA: Greenwood, 2013.

Zhou, Min, and Carl Bankston III. "Vietnamese Americans: Lessons in American History." Teaching Tolerance: A Project of the Southern Poverty Law Center. http://www.tolerance.org/sites/default/files/kits/vac_brief_history.pdf. Accessed January 17, 2017.

Zhu, Liping. *The Road to Chinese Exclusion: The Denver Riot, 1880 Election, and Rise of the West*. Lawrence: University Press of Kansas, 2013.

Zimmer, Kenyon. *Immigrants against the State: Yiddish and Italian Anarchism in America*. Urbana: University of Illinois Press, 2015.

Index